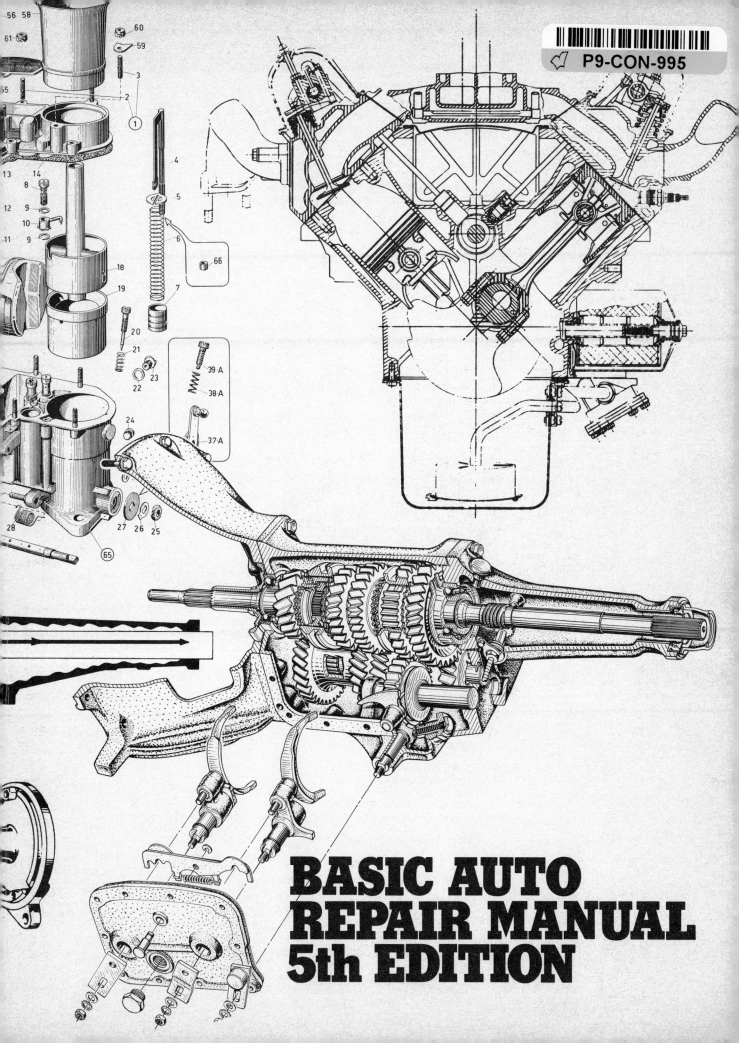

BASIC AUTO
REPAIR MANUAL
5th EDITION

Introduction

The subject of *Basic Auto Repair* is an involved one indeed. A book twice this size could be produced on any single make of American car. That's how complex today's automobiles have become. But rather than take the single-model approach to the mechanical nature of the beasts, this edition, like the four that have preceded it, encompasses the general repair and maintenance of all the U.S. cars that make up the bulk of today's traffic.

Because applying a "fix" to, say, a Ford product radiator is so nearly like the same chore on a Chevrolet (and on a Plymouth, and so forth), cooling systems are discussed in terms general enough to apply to each make, yet specific enough to guide you as you undertake an at-home repair of your very own car. The same treatment is given all the basic functions and components of the modern automobile, with a heavy smattering of individual how-to's on particular maintenance and repair steps where we felt they were necessary.

This updated version of *Basic Auto Repair* that you're holding in your hands has been tailored to suit the occasional tinkerer as well as the professional mechanic. So regardless of your automotive interest and/or background, this volume, together with a regular factory shop manual, will help you trace, solve and repair almost any automotive problem you're likely to encounter.

Spence Murray

SPECIALTY PUBLICATIONS DIVISION

Hans Tanner / Editorial Director
Erwin M. Rosen / Executive Editor
Robert I. Young / Art Director
Spencer Murray / Editor, Automotive
Al Hall / Editor, General Projects
Don Edgington / Editor, Outdoor Books
George E. Shultz / Editor, Spotlite Books
Don Whitt / Editor, Special Projects
Jeff Shifman / Editor, Research
Jon Jay / Technical Editor
Allen Bishop / Associate Editor
Jay Storer / Associate Editor
Mike Stensvold / Associate Editor
Harris R. Bierman / Associate Editor
Richard L. Busenkell / Associate Editor
Tom Senter / Associate Editor
Ann R. Cornog / Associate Editor
Lynn Anderson / Associate Editor
Ronda Brown / Associate Editor
Terry Parsons / Associate Editor
Chriss Ohliger / Editorial Assistant
Steve Hirsch / Artist, Design
Pat Taketa / Artist, Design
George Fukuda / Artist, Design
Don Wilson / Artist, Production Manager
Celeste Swayne-Courtney / Artist, Production
Dean Toji / Artist, Production
Salvatore Scorza / Artist, Production
Ralph Vindiola / Artist, Production
Mark Gold / Artist, illustration
Margaret Davies / Artist, Contributor
Angie Ullrich / Secretary
Al Michaelian / Research Librarian

BASIC AUTO REPAIR MANUAL NO. 5

Erwin M. Rosen / Associate Publisher
Spencer Murray / Editor
Robert I. Young / Art Director
Ann R. Cornog / Managing Editor
Kalton C. Lahue / Contributing Editor
Lynn Johnson / Contributing Editor
Mike Criss / Contributing Editor

COVER

Oldsmobile Division provided us with a full-size car cutaway of their Toronado to reveal some of the complexities of the modern automobile, most of which will require periodic maintenance and repair. Kalton C. Lahue photographed the three "hardware" shots, courtesy of Bob Ferris and Ken Valentine of Galpin Ford, as he did the bodyworking photo at Santa Monica City College.

BASIC AUTO REPAIR MANUAL NO. 5

Revision edited by Kalton C. Lahue and the Technical Editors of Petersen Publishing Co. Copyright © 1973 by Petersen Publishing Co., 8490 Sunset Blvd., Los Angeles, Calif. 90069. Phone: (213) 657-5100. All rights reserved. No part of this book may be reproduced without written permission. Printed in U.S.A.

LIBRARY OF CONGRESS CATALOG CARD NO: 73-79965
ISBN 0-8227-0008-5

PETERSEN PUBLISHING COMPANY

R.E.Petersen / Chairman of the Board
F.R. Waingrow / President
Robert E. Brown / V.P. Nat'l Advertising Director
Herb Metcalf / V.P. Circulation Director
Dick Day / V.P. Automotive Publications
Robert Andersen / Director, Manufacturing
Al Isaacs / Director, Graphics
Bob D'Olivo / Director, Photography
Spencer Nilson / Director, Administrative Services
Mitza B. Thompson / Director, Advertising Sales Administration

Larry Kent / Director, Corporate Merchandising
Ronald D. Salk / Director, Public Relations
William Porter / Director, Single Copy Sales
Jack Thompson / Director, Subscription Sales
Maria Cox / Manager, Data Processing Services
Mel Rawitsch / Manager, Manufacturing Planning
Robert Horton / Manager, Traffic
Harold Davis / Manager, Production
James J. Krenek / Manager, Purchasing

Contents

Contents

The Right Tools for the Job

A mechanic without tools is like a wheel without a tire. A wheel, thankfully, is satisfied with only one tire, but a mechanic never feels that he has enough tools. Part of being a mechanic is fascination with the sight of a full toolbox, a love of all the different sockets and extensions, handles and ratchets, and even some gadgets that haven't been used for so long that it's difficult to remember what car they were designed for, or even how they work.

The best advice we can give you about buying tools is to investigate before you buy even so much as a simple pair of pliers. Get as many catalogs as possible from the tool companies, and go to the retail stores so you can see and handle the merchandise. In many cases we have seen mechanics get started with a basic set of hand tools, only to discover later that another brand was much more appealing to them. The result was they switched to the other brand, and the money spent for the original basic set was wasted. It makes no difference whether you buy Snap-On, Proto, Sears' Craftsman, Ward's Power-Kraft, Mac, or any other brand. The important thing is to know about them all before you make that necessary purchase of your basic set.

In some brands you can save a lot of money by getting a set instead of individual tools. But beware of enormous sets that include everything from thread gauges to wheel pullers, with maybe a backscratcher thrown in. After all, you may find that you like one maker's socket sets, but not his pliers. And you may go to a third manufacturer for your screwdrivers, simply because you like the way they are made. Some of the small toolmakers do an excellent job on special-purpose tools for brakes, or engines, or electrical work. In many cases they are the only source for a special tool that is just what you need.

Major brand tools are not discounted to anybody. The backyard mechanic pays the same price as the guy who works on the line at a big car dealer. Some big-city hardware stores may have a line of hand tools that they discount, but such places are hard to find, and the amount you get off is only about 10%.

The best place to find different makes of tools is at an automotive parts store. The counterman is usually out of catalogs, but you can get the address of the factory from him and write for one. Some tools, including the best hand tools available, are not sold in retail stores, but only by wagon peddlers. The peddlers usually leave their calling cards all over town at the various independent garages and car dealers. Ask your local mechanic for the phone numbers of the various wagon peddlers that call on him.

Don't ignore the mail order houses, either. Sears and Ward's have excellent tools. Incidentally, their catalog price is usually less than you would have to pay in the retail store.

For the purpose of properly selecting and using the basic hand tools for fasteners, some knowledge of those fasteners—particularly the nuts and bolts—is very important to any type of repair work. It is not only a question of the proper wrench for the nut or bolt but of the proper bolt size and how tight it should be twisted.

UNDERSTANDING FASTENERS

Fasteners vary not only in a wide range of sizes and thread count, but also in the type of material from which they are made. Increased strength for a particular assembly is not always achieved by installing a larger bolt, but very often by the specified use of a stronger bolt material. Critically stressed parts of an automobile such as the suspension, steering and structural assembly generally use nuts and bolts of a higher tensile strength than those used just to hold accessories. Sheetmetal screws, for example, may look like some of the available wood screws, but they are treated for hardness and will withstand threading into a punched hole under stresses that just twist off wood screws.

Bolt and cap screws are easily identified by distinctive markings embossed on the heads which denote the type of ma-

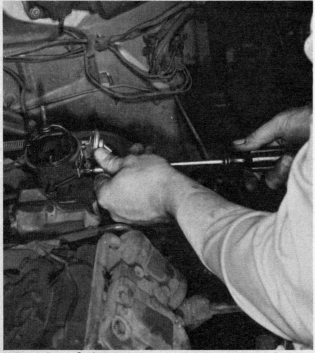

1. Removing a Carburetor

2. Toolboxes

terial and, therefore, the tensile strength range for proper torquing. The word "torque" will continue to crop up in specifications relating to everything from spark plugs to cylinder head nuts, and is a very important function of the strength of bolts and the pieces held together by them.

Before proceeding further with torque, it is best to clarify the method of identifying fasteners by strength rating. Bolt heads are embossed with a series of lines radiating outward. Plain-headed bolts without markings are the most common to the hardware store purchaser. They are graded as 1 or 2 by the SAE (Society of Automotive Engineers), and are adequate for most accessory fastening jobs requiring only low-carbon steel strength.

Generally specified for automotive use is the SAE grade 5, noted by three embossed lines on the head and with nearly double the tensile strength of the common low-carbon, plain-headed bolt. Slightly higher in strength are the grades 6 and 7 noted by 4- and 5-line markings respectively, and topping the commercial grades is the 6-liner for use in severe stress points and on heavy-duty trucks and construction equipment.

Carriage and stove bolts are not recommended as replacement for even the lowest SAE grade of bolts, although they have their place in the fabrication of many common items. Machine screws with special heads such as flat, fillister,

round, and pan designations are not usually marked except in aircraft grades.

Allen-head cap screws are unmarked, but they are usually grade 8 or better. Unfortunately, frequent use tends to round off the corners of the wrench or to strip out the head. If working space permits, you should change over to hex-headed cap screws. The strongest cap

screws are made for aircraft, but they are also the most expensive, unless you can find them in a surplus store.

Thread patterns, noted by the bolt size and a single number which means the number of threads per inch (4-40, 10-32, ¼-20, etc.) for machine screws, nuts and bolts, are important especially when the fastener is used in a threaded hole. All

1. Fifty bucks worth of hand tools should cover what the backyard mechanic needs to effect 90% of the repairs that would shape up the old clunker. A set of wrenches, a couple hammers, screwdrivers, pliers, bench tools and the "Basic Auto Repair Manual" can save the do-it-yourself hundreds of dollars in bills. A screwdriver is all that's needed to replace this choke vacuum actuator.

2. Multi-piece toolboxes usually find a home among the professionals. But many serious amateurs also tie up hundreds, even thousands of dollars in sets like these shown. Most packages include ¼, ⅜ and ½-in. drives, a full complement of ratchets, extensions, breaker bars, torque wrenches, sockets, speed handles, end wrenches, hammers, pliers, punches, drills and mikes.

3. Cap screws or bolts are available in varying head designs, all tailored to do a specific job. Some must be tightened by screwdrivers, others by various types of wrenches.

4. We call them bolts, nuts, washers, etc., but the trade refers to them as fasteners. Obviously they come in varying grades depending upon their use and/or need. High-stress areas— like the clutch or crank—require employment of a strong type of cap screw material. Low-stress areas— manifolds or carburetors—can use a lesser strength material.

5. Cap screws too have their design terminologies and characteristics. The better a mechanic understands the whys and wherefores of fasteners, the easier it will be for him to select the right grade and the right torque.

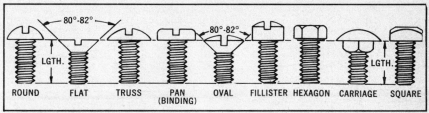

3. Cap Screw Head Designs

	ROUND	FLAT	TRUSS	PAN (BINDING)	OVAL	FILLISTER	HEXAGON	CARRIAGE	SQUARE

GRADE MARKINGS					
DEFINITION	No lines unmarked Indeterminate quality SAE Grades 0-1-2	3 Lines—common commercial quality Automotive & AN Bolts SAE Grade 5	4 Lines—Medium commercial quality Automotive & AN Bolts SAE Grade 6	5 Lines—rarely used SAE Grade 7	6 Lines—Best commercial quality N.A.S. & Aircraft Screws SAE Grade 8
MATERIAL	Low Carbon Steel	Med. Carbon Steel Tempered	Med. Carbon Steel Quenched & tempered	Med. Carbon Alloy Steel	Med. Carbon Alloy Steel Quenched & tempered
TENSILE STRENGTH	65,000 p.s.i.	120,000 p.s.i.	140,000 p.s.i.	140,000 p.s.i.	150,000 p.s.i.

GRADE MARKINGS					
DEFINITION	Supertanium	A-354-BD. A490	Socket Head Cap Screw Also N.A.S. Aircraft Std.	N.A.S. 144 Aircraft Std. MS 20000 Mil. Std.	N.A.S. 624 National Aircraft Standard Steel	Aircraft No Number Assigned Steel
MATERIAL	Special Alloy Steel Quenched & tempered	Med. Carbon Alloy Quenched & tempered	High Carbon Alloy Quenched & tempered	High Carbon Alloy Quenched & tempered	High Carbon Alloy Quenched & tempered	High Carbon Alloy Quenched & tempered
TENSILE STRENGTH	160,000 p.s.i. minimum	150,000 p.s.i.	160,000 p.s.i.	160,000 p.s.i.	180,000 p.s.i.	220,000 p.s.i.

4. Fastener Grade Marking Chart

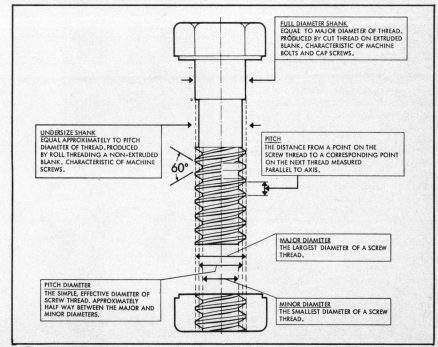

FULL DIAMETER SHANK
EQUAL TO MAJOR DIAMETER OF THREAD. PRODUCED BY CUT THREAD ON EXTRUDED BLANK. CHARACTERISTIC OF MACHINE BOLTS AND CAP SCREWS.

UNDERSIZE SHANK
EQUAL APPROXIMATELY TO PITCH DIAMETER OF THREAD. PRODUCED BY ROLL THREADING A NON-EXTRUDED BLANK. CHARACTERISTIC OF MACHINE SCREWS.

PITCH
THE DISTANCE FROM A POINT ON THE SCREW THREAD TO A CORRESPONDING POINT ON THE NEXT THREAD MEASURED PARALLEL TO AXIS.

MAJOR DIAMETER
THE LARGEST DIAMETER OF A SCREW THREAD.

PITCH DIAMETER
THE SIMPLE, EFFECTIVE DIAMETER OF SCREW THREAD. APPROXIMATELY HALF WAY BETWEEN THE MAJOR AND MINOR DIAMETERS.

MINOR DIAMETER
THE SMALLEST DIAMETER OF A SCREW THREAD.

5. Cap Screw Design

Right Tools for the Job

of the commonly used machine screws or bolts are made in two thread series, coarse and fine, and it is important that even though the bolt diameter is correct for the hole, the threads match those in the hole.

Internal threads and those on the bolt should always be clean and free of damaged or flattened sections before you attempt to assemble any part using threaded holes. Greater care must be taken if aluminum is involved. This applies to everything from installing spark plugs to assembling aluminum transmission cases. Even the poorest grade of steel bolt will cut its own thread in aluminum or soft steel if it has the wrong thread per inch pattern or if it is started into the hole improperly.

A good practice for any assembly is to first try all of the bolts *by finger effort only* into the threaded holes to check for both length and thread. Any doubt about the force required to thread the fasteners by finger pressure should be followed by an examination of both male and female thread condition. Slightly damaged threads on a bolt can be dressed up by filing with a slim 3-cornered file or a thread file, a handy tool in any mechanic's kit. These have eight different thread pattern filing sides and are reasonably priced, but worth a fortune when really needed.

Dressing up inside threads, if only slightly damaged, is best done by running the proper tap into the hole. While not absolutely necessary as part of the basic tool kit, a few taps in the most common sizes will come in handy especially when you are working on older cars that may have been badly repaired by the previous owner. Before getting into the total repair of damaged inside threads, it is best to consider the tools in common use for standard nuts and bolts.

END WRENCHES

Anyone looking at a set of standard open-end, box-end or combination wrenches will immediately notice how the total length increases with the size of the opening. This in itself is a sort of primitive built-in protection against overtightening as it limits the leverage and consequently the foot-pounds of torque that one can apply. It does not consider the strength of the individual, which can often mean a twisted-off bolt. Wrench sizes for American standard nuts and bolts are given in fractions of an inch and note the distance measured across the parallel flat sides of hexagon (6-sided) nuts and bolts.

Metric nuts and bolts are measured across the same dimension with the corresponding wrench size given in millimeters. British cars used to use the British standard system which is measured at the bolt shank diameter. A wrench marked 1/4 W (Whitworth) is made to fit a 1/4-in. bolt, even though the head dimension is 7/16-in. British cars now use American sizes.

Open-end wrenches exert their force against a pair of the parallel sides, and it is important that the proper size wrench

be used. Naturally, one too small will not even fit, but too large an open end will result in insufficient contact area to exert the proper force. It will burr the corners enough to impair the use of a wrench of the proper size, and make it impossible to fit a box-end or socket on the bolt head or nut.

Box-end wrenches and sockets apply their force on a small area on either side of the bolt or nut corners, but unlike the open-end tool, the force is applied to all six corners at once. These are the common 12-point type used on box-end and socket wrenches and are recommended for all general use. A set of combination open- and box-end wrenches is a good investment and will handle most general repair projects.

The adjustable-end wrench or "Crescent" is made by most tool manufacturers, including Crescent Tool Co., and is a very handy tool for the occasional mechanic for those jobs beyond the capacity of the average wrench set. A 10- or 12-in. adjustable will handle sizes slightly over 1 in., saving the need for an investment in an open/box-end set of the larger sizes. Adjustables also come in small editions with a maximum opening of ½-in., and there are click-stop models that hold the jaws firmly at preset positions. One of these, along with a good screwdriver and a pair of pliers, is nice to carry in the glove compartment just for on-the-road emergencies.

SOCKET WRENCHES

Socket wrenches are desirable for their adaptability to a variety of hard-to-reach places. Their speed when used with ratchet handles is a great aid in any mechanical work and no professional mechanic is without a full set of sizes, lengths, and adapters. Screwdriver and Allen screw bits increase the versatility of a socket/handle set and are ideally suited to applying great force in cramped spaces with the right-angle action of such a combination. In addition to these special ends, sockets for nuts and bolts are available in 4, 6, 8 and 12 points. The 4- and 8-point sockets are for square-headed fasteners, while the 6-pointers are mainly for power impact tool use on hex-nuts and bolts.

A common term used in connection with sockets, and the handles for them, is "drive." The connection between socket wrench and handle is by a square projection on the handle fitting into a similar hole in the drive end of the socket. The size of this connection is ¼-in., ⅜-in., etc., up to 1 in. in the standard and most commonly used tools. The size

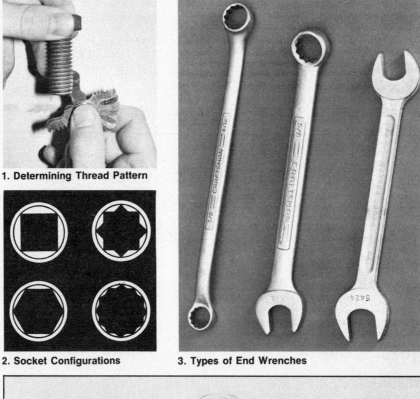

1. Determining Thread Pattern

2. Socket Configurations

3. Types of End Wrenches

4. Types of Nuts and Washers

1. Thread size and pattern is either coarse or fine and is best confirmed by the use of this simple thread gauge. In any automotive application, one must use the correct pattern and cap screw diameter. If not, you'll strip the threads or break the bolts.

2. Sockets encompass 4, 6, 8 and 12-point configurations. The 4- and 8-pointers are used when fasteners with square heads are encountered. The 6-point types must be employed with impact wrenches or in high torque situations so as not to round off the edge of the bolt head. However, most general repair work features the use of 12-point sockets.

3. The simple end wrench can be purchased as either a box-end (left), open-end (right) or a combination of the two (middle). Box-ends come in handy as a breaker or final tightener. The speedier open ends are better for hard-to-get-at places.

4. What applies to cap screws also applies to nuts and washers. They come in an infinite variety of shapes, sizes and grades. In top row (from left) is a standard, castellated, SPS Flex-lok, jamb, Cone-lock, L&S Stover lock and a nylon insert locknut. Below (from left) is a lock, external tooth and flat washer. To prevent galling, flat washers must be made of the same material as the nut, and the nut must be identical in grade to that of the cap screw.

5. A ratchet box-end wrench is handy in tight places as well as for general use. It speeds up the loosening/tightening process and seldom slips off the bolt head, saving you a lot of knuckle skin in the long run.

6. Every backyard Bignotti should have a couple of crescent wrenches—especially if he owns one of the new, foreign-built subcompacts with their metric bolts and nuts. Crescents will also save you the cost of buying large sockets and/or end wrenches.

7. Most socket sets (breaker bars, U-drives, extensions, ratchets, etc.) come in ¼, ⅜, and ½-in. drives. Small (¼-in.) drives are useful for electrical and body fastener work, the ⅜-in. drive comes in handy when working on the outside of the engine, and the larger ½-in. drive is usually employed in general engine overhaul work or suspension repairs.

8. Common torque-indicating wrenches include such units as (left to right), Continental American's round beam, which has a 100 ft.-lbs. torque capacity; Milbar's micrometer adjustable, which clicks when dialed-in reading is reached; S-K Tool's round beam model indicates from 0-150 ft.-lbs.; Milbar's dial unit, using a sensory dial indicator, calculates up to 600 in.-lbs. All are precision made.

9. This 8-in-1 wrench is a tool box space-saver. Swivel ball heads let you adjust angle for best leverage as well as for getting in and out of some of those really tight places.

5. Ratchet Type Box Wrench

6. Crescent Wrenches

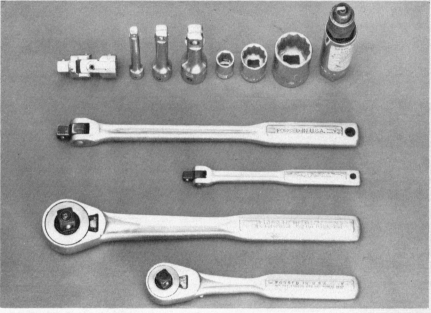

7. Socket Set

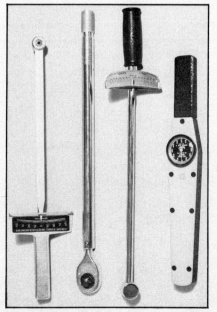

8. Torque Wrenches

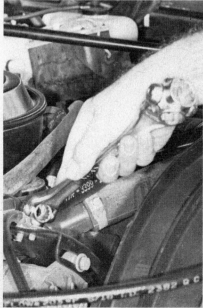

9. Multiple Box Wrench

Right Tools for the Job

of the drive is in proportion to the socket size, giving the strength needed for handle length and bolt size. Handles for socket drives come in a variety of models as to length, ratchet, swivel, screwdriver, speed and flexibility, with universal and step-down adapters for using sockets of a different drive size than the handle. There are also open and "crowfoot" wrenches, Allen or Phillips drive bits and ratchet spinner attachments for socket sets, making them a most versatile tool.

A good set of sockets is a must for precision work; it will save a lot of busted knuckles and damaged nut and bolt heads. Just about every part on an automobile held together by bolting has a specific degree of tightness or torque specifications for it. This torque setting is specified for both the tensile strength of the fastener and the required degree of fit or tension between the mating parts.

TORQUE AND TORQUE WRENCHES

Every type and grade of metal has a limit to which it can be safely stretched or stressed. There is an engineering phrase that says, "An over-torqued bolt is already half broken"—which is a good indication of just what degree of stretch fasteners of this type can take. Designers consider many things in selecting the proper size and material for a fastener. As engines, transmissions and suspension components become more complex, their efficiency becomes more and more dependent on just how the various parts are held together. Applying just the right amount of torque or stretch to the fasteners imparts the correct amount of pressure needed to hold the parts together without distortion.

In the case of aluminum and other soft metals, their ultimate strength governs the amount of torque rather than that of the steel bolt. Allowance for heat expansion or soft joints sealed by gaskets also

must be considered when applying torque, as too much pressure could damage or distort the two mating parts.

Tension is not to be confused with torque. Tension is the stretching force along the length of the bolt, or its degree of stretch. Torque is the force required on the bolt or nut to produce the desired degree of stretch in the fastener; it is measured in foot-pounds (ft.-lbs.) or inch-pounds (in.-lbs.). Torque is measured on the basis of a fundamental law of physics regarding leverage: Force times distance equals twist force or torque around a pivot point. If 1 lb. of force is exerted around the bolt or nut center at 1 ft. from that center, the torque is 1 ft.-lb. If the distance is measured in inches, then the torque is read as 12 in.-lbs.

Torque wrenches for applying the proper amount of torque to fasteners are available in four basic forms: The *dial type* incorporates a calibrated dial that indicates by pointer when the desired torque is being applied. The *clutch type* has settings calibrated on the handle with a knurled sleeve for setting to the desired torque (drive is disengaged or slips when proper torque is reached). *Direct reading pointer types* employ a calibrated scale with pointer rod attached to the handle head that indicates torque in direct readings on scale. The *click type* unit produces an audible sound when preset torque force is reached. Some models are available with reversible ratchet, allowing the same handle to be used for general assembly without the need for switching tools.

Sometimes adapters of various shapes must be used with a torque wrench to get around obstructions. If the adapter is in effect only an extension bar, with the drive and hex parts in line with each other, then the torque readings will not be affected. However, if the adapter is similar to an end wrench, in effect making the torque wrench longer, then the torque readings will have to be corrected, depending on how long the adapter is. As torque wrenches do have limits, they are made in a variety of sizes to accommodate all of the limits. Tiny ones

1. Dial indicator on Milbar torque wrench is shown hovering around the 120-in.-lbs. or 10-ft.-lbs. level. This sensitive tool is used in critical areas where precise tightening is mandatory.

2. The offset design of a distributor wrench is a big help in reaching those buried mounting bolts in today's overloaded engine compartments.

3. Restoring stripped threads (like blind spark plug holes), calls for drilling, tapping, then inserting Heli-Coil-type threads to restore the hole to its original size.

4. Breaking a cap screw off in a block or cylinder head always ends in a sweat. First try to remove the residual piece by tapping it with a chisel or a punch. It should unscrew from the hole. If that doesn't work, you can use an extractor or drill out the old bolt and re-thread the hole.

5. As basic to the toolbox as the screwdriver, pliers come in all shapes and sizes. For instance, we've shown (top row, from left) bent needle nose, and diagonal wire cutters; (bottom row, from left) lineman, a pair of double-jointed types and a needle nose.

6. Continental American's standard screwdriver set is ideal for most automotive work. It features both standard and Phillips head tips, various lengths and blade widths.

7. Spark plug-type tire pump fits into spark plug well and pumps up to 105 psi of clean air. A 16-ft. hose, connectors and pressure gauge make this an outstanding replacement for older hand pump.

8. No matter what you think, every mechanic needs his hammers. Claw type will pound 'n' pry; round end of the ball peen makes an excellent gasket shaper, and you can always use a soft-faced rubber or plastic headed hammer to tap in parts without marring their machined surfaces.

9. This 8-piece hex key set by Craftsman has just about every size from 2 to 10mm that you'll need for automotive work.

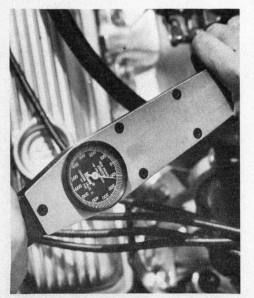

1. Torquing Bolts to Specs

2. Distributor Offset Wrench

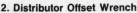

3. Heli-Coils

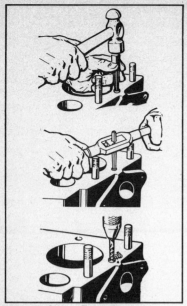

4. Using Screw Extractor

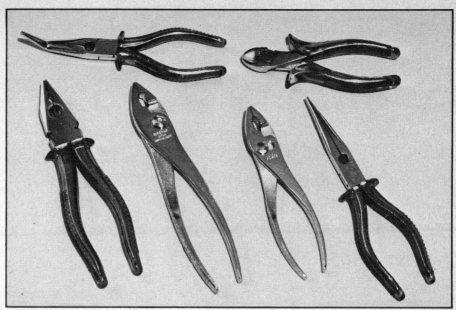

5. Plier Package

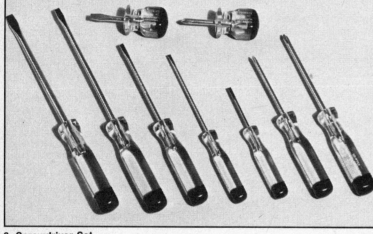

6. Screwdriver Set

7. Spark Plug Tire Pump

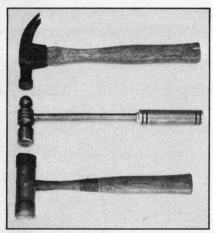

8. Types of Hammers

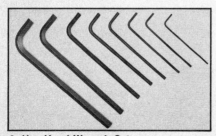

9. Hex Head Wrench Set

for setting fuel injectors have a limit of 150 in.-lbs., while larger handles with higher capacities are required for the 80-150 ft.-lbs. specified for main bearing caps, heads, etc. Heavy-duty ones used on industrial equipment go up to 6000 ft.-lbs. As a rough guide to selection of torque wrench range, here are a few general ratings and applicable common usages:

1) 0-80 ft.-lbs.—⅜- or ½-in. drive.

Spark plugs, intake and exhaust manifold, rocker arm brackets and covers, connecting rod cap bolts, transmission oil pan.

2) 10-150 ft.-lbs.—½-in. drive.

Main bearing caps, cylinder head bolts, main bearings, vibration dampener, transmission pump bolts, connecting rod bearings, power steering pump.

3) 100-500 ft.-lbs.—¾-in. drive.

Main bearing cap bolts, cylinder-head bolts, flywheel, pulley bolts and other jobs on big industrial and commercial equipment.

THREAD SAVERS

Breaking a bolt inside a threaded hole, or stripping the internal threads, are two major problems with fasteners that are sure to plague the amateur mechanic—

they occur quite often even to the trained professional. Stripping threads, especially in aluminum and quite often in the spark plug hole, does not mean the piece must be scrapped, thanks to several handy repair methods.

The two most popular devices for repairing damaged threads in blind holes, spark plug holes, or straight-through ones are the Heli-Coil, made by Heli-Coil Corp., Danbury, Conn., and the Slimsert by Proto Tool Co.

Both require the damaged hole to be drilled out, tapped properly, and then completed by the installation of the new thread assembly. Both are sold in complete kits to handle a variety of sizes and thread patterns, and have the advantage of restoring damaged holes to their original bolt and thread per inch size.

Broken bolts are another serious problem as they almost always break well inside the hole, eliminating the possibility of getting a hold on them with anything. With a little time and effort, and the proper screw extractors, they can be removed without damage to the part other than the cross threading or bottoming that caused the breakage in the first place.

Screw extractors are usually sold in sets, sized to remove anything from ¼-in.

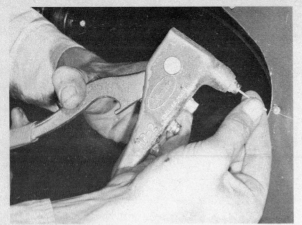
1. Pop Rivet Gun

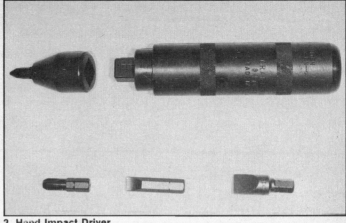
2. Hand Impact Driver

Right Tools for the Job

to 1-in. bolts or studs. They are fluted and tapered tools of high grade steel, sometimes with spiral fluting in a left-hand pattern.

For broken bolt removal it is necessary to drill a hole into the broken piece as near center as possible. The extractor is then driven or screwed into the hole and unscrewed while being held with a tap wrench. Penetrating oil on the broken part will often ease removal, and the internal threads should be examined and repaired before you proceed with any further assembly of the component.

Screw extractors are scorned by many automotive machinists, because they can break off, leaving a problem twice as bad as a simple broken bolt or stud. Broken extractors cannot be drilled out because they are so hard. Many broken bolts can be removed simply by tapping them with a sharp-pointed chisel so that they are unscrewed from the hole. If the bolt or stud has been in the hole a long time, as in an old engine block, the best and safest way to get it out is to drill a hole exactly in the middle of the bolt, and of the same diameter as the threads in the block. If done correctly, the only thing left in the block will be a spiral of thread that can be picked out with a chisel, leaving the threads in the block untouched.

SCREWDRIVERS

The screwdriver is such a basic tool that it hardly seems worth mentioning, but so many repair jobs have been butchered by the improper use of this tool that a few tips are in order. First, the slot in any screw has definite dimensions—length, width and depth. Like a bolt head or nut, the screw slot must be driven by a tool that uses all of the available bearing surface and does not slip. A close look at the blade of a new screwdriver will reveal that the sides near the end are parallel, just like those in the screw slot. When repairing or regrinding screwdriver blades, remember this: Tapered sides will just wedge the blade out of the slot, reducing the available force and damaging the slot itself. Don't use a big wide blade on a small screw, and don't try to operate a large screw slot with tiny narrow blades. Screws with Phillips heads, Allen heads

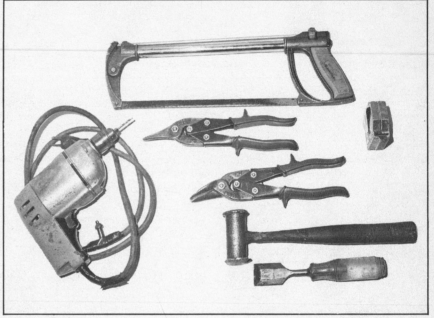
3. Bench Tools

or hollow hex heads should always be driven with the proper driving tool. Any attempts made with a single-bladed screwdriver can damage these openings to a point where removal is impossible even with the proper tool for the job.

PLIERS

Pliers are about as basic as the screwdriver and few homes are without a pair, but the sizes and shapes available will require some selectivity on the part of anyone starting to assemble a professional set of tools. One tool maker alone lists 29 different types of pliers in his catalog, with sub-selections under certain categories. No mechanic has or needs all of them, and a few carefully selected pieces will cover many jobs.

A good pair of double-jointed, straight-jaw pliers are always handy and some long-nosed ones for reaching into hard-to-get-at places will find ready use on many jobs. Be sure to include a set of diagonal wire cutters as they are indispensable when doing electrical wiring or setting cotter keys. There are also special pliers for brake springs, hose clamps, retaining rings, and the small nuts on distributors and voltage regulators which can be purchased as needed.

1. A hand pop rivet gun is a must if you plan to do any type of sheet-metal fabrication or panel reshaping.

2. Strike this hand impact driver with a hammer and up to 200 ft.-lbs. of pressure turns the bit up to 20°. It's also reversible for loosening frozen nuts, screws or bolts.

3. No mechanic's hand tool collection is complete unless it encompasses a bunch of bench goodies. Hack saws, tapes, an electric drill motor, tin snips, brass hammer and chisels are just a few things needed to make the job that much easier and better.

Two very handy tools are tne Vise-Grip (an adjustable locking plier that stays on when locked and also is capable of a very firm grip) and the parallel-jaw adjustable pliers with angled jaws that stay parallel in any degree of opening. This latter is often referred to as Channel-Lok or water pump pliers and is very handy for grabbing both round and square shapes firmly.

Specialty items that are nice to have but not really necessary are battery terminal and spark plug terminal pliers. The spark plug pliers are heavily insulated and allow the plug terminals to be removed while the engine is running without danger of shocking the user with high voltage.

HAMMERS

Often used with little discretion, hammers are a very important part of the mechanic's tool kit. There is a story that German mechanics forbid their apprentices to even have one in their kit, forcing the student to "fit it, don't bang it." A good ball-peen hammer of medium size, plus a soft-faced one for tapping parts into place without damaging them, are really necessary in most of today's automotive repair work. In addition, special hammers for bodywork are a must if any type of sheetmetal repair is attempted, and the handless hammer or bucking dolly in various shapes should be includ-

ed in the body repair tool kit to make the job easier.

With the multitude of service stations, each with a tire changing jig, it is rare that anyone peels tires off the rims or remounts them by hand anymore. But, just in case the need occurs, a heavy rubber mallet is a must for pounding tire beads back into the rim recess. A rubber mallet also comes in mighty handy when replacing wheel covers; it can assure a tight fit with little danger of denting the covers.

SAWS—FILES—BENCH TOOLS

For any kind of automotive repair work, where parts are removed from the car and refurbished at home, a good bench vise is indispensable. Naturally, it should be well mounted on a suitable work table or bench—not necessarily

large, but well anchored and capable of handling the usual pounding without giving way. The bench vise should be securely mounted and have at least 4-in. jaws with soft interchangeable inserts for holding parts that may scratch or be indented by sharp hard jaw faces.

A good hacksaw frame, one that will hold its shape and is adjustable for blades up to 12 ins. long, is needed in every tool kit. While they cost a bit more, the high-speed blades are a good investment as they last a long time. For general work one should have a selection of fine-toothed blades, 32 teeth per inch, for cutting harder steels, and some coarser ones in the 18-to-24-teeth-per-inch size for soft materials. One never knows when a bolt must be shortened or a bit of metal cut for a bracket.

Just about every saw cut must be finished off and a good file, in lieu of a

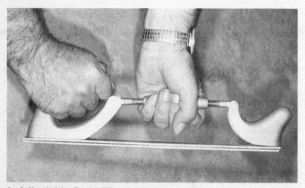

4. Adjustable Body File Holder

6. Filing Breaker Plate

4. If you plan on doing any metal work, this body file holder will come in handy. One like this Craftsman adjusts for concave, convex or straight filing; just turn the center post.

5. Files should be selected as to tooth—either fine or coarse. Small, fine files are used for delicate work, the large rasps for body repairs. Illustrated here is the basic rattail, flat, half-round and vixen . . . all well used.

6. Rattail file and a good bench vise will almost take the place of a juice-powered bench grinder.

7. Specialized tools, like these various types of valve spring compressors and a gasket scraper, aren't that expensive and are virtually indispensable should you plan to replace a blown head gasket or do your own valve job.

5. Various Types of Files

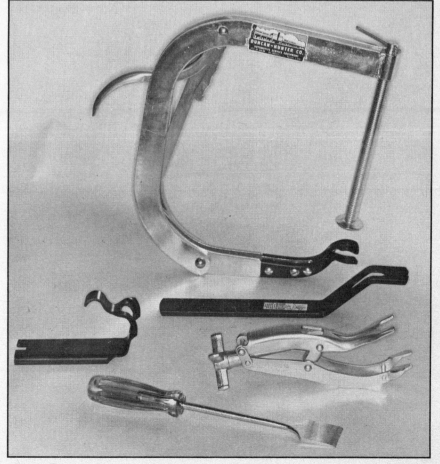

7. Specialized Tools

Right Tools for the Job

bench grinder, is the only answer. Files should be selected the same way as saw blades—some fine toothed, others on the coarse side for softer metals. Included in the file set should be a thin flat-point file for dressing up distributor contacts, plus some slim tapered 3-cornered ones and a round rat tail for cleaning out slots or enlarging and deburring drilled holes.

Any sheetmetal or body shop will require the need for metal shears or "tin snips," and the most versatile are a set of aviation-type shears sometimes called "dutchmen." A full set includes a straight cutter, and a left- and right-hand one since cutting curves is eased by using the one for the direction of the cut—i.e., left or right direction. These are also great for trimming exhaust tubing in the final fitting stages when making custom headers or exhaust systems to suit special needs.

If bodywork is your project, several additional special files should be added to the kit. These come in flat and half-rounded cross sections, have curved teeth more like a series of blades, and are used in a holder that curves them to suit conditions. Indispensable for smoothing or skinning sheetmetal or leaded portions of repaired sections, they are a valuable tool for any kind of bodywork, amateur or professional.

SPECIAL TOOLS

Many automotive assemblies and components require special tools to adjust or repair. One of the most specialized in this area is probably automatic transmission band adjustment. Universal sets for doing this type of work are available in complete form and include the necessary gauges, short-handled end wrenches, a band-adjusting T-handled tool, and complete torque setting chart for all types of automatics. A short-handled torque wrench is needed with a ¼-in. drive and a 0-150 ft.-lbs. range, but if such a tool is already a part of the kit, the additional pieces for doing such work can be purchased as needed.

Front suspension repair, especially wheel alignment work, will require special tools for certain cars due to the dif-

1. The machined surfaces between the cylinder head and intake manifold must be free of old gasket material and cinching compound if the new gasket is to seal properly. You can always use a large screwdriver or a putty knife for this cleaning operation, but a scraper is better.

2. Fully adjustable pullers are "the only way" to force the gear off the end of the crank. If you try it with a hammer, punch or chisel, you'll raise heck with the main bearings.

3. While water pump pliers will suffice, hose clamp pliers with specially milled jaws make pulling the rings off the hoses a snap.

4. If you plan to work under your car, you'll need a set of axle stands. Too many people have been killed or badly hurt trying to make a bumper jack take the place of stands or a hoist. Stands aren't expensive.

5. Drill motors, hones, wire brushes, stones, drills, etc., become an outfit a mechanic cannot afford to be without. Most quality ¼-in. drives will cost around $25-$30.

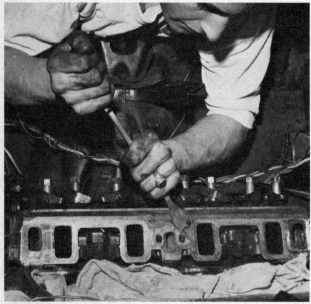

1. Scraping Cylinder Head

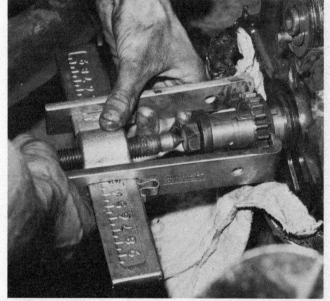

2. Pulling Crank Gear

3. Depressing Hose Clamp

4. Jack Stands

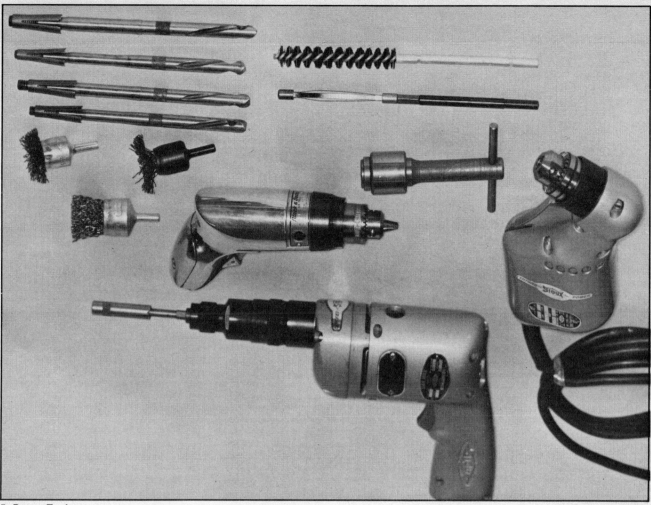

5. Power Tools

ficulty in getting standard wrenches into some of the tight spots. Most tool makers have such special tools designed for cars with these special requirements.

Similar special handle shapes are available for reaching hard-to-get-at hold-down bolts on both front- and rear-mounted distributors. While not absolutely necessary, they certainly can speed up access to these fasteners through the maze of ignition wires and other under-the-hood plumbing.

The correct bleeding and adjusting tools will make these repair and maintenance jobs a lot simpler, allowing better concentration on the work itself without knuckle busting. Valve adjusting for mechanical overhead systems is best done with a combo-tool that uses a ½-in. drive socket for loosening the lock nuts and a knurled knob that actuates a screwdriver down through the socket for turning the adjusting screw.

Anyone doing brake or fuel line work will need a tubing cutter and a double flaring tool. These will cut and flare properly all types of steel and copper tubing for hydraulic, fuel and oil lines and are the only things for a first-class job of cutting to size without distorting the tubing, and flaring properly for leak-proof and permanent joints.

Many a job has been bungled and expensive parts damaged because they were dismantled by pounding rather than by the use of a proper puller. There are a variety of these, both the screw-actuated type and the impact type. Timing gears, wheel hubs, harmonic balancers, axle shafts, bearings, steering wheels, blind pilot bearings, and even battery terminals often require the use of a special puller to separate them from their related shafts or mountings. In this classification are also stud removers, and while not employing exactly the same principles as a 2- or 3-jaw screw or impact puller, they operate by securely grasping the stud in a wedging manner, allowing it to be backed out in one piece by either socket handle drive or impact wrench.

In addition to the appropriate set of wrenches, sockets, etc., any engine overhauling—even a simple ring and valve job—will require a piston ring compressor of the adjustable type for inserting the newly ringed pistons without breaking the rings. Also included in this tool selection should be a valve guide cleaner, gasket and carbon scrapers, a valve lifter clamp for depressing the springs for removal of keepers, and a grinding tool for lapping the valves to the seats for a leakproof seal.

Glaze-breaking hones, ring groove cleaners, and small cylinder hones for brake overhauls will be necessary for the do-it-yourself mechanic as he expands his efforts into more complicated repair operations.

One can save a lot of money by checking first the tools needed for the job on a particular car and then shop-ping the parts supply houses for just the minimum required. Tool makers supply tools in kit form for various special parts of the car such as front end, transmissions, distributors, brake service, as well as bushing, seal installers, etc. Check these to see if the present tools will do the job before investing in tools that may only duplicate what is already in your kit.

POWER TOOLS

About the only power tool the home mechanic will find unlimited use for is a ¼- or ⅜-in. drill. These are available in a variety of qualities and prices, and those offered for the home mechanic are adequate for the average user for both drilling and honing. Industrial grades, made for the hard use of the professional, naturally cost more, but in recent years, many of the top power tool makers have designed power tools of all sorts well within the budget of the home craftsman. Try these before investing in extra heavy-duty industrial tools built to last several lifetimes of occasional use.

A good set of bits for the power drill will be a necessity, and the high-speed type is the best investment. There is not much point in buying a set larger than the chuck will accommodate, so govern the size of the set by this standard. Drills come in two basic sizes: number drills and fractional drills. The number drills go in sizes up to No. 1, the largest (.2280-in.), to the smallest, No. 80

Right Tools for the Job

(.0135-in.). There is a limit as to how small a drill can be safely used in a hand-held power drill, so this should be considered when selecting the set. There are also fractional drill sizes ranging from 1/16-in. to 1/2-in., in increments of 1/64th of an inch. The number drill series include letter sizes, A-B-C, etc., commonly used for tap drill holes larger than the No. 1. Whatever drill system is selected, purchase those that come in a metal case as this will aid in keeping the set complete and avoid loss—somewhere in the toolbox—of just the one you need.

If one has the budget and the need, he will find many uses for a bench grinder in the home shop. Sharpening tools, buffing, and wire brushing, to name a few, are easy jobs with a grinder.

Impact wrenches, mentioned earlier, come in both electric and air drive. For the latter, one needs a compressor and air storage tank, and if the shop is so equipped, say for spray painting, etc., then an air drive is a good investment. The smaller heavy-duty models are capable of tightening up to 200 ft.-lbs. of torque, while the equivalent electric drives impart up to 130 ft.-lbs. While standard ½-in. drive sockets can be used for lighter work, it is recommended that the special heavy-duty wrenches and adapters be used for impact wrenches because of the rather sharp blows imparted to the tools.

Body repair work or any kind of sheet-metal modifications will require a heavy-duty disc sander. These are used by professional body workers for everything from rough metal removal to final polishing of the painted and waxed surface. In addition, a vibrating-type sander for fine metal finishing and preparing bare or primed surfaces for painting is a must unless one is ready to spend needless hours doing these chores by hand.

TEST INSTRUMENTS AND MEASURING TOOLS

Every mechanic's toolbox should contain a set of flat steel feeler gauges, plus the round wire type for checking plug gaps. There are regular plug gap gauges that have all of the most common dimensions in addition to a device for bending the outside electrode. The flat feeler gauges are needed for point adjustment and valve rocker settings. For extensive repair and rebuilding of master and wheel hydraulic cylinders, an inside measuring kit is available consisting of a handle and a set of go, and no-go, gauges for determining the exact inside bore diameter of these cylinders.

Micrometers—inside, outside and depth —are needed for just about any major engine overhaul to accurately check bore, bearing diameters, and deck clearances. These will have to be purchased in sets, as no one tool will give the range of measurements needed for automotive work. Outside micrometers have only about 1 in. of range without special adapters, but some are available in sets that will handle everything from 1 to 4

1. Spark plug gapping tools should always feature an adjustment hook, round wire gauges and a fine tooth file. Forget tapping the side wire on the cement. Flat feeler gauges won't get an accurate reading.

2. Drill is perfect for chamfering oil holes or for removing flashing from the inside of a cylinder block.

3. Drill motors can power anything from bits to brushes. If you don't need 'em to cut some holes to mount a bracket, they'll come in handy for buffing out a lacquer paint job.

4. Impact wrenches are expensive, but are quick and efficient. Most amateurs rely upon electric models rather than the compressed air type. Sockets are 6-point types.

5. For anyone attempting to overhaul an engine, precision measuring devices such as inside, outside, and depth mikes are a must. Included in the precision toolbox should be a dial indicator, steel scale, and a vernier slide caliper.

6. The simple compression gauge or tester is used to measure how much chamber pressure engine can build. Pressure differential (from cylinder to cylinder), not total amount, is what's important . . . and so is how you hold the tester to the plug hole. The seal must be good or you'll receive a misleading reading.

7. No backyard tune-ups or engine timing should be attempted unless you have a strobe timing light.

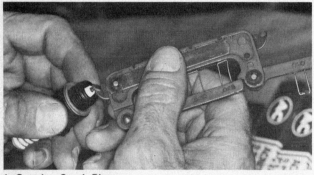

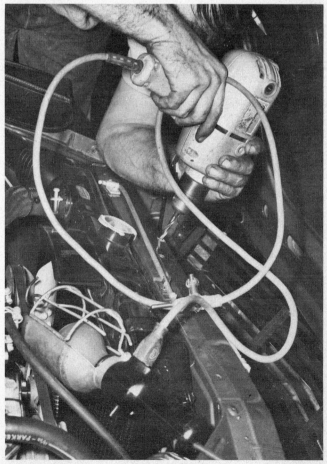

1. Gapping Spark Plugs

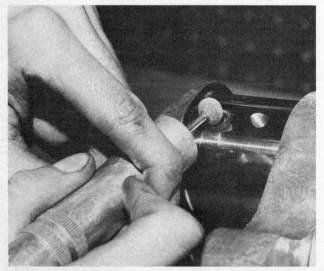

2. Chamfering Oil Holes

3. Drilling Holes

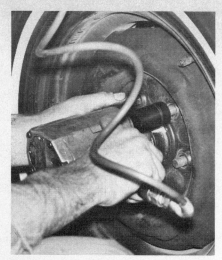

4. Removing Lug Nuts

5. Using Inside/Outside Mike

6. Testing Compression

ins. The same is true of inside micrometers and ones used for depth measurement. Learning how to read micrometers takes a bit of study so it is a good idea to become familiar in dealing with the .001-in. measurements before doing any serious work with them. Some micrometers have a built-in vernier so they can measure to tenths of thousandths. For quick measurements to thousandths, or even to tenths, a vernier caliper is handy to have.

Another measuring device is the brake drum and shoe gauge, which is used to detect both drum wear and diameter and to set up shoes on the backing plate. While this gauge is available from tool supply houses, most new car and brake repair shops will have it as a shop tool, not necessarily in the individual mechanic's kit. This is a modest cost tool that one should have for doing serious brake repair or overhaul.

There is a gauge or instrument for testing just about every component of an automobile. The list is long and mostly expensive: Automatic transmission oil pressure, vacuum, engine oil pressure, headlight candlepower, engine coolant temperature, fuel pressure, battery specific gravity, electrical resistance, voltage, current, engine speed, and on and on—an endless number of devices not including wheel alignment and balancing, that are available for automotive measuring, testing and repair work.

For serious engine tune-up and ignition work, the home mechanic's kit should include some kind of continuity tester for tracing out broken circuits, a voltmeter, and a power timing light. Simple volt/ohm ammeter and continuity testers can be purchased at radio supply houses, and many suppliers of automotive ignition testing equipment stock everything from simple meters to very sophisticated multiple units for checking everything electrical.

Continuity lights in the form of plastic-housed glow tubes with a probe and wire clip are modestly priced units that are worth the investment. One can make a simple test light by soldering a pair of wires to the proper contacts of a tail or parking light socket, terminating the loose ends to alligator clips or probes, and using a 12-volt bulb in the socket. This is an excellent light for setting ini-

7. Using Timing Light

tial spark timing by the "points-just-opening" method with the engine dead.

A strobe timing light is used for final ignition timing according to timing marks on the flywheel or vibration damper. They employ a flash or strobe tube that gets its trigger from the ignition high-voltage side. As the light flashes only on the high-voltage impulse, the timing marks apparently stand still while the engine is running, allowing an accurate visual setting of the distributor to the proper timing. One of these should be in every mechanic's tool kit for keeping the ignition in proper adjustment and diagnosing problems.

One of the handiest instruments for checking engine condition is the compression gauge. This comes in various forms, from the simplest one that is held in the spark plug hole while direct readings are noted on the scale, to the more expensive ones with flexible hose, screw-in spark plug fitting, and tell-tale needle that stays at the highest reading

until released. Both do a good job of reading the combustion chamber pressures; choice will depend on the size of your pocketbook.

Car clubs often find that pooling of funds allows the purchase of the more expensive instruments, justified by more use than the individual home mechanic would ever find practical unless he had unlimited funds. Some of the electrical analyzers are great time savers and allow more accurate adjustment of everything from dwell to fuel pump pressure.

One of the best ways to keep and protect a set of tools is to store them in a locked steel toolbox. Tools have a way of disappearing when left around loose, and a lock-type box of adequate size is a good investment. The choice is unlimited and goes all the way from a small kit to a large roll-away. Whatever the choice, anticipate that more tools will be added from time to time, so buy one larger than is needed at the moment and grow into it rather than out of it. ✦

Specifications--What They Mean

A specification can be anything from a description of the type of material used in upholstering fabrics to the amount of air pressure that goes in a tire. How you use specifications will depend to a great extent on the amount of training you have had in doing mechanical work, and also on your personality. If you feel that the men who designed and built the automobile in the first place were a bunch of stumblebums who didn't know what they were doing, then you probably will have very little respect for their specifications. A mechanic with that attitude is bound to have a lot of trouble with the cars he repairs. At the other extreme is the car repairman who feels that the Detroit engineers have set up the specifications as strict laws that cannot be violated in even the slightest degree. Strangely enough, the mechanic who has that attitude will also find repairing cars to be rather difficult.

The specifications were not laid down as the law of the automobile, but rather as guides to show the mechanic how the car was set up when it was brand new. A mechanic working in a new car dealer service department will follow the factory specifications as closely as possible, but when a car is 2 years old or 5 years old or 10 years old, it is not the same automobile that rolled off the end of the assembly line. The result is that a mechanic has to realize that a slight departure from the original factory specifications, based on the mechanic's own personal experience, may result in a better running automobile. Before you reach that point in experience, however, you must know how to read and understand the factory specs.

There are many types of specifications, and you'll find them published in a variety of formats. Probably the most general and yet the most familiar to the majority of car owners are those found in the Owner's Handbook. You may not have regarded such commonplace figures as tire inflation pressures, crankcase and cooling system capacities, etc. as factory specifications, but they are. So if the mere mention of the word "specifications" conjures up visions of incomprehensible data, set your mind at ease and follow along as we explore the world of specifications—where to find them and what to do once you've got them.

If you've done any work at all under the hood and your car is a recent model, you've probably noticed a label, sticker, or decal marked Vehicle Emission Control Information. While you might not have thought of it as such, this is really a basic spec chart complete with instructions on how to interpret and apply the information it contains. With nothing more than this chart and a few simple tools, you can keep your engine tuned to

1. Checking Valve Lash

2. Rod Side Clearance

1. Clearances can be quite important on stock engine setups; on high-performance machinery they are very critical. Here rocker arm adjustment is being checked for valve lash with feeler gauge and indicator dial.

2. Rod side clearance is checked on assembly in block. If it's too close, the rods should be switched about or replaced, or the sides must be ground sufficiently to fall within the recommended factory spec range.

3. Checking installed valve springs for equal height and pressure is an important step in setting up valve action for high-rpm operation.

4. Assembled inside mike has a 2.5 to 3.5-in. rod and .5-in. sleeve, making starting point 3.0 ins. Numbered lines on hub (1) are tenths; spaces between (2) are each .025-in. Numbers on thimble (3) are in thousandths of an inch (reading shows between .010-.011.). The total measurement indicated here is 3.260 ins.

5. Rod bore is measured with inside micrometer. Extension handle on this mike is just an easy way to hold it; it cannot be used to adjust the mike.

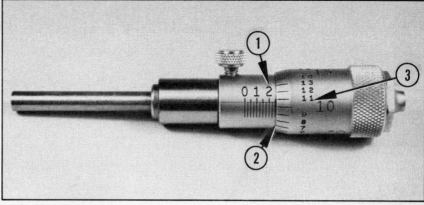

3. Checking Valve Spring Height

4. "Inside" Micrometer

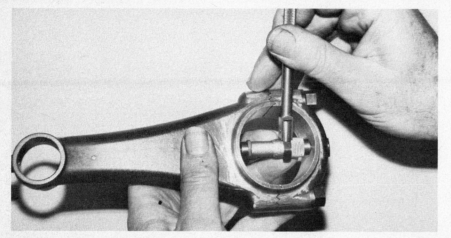

5. Measuring Rod Big End Bore

day's production which is in the thousands of units, and with hundreds of parts involved in each unit, the law of averages sees to it that there will be "tight" fits, "loose" fits and very occasionally, an "ideal" fit. This is the reason why one man's car will go a few miles faster and get a few more miles per gallon than the identical car belonging to his neighbor. It is also the reason why skilled racing mechanics can extract upwards of 600 hp from a "stock" engine that is rated at maybe 400 hp by the factory. They painstakingly "blueprint" every part, honing it to its precisely ideal tolerance—and the resulting collection of parts sings like no engine ever to leave the factories in Detroit.

SAMPLE ENGINE DATA

To give you an idea how to interpret specs, we have reprinted the accompanying chart verbatim from the 1973 Chevrolet factory shop manual. It shows engine data for a group of engines used in Chevrolet cars and trucks. Where an explanation seems necessary, the numbers alongside each item are keyed to the following text.

1) Horsepower and torque are measured by the factory under standardized conditions, and the figures "claimed" are those for the most favorable engine speed. A higher engine speed won't necessarily result in a higher horsepower or torque unless cam configuration and other components are altered. We say "claimed" because auto makers have in the past made free use of an "educated pencil" in assigning horsepower figures to their engines. In 1972, this situation was reversed, with the manufacturers using "net" figures that are decidedly on the pessimistic side to please the government safety bureaucrats and insurance companies.

2) Bore and stroke dimensions govern engine displacement. Usually you can overbore up to .030-in. without weakening the block structure, and it is common hot rod practice to "stroke" the engine by welding and regrinding the crankshaft connecting rod journals, and thus increase the distance traveled by the piston. Either or both of these procedures will increase the displacement and, thus, the power output.

3) The higher the compression ratio, the greater the pressure in the combustion chamber, and the greater the horse-

factory settings. But many specs are a good deal more exotic; they require that you have a knowledge of exactly where they can be located, as well as a deeper understanding of what makes your car tick.

SOURCES FOR SPECS

There are many sources for factory specifications. Independent companies produce repair manuals that have specs, and many parts companies give out booklets of specifications so that their parts will be installed correctly. The original specifications for all cars are printed by the car maker in what is called the "Shop Manual." Every year about the time that the new cars come out, a new "shop manual" is issued to be used any time that year's car is worked on.

The unfortunate thing about shop manuals is that, in most cases, they are printed before any of the new cars actually hit the street. The result is that there are many changes in specifications and repair procedures during the model year that do not appear in the shop manual. The manufacturer takes care of this—as far his own dealers and repair facilities are concerned—by issuing service bulletins on a regular basis.

Some of the manufacturers do not care who does the repairs on their cars, just so they are done correctly. They will send their service bulletins to any legitimate repair facility. Other manufacturers consider their service bulletins in the same light as top secret war communiques, and will not allow anyone out-

side of their own organizations to see them. This attitude works a definite hardship on the independent garage or service station who has new car customers. If the service bulletins were distributed to all repair outlets, it would be great for the trade, but what good would it do you as an individual car owner who wants to fix his car on a Saturday afternoon? Unfortunately there is no way at present for a car owner to obtain service bulletins, either for pay or for free. But you can buy all the service manuals that you want, even going back as far as 15 years.

If you are interested in factory service manuals, the address to write for them is usually in the back of the owner's manual that comes in the glove compartment of your car; or you can get the address from any dealer who sells the make of car you are interested in. Now let's take a look at what some of the specifications mean.

Dimensions are directly related to performance because of a compromise necessary in mass production known as tolerances. If every moving part had to perfectly fit its mating surface, the car makers wouldn't be able to produce 9 million cars a year. Therefore, tolerances are allowed which compensate for the imperfections inherent in both man and machine without seriously affecting the proper function of the car. For example, in a popular current V-8 engine, the maker specifies a tolerable variance of from .0007 to .0027-in. in the clearance between the connecting rod bearings and the crankshaft. In the course of a

Specifications

power output. Ratios over 8.5:1 usually require premium high-octane gasoline.

4) Firing order alone is not enough to enable you to run the wires from the distributor cap to the spark plugs correctly. You must also have the cylinder numbering, which is not given here. Sixes are numbered front to rear, consecutively. General Motors V-8's have the evens on the right and the odds on the left. Ford products have 1 to 4 on the right, and 5 to 8 on the left. Cylinder numbering is sometimes embossed on the intake manifold right above each cylinder.

5) Bore diameter on these engines varies about .003-in., but piston clearance in the bore is in most cases considerably less than that. (Pistons come in different sizes and are select-fitted to each bore.) Small shops do not have the luxury of an unlimited supply of different size pistons, so when they rebuild an engine they simply buy one set of pistons and bore each cylinder to fit a particular piston.

6) Throughout the chart, specs are listed as either "production" or "service." The "service" dimension is a wear limit. If it is exceeded, the part must be reconditioned or replaced.

7) Taper in the cylinder bore is extremely hard on the rings; it causes them to flex and wear out as the piston strokes up and down. Measuring taper on the thrust and relief sides of the bore is like splitting hairs. The relief sides of the bore are the front and rear, 90° from the thrust sides where the piston skirt slides. Excessive taper requires a cylinder rebore.

8) If piston clearance exceeds the service wear limit, the engine will have to be overhauled or rebuilt. There are several ways to get the piston clearance within limits. The old pistons can be knurled; new pistons can be fitted; or the cylinders can be bored to fit some new pistons.

9) Piston ring groove clearance is the difference between the vertical thickness of the ring and the vertical measurement of the groove. If the rings are too tight in the groove they will not be free to put pressure on the cylinder wall. If they're too loose, combustion pressure or oil will find its way around the back side of the ring, and the result will be lower performance. Ring gap is not critical, as shown by the great tolerance, but gaps too close may allow ring ends to butt, which can ruin the rings. Service wear limit is found by adding the figure shown to the production high limit, which in the case of groove clearance on the 307 2nd ring would be .0032 plus .001, for a total of .0042-in.

10) Clearance refers to clearance between the piston pin and the pin bosses. The interference fit specified in the rod means that the pin is larger than the hole in the rod by the dimension shown, which results in a press fit.

11) Main bearing journals are numbered from front to back. Note that there is about .001-in. tolerance on the journal size. A crank ground to the low end of the specs would have more clearance in the bearings, and would be a freer turn-

SPECIFICATIONS

VEHICLE IDENTIFICATION NUMBER LOCATION

Your vehicle identification number is stamped on a metal tab located on the driver's side of vehicle on the pillar post, visible through the windshield. This is the official number that is used for car title registration purposes.

VEHICLE SPECIFICATIONS

DIMENSIONS AND WEIGHT

Wheelbase	100.8 inches
Overall length	167.8 inches
Overall width	64.8 inches
Overall height	50.7 inches
Turning circle	34 ft.
Ground clearance	5.0 inches
Curb weight: 2000 CC Std. Transmission	2266 pounds
Auto. Transmission	2299 pounds
2600 CC Std. Transmission	2293 pounds
Auto. Transmission	2326 pounds

ENGINE SPECIFICATIONS

Refer to the "Emission System Warranty and Maintenance Schedules" Booklet for the Engine Specifications.

ENGINE LUBRICATION	2000 CC	2600 CC
Oil Pan Capacity—Without Filter	3.5 US Quarts	4.0 US Quarts
—With Filter	4.0 US Quarts	4.5 US Quarts
Oil Pressure	34 Min. psi @2000 RPM	40 Min. psi @ 2000 RPM
FUEL SYSTEM		
Tank Capacity	12 US Gallons	
Fuel Pump	Mechanical Diaphragm	
CARBURETOR		
Type	Weber — Two Venturi	
COOLING SYSTEM		
Type	Pressure Vented (13 psi)	
Thermostat	Wax Capsular Open at 185–192°F	Wax Capsular Open at 183–190°F
Capacity (with Heater)	6.5 US Quarts	8.2 Quarts (Std.) 8.4 Quarts (H.D.)
CLUTCH		
Type	Single Disc	
Diameter (inches)	8.5	9.5

1. Typical Manual Specs

ing crank. Worn cranks are customarily reground .010, .020, or .030-in. undersize, and used with thicker bearings.

12) Main bearing (and rod bearing) clearance is usually controlled by the diameter of the crank journals, because bearings usually come in one standard size. However, some manufacturers make bearings that vary by tenths of thousandths, allowing clearance to be controlled by select-fitting. Note the reduced clearance on the front main, and increased clearance on the rear. The front main has to be tighter or it may knock before oil pressure rises when the engine is started up, due to load of belt-driven accessories on the front pulley. Rear main has increased clearance for

1. Capri owner's manual contains general specs of concern to all drivers.

more oil flow, because it is heavily loaded by the power flow and needs oil.

13) "Crankpin" means the same as "rod journal." The same methods of obtaining clearance apply here as on main bearings.

14) Lobe lift is different from valve lift. Lobe lift can be measured on the cam with a micrometer. Valve lift is usually greater than lobe lift, because of rocker arm ratio.

15) Hydraulic lifters have an internal spring that takes up the play in the valve train when the valve is closed. "Zero lash" means that the adjusting screw in

VEHICLE SPECIFICATIONS (Cont'd)

MANUAL TRANSMISSION	2000 CC	2600 CC
Type		4 Speeds Forward One Reverse (Fully Synchronized in all Forward Gears).
Lubricant Capacity		2.8 US Pints
Lubricant		SAE 80 E.P.
Ratios (Overall)		First – 3.65
		Second – 1.97
		Third – 1.37
		Fourth – 1.00
		Reverse – 3.66
AUTOMATIC TRANSMISSION		
Type		C 4
Lubricant Capacity		14.80 US Pints
Lubricant		12.50 US Pints
REAR AXLE		
Type		Rigid Axle with Radius Arms
Ratios	3.44	3.22
Lubricant Capacity		2.32 US Pints
Lubricant		ESW-M2C105-B
STEERING GEAR		
Type		Rack and Pinion
Lubricant Capacity		0.25 US Pints
Lubricant		M2C-28B SAE 90
FRONT SUSPENSION		
Type		McPherson Strut
Toe in		0 to 1/4"
Track (inches) – Front		53.0
– Rear		52.0
REAR SUSPENSION		
Type		Semi Elliptic Leaf Springs with Radius Arms
BRAKES		
Dual Line System		Power Assisted
Front		Disc
Rear		Drum
Parking Brake		Mechanical (only rear)
Disc Diameter (inches)		9.62
Fluid		ESA-M6C 25–A
Rear Drum Diameter (inches)		9.00
WHEELS		
Type		5J x 13
TIRES		
Standard	165–SR x 13 Radial Ply	185–70 HRX x 13 Radial Ply
Optional	185–70 SR x 13 Radial Ply	– – – –

the rocker arm is turned down until the pushrod is just starting to compress the lifter spring. One turn additional puts the valve train within the lifter's operating range. If the rocker arm does not have an adjusting screw, this job must be done by changing to different length pushrods.

16) Face and seat angles are always measured from the horizontal. The increased angle on the seat insures that the upper edge of the seat will meet the valve with line contact, which has less tendency to leak than a seat that meets the valve squarely over its whole face. After a few miles, the valves pound in and seat over the whole face.

17) Wide valve seats cool the valve better, but have more tendency to leak. Narrow seats seal better, but they pound out easily. Seats are probably going to get wider in years to come, so they will live longer with unleaded gasoline.

18) Stem clearance is not critical, except that excessive clearance can allow too much oil to be sucked down the guides into the combustion chamber. Worn guides can be renewed several ways: They can be reamed out, which requires the use of valves with oversize stems; they can have bronze inserts installed and used with standard size valves; or, in some cases, the guides can be replaced.

19) Valve spring pressure is checked on a test fixture at the indicated length

in inches. A bathroom scale and a drill press work fine, too. Weak springs must be discarded. Note that the installed height is equal to the "spring closed" checking dimension. If installed height is too much, spring pressure will be low, and valves may leak and burn. Too little height increases spring pressure, and can result in a worn out cam lobe or a bent pushrod from coil bind. When seats and valves are ground, installed height increases, and must be brought back to specs with special washers installed between the spring and the head.

Next to a good engine tune-up, most cars on the road today could use a front-wheel alignment check. And you'd probably find about 50% of all those over one year old sadly lacking when compared to factory specifications. Front-wheel alignment is really a very simple matter, but the specialized equipment necessary to do the job properly is seldom found outside a repair shop. Yet a knowledge of what's involved can be of help to anyone who takes the time to work on his own car.

The three adjustments involved in wheel alignment are caster, camber, and toe. Caster is the tilt (front or back) of the top of the wheel spindle; positive caster is tilt to the rear, negative caster is tilt to the front. Camber is the amount of tilt at the top of the wheel; outward tilt is positive camber, inward tilt is negative camber. Toe is the difference between the measurement at the extreme front and extreme rear of the front wheels. If the front measurement exceeds that of the rear, it's called toe-out; when the rear exceeds the front, it's known as toe-in. The accompanying specifications provided the minimum and maximum allowable distances for 1972 Fords when checked under curb load conditions.

GEAR AND AXLE RATIOS

Normally, a customer has no choice in the gear ratios of an automatic transmission unless he has the unit rebuilt and "blueprinted" to his preferred specs by an independent specialist. A choice is sometimes offered in the lower gear ratios of 3- and 4-speed manual transmissions that can alter acceleration potential. If there is a pronounced spread between the lower ratios of a transmission, the unit is known as a "wide ratio," and is probably more suitable for normal driving. Conversely, a lesser spread is known as a "close ratio," and is the one to be preferred for road racing or performance cars. In any case, the final or "high" gear is always a 1:1 ratio except, of course, in the case of an overdrive-equipped transmission.

Practically all auto makers, on the other hand, offer a fairly wide choice of rear-end gears. These can range from as "high" as 2.5:1 to as "low" as 4.5:1 on modern cars. The terminology is admittedly confusing, but the word "high" as used here means a high car speed in relation to engine rpm, a combination that will give greater economy and possibly speed (depending upon engine size) but less acceleration potential. "Low" is the opposite condition. A practical gear for street use with a medium-sized V-8 engine is around 3.5:1, or for fast accel-

Specifications

eration 4.11:1. As the engine increases in displacement and, thus, torque output, gearing can drop to 2.5 or so and still produce equivalent acceleration. Also, other factors that must be considered in the choice of rear-end gears are the weight of the car and whether or not you plan to tow trailers. In general, the more load, the "lower" the gear required.

Another way to describe gearing is to use the word ratio. A "high" gear such as the 2.5 described above, would be called a "low-ratio" gear. If you had a set of 4.11's in the rear end, they could be called "high-ratio" gears or, if you like the other terminology, "low gears." Admittedly, it can be confusing, but in one case we are about the numerical value of the ratio, so the bigger the number, the higher the ratio, as with the 4.11's.

But in the other case we are describing the performance of the gears, which have lots of power at low speeds because they let the car get moving easier. So we call the set of 4.11 gears a low gear, and a 2.5 gear-set would be a high gear.

Every so often someone comes out with a new specification, or at least one that you never heard of before. A knowledge of basic specs will help, because the new dimension or tolerance can not really be much different from the basic specs you know so well, if you really know them.

SPECIFICATIONS—1971 CHEVROLET ENGINES

	GENERAL DATA:				In Line			V8		
	Type									
	Displacement (cu. in.)				250	292	307		350	402
1	Horsepower @ rpm				145 @ 4200	165 @ 4000	200 @ 4600	215 @ 4800	250 @ 4600	300 @ 4800
	Torque @ rpm				230 @ 1600	270 @ 1600	300 @ 2400	305 @ 2800	350 @ 3000	400 @ 3200
2	Bore				3-7/8		3-7/8		4	4-1/8
3	Stroke				3.53	4.12	3.25		3.48	3.76
	Compression Ratio				8.5:1	8.0:1	8.5:1		8.5:1	8.5:1
4	Firing Order				1 - 5 - 3 - 6 - 2 - 4		1 - 8 - 4 - 3 - 6 - 5 - 7 - 2			
	CYLINDER BORE:									
5	Diameter				3.8745 - 3.8775		3.8745 - 3.8775		3.9995 - 4.0025	4.1246 - 4.1274
6	Out of Round	Production			.0005 Max.		.001 Max.			
		Service			.002 Max.					
7	Taper	Production	Thrust Side		.0005 Max.				.001 Max.	
			Relief Side		.0005 Max.					
		Service			.005 Max.					
	PISTON:									
8	Clearance	Production			.0005 - .0015	.0025 - .0031	.0012 - .0018		.0007 - .0013	.0018 - .0026
		Service			.0025 Max.	.0045 Max.	.0032 Max.		.0027 Max.	.0045 Max.
	PISTON RING:									
9	COMPRESSION	Clearance Groove	Production	Top	.0012 - .0027	.0020 - .0040	.0012 - .0027		.0012 - .0032	.0017 - .0032
				2nd	.0012 - .0032		.0012 - .0032			
			Service		Hi Limit Production +.001					
		Gap	Production	Top			.010 - .020			
				2nd		.010 - .020			.013 - .025	.010 - .020
			Service		Hi Limit Production +.01					
	OIL	Groove Clearance	Production		.005 Max.	.005 - .0055	.005 Max.		.002 - .007	.0005 - .0065
			Service		Hi Limit Production +.001					
		Gap	Production		.015 - .055					.010 - .030
			Service		Hi Limit Production +.01					
	PISTON PIN:									
10	Diameter				.9270 - .9273				.9895 - .9898	
	Clearance	Production			.00015 - .00025				.00025 - .00035	
		Service			.001 (Max.)					
	Fit in Rod				.0008" - .0016 Interference					
	CRANKSHAFT:									
11	Main Journal	Diameter			All 2.2983 - 2.2993		#1-2-3-4 2.4484 - 2.4493			#1-2 2.7487 - 2.7496
							#5 2.4479 - 2.4488			#3-4 2.7481 - 2.7490
										#5 2.7473 - 2.7483
		Taper	Production		.0002 (Max.)					
			Service		.001 (Max.)					
		Out of Round	Production		.0002 (Max.)					
			Service		.001 (Max.)					
12	Main Bearing Clearance	Production			All .0003 – .0029	All .0008 – .0034	#1 .0008 - .0020			#1 .0007 - .0019
							#2-3-4 .0011 - .0023			#2-3-4 .0013 - .0025
							#5 .0017 - .0033			#5 .0019 - .0033
		Service			#1 - .002 (Max.) All Others .0035 (Max.)					
	Crankshaft End Play				.002 - .006					.006 - .010
13	Crank-pin	Diameter			1.999 - 1.2000	2.099 - 2.100	2.199 - 2.200			2.1985 - 2.1995
		Taper	Production		.0003 (Max.)					
			Service		.001 (Max.)					
		Out of Round	Production		.0002 (Max.)					
			Service		.001 (Max.)					
	Rod Bearing Clearance	Production			.0007 - .0027		.0013 - .0035			.0009 - .0025
		Service			.0035 (Max.)					
	Rod Side Clearance				.0009 - .0014		.008 - .014			.013 - .023
	CAMSHAFT:									
14	Lobe Lift ± .002"	Intake			.2217	.2315	.2600			.2343
		Exhaust			.2217	.2315	.2733			.2343
	Journal Diameter				1.8682 - 1.8692					1.9482 - 1.9492
	Camshaft Runout				.0015 Max.					
	VALVE SYSTEM:									
	Lifter				Hydraulic					
	Rocker Arm Ratio				1.75:1		1.50:1			1.70:1
15	Valve Lash	Intake			One Turn Down From Zero Lash					
		Exhaust								
16	Face Angle (Int. & Exh.)				45°					
	Seat Angle (Int. & Exh.)				46°					
	Seat Runout (Int. & Exh.)				.002 (Max.)					
17	Seat Width	Intake			1/32 - 1/16					
		Exhaust			1/16 - 3/32					
18	Stem Clearance	Production	Int.		.0010 - .0027					
			Exh.		.0015 - .0032		.0010 - .0027			.0012 - .0029
		Service			Hi Limit Production +.001 Intake - +.002 Exhaust					
19	Valve Spring (Outer)	Free Length			1.90		2.03			2.12
		Pressure lbs. @ in.	Closed		55-64 @ 1.66	85-93 @ 1.69	76-84 @ 1.70			69-81 @ 1.88
			Open		180-192 @ 1.27	174-184 @ 1.30	194-206 @ 1.25			228-252 @ 1.38
		Installed Height ± 1/32"			1-21/32	1-5/8	1-23/32			1-7/8
	Valve Spring (Inner)	Free Length			—					2.06
		Pressure lbs. @ in.	Closed		—					26-34 @ 1.78
			Open		—					81-99 @ 1.28
		Installed Height ± 1/32"								1-25/32
	Damper	Free Length			—		1.94			—
		Approx. # of Coils			—		4			—

TUNE-UP SPECIFICATIONS

ENGINE AND CODE (Code is on Oil Filler Pipe V-8)	IGNITION TIMING L-6 33° DWELL V-8 30° DWELL	SPARK PLUG TYPE & GAP	SOLENOID SCREW † (RPM)	SLOW IDLE CARBURETOR SCREW (RPM)▲	FAST IDLE RPM ▲	CARBURETOR IDENTIFICATION 7043	EMISSION CONTROL DEVICES	EGR VALVE MODEL	TUNE-UP LABEL CODE	SPARK DELAY DEVICE	DISTRIBUTOR MODEL	DISTRIBUTOR VACUUM MODEL	VACUUM ADVANCE @INCHES OF VACUUM	VACUUM AND MECHANICAL ADVANCE @DISTRIBUTOR RPM
250 CU. IN. 1 BBL. L-6 ENG. CODES (L-22) CCC, (CCD CALIF) M.T. CCA, (CCB CALIF) A.T. OMEGA	6° @ 700 / 6° @ 600	R46TS .035" GAP / .035" GAP R46TS	700 (N) / 600 (DR)	*450 (N) / *450 (PARK)	PRESET / PRESET	017 (MT) / 014 (A.T.)	C.E.C., C.C.S. P.C.V. A.I.R. E.G.R. / C.C.S. P.C.V.	7035171 / 7035169	WB	NO / NO	1110499	1973428	START 6-8 IN. HG. / 12" 14.5-15.5 IN. HG.	0° 930 RPM / 2° 1270 RPM / 14° 2300 RPM / 24° 4100 RPM
350 CU. IN. 2BBL. V-8 ENG. CODES (L-32 A.T.) QP, QQ, QS, QT OMEGA & CUTLASS	14° @ 1100	R46S .040" GAP	700 (DR)	550 (PARK)	900 (PARK)	•158 OMEGA •154 CUTLASS	C.C.S. E.G.R. P.C.V. / T.V.S. P.C.V.	7040497	OA	NO	1112226	1973468	START 10" 3.5-4.5 IN. HG. 12-13 IN. HG.	0-2° 400 RPM / 8-10° 1050 RPM / 14-16° 2000 RPM
350 CU. IN. 2BBL. V-8 ENG. CODES (L-33 A.T.) QN, QO 88	12° @ 1100	R46S .040" GAP	700 (DR)	550 (PARK)	900 (PARK)	•152	C.C.S. E.G.R. P.C.V. / T.V.S. P.C.V.	7040452	OB	NO	1112226	1973468	START 10" 3.5-4.5 IN. HG. 12-13 IN. HG.	0-2° 400 RPM / 8-10° 1050 RPM / 14-16° 2000 RPM
350 CU. IN. 4BBL. V-8 ENG. CODES (L-34 EXC. WGN. A.T.) QA, QB, QJ, QK-OMEGA & CUTLASS	12° @ 1100	R46S .040" GAP	650 (DR)	550 (PARK)	1000 (PARK)	•255 OMEGA •250 CUTLASS	C.C.S. E.G.R. P.C.V. / T.V.S. P.C.V.	7040452	OC	YES "V"	1112195	1973453	START 8" 5-7 IN. HG. 10-12 IN. HG.	0-2° 400 RPM / 8-10° 1050 RPM / 14-16° 2000 RPM
350 CU. IN. 4BBL. V-8 ENG. CODES (L-34 WGN. A.T.) QU, QV VISTA CRUISER	10° @ 1100	R46S .040" GAP	650 (DR)	550 (PARK)	1000 (PARK)	•256	C.C.S. E.G.R. P.C.V. / T.V.S. P.C.V.	7030963	OP	YES "V"	1112225	1973453	START 8 5-7 IN. HG. 10-12 IN. HG.	0-2° 380 RPM / 5-7° 550 RPM / 11-13° 1050 RPM / 17-19° 2000 RPM
350 CU. IN. 4BBL. V-8 ENG. CODES (L-34 M.T.) OMEGA QC, QD, QE, QL CUTLASS & V.C.	8° @ 1100	R45S .040" GAP	1100 (N)	650 (N)	1100 (N)	•255 OMEGA •257 CUTLASS	C.C.S. E.G.R. P.C.V. / T.V.S. P.C.V.	7040350 V.C. 7040528	OM	NO	1112222	1973453	START 8" 5-7 IN. HG. 10-12 IN. HG.	0-2° 485 RPM / 8-11° 1000 RPM / 14-16° 2000 RPM
455 CU. IN. 4BBL. V-8 ENG. CODES (L-75 M.T.) UD CUTLASS	10° @ 1100	R45S .040" GAP	1000 (N)	750 (N)	1100 (N)	•253	C.C.S. E.G.R. P.C.V. / T.V.S. P.C.V.	7040350	OJ	YES "V"	1112197	1973232	START 9" 7-9 IN. HG. 15-16.6 IN. HG.	0-2° 540 RPM / 5-7° 1000 RPM / 9-11° 1800 RPM
455 CU. IN. 4BBL. V-8 (L-74 & L-75) ENG. CODES UA, UB, US, UT (A.T.) CUTLASS, 88 & 98	8° @ 1100	R46S .040" GAP	650 (DR)	550 (PARK)	1000 (PARK)	•251	C.C.S. E.G.R. P.C.V. / T.V.S. P.C.V.	7040452	OD	YES "V"	1112197	1973232	START 9" 7-9 IN. HG. 15-16.6 IN. HG.	0-2° 540 RPM / 5-7° 1000 RPM / 9-11° 1800 RPM
455 CU. IN. 4BBL. V-8 (L-78 A.T.) ENG. CODES UU, UV TORONADO	8° @ 1100	R46S .040" GAP	650 (DR)	550 (PARK)	1000 (PARK)	•252	C.C.S. E.G.R. P.C.V. / T.V.S. P.C.V.	7040452	OS	YES "V"	1112198	1973466	START 9" 7-9 IN. HG. 12-14 IN. HG.	0-2° 575 RPM / 3.5-5.5° 1000 RPM / 7-9° 1700 RPM

C.E.C. = Combined Emission Control Valve
A.I.R. = Air Injection Reactor
E.G.R. = Exhaust Gas Recirculation
C.C.S. = Controlled Combustion System
T.V.S. = Thermal Vacuum Switch
P.C.V. = Positive Crankcase Ventilation

† Turn Idle Stop Solenoid In or Out To Adjust Slow Idle RPM (Solenoid Energized)
▲ Turn 1/8" Hex Screw To Adjust Low (Shutoff) Idle. (Solenoid De-Energized)
▲ With E.G.R. Vacuum Hose Removed and Plugged
V = Vacuum Device
• Solenoid De-Energized
*Choke Set At Index
*Choke Set One Notch Rich

FRONT OF ENGINE

FRONT OF ENGINE

VEHICLE EMISSION CONTROL INFORMATION

OP GM 301 350 CU. IN. 4 BBL. CARB.

OLDSMOBILE DIVISION • GENERAL MOTORS CORP.

MAKE ADJUSTMENTS WITH ENGINE AT NORMAL OPERATING TEMPERATURE, CHOKE OPEN AND AIR CONDITIONING OFF. PLUG DISCONNECTED VACUUM FITTINGS AND/OR HOSES. SET PARKING BRAKE AND BLOCK DRIVE WHEELS.

1. DISCONNECT AND PLUG CARB. HOSES FROM VAPOR CANISTER, E.G.R. VALVE AND DISTR. VACUUM UNIT.
2. SET DWELL. SET TIMING AT SPECIFIED RPM.
3. ADJUST SOLENOID (ENERGIZED) SCREW TO SPECIFIED RPM.
4. ADJUST CARBURETOR SPEED SCREW (SOLENOID DE-ENERGIZED) TO SPECIFIED RPM.
5. WITH TRANSMISSION IN PARK ADJUST FAST IDLE SCREW TO SPECIFIED RPM ON LOW STEP OF CAM (NO E.G.R.)
6. RECONNECT DISTR., CANISTER AND E.G.R. VALVE HOSES.

SEE OLDSMOBILE SERVICE MANUAL FOR ADDITIONAL INFORMATION
FUEL REQUIREMENTS—USE 91 OCTANE OR HIGHER
THIS LABEL USED WITH ENGINE CODE: QU , QV

C.C.S.—E.G.R. EXHAUST EMISSION CONTROL

DWELL	30°
TIMING (DEG. BTDC @ RPM)	10° @ 1100
SPARK PLUGS GAP	AC R 46 S1
SOLENOID SCREW (RPM)	650 (IN DRIVE)
CARBURETOR SCREW (RPM)	550 (IN PARK)
FAST IDLE SCREW (RPM)	1000 (IN PARK)
CHOKE SETTING	INDEX

TIMING MARK   FAST IDLE SCREW

IDLE MIXTURE PRESET—DO NOT REMOVE CAPS.
IF CARBURETOR IS REPAIRED AND IDLE EXCEEDS 1% CO, RESET IDLE TO .3% CO.
REMOVAL OF MIXTURE CAPS AND ALTERING TO OTHER THAN CO SETTING MAY VIOLATE FEDERAL AND/OR CALIFORNIA AND OTHER STATE LAWS.
THIS VEHICLE CONFORMS TO U.S. EPA AND WHERE APPLICABLE, CALIFORNIA REGULATIONS FOR 1973 MODEL YEAR NEW MOTOR VEHICLES.

BEFORE AFT

Part No. 41432I

Where to Get Parts

The buying of parts for an automobile is considerably different now than it was way back when. In the old days, mechanics used to fix things. Wages were very low—perhaps as low as $2 or $3 a day in some cases. From both a time and money standpoint, it was practical to remove a unit from a car, give it to a mechanic and let him spend several hours tearing it apart, replacing the small piece that had broken or worn out, and then reassembling the unit. With the rise in wages, to the point where shop time in some garages now costs as much as $15 an hour, it just isn't practical to pay a mechanic to fix anything. Now, most of the fixing is done on an assembly line in some factory. The repaired or rebuilt units are furnished to repair garages, and all the mechanic does is make a replacement.

In many cases, this replacement philosophy applies to new parts also. Assembly lines are so efficient nowadays that new parts can be built almost as cheaply as the rebuilder can renew an old part. The result is that there is a definite competition between new and rebuilt parts, with new parts frequently coming out the winner, because their cost is very close to that of a rebuilt item.

The replace-instead-of-repair situation can be exasperating to a competent home mechanic. He knows what part is worn out inside the unit he wants to fix, but he can't buy it at the parts house, and is therefore forced to buy the complete unit, spending much more money than he would have spent if he could obtain the individual parts. The replacement philosophy has gone so far that some units are not rebuildable under any circumstances. Most of the late fuel pumps, for example, are sealed. You can't even take them apart. When one goes bad, you throw it away and put on a new one. For that reason, we have not shown in this book how to rebuild certain parts such as a water pump, because we know that it is extremely difficult to find water pump rebuilding kits nowadays. You are forced to replace the worn-out pump with either a rebuilt or a new one.

We'll get into the advantages and disadvantages of new versus rebuilt parts a little later, but this list of rebuilt items in order of sales popularity will give you an idea of what commercial garages have found practical to replace as an assembly rather than overhaul themselves: generators, starters, brake shoes, fuel pumps, clutch pressure plates, clutch discs, starter drives, water pumps, carburetors, connecting rods, armatures, crankshafts, complete engines, solenoids, voltage regulators, power brake parts, oil pumps, brake cylinders, shock absorbers and transmissions. This order of popularity is an indication of both the frequency of failure and the degree of difficulty in making individual repairs. The latter is not so much a measure of complexity but the type of assembly required: e.g., a generator or alternator has many parts that are soldered or glued together and thus lends itself to production line rebuilding.

The main sources for parts are new-car dealers and automotive parts houses (jobbers). If you go to the dealer you will only be able to buy parts for his make of car, whereas the jobber has parts for all makes. However, there are parts called dealer items that have such a narrow application that the jobber doesn't carry them. They are available only from the dealer.

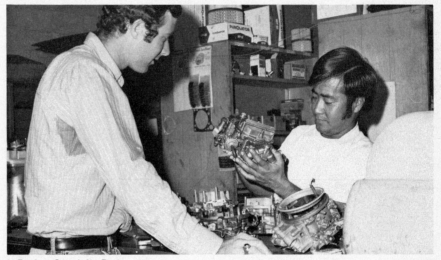

1. Buying Specialty Parts

2. Double-Checking New Parts

| | X 0 2 9 J 8 G 1 0 0 0 0 1 | | | | | |
	CHRYSLER CORPORATION					
1st Digit	**2nd Digit**	**3rd & 4th Digit**	**5th Digit**	**6th Digit**	**7th Digit**
Car Make	Model	Body Style	Engine Ident. Displacement	Year	Assembly Plant
L—Dart	L—Low	21—2 Door Sedan	A—170 Cu. In.	8-1968	A—Lynch Road
	H—High	23—2 Door Hardtop	B—225 Cu. In.		B—Hamtramck
W—Coronet	M—Medium	27—Convertible	C—Spec. (6 cyl.)		C—Jefferson
	P—Premium	29—Charger	D—273 Cu. In. Std.		D—Belvidere
X—Charger	K—Police	41—4 Door Sedan	F—318 Cu. In. Std.		E—Los Angeles
	T—Taxi	43—4 Door Hardtop	G—383 Cu. In. Std.		F—Newark
	S—Special	45—6 Pass. Sta. Wgn.	H—383 Cu. In. H.P.		G—St. Louis
	O—Super Stock	46—9 Pass. Sta. Wgn.	J—426 Cu. In. Hemi		R—Windsor
			K—440 Cu. In. Std.		
			L—440 Cu. In. H.P.		
			M—Spec. (8 cyl.)		
			P—340 Cu. In.		

3. Typical Identification Plate Code

4. Buying Original Equipment Parts

Besides dealers and jobbers, there are many other sources for parts. General automotive stores, hardware stores, department stores, wrecking yards, and mail order companies are all good sources, but none of them has the complete selection carried by the dealer or the jobber.

If a week or so's delay in obtaining the needed part won't inconvenience you, a very practical source for quality merchandise is to order it by mail or by phone from the nearest catalog order center operated by Sears, Ward or Spiegel. Sears has a special automotive catalog available free for the asking. Then, J. C. Whitney and Honest Charley have extensive catalogs listing replacement parts as well as hot rod items.

IDENTIFYING THE PART

If you bought your car new, you of course know its specifications in detail or at least they will be listed on your copy of the order form, if you still have

1. Specialty parts dealers can often provide items for specialized applications which may not be readily available from general parts houses, dealerships, mail order firms, etc. Selection, immediate availability and guarantee are prime considerations in selecting a parts source.

2. Precise identification of specific parts to fit particular system components is often best done by taking the old unit to the parts-buying source for a direct double-check.

3. Detailed description of a car model and its engine is necessary for identifying the specific item being sought. Chrysler Corp. identification plate code will list the car series, model, body style, engine, year of manufacture, assembly plant.

4. Original equipment replacement parts can be bought at independent parts stores as well as car dealers. They're often preferred by car owners who like "brand-name" reassurance.

5. New or rebuilt engines can be purchased through new car agencies and garages, and sometimes parts houses. Better companies will usually offer a warranty, something that's lacking in a wrecking yard "as is" deal.

5. Remanufactured Engines

it. Detailed information, however, will generally be missing in most used car transactions. You will know the model designation, year, the fact that it's a V-8 or not and whether or not it is equipped with an automatic transmission. Still, this is not enough information upon which to base the purchase of many parts. For example, a 361-in. V-8 was standard in Chrysler Newports of the early '60's, but a 383-in. V-8, identical in outward appearance and dimensions, was optional. Current MoPar twins include the 318- and 340-in. V-8's used in many Plymouth and Dodge models. Similar situations exist in GM divisions, FoMoCo and American Motors. Obviously, many internal parts are not interchangeable on these engines because the bore and stroke differ. These factors, in turn, may or may not dictate differences in fuel, ignition and drivetrain components. Lastly, since auto makers don't like to rely on a single source of supply for a component they may, like Ford, make some of their own carburetors and buy the rest of their requirements on the outside, in this case Holley. On a given model, these units are generally interchangeable as an assembly but their components are different and cannot be interchanged.

DEFINING YOUR CAR

All auto makers, past and present, have permanently affixed to the vehicle one or more sets of code numbers that together define exactly the specifications and major items of optional equipment that were included when it was built. Changes made by the original or subsequent owners will not be reflected in these codes. Sometimes decoding information is included in the owner's manual; in all cases it will be found in the first few pages of the applicable shop manual that is available for purchase at prices ranging from $5 to $10 directly from the factory. Information on how to order these manuals (they are available for older cars) is available at the new car dealer, and it's worth noting here that you can make the best use of the book you are now reading by supplementing it with the specific information contained in the shop manual for your make and model.

Coding systems used vary from make to make, and sometimes within a make,

from year to year. On some models the plate is located on the dash panel in the left corner where it is visible through the windshield. On others, you'll find it on the left front door post or on the firewall. On a 1968 Dodge with the number XO29J8G-100001, the first digit is a letter that defines the make, the letter "X" in this instance standing for Charger. The second digit indicates various degrees of luxury, performance or special usage. The sample shows "O" which stands for Super Stock, an important bit of information because that designation indicates the presence of special equipment packages such as heavy-duty suspension, cooling and powertrain systems. The table shows how this second letter is coded in no particular order of the alphabet.

Low through Premium ("L" and "P," respectively) are indications of trim luxury and the rest, special purpose designations. The third and fourth digits tell body style. Note that our sample Charger carries a different number than the standard 2-door hardtop. The fifth digit is a letter code for engine type and displacement, the "J" in our sample standing for the 426-in. Hemi. Next comes the number "8" to indicate the model year, 1968. Finally, the seventh digit shows the assembly location, an item unimportant to the owner except if our sample had shown "R" for Windsor, Ontario, Canada. Many of the auto makers have Canadian assembly plants, and a Canadian-built car may contain parts that vary in detail from their U.S. equivalents. However, Super Stock Chargers aren't assembled there so our completed identification plate reads "X O 29 J 8 G—100001." These last six numbers would indicate that you own the first 1968 Charger built. This sample identification, incidentally, would also be the one used for licensing purposes in most states.

Even with this relatively complete system used by Dodge, there is still quite a bit of information missing. Some of it will be found on an auxiliary body-number plate located, in the case of our sample Charger, on the left front wheel house. These codes, too, vary from make to make, but the system currently used by Dodge is indicated as an example.

If you know how to interpret the identification code for your car, you'll be

Where to Get Parts

able to order parts for it with accuracy. This assumes, of course, that you can accurately describe the function of the needed part to the counterman or better yet, bring the old one with you for positive identification.

PART NOMENCLATURE

The average modern car contains about 15,000 separate parts, and at a given time anywhere from 50% to 75% of these will have application on previous models, depending upon whether it is the policy of that auto maker to make frequent engineering and/or styling changes. Chevrolet, for example, revises its cars in more detail from year to year than does American Motors. There is also a considerable degree of joint usage between makes made by the same parent company.

Internal body parts, transmissions, differentials and suspension components are all widely shared. The parts with a specific application to a single line are usually identification features such as trim, external body panels, instruments and the like.

Ford, Chrysler and American Motors catalog and sell parts on a corporate basis. Thus, any part shared by Ford and Mercury would carry the same number at both dealerships, and the same would be true of Dodge and Chrysler-Plymouth. General Motors, however, is somewhat more complicated. Except for internal body components and in a few isolated instances, engines and transmissions, there is far less sharing between divisions. And when they do, the part numbers will be different. For example, both Buick and Oldsmobile have offered a Chevrolet-built L-6 engine in their low-line intermediates, but every part in this engine carries a Buick or Oldsmobile

part number as well as a Chevrolet number, depending upon the make of car in which it is installed. GM accessory divisions such as United-Delco and Harrison Radiator, on the other hand, carry their own specific part number, regardless of interchangeability.

There once was a day when a certain model Carter carburetor or Bower bearing would fit in a dozen different makes of cars. An interchange manual was worth its weight in diamonds, and "The Hollander" was the one to have.

Nowadays such easy interchangeability doesn't exist, but there is still enough similarity between parts that the Hollander manual is a good tool to own. It costs $43.50, covers U.S. cars from '61-'71, and is available from Hollander Publishing Co., 12320 Wayzata Blvd., Minnetonka, Minn. 55343. The Hollander's primary use is in wrecking yards, where a sale might be lost if the counterman didn't know that a certain Chevrolet part will also fit a Pontiac. For car nuts who just want to have a Hollander, the publisher has older editions for a lower price.

You can see now why you just can't go down to the dealer, much less the independent jobber, and ask for a "widget that fits on the whats-it" for your 1967 Chevy. You have to say "I need an automatic choke temperature sensing unit for the 4-bbl. Rochester on my 1967/SS-396 to replace the old one I have here that's stamped part No. 000001." The counterman will still consult one of his catalogs because he might have to say, "There's been a running change on that part. I'll give you part No. 000002 which will fit right in if you use this adapter No. 10000001, and you should have no more trouble." An independent jobber, selling non-official replacements, may or may not know of this change. Be as specific as you can to save both your time and that of the counterman.

WHERE TO BUY PARTS

As we have mentioned earlier, the main sources for automotive parts are the car dealer, the independent jobber, the automotive chain store, the mail order house and the wrecking yard. These are not listed in order of preference because there are advantages and disadvantages with each source.

No rule can be made in choosing between the car dealer or a jobber as a parts source. The car dealer is the only source for some parts. Jobbers and other outlets compete with the dealer in the marketplace. You should consider all outlets for parts and buy wherever you find satisfaction.

Of course, if you own a car that is no longer manufactured, like a Studebaker or Kaiser, the jobber and mail order house are your only sources for new parts. Many people think there is a law requiring auto companies to make parts available for a certain number of years after they discontinue a model or go out of business. There is no such law. The left-over parts are bought up by brokers strictly on the basis of how many Kaisers, Edsels, Studebakers or whatever are still on the road and as long as there is a demand, there will be a supply through jobber and mail order channels. Sometimes this demand causes a car to be in a sense, reborn. You can, for example, practically assemble a brand new Model "T" or "A" Ford from the catalogs of Sears or J. C. Whitney, though it's doubtful that any part would be available for these cars at a Ford dealership.

Chain stores like the Pep Boys, Western Auto, J. C. Penney or the auto departments at Sears and Ward retail stores generally limit their replacement parts stock to fast moving items like plugs, points, fan belts, perhaps a few varieties of voltage regulators and horn relays, and anything that has a universal fit like sealed-beam headlight units.

1. Parts at Swap Meet

Mail order, as we've said, takes a little time but is an entirely satisfactory way of buying parts. The Sears, Ward, Spiegel, J. C. Whitney and Honest Charley catalogs are amazingly complete; all of them stock parts for a wide variety of imported cars. A further advantage is that these firms "guarantee satisfaction or your money back," a protection that may or may not exist when dealing with a car dealer or jobber.

Address requests for automotive catalogs to:

Sears Roebuck and Co.
Local catalog order center

Montgomery Ward and Co.
Local catalog order center

Spiegel Inc.
Chicago, Illinois 60609

J. C. Whitney & Co.
1917 Archer Ave.
Chicago, Illinois 60616

Honest Charley Inc.
108 Honest St.
(P.O. Box 8535)
Chattanooga, Tenn. 37411

NEW VS. REBUILT PARTS

You can get into some heated arguments over which is better—a brand-new part or one that has been rebuilt or has been reconditioned. The quality of any automotive unit depends upon the inspection procedures that are supposed to eliminate all the faulty parts. There isn't a machine or a man that is perfect. No matter how hard a manufacturer or a rebuilder tries, a certain percentage of the parts he has on hand will be defective. Most of the defective parts will be eliminated by inspection, but some of them will definitely turn up in completely assembled units at the end of his assembly line. The manufacturer and rebuilder know this, so they perform tests on the completed units to weed out the bad apples. The big question is: Do they test every unit, 1 out of 10, or 1 out of 100, or none? There are some manufacturers who don't look at anything after it comes off the end of the line. They figure that if it's bad enough, the ultimate user—you and I—will bring it back to the store where he bought it, and either get his money back or get another part. Fortunately, there are not many rebuilders or manufacturers with that attitude. The only way you can protect yourself from such fast buck artists is by relying on

1. For that unusual part needed for a scratch-built model or a restoration job, a swap meet may very well turn up some hard-to-find items.

2. With the high degree of interchangeability built into many factory parts, it is often possible to substitute a heavy-duty part for a stock item when making repairs—if you know the correct part numbers. Shown here are three kinds of rods for big-block Chevy engines (from left): standard, high-performance, and "super" high-performance.

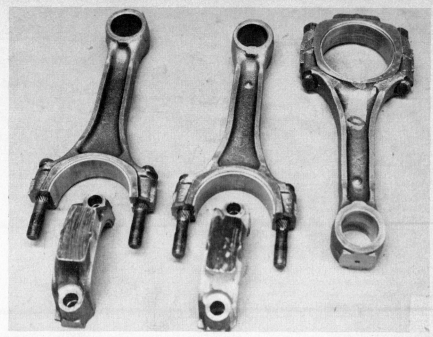

2. Different Types of Rods

your own experience and the experience of other people who have purchased parts. If a mechanic tells you that he has had bad luck with a certain brand of either new or rebuilt parts, then by all means stay away from that brand.

You should also listen to a mechanic's recommendation for good parts. Some shops have been using a certain line of new or rebuilt merchandise for many years with a very low comeback rate. Those are the parts that you should use on your car.

If there is no one from whom you can get advice, then the safest way to go is to use what are known as "original equipment" parts. The theory behind using original equipment parts is that if the car maker thought the parts were good enough for him, then they certainly should be good enough for you and me as replacements. Examples of original equipment parts would be Delco-Remy electric parts and units on General Motors cars, Autolite electrical units on Ford products, and Holley carburetor parts on Holley carburetors. In many cases, it is not necessary to go to the new car dealer to get your original equipment parts. Most of the parts manufacturers who supply the original equipment units to the car maker and his dealers also sell through independent parts stores. For example, all General Motors cars are equipped with AC fuel system parts, but you can buy AC units at almost any auto parts store.

THE ROLE OF THE WRECKING YARD

Members of the National Auto and Truck Wreckers Association (NATWA) don't like to be referred to as operators of junkyards. Their main function today is to supply the nation's steel mills with the 50% content of scrap steel needed to blend with the fresh pig iron in each charge of the furnace. In addition, about 70 lbs. of aluminum, 35 lbs. of copper, 30 lbs. of zinc, 20 lbs. of lead and 180

lbs. of rubber are similarly salvaged from each wreck, new or old, and ultimately reused.

All yard operators strip some fast-moving or valuable parts from a wreck and stock them for resale. Examples would be undamaged components from an air-conditioning system; batteries, tires and even engines and transmissions from late-model wrecks; and intact sheetmetal parts like hoods, trunk lids, bumpers and grilles. The biggest operators are tied together by a regional teletype system so that if one doesn't have the part, it can be determined in seconds whether anybody has it. In fact, if your needs are put on teletype and no one has the part, odds are that in a few days an accident will happen that will enable your order to be filled. A late-model wreck, is by no means "junk." It will return at least $500 if properly salvaged. Then, there are still countless rural yards that fill a cow pasture with derelict cars and let you prowl around until you find the part you want. These are self-service stores in the true sense because you do your own dismantling, but it's a fascinating way to spend a Saturday afternoon.

The yards that cater to retail customers will generally be quite obvious because there will be a building to house the binned and inventoried small parts and outdoor display racks for the larger items. You must remember, though, that while the part may look serviceable, there is no guarantee that it is, because the yard operator, with the sometime exception of complete engines, doesn't check their function. Therefore, if you wanted to replace a damaged radiator on your late-model car, go search the yards for a low-mileage identical model that's been totalled from the rear. For older cars, the salvage radiator may be no better than the one you want to replace. The bigger yards know what they can get for an item so there is no sense in haggling. In the do-it-yourself lots, though, start with an offer.

Accessory Fix-it Tips

A car that doesn't have any of its accessories working is not much of a car. When the windshield wipers, the air conditioning, the heater, horns, or the cigarette lighter don't work, you really only have part of an automobile. A little knowledge of the weak points in accessory units will give you a pretty good clue as to where to look and what is required to fix them. In most cases, you can even fix them yourself.

There's one accessory, however, that you should not attempt to fix, because it can be dangerous. That is the air-conditioning unit. The liquid contained in an air-conditioning system can cause severe frostbite if it splashes on your skin; and if it hits you in the eye, it can freeze the eyeball and cause blindness. You can see why we don't recommend that you play around with your air-conditioning system, but it would be a good idea if you knew how it worked and perhaps were able to do a certain amount of diagnosis that you could pass on to the air-conditioning serviceman you choose to do the repairs. So let's take a look at air conditioning first.

AIR CONDITIONING

Nobody really knows how an air condi-tioner works; it works according to laws of nature. Water boils at 212° F., just because it does. It's one of those things that you can't explain, you just have to accept. The theory of air conditioning is based on a similar law of nature. You must accept the fact that when a substance evaporates—which, of course, means changing from a liquid to a gaseous state—it absorbs heat. Another way of stating this is that it takes a certain amount of heat to make a substance go from the liquid to the gaseous state. Either way you look at it, whenever a liquid evaporates and becomes a gas, a certain amount of heat is necessary to do the job. Pour some water on your hand and your skin will feel cool. It's because the water evaporates into the air, and in so doing, absorbs heat from your hand. Do it with alcohol and you will find that your skin becomes quite a bit cooler than with water. It's because the alcohol absorbs more heat when changing from a liquid to a gas.

If the absorption of heat will change a substance from liquid to gas, then it's reasonable to assume that if the substance gives up heat, it will change from a gas back to a liquid. About this time you should be getting a glimmer of how the air-conditioning system in your car works. All you need is some kind of liquid that you can evaporate in the passenger compartment. The liquid will, of course, pick up heat when it evaporates, thus cooling the air around the passengers. Then if you take the gas that results and cool it enough by blowing air over it so that it condenses back to a liquid, you have completed a full air-conditioning cycle and you can start all over again with the same liquid, evaporating it in the passenger compartment to cool the air.

The marvelous liquid that is used in an air-conditioning system to do this terrific job is called Refrigerant 12 or R-12. You have probably heard it referred to as Freon. Strictly speaking, Freon is only the trade name of the Refrigerant 12 that is sold by DuPont.

If you have the cycle of evaporation and condensation firmly in your mind—that the R-12 absorbs heat when it evaporates and gives off heat when it condenses—then we can take a look at the mechanical components of the air-conditioning system and see how they make the R-12 do its work. The R-12 is circulated through the air-conditioning system by the compressor that is mounted on the engine and driven by a belt from the engine crankshaft. You won't

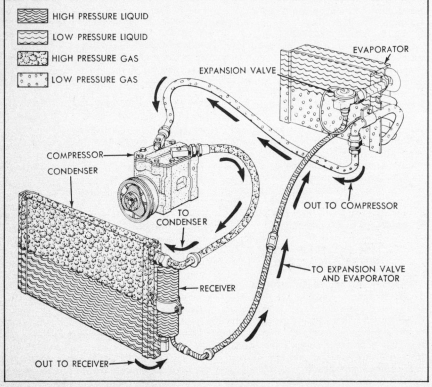

1. Typical Air-Conditioning System

HIGH PRESSURE LIQUID

LOW PRESSURE LIQUID

HIGH PRESSURE GAS

LOW PRESSURE GAS

EVAPORATOR

EXPANSION VALVE

COMPRESSOR

CONDENSER

TO CONDENSER

OUT TO COMPRESSOR

TO EXPANSION VALVE AND EVAPORATOR

RECEIVER

OUT TO RECEIVER

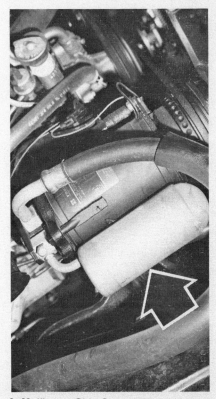

2. Muffler on Olds Compressor

have any trouble recognizing the compressor on an engine. Just lift the hood and look for the biggest and ugliest hunk of iron that you can find.

The easiest way to understand the compressor is to consider it nothing more or less than a simple pump. From the compressor, the R-12 is pumped to the condenser, which is usually mounted in front of the radiator. From the condenser, the R-12 goes to the receiver-dryer, then to the expansion valve which controls the flow, then to the evaporator and back to the compressor. The evaporator is in the passenger compartment, of course, because that is where we want the R-12 to absorb heat when it evaporates. The condenser is out in front of the radiator in the main airflow, because we want it in the coolest place we can find, so that the R-12 can get rid of the heat.

When the R-12 comes out of the evaporator, it is a gas and it goes from there directly to the compressor. Therefore, the compressor is pumping gas only. It compresses the gas and forces it into the condenser, where the gas gives up heat to the air that is flowing through the

1. The refrigerant, called R-12, in a typical air-conditioning system is constantly changing from a liquid to a gas and back again under conditions of high and low pressure.

2. The large silver canister beside the compressor on this '72 Olds is a muffler. It helps cut down noises from the compressor and also helps minimize line vibrations.

3. Old-style GM compressor, with the piston rods connecting the socket plate to the pistons. Later models have longer pistons, without rods.

condenser fins. With this release of heat, the gas condenses to a liquid and flows to the receiver-dryer, the expansion valve, and into the evaporator again.

The expansion valve is necessary because there must be some way of controlling the flow of liquid into the evaporator. Without the control, liquid R-12 could flow through the evaporator faster than it could change from a liquid to a gas. The expansion valve controls the flow by sensing the temperature of the R-12 as it leaves the evaporator. A sensing bulb, connected to the expansion valve with a capillary tube, tells the expansion valve when to open and when to close. If the gas flowing out of the evaporator coil is too hot, the expansion valve will open and allow more R-12 to come in. If the gas is too cold, it means that the R-12 is flowing through so fast that it can't pick up the heat. In that case, the expansion valve cuts down the rate of flow.

If the expansion valve goes bad and allows liquid R-12 to flow out of the evaporator and get into the compressor, it can really ruin things. A liquid is not compressible, but the compressor does not know this and will try to compress it anyway. The result can be a mess and very expensive to fix.

When the expansion valve cuts down on the flow of liquid R-12, there has to be some place for the liquid to go, because the compressor is pumping continuously. This is where the receiver-dryer comes in. It is mounted between the condenser and the expansion valve. The receiver-dryer is a small tank with an inlet at the top and the outlet attached to a dip tube that goes to the bottom. When the expansion valve allows a lot of R-12 to pass, the level of liquid R-12 in the receiver-dryer goes down. The space

that was taken up by the liquid is now filled with gas. This situation occurs because the condenser cannot condense the gas into a liquid fast enough when the flow is too great.

The receiver-dryer takes care of the situation very well, however. When the expansion valve slows down the flow, the condenser will do its job better, and the gas in the receiver-dryer will be displaced by liquid R-12.

The basic air-conditioning system is really very simple. The controls that are added to the basic system to make it work better are where we run into some complication. Our air-conditioning units today use a clutch on the compressor pulley to turn the compressor on and off. The belt from the engine drives the pulley at all times, but the clutch is magnetically actuated so that it can engage or disengage the pulley from the compressor shaft. Occasionally the clutch plate will develop slippage—it moves into position when actuated and engages the pulley, but the pulley cannot drive it.

Some air-conditioning units use what is known as the clutch cycling method to control temperature. If the temperature gets too cold, they disengage the magnetic clutch so that the compressor shuts down. Of course, this stops the flow of R-12 so that nothing happens anymore. Other manufacturers leave the compressor clutch engaged anytime the air-conditioning unit is on. They control the flow of R-12 with additional valves that sense temperature and allow the R-12 to double back from the pressure to the suction side of the compressor.

The situation really gets complicated when the heater is hooked to the system for completely automatic temperature control. Those units will turn either the heater or air conditioner on or off when-

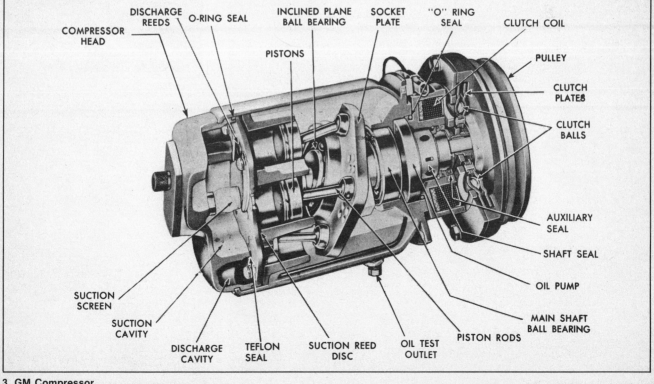

3. GM Compressor

Accessory Fix-it Tips

ever necessary to control the temperature in the car without any need for the driver to do anything except set the temperature he wants to maintain.

In checking out an air-conditioning system, the first thing to do is to have the engine running and observe the compressor while someone inside the car turns the air conditioner on and off. You should be able to see the compressor engage and disengage the pulley from the compressor shaft. If the compressor is working, look for the sight glass which is either on top of the receiver-dryer or in the line leading to it. The sight glass will probably be so covered with dust and dirt that you can't see anything. Wipe it off and observe the flow of liquid refrigerant.

Don't worry about any bubbles that appear when the compressor is first started; they should go away as the system gets operating. In fact, bubbles in the sight glass do not always indicate a low refrigerant level in the system. If the system is at a control point, bubbles may appear even when it's fully charged. A certain amount of foaming is also normal if the outside air temperature is 70°F or below. But if you do see bubbles in the sight glass, and they continue after the system has been in operation for several minutes, head for an air-conditioner service outlet and have it checked out—odds are that you will need an R-12 recharge and perhaps even repairs for minor leaks.

A system that is low on refrigerant does not necessarily mean that a leak has to be fixed somewhere. If you have to have the system charged once every five years, then it would be silly to look for such a minor leak. However, if every three months the system is bad because the refrigerant is leaking out, then you had better get your serviceman to find the leak or you might as well plan on doing a lot of recharging. Sometimes, the system works no better after servicing. In this case, it's likely that dirt, air, or moisture were allowed to get into the lines. As efficient air conditioner operation depends upon the pressure/temperature relationship of pure R-12, any contamination introduced alters this relationship and the system cannot function properly.

The electrical part of the air-conditioning system is the easiest to fix. If you don't get any air coming through the evaporator, look for a blower fuse that is burned out. It could even be a bad blower switch. If the compressor is not working, check for a blown fuse near the compressor on top of the engine. A check of a wiring diagram for your air-conditioning system will help you to locate fuses. The wiring diagram can be found in the shop manual for your car.

Many times a case of low cooling is not the fault of the air conditioner at all. Most cars have many air ducts or places where outside air can leak in. A leak in any location will allow hot outside air to enter, so that no matter how hard the air conditioner works, it can't keep up. To find leaks, drive at freeway speeds and have a friend put his hand in front of all the ducts and possible leaks. Fixing the leaks with tape is no problem, once you have located them.

CLOCK

Practically all modern automobile clocks are of the electrically wound, mechanical type. Late models are equipped with an adjustment feature that speeds up or slows down the clock whenever the time is reset by hand. Earlier models have an adjustment lever which can be moved slightly in the direction of "S" or "F". After a few such adjustments the clock should maintain reasonably accurate time.

Automotive clocks have been unfairly accused of being the most unreliable part of the car. We say "unfairly" because while no one seems to question the wisdom of taking his wristwatch to the jeweler once a year for a routine cleaning, equivalent care is rarely given the clock in a car. The lubricant in the mechanism has the same tendency to form gum after long periods, and the unit is subjected to road shocks and extremes of temperature. Thus, the automobile clock should be given routine service like any other timepiece.

The clock is always connected to the "hot" side of the ignition switch so that there is a current source for the winding mechanism whether the car is in use or not. If the unit is remote from the instrument cluster, there will be another wire leading from the illuminating bulb in the clock to the main light switch. Both of these circuits are grounded through the screws attaching the clock case to the

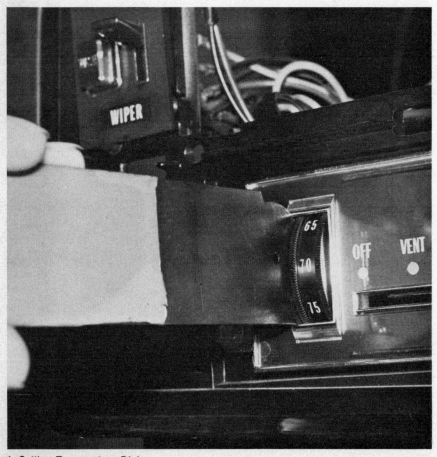

1. Setting Temperature Dial

2. Ford Sight Glass

3. Dust Cap on Plymouth Sight Glass

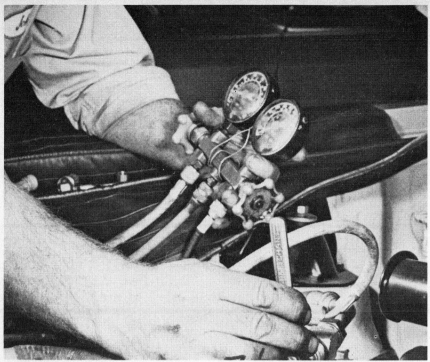

4. Charging the System

5. Printed Circuit Switch

1. *Setting the temperature control dial on a GM Climate Control is done with a special tool that holds the shaft while you turn the dial.*

2. *Ford sight glass is in the line, instead of being on top of the dryer-receiver. A continuous stream of bubbles in the sight glass indicates the system needs a charge.*

3. *The sight glass on most cars gets covered with dirt in time, so you'll have to clean it off to check for bubbles in the system. This Plymouth, though, has a dust cap.*

4. *Your air-conditioning system can be recharged at any garage that does a.c. work. A checkout of the system and an R-12 recharge costs $10-$15.*

5. *Late-model Buicks have a printed circuit switch, controlled by a vacuum diaphragm working against a long spring (arrow).*

panel so if the clock is inoperative, the tightness of these screws is the first item to check. The clock may be removed for repairs by unfastening these screws and the connecting wires. If the clock is part of the instrument cluster itself, the entire cluster must usually be removed to gain access to the clock. Some of the more modern clusters have printed or "bread board" circuitry, and the electrical connections are automatically made when the clock is positioned correctly in its mounting.

Generally speaking, two things can go wrong with an automotive clock. Either the clock movement stops operating, or the winding mechanism gets gummed up so that it doesn't work and blows a fuse. When you put a new fuse in, it will blow immediately. This is usually caused by a lack of lubrication or a gumming of the old lubrication in the winding mechanism. To fix the winding mechanism you will have to take the clock housing

itself apart, but it is not necessary to do anything to the works. A little oil in the right spot, which is obvious on inspection, and you will eliminate the fuse blowing. If it turns out that the clock problem is in the works itself, take it to a watchmaker so you can get professional repairs.

AUTOMATIC SPEED CONTROL

In a typical system, the desired speed is dialed on a gauge, sometimes incorporated in the speedometer. When the driver wishes this speed to be automatically maintained, he pushes the "speed set" button located in the tip of the turn indicator control on some cars. The unit will maintain this speed regardless of terrain, adding to or cutting back on the throttle opening automatically as is required. However, it has no way of telling that you are bearing down on a slow truck or coming up on an intersection. This information you feed into it by stepping lightly or otherwise on the brake. This action, sensed by an electro-vacuum switch in the system, deactivates the control until such time as you twirl the "resume-speed" switch.

Some older systems do not have the "resume-speed" switch. These return the car to automatic control as soon as the driver brings the vehicle back to the pre-selected speed. The tell-tale sign that the control has taken over is a pronounced stiffening of the accelerator pedal. You can override this to go faster, though the pressure on the pedal required is uncomfortable for any period longer than passing another car, but you cannot override it to go slower unless you de-activate the system with the brake.

Due to the safety hazard that could be created by any error in the adjustment or repair of a component in an automatic speed control system, it is recommended that this system be serviced only by a factory-trained mechanic.

AUTOMATIC HEADLIGHT DIMMERS

Headlight dimmers used to be very obvious. The photocell setup was on the top of the dash behind the windshield and looked very much like a gunsight or aiming device for the car. Late models all have the photo tube mounted in the grille or leading edge of the fender. It's not as prominent in that position but it is much more susceptible to dust and road grime. Many problems with the headlight dimmer can be solved simply by wiping off the front of the photocell.

Some cars have an on-off control in the headlight switch but in most models the only control is the foot-operated dimmer switch. One position of the dimmer switch puts the headlight control on automatic. The other position will keep the headlights on low beam at all times. There is a third position built into the foot switch which allows the driver to override the control and obtain high beam in bright areas or during daylight. This third position is activated by depressing the foot switch just until resistance is felt. When the driver takes his foot off

Accessory Fix-it Tips

the switch, the headlights will go back to low beam.

The system consists of a photo-electric cell and amplifier, usually housed as one unit on top of the instrument panel or on the left front fender; a power relay; a manual override foot switch to replace the conventional dimmer; and the vernier switch that lets the driver adjust sensitivity within the limits of the basic factory-set calibration. Horizontal aim on most dash-mounted models may be adjusted by turning the pivot pin accessible on the outside of the case. The unit should be aimed as parallel as is visually possible to the centerline of the car. Vertical aiming requires removal of the case, which on some models will expose a bubble-type leveling gauge built into the sensing unit. While aiming vertically, the car must be on an absolutely level surface, the tires inflated properly and no load other than a half tank of gas.

HEATER/DEFROSTER

Basic differences in the design of relatively modern heaters and their associated defroster units are limited to the point of air intake and whether the various controls are actuated mechanically or by vacuum. All except those used on air-cooled cars utilize a core (basically a miniature radiator) to extract heat from the engine coolant and a fan to distribute the heated air through ducts. The most desirable but more expensive location for the fresh-air inlet is in the top surface of the cowl just forward of the windshield. The alternate location just behind the right side of the grille is bad in heavy traffic because it picks up carbon monoxide and other noxious fumes from the car ahead. Though more expensive, vacuum-actuated controls are preferable to mechanical because their

1. Getting at the clock's attaching screws will probably be the hardest part of removing your clock. On this late Chrysler, like most cars, the time spindle comes out the front, while the clock comes out from the back of the instrument panel.

2. Repair or replacement of most clocks on late-model cars requires that you pull the entire dash. To replace this '70 Buick clock unit, many dealers will charge the equivalent of 4 hrs. labor. For '73 Buick has gone back to the front-mounted clock removed by prying loose the trim panel that surrounds it.

3. Check your factory service manual before attempting this, but on older cars the clock's attaching screws often are exposed at the front of the dash once the dash trim is removed.

4. Cars with sporty interiors like Mustang and Cougar often have the clock mounted down on the console, which makes getting at the clock a little easier than working behind a cramped dashboard.

5. The brake switch and vacuum lines are important parts in an automatic speed control system. Malfunctions in these components can cause a runaway!

1. Typical Rear-Mounted Clock

2. '70 Buick Clock Unit

3. Front-Mounted Clock

action is more precise and there is considerably less linkage to get out of adjustment.

HEATER SERVICING

Servicing any of the more modern heater/defroster designs is one of the meanest jobs (perhaps second only to windshield wiper linkage) on the car, helped in only a few rare instances where the blower motor and fan are accessible through the engine side of the cowl. Fortunately, very little will go wrong with the heater/defroster system.

There are two ways of controlling the heat: with a water valve or air doors. A water valve usually has a thermostat built into it. When you move the control valve to "Hot," you are doing nothing more than turning up the thermostat. In the air-door system, water flows through the heater core at all times, and the doors direct the air either through or around the heater, or both, in varying

degrees. There is usually no thermostat in this system. You set the doors where you want them to get the right amount of heat.

Assuming the blower motor is working, heater malfunctions generally fall into these categories: 1) no heat, 2) heat all the time, and 3) not enough heat. Let's deal with the latter symptom first because it is frequently caused by malfunction outside of the system or even unfamiliarity on the part of the operator. Cable-actuated heating systems are found on most compact and intermediate-size cars. The somewhat more elaborate vacuum-actuated system is used on more expensive cars.

In the cable-controlled model, a lever control actuates the air door in the ductwork to direct the airflow almost entirely to the interior of the car or almost entirely to the defroster outlets. The position marked "Heat" usually routes 80% of the heated air to the interior and 20% to the defroster outlets. Another lever controls the degree of heat, from none to maximum, by actuating another door in the ductwork which determines how much of the incoming air is routed through the heater coil. A multi-position switch determines the speed of the fan. The fan is necessary in traffic but at highway speeds there is a ram effect from the incoming air and operation of the fan is no longer necessary.

Thus, the basics in operating this type of heater are deciding how you want to divide the incoming air, how hot it should be, and whether or not it needs a boost from the fan. Fresh-air ventilation is handled manually on either side, usually by direct controls mounted in the kickpads or under each side of the instrument panel. These outlets should not be used when heated air is desired. As to windows, you have to experiment with them or consult the operator's manual.

The vacuum control system works the same way except that you can't alter the heater-to-defroster airflow ratio of 80-20 or vice versa. The fresh-air vents are controlled by pushbutton and in most cases only one button may be operational at a time. The heat control and fanspeed selector are common to both systems. If pushbuttons are not present, check whether your system is vacuum or mechanical by looking for a vacuum line leading from the intake manifold to the general area of the heater. Make sure this line is free of cracks and securely seated on its nipples at both ends.

If it's not operation of the controls that is causing the problem, it may be the thermostat or water pump in the cooling system. A thermostat stuck open will result in little heat from the heating system and little heat in the engine. Double-check this, plus your knowledge of the system's operational controls, before troubleshooting.

If the vacuum or mechanical valve that controls the flow of coolant through the heater coil is sticking in a partial or fully open position, the symptom is a constant flow of heat from the heater outlets. Conversely, if it is stuck closed, no heat can be obtained. A malfunction of the mechanical type of valve will almost always evidence itself in the form of stiff,

non-positive control operation. The operation of a vacuum valve is generally audible. You can turn off the engine to check its operation because there should be enough vacuum in reserve for one cycle. If you don't hear it click into position, suspect the valve. If the air-door valve is sticking open, there will be a flow of cold air from the heater or defroster outlets when the heater is turned off. If it is sticking in a partially or fully closed position, little or no heat will result. Symptoms of these valves sticking are the same as described above for both types of controls.

Unfortunately, replacement of either valve usually requires removal and disas-

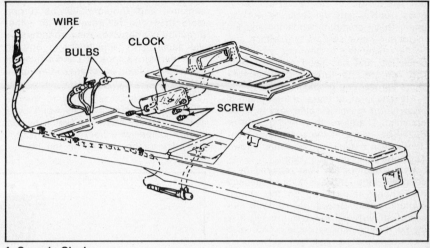

4. Console Clock

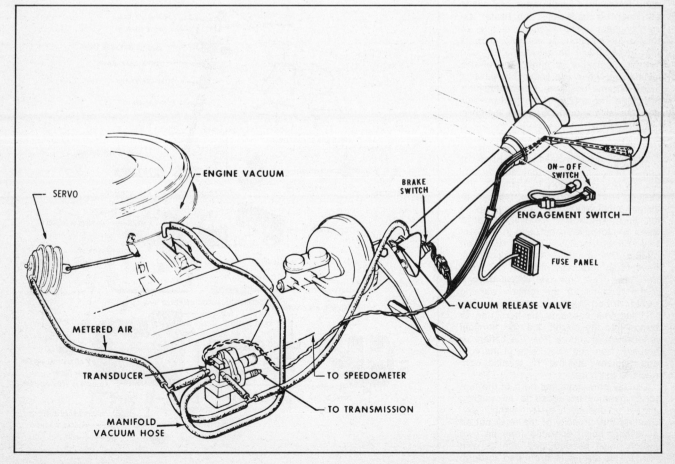

5. Oldsmobile Cruise Control

Accessory Fix-it Tips

sembly of the entire heater. Except for noting that the engine coolant should first be drained below the level of the heater, it is impractical to give step-by-step procedures for removal of the heater due to the fact that the design for each make and model of car is different. You must first remove obvious obstructions such as the radio (see section in this chapter) and glove compartment box. Wires and cable leading to the system should be disconnected, and also the hoses at their attaching point on the engine side of the cowl. Note that in addition to the power lead to the fan, there will also be a separate wire to ground the fan motor to the car structure. A good trouble light will facilitate working under these cramped conditions and aid in locating the screws that attach the heater assembly to the car structure. Once the unit has been removed from the vehicle, its further disassembly should present no problem.

Prevention of air leaks in the system is important if maximum efficiency is to be obtained. Therefore, there will be one or more sequences in the assembly procedure where a caulking compound known as "body seal" must be used.

Heater motors are best repaired by a specialty shop, and a leaking or blocked core should be replaced. So, too, should malfunctioning vacuum valves. With mechanical valves, the trouble usually stems from a kinked cable which also must be replaced. Attempts to "unkink" these are usually unsuccessful. Adjustment is provided at the attaching points and may be made after the heater assembly has been installed. A rule of thumb for mechanical control action is that there should be between 1/16- and 1/8-in. clearance at either end of the lever travel when the applicable valve is in its extreme positions. When attaching the cable, the setting of the control lever and the valve should, of course, match.

HORNS

The horn system on a car consists of one or more horns, a relay and an actuating ring or button to complete the circuit. The function of the relay is to deliver a full ration of electric energy to the horn; without it, excessively large wires would have to be used in the system. All horn relays, except those on 1968 or later model General Motors cars, have three terminals marked "S," "B," and "H." The new GM relays have a fourth terminal for the ignition warning buzzer incorporated in the relay. The "S" terminal connects the horn ring or button into the circuit; the "B" terminal is the current source from the battery or actually, from the "hot" side of the voltage regulator; and the "H" terminal connects to the horn.

Usually one additional horn of the factory type may be added to an existing single- or dual-horn system without exceeding the capacity of the relay but an accessory horn, operated from its own switch, must be equipped with its own relay. The circuit is grounded through the horn mountings and at the steering

wheel column. When the horn button or ring is pushed, it grounds or completes the circuit, the electromagnet in the relay is energized and makes contact, and the horns blow. When the circuit is not energized, a spring on the electromagnet keeps the contact open.

A horn with a harsh or tinny sound may only need adjustment. The method of adjustment varies by make. In the Sparton, Autolite and Prestolite horns used on Ford, American Motors and Chrysler cars, the adjusting screw or nut should be turned counterclockwise until no tone is heard. Then the adjustment is turned clockwise, ¼-turn at a time, until the desired mellow sound is achieved. In the Delco-Remy horns used on General Motors cars, the adjusting screw is more sensitive and should never be turned more than one full revolution in either direction. Otherwise, the procedure is the same. This adjustment is only to clear the horn's tone; it cannot raise or lower the pitch or change the basic note.

The horn circuit is simple to troubleshoot. If one or both horns won't blow, first bypass the relay and switch by running a jumper wire from the "B" post in the relay to the terminal in the horn. If

the horn then blows, the trouble lies in the relay or switch. If the horn doesn't blow, try tapping it—dirt may have lodged in the contact. If it blows only when tapped, it may be badly out of adjustment and the procedures described above should be followed.

On older cars, the no-blow problem is usually caused by a bad ground from rust under the horn mounting. Cleaning the rust away until you get a bright metal mounting won't always cure it, either, because the fender panel that the horn is mounted to might have its own bad ground from rust. A quick way to find out if the horn is any good at all is to run a ground wire from the body of the horn back to the ground battery post. If the horn works, you know you have a ground problem and some cleanup work to do.

A faulty horn is easier to replace than to repair, but before this, isolate the relay from the switch. Connect the jumper wire from the "B" terminal to the "H" terminal. If the horn blows, the relay is defective and should be replaced. To check the switch on the steering wheel with a relay that is known to be functioning, run the jumper wire from the "S" terminal to ground. If the horns blow, the

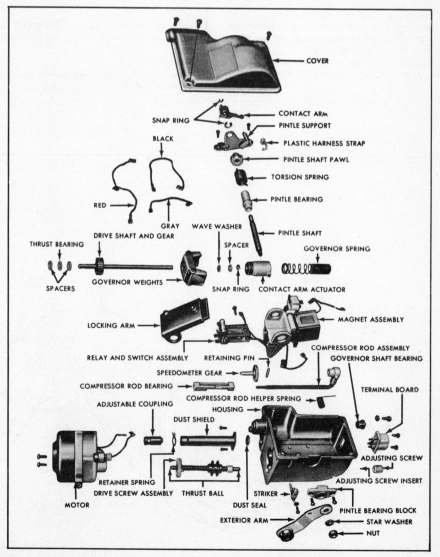

1. Speed Control Servo Unit

1. *We doubt you'll ever take one apart, but this shows how control is designed. This is a late GM type. Note governor weights (center) that maintain throttle opening once the system has been set.*

2. *Older GM system had phototube mounted above dash like gunsight.*

3. *Later GM models mount the tube behind the grille. The system often is combined with sentinel system that turns the headlights off.*

2. Early-Model Headlight Dimmer

switch should be checked for dirt or faulty connections at the horn ring. Most rings may be removed by turning the decorative center plate to the left and removing it. This exposes the attaching screws for the ring which in turn may be removed for access to the switch. Switches, also, are easier to replace than repair.

ACCESSORY HORNS

There is a wide variety of accessory horns on the market, ranging from genuine, truck-type units actuated by compressed air to novelties that imitate such sounds as Bermuda bells and a mustang's whinny. The true compressed-air installation is relatively expensive as it requires a belt-driven compressor, smaller but similar to the ones used in air-conditioning systems. Somewhat cheaper are the electrically actuated compressors (or vacuum pumps, depending on the system), but some are a little short on power and consequently the note may be a rather poor imitation of the real thing. Still other accessory installations are operated by cylinders of compressed gas which must be replaced periodically. The latter two types are relatively easy to install as the system is completely sepa-

rate from the standard factory installation. Mail order houses like J. C. Whitney and Vilem B. Haan list all types of horns and the units come with complete installation instructions.

One particular type should be purchased with caution. This imitates the standard European "hee-haw" emergency signal which is now being adopted by some American police, fire, and ambulance operations. Any horn on a passenger car that even resembles an emergency warning is illegal in all states. A louder than normal sound, however, usually is not.

LOCKS

If you have to replace an ignition key lock or door lock, it's best to avoid buying a replacement lock cylinder that is already coded because you'll end up with the nuisance of a different set of keys for each lock. A locksmith can sometimes adapt a key to work in both the old and the new lock, but this makes them a lot less pick-proof. The best method is to buy an uncoded replacement cylinder and have the locksmith file the tumblers to fit the existing key.

A door lock is easy to remove and replace once access to it is gained by re-

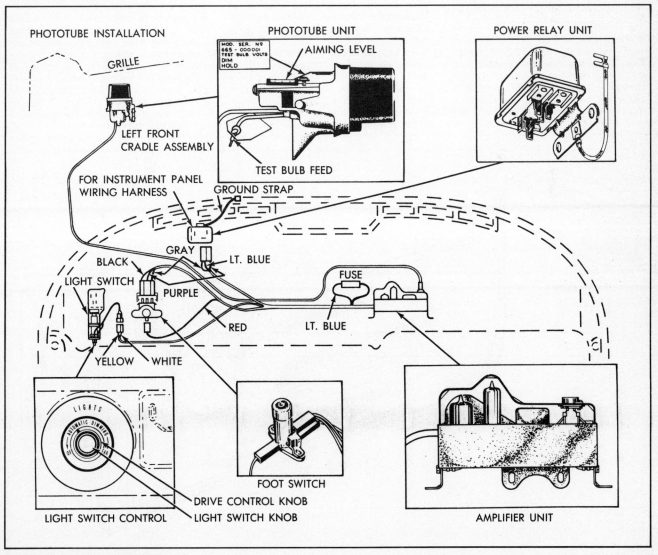

3. Grille-Mounted Headlight Dimmer

Accessory Fix-it Tips

moving the door trim panel. In practically all designs, the panel is held by a retaining clip on the inside of the door sheet-metal which can be sprung off with a screwdriver. This clip will be found there whether the lock is in the door handle or separate from it. The lock assembly then slides out of its socket or housing in the door. The replacement assembly consists of a lock cylinder and a dust cover. The latter must be crimped to hold it in place before installation in the housing. A new cylinder should be lubricated, but this may be done after the job is buttoned up simply by coating the key with a light graphite and working the lock a few times.

Trunk lock replacement is done in the same manner, speeded, of course, by the lack of upholstery in that area. The lock in the tailgate of a station wagon may be reached by removing the window molding and trim panel and manipulating the glass electrically or by crank out of the way. Exercise caution here because when the glass is fully extended in a tailgate that is open, it is free to fall out of its retaining channels in most designs. To operate an electric window with the tailgate open, press the spring ground with your finger and have a partner actuate the control switch which is located in the driver's compartment.

Power locks, whether for the doors or trunk, are vacuum actuated. Although these locks may use the same vacuum source as other more commonly installed accessory components such as vacuum-controlled heater and air-conditioning valves—and the vacuum lines connecting these accessories may be shared in the

interest of economy and saving clutter—each will have its own vacuum reservoir. These are usually located under the hood on the left fender. Most designs have a separate switch, usually in the glove compartment, through which the vacuum line for the trunk lock is routed.

Except for binding in the actuating cylinder, about the only malfunction possible in these systems is a crimped or leaking vacuum supply hose. It is easy to isolate the hose involved. With the engine idling, disconnect a vacuum supply hose to an accessory known to be working, place your fingertip over the end and feel the degree of suction. Anything less than full engine vacuum in the suspected hose indicates a crimp or leak. You may locate a crimp by observing the hose throughout its length; a leak may also be located by repeating this check at each connecting point or T-fitting. A leaking hose may be temporarily taped until replacement is convenient. If all vacuum-operated accessories are malfunctioning, the leak will be between the source of supply on the intake manifold and the first reservoir in the line. Further evidence can be found in a faster than usual, loping idle.

The simplest type of "power" trunk lock is a cable with one end attached to a pull knob located in the glove compartment and the other to a catch release on the trunk lid. Universal kits may be bought at most auto parts stores or through mail order houses. The regular trunk lock, of course, must either be left unlocked or removed entirely. Body shops will fill in the resulting hole for a very small charge. Hiding the trunk lock switch in the glove compartment delays even a serious thief because he has to jimmy one more lock.

CIGARETTE LIGHTER

A cigarette lighter consists of a removable element and a socket or plug. The plug is connected to the "hot" side of the ignition switch via the fuse box. In some installations, interior courtesy lights share the same 20-amp fuse, but in many designs there is a cartridge type fuse on the back of the lighter. As the plug is always "hot," it is a convenient source of power for accessories such as a trouble light, vacuum cleaner and coffee maker as well as the lighter element.

When the element is pushed in, the coiled resistance wire in it receives current and begins to heat. In 10 to 14 secs. the heat is sufficient to cause bimetallic grips in the socket to expand and release the element for use. They expand only a certain amount, however, because they also have a secondary gripping point to prevent the spring-loaded element from popping clear of its socket and causing a fire hazard. If this does occur, the socket is faulty and must be replaced as a unit.

The most common cause of lighter failure is a burned out fuse. If the fuse block has a slot marked "ltr" or something similar, try putting in a new fuse that you know is good. If you still don't get current to the lighter, check at the back of the lighter socket for a cartridge fuse. If you have current to the lighter socket (check with a test light) but the lighter still won't work, the trouble is probably a burned out element. New elements are available, but be sure the prongs are the same as your old one, or it might not fit the socket. There are several different designs.

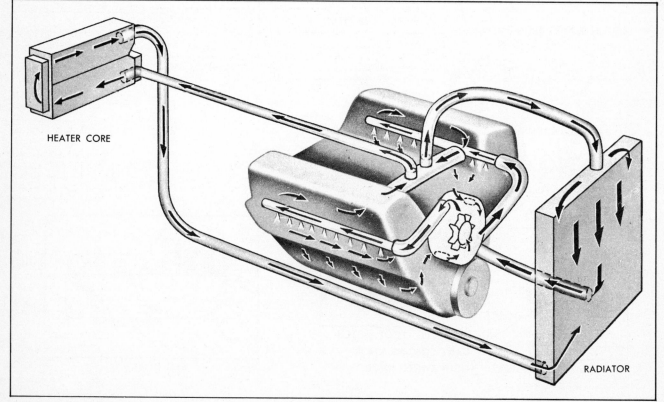

HEATER CORE

RADIATOR

1. Coolant Circulation

RADIO

There are four basic types of radios installed in modern cars, and in recent years they have been fully transistorized. These are AM with or without pushbuttons, AM/FM, AM/FM stereo and AM incorporating a stereo tape player. Repairing any of these receivers is beyond the scope of this book, but there are many checks and adjustments which may be made on items other than the receiver that are very often the cause of the trouble. If after these checks the trouble is pinpointed to the receiver, you can remove and install it yourself and save that labor cost. Receiver repairs and particularly warranty work should be done by an authorized shop. None of the car makers builds its own radio although it will put its own name on the unit. Usually, however, the actual maker will be noted on the receiver case or you can call the car dealer and ask for the name of the authorized repair station.

A basic adjustment is antenna trimming which must be done whenever the receiver is installed after removal for repairs. The serviceman trims to his own antenna which may not have the same characteristics as the one on your car. Locations of the trimming screw vary but it is often found hidden under the tuning knob, or on the side of the radio under the instrument panel. Let the radio play for 15 mins. to warm it, set the antenna between 31 and 40 ins. and select a weak but clear station as close as possible to 1400 kc. Remove the tuning knob or otherwise expose the trimming screw. With a screwdriver turn the trimming screw in small steps in both directions to where a setting is found with the strongest signal. Replace the knob and the job is done until the next time the receiver or antenna is disturbed.

NOISE SUPPRESSORS

Capacitors to suppress radio interference are normally located at or in the alternator or generator, on the "B" terminal of the ignition coil, on the voltage regulator, on the fuse block and some-

1. Here's the flow in a typical heater system. Note that heater water flows from the bottom to the top of heater core. If your heater isn't working very well, you may have put the hoses on the wrong way.

2. A heater core is really just a small radiator. Very little ever goes wrong with one; being on the firewall or under the dash, it isn't subjected to the flying stones and careless wrench-handling that your regular radiator is. If you do start getting leaks in one, just take it out and bring it to a radiator shop.

3. Many new cars have an optional rear window defroster that is a set of wires built into the glass. There are no moving parts, and it does the job without any blower noises.

4. Vacuum-operated water valves like this '71 Plymouth unit are relatively trouble-free, as there are no cables to bind or need adjustment.

2. Heater Core

3. Electric Rear Window Defroster

4. Vacuum-Controlled Water Valve

times on certain power accessories. The connections to these may corrode or come loose, but the capacitor itself seldom "wears out." If the capacitors are suspect, but you've determined that all of their connections are tight and clean, it is cheaper from a time standpoint to replace all of them rather than to try to isolate the offending item. Before doing this, however, inspect the spark plug wires. One or more old, leaking plug wires can cause radio static very similar in sound to a defective capacitor. Then determine if the static occurs only when the car is moving. In this case, the trouble is likely caused by either the front wheels or tires. To isolate one of these from the other, drive on a smooth road and drag the brakes slightly. If the static stops, the problem is in the front wheels; if it continues, it is the tires.

To cure front wheel static, install a collector spring and dust cap in each wheel. For tire static, radio shops have a powder available that must be injected into the tire with a special gun. Another cause of static when the car is in motion but not when standing still is a missing ball tip on the antenna.

ANTENNAS

A typical manual antenna may be readily removed for repair or replacement. Power antennas, except for tightening and cleaning, are best left to a specialized shop. Antennas should be kept clean at all times but not waxed. An occasional wipe with an oil moistened cloth is all that is necessary for lubrication of the power type. The quick check for antenna problems is to borrow one that is known to be good, plug it into the radio and hold it out the window of the car with, of course, a wire connection to any convenient ground. If the radio now plays, or plays better, the existing antenna should be repaired or replaced. If the radio gains volume when you touch an installed antenna, it is an indication of a poor ground.

RADIO REMOVAL

The receiver is supported primarily by attachment points at the two control knobs. There may be one or more supporting brackets at the rear of the unit. The attaching sleeve screws are behind the control knobs and of course the power, ground, speaker and antenna wires must be disconnected. On some air-conditioned cars it may be necessary to remove a portion of the duct work to allow clearance for radio removal. Repairs to the receiver should not be attempted by anyone but specially trained personnel.

Accessory Fix-it Tips

SEATS

Since the invention of the adjustable front seat, manual or power, the cushions of necessity became an integral part of the seat frame, which in turn is attached to the floorpan through the adjusting mechanism.

The adjuster is mounted to the floorpan by only two bolts, but alternate holes are provided in the adjuster for each of the bolts, one on either side of the center hole used by the factory. With the car on a hoist, these bolts may be removed and repositioned as desired to change the base of adjustment without removing the seat from the car. For changing the vertical base of adjustment, shims in these bolts may be removed or added as desired. For fore-and-aft change of permanent adjustment, the satellite track on the other side of the seat should use the same holes. In a change in the vertical, the number of shims on each side should match to prevent an uncomfortable tilt and possible binding of the seat in its slides.

Worn parts in the adjusting mechanism may be replaced by removal of the attaching bolts, which frees the assembly from the seat frame and allows it to be removed for bench maintenance. Each manufacturer's design varies in detail but the parts are straightforward and easy to work with.

Seatback latches are now required on all non-rigid seatbacks by the Federal government. Some use a much more elaborate mechanism that combines this latch with a reclining feature. In this design, the front seatback may be removed without disturbing the cushion or frame. The rear seat cushion is held in place by tabs and may be readily removed. The removal of the rear seatback may, in some cases, require loosening of the attaching points for the package shelf (accessible through the trunk) and possibly

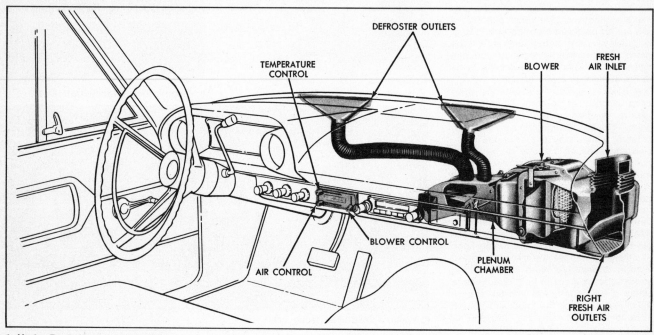

1. Under-Dash Heater Installation

1. On most modern cars the heater is in combination with the defrosting and sometimes the air-conditioning systems. Some types, as here, mount under the dash, others on firewall.

2. Getting at the horn switch on most late cars with 2-spoke wheels means removing trim cover (usually padded).

3. About the only test you can make on a horn is for current draw. Hook up a voltmeter and ammeter as shown. The normal current draw for a dual-horn car is between 4 and 6 amps.

4. On most cars the door panel must be removed to get at the door lock, but on this '63 Ford you merely pry the retaining clip (arrow) out and pull the lock from the outside.

5. Once the lock is outside the door, a screwdriver can be used to pop off the retaining C-clip, and the lock is off and ready to be fixed or changed.

6. Cadillac has a vacuum-controlled trunk lock that shuts automatically when the lid is pushed down. Arrow points to roller that is the control mechanism. Trunk may be opened with key or by button in glove compartment.

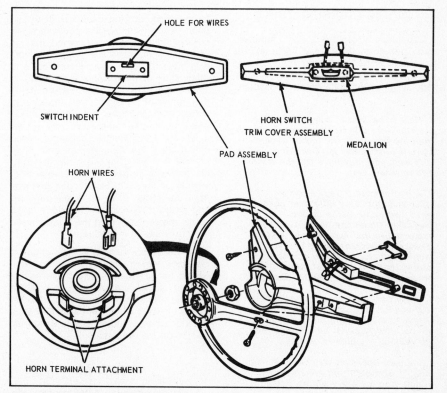

2. Two-Spoke Wheel and Horn Switch

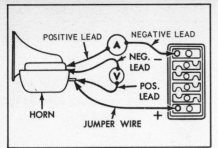

3. Testing Horn For Current Draw

rear window moldings. In either case, the procedures involve only the loosening of attaching screws.

The motor of an electric seat should be serviced by a specialized shop. The wiring here is uncomplicated because the switch is adjacent to the motor, but the circuit is routed through the fuse block from the power source.

MANUAL AND POWER WINDOWS

For economic and safety reasons, two types of "shatter-proof" glass are used in an automobile. The side and back windows are usually made from tempered glass which has the characteristic of fragmenting entirely into relatively harmless particles when broken. Sometimes the sheet doesn't disintegrate but visibility through it is reduced to near zero. For this reason another type of glass, called laminated, is used in windshields. As the name implies, this is a sandwich composed of two layers of glass separated by transparent plastic. The plastic isolates breaks, and visibility is maintained if the window is impacted.

Replacement glass for side windows may be of either type. Tempered glass must be cut to shape before the tempering process, so a glass shop will generally stock pre-cut forms for the most popular cars and cut laminated glass on a custom basis to fit rarer makes and body styles. Glass removal and replacement must be preceded by at least partial disassembly of the winding mechanism which, in turn, requires removal of the interior handles and upholstery trim panels.

WINDOW ADJUSTMENTS

There are adjustments you can make to compensate for normal wear. A common problem is a loose vent window (of the non-crank type) that won't keep its position against the airstream. A lower pivot nut at the bottom of the window regulates the tension, and you can get at this nut to tighten it by removing the inner window-to-door molding.

Adjustments to the regulating mechanism of any of the main side windows requires removal of the trim panel. First remove the window-to-door molding and the arm rest. Both of these items are attached with sheetmetal screws, although in the case of the arm rest, the screw heads may be hidden under plastic covers. Next, remove the inner door and window handles. Unfortunately, some of these require special tools. The trim itself is attached to the door struc-

4. Removing Lock Retaining Clip

5. Removing Lock Cylinder

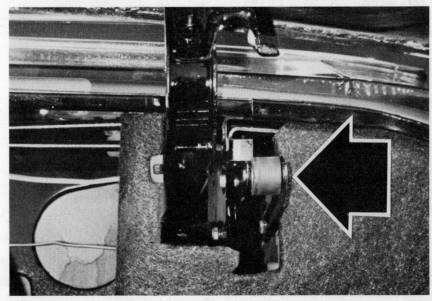

6. Cadillac Trunk Latch

Accessory Fix-it Tips

ture by various types of clips that can be pried out with a screwdriver.

Most window adjustments can compensate for normal wear or correct leaks and wind whistle caused by misaligned glass, and are self-explanatory.

Anytime the trim panel is removed from the door, it is a good idea to lubricate the gears at various rubbing points of the window regulator with a heavy grease that will not run off and stain upholstery in hot weather.

1. If your doors don't fit or latch properly, the door may be just out of alignment. It can be realigned by loosening the screws on this striker plate for readjustment.

2. Some elements can be changed by unscrewing them from the knob, but you must push the sleeve back and grab the end of the element itself in order to unscrew it.

3. With the element unscrewed, the whole thing comes apart easily. The replacement element must be the same size and shape or it won't fit into the dash receptacle. Elements seldom go bad. Look for a blown fuse first, either at fuse block or lighter.

4. Cartridge fuse screws onto the rear of many lighters. Check for continuity with a test light. If it's blown, you have to replace it.

5. Removing lighter shell shows prongs that grab end of the element. Both the internal (top) and external types are used. They're not interchangeable.

6. Collar on this Ford lighter picks up light from behind the instrument panel to illuminate "lighter" sign. Element is covered by ash guard.

7. Here are several of the methods the factories use to eliminate static in radios. Suppression capacitors can be installed on the coil, generator and other electrical components; GM cars use a metal shield over the ignition points; spring-loaded dust caps can be used on the wheels; and most cars in recent years have used metal ground clips between the hood and the cowl.

8. Seats are hard to work on because the cushions cover up the works. If you remove the cushion, your chances of fixing the seat are better.

9. It's a sign of the times, but you see quite a few of these antennas made from coat hangers because someone vandalized the antenna. They work, but not too well.

10. Don't forget switch as a source of trouble on electric seats. If the seat works only when you wiggle the switch, you may have bad contacts.

11. At left is the mechanism for a GM 4-way power seat. For comparison, the model at right is a 6-way, which has the extra vertical gear nuts that raise and lower the seat.

1. Door Lock Striker Plate

2. Removing Element

3. Disassembled Lighter

4. Cartridge Fuse

5. Element Construction

6. Illuminating Collar

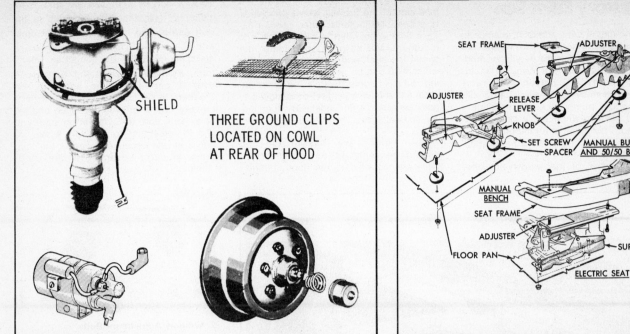

SHIELD

THREE GROUND CLIPS
LOCATED ON COWL
AT REAR OF HOOD

7. Static Suppressors

SEAT FRAME | ADJUSTER
ADJUSTER | RELEASE LEVER | KNOB | SET SCREW | SPACER | MANUAL BUCKET AND 50/50 BENCH
MANUAL BENCH | SEAT FRAME | ADJUSTER | SUPPORT
FLOOR PAN | ELECTRIC SEAT

8. Seat Mounting Mechanisms

ELECTRIC WINDOWS

Replacement or lubrication of the separate, permanent magnet-type motors that operate each window requires removal of the regulating mechanism. We have advised against the owner-mechanic attempting this for reasons described above. If you do go ahead, the regulator assembly must be held in a vise when the motor is removed from it to prevent the assist spring from unwinding. If the master switch is malfunctioning, it must be replaced as a unit. The window circuit utilizes a circuit breaker with the current source being the ammeter.

WINDSHIELD WASHERS AND WIPERS

Windshield washers fall into three general categories. The simplest type is a foot-operated pump mounted on the floorboard or cowl on the left side above the headlamp dimmer. It is connected by hoses to the fluid reservoir in the engine compartment and to the nozzles. The simplest electric type is at the bottom or adjacent to the fluid reservoir and is actuated by a switch incorporated in or adjacent to the wiper control. A "deluxe" type of pump is part of the windshield wiper motor and when actuated, also operates the wipers for a predetermined number of strokes.

Chemicals are sold in all service stations for mixing with water in the system. In winter the chemical acts as an antifreeze, with the degree of protection determined by the graduations on the bottle. The antifreeze not only keeps the solution from freezing in the bottle and breaking it, but prevents the solution from freezing solid when it hits the ice cold windshield. A partially frozen solution can create enough load to burn out the pump motor. In the summer, a solution of chemicals and water improves cleaning action to cut those bugs off the glass.

9. Homemade Antenna   **10. Dash Control for Six-Way Seat**

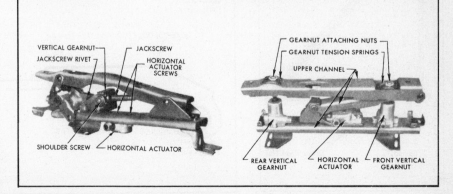

VERTICAL GEARNUT | JACKSCREW | GEARNUT ATTACHING NUTS
JACKSCREW RIVET | HORIZONTAL ACTUATOR SCREWS | GEARNUT TENSION SPRINGS
UPPER CHANNEL
SHOULDER SCREW | HORIZONTAL ACTUATOR | REAR VERTICAL GEARNUT | HORIZONTAL ACTUATOR | FRONT VERTICAL GEARNUT

11. Four-Way and Six-Way Adjusters

Accessory Fix-it Tips

In late-model cars, Rambler is alone in still using a vacuum-driven windshield wiper and this is only for 6-cylinder models. All others have a one- or multi-speed electrically driven system. A vacuum-driven system requires an auxiliary vacuum pump to keep the wipers moving steadily when the engine is under load. This pump is an integral part of the fuel pump on most cars equipped with vacuum wipers.

The location of the windshield wiper motor varies. Sometimes it is on the engine side of the firewall where it is readily accessible. In some other cars an access hole is provided in the firewall, and in others, the strip of body metal between the back end of the hood and the windshield can be removed to give working room. In some designs the entire instrument cluster must first be removed to gain access to the windshield wiper motor and linkage.

Foot pumps are inexpensive and should be replaced as an assembly. They are mounted to the floor pan with several screws with spacers and a retainer to give the mount rigidity in the soft carpet and mat. Replacement electric pumps are similarly easy to install and can generally be bought in rebuilt form. Ejection nozzles tend to corrode over a period of time and may be cleaned by a careful reaming with a hand-held drill bit. Aiming these nozzles is a "cut and try" operation and you should remember to aim low when the car is at rest because at speed, the fluid tends to carry up and over the windshield.

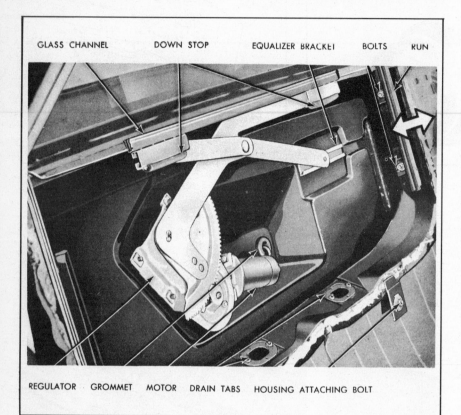

GLASS CHANNEL   DOWN STOP   EQUALIZER BRACKET   BOLTS   RUN

REGULATOR   GROMMET   MOTOR   DRAIN TABS   HOUSING ATTACHING BOLT

1. Power Window Mechanism

2. Window Adjustment Bolts

3. Window Channel Adjustment Points

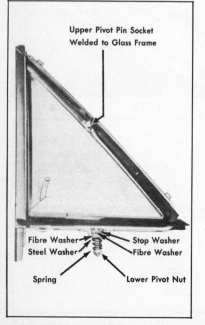

Upper Pivot Pin Socket Welded to Glass Frame

Fibre Washer   Stop Washer
Steel Washer   Fibre Washer

Spring   Lower Pivot Nut

4. Vent Window Assembly

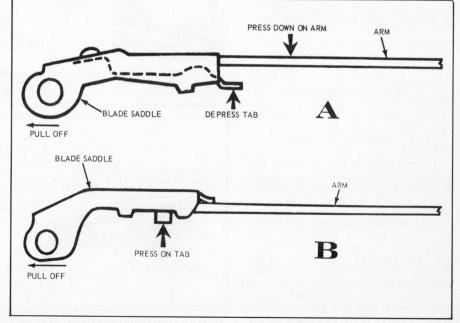

PRESS DOWN ON ARM   ARM

BLADE SADDLE   DEPRESS TAB   **A**

PULL OFF

BLADE SADDLE

ARM

PRESS ON TAB   **B**

PULL OFF

5. Bayonet-Type Wiper Blades

WIPER MOTOR AND LINKAGE MAINTENANCE

Most wear in the linkage can fortunately be compensated for by adjusting the position of the wiper arms. Most are attached to their shafts by a conventional cap bolt. If no bolt is evident, a special tool, varying by the make of the car, is required to remove the wiper arm without damaging it.

Replacement wiper blades are obtainable in any service station. In newer designs only the rubber is replaced; older cars require a complete blade assembly. Extreme care should be taken not to bend the wiper arm when replacing a blade because it takes only a slight misalignment to cause metal to contact glass and the result is a permanently marred windshield.

The decision as to whether you should attempt to work on the linkage and motor or buy this service depends entirely upon its accessibility. Once you get at it, there is nothing very complicated about the assembly, and wear points are quite evident by their sloppiness. Unlike most other assemblies on the car, wiper linkage parts are sold separately. When you find the worn part, bring it with you to the dealer's parts counter so you can be sure you get the right replacement.

The easiest way to fix an electric wiper motor is by replacing it. New motors are rather expensive, but you can get good bargains on used ones in wrecking yards if you are willing to remove it from a wrecked car yourself. Vacuum wiper motors can usually be made to work, even though they haven't operated for years; simply squirt a little oil into the motor and work the shaft back and forth so that the oil lubricates the mechanism. A vacuum wiper rejuvenated by this method will certainly not have the power and speed of a completely overhauled or new unit, but at least it will work.

6. Removing Wiper Arm

7. Wiper Shaft Spline

8. Windshield Washer Assembly

1. Take care in repairing a motor for a power window, as the spring in the regulator is extra powerful. Motor and regulator should be removed as a unit. The regulator should be clamped in a vise, so the gears can't move, before you loosen the motor.

2. If adjustment is not obvious, mark the position of the bolts as they are, then loosen them for adjustments.

3. Slotted hole behind clamp bolt is to allow adjustment of window channel. To get to these adjustments, you have to remove the interior trim panel.

4. Loose, floppy, hand-operated wind wings (vent windows) are usually a result of loose springs on post.

5. Two of the most common wiper blade types are the Trico (A) and the Anco (B). Both of those shown are bayonet type; there are pin-types also.

6,7. A little tab under the wiper arm must be lifted to remove the arm. You can slip it off with a screwdriver. Arms will go back on the splined part in any position. If the blades don't stop in the right position or hit the window frame, you can reposition arm.

8. A windshield washer consists of a reservoir for the water/detergent mix, usually a plastic bag or box, and a small motor which pumps the fluid up through the hoses onto the windshield.

9. Most wiper motors attach to the firewall, with the linkage to the wiper arms being under the dashboard.

10. This is a late Ford wiper motor, which has the park switch adjustment inside the wiper. You should have a shop manual to go by if you're going to disassemble an electric wiper.

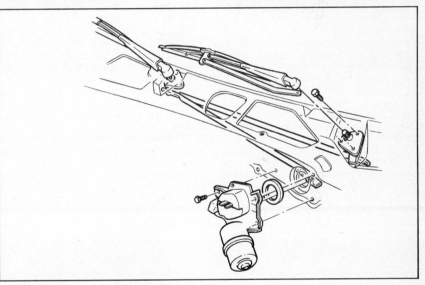

9. Wiper Motor and Linkage

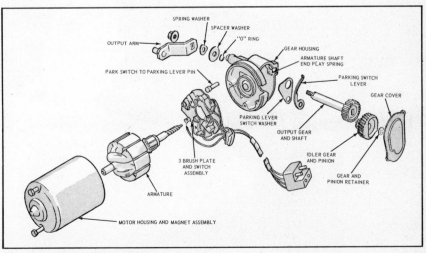

10. Disassembled Wiper Motor

Lubrication

Nobody, except perhaps a small boy, finds any particular pleasure in getting dirty. It isn't so bad if only your hands get dirty when working on your car, but when you get grease on your shoulders and in your hair and maybe down the middle of your back from crawling around underneath while doing a grease job, it's no wonder that most lube jobs are done in service stations while the owner just stands and watches. Paying somebody else to do your oil changes and lubrication can be expensive—not only because you are paying for their labor, but because you are giving them full price or even more for the oil and other parts that they use. A good lever-type grease gun can be purchased from Sears or Ward for a few dollars, and almost all discount stores have greases and oils. If you don't mind a distasteful job, you can save quite a bit of money by doing the oil changes and lube jobs yourself.

Lubrication and general maintenance work should be performed on a "mileage" or "time" basis. Either one or both can be utilized according to driving habits. Simply put, if you don't drive enough miles within a certain time period, say 90 days, the service should still be performed to keep your car in top running condition.

In recent years, all of the automobile manufacturers have extended both time and mileage service intervals with much improved components—filters, corrosion-resistant coatings and permanently lubricated joints. However, due to the differing geographical conditions in the U.S. (cold, heat, dust, moisture), certain components need more frequent servicing than others. Keeping this in mind, you will want to adjust (for some items) the service interval suggested in the lubrication and maintenance chart to suit your car's needs. Trailer towing would also come under this adjustment. It is true that a careful lubrication and maintenance program—one that you stick to—will keep your car looking and running like new for many years.

ENGINE OIL TYPES

The type or grade of engine oil and the regularity of engine oil changes will affect engine operation, wear, and combustion chamber deposits. Oil viscosity will affect oil economy and ease of starting. Many people think that a higher viscosity oil, such as 30 wt. or 40 wt., is a "better" oil than 10 or 20 wt. The weight of the oil has nothing to do with its quality. All that the weight numbers indicate is the thickness or fluidity of the oil, from the extremely thin oils of 5 or 10 wt., up to 90 or 140 for gears, and on up to 200 wt. or beyond, which is so thick you can't pour it.

There are four harmful deposits which can form in the crankcase of an engine: sludge, varnish, moisture, and acids. The formation of these deposits largely depends on the quality of oil and the additives therein, and the type of driving conditions. They form under both high- and low-speed driving conditions, but generally form more rapidly in cold weather under short-trip or city traffic conditions. As far as motor oil is concerned, consider these as severe operating conditions.

Formation of these deposits can be substantially reduced by using quality oils that contain the correct type and quantity of additives. Sludge is reduced by additives having detergent dispersing characteristics. Varnish deposits are reduced by oxidation inhibitors, and bearing corrosion is eliminated by corrosion-preventive additives.

To minimize the formation of these harmful deposits, and to assure the use of the oil best suited for present-day operating conditions, the automobile manufacturers have developed a series of sequence tests designed to evaluate the ability of any oil to properly lubricate automobile engines.

For many years, oils were graded ML, MM, or MS, for Motor Light, Medium, and Severe. MS was the best oil, because it would stand up under severe service, but it wasn't *the* best MS oil unless it had a statement on the can which verified that it had passed the car makers' sequence tests.

Now, there is a new rating system, with five classifications.

SA oils are non-detergent, with no performance requirements. This classification includes not only high-quality non-detergent oils put out by major companies, but also the dregs from the local

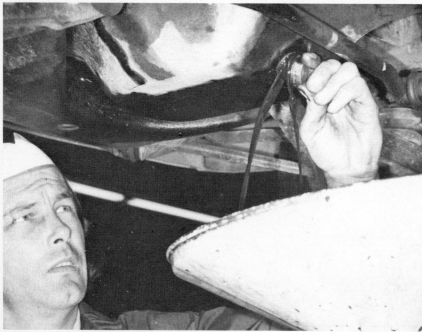

1. Removing Drain Plug

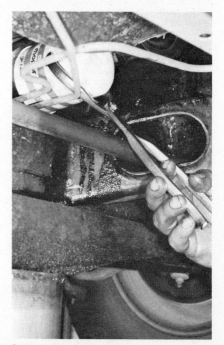

2. Cinching Down Filter

tar pit. If you want a good non-detergent oil, you will have to rely on the reputation of the maker.

SB oils have a few additives that protect against scuffing, bearing corrosion, and oil oxidation. These oils give only minimum protection.

SC oils are better. They have additives that protect against high- and low- temperature deposits, rust, wear, and corrosion.

SD oils are the next best. They protect against all the conditions that the other oils do, only more so. If a car maker recommends SC oil, you will be giving your engine greater protection by using SD oil.

Until late in 1971, SD oil was thought to be the best oil available, but then the strange cases of oil thickening showed up. It seems that increased engine temperatures caused by running lean to control emissions, when coupled with trailer towing or other heavy load operation at high speeds, can heat the oil so that it oxidizes, leaving nothing but a gooey mess that the oil pump can't pick up out of the pan. The result is a thoroughly destroyed crankshaft and bearings, maybe even a seized engine. To combat this, the oil makers have hurriedly come out with SE grade oil. It is now the best oil you can get, at least until some new problem comes up that it can't cope with.

Just in case you see them on the can, let's also go through the oil classifications for diesel use. The old classes were DG, DM, and DS, for Diesel General, Diesel Medium, and Diesel Severe. New diesel classifications are as follows:

CA oils are for light-duty diesel engine service. These oils will give protection from bearing corrosion and high temper-

1. Your car represents a pretty healthy hunk of bread. Obviously it makes good "cents" to see that all of its moving parts are properly maintained and well lubricated. Most of us tend to sub out our maintenance work to keep our hands from getting dirty, but we can all save a considerable piece of change by investing in a few tools, some oil, grease and body lube—and do it ourselves.

2. There are several types of band wrenches and pliers available that are designed to loosen and tighten throwaway oil filters. Once the filter is in place, let the engine run until it reaches operating temperature. Then check around the edge. Tighten further if it leaks.

3. Chassis lubrication diagrams—such as for this '68 Chevy—can be found in any dealer's service manual. It allows the car's owner to see where the lubrication points are, the location of the oil and fluid reservoirs, and when they should be checked, refilled and/or replaced.

4. Lubrication is a matter of either mileage or time intervals. For example, if your car has seen 2 months or 2000 miles go by, it's time to lube the water pump, check the steering gear, change the oil and filter.

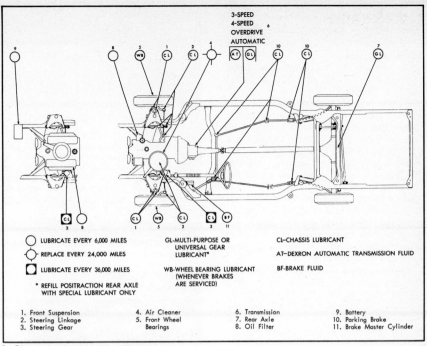

LUBRICATE EVERY 6,000 MILES
REPLACE EVERY 24,000 MILES
LUBRICATE EVERY 36,000 MILES

* REFILL POSITRACTION REAR AXLE WITH SPECIAL LUBRICANT ONLY

GL-MULTI-PURPOSE OR UNIVERSAL GEAR LUBRICANT*
WB-WHEEL BEARING LUBRICANT (WHENEVER BRAKES ARE SERVICED)

CL-CHASSIS LUBRICANT
AT-DEXRON AUTOMATIC TRANSMISSION FLUID
BF-BRAKE FLUID

1. Front Suspension
2. Steering Linkage
3. Steering Gear
4. Air Cleaner
5. Front Wheel Bearings
6. Transmission
7. Rear Axle
8. Oil Filter
9. Battery
10. Parking Brake
11. Brake Master Cylinder

3. Chevrolet Lubrication Diagram

Quick-Reference Maintenance and Lubrication Guide

Service at indicated time and/or mileage intervals	Fuel Stop	2000 (2 mo)	4000	5000	6000 (6 mo)	10,000	12,000 (12 mo)	24,000 (24 mo)	36,000 (36 mo)
Check engine oil level	X								
Check radiator coolant level (remove cap on cold engine only)	X								
Check battery liquid level	X								
Check windshield washer reservoir level	X								
Lubricate generator cup(s)		X							
Lubricate distributor cup		X							
Lubricate water pump(s) if equipped with grease fittings		X							
Change engine oil and filter			X						
Check tire air pressure			X						
Lubricate front suspension on older types			X						
Lubricate exhaust manifold valve			X						
Check brake master cylinder fluid level			X						
Check hydraulic clutch master cylinder fluid level			X						
Check automatic transmission oil level			X						
Check power steering fluid reservoir			X						
Check steering gear lubricant level			X						
Clean and lubricate oil wetted wire mesh air cleaner[1]			X						
Clean and lubricate oil filler cap[1]			X						
Perform minor engine tune-up				X					
Check and clean crankcase ventilation system					X				
Check manual transmission lubricant level (early type)					X				
Check manual transmission lubricant level (full synchromesh type)							X		
Check rear axle lubricant level (early)					X				
Check rear axle lubricant level (late)								X	
Lubricate transmission, clutch and brake linkage					X				
Adjust clutch pedal travel					X				
Lubricate universal joints with grease fittings					X				
Lubricate universal joints without grease fittings								X	
Perform brake adjustment[2]					X				
Clean body and door drain holes					X				
Rotate tires					X				
Clean dry-type air cleaner[1]					X				
Replace dry-type air cleaner[1]							X		
Clean polyurethane type air cleaner[1]					X				
Perform body lubrication (hinges, striker plates, etc.)					X				
Inspect brake hoses					X				
Check accessory drive(s) belt tension					X				
Perform major engine tune-up						X			
Clean and refill oil bath type air cleaner[1]						X			
Clean and lubricate accelerator linkage						X			
Clean and repack front wheel bearings							X		
Lubricate dash controls and seat tracks							X		
Major brake adjustment (remove drums, clean dust, lube pivots, etc.)							X		
Check headlight adjustment							X		
Check front-end alignment[2]							X		
Clean battery terminals[2]							X		
Check air-conditioning system (bolts, hose condition, sight gauge)							X		
Replace P.C.V. valves and clean hoses							X		
Inspect cooling system[2]							X		
Lubricate slip yoke (automatic transmission models)							X		
Change automatic transmission fluid								X	
Check shock absorbers and bushings								X	
Replace spring leaf inserts (small pads between leaves)								X	
Check convertible top operation								X	
Lubricate speedometer cable									X
Lubricate long-life front suspension									X

1 Perform this service more frequently in dusty areas   2 More frequently if necessary

NOTE: The above time and/or mileage servicing intervals are averages based on recommendations from various automotive sources, and are designed to serve primarily as a guide. Wherever possible, it is desirable to refer to specific car manufacturer shop manuals for factory-prescribed servicing intervals and procedures, particularly during warranty coverage periods. Unusual operating conditions—such as extreme heat or cold, extended trailer towing, dusty environment, excessive moisture, etc.—may demand more frequent servicing, which may also be the case with older, higher mileage cars.

4. Maintenance and Lubrication Guide

Lubrication

ature deposits, but only if high quality diesel fuel is used.

CB oils are for moderate-duty diesel engine service. They are a little bit better than the CA oils.

CC oils are a step better than CB oils. Lightly supercharged diesel engines should use these oils for protection from high temperature deposits. CC oils are also recommended in some gasoline engines. When used in gasoline engines, CC oils are roughly equivalent to SC classification oils.

CD oils are the best for diesel, but they are definitely not recommended for passenger cars. They are too high in additive content to work well with gasoline engine spark plugs. In diesel engines there are no plugs to worry about.

It will be some time before all the cartons and containers with the old grading system have disappeared. If your car is supposed to use SC or SD oil, but you can't find any, then you should use MS oil that has passed the sequence tests.

ENGINE OIL VISCOSITY

SAE oil viscosity numbers, we repeat, indicate only the viscosity or thickness of the oil and *do not* indicate other properties or quality.

The lower SAE numbers, such as SAE 5W and SAE 10W (Winter), are light-body oils and are recommended for cold weather use. They provide easy starting and instant lubrication. The higher SAE viscosity numbers such as SAE 20, SAE 30, etc., are heavier-body oils and are recommended to provide adequate lubrication under high-operating-temperature conditions.

Oils are also available which are designed to combine the easy starting characteristics of the lower SAE numbers with the hot weather operating characteristics of the higher SAE numbers. These are called "multi-viscosity oils" and run SAE 5W-20, SAE 10W-20, SAE 10W-30, etc.

Engine oil should be selected to give the best performance under the climatic and driving conditions in the area in which your car is driven. When the crankcase is drained and refilled, the new engine oil should be selected not on the basis of the existing temperature at the time of the oil change, but on the lowest temperature anticipated for the period during which the oil will be used. The following chart will serve as a guide for the selection of the correct SAE viscosity numbers under different atmospheric conditions.

Lowest anticipated temperature	Recommended SAE viscosity	Recommended SAE multi-viscosity
Consistently above 32°F.	SAE 30 or 40	SAE 10W-30 or SAE 20W-40
0°F. to 32°F.	SAE 10W or SAE 20W	SAE 10W-30 or SAE 10W-40
Below 0°F.	SAE 5W or SAE 10W	SAE 5W-20 or SAE 5W-10

The above recommendations are for engines in good condition. If your engine

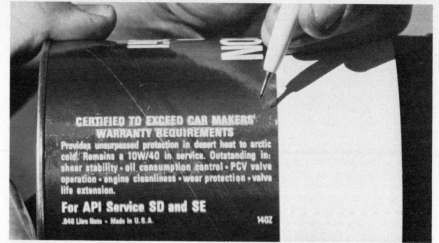
1. Determining Oil Properties

2. Lubricating Filter Gasket

3. Bypass-Type Filter Element

4. Cinching Down Filter Can

is clanking, or using oil, it's a good idea to go to a higher viscosity, such as 40 or 50 wt. The heavier oil will result in less oil consumption, and may keep the engine together longer because it fills in the excessive space between parts caused by wear.

CHANGING OIL

While motor oil does not lose its "oiliness," it does wear out as its additives are used up in performing their function. That is one particular disadvantage of multi-viscosity oil, which is really more additive than oil. It must be changed regularly. The oil in the crankcase, while performing its many functions to protect the engine from harmful effects of contamination, becomes more and more loaded with these waste products, not all of which can be trapped by a filter. Oil filters help if properly maintained, but they don't prevent varnish deposits, sludge, or corrosive wear caused by liquid contaminants which will pass through the filter. There is only one sure way to remove contaminated oil from your engine, and that is by changing the oil on a regular basis before the additives are depleted. Adding makeup oil to a crankcase of dirty oil is no substitute for draining and refilling. Today, as always, 3 qts. of dirty oil and 2 qts. of clean oil make 5 qts. of dirty oil.

Automobile manufacturers vary slightly on their recommendations of oil change intervals. And today's new car standards are not retroactive to older model cars. Therefore, engine oil and filter should be changed every 90 days or 3000 miles, whichever occurs first. These figures apply to almost all driving conditions and are well within the manufacturer's recommendations and those of the American Petroleum Institute.

It's advisable to drain the crankcase only after the engine has reached normal operating temperature. The benefit of draining is, to a large extent, lost if the crankcase is drained when the engine is cold, as some of the suspended contaminants will cling to the sides of the engine block and oil pan and will not drain out readily with cold, slow-moving oil. Allow sufficient time for the oil to drain out and replace the plug carefully, starting the threads by hand so as not to strip the oil pan. Oil pan plugs should be torqued 30 to 40 ft.-lbs. After changing the oil and the filter, do not accelerate the engine beyond idle until the oil light goes out or the pressure gauge reads above 20 lbs. of pressure.

Flushing the crankcase with oils or solvent solutions other than a good grade SAE 10W oil is not recommended. If flushing is necessary due to contamination, fill the crankcase with 3 qts. of SAE 10W oil (4 qts. with filter) and idle the engine at 1000 rpm until the oil is hot; then drain the pan and filter immediately after stopping the engine. Install a new filter and the correct grade and quantity of engine oil.

The engine oil dipstick is marked "full" and "add oil." These notations are marked with broad lines and arrows so that you will know exactly how much oil is in the crankcase and how much you should add if necessary. Never let the oil level go below the lower mark and never overfill the crankcase. Before adding oil, wait until the oil level reading is just below the "add 1 qt." line. Also, if the car has been driven, you will avoid a false reading if you allow a few minutes for the oil to drain back to the crankcase before checking the oil level.

OIL FILTERS

There are two types of oil filter systems: full-flow and bypass. In the full-flow type, the oil filter is in the system between the oil pump and the engine so that all the oil has to go through the filter before it reaches the engine. When flow through the filter is restricted by dirt (which means the filter is doing its job), a valve in the filter (or in the engine block) opens up and allows the oil to go around the filter. Most people don't realize that the valve also opens when the oil is cold, because cold oil is too thick to pass through the filter element. The valve can also open during high-speed operation, because so much oil is being pumped that the filter element can't accept it all.

In the bypass filter system, the filter is on a separate line. Oil goes from the pump to the filter, and then dumps back into the pan. A bypass filter can be removed, and the line plugged, without affecting the operation of the oiling system. On many older cars, the bypass filter was an accessory added by the dealer if the owner wanted it. Bypass filters are supposedly obsolete, inefficient, and unnecessary. But when you consider how much of the time a full-flow filter is

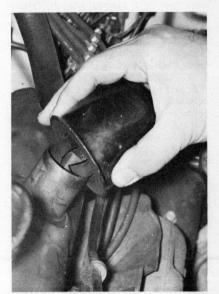

5. Pulling Breather Cap

1. Oil types and viscosity properties are found printed on the back of the can. Weight and classification (10W-40, SD, SE) shows this grade of oil will protect the engine's moving parts in a wide variety of driving conditions. Check factory recommendations for your particular car and the climatic changes it will be subjected to before you replace your oil.

2. The neoprene gasket must be lubricated with engine oil before filter element is installed. Element is torqued to a recommended 25 ft.-lbs.

3. Elements for the older bypass-type filters are usually made of coarse fiber to provide a high oil flow and cellulose fibers to give good filtration. Element is thrown away when the engine oil is changed.

4. Filter can should be cleaned in solvent, filled with new oil and the cartridge replaced before it's tightened. Care must be taken not to under- or overtorque. Too much will warp can or break gasket; too little won't allow can to seal properly.

5. The steel mesh in the breather cap must be checked and cleaned before you add new oil. Plugged breather can have a bad effect on crankcase ventilation.

6. Most manufacturers of automatic transmissions advise that the ATF (automatic transmission fluid) be changed every 24 months or 24,000 miles, whichever arrives first. Most drain plugs are located in the pan.

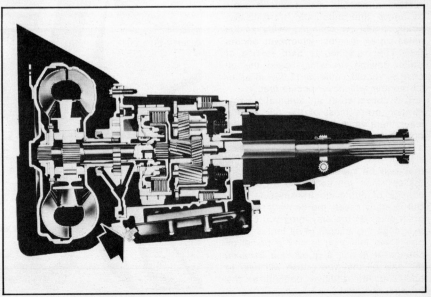

6. Automatic Trans Drain Plug

Lubrication

actually bypassing the oil, then the old bypass filter doesn't look so bad. Any filtration is better than none; your engine needs the protection.

Most late model cars use a "can"-type filter that screws onto a special mounting bracket attached to the engine. To change it, you merely unscrew it and throw it away. A complete new element is then screwed on in its place. Before attaching this type of element, wipe gasket area of base clean, coat the neoprene gasket with engine oil, and screw the filter can onto its base until the gasket is firmly against the sealing surface. From that point, turn the filter can an additional ½-turn.

Most filter makers consider that anything beyond a ¾-turn will result in the need to use blasting powder to get the filter off when it comes time to change it. But Chevrolet has experienced some leaks when following the ¾-turn rule. They recommend 25 ft.-lbs., which is equivalent to between 1 and 1⅔ turns.

Some throwaway filters have fluted ends that fit a special wrench. Others have a hex so you can use ordinary socket wrenches. Some filters have only a smooth can, so you must use one of those wrenches that looks like a kitchen jar opener and is sold in all the auto supply stores.

Earlier filters are contained in a steel can which also mounts on the engine in either a top or underneath mounting position. The top-mounted filters have a lid that you can remove by unscrewing a bolt. Then lift the filter element out. On filters mounted under the engine, the whole can and filter element is removed when the bolt is loosened. In either case, the filter element is thrown out, the container can wiped clean, and a new element replaced.

Remember, the filter holds 1 qt. of oil. Therefore, if you change the filter when you change the oil, you will need to add an extra quart of oil to fill the crankcase.

AUTOMATIC TRANSMISSIONS

Most automobile manufacturers seem to agree that automatic transmission fluids should be changed every 24,000 miles or 24 months, whichever occurs first. The exception is hard service or trailer towing, in which case the oil change should come at 12,000 miles or 12 months, whichever occurs first.

The converter in an automatic transmission holds most of the fluid and it stays there when the transmission is not operating. Draining the pan will only get a few quarts of fluid out of the transmission. If the converter has a drain plug that can be reached from underneath the car, then you can make a complete change of automatic transmission fluid. But in many cases, the converter has no drain plug. So the only thing you can do is change the amount of oil that is in the pan. Even though it is only a partial oil change, it is still a good idea because the new oil that you put in will help to build up the additive content of the transmission fluid.

As mentioned earlier, to check the flu-

id level in an automatic transmission, the engine must be at normal operating temperature. The check must be made with the engine idling and the selector lever in "P" (Park) position. When the fluid is hot, the level should be in the "add 1 pint" mark. *Caution: Do not fill above the "full" mark as this will cause foaming and will result in improper operation.* If it is necessary to check the fluid level when the transmission is cold, fluid level should be at, or slightly below the "add 1 pint" mark. If it's below this mark, add just enough oil to bring it up to the "add 1 pint" mark. This avoids overfilling.

For many years, the only kind of automatic transmission fluid available was Type A, sometimes called Suffix A. In recent years, Ford came out with their own fluid called Type F, which is now available from all fluid manufacturers. Type F is the only fluid that should be used in any Ford product automatic transmission. This includes the older transmissions for which Type A was originally recommended. Some of the early Chrysler, DeSoto, Dodge or Plymouth automatic transmissions were of a different design, actually amounting to a manual transmission that was hydraulically shift-

ed. Most of those old units, including the one called Fluid Drive, were filled with engine oil. Before adding any kind of fluid to any transmission, check the factory specifications to be sure you're adding the right fluid.

Due to severe engine overheating or heavy-duty towing, the transmission fluid should be checked to determine if the fluid has deteriorated. Deteriorated fluid, if allowed to remain in the transmission, will cause early transmission failure. To check for fluid deterioration, wipe a small amount of fluid off the dipstick with your fingers. If it smells like burnt toast, replace it.

STANDARD TRANSMISSION

Most auto manufacturers state that regular transmission oil changes are not necessary on late-model cars whose operation is classified as normal service for passenger cars. This is difficult to go along with and it certainly is not true for the older models. No one is absolutely perfect at shifting, and every time there is a clashing of gears—or even the normal wear of transmission parts—there are bound to be metal particles suspend-

1. Checking Trans Dip Stick

2. Manual Trans Drain Plug

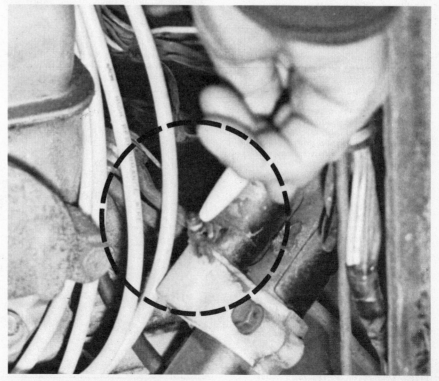

3. Shift Linkage Grease Fitting

ed in the oil. And there is no filter in the transmission to catch these metal particles. Therefore, transmission oil on early model cars should be changed every 6 months or 6000 miles. On newer cars with full synchromesh gears, change the oil every 12 months or 12,000 miles. On some late-model cars there is no drain plug; on others a drain plug is provided at the bottom or low on the side of the transmission for this purpose. If no drain plug is provided, a suction pump must be used to remove the oil.

SAE 90 viscosity grade oil is recommended for year-round use; however, SAE 80 may be used when low temperatures are encountered. Good quality multi-purpose lubricants are defined by the number MIL-L-2105B. Except for checking fluid level at engine oil change intervals and draining the oil, there is no maintenance on the transmission other than lubricating the gearshift mechanism. A 30 wt. engine oil is excellent for this purpose, and you should wipe all the pivot points clean before oiling. Some older cars have a grease fitting on the steering column to lubricate the shift levers and linkage.

Many lubricant manufacturers now make multi-viscosity transmission lubes as well as engine oils. In some cases, it is difficult to find single-viscosity transmission lube such as 80 or 90. The 90-140 that most stations carry now seems to work just as well as the old single-viscosity grades.

STANDARD AND LIMITED-SLIP REAR AXLES

On most late-model cars you will not find a drain plug at the rear axle. Late-

1. Fluid level and smell are both important when you eyeball the trans dipstick. Too much or too little fluid can drastically affect the performance of the unit. And so can overheating. If fluid is acrid or extremely pungent, it has been subjected to severe heat and must be changed.

2. Manual transmissions should have their 90-wt. oil replaced every 6 months or 6000 miles. Gear or synchromesh particles, held in suspension by the thick oil, quickly increase unwanted gear and synchromesh wear.

3. The shifting linkage on older cars have "Zerk" fittings which need to be zapped with grease annually.

4. Low-cost, hand-operated grease guns, although not as fast, will do every bit as good a job as the air-operated ones found in gas stations or dealer's repair shops. Many outfits come complete with swivel heads for difficult-to-reach fittings.

5. The oil level in the third member should be checked only after it has achieved running temperature. "Posi"-type units require a special limited-slip differential lubrication to keep the clutches from chattering.

6. Late model cars are equipped with threaded metal plugs (A) instead of grease fittings (B) The plugs are removed at lube intervals and replaced with the Zerk fitting.

model cars may go 2 years or 24,000 miles before the fluid should be changed. Older model cars should have their oil changed every 6 months or 6000 miles, whichever occurs first.

Again, the oil level should be checked with the fluid hot, and it should be up to the bottom of the filler plug. If checked cold, it should be ½-in. below the filler plug. Also, SAE 90 viscosity grade oil that meets MIL-L-2105B standards should be used. *Caution: Straight mineral oil gear lubricant should not be used in hypoid rear axles.*

Positive traction rear axles use a special lubricant intended for limited-slip differentials. Some oil companies have a high-quality, multi-purpose gear lubricant that can be used in all types of rear axles; however, if the wrong lubricant is used, no harm will be done except that you will feel a chattering on the turns. If this happens, suction the wrong lubricant out and replace it with the correct anti-slip fluid. Allow about 50 miles of driving for the correct fluid to work its way in between the clutch plates. Turn-

ing from right to left will help work it in by exposing plates to the oil.

If the rear axle is submerged in water, such as on a boat launching ramp where water can enter the axle vent, and contamination is suspected or evident, replace the lubricant immediately to avoid early axle failure.

CHASSIS

Between 1961 and 1963, American automobile manufacturers introduced what is called "long-life" front-end ball joints that only require lubrication every 3 years or 36,000 miles, whichever occurs first. These semi-permanently lubricated ball joints should be inspected every 6 months—or whenever the car is serviced—for signs of damage to seals, which can result in loss or contamination of lubricant. The special seals at each joint are the key to this extended lubrication period, and if they become damaged in any way they must be replaced and the joint lubricated.

It's easy to tell if your car has the

4. Hand-Operated Grease Gun

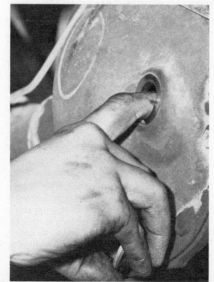

5. Determining Rear End Oil Level

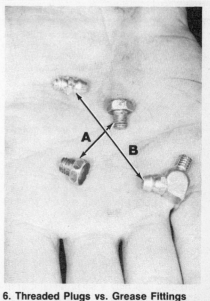

6. Threaded Plugs vs. Grease Fittings

Lubrication

long-life ball joints: the car will not have any grease fittings. Instead you'll find a tiny threaded metal plug. The procedure for lubricating these new type ball joints is to remove the plug and screw in a special grease gun fitting. Stop filling when lubricant begins to flow from bleed area at base or at top of seal, or if seal begins to "balloon." Remove the grease fitting and reinstall the plug.

The only types of lubricant that should be used in these semi-permanently lubricated joints are moly-disulfide greases. They are long lasting and highly waterproof.

Cars without the long-life ball joints should be lubricated every 60 days or 4000 miles. These joints have what are called Zerk fittings installed at each lubrication point, and if you expect to have a trouble-free front end and one that is safe, you must lubricate these joints regularly. The reason is that these Zerk fittings, even though they have a ball-check valve that doesn't let grease leak out, do let in a small amount of dirt and water. Also a certain amount of dirt and moisture works its way in at the joint. To get rid of this dirty grease, it's necessary to flush it out with new grease periodically before it does any damage. All Zerk fittings must be wiped clean before injecting any new lubricant.

While it's possible that you may want to lubricate your own car with a hand-operated grease gun, it's easier and faster in a service station with a high-pressure grease gun. Also, a service station or car dealer will have a complete lubrication chart (number of fittings, location, types of lubricant and refill quantities) on every car so that you can be sure of a thorough job. There are exceptions to this if you have replaced any factory parts that did not have a lubrication fitting with one that does. An example might be universal joints or idler arm, in which case you must make the attendant aware of the change, so that he does not miss properly lubricating it.

Other chassis pivot points such as rubber shock absorber bushings, spring leaf bushings and leaf liners or pads, and anti-sway bars do not require lubrication. They are made to run dry and if they wear out, they should be replaced. However, after many years and miles of use they sometimes get squeaky; then, and only then, should they be lubricated with a special rubber lubricant spray. Be sure to mention this to your dealer too, as they sometimes make it a point to spray only older cars.

Clutch, brake and parking brake linkages should also be lubricated about every 6 months. Wipe all the pivot points clean and lube with 30 weight engine oil. Lubricate pivot points inside car sparingly so as not to cause dripping which will stain upholstery.

On some older cars (especially Ford products '32-'48) it is necessary to lubricate the clutch throwout bearing shaft, and a Zerk fitting is provided for this purpose. Use only a small amount of lubricant, as excessive grease may work

1. Locating Metal Plugs

3. Tightening the Zerk Fitting

its way onto the clutch and cause it to slip when engaged.

UNIVERSAL JOINTS

Most cars, except some of the late models, will have lubrication fittings at the driveshaft universal joints. They should be lubricated every 4 months or 6000 miles, but sparingly and very carefully so as not to pump out the seals. On cars with torque tube drive there is only one fitting, and that is where the driveshaft meets the transmission output shaft at the ball joint. This joint must also be lubricated carefully so as not to damage the rear transmission oil seal.

On some late-model cars without lubrication fittings on the universal joints, the manufacturers say that lubrication is not necessary for the life of the joint and that only periodic inspection is necessary to check for leaking seals, in which case either the seal may be replaced or the complete universal joint.

Because auto manufacturers vary so widely on universal joint lubrication, it's best to consult your owner's manual to

2. Removing Plugs

4. Wiping Off Zerk Fitting

see if lubrication is advisable for your make, year and model. If there is no universal joint grease fitting and lubrication is advisable, it should be done every 2 years or 24,000 miles. To lubricate this type of joint it is necessary to remove the driveshaft and disassemble the U-joints as if you were going to renew the bearings. (That operation is described in the chapter on driveshafts.)

STEERING GEAR

The lubrication installed in the steering gear at time of assembly is a high-quality product, and regular or seasonal changes are not normally required.

Steering gear oil level should be checked at every engine oil change interval; its normal level is up to the filler plug. Some steering boxes use grease instead of oil. Your owner's manual or local lubrication expert will tell you which should be used.

POWER STEERING

Check the power steering reservoir level at every engine oil change. The

5. Lubing Rubber-Mounted Pivot Points

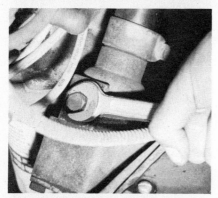

6. Loosening Screw on Steering Box

1. The threaded metal plugs are found installed on semi-permanently lubricated ball joints. Clean away all dirt and grease before removing.

2. A small socket wrench works best for plug removal. Some shops will replace the plugs after greasing the car; you're ahead of the game if you leave the Zerk fitting in.

3. Screw the Zerk fitting in by hand as far as it will go, then tighten snugly with an open end wrench. Using the angle fitting on top of the ball joint makes greasing a bit easier. The straight fitting works fine on the bottom of the ball joint.

4. All Zerk fittings must be wiped free of old grease or road scum build-up before fresh grease is added. The accumulation will contaminate the fresh grease if this isn't done.

5. Rubber-mounted pivot points on shocks, springs, torsion bars, etc., are lubricated with a silicone-based rubber lube applied with a squirt can, but only if they are squeaking. Otherwise they should be left dry so they won't slip and wear out.

6. The oil or grease level in the steering gear—normally up to the filler plug—must be checked at the same time you change oil and filter.

reservoir will either have a dipstick for measurement, a *full* mark on the housing or a notation on the cap to *fill* to ¼-in. *below* top.

Most power steering units use automatic transmission fluid, but special power steering fluid is available, and the units seem to work a little bit better on it. Both special steering fluid and the auto trans fluid will mix compatibly, so there is no necessity for emptying the system when adding fluid. Do not overfill any power steering unit. Overfilling can cause pressure to build up that would blow the seals in the pump.

WHEEL BEARINGS

Front wheel bearings are one of the most important lubrication points on a car and yet one of the most neglected. It is highly imperative that they be cleaned, repacked and the seals inspected every 12 months or 12,000 miles. This includes all cars, both old and late models regardless of make.

To lubricate the front wheel bearings, it's necessary to remove the wheel and hub assembly.

The condition of ball and roller type bearings that have been in service cannot be judged until they are thoroughly cleaned. There is always enough dirt present to affect the "feel" of the bearing and give the impression that they are rough.

Bearings with seals or shields on both ends should not be washed in solvent since there is no way to replenish the grease supply. This type is merely wiped clean and checked for a rough or noisy "feeling."

Unsealed bearings should be washed thoroughly in clean solvent which has not been used for other parts. Slosh the bearings up and down rapidly in the solvent to flush out all dirt and metal particles. It may be necessary to soak hardened dirt and lubricant from bearings; however, do not let them touch the bot-

tom of the pan and pick up any dirt that may have settled there.

After washing, blow out the bearings with clean dry air, directing the air stream squarely into the open side. Hold the inner race and turn the outer race slowly by hand. *Never spin the bearings with air pressure.* It's not only hard on the bearing, but dangerous. That bearing will spin at several thousand rpm, enough to make it disintegrate like a fragmentation grenade, and you know what damage they can do.

Most dealers with service stations have a pressure packing tool that forces the lubricant throughout the bearing. This is the best way; however, it may be done by hand by carefully pushing the grease down in between the balls or rollers. It takes time to do this, and you must work the grease in from all open sides.

Rear wheel bearings get their lubrication by "splash" from the rear axle gears, although some very old cars have a lubrication fitting at the ends of the axle housing. Check this out. Also, they only require one quick shot of lubricant so as not to damage the seals or force lubricant into the braking surface areas.

AIR CLEANERS

There are four main types of carburetor air cleaners in use today: the dry replaceable paper element, the oil-wetted wire mesh air cleaner, oil-wetted polyurethane, and the oil bath type.

The dry replaceable paper type should be cleaned every 6000 miles and replaced every 12,000 miles or 12 months. To clean this type of filter, drop it repeatedly and squarely on a clean, flat surface until all loose dust has been removed. Turn element over and repeat process. Air blast cleaning is okay if done very carefully. Now visually inspect the element for any breaks or holes in the fiber and replace if any dust leaks are found. Before installing element, wipe all dust from interior of air cleaner and install element by turning 180° from removal position. When element and cover are in place, tighten wing nut securely by hand to insure a good seal.

Oil-wetted wire mesh cleaners must be cleaned every 4000 miles. This type is washed in clean solvent by sloshing up and down and then setting aside to drain dry. Oil the element liberally with 30 wt. engine oil, allow excess to drain off, and reinstall your element.

The polyurethane type filter is washed in clean solvent and squeezed dry. Soak in 30 wt. engine oil and replace element. This type of element may be cleaned every 6000 miles in most areas.

Oil bath air cleaners are serviced by emptying the oil reservoir and washing the entire unit in clean solvent every 10,000 miles. The reservoir is then refilled with 30 wt. engine oil to the level indicated on the unit. Some oil baths also have a wire mesh filter which is serviced as outlined for this particular type.

Never dunk an entire air cleaner in solvent. You may think you are going to get it really clean, but all you will do is get solvent inside the air chamber, and it will take you about 2 weeks of rich run-

Lubrication

ning on your car before all the stuff evaporates.

Oil filler caps with mesh breathers should be washed every 4000 miles with solvent. Slosh the cap up and down in the solvent rapidly and tap squarely on a flat surface until all dirt is removed. Allow cap to drain until dry and lubricate with 30 wt. engine oil.

On late-model emission-controlled cars, the breather mesh that used to be in the oil filler cap is now in the air cleaner at the end of a hose running from the sealed filler cap. The reason for the breather mesh inside the air cleaner is not to protect the engine, but to keep oil fumes off the air cleaner element. Clean the breather mesh in solvent, but leave it dry when you replace it.

GENERATORS AND ALTERNATORS

Most generators have oil cups at one or both ends of the housing. These cups should get 2 or 3 drops of 30 wt. oil every 2000 miles or at engine oil change interval.

Alternators are equipped with sealed bearings and lubrication is not possible. If a bearing goes bad (usually from water, so cover vent holes when washing or steam cleaning your engine), it must be replaced. No other maintenance is necessary except wiping dust from vents.

DISTRIBUTOR

Most distributors, except on late-model cars, have an oil cup outside the housing. This should be filled every 2000 miles or at engine oil change interval with 30 wt. oil. Many distributors have a felt wick underneath the rotor. A few drops of oil on the wick will keep it moist so that the breaker cam will move freely on the shaft. However, the wick does not lubricate the advance weights. They should be checked whenever the points are going to be replaced.

WATER PUMP

Almost all water pumps have sealed bearings which never need service for the life of the pump. When the bearing goes bad the pump is replaced. However, preventive maintenance means adding a can of Rust Inhibitor and Water Pump Lubricant to your radiator every 6 months, unless you are running antifreeze. In that case, the antifreeze is all you need. Adding rust inhibitor to the antifreeze might prolong the life of the water pump, but in our experience it lowers the boiling point of the coolant enough to cause boiling over and coolant loss.

Some older cars have a grease fitting on the water pump, and this type should be lubricated every 2000 miles or at engine oil change with special water pump grease. It's waterproof.

EXHAUST MANIFOLD VALVE

The exhaust manifold valve should be lubricated at every engine oil change to keep it operating properly. Any sticking of this valve will impair engine efficiency. Lubricate both sides of the shaft with a mixture of graphite and kerosene, or you can purchase special exhaust manifold valve lubricant at a parts store.

ACCELERATOR LINKAGE

All the pivot points in the accelerator linkage should be lubricated at the 10,000-mile mark when the engine tune-up is performed. It's not difficult to understand that smooth operation of the accelerator linkage is important to safety and control of your car. Use 30 wt. engine oil on all pivots and grease on all sliding arms. Some car makers suggest keeping linkage dry, so it won't pick up dirt and wear faster.

SPEEDOMETER CABLE

To service a noisy speedometer cable, disconnect the cable at the speedometer head and remove the shaft. Clean the shaft thoroughly and then lubricate. Insert the shaft back in the cable, being careful not to let it touch the ground and pick up any dirt. Wipe the excess lubricant from the end of the cable and reconnect to the speedometer head.

CONTROLS AND SEATS

Once a year do a little spring lubing

1. Determining Fluid Level

2. Greasing Wheel Bearing

3. Cleaning Paper Air Cleaner Element

inside the car. Dash control knobs that you push and pull should be wiped clean (remove any rust spots with crocus cloth) and lightly lube with grease. Push the knob in and out to work in the lubricant. Also lubricate the open cable ends where they attach to the heater, the air conditioner, windshield wiper, fresh air intakes, etc. And don't forget the seat tracks. It's always annoying and diffucult to try to adjust a seat that won't slide smoothly. Lubricating power seats is especially important.

BODY LUBRICATION

Don't forget there are literally hundreds of body parts that need regular lubrication too, and they should be serviced every 6 months to keep your car in top condition.

All rotating parts and hinge pins are to be lubricated with 30 wt. engine oil. All sliding and rubbing contact parts are lubed with grease. The only exceptions to this are the door and tailgate striker plates and bolts, and the ends of the sunshade rods which require non-staining stick-type lubricant—and the door key locks which use powdered graphite.

Accumulated dirt, dust and old lubricant should always be wiped off before applying new lubrication. Then operate the mechanism to work it in, wiping off any excess. All rubber moldings should be lubed with a special rubber lubricant to keep them from weather cracking and prolong their life. Rubber lubricant soaks into rubber and soon disappears. We have been experimenting with silicone (either spray or grease) and find that it does an excellent job of protecting rubber parts from deterioration.

Start at the front and work your way back. Lubricate the hood latch, release

1. Like the steering gear, the fluid level in the power steering reservoir must be looked at every 3 months or 3000 miles. Don't overfill reservoir.

2. Repacking the wheel bearings can be done by man or machine. Some use a bearing packing tool to force the grease between the rollers or balls. The hand method means you must put a large dab of grease in the palm of your cupped hand and stroke the bearing over the material, forcing it in between the balls or rollers.

3. Paper air filter elements are prone to disintegration when compressed air is blown over the surface to remove loose dust. It's easier to go out and buy a fresh element.

4. From the generator we'll move to the distributor. Most have an oil cup on the outside of the housing which needs a drop or two of 30-wt.

5. The moving parts attached to the car's body require periodic servicing. Work your way back from the front, catching the hood latch, release cable, safety catch, etc., then on to the door latches, hinges, striker plates, trunk lid catch, key lock and trunk hinges.

6. If it moves, don't salute it, lube it! All pivot points in the throttle linkage require the oil treatment every 10,000 miles.

cable and safety mechanism and the hood hinges. The doors are next—striker plates, door locks, striker rotor, hinges and hold-open mechanism and/or torque rods, the latching mechanism and key lock. If you have a station wagon or pickup, don't forget the tailgate hinges, lock and support rods. And way out back, put a little lubrication on the gas cap cover door hinges. If you have a convertible, you'll want to do the folding top mechanism, but apply it sparingly (have a rag handy) so as not to get any lubricant on top of upholstery. Oil frequently seeps out onto the paint a few days after lubing door hinges and other body parts, so use just as little oil as possible, unless you want to be a traveling advertisement for 3-in-1.

We'll leave the window regulators up

to you. Normally, they will probably never need care unless you have an older car, or trouble develops inside the door panel. But if it's difficult to turn the window crank, remove the upholstery panel and determine the cause. It may just need aligning and lubrication. By servicing it now, before it breaks entirely, you'll save some money.

To remind you of your regular lubrication and maintenance program, the accompanying chart will tell you at a glance the items that need service on a "mileage" and "time interval" basis. As previously mentioned, some of the items will need adjustment according to your driving habits and geographical location. Stick to it and your car will always be in top condition and serve you reliably.

4. Oiling Distributor

5. Greasing Hood Latch

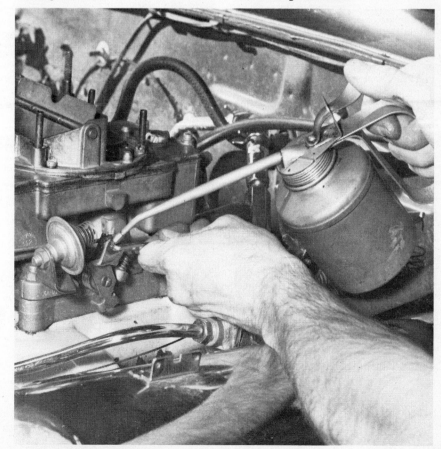
6. Lubricating Throttle Linkage

Tuning Your Engine

Ever since somebody coined the word "tune-up" it has been used and abused so much that nobody really knows what it means anymore. Probably the main reason is that nobody knew what the guy meant when he conceived the term in the first place. If we ever meet him, we will certainly ask.

Because a tune-up varies so much, depending upon what garage or what mechanic is doing the work, we can only tell you what we feel a tune-up should include. We have known garages that included a check of the brake fluid and a windshield cleaning in their regular tune-up procedure. There's certainly nothing wrong with that, but what we will deal with here are just the bare necessities in what we consider a basic tune-up.

AIR CLEANER

Much of a tune-up involves using your naked eye to look for parts that are out of adjustment, worn out, or just plain dirty. For instance, the first thing that is usually done in any tune-up is to remove the air cleaner. We do this for a couple reasons. The most obvious is to get the cleaner out of the way so we can work on the engine. The other is to examine the filters that are inside it to see if they are in need of replacement.

If your car has the type of filter that traps dirt because it is moistened with oil, then all you have to do is wash it out in solvent, put some clean oil on it, and it's ready to go back on the car. Incidentally, if you should be washing any of the old-fashioned air cleaners that have a large silencing chamber, do not submerge them in a bucket of solvent, because the solvent will run inside the silencing chamber where you can't pour it out. It will take about two weeks to evaporate out of there, and all during that time your car will be running rich because of the solvent fumes.

Many cars today use the dry type of air cleaner element made out of folded paper. You don't need any fancy testing rigs to determine if it is good. Just hold the element up to a naked light bulb and you can see if it's clean or not. On late model cars, there is another filter inside the air cleaner can that stops oil fumes coming from the hose that connects to one of the rocker covers. That filter should be washed out and reinstalled.

GUM AND VARNISH SOLVENT

Removing the air cleaner exposes the top of the carburetor. So this is an excellent time, before you touch anything else on the engine, to feed some tune-up solvent through the carburetor with the engine running at a fast idle. This is a step that is seldom done in commercial garages because it smokes up the neighborhood and it takes a lot of time. However, it is probably the most important part of the whole tune-up. It must be done before the tune-up is started, not afterwards. The tune-up solvent does a good job of loosening up carbon accumulations in the cylinders. The carbon starts flying around and one of the first places it lands is on the spark plug. Sometimes the loosened carbon will foul the plugs so badly that they can't be cleaned and reused. So the only way to do it is when you know you are going to change the old plugs anyway.

When feeding the tune-up solvent through the carburetor the basic idea is to feed it as fast as you can without killing the engine. It amounts to a delicate balance between one hand holding the throttle and the other tipping the can. When you get down to the last part of the solvent, let it all run in so that the engine is flooded and dies. Then let the car sit a while so that the solvent will have a chance to work on the combustion chamber deposits. The final step is the blowout. Drive the car slowly and accelerate from zero to 30 at wide-open throttle a few times. Continue until all the smoke is gone and you can see out the rear window once again.

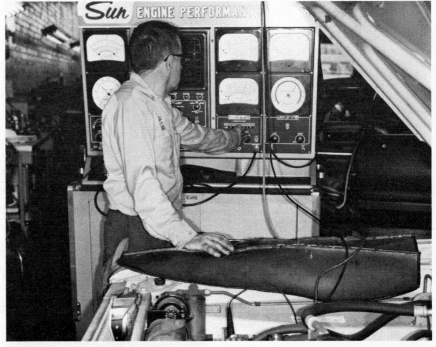

1. Professional Tune-Up Equipment

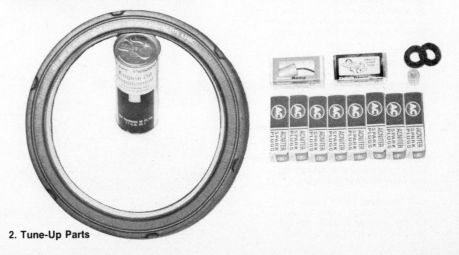

2. Tune-Up Parts

3. Cleaning Battery Posts

4. Cleaning Cable Ends

5. Emission and Tuning Specs

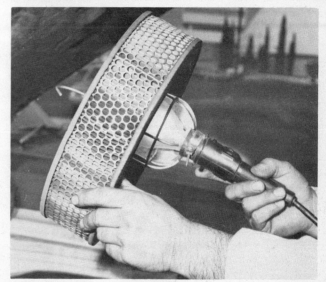

6. Checking Paper Air Cleaner Element

1. Much exotic new professional tuning equipment has been developed over recent years, but do-it-at-homer can still do the job himself, though it will take longer than for a pro.

2. Parts used in most basic tune-ups include air and fuel filters, spark plugs, point set and condenser.

3. Cleaning battery posts is a snap with this dual-purpose tool by Snap-on. Leading edge on heavy gauge snap ring does the trick nicely.

4. With its six metal blades embedded in plastic, Snap-on battery tool has wide edge on older wire brush terminal cleaner; this one really does the job quickly and cleanly.

5. On the newer cars with the smog systems, special tuning information is on a label in engine compartment.

6. A dirty air cleaner element can cut your gas mileage considerably. You can check the condition of one by shining a droplight through the back. If light won't go through, then you should replace the element.

7. If you have access to an air hose you can blow (from the inside) some of the loose dirt out of an air cleaner and recheck with droplight.

CRANKING VOLTAGE

Cranking voltage at the battery terminal of the ignition coil should also be checked before you proceed any further with the tune-up. If while making the cranking voltage test you use a tachometer or your good ear to tell if the engine is being cranked at a normally fast cranking speed, then you have checked the battery, the generator, the starter, the ignition switch and the wiring in just a few seconds.

If that doesn't sound right to you, let's analyze it. When the cranking speed of the engine is normal, you know that the starter and the battery are good. If the coil is receiving at least 9 volts, you know that the wiring from the battery through the ignition switch to the coil must be good. How about the generator? Well, if the battery cranks the engine normally and supplies normal voltage to the coil, it must be adequately charged. And if it is charged, it follows that the generator has to be OK.

The cranking voltage test is done with a remote starter button which is connected to a terminal on the starter solenoid so that you can operate the starter directly from the battery. On some cars, you can't reach the solenoid, so the way

7. Cleaning Dry-type Element

to do it is to use an ice pick to connect with the wire that runs from the solenoid to a plug on the firewall. The procedure varies with the make of car. If you have trouble and can't seem to get the starter to work with a remote starter button, the easy way to do it is to just sit in the car and use the normal ignition switch. Position your voltmeter so that you can see it through the windshield during cranking, and the job's done. Remember that the voltmeter goes to the battery terminal of the coil, not to the distributor side. To keep the car from starting so that the engine will crank long enough to get a good reading on the voltmeter, you

Tuning Your Engine

should pull the wire out of the center tower of the distributor cap and use a short jumper lead to ground it to the engine. Another way of keeping the engine from starting is to either disconnect or ground the wire to the points. Be very careful you don't ground the wrong wire, or you will burn up the ignition switch, and maybe the car, too.

The battery only puts out a little over 9 volts during cranking because of a phenomenon known as voltage fall-off. Were you ever in an old house where the lights used to dim every time the refrigerator went on? A similar thing happens when the battery is operating the starter. A tremendous amount of current is flowing out of the battery, which causes the battery voltage to drop. We expect a certain amount of voltage fall-off, so long as it's not too much. If the voltage falls off too much, we know that the battery is weak or worn out, or there's a bad cable connection, etc. We check the voltage at the battery terminal of the coil because that is the most important point. If you don't have sufficient voltage there, you don't get any spark.

If you don't get at least 9 volts at the coil during cranking, the first thing to check is the battery. A 12-volt battery should put out approximately 12.6 volts when it's not running anything. If it only puts out an even 12 volts, it is low. If you don't have a voltmeter, you can't very well check cranking voltage, but you can listen to the cranking speed, and that will tell you quite a bit in itself.

TUNE-UP EQUIPMENT

A tune-up is only necessary once a year or every 12,000 miles. So it's hard to justify purchase of a voltmeter or other tune-up equipment if you are only going to use it once a year. However, with the cost of labor skyrocketing these days, you will find that buying a tune-up in a garage will cost you more than buying all your own tune-up equipment and parts and doing the job yourself.

Only a few pieces of equipment are necessary in order to do a tune-up. It would be nice if you had a timing light, a tachometer, a dwell meter, a remote start button, and a compression gauge. The only one that you really need is the timing light. Sure, it is possible to set timing statically, but on a modern engine there is too much chance for error, and the recommended way is to use a light while the engine is running. The tachometer you can do without, because you can pay a garage man a couple of dollars to set the idle speed for you. The dwell meter is not necessary if you have a specification book which will tell you what the point gap should be, and you can set that with a feeler gauge. The remote start button, as we have already pointed out, can be eliminated by using the key switch on the instrument panel.

You may feel that it is absolutely necessary to take a compression check, but it isn't. A garage man takes a compression check only because he has to guarantee his work. He knows that tuning of a car with poor compression is not done because the car should first have a ring and valve job. But even the most horrible old clunker will run better if it has the timing set, points gapped correctly, and the spark plugs either cleaned or replaced.

When you do the tune-up yourself, you don't have to guarantee it to anyone. You just want your car to run better and it will not matter what the compression is. Taking a compression check on your own car will, in many cases, just make you feel bad, because you'll find out some disappointing news that you didn't know before. However, if you are buying a car or checking out somebody else's car, then by all means make a compression check because it will tell you the condition of the engine.

1. Pulling PCV Valve

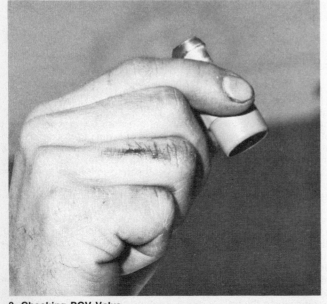

2. Checking PCV Valve

3. Echlin PCV Valve Tester

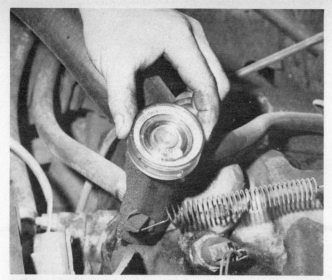

4. Testing Running Engine

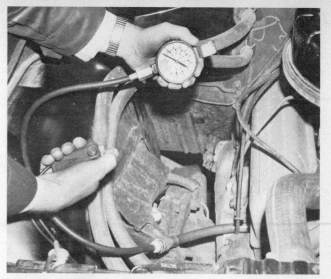

5. Making Compression Check

6. Heat Riser Valve

7. Fuel Line Filter

TIMING LIGHT TESTS

If you do have a certain amount of equipment, you should use it to take measurements before you start doing the tune-up so that you will have some basis for making adjustments afterwards. It is entirely possible that the ignition timing or the idle speed is not set to stock specifications. Maybe the idle speed is set a little faster so the engine won't die. Or maybe the timing is retarded a little to take care of cheaper gas, or advanced a little to give more acceleration. If you don't check timing and idle speed before you start fiddling with the distributor, there is no way—after you get the engine running again—that you can get it back to where it was.

Suppose you check an engine that has the ignition timing set 4° advanced from where it is supposed to be. If it runs well, and it doesn't ping, you'd better leave it there because the last guy who set it probably knew what he was doing. Any time you touch the points you automatically change the ignition timing. So if you dive right in to replace them without checking the timing first, you may find that you are experimenting for three weeks afterwards trying to get the timing

set to a position that will give the performance you had before you changed the points.

With a timing light, you can also check the vacuum and centrifugal advance curves in the distributor very easily. With everything hooked up normally, all you have to do is run the engine up slowly to about 2000 rpm and watch the timing marks move on the front pulley as you shine the timing light on them. As you open the throttle to run the speed up, the vacuum advance will change the position of the marks, and you can see what's happening right on the front pulley. Pull the vacuum advance line off the distributor and then you can check the centrifugal advance. Of course, you are not accurately measuring the advance when you are doing this, but at least you can get an indication that both vacuum and centrifugal advance are working to some degree.

There are timing lights on the market that have an adjustable electronic delay. With them you can actually measure the amount of advance you are getting on the front pulley, because turning the little knob on the light will bring the marks back in line with each other. It's a slick unit but it's very expensive and not too

1. The PCV valves in your rocker covers or carburetor need to be removed and checked once or twice each year for clogging.

2. By shaking the smog valve, you can hear if the inner element is free. If it rattles, OK; if it doesn't, it's clogged and should be replaced with a new one.

3. Smog valve checkers like these are available inexpensively at most auto parts houses.

4. Holding the checker on the oil filler tube while the engine is running tells you whether system is working or not.

5. Before doing a tune-up, it may be a good idea to make a compression check. It will tell you if there are any major engine problems such as worn rings or valves.

6. It's very important to check for free operation of your heat riser in the exhaust manifold. If it isn't free, spray it with some solvent or choke cleaner.

7. There's usually a fuel filter in the gas line or carburetor that should be replaced periodically.

Tuning Your Engine

practical for home use. Your best bet is to check it as we have suggested and if you see the marks jump around, or if it appears that you're not getting enough advance, pull the distributor out and take it down to a garage so that they can set it on the distributor machine.

TUNE-UP PROCEDURE

Now we're ready to start the actual tune-up, so we shut the engine off, pull the smog valve and drop it in a bucket of carburetor cleaner. Remove the plugs and take a look at each one, keeping them arranged on the fender or on a bench so that you can remember from which cylinder each one originally came.

Reading spark plugs is not too difficult after you have looked at a few. If they're as black as a coal bin, they are fouled. A kind of dull white to light brown on the plug porcelain is fine. This depends a lot on the year of the car. Late-model cars run so lean that their spark plugs will be just about pure white almost any time you look at them. Modern combustion chambers can run the plugs that white because the plug position in the cylinder is such that the incoming fuel keeps it from burning up. Unless you have a problem with plug fouling, you should use the same heat range plug that came in the engine or its equivalent in another manufacturer's line.

We might mention here about the "rebuilt" spark plugs that you see in grocery stores, drug stores and just about every place except where they sell auto parts. Most of those plugs say "rebuilt" on the package. We don't know what their definition of rebuilt is, but we do know that the rebuilding we have observed consisted only of sandblasting the plugs to clean them. The sandblaster that they use is extremely powerful, much more so than you would find in any service station or auto repair shop. We have used the rebuilt plugs and found in our own experience that they

foul much quicker than new or normally sandblasted plugs.

One reason that the rebuilt plugs have prospered is the difficulty of getting anybody to clean spark plugs these days. Most service stations and garages have a plug cleaner somewhere off in the corner that is either broken or hasn't been used for 15 years. There is nothing wrong with cleaning plugs in a normal sandblast cleaner. If they will come

clean, the center electrode should be filed to a sharp edge, the gap reset, and they can then be used over again. If the porcelains will not come clean because of splash fouling or other deposits that won't come off, the plugs should be thrown away.

With the plugs out, you should now make a compression check if you're going to do it at all. Then it's time to remove the old points and install new

1. Freeing Choke

2. Blowing Out Carbon Deposits

3. Normal Plug

4. Oil-Fouled Plugs

ones. We recommend that you put the points in without removing the distributor from the car. You may have to crawl over the fender and lean on top of the sharp points of the engine in a very uncomfortable position, but installing points in the car will get you into a lot less

1. If you get a lot of black smoke from your tailpipe in the morning, maybe your choke is sticking. Spray lubricant for freeing chokes is available in spray or squirt cans.

2. Pouring a little Chemtool into the carburetor while the engine is running helps to clean out the motor by dissolving carbon and deposits.

3. Light tan or gray-colored ash deposits and some electrode wear are typical of a normal plug. If the porcelain is extremely white, the engine may be running too lean.

4. If the deposits are black and heavy, the trouble is probably that of excessive oil in the cylinders. However, it could also be caused by flooding of the carburetor.

5. Here's the best advertisement for blowing out an engine before you tune it up. That way, the splash fouling will occur on the old plugs.

6. You will see a broken insulator like this every once in a while. It is caused by severe detonation, or it could be caused by pressure on the center electrode when gapping plug.

7. These dry, fluffy black deposits may be caused by a rich mixture, which may in turn be caused by a clogged air cleaner or sticky choke. If only one plug is fouled, suspect the electrical circuit to that plug, the plug itself, or that cylinder.

8. Plugs do wear out. If there is a lot of wear on the electrodes and the insulator looks pitted, it's time to replace the plug.

9. Flaky, white or yellow deposit is caused by scavenger additives in the gasoline. These deposits will easily come off in a plug cleaner.

trouble than pulling the distributor and then trying to get the thing properly timed when you put it back in. In a commercial garage it's a different proposition. They want to check the vacuum and centrifugal advance curves, so they may pull the distributor and test-run it on their machine.

You can tell a lot about the vacuum and centrifugal advance difficulties you may be having just by looking at the distributor parts. If you have a Delco distributor with the weights up on top where they are easily seen, check to see if the weights move freely back and forth and that the springs are not rusty or broken. You can check the vacuum advance just by sucking on the end of it and watching to see if the breaker plate moves back and forth. If it doesn't, there's a hole somewhere and you'd better get a new vacuum advance unit.

If you haven't put points in a distributor before, move very slowly when removing the old points. You want to get the new ones back in exactly the same position with all the screws in the same place and all the leads positioned exactly where they were before. There's a lot of movement that goes on underneath the distributor cap. If everything isn't in the right place, things can get all tangled up, and then it's no spark.

New points are usually lined up fairly well, and there are thousands of mechanics all over the country who don't even look at them before they put them in. But it's a good idea to check the points' alignment because they will last a lot longer if you do. The idea is to have the point faces meet squarely so that in the case of conventional points, the only contact is exactly in the center. If you have the points with the hole in the middle, then the contact is a full circle rather than a single point. Point alignment

5. Splash Fouling

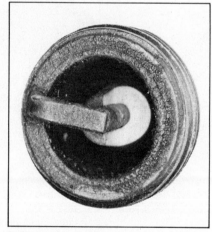

6. Chipped Insulator

7. Carbon-Fouled Plug

8. Worn-Out Plug

9. Scavenger Deposits

Tuning Your Engine

can be checked by looking through the points parallel to their surfaces with a white card held behind them. You can easily see if they are twisted at all. To line them up, bend only the stationary point until the contact faces meet squarely.

The design of the points will determine whether you do point alignment before the points are put in the distributor or afterwards. On a General Motors V-8, the point assembly is made in one piece so you can do the alignment while you're holding the points in your hand. Some other cars have the points in two pieces with the pivot post mounted on the distributor breaker plate. To align those points you have to have them mounted on the breaker plate in their normal position before attempting to bend the stationary point. You can use ordinary pliers to bend the stationary point, but you might slip and ruin something. A special tool with a hook end is much easier to use.

What you do with the points after they are installed will depend upon your make of car. In a Delco distributor with an Allen head set screw you don't do anything because the point gap will be set after the engine is running. Most other cars require that you use a feeler gauge to set the actual point gap in thousandths of an inch. When you check the gap, be sure that the rubbing block of the points is at the high spot on one of the cam lobes. If you feel like checking things out, measure the point gap on several cam lobes. You'll find that it varies a couple of thousandths. Nothing's perfect these days.

To get the cam lobe exactly under the point rubbing block, you can turn the engine over by pulling on the fan belt. You have the plugs out so it should turn easily. Another way is to "bump" the engine with a remote starter button. The easiest and most accurate way is to loosen the distributor hold-down bolt and turn the body of the distributor either way until you get what you want. After the gap is set, move the distributor body back

where it was, so that the engine will start easily.

After installing the points, check the gap on the new plugs. Put a drop of oil on the threads of each plug and then thread it home. If the spark plug wires are all mixed up and you can't figure out which ones go on which plugs, the only way to check it out is by firing order. You can usually find at least one plug wire that you know is on the right plug. Trace that wire back to the cap and then follow the firing order around the cap in the direction that the rotor revolves. This will tell you to which spark plug each wire should go. On most distributor caps, No. 1 is marked so that you have a starting point for your firing order.

With the plugs in and the wires on, the engine is almost all put together but you're not ready to start it up yet. A good tune-up involves more than just points and plugs. Somewhere in the exhaust manifold you may find a small flapper valve. It's called the heat riser valve and it's responsible for giving good warmup when you first start your car.

1. Pre-ignition Damage

2. Burned Electrodes

3. Mechanical Damage

4. Bent Side Electrode

The heat riser valve has a spring to hold it in the closed position. It is forced open by exhaust gas pressure when the engine is running at high rpm. The valve should move easily when you touch it and the spring should return it to the closed position when you let go.

What the heat riser valve does is force the exhaust gases through a passageway underneath the carburetor before they can go out through the exhaust system to the muffler. Some cars (mostly Fords) do not have a heat riser valve. They get heat to the manifold by circulating radiator water through a passageway under the carburetor. Late-model cars using temperature controlled air cleaners do not have the valves either; but they do have a flapper valve in the air cleaner snout that gives the engine hot air off the exhaust manifold or cool air from under the hood, depending on the temperature. A quick check for the flapper valve is to move it with your finger to see if it's free. If you want to check it out thoroughly, you can watch it move as the engine warms up.

Cleaning battery terminals is also part of the basic tune-up. You should remove them from the posts, scrape away any corrosion that you find, grease the terminals to prevent future corrosion, and then make sure they are good and tight when they go back on.

The fuel filter is another part of basic tune-up. It should definitely be replaced whether it is the inline type or a little insert that goes in the carburetor inlet.

Now that you've done all those chores, it's time to rescue the smog valve out of

1. A plug has to get pretty hot to melt the electrodes like this. It could be caused by lean mixture, an air leak or even crossfire from another spark plug wire.

2. These electrodes have been hot, but not hot enough to melt away. The plug could be the wrong heat range or the trouble could be caused by spark timing or low-octane fuel.

3. Everything's slightly bent out of shape here because of a nut or washer bouncing around in the cylinder. Changing the plug will not solve the problem until the foreign matter is removed from the engine.

4. Some plier-type gapping tools will bend the side electrode like this, which doesn't necessarily ruin the plug, but the same tools also put pressure on the center electrode. This pressure may push the center electrode right out of the plug.

5. Spark plug cleaning machines are really just small sandblasters. You can get thousands of extra miles out of your plugs by cleaning them, but only if they are undamaged as well as in need of cleaning and regapping.

6. Most spark plug gap gauges have an electrode bender as part of the tool, to adjust the gap to specs by bending the side electrode.

7. When cleaning and gapping old plugs, you should pull back the side electrode so you can get a thin file in to file the center electrode flat.

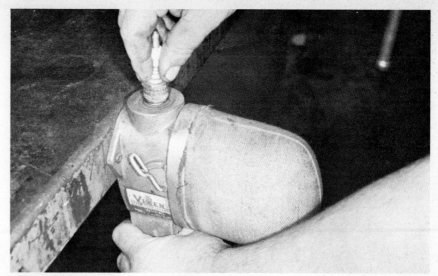

5. Spark Plug Cleaner

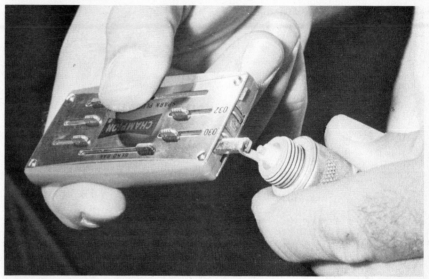

6. Bending Side Electrode

the carburetor cleaner, wash it out in cleaning solvent and put it back on. Some manufacturers do not want you to clean smog valves. They would rather you replace them. Strictly speaking, they are correct because most smog valves cannot be taken apart to make sure they are clean. But if you can hear the little jiggle-pin rattling in there, you can be pretty sure that the valve is going to operate correctly.

Now's the time to fire up the engine, but check your timing light hookup first. It's much less shocking if you hook it up with the engine dead. On Ford and Chrysler products you will already have set your point gap so you don't have to worry about that. But on a Delco-Remy distributor the point gap is set after the engine is running. If you have a dwell meter, set it to 30° and forget about it. But you don't need a dwell meter with a Delco distributor. Use an Allen wrench or one of the special little wrenches with a cable handle that you can buy in most auto parts stores. Lift the window in the side of the distributor cap and turn the Allen screw clockwise until the engine starts to misfire. Sometimes the engine will just flat die without even giving a hint of misfiring. In either case back off counterclockwise ½-turn and your dis-

tributor point dwell will be set perfectly at 30°. Check it with a dwell meter if you want to, but it isn't necessary.

The procedure of backing off ½-turn has been standard for some time, but it has been found that spring tension can cause the screw to move a little later on, if the final turning movement is in a counterclockwise direction. The latest recommendations now call for backing off one turn and then going clockwise ½-turn so that the last movement is

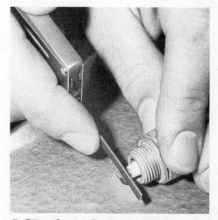

7. Filing Center Electrode Flat

Tuning Your Engine

against the spring tension rather than backing away from it.

You must remember to adjust the initial timing after you adjust the dwell. Any change of point gap will change timing, so you must make your timing setting last. To check the timing, loosen the clamp bolt at the base of the distributor and turn the whole distributor while the engine is running to get the timing marks to line up under the timing light. The timing light must be hooked to No. 1 cylinder, of course, and the vacuum advance hose should be disconnected so that there is no chance for the vacuum to affect the initial timing. Also, you must have the engine speed at a normal idle. If the engine is idling too fast, the centrifugal advance will start to take over and your timing setting will be all out of whack. After the timing is set according to specifications, it's a good idea to make a final check of both centrifugal and vacuum advance by watching the timing marks under the light as you rev up the engine. Then the idle mixture and speed settings should be made. The carburetor should be checked to see if the choke is free. The choke unloader should be working properly. The fast idle mechanism should give the right speed, and the anti-stall dash pot—if it has one—should keep the engine from stalling when you let the

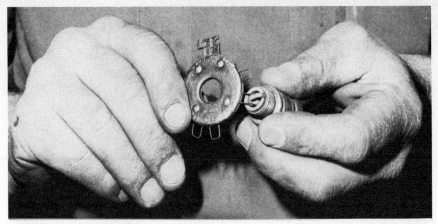
1. Round Wire Plug Gapper

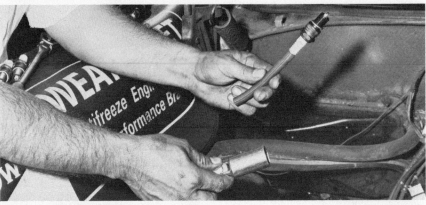
2. Hose for Starting Plugs

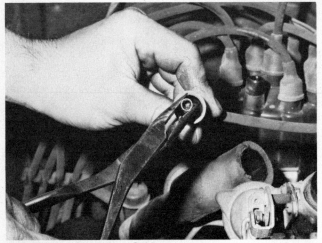
3. Tightening Spark Plug Cables

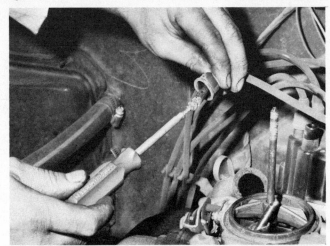
4. Cleaning Cable Ends

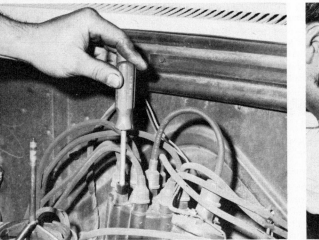
5. Cleaning Distributor Terminals

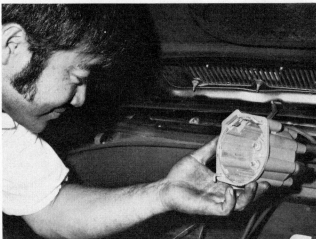
6. Inspecting Cap

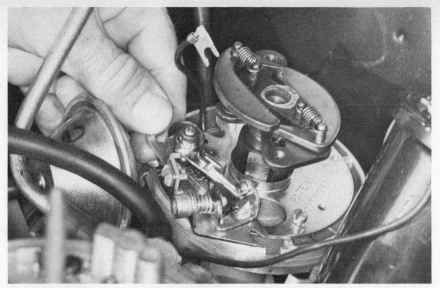

7. Installing Points

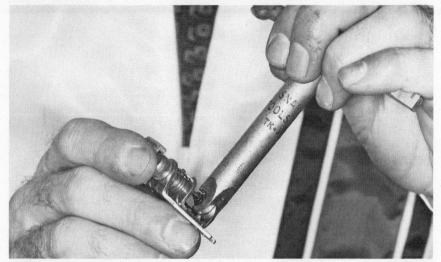

8. Point Aligning Tool

throttle snap shut. Your basic tune-up is now complete.

Other tasks that are sometimes included at extra cost in the tune-up are an overhaul of the carburetor, a check of alternator output and voltage settings, a battery breakdown test, a starter draw test, an oscilloscope test of the ignition, a check of air/fuel ratio at the tailpipe, an exhaust emission test, and many other tests until you end up having everything on the car replaced except the hood ornament. A lot of the tests are good. We personally feel that an oscilloscope is the greatest thing since sliced bread, and a check of air/fuel ratio or emissions is the only way to go. But when you are working on your own car you have to be practical. You can't go out and buy $500 worth of equipment when you only have one car to work on. So what do you do if you want those other tests made? You go to a garage. That's what we'll talk about next.

HAVING A GARAGE TUNE-UP

The question most often asked is, "Where can I go to get a 'good' tune-up?" Unfortunately, there is no pat answer. It's difficult to recommend any particular place unless you have had some

kind of personal contact with the establishment. And this is often impractical or impossible, especially when you have any number of different garages to choose from. Anyone who cares about his car wants to know that whoever works on it will be careful and dependable. Also that the price of repair is reasonable and that he won't be charged for unnecessary repairs or parts. So, the choice of a garage is very important.

The best way to narrow down the selection of garages and service stations is to ask friends and neighbors where they go for tune-ups and repairs and what they think of the work and service. The next step is to look over the work that was performed and see that it was done neatly and that the engine compartment was left clean. If they replaced the points, see if they cleaned the old grease off the distributor cam and then regreased it. It's a little thing, admittedly, but it's important if you want the job to be a lasting one.

At this point, if you have one or two shops in mind, visit them personally. Look over the work they're doing, what they have in the way of tools and equipment, and whether the shop is kept neat and clean. These are all important indications as to the type of work you can

expect from this shop. If you're satisfied so far, the next step is to talk to the manager. See if he takes a genuine interest in you, your car and your problem. If so, this is a good place to start.

In almost every town there is always talk of an "old-timer" who can tell exactly what's the matter with your car as you turn into his driveway and before the turn indicator shuts off. In some cases this is true—though maybe not quite that fast. This fellow is the type who grew up with automobiles and never worked at anything else. He's been up against every problem there ever was and knows every part inside and out—mainly because in his time he has had to rebuild the parts himself. There was no such thing as inexpensive rebuilt parts, and to buy a new part was costly. And certainly, there was no electronic tune-up equipment. This type of person is fading out of the picture. Age, and the fact that labor is so expensive, make it cheaper to install a rebuilt or new part instead of fixing the old existing one.

The modern garage or repair shop of today is based on their mechanics' ability to tell what is wrong and replace the part. By this replacing of parts they can bring your car up to good running condition as usually defined by "factory specifications."

WHAT IS A DIAGNOSTIC CENTER?

A modern diagnostic center is a highly organized method of testing, checking

1. A flat feeler gauge may throw your gapping off, so the best gapper for plugs is the round wire type.

2. When reinstalling plugs in the engine, a short piece of rubber hose can be used to hold the plug while you start it into the threads. It's safer than starting them with wrench.

3. If the spark plug ends of your secondary ignition wires are loose on the plugs, you can get a better connection by tightening the ends with needle-nose pliers.

4. A small wire brush like this K-D #103 is useful in a tune-up for cleaning the ends of your spark plug cables and the terminals in your distributor cap.

5. Some tuners may miss possibility of corrosion buildup inside distributor cap terminals. This tool has wire brush on end for cleaning these hard-to-get-at places.

6. The inside of your distributor cap should be checked carefully for corrosion on the terminals or any carbon "tracks" around cracks.

7. Everyone can understand a spark plug replacement, but some amateur mechanics are wary of replacing their own points and condenser. It's not really that complicated, though.

8. Proper alignment of the point arm is vital to a good tune, but you must remember you can only bend the stationary point, with a tool like this. The GM-type point like this can be adjusted off the car.

Tuning Your Engine

and analyzing every safety and performance factor of a motor vehicle. All tests are conducted with sophisticated electronic and dynamic equipment and instruments with a degree of accuracy never before attained in the servicing of automobiles.

The first true diagnostic center was opened by Mobil Oil Co. in 1962. Since then, Mobil has expanded to more operations located in various parts of the U.S. Also in the intervening years, other major oil companies, automobile dealers and independent repair shops have opened diagnostic centers. And many more are in the planning or construction

stages. A diagnostic center may be simple or elaborate—as small as one or two bays, or as large as a 6-station lane. However, the tests and inspections are common to all. Only the number of cars able to be checked during a given length of time changes with the size of the shop. You'll find it best to make an appointment in advance if you decide to have your car checked.

The most important service a diagnostic center does is to take the guesswork out of locating vehicle malfunctions. In difficult cases it can save you many more times the cost of the diagnosis. Basically, it tests a car through its complete speed and power range while it is hooked up to sensitive electronic gear. The chassis dynamometer can accurate-

ly simulate any type of road operating conditions such as acceleration, cruise, high speed and uphill pull. For instance, if you have a complaint of "missing" at 50 mph or poor acceleration, the trouble can be diagnosed accurately and quickly right in the shop and under almost the same conditions you experienced while driving your car on the road. An additional benefit of chassis dynamometer operation is that the complete driveline of the vehicle can be tested without leaving the shop. This includes clutch, transmission (manual or automatic) and differential.

Clayton Manufacturing Co., one of the leading manufacturers of chassis dynamometers, provides a vehicle Performance Guide chart to diagnostic centers

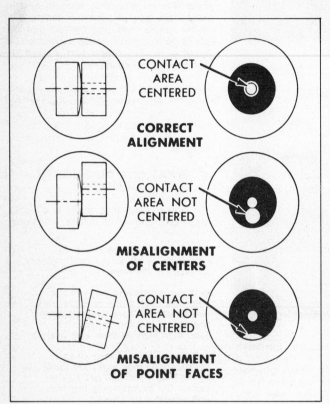

1. Point Alignment

2. Greasing Distributor Cam

3. Greasing Distributor

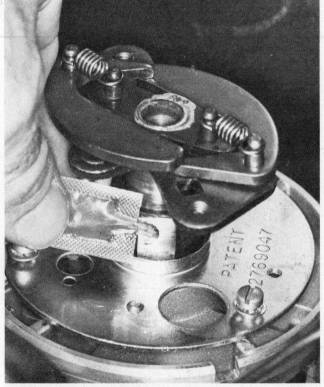

4. Advance Weights

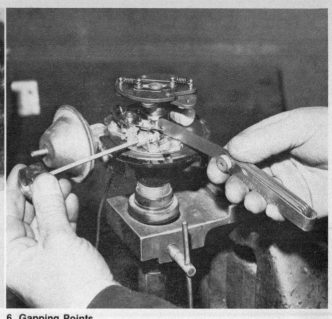

5. Distributor, Testing Machine

6. Gapping Points

1. Getting the right alignment on the points assures that the contact pattern will be centered.

2. When installing new points, one spot you should be sure to lubricate with a small dab of grease is the distributor cam.

3. Other points that should get the clean 'n' lube treatment include the pivots for the advance weights.

4. For proper operation of the distributor, both the distributor cam and the centrifugal advance weights (the part being held up) should be cleaned of any rust or old grease.

5,6. Garages and tune-up shops use sophisticated gear for checking and adjusting distributors, but you can set points with just hand tools and a clean feeler gauge.

7. A portable instrument very handy for on-the-car testing is a tach and dwell meter, useful for setting idle and checking distributor dwell angle.

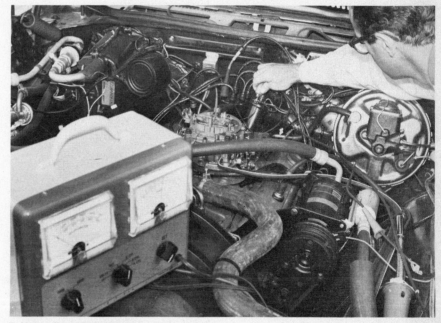

7. Using Tach-Dwell Meter

where their equipment is used. A diagnostic center will use this "road horsepower" guide as a "base line" with which to compare your car's performance. After a center has been in operation for a while, these guide charts may be changed due to geographic location. If a new car dealership performs many tests on one make, it gets to know these cars intimately and has very intimate guide lines. Also, the dealership technicians become highly skilled at testing and diagnosing a particular make. This is not to say, however, that an independent diagnostic center cannot do an equally good job.

Upon entering a diagnostic center, you will notice that it is a very clean, well organized and brightly lighted shop. Most centers are glass enclosed so you can see what is being done to your car. Moreover, you may find additional gauges in your viewing area which are duplicates of those being used by the technician. For the most part, the gauge

readings may not mean much unless there is an audible description of just what is taking place at that particular time. Some centers have a speaker system, while others utilize a brief written description next to the gauge.

Do not get the idea that a diagnostic center is the same as a dyno tuning shop. Much of the equipment is similar and some of the tests are the same, but the big difference is in the work performed and the end results. The function of a diagnostic center is to work to factory specifications, and nothing more. Diagnostic center equipment tests and evaluates the performance of your car's engine and tells the operator what work needs to be done to return your car to a satisfactory operating condition as established by the manufacturer. In other words, plugs (gap and heat range), points (gap and dwell), coil, timing, advance, etc. are all set according to and checked for working to factory specifications. Nothing is altered internally,

nor is there any deviation from the program of testing. As a rule, when this close-tolerance tune-up work is performed by a diagnostic center you should notice an improvement in performance, mainly because most cars are operating at a very minimal condition.

Diagnostic operations have been the center of considerable controversy since they started popping up everywhere. Small independent garagemen will tell you that the diagnostic center is a production line designed to sell parts and services, and that frequently the work done is not really needed at all.

Diagnostic center personnel, in turn, say that the small independent garageman does not have a dynamometer and other necessary equipment to make a complete test of your car.

The new car dealer then gets into the act by claiming that he is the only one who is in close touch with the factory and, therefore, he is the only one who knows how your car should run.

Tuning Your Engine

All of these factions are correct to a degree. Actually, it really doesn't matter where you take your car for service. What does matter is the honesty, capability and knowledge of the people who work on your car regardless of what type of establishment they work in. If you find a place that keeps your car in good condition, to your satisfaction, then stick with it—whether it is a 1-pump service station, an independent garage, a new car dealer, or a million dollar diagnostic center.

HOT ROD TUNE-UP

The old adage "If one's good, two's better and three's a gas" just isn't true in performance tuning any basically stock or near-stock engine. Today, in most cases, the factory stock parts are more than adequate in giving you all the horsepower that's on tap right up to 6500 rpm.

If you decide to modify your car, you should realize what you're getting into—not only from a standpoint of dirty hands but also from a legal angle. In some cases you may actually be breaking laws by modifying your car. A simple change from resistor-type spark plug wires to the solid metallic non resistor type could be in violation of a federal public law which states that in time of emergency, ignition radiation that interferes with radio or television broadcasts is illegal. That is why all of the car makers put resistor wires on new cars. Not that there is any law against the solid core wires, but the car makers do not want to be accused of contributing to a situation wherein all of the airplanes in the country might have trouble transmitting in case of a national emergency.

What about other modifications that affect the smog controls? In that case it presently depends upon your state law. The Federal emissions control legislation currently applies only to cars before they are first sold, except in certain specific

1. Handheld Meter

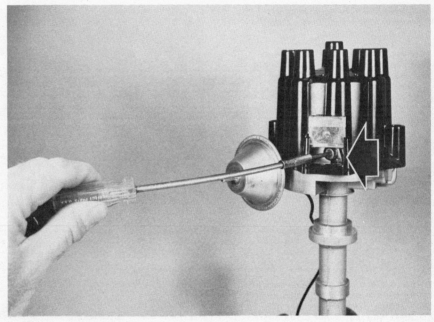

2. Adjusting GM Distributor

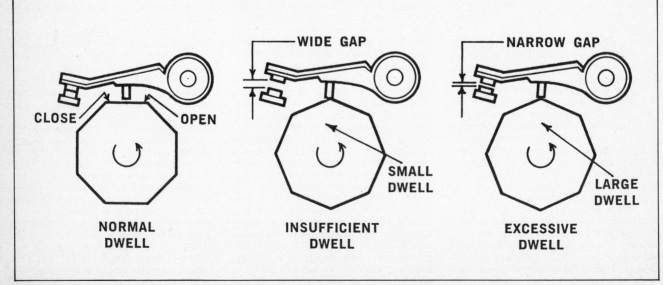

3. Dwell vs. Point Gap

instances that apply to new-car dealers only. However, if your state has passed no specific laws against modifications that would affect smog controls, you're on safe ground.

Some states (and California is an excellent example) have specific laws that

1. Handheld tach and dwell meters are relatively inexpensive at most auto parts stores and well within the reach of the "weekend" mechanic.

2. General Motors distributors from 1957 up have a "window" (arrow) through which points can be adjusted while the engine is running.

3. "Cam angle," "dwell," and "coil saturation" are all determined by the gap of the distributor's breaker points. Careful work with a flat feeler gauge or electronic dwell meter will set you up to specs.

4. When setting the timing, the idle speed should be set low enough so the centrifugal advance doesn't come in, and the vacuum line should be pulled from the distributor (arrow) and plugged with a pencil or wooden golf tee. This keeps vacuum advance at idle from influencing the setting.

5. One of the most useful tune-up tools is a timing light. Inexpensive neon units ($5-$10) work but require some darkness to be able to see the light on the engine's timing marks. Power timing lights like this one are powered by the car's battery and can be used in broad daylight. Take care in moving the timing light in close that you don't hit the fan!

'72-73 VACUUM READINGS ARE LOWEST EVER

If you like to use a vacuum gauge for checking your engine, you are in for a surprise when you hook one up to a late-model car. For many years we have expected 18-21 ins. of hg. vacuum at idle. Anything less meant the valves were leaking, the rings were shot, or any of dozens of ailments. The only exceptions were high performance cars with a lot of overlap in the valve timing. In 1970 and '71, the retarded ignition timing, that was used to cut down on emissions, gave vacuum readings at idle of only 15 ins. of hg. on many cars. For '72, valve timing overlap was increased to control nitrogen oxide emissions, and some cars even recirculate the exhaust gas. The result is vacuum readings so low you won't believe your gauge. Many '72's and '73's idle at 13 ins. of hg. So if you check a late engine for idle vacuum and get a low reading, don't start tearing it down to do an overhaul until you check the vacuum above idle, or even while driving the car. You'll probably find that the vacuum is good at speeds above idle. If it isn't, make a compression test or cylinder leakage test to be sure the problem is really inside the engine before you tear it down.

---

make it illegal to do any modifications whatsoever that would affect emissions. This includes timing changes, carburetion changes or just about anything that you could do to the engine. If you live in a state that has such laws, it is your responsibility to find out if you're breaking the law.

There currently is no law against modifying your car for drag strip use or any other use that is off the public highways (it's only a matter of time before someone suggests it seriously). Presently, you can do anything that you want to on the drag strip to conform to strip or association rules just as long as you change it back to stock before you hit the road again.

The best thing you can do to your engine is experiment. Have you ever run .020-in. plug gaps? If you haven't, how do you know it isn't a good thing to do?

Have you ever tried bigger jets or smaller jets? How about spark advance or initial timing? The only difference between you and Ed Pink is that Pink has tried everything in the world. He knows what will give more horsepower and what won't, so he sticks with the things that will.

In addition to experimenting, you must keep records. Write down everything you do to your car. Every change you make should be recorded, including the results of the change. Slowly, you will eliminate all the wrong guesses, and your car will start performing better. Sounds like a lot of work, doesn't it? We don't know a single lazy person who has ever made a car run well. Most tuners work around the clock, constantly searching for perfection. But they have the satisfaction of knowing they have made a car run well. We hope that you will experience that feeling too.

4. Vacuum Advance Hose

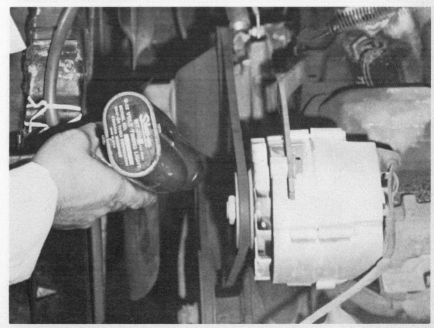

5. Timing the Engine

Understanding Emission Control Systems

During the past decade, the automobile has become a political football and it seems that almost everyone who has some kind of axe to grind (and there are many who do) has taken up the cudgel against Henry's greatest achievement. Safety experts condemn it, and so the government moves with a heavy hand into automotive design; pollution authorities blame it for the ever-increasing black cloud that hangs ominously over much of the nation's urban areas, and so the government dictates by *fiat* what the engine can discharge into the atmosphere. Motorists grumble about the lack of power, poor operation, and increased amount of fuel required to run each new-model-year's engines. As the legislative timetable for engine "cleanup" runs out, Detroit hedges in seeking new answers to the problem, and a California legislator seeking an answer to the recently discovered national energy "crisis" introduces a measure that, if enacted, would require each auto manufacturer to not only meet his state's emission requirements but also guarantee the owner a minimum of 15 mpg.

While the whole world seems to have gone mad, the smog problem worsens every year despite everything that's being done to control it. Smog first started in Los Angeles, but now there's eye irritation to some extent in all large (and many small) cities in the United States. It affects our breathing and can even cause death. Scientists tell us that the country loses millions every year from damage to plants and farm animals caused by smog. Whether you agree with their analysis that a photochemical reaction in sunlight between hydrocarbons and oxides of nitrogen that come out of the automobile crankcase and exhaust pipe is the main cause of smog (and many don't), the important thing is that laws have been passed to control such emissions from cars.

The average driver who never looks under the hood of his/her car isn't too concerned about the matter because he/she leaves such problems up to a mechanic. But the hot rodder and those who work on their own cars must study the law, understand it, and abide by it. The days when engine modifications could be freely made are gone forever. Today, you must know the federal and state laws that apply where you live and you must also comply with them. And if you make an engine modification that's illegal, you can be fined or denied a renewal of your license plates or tabs for your car.

Since all this smog business began in California, let's examine the situation in that state. If you live outside California, don't make the mistake of thinking that the same thing can't happen in your state. It can and probably will sooner or later, even if you have never shed a smog-caused tear or seen the kind of ugly brown haze that settles across the Los Angeles Basin.

Most people think that the only thing that blows out of an automobile crankcase breather is oil smoke, but that's not quite true. The hydrocarbons that cause smog are basically unburned gasoline and are emitted from the breather and the car's tailpipe. So let's take a look at crankcase devices to begin with, then we'll get into exhaust controls proper.

No piston ring has ever been manufactured that provides a positive seal between the piston and the cylinder wall; they all leak, even when brand new. Prove it to yourself by screwing an ordinary pressure gauge (without the valve) into the spark plug hole. Crank the engine over until the piston is on TDC at the end of the compression stroke, then stop. The pressure rises as the piston goes up, reaching a maximum at the top of the stroke. Now watch the pressure gauge after the piston stops and you'll see that it only takes a few seconds for the pressure to leak away. And where does it go? Between the cylinder wall and rings, that's where. When the engine is running, this leakage takes place fast enough to build up pressure in the crankcase.

It happens because the combustion in the chamber doesn't burn all of the fuel; most of the time, it only burns that which is atomized. The remainder clings to the combustion chamber sides and cylinder walls, and so it doesn't burn. More spe-

1. Hose connecting air cleaner to rocker cover identifies this as a closed crankcase ventilation system.

2. When the spring-loaded PCV valve is in closed position (shown), engine is either off or in vacuum situation. As vacuum increases, valve moves against spring to allow flow. Spring must be tailored to fit a particular engine, as some pull more vacuum than others; you need correct smog valve if your engine is to idle right.

1. Closed Crankcase System

To Crankcase Connector — To Carburetor Insulator — Spring — Valve — Connector

2. PCV Valve

cifically, the fuel gets into that small space between the top of the piston and the cylinder wall.

When combustion takes place, the force of the burning gases pushes the piston down to make everything work, but that same force also pushes the unburned fuel down past the rings and into the crankcase. A scientific analysis of these blowby gases has found them to be mainly unburned gasoline. Now, if this unburned gas was allowed to build up in the oil pan, it's easy to visualize what would happen. Before long, the oil would contain so much gasoline that it would no longer work as a lubricant.

These blowby gases are also responsible for the varnish, sludge, and acid that begins to eat at the bearing metal.

Automotive engineers recognized the problem long before the politicians discovered smog, and they tried to get the vapors out of the crankcase, but without too much success. To do this, almost every manufacturer settled on a road draft system. A tube connected to the crankcase extended below it so that the draft of air flowing underneath the car would create a slight suction at the end of the tube, drawing the vapors out of the crankcase. Naturally, there has to be a hole somewhere else on the engine

where fresh air can enter. This was usually placed in the oil filler cap and there was some kind of an oil-wetted mesh inside the cap to keep dust out of the engine.

As long as the car was traveling fast enough to cause a draft on the tube, the system worked pretty well, but at speeds below 25 mph, it didn't work at all, other than to let the crankcase vent itself just from pressure of the gases. Delivery trucks went for days without ever going over 25 mph but they weren't alone with the problem; boats had their share of problems too. It's a little difficult to create a road draft when you don't even

Typical PCV Valve Locations

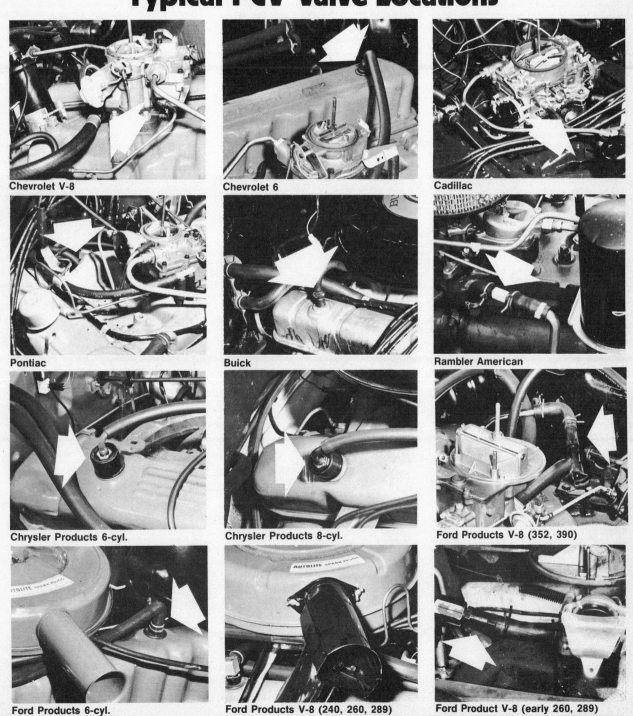

Chevrolet V-8

Chevrolet 6

Cadillac

Pontiac

Buick

Rambler American

Chrysler Products 6-cyl.

Chrysler Products 8-cyl.

Ford Products V-8 (352, 390)

Ford Products 6-cyl.

Ford Products V-8 (240, 260, 289)

Ford Product V-8 (early 260, 289)

Emission Control

have a road on which to travel. So, the problem is not really new—positive crankcase ventilators of various types have been used for many years on vehicles operating under such special conditions.

CRANKCASE DEVICES

There are four types of crankcase devices, usually called PCV (Positive Crankcase Ventilation) systems. In all PCV systems, the road draft tube is either nonexistent or plugged. Type 1 has a hose running from the crankcase through a valve to the intake manifold. Manifold vacuum sucks the vapors out of the crankcase and into the intake manifold where they are carried into the combustion chamber and burned, with fresh air entering through the oil filler cap. The vacuum connection to the crankcase does not necessarily have to be directly on the crankcase; it can be practically anywhere on the engine depending upon how the system was designed. But regardless of where it's located, the purpose is the same.

In a Type 1 system, the PCV valve can have either a fixed orifice or a spring-loaded plunger. Six-cylinder engines usually have the fixed orifice, and V-8's have the plunger. If the engine has an intake manifold explosion or "backfire," the spring plus the force of the backfire closes the valve to prevent flame from getting into the crankcase and causing an explosion. But when the engine is under high-vacuum conditions such as idle or deceleration, the plunger moves against spring pressure to a minimum flow position. And when the engine is under low vacuum or a partial load, the spring moves the plunger to a central position for maximum flow.

Under wide-open throttle conditions with zero vacuum, the spring closes the valve, but the blowby gases are still sailing past the rings into the crankcase. The only place they can go under this condition is out through the oil filler cap. The same thing happens on the fixed orifice system, since there's no vacuum to draw the gases into the intake manifold. So Type 1 is not perfect, because it allows the gases to escape into the air at zero vacuum.

Much the same as Type 1, the Type 2 system uses a special PCV valve and oil filler cap. The valve is a diaphragm type that regulates the amount of flow according to crankcase vacuum. If the crankcase is under pressure most of the time (as it would be on a worn engine), the valve opens up to take care of the blowby gases.

The Type 2 oil filler cap uses a calibrated hole, large enough to let in fresh air but small enough to keep the crankcase under vacuum. Type 2 systems can be installed only on engines with a "tight" crankcase, as any leaks that allow air to enter the crankcase will cause the valve to open wide, creating a condition that may lean the fuel mixture to a dangerous level.

Type 3 is the same kind of breather that home mechanics have used for years to cure a bad case of excessive crankcase smoking. It's simply a tube from the crankcase to the air cleaner that lets fresh air enter the engine via the oil filler cap, through the tube into the carburetor and then into the engine. Since blowby gases are mainly unburned gas, this system tends to richen the mixture, a fact that must be taken into account when designing the carb.

Type 4 is a combination of Types 1 and 3, and it's sometimes called a CCV (Closed Crankcase Ventilation) system. A sealed oil filler cap prevents crankcase gases from escaping under zero vacuum conditions as it would with Type 1. A tube from the air cleaner goes to the rocker cover, carrying fresh air down

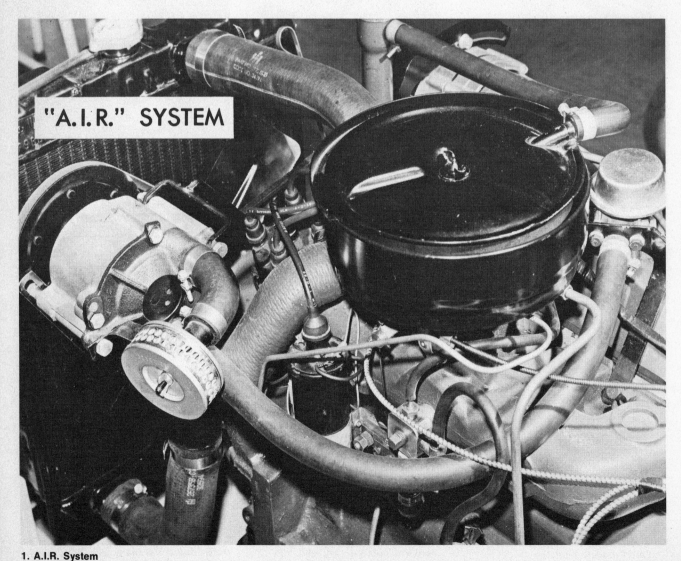

"A.I.R." SYSTEM

1. A.I.R. System

1. *Everyone complained about the complexity of "plumbing" on this early air-injection system, not realizing that this rather simple system was just the beginning.*

2. *Anti-backfire valve is controlled by engine vacuum. When engine is decelerating at high vacuum, anti-backfire valve is actuated and relieves pump pressure so that no air is pumped into exhaust manifold.*

3. *Some early air pumps used a large external filter to help muffle the noise of air pump operation as well as filter incoming air.*

4. *Late-model air pumps use a diverter valve to prevent excessive system pressure from causing a backfire. Filter is an integral part of pump on this Delco unit (arrow).*

into the crankcase. From that point, blowby gases go through the hose into the PCV valve and into the manifold, just as in a Type 1 system.

When the Type 4 system is under zero vacuum, there's no suction on the crankcase (just as in Type 1), but the gases go from the rocker cover through the hose into the air cleaner, where they're drawn into the engine. If an engine has a lot of blowby, some of the gases will pass into the air cleaner at all times. The resulting oil fumes will ruin a dry paper element in a short time. The remedy here is to fix the engine so that it does not blowby as much, or change to an oil-wetted element.

That's a brief rundown of the four types of crankcase devices, and as you see, they aren't really difficult to understand. It's amazing that something as simple could have caused as great an uproar as it did among car owners and mechanics alike when Type 1 devices were factory-installed on all new cars sold in California in 1961. Problems arose at that time because few people understood just how the things worked,

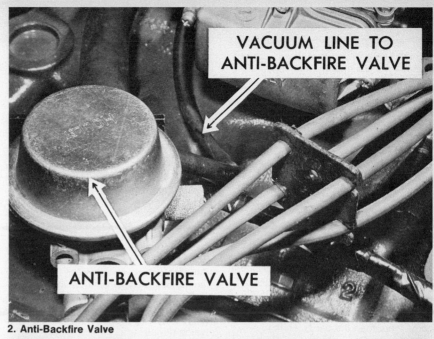

VACUUM LINE TO ANTI-BACKFIRE VALVE

ANTI-BACKFIRE VALVE

2. Anti-Backfire Valve

AIR PUMP AND FILTER

3. Air Pump and Filter

4. Diverter Valve

Emission Control

and there were some cases of poor design that aggravated matters. But the manufacturers cleared that up and so smog valves settled down to their job.

The uproar began all over again in 1963-64 when the new cars were equipped with a Type 4 system instead of Type 1, and devices were required by law on some used cars. The used car scene was really a bad one, as mechanics and car owners didn't always follow instructions when installing the devices. One source of trouble was the installation of a crankcase device on a worn-out engine. In such a case, the device could cause plug fouling, along with other complications. But the law simply stated that such a device *would* be put on a car, with no provision for the fact that once it was installed, the car might not run properly. The only solution with a worn engine is to junk the car, or to do a ring and valve job, which can often cost more than the car is worth.

But in all fairness, we must point out that if an engine is worn so badly that it won't accept any crankcase devices,

then it must really be in terrible condition. There's no such thing in California as an exemption for worn engines—the car must comply with the law or it can't be operated on public streets—it's that simple. This may seem unfair but there are many states where a cracked windshield, bald tires, or a brake pedal that goes down too far will result in our being unable to drive the car until it's fixed—and fixing those cars may also cost more than they're worth.

Occasionally, a smog device is installed and the car runs rough, or a smog valve is changed and the car won't idle without shaking you off the seat. This can be caused by installing the wrong valve or system for that particular engine. You just can't make up a smog device from tubing, hose, and a few other available parts. The entire device must be designed to fit and be approved for that particular engine by the proper authorities. It must also be installed exactly as instructed, with the tune-up performed according to specifications or the engine won't perform, smog device or no smog device.

Do smog devices do any good? Well, they do a better job of crankcase ventilation than any road draft tube ever did,

resulting in less oil contamination and a longer lasting engine. Crankcase systems do cause slightly increased intake valve and intake manifold deposits, but the increase is so slight that authorities claim it won't hurt an engine.

Maintenance of the crankcase device is important. If the valve or hoses are allowed to plug up, damage to the engine can result. Some car manufacturers say that the system should be checked at every oil change; others recommend cleaning or replacing the valve once a year or every 12,000 miles. Checking the valve is simple. It should be clean, and the plunger should be free so that it rattles. If it's the fixed-orifice type, the hole should be clear of all obstructions, as should any hoses. Any flashback screens in the hoses should also be clean. The Type 2 valve is never cleaned, but a simple test of mouth suction will tell you if it's OK.

Different systems are found on different year models. While there are exceptions, you'll usually find the following: California models 1961-63½ have factory-installed Type 1 systems. California models 1963½ and later have factory-installed Type 4 systems. Prior to 1963, cars sold outside California had no

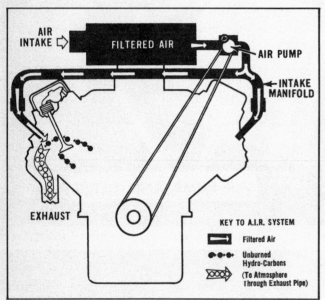

1. How A.I.R. Works

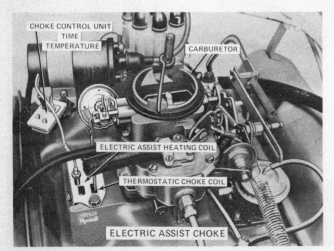

2. Chrysler Electric Assist Choke

3. Limiter Caps

1. Unburned hydrocarbons enter the exhaust manifold and are burned near the valve when air from AIR pump hits them. Exhaust manifold or entire exhaust system can get much hotter than it would without pump.

2. Chrysler Corp. has equipped all its 1973 engines with an electric assist choke to reduce emission during starting and warm-up. Heater element is located in choke well and is completely covered with a nonconductive insulation. Time/temperature control unit operates heater.

3. Black limiter caps on carb idle mixture screws are one part of ignition-induction system. If original black caps have to be removed during carb overhaul or adjustment, they are replaced with red ones that indicate an alteration has been made.

4. Ford's electric choke heater is contained in the thermostatic choke spring and draws power by direct tap from alternator. A bimetallic disc acts as control switch.

5. Orifice Spark Advance Control (OSAC) is latest Chrysler Corp. device to delay vacuum advance during acceleration. Delay is accomplished by restricting airflow from distributor advance chamber to carb port. Special thermal cutoff device incorporated in the OSAC valve assures satisfactory driveability when outside temperature is below 58° F.

4. Ford Electric Choke

crankcase system; 1963-67 cars manufactured for sale outside California have Type 1 systems, and from 1968 on, the Type 4 system has been used nationwide.

If your car came with a crankcase device, than you must not remove it under penalty of California law, unless for the purpose of putting a used car device in its place. If your car did not come equipped with a device, there are certain situations that will require you to install one. It all depends upon the year and model of the car and where it's registered, in most cases. Models from 1955 to 1962 must have a crankcase device if their ownership is transferred to someone who lives in a county that requires it. This doesn't mean that the new owner can then remove the device once the car has been registered under his name. After installation of a crankcase device, you're breaking the law if you take it off.

Some exceptions have been provided in the law for certain types of engines, but these are gradually being closed. Motorcycles are also exempted. We won't go into all of the technical details pertaining to California law here, as the idea is only to give you general knowledge of the California situation and what you might expect in your own state. Now let's get into exhaust controls and find out how they work.

EXHAUST CONTROL SYSTEMS

If hydrocarbons are mostly unburned gasoline, then it follows that when the engine is putting out hydrocarbons, it's running with a rich mixture. If the engine could be made to run on a leaner mixture, it wouldn't cause nearly as much

5. OSAC System

Emission Control

pollution as it does with the richer one. The problem is to find out whether a particular engine is running rich or lean. This is done with the use of an exhaust gas analyzer, a test instrument manufactured by tune-up equipment makers. These analyzers have been around for many years now, but basically they all work the same—by measuring the thermal conductivity of the exhaust gas, which is directly related to how rich the engine is running.

The analyzer meter gives its reading in an air/fuel ratio, which may range anywhere from 11:1 up to 15:1. If the meter read 12.5:1, it would mean that the engine was running on a mixture with an air/fuel ratio of 12½ lbs. of air to 1 lb. of fuel. A rich mixture is one that contains an excess amount of fuel, and a lean mixture, of course, is just the reverse. Any reading near the 15:1 end of the scale is lean, and a reading on the 11:1 end of the scale is rich. An engine can run as rich as 8:1, but only if you're wealthy and the gas pumps are spaced close together. The leanest the analyzer will measure is 15:1.

Most engines without exhaust emission controls run about 12:1 at idle and at cruising speed, they usually lean out to somewhere around 14:1. The richer mixture at idle is necessary because some exhaust gas remains in the combustion chamber at idle speed. Engines also run rich on deceleration, but under most other operating conditions, they'll run sufficiently lean to avoid overly polluting the air. So the problem really narrows down to an elimination of the rich mixture during idle and deceleration. There are two ways to do this within the confines of the present state-of-the-art—with either an air injection system or an ignition-induction system.

AIR INJECTION SYSTEM

Essentially, the air injection system is little more than an engine-driven pump that transfers air from outside the engine into the exhaust passage close to the exhaust valves. As the unburned fuel comes out of the exhaust valves, it combines with the fresh air provided by the pump and actually burns right in the exhaust passage. This means that the exhaust system gets considerably warmer than it would without the pump system, and it also means that there has to be a lot more "plumbing" to handle air movement cluttering up the engine compartment.

Authorities claim that a warmer exhaust system can be beneficial in that it may eliminate condensation in the muffler (the major cause of mufflers falling apart), but not enough statistics are in to make any really definitive statement about this yet. Even though air pumps have been used for several years, mufflers seem to fall to pieces just as rapidly, if not more so, than before. And mechanics who work primarily on the small 4-cylinder engines used in Pinto, Vega, and the import cars will tell you that those with air-injection systems tend to have a much shorter exhaust valve life.

That cluttered exhaust control mess in

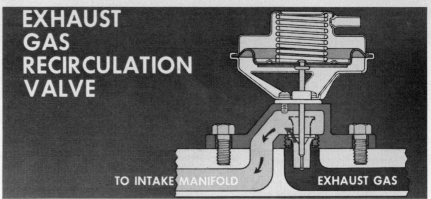

EXHAUST GAS RECIRCULATION VALVE

TO INTAKE MANIFOLD   EXHAUST GAS

1. How EGR Works

the engine compartment is something we have to live with, and since it seems to get worse every year, let's take a look at exactly how an air-injection system works. Mounted at the front of the engine, the air pump is driven off the front pulley by a belt. All pumps draw their air from the engine compartment, but different manufacturers have take different approaches; some pumps use a filter on their air intake and others receive the air from the clean side of the carburetor air cleaner.

Various methods are used to move the air from the pump to the exhaust valve. The air travels (under pressure of about 1 psi) from the pump to a manifold on each cylinder head. Then it moves into the injection tubes that direct the air to the underside of each exhaust valve. Some engines like Buick use a passageway cast into the cylinder head instead of an external manifold. Chevrolet V-8's have the injection tubes entering the exhaust manifold and from there they go up the passageway to the exhaust valve.

All air-injection systems have check valves with a one-way diaphragm to prevent the hot exhaust gas from backing up in the system to the pump in case of high exhaust-system pressure, pump belt failure, or air hose rupture. All late models use a diverter valve that prevents excessive pressure in the system from causing a backfire. It does this by sensing sudden increases in intake manifold vacuum, causing the valve to open and let air from the pump vent outside. A pressure relief valve is contained in the same housing. Early models used a by-pass valve which performed the same function as a diverter valve. Pump relief was provided by a second valve in the air pump itself.

The diverter or anti-backfire valve works by sending the air output from the pump directly into the intake manifold instead of into the injector tubes. This leans out the excessively rich mixture that occurs just after you lift your foot from the gas. If this mixture were not leaned out, it would explode in the exhaust system, causing a loud noise from the tailpipe. Some anti-backfire valves dump atmospheric air into the intake manifold instead of pump air. Other types don't dump air into the manifold but allow the pump air to exhaust into the carburetor air cleaner instead. This effectively cancels any airflow through the injector tubes, and silences the sound of the exhausting air. Design of the backfire valve depends upon who's

1. EGR valve acts as one-way switch routing exhaust gases to intake manifold except during idle/deceleration condition, when addition of gases to incoming air/fuel mixture would cause rough engine operation.

2. All 1973 cars use an EGR system. One arrangement is Chrysler's Proportional Exhaust Gas Recirculation, which incorporates an EGR valve and sophisticated vacuum sensing to assure proper flow of exhaust gases.

sitting at the drawing board and what he feels is necessary to stop the engine from backfiring.

The backfire valve only operates to eliminate backfire just after the driver removes his foot from the pedal; after that, the air-injection system returns to normal operation whether you put your foot back on the gas or leave it off. These diverter valves can cause some strange things to happen when the car is started. Since the valve is controlled by engine vacuum, it takes a couple of seconds for the vacuum to build up. Until it does, the type of valve that dumps air into the manifold is wide open, allowing outside air to enter. Some engines may shake like jello until the vacuum builds up sufficiently to close the valve. This doesn't really do any harm to the engine or anything else, but it sure makes the unknowing driver wonder just what's going on under the hood and it's likely to send the little woman to the nearest searvice station in tears.

If the air injection system consisted of just the pump and its corresponding plumbing, things would be fine. But it also requires changes in the carburetor, distributor, cooling system, and many internal changes in the engine proper. This means that it's impossible to use the air-injection system from one engine on another. It might be possible to design a universal system, but the cost would be fantastically high and would probably involve changing everything on the engine except the crank, block, and rods. And who could get the Big Three to cooperate on such a project? Like all other smog controls installed to date, the air-injection system is really an emergency system hung on the car's engine because nothing else that would drop the emissions to the level specified by the politicians was available. Air injection will be around for a long time yet, for despite those who placed their money on the ignition-induction system as an alter-

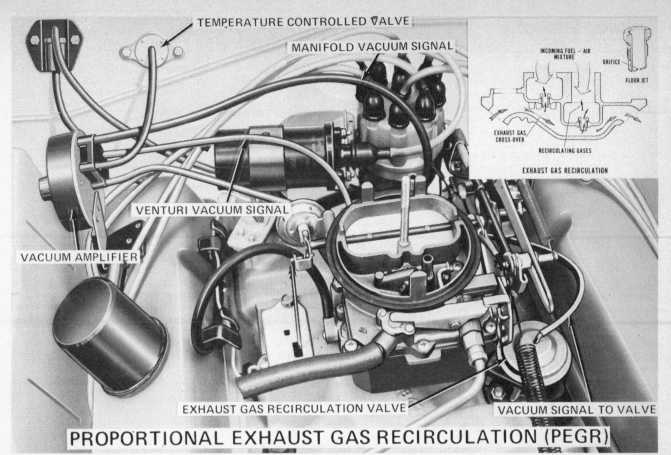

TEMPERATURE CONTROLLED VALVE

MANIFOLD VACUUM SIGNAL

INCOMING FUEL – AIR MIXTURE

ORIFICE

FLOOR JET

EXHAUST GAS CROSS-OVER

RECIRCULATING GASES

EXHAUST GAS RECIRCULATION

VENTURI VACUUM SIGNAL

VACUUM AMPLIFIER

EXHAUST GAS RECIRCULATION VALVE

VACUUM SIGNAL TO VALVE

PROPORTIONAL EXHAUST GAS RECIRCULATION (PEGR)

2. Chrysler EGR System

native, manufacturers are discovering that with many engines, meeting the 1975 specifications requires a combination of the two.

IGNITION-INDUCTION SYSTEM

The ignition-induction system was pioneered by Chrysler Corporation, who installed its Clean Air Package (CAP) on 2000 of the 1963 Plymouths. As these cars were sold only to fleet accounts in the Los Angeles area, a careful check on how they performed was feasible and led to approval of the CAP system in November 1964. This exhaust emission system worked so well that similar systems have now been adopted by the competition (sometimes from sheer desperation) and ignition-induction is used on many new cars.

Sometimes called an "engine modification system," ignition-induction reduces emissions at idle by using a carburetor that's set lean. On some cars, the idle mixture screws are installed with a pin in the throttle body to prevent anyone from backing them out to obtain a richer mixture. If the screws are backed out with force, they break, and the carburetor must be removed from the engine. The pins and screws are then replaced with parts from a special kit. Other cars use idle mixture screws with limiter caps that butt against the carburetor to prevent the screws from being turned beyond a certain point. Still, other carburetors don't use limiters because their idle mixture needles were designed so that the mixture cannot richen excessively, even if the screws are backed out.

If a lean mixture is all that's required

to reduce emissions, it then follows that adjusting the carburetor on the lean side will do the trick, or will it? The only problem here is that the engine won't run. Exhaust dilution of the mixture at idle requires an air/fuel ratio of about 12:1. The mixture is also very thin because it's under a high vacuum. Both problems can be overcome by opening the throttle wide enough to get a denser mixture and more flow to scavenge some of the exhaust gases from the cylinder so that the engine will run at 14:1. The result is fewer emissions, but the engine is idling so rapidly you can't hold it down. Without touching the idle mixture or mixture adjustment, retarding the spark is the only other way to get engine speed down to a normal idle.

And that's just what Chrysler did; all CAP engines have an initial spark setting that's retarded as much as 15° from normal; this is accomplished by a ported spark. When the throttle is closed, the spark port is above the throttle plate. Since there's no vacuum on the advance diaphragm, the distributor goes into full retard. But when the throttle plate is opened, the spark port is uncovered and the vacuum diaphragm advances the spark up to a conventional setting.

With this system, the spark is retarded during deceleration, because the throttle plate is closed at that time. The designers discovered that the only way to reduce emissions during deceleration was to advance the spark. This is done by placing a little spark valve in the line between the carburetor and the vacuum advance diaphragm and connected to manifold vacuum. Whenever you lift your foot, this spark valve sends full manifold

vacuum to the distributor advance diaphragm, which then advances the spark. The spark valve will hold the distributor in full advance position as long as the deceleration continues, even if the car is going downhill from here to you know where. But as soon as manifold vacuum drops below about 21 ins. (the figure is lower on '72-'73 models), the spark valve changes the distributor back to carburetor vacuum and the distributor works normally again.

The CAP system has been modified by other manufacturers so that it works a bit differently, but does the same thing. Some designs do not use the spark valve because their carburetors do not go rich during deceleration; others use the spark valve but their purpose is to eliminate exhaust popping, not to lower unacceptable emissions. The Chrysler distributor has one vacuum diaphragm to advance the spark all the way from retard position to full advance. Some Ford engines use a dual diaphragm with two hose connections, while Pontiac uses a single diaphragm with two hose connections. One hose goes to carburetor vacuum and the other to manifold vacuum. The carburetor vacuum hose controls the distributor in the normal way, but the manifold vacuum hose pulls the breaker plate to the retard position during idle and deceleration.

Actually, this is exactly opposite to the CAP system, which goes to full advance during deceleration. Ford and Pontiac were able to get away with this on some of their engines because of changes in combustion chambers, cam timing, stroke length, and other internal modifications. But it didn't work on all engines

Emission Control

in their lines, so you'll find some that continue to use the spark advance valve. A similar situation exists on late-model Chrysler Corporation cars. Some engines use a spark advance valve and some don't. As you can see, there's no such thing these days as simply setting the idle speed and letting it go at that; a tune-up man has to understand the system he's working on and how it affects the engine. And he must be sure that he has the exact specifications for the engine he's tuning.

Some late-model Chrysler product carburetors have an idle speed adjustment screw that seats against a little metal contact on their side, with a wire running to a solenoid mounted on the side of the distributor. When the throttle is in the curb-idle position, the idle-speed screw touches the contact, retarding the spark. If the carburetor also happens to be equipped with an anti-dieseling solenoid, then the contact for the screw is located at the end of the solenoid plunger.

What the solenoid retard does is to bring the spark to a retarded position to slow the engine down for an idle at a reasonable speed. The solenoid is just a small electromagnet mounted on the distributor vacuum advance chamber. It exerts a small amount of pull on the rod that links the vacuum diaphragm with the breaker plate. The old system of ported spark and a long throw on the single vacuum diaphragm worked very well for Chrysler, but the distributor solenoid modulator (DSM) did an even better job, because it allows advanced timing during a cold start. When cold-starting an engine, the fast idle cam holds the idle-speed screw away from the retard solenoid contact. A cold engine needs all the help it can get and the slight spark advance (about 5.5°) comes in handy for quicker starting. As soon as the engine warms up, the choke opens, the fast-idle cam goes off, and then whenever the throttle is let down to the idle position, the solenoid is energized and retards the spark to keep the idle speed at a reasonable level. Along with other changes, this system was modified on 1972 models to receive its power from the starter relay. Thus, the distribu-

tor solenoid now works only during engine cranking, and advances the spark 7.5° for better starting. Simplification of the system was made possible by the introduction of Chrysler's electronic ignition system.

Chrysler also added an electric assist choke system to its entire engine line in 1973. This system was designed to provide a quicker choke opening at temperatures above 63° F and a slower opening below 63° F. Ford uses a temperature-sensitive bimetallic disc as a switch to control the ceramic heater within the thermostatic spring of the choke on its 4300 4-bbl. This electric choke draws power constantly from a center tap on the alternator, but the disc switch remains open and no current is supplied until underhood temperatures reach 60° F, when the switch closes. Current supplied to the ceramic heater causes the thermostatic spring to pull the choke plates open within 1.5 mins.

Chrysler's original CAP system has now been changed to CAS (Cleaner Air System). The changes involved were many and subtle ones inside the engine where they made a considerable differ-

1. Chrysler EGR Valve

1. EGR valve location differs from engine to engine. Valve is not repairable and must be replaced if not working properly. Dodge 198- and 225-cu.-in. engines have unit mounted on intake manifold, where valve stem action is easily visible.

2. Ford's EGR system is considerably more complex than that of other manufacturers. An internally-channeled spacer unit fits between intake manifold and carb, and has valve mounted at its back. Depending upon engine, the valve may be a poppet, modulating, or tapered-stem type.

3. Pinto equipped with 2000cc engine and manual transmission uses a Decel valve for 1973. Mounted on intake manifold, the valve meters extra fuel/air during deceleration to permit more complete combustion.

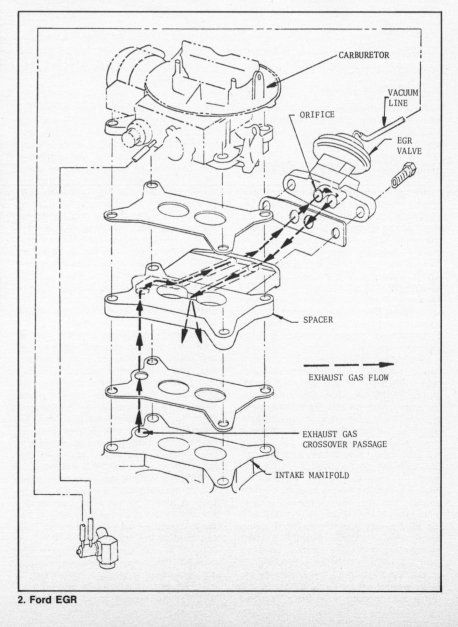

2. Ford EGR

ence in emissions, but very little change in servicing. Some strange things were done with the controls on some of the carburetors. There are 4-bbls. with single idle-mixture screws similar to some old Holley designs. Some carburetors have a bypass airflow (nonadjustable) that directs air below the throttle valve to break up raw fuel. But even with its advanced thinking behind CAP and CAS, Chrysler found it necessary to resort to an air pump system in addition to the ignition-induction system in order to make certain engines in its line conform to standards for 1973.

A temperature-sensitive, vacuum control valve is used on many cars. This screws into the water jacket and is connected between the distributor, carburetor, and the intake manifold. The source for the distributor vacuum-advance unit is the port above the throttle plate, resulting in no spark advance at idle. As the retarded spark at idle may cause an engine to overheat in heavy traffic, the control valve senses excessive heat and changes vacuum source from the spark port in the carburetor to full intake manifold vacuum, causing the spark to advance and speeding up the engine to help overcome the heating condition. This thermo switch is not really much

different from the old air-conditioning idle speed-up solenoid used on many early air-conditioned engines.

But if you think that Chrysler Corporation's solenoid retard is complicated, take a look at Ford's Electronic Spark Control (ESC) system. A speed sensor hooks into the speedometer cable to control the spark advance according to the car's speed. There's no spark advance at all until the engine reaches about 23 mph on acceleration, when spark advance works normally. On deceleration, the distributor modulator valve shuts off the vacuum to the advance unit as the vehicle speed drops to approximately 18 mph, and the spark is allowed to retard. The electronic module works in conjunction with the usual dual-diaphragm Ford vacuum-advance unit. The diaphragm closest to the distributor is for retard and is connected to manifold vacuum; the other connects to the spark port on the carburetor above the throttle plate. This ESC system is entirely separate from the electronic rpm limiter appearing on some Ford products; the two units have no connection and could be used on the same engine if Ford wanted to install them that way.

GM and Chrysler also have spark control systems. The GM system is called

Transmission Controlled Spark (TCS). A switch in the transmission connects to a solenoid that controls the vacuum applied to the distributor diaphragm, resulting in the elimination of vacuum spark advance in all lower gears. On a 4-speed box, you'll get vacuum spark advance in 3rd and 4th gears, but only in top gear with all other transmissions.

COMBINATION EMISSION CONTROL VALVE

Chevrolet eliminated the TCS solenoid in 1971 in favor of a vacuum-electric gadget called a Combination Emission Control (CEC) valve. This looks very much like an anti-dieseling solenoid, but it doesn't do the same job. Unfortunately, it occupies the same space on the carburetor, so many mechanics have probably used the CEC valve plunger to set curb idle. Just for the record, never use a CEC valve plunger to set the curb idle; the normal throttle-cracking screw on the carburetor is the proper route to go.

CEC does exactly the same thing with vacuum spark-advance as a TCS system, but an additional function opens the throttle on deceleration. If the throttle is allowed to close to the curb idle position

3. Pinto 2000 Decel Valve

Emission Control

during deceleration, a high vacuum results and pulls in huge amounts of raw fuel through the carburetor idle system. But keeping the throttle at a slightly greater opening reduces the vacuum, creating fewer emissions because the mixture is not as rich.

CEC does both tasks at the same time, so that whenever there's vacuum spark elimination, you also have a greater throttle opening on deceleration. The CEC valve can do both at once as it has a long plunger, one end of which shuts off vacuum to the distributor while the other end moves away from the throttle linkage. When the transmission shifts into top gear, electricity flows to the solenoid coil in the CEC valve, moving the plunger out. This movement uncovers a hole to allow vacuum to the distributor and at the same time, the end of the plunger moves out to prevent the throttle from closing completely.

Additional controls complicate the CEC valve. A temperature switch cancels the whole operation to allow vacuum advance below 82° F. A time-delay relay cancels the CEC valve for 15 secs. after turning on the ignition switch to provide vacuum advance for easier drive-away and fewer stalling-after-start problems. Curb idle on CEC valve carburetors is set with the throttle-cracking screw, as we said earlier. Deceleration idle setting (considerably higher) is set with the CEC valve plunger in the energized position. If curb idle is set with the CEC valve plunger, the throttle will be held open too far on deceleration, giving you quite a surprise when you take your foot off the gas and the car keeps right on going. The vacuum hose connection on the CEC valve differentiates it from the ordinary anti-dieseling solenoid, which has no hose.

Because the throttle is automatically

held open on deceleration, it isn't necessary to idle the '71-'73 cars as fast as in the past, and so idle specs have dropped 50-100 rpm, making anti-dieseling solenoids unnecessary in many cases. As air-conditioning demands faster idling, which leads to dieseling, a solid-state time device on air-conditioned Chevrolets holds the compressor on for 3 secs. after the engine is turned off. This extra load slows the engine down and keeps it from dieseling.

NOx SYSTEM

Installed on all California cars in 1971 (and nationally in 1972), Chrysler's Nitrogen Oxide (NOx) system takes the place of the previously mentioned solenoid-controlled spark advance. In case you haven't heard about NOx, it's the stuff that makes your eyes smart so badly on a smoggy day in L.A. As initial efforts toward emission control concentrated on hydrocarbons, little attention was paid to NOx emissions, resulting in a lessening of hydrocarbons but an increase in NOx in L.A. Chrysler's approach to NOx control was rather sophisticated, using a special camshaft with increased overlap. This overlap produces more exhaust gas contamination in the cylinder, which reduces peak combustion chamber temperatures, the primary cause of NOx emission. Along with a camshaft, the engines are equipped with a 185±thermostat, a move directly opposite to that made to reduce hydrocarbons, which resulted in the use of 195± thermostats. Because of the many other changes made, this doesn't mean that hydrocarbon emissions will increase, but you can see a rather complicated interplay of forces at work here. The lean mixtures necessary to bring hydrocarbons under control resulted in higher combustion chamber temperatures, and so an increase in NOx emission.

Until the 1973 model year, the heart of Chrysler's NOx system was a solenoid

vacuum valve that controlled vacuum spark advance. On manual transmission cars, this valve is connected to a transmission switch to eliminate vacuum advance in all but top gear. In any other gear position, the valve is energized, shutting off vacuum to the distributor. In high gear, the transmission switch breaks the electrical circuit to the solenoid, the spring in the valve opens the passageway, and vacuum is allowed to advance the spark. The only additional control on manual transmission cars is a thermal switch mounted on the firewall to sense the temperature in the fresh air cowl inlet. Below 70±° F, the thermal switch breaks the circuit to the solenoid valve which allows normal vacuum spark advance; above that temperature, the thermal switch makes the connection and allows the NOx system to operate as described above.

Automatic transmission cars are different—they have an increased-overlap cam, a 185° F thermostat, and solenoid vacuum valve, but the control mode is different. A control module, vacuum switch, thermal switch, and speed switch all work together to tell the solenoid when to turn distributor vacuum on or off.

Chrysler NOx control on the '73 line is handled by a temperature actuated Orifice Spark Advance Control (OSAC) and Exhaust Gas Recirculation (EGR) system instead of the solenoid vacuum valve. When going from idle to partial throttle, a small opening in the OSAC valve delays the change in ported vacuum to the distributor by about 17 secs., but when reversing the sequence (part throttle to idle), the change is instantaneous. As vacuum is provided by a tap just above the carburetor throttle plates, manifold vacuum is not present under idle conditions, but as soon as the throttle plates open slightly, the system kicks into operation, provided the temperature is 58° F or higher. EGR (see Exhaust Systems) is handled on Chrysler Corporation cars by

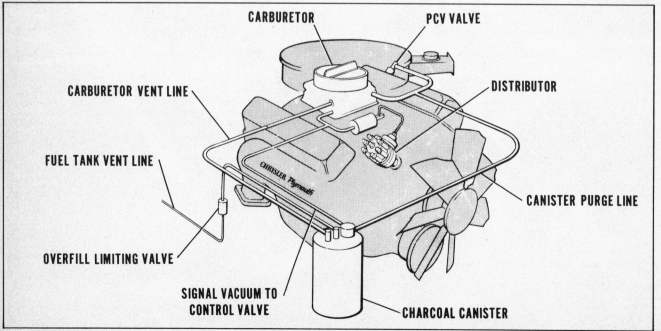

CARBURETOR   PCV VALVE

CARBURETOR VENT LINE

DISTRIBUTOR

FUEL TANK VENT LINE

CANISTER PURGE LINE

OVERFILL LIMITING VALVE

SIGNAL VACUUM TO CONTROL VALVE

CHARCOAL CANISTER

CHRYSLER Plymouth

1. Vapor Control System

either a ported vacuum control, a venturi vacuum control, or a floor jet system, depending upon the engine involved, but the end result is the same—a predetermined amount of hot exhaust gases are recirculated to dilute the incoming air/fuel mixture and to lower the combustion temperature, thus reducing NOx emissions.

Ford's approach to EGR is tied into the engine coolant temperature as the actuating device, instead of the air temperature as used on GM and Chrysler cars. While the end result is the same as these other systems, Ford's is rather complicated in that the coolant temperature can be 60°, 95° or 125° F, depending upon the engine application involved. Ford also uses three different types of EGR valves; a poppet, a modulating, and a tapered-stem, again depending upon application. The temperature control device that activates the Ford EGR system is a vacuum switch similar to the distributor vacuum control valve used in 1972. To eliminate the add-on piping system used in other EGR designs, exhaust gases are picked up from the exhaust crossover passage in the intake manifold and routed through a thick carburetor spacer to the EGR valve which meters the gases back through another passage in the spacer. This means that the exhaust gases are directed to the primary bores where they dilute with the incoming air/fuel mixture headed for the combustion chambers. As vacuum for EGR operation comes from the carburetor's primary bore in this system, you'll find two vacuum ports on the carburetor, one for EGR control and one for the distributor spark advance.

Ongoing production changes have modified some Ford carburetors to use a single port for both applications. A more complicated version of this system was necessary to produce acceptable engine operation at high-speed cruise conditions. This high-speed modulator subsystem is used on the 351-C, 400, 429 and 460-cu.-in. engines and is similar in concept, components, and operation to the ESC system—Henry wouldn't recognize his infernal combustion machine if he could see how complex it's all become these days.

Beginning in 1970 with California cars and in 1971 nationwide, an additional system entirely separate from the exhaust and crankcase emission controls was added by manufacturers to reroute any gasoline vapors that might escape from either the fuel tank or carburetor. Except for a line going to the engine crankcase, the fuel tank is completely sealed. Vapors move along the line and are stored in the crankcase until the engine is started; then they are sucked into

the intake manifold and burned. To keep liquid fuel from getting up to the crankcase, a vapor separator on top of the gas tank sends all the liquid fuel back to the tank where it belongs. Some vapor control systems use a canister filled with activated carbon to trap the vapors instead of letting them enter the crankcase. The carburetor float bowl also connects to the crankcase or the carbon canister (whichever is used), so that vapor from the float bowl will not escape into the atmosphere.

And where do we go from here? Well, it's another big leap in the coming months to meet the 1975 emission standards, unless the government relents and allows the manufacturers the extra year they insist is necessary. In the meantime, critics wonder why Detroit has not embraced the rotary engine, and legislators are turning their attention to the millions of used cars on the road that met standards when they were new, but are far from the 1975 levels. Some states like California are passing legislation requiring that additional devices be placed on used cars. One thing is certain, however. You can only expect emission control systems to get more complicated while exacting a heavy toll on performance and gasoline mileage. And if government agencies ever decide to put teeth into the legislation and establish a uniform system of enforcement, the do-it-yourselfer is virtually out of business. In the meantime, we're sitting right on the horns of a gigantic dilemma—will we as a nation pay the price for clean air, or are we content to look the other way and pretend that the polluted air doesn't exist? Only time will tell. ⚜

1. Late-model vapor control systems use a charcoal canister that traps fuel vapor which would otherwise escape from fuel tank or carb bowl. A vacuum-operated valve on top of canister channels vapor flow to engine.

2. FoMoCo uses a fuel vapor return system with certain engines to reduce amount of vapor entering carb. On 1973 Gran Torino, it's hard to get at unless car is on hoist.

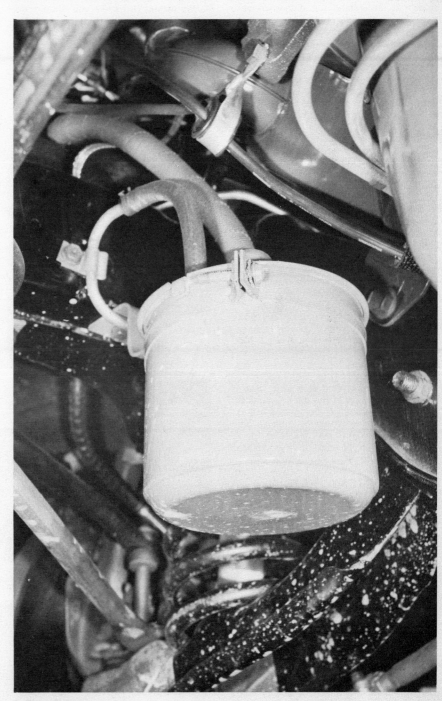

2. Ford Canister

Starting System

It happens all the time. Somebody calls up a garage and says, "My car won't start." The garage man immediately comes back with, "Will it turn over?" And the owner answers, "Yeah, if I drive it off a cliff, but what's that got to do with it not starting?"

Right there is the basis for a beautiful argument, all because the car owner does not understand the difference between a car that won't start and one that won't turn over, or crank. The starting system might be in beautiful shape with a battery powerful enough to light up New York City. When the key is twisted to the start position, the engine spins faster than it does when you're driving down the road. But it doesn't start.

Then there's the situation where the battery and starter give a few weak gasps and then everything is as quiet as a calm day in the desert. In this case we say that the engine will not turn over or won't crank. We don't know if it won't start because we can't crank it to find out.

Most of the problems with the starting system are caused by the battery. Not that the battery is a weak point. It's just that it only lasts so long—and that usually isn't long enough. Suppose your car won't crank some morning. Is there any way that you can tell what is the matter? You bet there is. You can pinpoint the problem by turning on the headlights. If they are normally bright, it's likely that the battery is OK. But if they're dimmer than a candle flame in a high wind, the trouble is almost certainly in the battery or its connections.

Let's assume that your car's headlights are very dim. The next step is to determine the condition of the car's battery. If the charging system is doing its job and the battery still tests weaker than an old dry cell, you'd better start shopping for a replacement. Don't wait for a complete battery failure.

BATTERY TESTS

Several tests can be made to find out if your starting system is doing its job. The easiest and most practical is to check starting voltage at the battery terminal of the coil while the engine is cranking. You should get at least 4½ volts on a 6-volt system, or 9 volts on a 12-volt system. You should check cranking speed of the engine at the same time, either with a tachometer or a well trained ear. If the cranking voltage and speed are above the minimum specifications (published in factory shop manuals), then there is likely nothing wrong with the starting system.

If all is not well with the cranking test, the next step is a check of battery voltage while the battery is not doing any-thing. It's called an open circuit voltage test, because all the circuits connected to the battery are disconnected, or turned off. Anything above 12.5 volts is considered OK. A 6-volter is OK at about 6.2 volts.

Suppose some of the above tests are marginal. Then the thing to do is to make a high-rate discharge test with a battery-starter tester. However, you should not make this test if the battery is undercharged. Charge it up first, until the open circuit voltage is above 12.5 volts. If it won't charge up to that level, you know you have a defective battery. The high rate discharge test is made by drawing three times the ampere-hour rating out of the battery while observing the voltage. For example, a 60 ampere-hour battery (20-hr. rating) should be tested at 180 amps. If the voltage on a 6-volt battery stays above 4.8 and on a 12-volt battery above 9.6, then all is wonderful in batteryland. If it won't, get rid of the battery; you're flirting with a no-start situation.

Suppose the battery checks OK, but you know the car won't start because you had to take the bus to work yesterday. In that situation it might be a good idea to buy a monthly pass for the bus. But the situation is not that desperate. You know the battery is OK, so the trouble must be in the starter. If you want to check it, a battery-starter tester will measure the amount of current the starter is drawing. If it's drawing in excess of specifications, that's proof that the time has

1. Portable Battery Charger

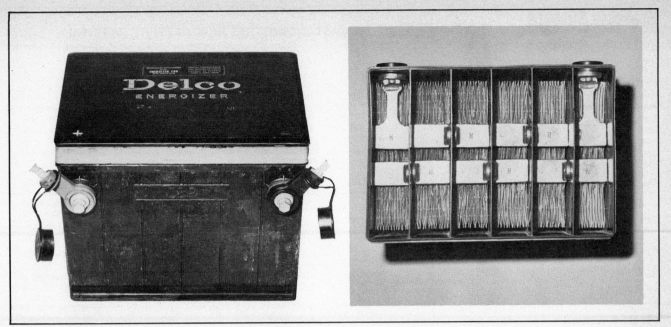

2. Non-Fill Battery

1. A portable battery charger can return its cost in a short time. This Sears unit can be used as a 50-amp booster or 10-amp charger that automatically reduces its power flow to 5 amps as battery nears full charge.

2. The new Delco-Energizer battery is permanently liquified and sealed at the factory. The owner of this optional electrical storehouse will never have to worry about filling the cells. Vaporized electrolyte is trapped in a baffled tank above the cells where it condenses and returns to the main body of battery fluid.

come to put on your old clothes and take the starter off the engine.

Battery testing used to be a lot easier when the cell connectors were exposed on the top of the battery. Then you could test each cell with a voltmeter or a load tester.

The internal cell connectors that are now an almost universal feature of automotive battery construction do not permit access to the poles of the individual cells. *(No attempt should ever be made to jab voltmeter prongs through the cases of such hardtop batteries.)*

High-discharge tests provide useful information only after the battery has been charged, and are therefore of little value in troubleshooting. In fact, if the battery does not have at least a 50% charge, such tests can seriously damage the battery.

Hydrometer testing is a better means of checking cell condition—particularly for the backyard mechanic. Battery-testing hydrometers can be purchased for as little as 50 cents, and really excellent instruments sell for under $3 in many automotive supply stores.

In using the hydrometer, all the filler caps are first removed from the battery top and the tube on the tip of the tester inserted in turn into each cell. By squeezing the rubber bulb and releasing it, a quantity of the battery's water-and-acid mixture is drawn up into the glass barrel of the instrument. Inside the hydrometer barrel is a weighted float with

numbers on it. The numbers on the scale read from 1.300 to about 1.100 and indicate the comparative weight or density of the solution. The reading is taken at the surface of the liquid in the tube.

A fully charged cell will test between 1.275 and 1.280, while a cell in good condition may be anywhere between 1.280 and 1.250. A cell in only "fair" condition will produce a reading between 1.250 and 1.225. Any reading below 1.225 indicates a poor charge and, if a cell is found to be below 1.150, the battery is for all practical purposes dead.

If the cells test in the "poor" range the battery must be given a recharge. This can be done at a service station or with one of the popular little "trickle" battery chargers that have become popular for home use. By testing the cells during charging it is possible to tell when the process is complete. As stated above, a fully charged cell will test at 1.275 to 1.280 (or even 1.300). A half-charged cell will read from 1.200 to 1.225 and isn't ideal.

If any cell is lower than the others by .050 or more, that cell is shorted and the battery's days are numbered. Also, if charging can no longer bring the cells of the battery up to at least a 50% charge (about 1.200), the battery is really shot and should be replaced immediately.

Hydrometer testing should also be a part of the routine servicing that you give your car. By testing the battery every 2 or 3 weeks, most battery trouble can be headed off before it has had time to become serious.

To get the most accurate picture of the battery's health, the hydrometer tests should be made under proper conditions. Never take readings after adding water to the cells or after a long, high-speed trip. The best readings are obtained 2 or 3 days after water has been added and the car has been driven in normal service. To make the test, the car should have been left standing for several hours or overnight. The engine is then started, switched off, and the battery giv-

en about 5 mins. to "recover." The cells are then tested with the hydrometer. Readings taken at this time will give the truest picture of the battery's actual condition.

It should be noted that temperature has a definite effect on the readings you will get with your hydrometer, due to the fact that the density (specific gravity) of the battery electrolyte changes with the temperature. When the battery is hot (in summer), the hydrometer readings will be lower; when the battery is cold (in winter), the hydrometer readings will be higher.

Readings are considered to be correct when the temperature of the battery liquid is 80° F. For every 10° above 80° you must add .004 to the original reading; for every 10° below 80° you must subtract .004. Thus, a cell that produces a reading of 1.225 might appear to be in fair condition, but if the temperature of the fluid is only 40°, the correct measurement would be equal to only 1.209—a poor figure. For accurate readings, you can measure the temperature of the battery acid before testing it. In fact, a few of the more expensive hydrometers have a thermometer built-in for this purpose.

Besides making tests, there is another way to keep an eye on the condition of your car's battery. Most present-day cars have the so-called "idiot lights" to indicate a lack of battery charging rather than the more accurate—and, of course, expensive—ammeter. The trouble with the idiot light system is that it does not tell the driver if his battery is being overcharged.

Overcharging can be very harmful to an automobile battery. The best way to detect it—short of installing an ammeter—is to make a frequent check of the water level in the battery's cells. Normally, an automotive battery requires water only four or five times per year (hot climates excepted), but if yours seems thirstier than a sun-dried sponge, it's time to check the voltage regulator before trouble develops.

Starting System

Low battery electrolyte is caused by a high charging rate because the excessive charging heats up the battery, thus evaporating the water. High charging rate comes directly from a voltage regulator that is set too high, not from the current regulator. Six-volt regulators should keep the voltage below approximately 7.2, and the 12-volt systems below 14.2. Higher voltages are permitted if they are necessary to keep the battery charged.

BATTERY CABLES AND CONNECTIONS

Of course your "headlight test" might have turned out differently. Let's suppose that the lights were quite bright and that a hydrometer test proved the battery to be in top shape—yet, when you try to crank the engine, the lights go completely out. If this is the case, the trouble is probably a bad battery cable connection.

The battery terminals are the first thing to check. As pointed out earlier, these are often subject to looseness and acid corrosion. In an emergency, you can often get started by having someone press the tip of a screwdriver into the joint between the cable terminal and the battery post. The permanent cure is to get the

BATTERY EFFICIENCY AT VARIOUS TEMPERATURES	
Temperature	Efficiency of a Fully Charged Battery
80°F.	100%
50°F.	82%
30°F.	64%
20°F.	58%
10°F.	50%
0°F.	40%
−10°F.	33%

UNDERSTANDING THE NEW BATTERY RATINGS

PHYSICAL SIZE	Battery size does not necessarily indicate quality, but it's important for replacement fit. The best battery in the world won't do any good if it doesn't fit into the battery box in your car.
AMPERE-HOURS	A measurement of the amount of amperes the battery will put out for 20 hrs., ending up with 1.75 volts per cell. For example, a battery that will put out 5 amps for 20 hrs. (5×20) is a 100-amp-hr. battery. This 20-hr. rating is being discontinued in favor of the "reserve capacity" rating.
RESERVE CAPACITY	This new rating gives the number of minutes that the battery will sustain a 25-amp discharge at 80° F. and still remain above 10.5 volts. This standard gives you a rough idea of how long you could run everything in the car (about a 25-amp load on most cars) if the charging system went dead. The higher the rating, the better the battery.
0° CRANKING POWER	Given in voltage and minutes. A 150 or 300-amp load (depending on the capacity of the battery) is applied to the battery in 0° air temperature, and the voltage is measured after 5 secs. The number of minutes in the ratings is how long it takes the battery to fall to about 5 volts (specifications vary) with the same load. In both cases, the higher the reading, the better the battery. This 0° cranking power rating is being discontinued in favor of the "cold cranking power" rating.
COLD CRANKING POWER	A new rating giving the amount, in amperes, that a battery can put out at 0° F. for 30 secs. In making the test, the load on the battery is adjusted until the battery voltage drops to 7.2 (12-volt battery) and then the ampere flow is measured over the 30-sec. period. The higher the rating, the better the battery.
NUMBER OF PLATES	More plates mean more active material for producing power. However, if the plates are extremely small, a battery might have a high number of plates, and still have comparatively low power. Plates are made by applying lead to a grid, so they're sometimes called grids.
MONTHS OF GUARANTEE	Can be used to figure the cost-per-month of owning the battery. This month-guarantee figure can be misleading. A battery might be guaranteed for several years, but in the last year of its guarantee it might not have the power to light a dome lamp. Therefore, it is wrong to suppose that just because a battery is guaranteed for several years, you won't have to buy another battery until that time is up. Life of a battery depends on how hard you work it, how well you keep it charged and full of water, and how it was originally constructed. Generally, the higher capacity (and higher priced) batteries will last longer.

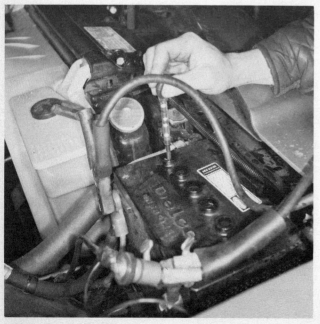

1. Using Battery Tester

2. Measuring Battery Condition

cables into good electrical contact with the battery.

The boltless clamps used to attach cables to the battery posts on many late-model American cars are easily damaged by corrosion. Many starting problems originate right here. If the cast-in spring on these terminals has been eaten away by corrosion, the clamp must be replaced. Bolt-on types sometimes become so corroded that the bolt must be cut with a hacksaw in order to free the terminal clamp from the battery post. New bolts for these are available separately, which can save you the trouble and expense of installing a complete new cable terminal.

If the cable connections are corroded solidly onto the battery posts, a battery terminal puller should be used to remove them. These inexpensive tools work by pulling the cables straight off the post. Trying to remove frozen clamps by twisting or hammering on the terminals can cause serious damage by breaking the post's internal connection with the battery plates. Even cars that have shown no particular starting system weakness can often have their starting ability improved by removing the cable connections, brightening the terminals with emery cloth, and reinstalling them tightly. This is an especially good precaution before winter arrives.

The cables that connect the battery to the starter and to the chassis of the car are much heavier than any other wiring in the automobile. This is because the amount of current they must carry is much greater. The heavy flow of electricity necessary to start an engine would burn up ordinary wires as quickly as a burning fuse. Should some of the strands of wire forming these cables be broken, a greater load is thrown onto those that remain. Such breaks usually occur near the terminals and, quite often, spilled battery acid is to blame for the damage. If this appears to be a possible cause for insufficient current reaching the starter, or if terminals themselves

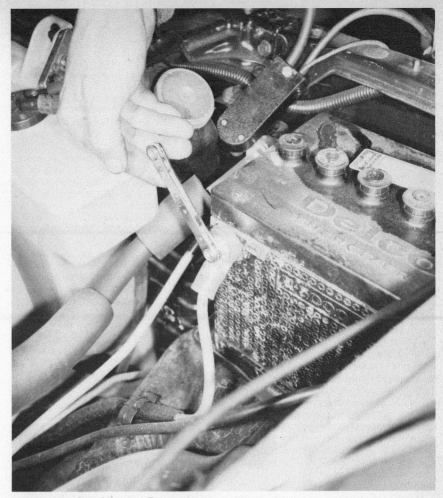

3. Removing Side-Mounted Terminals

1. Thexton Hydro-mite battery tester is temperature-corrected to give accurate readings of battery condition. Each floating ball indicates 25% of charge; if all four float, the battery is fully charged.

2. A battery's condition can be evaluated in many ways. Most pros have testers like this Allen Battery-Starter unit. Testers like this allow the mechanic to measure the voltage level when 3 times the rated ampere-hour of the battery is drawn out. If the battery "lives" up to its rating, then a no-start problem could lie in such diverse areas as bad terminal connections, ignition or starting switches, solenoid or starter motor, or breaks in the wire.

3. Standard Delco Energizer has vent caps and must be filled periodically like any other battery. Treat its terminals with care; a 5/16-in. wrench fits cable connector and should be used to avoid rounding its corners. Tighten at 15 to 20-in.-lbs. only; if connector is tightened too much, it'll break the internal seal and cause battery failure.

are in poor condition, the terminals can be removed from the cable, the damaged portion can be cut off, and the terminal—or its replacement—installed.

Usually, the terminals supplied by the car maker are either soldered or crimped onto the cable. Soldered terminals can be removed by heating them with a propane torch or over a gas burner. A damp cloth should be wrapped around the cable's insulation to keep it from accidentally being barbecued. Crimped-on terminals must be cut off, discarded, and new terminals installed in their place. Replacement terminals are available which require no soldering to attach them to the cable. A portion of the insulation is simply stripped from the cable and the terminal secured in the correct place by tightening two small screws or bolts.

On some cars the ground cable connects the battery directly to the engine block. On others, the battery is grounded to the car's body and another ground strap—often located between the engine and the firewall or between the transmission and the frame—connects the engine block with the chassis. Any of these connections can provide a source of potential trouble. If there is poor electrical contact at these points due to paint, corrosion, dirt or loose connections, starting problems are as certain as a cold winter in Minnesota. A reconditioned used car that has had the engine steam-cleaned and repainted sometimes will have paint on the engine block under the ground

cable terminal. This can also happen on new cars. All such ground connections should be removed from the engine or body, the mating surfaces brightened with emery cloth, and the connections re-bolted tightly together. *Poor ground contact has often been the cause of hard-to-trace car troubles.*

The battery's "hot" cable may pass through one or two switches or solenoids before reaching the starter. Follow this cable all the way to the starter and see that all connections are clean and tight. Insulation may also be worn from the cable in spots—particularly on long cables that may pass under the car. This can allow a short circuit to take place should the bare wire come into contact with the car's frame or any other grounded part. Not only would this lead to more fireworks than a flame in a gunpowder factory, it could discharge the battery to a big, fat, permanent zero. Repairing the insulation temporarily involves nothing more than wrapping the worn spot with a few inches of plastic electrical tape. This repair can later be made more durable by applying a coat of liquid rubber compound over the tape.

SOLENOID AND STARTING SWITCH

If the car doesn't crank, but the lights remain bright, or if they dim only slightly when the starter is switched on during the "headlight test," look for trouble in the magnetic starter switch or solenoid.

Starting System

In fact, if the trouble is in the solenoid, the starter may not run at all, or may run without turning the engine.

Two types of starters are used on late-model automobiles. American Motors cars, Plymouths from the late 1950's and early 1960's, Studebakers, and many Ford products have *Bendix drive* starters. GM cars, Chrysler products including late Plymouths, VW's, and many of the later FoMoCo models employ *overrunning-clutch* types. The latter have a solenoid mounted directly on top of the starter which pushes the starter pinion gear into mesh with the engine's flywheel ring gear during the starting operation. Bendix drive starters have a pinion gear that is mounted on the starter shaft in such a way that it is thrust into engagement with the flywheel ring gear by the starter motor's rapid speed buildup. But Ford's positive-engagement starter uses the magnetic force of the starter itself to engage the starter drive and needs no separate solenoid to assist it in its function.

In cars with Bendix drive starters the solenoid is actually only a magnetic switch that connects the starter to the battery. Since it has only an electrical function, it need not be mounted on the starter, although sometimes it is. The solenoids of overrunning-clutch starters must, however, be mounted on the starter because in addition to connecting the battery to the starter, they must move the starter pinion gear into engagement with the engine's flywheel.

When the ignition is turned to the "start" position, or when the starter button is pushed, current is not sent directly to the starter. Instead, it energizes the solenoid (in Ford or GM products), which in turn connects the heavy "hot" cable of the battery to the starting motor windings. Chrysler products are slightly different. They use an additional gadget called a starter relay, mounted on the firewall in the engine compartment. In the Chrysler system, the ignition switch energizes the relay, then the relay energizes the solenoid, and finally, the solenoid makes the connection between the battery and the starter.

Solenoids can be tested without removing the unit from the car.

Using the following simple jumper cable test you can quickly condemn or exonerate the solenoid as the source of the trouble.

1) Carefully (sparks may fly and a lot of heat can be generated) connect the two large terminals of the solenoid with a heavy jumper cable. The starter should turn the engine normally. If it does not, the trouble is not in the solenoid.

2) By attaching the jumper cable between the "hot" terminal of the battery and the correct small terminal of the solenoid, it should be possible to make the starter operate normally. On some early Chrysler products, touching a hot lead to the wrong small terminal will burn up the neutral safety switch. The terminal to avoid is the one with a wire running down to sythe transmission. If in doubt, disconnect both small leads from the solenoid, then connect a hot lead to

one small post and ground the other. If the starter operates, the trouble is *not* in the solenoid, but in the ignition switch, starter button, automatic transmission "neutral" switch, or it could be in the wires connecting these controls with the solenoid.

The magnetic switch (often called a solenoid) on Ford cars with all types of starters usually has two small terminals. The "hot" jumper should be connected to the one closest to the large terminal whose cables go to the battery.

3) If connecting the "hot" side of the battery to the solenoid's small terminal causes the starter to run, but does not turn the engine, the trouble is in the starter drive mechanism.

4) Assuming that the battery tests OK, and none of these tests gets a reaction from the starter, try connecting a heavy jumper cable directly between the battery's "hot" side and the solenoid terminal that leads to the starter or to the terminal on the starter itself. If this does not cause the starter motor to run, the trouble is in the starter—not the solenoid.

When making the above tests it is neither desirable nor necessary to have the ignition turned on. However, when using jumper cables there is always a chance for accidental contact with other electrical connections. For this reason, it is *always* advisable to disconnect transistor ignition systems and alternators before making jumper cable tests, since accidental shorts can destroy these units instantly.

You must also be extremely careful about making any sparks near a battery.

Whenever a battery is being charged, hydrogen gas is created in the cells above the electrolyte. This gas can stay there a long time, even when the car is not being operated. All it takes is one spark to set it off, and you have an exploded battery, with everything nearby drenched with sulphuric acid. When connecting jumper cables, make the connection to the hot battery post first, then connect the ground jumper to someplace away from the battery, such as the engine block. If any sparks fly when you connect the ground, they will be far enough away from the battery to keep from blowing it up.

If the tests do prove the trouble to be

1. Any do-it-yourselfer can easily afford an inexpensive "trickle" charger to augment his lack of taking long, battery-charging trips. These units, however, cannot rectify the problem of a "used up" battery or a malfunctioning voltage regulator.

2. S-K battery pliers, with their thin jaws set at a 30° angle, will go a long way to end the threat of rounding off the flats on the nut of a battery terminal. Never pound or violently twist the terminal to free it from the post. Chances are you'll damage or break internal connection.

3. Some motorists have experienced hard starting problems which were ultimately traced to poorly grounded battery and/or starter motor. Always make sure the battery and starter ground strap is securely attached to your car's frame.

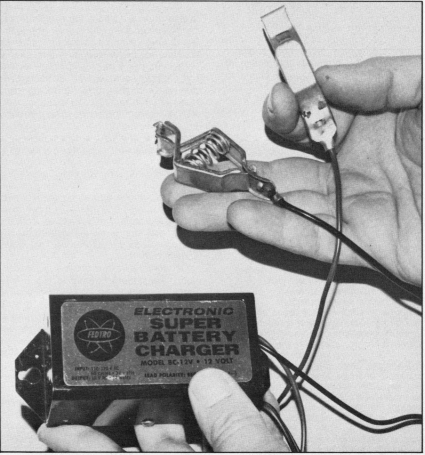

1. Trickle Charger

2. Battery Pliers

3. Battery Ground Strap

in the starter solenoid or magnetic switch, the only repair practical in some cases is to replace the entire unit since they may be sealed assemblies. However many units, such as the Delco solenoids on GM cars and many Ford trucks—as well as some of the magnetic switches used by Plymouth—*can* be disassembled. In these, the internal contacts can be examined and repaired. If the contacts are in good condition and the plunger works freely, the solenoid *should* work. If it does not—sorry, the windings are probably burned out.The exact condition of the windings can be checked with an ohmmeter or with a battery-powered tester.

To repair the starter solenoid on a 4- or a 6-cylinder inline engine it is not always necessary to remove the unit from the car, but on most V-8's the solenoid is otherwise inaccessible. In some cases it's necessary to remove the starter before you can get at the solenoid at all.

SOLENOID REPAIR

Firewall-mounted solenoids must be replaced, but the type that is mounted on the starting motor can be repaired.

If the solenoid is coated with grease and road dirt, it should be thoroughly cleaned before removing the cover from the contact points. Otherwise, dirt may get onto the contacts to cause trouble later. Except to remove the battery cable and the small wire from the dashboard starter control, it is not necessary to take any of the other nuts and washers off the terminals. In most cases there is just one small screw that holds the dust cover in place. After removing it, the cover can be lifted off the solenoid's contact assembly. Some late Delco solenoids

have two screws holding the cover in place. The cover on these also contains the stationary contacts, so remove it very carefully.

If they are not attached to the cover itself, the contacts can be dismounted from the body of the solenoid by undoing two small screws. Once these are out, the stationary contact assembly can be lifted and pushed to one side while still connected to the wires that enter the body of the solenoid. The assembly can be further dismantled by taking off the nuts holding the contacts, but this is only necessary if you have purchased a rebuild kit that contains new contacts.

The contact disc—a large brass washer that moves against the stationary contacts—can become quite pitted and worn, as can the stationary contact to which the battery cable is attached. If the battery contact and the contact disc are not badly burned, but only coated with dirt and deposits, they can be sanded or filed smooth. However, if the contacts are causing starting troubles, it is likely that they are worn quite badly. In most of these solenoids it is not necessary to file the contact surfaces flat nor to replace the parts. By simply removing a snap retainer, the contact disc can be taken from its shaft and turned over. This puts the "new" side of the disc toward the contacts. Similarly, the battery contact retaining nut can be loosened about 3/16-in. and the contact rotated 180° to put its "good" side under the contact disc. The other contact cannot be turned since one of the wires leading to the solenoid windings is welded onto it. However, this contact seldom wears as badly as the other, and it can quite easily be restored to like-new condition by a few strokes with a file. Complete

contact assemblies and solenoid rebuild kits are also available at very moderate cost at auto parts dealers.

If your jumper cable tests seem to indicate that there is a burned-out winding in a starter-mounted solenoid, always remove the dust cover and check the wires connecting the windings to the contacts. In a few cases what have appeared to be burned-out solenoids were able to be returned to service after a simple wire repair. It's always best to check this before tossing the unit into the trash can.

When reassembling the solenoid, make certain that the contact shaft and the plunger work smoothly. A binding contact can produce a no-start just as quickly as a flat battery. If the plunger has been left attached to the starter drive, don't tighten the bolts that hold the solenoid until it has been aligned to allow the plunger to move effortlessly.

After cleaning and reassembling the solenoid, ground the case and connect the small terminal to the "hot" side of the battery. There should be a click as the solenoid coil moves the plunger into "contact" position and another click when the connection is broken and the spring causes the plunger to retract. If there is no click, the windings are defective, which means a new solenoid must be installed.

STARTING SWITCH TROUBLES

If the car's solenoid checks out all right, but trouble is indicated in the circuit that connects the dash control to the solenoid's small terminal, there are a number of possible malfunctions to be considered. The most likely trouble spot is the ignition switch itself in cars

Starting System

equipped with "key" starter controls. This switch is used at least twice every time you drive your car. Consequently, considerable wear can take place—especially if the lock and cylinder are never lubricated. Key-starter switches are sealed units which must be replaced in their entirety.

If you suspect that the reason for a no-crank condition is the key switch, disconnect the plug at the back of the switch and connect a jumper between the hot terminal and the terminal that operates the starter. If your no-crank condition disappears with the starter suddenly springing to life, you know that the problem was in the key switch. A wiring diagram will help you find the right terminals and wires without having to trace the wires from one end to the other.

To remove the ignition switch from the dashboard, any individual wires should be carefully disconnected from the back of the switch and labeled to facilitate their installation on the new unit. If there is a plug, free the locking tangs and unplug it. The ground cable should be disconnected from the battery to prevent shorts during the switch-changing job. After the wires have been disconnected the switch can be removed from the dash. This is done by unscrewing the retaining ring that surrounds the lock cylinder. A special wrench will fit the slots in the ring, or pliers may work. Care should be exercised to avoid marring the dash or the ring. It isn't necessary to change the key and tumbler portion of the switch. It can be inserted into the new switch. But in some designs you have to remove the tumbler barrel before you can unscrew the retaining ring from the instrument panel. The clue is a small hole in the front face of the switch near the keyhole. Shove the end of a paper clip into the hole while you turn the key, and the whole key and locking mechanism will come out into your hand. Then you can unscrew the retaining ring and remove the body of the switch.

Installing the new switch is simply a reversal of the removal operation. If the terminals on the wires are corroded, they should be brightened with abrasive cloth before reconnecting them.

Battery current is supplied to the starter button or ignition switch by a wire that first passes through the ammeter, or perhaps a circuit breaker, relay, or junction block. Locate the "hot" wire behind the ignition or starter button and trace it to determine if it comes from the ammeter or any other electrical unit. By attaching your jumper to both terminals of each component you can bypass them temporarily. If the key or starter button operates the starter normally with the jumper in place, but not with it disconnected, then the trouble is an open circuit in the electrical unit being bypassed.

If one of these units is the source of your trouble it will probably have to be replaced. The jumper wire can be temporarily left connected across the terminals so that the car can be driven until a replacement part is located and then installed.

Late-model cars have the ignition "switch" in the steering column. If you suspect a bad switch, the column-mounted cars can either be a blessing or a chamber of horrors. To find out if your particular car is a blessing, look on the steering column between the instrument panel and the floorboards. If you're lucky, you will find your ignition switch mounted on the column with two bolts, and connected by a rod to the key lock up near the steering wheel. Removing the switch is easy, because the wiring unplugs and the two bolts are all that holds the switch in place. The switch mounting holes are slotted so you can get the switch slide in the same position as the lock.

Chevys are a special case. Their ignition switch is on the lower part of the column, but not low enough to remove it without dropping the column. That's right, you have to take off the two nuts that hold the column to the dash and lower the column until the steering wheel rests on a block that you have placed on the seat. Without the block, the column might come down far enough to break off the little string that runs up to the shift indicator. Once you get the column down, it's obvious how the switch comes off.

If you don't have the switch on the lower part of the steering column, then your personal chamber of horrors is that complicated area under the steering wheel. The wheel must be removed, and sometimes part of the top end of the column, in order to get the switch out. It's not an impossible job, but we suggest you have the shop manual for your car before you tackle it.

Another potential trouble spot is the "neutral safety" switch found on cars with automatic transmissions. The purpose of this switch is to make it impossible to start the car unless the selector is in the "N" or "P" position. Needless to say, this switch also receives a great deal of wear. Also, since it is frequently located at the lower end of the steering column or under the car, road splashes can eventually take their toll. Many cars have the neutral safety switch conveniently mounted on the steering column

1. The best way to break 'em free from each other is to first loosen nut, then use a cable puller to lift offending terminal off the post.

2. Some no-start situations can be attributed to terminal looseness or acid corrosion. Baking soda and water will clean off most of the buildup, but you'll need a stiff wire terminal cleaning brush to finish the job.

3. Spreader pliers should be used to increase the inside diameter of a terminal so it will fit over post.

1. Cable Puller

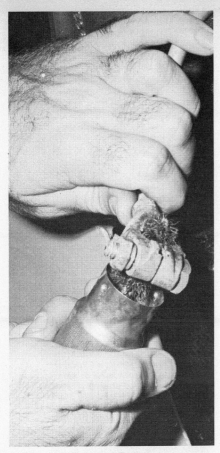

2. Cleaning Corroded Terminal

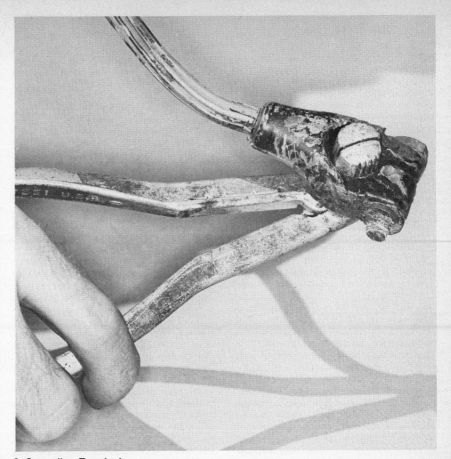

3. Spreading Terminal

just below the instrument panel. The switch holes are slotted so you can get it in the right position to allow the car to start in park or neutral only. On some automatic transmissions—such as on Chrysler Corp. cars—the neutral safety switch is located on the transmission itself and can be reached only from under the car. After bypassing the switch with a jumper (making sure the transmission selector is in neutral or park position), it should be possible to start the engine normally if the trouble is in the neutral switch.

Although it is the most likely suspect, the neutral switch itself may not be the actual culprit. An incorrectly adjusted shift linkage can produce the same symptoms. Neutral switches that work off the end of the selector shaft can be checked for improper action of the transmission linkage. However, about all you can do with the "plug" type switches on Chrysler Corp. cars is replace them—since that's where the trouble usually is. Then if the new switch doesn't work, but the jump wire will, you'll have to get the shift linkage adjusted at a transmission shop.

Neutral safety switches that screw directly into the transmission are made with a hex that allows them to be removed with a thinwall socket. Those that mount at the end of the steering column or are actuated by the linkage arms on the transmission are detached by the removal of two or three screws.

STARTER DRIVE DIAGNOSIS

If the starter motor runs normally when the dashboard control is actuated but fails to turn the engine, the trouble lies in the starter drive assembly. There are several other symptoms of drive trouble in addition to this, however. Horrible grinding noises accompanying starter operation are reason for immediate attention. Continuing to use the car will only lead to further damage to the starter drive and to the teeth of the flywheel ring gear. If there is a grinding sound, but the engine does not turn, it could mean that the engine or transmission will have to be pulled and the flywheel gear replaced, but the trouble could also be merely a broken overrunning clutch, in which case you could make the repair.

Sometimes the starter drive pinion gear will jam in the engaged position. If the car's engine is running you'll probably be able to hear an unusual noise which is the starter or starter gear being driven by the engine. If the drive jams during starting, the engine probably will not turn but a groaning or humming sound will be heard from the starter as though it was trying to turn the engine but lacks the power. Bendix drive starters are far more likely to jam than positive-engagement types. A jammed drive can be freed by putting the transmission into high gear and rocking the car forward and backward. This is not possible with an automatic transmission of course, and the starter must be removed to free the drive.

STARTER REMOVAL

If the drive assembly is not functioning properly, it will be necessary to remove the starter from the car on all but a very few engines. Even then it is usually far easier to make repairs with the starter out and on the work bench.

Start by disconnecting the battery, then the cables and wires from the starter or solenoid terminals. Locate the bolts that mount the starter on the flywheel housing (*not* the long bolts holding the starter together) and remove them. Undo the bolts under the starter first and those holding the top of the starter last. When the last bolt is almost out, the starter should be supported in some way to keep it from falling. It may be necessary to tilt the starter slightly to clear the starter drive around the flywheel.

On some V-8's it is necessary to remove the exhaust pipe or jack up the frame slightly so that the starter will clear the upper front suspension arm as the starter is withdrawn. After the starter is out, look into the opening in the flywheel housing and inspect the condition of the ring gear. The flywheel may be turned by prying with a large screwdriver. If it is stripped or broken the car will have to go to a garage for repairs.

STARTER DRIVE REMOVAL

Starters with Bendix drive need not be further disassembled when you work on the drive assembly unless there is a separate housing surrounding the drive and pinion as on some Ford-Autolite models. Delco, and other positive engagement starters, must have the long bolts that pass through the starter taken loose and the housing surrounding the drive assembly removed. It is also mandatory that the starting drive actuating lever be unbolted to allow the drive assembly to slide off the starter shaft. The solenoid

Starting System

need not be dismounted from the starter for removal.

The Bendix drive assembly found on American-made starters is held in position on the armature shaft by a locking screw and two keys. Using a large screwdriver, compress the starter drive spring slightly at the end toward the starter motor. It is then possible to get at the locking screw and remove it. Some very early Ford starter drives can also be taken apart and individual parts can be replaced.

STARTER DRIVE INSPECTION

Whether the drive is an overrunning-clutch or Bendix type, the first thing to look for is broken or cracked springs. The overrunning clutch should be checked for proper action. It should be possible to turn the pinion gear clockwise (counterclockwise on VW's), but not in the opposite direction. Inspect the bushings inside the drive assembly. If they are badly worn the drive may bind or slip out of engagement.

All Bendix drives should be checked to see that the pinion gear turns smoothly as it slides in and out on its spiral-cut "worm." By looking inside, you may be able to locate small broken pieces that indicate an internal failure. It is extremely important that the drive assembly operates without the slightest binding.

Inspect the pinion gear for burrs and worn or chipped teeth. Also, look for bent tangs on the drive spring.

In many cases, starter drive trouble is due only to dirt and old grease preventing proper operation. However, overrunning clutches on U.S. and VW cars should *never* be cleaned with solvent, since they are packed with a special long-life grease at the factory. Solvent cleaning would remove this.

Bendix drives should be cleaned in kerosene but no additional lubrication applied, since oil on the "worm" could attract dirt and grit which would interfere with its smooth operation. If the worm is cleaned in solvent, then a light oil mist should be applied to the worm.

Unfortunately, all recent American starter drives—both Bendix and overrunning-clutch types—are serviced only as complete units. Any broken, worn, or damaged parts mean replacement of the entire assembly.

When a new overrunning-clutch drive assembly is installed, make certain that the starter shaft is clean and free of rust and corrosion. This will contribute to smooth action and a longer life for the new part. Rust spots can be polished away with fine steel wool and crocus cloth.

After the drive assembly and the starter have been put back together, check to see that the parts work correctly and effortlessly before reinstalling the starter on the engine.

It should be noted that the Bendix-type "Folo-Thru" starter drives on Ford cars have an internal lock pin that keeps the pinion from moving on the worm once it reaches full-engaged position. This pin will not disengage unless the starter is

mounted on the engine and the engine speed reaches 310-390 rpm. Occasionally, a person who is not aware of this thinks that the drive unit is faulty because the pinion does not retract by hand, but it is perfectly normal.

STARTER MOTOR

Until now we have only talked about those parts of the starting system that *control* the starting operation. Now it's time to take a look at the part that does the actual work—the starter motor. Starter motors are normally a very dependable part, and most of the common troubles that interfere with their operation are elsewhere in the system. The types of troubles that strike the motor itself are likely to be simply the result of normal wear. Most such problems are capable of being coped with by the backyard mechanic. However, starters that have operated under some abnormal conditions can have certain internal electrical defects that call for the attention of a trained service man. You can usually save money in such cases by simply turning the starter in on a rebuilt one. Still, you should know how to check out the starter if for no other reason than to know if it should be scrapped.

There are three or four tests you can make of starter efficiency, with the starter off the car. We assume you have already checked cranking voltage, cranking speed, and starter current draw, and found something wrong. Or maybe you suspect something is wrong, but you don't have the equipment to check it out. In either case, let's get the starter off the car and take a look at it.

The first test is to rotate the armature by hand and feel for any dragging. Many starters fail because the bushings or bearings wear and allow the armature to drag on the fields. If the armature does not spin freely, then you've found the problem.

The second "test" is to check for worn bearings. Wiggle the shaft from side to side. If there seems to be a considerable looseness, try rotating the shaft while at the same time exerting heavy side pressure. If there is extreme binding

or mechanical interference, the bearings will need attention.

On some starters, the bushings that support the starter shaft cannot be replaced and an entire new end plate must be obtained. However, in most cases the bushings are removable. The bushing at the flywheel end of the starter can be quite easily driven out with a piece of round steel somewhat larger than the starter shaft or with a regular bushing driving tool. A new bushing can then be installed in its place. Lubricate the outside of the new bushing so that it will go into place with a minimum of binding. A

1. Troubleshooting your starting system (like on this Ford) isn't hard, if you know what you're looking for and where to place a heavy-duty jumper cable. (1) Your solenoid is OK if, when you "jump" the two large terminals on the starter switch, the starter works normally. (2) When you connect the hot side of the battery (+post) to the small terminal (S) of the solenoid and your starter works, you have problems in the ignition switch, starter button, neutral safety switch, or wiring. (3) If when you attach the jumper cable from the hot side of the battery to the starter side of the ignition switch and the starter motor turns, you've got problems in the ignition switch area. (4) If a jumper placed here allows the ignition switch to start the car normally, you've got troubles in the wire to the switch. By the way, if your starter motor clicks as if the battery is dead (but you know it's fully charged) yet finally makes contact and lights your engine off, either your solenoid or switch is going away and should be replaced soon.

2. These are the two basic external types of solenoids or starting switches. At bottom is GM unit, attached to the top of the Delco-Remy starter. The one at the top is a Ford starter switch, usually placed somewhere on the firewall.

3. Many Ford ignition switches look like this. When plugging in the connector, make sure the locking tabs are fully engaged.

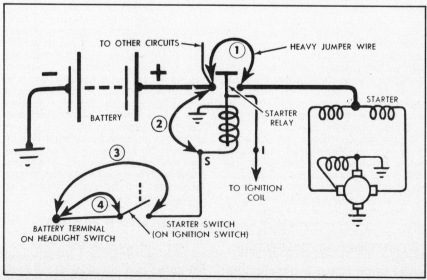

1. Troubleshooting Ford System

block of wood should be held against the end of the bushing (if a bushing driver is not available) and tapped *lightly* with a hammer until the new bushing is seated. The bushing in the other end of the starter presents more problems since the bearing end is capped and the bushing cannot be driven out. Some starters have a removable bearing cap that must be replaced along with the bushing, but in most starters the bushing must be cut out with a hammer and a small sharp cold chisel before the new one can be put in. There are tools available that thread themselves into these bushings so

that they can be pulled out, but at $10 you'd spend more on the tool than you'd save by not buying an entire end plate which has a new bushing in it. Always have the new bushings on hand before taking out the old ones. Replacements may not be available for your particular starter.

Finally, a starter "no-load" test should be performed before disassembling the starter—providing all seems normal when turning the armature shaft by hand. The no-load test is a bench test only and cannot be made with the starter mounted on the car. It also requires an amme-

ter which will register up to 200 amps for Bendix drive starters and up to 500 amps for Ford positive-engagement overrunning-clutch types. The positive engagement Ford starter has an initial high current demand because the drive is being actuated by the starter's windings.

With the starter running, the ammeter should indicate approximately 0-80 amperes, according to the car maker's specifications. This should be the *maximum* for a 12-volt system. Higher readings indicate such faults as shorted windings, a rubbing armature, tight bushings or a bent armature shaft. If the starter fails to run and the ammeter registers zero, the trouble is likely open windings or worn-out brushes.

You can perform the same test *without* an ammeter by simply using two jumper cables. Connect the positive cable to the starter terminal and the negative cable to the starter frame. This should be reversed if the starter is from a car with positive ground. Of course, you will not be able to check for shorted windings as you would with an ammeter, but you will find out if the starter runs at all. Also, if it seems to turn slowly, a bent shaft, tight bushings, or rubbing armature can usually be detected. If these conditions are not present, the slow running just *might* be the tip-off that there's an armature short.

In the days of manual transmission cars, it was easy to perform a starter lock test by putting the car in gear, applying the brake, and operating the starter. A certain amount of current would flow through the starter, and it could be measured with an ammeter, then compared with specifications. In these days of automatic transmissions, the lock test can only be done on a starter test bench, and they are scarcer than males at a Women's Lib meeting.

STARTER MOTOR DISASSEMBLY

The same long through-bolts that release the drive housing also allow the starter to be opened up once they are loosened and taken out.

After the through-bolts are out, you will be able to remove both ends from the starter motor. The drive assembly must also be removed as described earlier. The other end plate contains the brush holders, and therefore the brushes must be lifted out before the end plate can be taken off. This is also a necessary operation prior to replacing the bushings in the end plate. The two ground brushes can have their wires unscrewed from the starter frame and the brushes left on the end plate if desired. The brushes on Delco starters are attached to the brush holders with screws. After the end plate is off, the brush holders and springs should be removed from it and the mating surfaces cleaned thoroughly before the new brushes are put in. A word of caution: *do not* clean inside of case with solvent as it will damage armature and field coil insulation. Merely wipe off with a clean cloth.

If the commutator was not checked earlier, it must be supported on "vee" blocks and rotated against a dial indica-

2. Solenoid and Starter Relay Switch

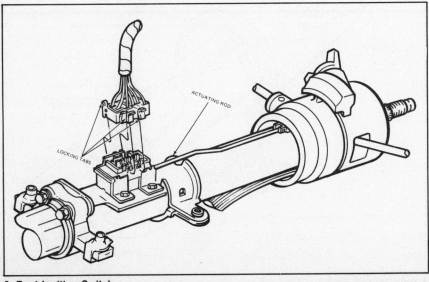

3. Ford Ignition Switch

tor or a reference block that can have the clearance checked with a feeler gauge. If the commutator is found to be eccentric, the armature must be chucked in a lathe and *very light* cuts made across the face of the commutator until it is once again round and concentric with the shaft in its center. After turning the commutator on Delco starters, the mica strips separating the brass segments of the commutator should be under 1/32-in. using a section of hacksaw blade. The undercutting should also be about .002 wider than the insulation strips. On Autolite starters, the commutator is polished with #00 or #000 sandpaper to remove all burrs left by the turning operation. Autolite also recommends not undercutting the mica, but make certain that no brass particles are left on the insulation strips between the segments. If you do not have a lathe available, the armature can be taken to an automotive machine shop to have the work done. There are also some special tools made for turning commutators and undercutting mica. They take the place of a lathe and do an excellent job if used correctly.

STARTER BRUSH REPLACEMENT

Brushes should be replaced if they are not making good contact with the commutator or whenever they have worn down to a length of 5/16-in. Always install a complete set at one time to equalize wear.

After removing the brushes from their holders and the end plate from the starter, the armature can be taken out. The old brushes may then be removed. This calls for some work with a soldering iron, since the four new brushes must be soldered to the field and ground wires in place of the old ones. On Autolite starters, the two ground brushes sometimes do not require unsoldering since the new brushes come with the wire already attached. These can simply be screwed onto the terminal. All carbon, grease and dirt should be cleaned from the end plate, and if the insulation barrier between the field brush holders and the end plate is cracked or broken, the entire end plate should be replaced.

The new brushes may now be soldered onto the correct wires. Any flux that remains from the soldering job should be cleaned off with baking soda and water.

How to insert the brushes into the starter will be obvious after you have made a couple of false starts. In general, starters without slots in the frame must have the brushes in place before the armature is inserted. When the starter has slots, then the end plate and armature are installed, and the brushes put into their holders through the slots. The brushes must pivot freely or slide freely, whichever method is used, so that they will have good, firm contact with the commutator.

The ground wires should be reconnected in their original places before the end plate is completely in place. Be careful not to pinch the brush leads between the end plate and the frame. Also, if there is not a dowel or notch to locate the correct position of the plate on the frame, mark the plate and frame when taking the starter apart so that they can be reassembled in their proper relationship. Once the starter ends are in place, the two through-bolts can be inserted and tightened.

If electrical trouble exists within the windings of the armature or field coils, the repair is definitely not one to be attempted at home. In fact, having the starter rewound by an automotive electrician would be more expensive than simply replacing the starter with a rebuilt one. New armatures and field coils are available from new car dealers' parts departments, but the cost is sometimes equal to that of a rebuilt starter at an independent parts store. Therefore, the main value of the following tests to home mechanics is (1) to determine if the starter really needs replacement, (2) to pinpoint the trouble so that you can replace the starter's armature or frame with a used part, and (3) to test used components to make sure that they are serviceable.

Tests for grounded circuits in field windings and armatures can be made with a voltmeter and the car's battery, a self-powered ohmmeter, or a simple battery-operated test light. By connecting one test lead to the shaft and touching the other to the commutator, you can quickly detect grounded circuits in an armature. If any current passes through to the shaft, as indicated by a voltmeter reading or by the test lamp lighting, the armature is defective. The trouble was probably caused by failure of the winding insulation. The only practical repair is to replace the armature—if this is economically possible. Otherwise install a rebuilt starter. A device known as a "growler" is sometimes used to test armatures for shorted windings.

An open circuit in the armature can often be detected by examining the commutator for signs of burning. The burned place is caused by an electrical arc that is formed each time the commutator segment connected to the open-circuit winding passes under a brush rubbing surface.

The field coils can also be tested for grounded circuits using a voltmeter or test light. The same hookup is used as in testing the armature. The field brushes *must not* be in contact with the starter frame during the test. One lead from the battery is connected to the starter terminal, and the lead from the voltmeter or test lamp is touched to the starter frame. If the voltmeter shows a reading or if the test light comes on, it is an indication that the field windings are grounded.

Open circuits can be tested by attaching the battery lead to the starter terminal, and the voltmeter or test lamp lead to each of the field brushes in turn. Do not test the ground brush. If one or all of the brushes fails to light the test lamp or produce a full voltmeter reading, the field coils have an open circuit. If an open circuit is located, the wire leading from the brush to the coil should be checked for breaks. If the open spot is in the windings themselves, you will either have to get the field coils replaced by an automotive electrician or turn the starter in on a replacement.

Summing it up, let's remember that internal starter troubles are generally as rare as free samples at a U.S. mint. However, some makes do have starting motor problems because their starters are too small for the job they have to do. The trouble usually shows up as a drag-

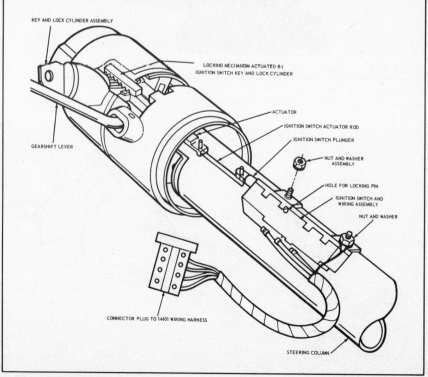

KEY AND LOCK CYLINDER ASSEMBLY

LOCKING MECHANISM ACTUATED BY IGNITION SWITCH KEY AND LOCK CYLINDER

ACTUATOR

IGNITION SWITCH ACTUATOR ROD

IGNITION SWITCH PLUNGER

NUT AND WASHER ASSEMBLY

HOLE FOR LOCKING PIN

IGNITION SWITCH AND WIRING ASSEMBLY

NUT AND WASHER

GEARSHIFT LEVER

CONNECTOR PLUG TO 14401 WIRING HARNESS

STEERING COLUMN

1. Ford Ignition Switch

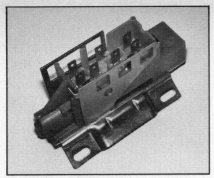

2. Chevrolet Ignition Switch

1. Many late-model cars with locking steering columns have their ignition switch low on the steering column, as on this Ford.

2. A Chevrolet ignition switch, which is typical of GM cars. The steering must be lowered to get the switch off the column.

3. Major pieces shown in this view of a disassembled Ford starter (late model) are, top: commutator and starter drive and long bolts; center: pole shoe cover, shifter forks, and starter drive housing; bottom row, from left: starter cover band and end plate assembly.

3. Late Ford Starter

ging armature from worn bearings or bushings. Open-circuited or shorted armatures can result, too.

Many short trips cause a starter to be used more than normally. On long trips a starter might be used only once a day. The type of driving has a lot to do with how long the starting system will be trouble-free, just like everything else on a car.

Before you perform any exploratory surgery on the starter motor itself, be very certain that the other parts of the starting system have been thoroughly tested and inspected. Furthermore, many starter troubles have been licked just by taking the starter apart and cleaning it. This is something to remember when installing a used starter. Clean it before you hang it on the engine and you're much more likely to be satisfied with your "bargain" replacement.

HARD-STARTING CAUSES

Sometimes the starting system gets blamed for trouble that isn't really its fault. More than one amateur mechanic has ended up with a dismantled starter in his lap while the real trouble lurked in the engine room. While these things are not, strictly speaking, starting system troubles, we'll list them here so that you'll at least be warned and on the lookout should your starter fail to turn the engine over some bright and sunny day.

1) Hydrostatic lock occurs when a cylinder becomes filled with water. (Or, in rare instances, gasoline or oil.) Liquids will not compress—that's what makes hydraulic brakes possible—and if there is a greater volume of water in a cylinder on its compression stroke than the combustion chamber can hold, the engine will not turn. The usual cause is a leaking head gasket or a cracked cylinder head.

2) Oil rundown is a condition that usually strikes the turnpike traveler. After bombing along at 75 or 80 mph for 3 or 4 hrs., the oil in an engine can get pretty thin and watery—especially if it is some kind of 30¢-per-quart "cheapie," or hasn't been changed since the election of '68. The trouble starts when you pull into a service station for gas. After your tank has been filled and the windshield scrubbed you prepare to continue on your happy way, but the starter will hardly turn the engine! It sounds as though the battery has run down—a highly improbable condition on a long high-speed trip. The real trouble is that your hot, thin oil has run right off the cylinder walls, leaving them as dry and unlubricated as scorched sandpaper.

Don't let some "sharpie" sell you a battery—save your dough for an oil change. To get started, just take off the air cleaner and pour some SAE 10 engine oil into the carb intake while someone else runs the starter. The cranking speed will soon increase and the engine should fire right up.

3) Heavy oil can place a tremendous load on the starter in cold weather. If you still have SAE 30 in the engine when the first cold blast of winter arrives, don't blame your misery on the starting system. With the temperature at 10° or 15° below the freezing point, even the best starting system probably won't budge an engine that's been sitting out all night with a crankcase full of summer-grade oil.

4) Carbon buildup in the combustion chambers can both increase the effective compression ratio of an engine and, when heated to incandescence by a high-speed run, convert your engine into a "diesel." Carbon particles may remain glowing coals for many minutes after the engine is switched off. When you try to restart the engine, the increased compression and the glowing carbon cause the fuel to ignite before the spark plugs fire. Since ignition is taking place long before the pistons near the top of their stroke, the engine tries to run backward, fighting the starter. Lots of people have spent money on their starting system trying to cure this before finally pulling off the heads to get rid of all that carbon.

Excessive initial spark advance or a defective distributor can cause symptoms similar to those produced by carbon buildup; however, this will also cause trouble when the engine is cold.

5) Mechanical interference is another possible source of starting trouble. It's usually the result of improperly done tune-up or repair work—such as installing the camshaft 180° from its correct position.

If you have been working on the car, and it then refuses to start, check on your own work before condemning the starter.

6) Antifreeze lockup will call a halt to engine cranking just as quickly as a mechanical lockup. Antifreeze is not a lubricant. When it seeps through a head gasket and gets on the cylinder walls, the pistons and cylinders like each other so well that they are inseparable. This problem usually shows up on the first attempt to start in the morning, after the antifreeze has had all night to do its seeping. The test is to drain the cooling system and fill it with water only. Usually, the cranking problem will go away. You should then put a good sealer in the cooling system and then just refill it with antifreeze.

In some cases the antifreeze contaminates the engine so badly that merely draining the cooling system will not help. In that unhappy situation you have to use a compound known as Butyl Cellosolve in the oil. It will pick up the antifreeze from the engine, if you follow directions on the package.

7) Piston seizure, similar to oil rundown, can also cause a no-crank condition. If the cooling system is partially

Starting System

clogged around the cylinders, local hot spots develop which expand the cylinders unevenly. If magnified, the cylinder surface might look like a plowed field. The hillocks grab hold of the piston and won't let it move in the cylinder. It will happen every time the engine gets up to operating temperature. Let it cool, and the engine will start normally. A thorough cooling system cleaning will get rid of this problem. We have seen some people cure it by putting in high-powered starters and heavy-duty batteries, but that's like putting a cork in your tailpipe to stop exhaust smoke. It may cover up the problem temporarily, but it won't cure it.

MORE STARTING POWER

The stock starting systems on most cars were designed to do their job on stock engines. Some of the last 6-volt systems were hardly up to their work even then! As soon as you start boosting compression ratios and fiddling with ignition and valve timing, you're making the starting system's life a little more fraught with drudgery.

There are no "hopped-up" starter motors marketed at the local speed shop, but there is something almost as good waiting at the nearest parts store or wrecking yard; namely a truck starter. Most of the standard blocks used in passenger cars also get punched out and draped with different accessories for use in trucks. In most cases the heavy-duty "commercial" starters will bolt right onto them. You can usually find out "what'll fit what" by checking the exploded view drawings in the dealer's parts catalog.

Commercial starters have a greater current demand than those found on standard cars and, therefore, depend on a more powerful battery. This is something that should be considered anyway when planning a starting system for your "rod."

Cars that were originally built with a 6-volt electrical system can have their starter changed to a more powerful 12-volt number without completely rewiring the car and throwing out all 6-volt instruments and accessories. The answer is a "6-12" starter-electrical system. The heart of the system is an automatic voltage converter switch such as the Orpin unit. All you do is add a second 6-volt battery and wire the batteries and starter into the switch according to the directions. This system will automatically shoot 12 volts to the starter for cranking the engine without increasing the voltage to the rest of the electrical system.

There are also several conversion kits that permit using entire 12-volt engines in 6-volt cars and 6-volt engines in 12-volt cars. The 6-volt starters can be fitted to engines that originally had 12-volt jobs, but converting a 6-volt system to 12 volts will get you much more reliable starts than a 12-to-6 starter swap.

This should give you a good idea of just what takes place in a modern-day automotive starting system. Starting systems have come a long way since the day of the crank, but they still aren't so overly complicated that the home mechanic can't service them. This is especially true in preventive maintenance, which includes battery terminal cleaning and checkups, tightening connections and inspection of wiring. This is all part of good-car-care that will result in dependable transportation for you—from the very start. 🎬

1. Delco-Remy starters have changed very little over the years. Recent models have had two distinguishing features added to them: non-reversible solenoid contacts and a fully enclosed drive housing.

2. Worn brushes can cause a no-start problem. Pin retains entire assembly, which, when removed, allows brushes to be replaced.

3. Brushes are attached to holders with small screws. No solder needed. Disassemble one pair of brushes at a time. Use other pair as an example.

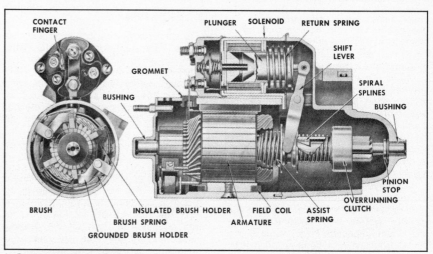

1. Cutaway of Delco-Remy Starter

CONTACT FINGER — GROMMET — BUSHING — BRUSH — BRUSH SPRING — GROUNDED BRUSH HOLDER — INSULATED BRUSH HOLDER — PLUNGER — SOLENOID — RETURN SPRING — SHIFT LEVER — SPIRAL SPLINES — BUSHING — PINION STOP — OVERRUNNING CLUTCH — ASSIST SPRING — FIELD COIL — ARMATURE

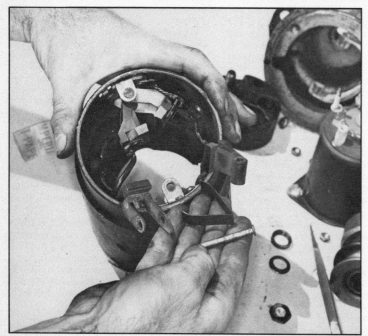

2. Worn Brushes

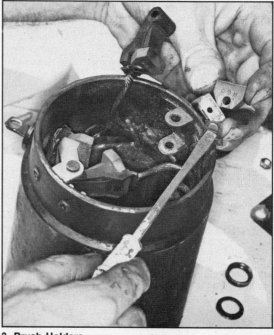

3. Brush Holders

1. Solenoid disconnect is done from under hood. On some late-model cars, plumbing is heavy, so you'd do better to work from underneath.

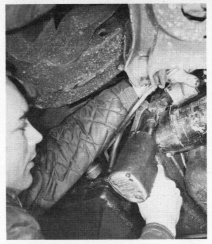

2. Once solenoid is disconnected, removal of two bolts will allow starter to be pulled. Bolt location differs from year to year and car to car.

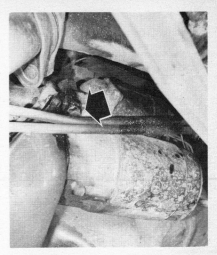

3. Starting motor removal from majority of GM cars is best accomplished from underneath. There's another bolt on the side opposite from the one marked.

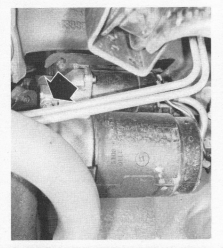

4. Dual exhaust on same GM car as in photo #3 shows how access to starting motor can vary, depending upon the particular car and how it's equipped.

5. FoMoCo starting motor is mounted to flywheel housing with two horizontal bolts. Access on '73 Ford LTD is exceptionally easy compared to many cars.

6. Here's a late-model T-Bird starter mounted exactly as in LTD, but note how access is obscured by crossarms and suspension linkage.

7. Getting at this '73 Valiant starter is no picnic. Steering linkage and dual exhaust pipes hamper removal of the lower bolt, making removal tedious.

8. Lower bolt on this '72 Le Baron is difficult to get to. Upper bolt on Chrysler Corp. V-8's is reached from under hood, with equal difficulty.

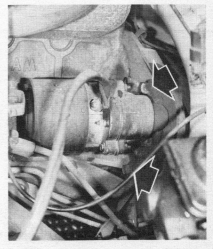

9. Easiest starter to remove is that on a Chrysler Corp. Slant-6. As on this '72 Duster, the starter comes out easily from under the hood.

HOW-TO: Ford Starter Teardown

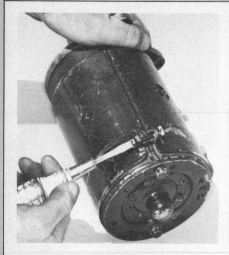

1. Ford starters can best be removed by disconnecting starter cable at relay (drop steering idler arm on Montego), take off mounting bolts.

2. To disassemble this Ford starter, loosen and remove the brush cover band, starter drive plunger lever cover and the cork gasket under it.

3. Next insert needle nose pliers and a hook made from a large cotter key, and lift out the brushes so the end plate can be taken off.

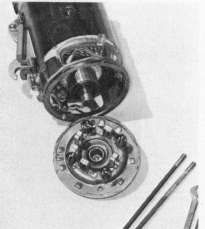

4. With the brushes now out of the way, you can fully remove through-bolts and pull off the starter end plate with the brush springs on it.

5. Extract pivot pin which retains lever. Now is a good time to look at the contacts at the other end of the lever to be sure they are OK.

6. Starter gear plunger lever can now be lifted out. Remove armature. Use brush or air to clean field, coils, armature shaft, brush end plate, etc.

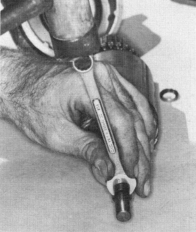

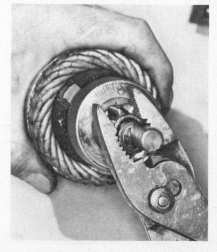

7. Inspect pole shoes to see if the armature has been rubbing them. If it has, the armature bearings have gone away, and shaft has sagged out.

8. If starter drive gear assembly is to be reused, remove stop ring retainer and the stop ring from the end of armature shaft; remove drive.

9. Place the drive gear assembly on the new armature with new stop ring. Install the fiber thrust washer on commutator end of armature shaft.

1. To disassemble, check Delco-Remy starter, remove through-bolts off commutator end frame, then pull motor connector strap terminal screw.

2. Slide field housing away from lever and nose housing. If solenoid is OK, and you're just checking armature, leave solenoid alone.

3. Once armature is out of field housing, check commutator. If it's grooved, rough, or out-of-round, it must be turned down smooth.

4. If armature touched or rubbed against field coils, chances are bushings in commutator end frame are gone and should be changed.

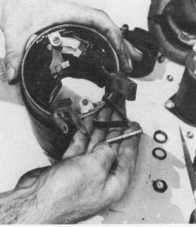

5. Worn brushes can cause a no-start problem. A pin retains entire assembly, which, when removed, allows brushes to be replaced.

6. Brushes are attached to holders with small screws. No solder needed. Disassemble one pair of brushes at a time, use other pair as example.

7. Drive is kept on armature shaft by three pieces. First take thrust collar off end of shaft. Note flange goes toward body of armature.

8. Next, retainer must be driven back along armature shaft. Use a deep socket and plastic-head hammer; don't punch it off with a ball peen.

9. Once snap ring is exposed, remove it with two screwdrivers. Drive assembly can be slid off armature shaft and replaced, if necessary.

HOW-TO: Chrysler Starter Teardown

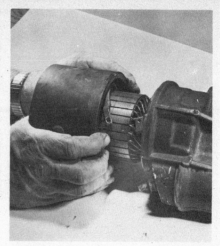

1. Begin removing MoPar starter by disconnecting battery ground strap, hot cable from starter, and solenoid lead wires at solenoid terminals.

2. Remove stud nut (bolt holding starter to bellhousing); slide trans oil cooler tube bracket off stud prior to removing starter, end head.

3. With long bolts removed, you can pull frame off to expose terminal screw, wrapped wire connection of shunt field at brush terminal.

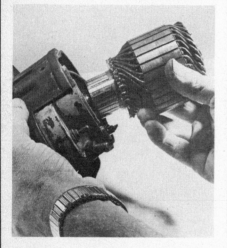

4. Armature can now be pulled up and out of gear housing, starter frame and field assembly. Then remove the steel and fiber thrust washers.

5. Extract brush holder plate screw before taking off steel insulation washers from solenoid. Remove brush hold plate (with brushes) as unit.

6. Now, solenoid/brush assembly can be pulled from gear housing well, the nut, steel washer and sealing washer from battery terminal.

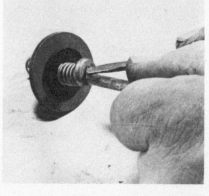

7. After nut on solenoid terminal is off, solenoid lead wire to brush terminal post must be unsoldered so solenoid assembly can be removed.

8. Brass washer contact disc that makes the electrical connection between the battery and starter, is subjected to pitting tend/or burning.

9. The contact disc can be removed, replaced or reversed by releasing it from contact stud, plunger. Pop off snap retainer holding it on plunger.

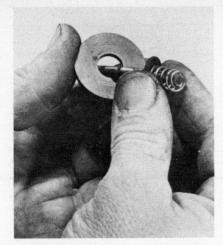

10. After removing the contact disc, turn it over and return it to the plunger. This new, fresh side saves you from buying a new contact disc.

11. In order to get at the starter drive, all you have to do is grab one of your trusty screwdrivers and pry off the dust cover.

12. Release U-shaped retainer that positions driven gear on pinion shaft. Be careful; retainer is under pressure and can spring away.

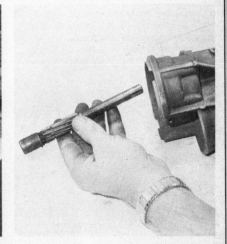

13. Retainer ring on front of pinion shaft can now be released. Don't use a spreader any larger than shaft's O.D. or ring can be damaged.

14. Tap pinion shaft toward rear of housing. Extract retaining ring, thrust washer, clutch, pinion (shifter forks, nylon actuators) as unit.

15. With pinion shaft removed from rear of the starter housing, check it carefully for any burrs, cracks or other signs of wear or damage.

16. Large friction washer on driven gear is subjected to wear because it absorbs shock of large gear being driven to rear of the housing.

17. Clutch assembly can be removed as well as the clutch shifting fork assembly. Do not soak in solvent; wipe all pieces with a clean cloth.

18. Check the wiring on inside of field for breaks or signs of burning. Make sure screws that hold pole shoes in are good and snug.

Ignition System

The ignition of an internal combustion engine has very probably had more development work done on it than any other part of an automobile. Even so, it is still a long way from being perfect. Just in the past few years we have seen transistor ignitions appear that weren't much good and capacitor discharge ignitions come on the scene that were a lot better. The ignition has a very difficult job to do.

As the entire purpose of the ignition is to fire the fuel/air mixture compressed in the engine combustion chamber, with only a storage battery as power source, the system's basic functions are quite clear: 1) Convert the relatively low voltage of the storage battery to the high voltage needed to fire the plugs, and 2) Control the timing of the firing to suit varying engine speeds and loads.

The ignition system has two electrical circuits. One, operating on battery current and controlled by the ignition switch and distributor points, is called the *primary* circuit. The *secondary* circuit carries high voltage current induced in the coil and consists of a high tension cable between the coil and distributor, the distributor rotor and cap, the spark plug cables and the spark plugs.

When the ignition switch is turned on, the current flows from the battery through the switch to the coil primary windings, then to the distributor points which are connected to ground. Any time that the distributor points are closed there is a continuous flow of current from the battery through the ignition switch through the coil primary and through the points. This flow of current through the coil primary creates a magnetic field which stays there as long as current is flowing. As the engine rotates, the distributor cam pushes the points apart, which breaks the primary circuit and stops the flow of current. When the current flow ceases, the magnetic field in the coil collapses—which creates a high voltage in the secondary windings in the coil. The secondary windings are connected to the spark plugs so that the high voltage can jump the spark plug gap, thus firing the mixture and making the engine run. The distributor cam is timed to the engine so that it opens the points at exactly the right moment, when the combustion chamber is full with the fresh charge of fuel/air mixture.

A condenser is connected between the coil primary and the points. The condenser's purpose is to assist in the quick collapse of the magnetic field in the coil. Many textbooks state that the condenser is in the circuit to keep the points from pitting. If that were all the condenser did, you could remove it and the car would still run. We have never found an engine with battery ignition that would

1. Racing Plug Check

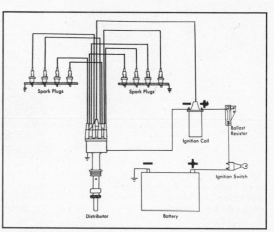

3. Condenser Inside Housing

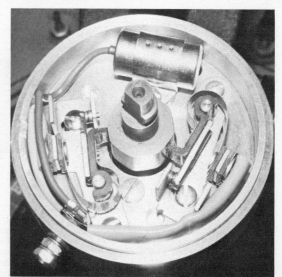

2. Battery Ignition Circuit

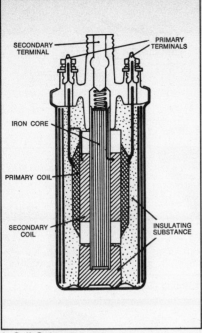

4. Coil Cutaway

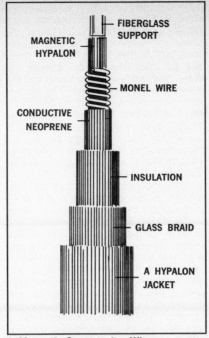

5. Magnetic Suppression Wire

6. Conventional Cable

7. Carbon Resistance Cable

8. Belden #7300 Cable

9. Lacquered Wire Cable

run without a condenser. So this proves, at least to us, that the condenser does much more than just keep the points from pitting. Now that we have a general idea of how the ignition system works, let's look at the various components.

THE COIL

An automotive coil is an induction transformer not much different from the little transformers that are used to run toy trains. A train transformer takes 110 volts out of the wall outlet and converts it to a safe low voltage so that your hair doesn't stand on end every time you touch the tracks. The ignition coil works the other way around. It takes the 12 volts that is available at the battery and changes it to 10,000 or 20,000 or even 30,000 volts, whatever is needed to jump the particular gap at the spark plug.

Every modern coil has three terminals—two small threaded posts for the primary and a large center tower which is the connection for the secondary. Inside the coil is an iron core with the primary and secondary windings wound around it. The ratio of turns between the primary and secondary windings determines how big the step-up in voltage is between the battery voltage and secondary voltage. Because the step-up is from comparatively low battery voltage to very high spark plug voltage, the primary has relatively few turns and the secondary has many.

Current flow in the secondary is created in the coil and flows out along the secondary lead to the distributor and then to the spark plugs. If you study electrical circuitry, you will be told that all current must return to its source in order to make a complete circuit. If the circuit is broken anywhere the current will not flow. The theory works fine with low voltage but it is a source of embarrassment to many automotive instructors when they attempt to explain the path of ignition system secondary voltage. One end of the secondary winding goes out

to the spark plug. The other end may be grounded to the coil can, or in most cases is grounded to the primary windings. The standard explanation of the secondary current flow is that it goes out through the spark plug wire, jumps the gap at the plug and then returns through a ground path into the battery and back through the primary windings. It may be very convenient to explain secondary current flow in this manner but the theory just doesn't hold water when you analyze it.

The next time somebody tells you the secondary current has to have a return path through the coil winding, ask him to reach over and touch a bare spark plug wire tip while the engine is running. He probably will refuse because he knows that the secondary current will go into his body, which can in no way be a return path to the coil windings. If you want to experiment even further, get a long spark plug wire and plug it into one distributor tower with the engine running. Walk around with the wire in your hand and touch it to various objects. You will find that the spark will jump to just about anything. In fact it will jump to any mass of electrons big enough to attract it.

When removing or installing primary wiring connections to the coil, be sure to observe proper polarity. These connections are marked either positive (+) and negative (-), or "batt." (battery) and "dist." (distributor). Most cars are currently using 12-volt ignition systems with negative ground, but earlier Fords to 1956 with 6-volt systems used positive ground. When replacing coils it is important to use only those that match the rating and polarity of the system. Reversing polarity or using the improper voltage-rated coil will result in poor voltage output and insufficient power to fire the plugs.

CONDENSER

The condenser is attached across the breaker points of the distributor. Some

1. Many advances in ignition design have come from racing applications. Reading plug condition after a run helps engineers determine sources of power loss and what adjustments are needed to improve engine efficiency.

2. Simplified ignition circuit shows basic components in primary and secondary circuits.

3. The condenser (also called the "capacitor") can be either inside or outside the distributor housing. It stores primary circuit energy when the points are open and hastens the collapse of the magnetic field in the coil.

4. Cutaway of typical coil shows primary and secondary windings with insulation. Iron core is necessary to create magnetic field.

5. Magnetic suppression wire has a complicated construction.

6. Here's the wire that practically every mechanic is familiar with—good ol' metallic core with rubber insulation, neoprene outer covering.

7. This "whisk broom" is really the inner core of one brand of resistance spark plug wire. The filaments are impregnated with carbon and encased in a nylon sheath.

8. Belden IRS has a 1-piece tubular conductor with a strengthening nylon cord through its center and rubber insulation with a neoprene sheath.

9. This is really old stuff— metallic wire, with rubber for insulation, is further coated with a mixture of cotton and lacquer.

Ignition System

distributors have the condenser installed inside the housing, others are externally mounted. In either case it has only one lead wire, the other connection being the outer case or mounting bracket which is grounded. The wire lead is connected to the coil primary usually at the same place as the wire from the coil to the distributor points. The condenser is a very important part of the point switching system and is in the circuit to speed up collapse of the magnetic field in the coil. It is, in effect, a small storage tank with capacity that is balanced to the circuit.

Condensers develop internal leaks that disturb this balance, the effects of which show up in the form of metal transfer on the points themselves. Even a new condenser in perfect condition will cause this metal transfer if it is not of the proper capacity. Condensers are rated in microfarads (mfds.), which can be measured with a condenser tester.

Condenser capacity usually runs from .21 to .25 mfds. If you have a problem of rapid point pitting on a particular car, it is possible to reduce the pitting by selecting the proper capacity condenser. Condenser selection according to capacity is rarely done nowadays because of the amount of time it takes.

Examination of the points will indicate over- or under-capacity of the condenser by applying the "minus-minus-minus" rule: *If the minus (negative) point is minus metal (pitted), then the condenser is minus capacity.* Increasing condenser capacity would correct the condition. Conversely, if the pit were on the positive point, then the condenser would have too much capacity, and another condenser with less capacity would be the solution. This applies to both 6- and 12-volt systems, with either negative or positive ground.

Few mechanics bother to test condensers—it's easier to put in a new one. However, many apparent cases of low-capacity condenser damage result from poor ground contact between the condenser case and the distributor. A new condenser won't help unless the mounting area is kept clean and bright.

Delco introduced a new unitary points/condenser unit for use on some '72 GM cars. Mounted on the points, the condenser is connected to the insulated point arm by two thin ribbons of metal that flex each time the points open and close. With no wire lead connecting the points and condenser, there's much less radio interference and no need to use a metal shield over the points. But as this design is somewhat more complex to make than the older separate points/condenser, the manufacturer believed he was justified in asking a higher price for replacement units.

When the price commission took exception to the replacement unit price and insisted that it be reduced, Delco simply removed it from the market, and so what started out as an improvement in the ignition system turned into just one more small example of govermental interference in automotive design, with the customer coming out on the short end, as usual. To replace the points and condenser in this distributor now, it's necessary to install a new breaker plate first, because the one originally supplied with the unit has no hole for condenser installation. A conversion kit is available through GM dealers complete with new breaker plate, but its installation adds $15-$20 to the customer's bill for the initial tune-up.

SECONDARY WIRING

The secondary or high-voltage wiring—those connections from coil tower to center of distributor and the individual ones from distributor to spark plugs—differ a great deal in construction and capacity from those used to carry the current from battery to coil (primary wiring).

Unlike the primary wire, cable used in the secondary circuit must be heavily insulated to contain the high voltage current it carries. Most cars have cables sheathed with Hypalon insulation. This has good resistance to oil damage but withstands the higher underhood temperatures of today's cars better than the neoprene insulation which was used in the past. If you replace the spark cables, stay away from glossy plastic-insulated

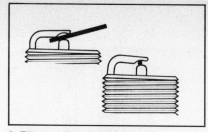

4. Effect of Flat Gauge

5. Using Gap Gauge

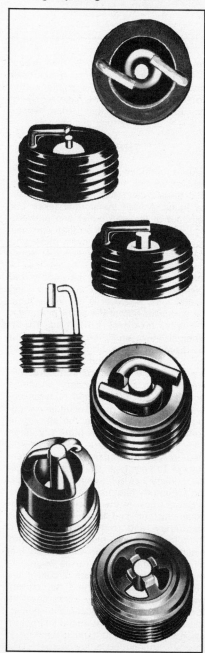

6. Electrode Types

1. Lump Resistor

2. Defective Plug Boot

3. Checking Wiring Resistance

1. If you don't have resistor wires but want to cut down on radio interference, insert this lump-type resistor between the coil and distributor. Resistance is about 10,000 ohms.

2. Plug boots that cover the plug can sometimes be the catalyst producing flashover. Plug insulator is ruined by carbon track. Both plug and boot must be replaced.

3. All ignition wiring, resistance type or otherwise, can be checked with an ohmmeter. Extremely high reading reveals defective wires.

4. No matter how careful you are, you just can't gap plugs with a flat feeler gauge. You must use a round wire gauge.

5. If the spark plug gauge will pass through the gap with a slight amount of friction, then you can be sure that the gap is correct.

6. Spark plug ground electrodes come in many different shapes and sizes. The multiple-electrode designs are good only on industrial and aircraft engines that operate at constant rpm. They have a tendency to foul if used in a car where the engine is idled in heavy traffic.

7. Champion gap tool is handy, since individual gap gauges are retractable. Gapper is less likely to make a mistake with this setup.

8. Core bridging—buildup of combustion chamber deposits between insulator and shell—is caused by poor oil or bad oil control.

9. Combustion chamber deposits can also lodge between the electrodes, thus shorting out the plug. Cleaning and regapping are the answer.

10. This is what can happen when dirt, dust, and sand enter with the fuel/air mixture. Ineffective air cleaner and bad intake gasket or loose bolts are usually the cause.

11. Fast acceleration after prolonged low-speed driving can produce a hard, glassy brown coating on the insulator tip and electrode. Glaze is conductive and can ruin plugs.

12. If you were to cut away the outer shell of the plug, this is what a dirty insulator would look like. Sandblaster will remove this.

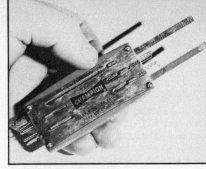

7. Champion Gap Tool

8. Core Bridging

9. Gap Bridging

10. Silicone Deposits

11. High-Speed Glazing

12. Carbon Fouled Plug

wire with "poly" or "vin" in their trade names. Some of these are transparent and look good on show cars, but their polyvinyl chloride insulation melts easily near a hot exhaust manifold. A silicone rubber insulation is used on cables designed for maximum heat resistance. Belden 7770, Autolite 7SH, and cables sold under the generic name "7SH" in speed shops are examples. They will usually operate continously at 450° F. without failure.

All cars now use resistance type high tension cable, but some of it isn't very resistant to internal breaks and burnouts. The conductor is usually a nylon or glass fiber string impregnated with carbon—at least on production cars.

If you're careful to pull on the plug connector and not the wire when re-

moving the cables from the spark plugs, the factory installed resistance cable can last a long time. However, many resistance cables have a soft "fluffy" conductor which fails to provide good contact for the terminals. The result is often a tiny spark which arcs between the carbon impregnated yarn and the terminal. The heat eventually burns away the conductor and produces an ignition failure.

Because of burnouts and breaks caused by careless handling, resistance cable has gotten a bad name with many car owners. It should not be replaced with metallic conductor cable, however—for the sake of your spark plugs and the neighbors' TV. Instead, replace the factory cable with one of the reliable brands of resistance cable.

If for some reason you must use me-

tallic conductor cable, it's necessary to add resistance to the stock ignition system if you are to avoid rapid spark plug gap growth due to electrical erosion. The usual method is to use plug connectors with built-in resistance or a "lump" type resistor at the distributor cap. These are available from radio shops. The use of resistor plugs will do a half-way job on solving the problem.

Lump resistors come as little plastic tubes with screws in each end. Cut the wire (metallic wire only) between the secondary coil and distributor and screw one in place. You can also buy resistors that go on each spark plug, but their durability, in our experience, has not been too good. Several companies now sell magnetic suppression wire, which has very low resistance, but excellent

Ignition System

suppression. Whittaker makes wire sets with lump resistors in each plug connector, attached to metallic wires. That way the wires are more durable, but you still have the resistance built in.

All wires, whether metallic or resistance types, should be checked with an ohmmeter. If the resistance of any one wire is above 40,000 ohms, suspect a bad wire. But before you condemn it, measure a new wire of the same type for comparison. Resistance specifications for wire vary several thousand ohms, depending on the manufacturer. While checking with the ohmmeter, flex the wire to see if there are any breaks in it. If the ohmmeter jumps to infinity, there is definitely a break. Don't worry about an increase of a few thousand ohms as you flex the wire. That's normal with carbon-string wires.

You may wonder why the new car makers continue to use carbon string wire when all the aftermarket companies are promoting other types of resistance wire. The main reason is that carbon string wire is the only type that provides maximum suppression. The other wire designs have good suppression, but they don't quite keep the interference level down to what you get with carbon string wire.

SPARK PLUGS

Often termed the barometer of engine condition, the spark plugs have one main function: to fire properly under all normal engine operating conditions.

The art of "reading" a plug to determine engine operating efficiency is also covered in the tune-up chapter, but as part of the ignition system alone, there are certain tell-tale points that are important to "lighting the fire."

First, you'll need the correct plug for your engine. This is usually just a matter of walking into the parts store and telling them what kind of car you drive. They'll check a chart prepared by the spark plug company and give you the right plug—hopefully. Mistakes are occasionally made, so it's important to know a bit about spark plug design to protect yourself from accidents.

It's impossible to put an 18mm (thread diameter) plug into a 14mm hole, but a plug with the wrong *reach* could be installed. Reach refers to the length of the threaded portion of the plug shell. Always check the reach of the new plugs against that of the old. Installing a plug with a ¾-in. reach in an engine made for ⅜-in. reach spark plugs could bend the valves or knock holes in the pistons. Installing a short reach plug in a deep hole won't cause mechanical damage, but it'll mean a definite power loss and very quick fouling or burning of the spark plugs.

1. This plug insulator is not properly cleaned. A good sandblaster will remove all the deposits so that the insulator is white.

2. Detonation can not only ruin pistons, but also spark plugs. The ground electrode was snapped off clean by the force of detonation.

3. A dirty insulator top can cause flashover, and a dead cylinder. Clean upper insulator with a rag and solvent only, never sandblasting.

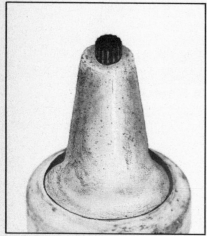

1. Improperly Cleaned Insulator

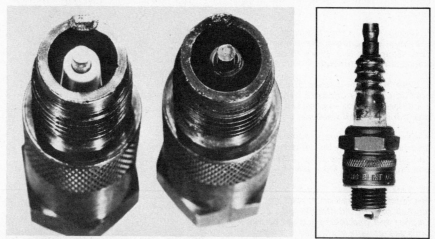

2. Detonation Damage

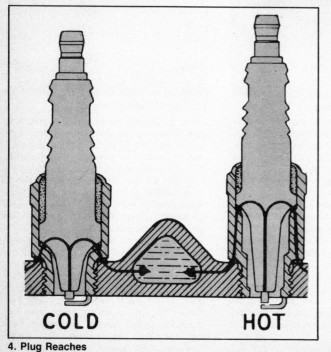

3. Dirty Insulator Top

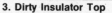

COLD   HOT

4. Plug Reaches

PREIGNITION REGION

OXIDE FOULING & ELECTRODE BURNING

FAHRENHEIT

IDEAL TIP TEMPERATURE RANGE

1700
1500
1000
750
500

CARBON & OIL FOULING REGION

5. Hot and Cold Plugs

6. Top Types

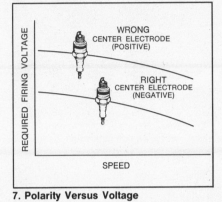

7. Polarity Versus Voltage

8. Test Lab

4. The plug with the longer nose will run hotter because the heat cannot get to the cooling water as easily. The hot plug will stay clean longer, but it may burn up too.

5. Fouled plug at bottom is too "cold." Plug at top shows signs of overheating, with the possibility of preignition damage. Condition of plug in the middle shows proper heat range choice for particular use.

6. When selecting plug connectors, make sure they'll fit the plug you intend to use. Some connectors require that the terminal nut be taken off, as is possible with plug at right. Terminal at left is solid.

7. Wrong coil polarity requires a higher voltage to fire the plug, and a greater chance for misfire. Plug should have negative polarity.

8. In the Champion Spark Plug lab, a wire leads to each plug for exact temperature readings. Engine vacuum and spark timing are also read.

It is also imperative that a spark plug of the proper heat range be used. If a plug is too "cold" for your engine, it will not retain enough combustion chamber heat to burn fouling deposits off its firing end. If the plug is too "hot," it will retain excessive combustion chamber heat. This can be extremely dangerous. Not only do overheated plugs wear out quicker, but they may become incandescent and ignite the fuel/air mixture in the cylinders before the spark actually fires. This is called preignition and, if sustained, can destroy pistons or even an engine.

You can tell whether a plug is of the proper heat range by comparing its number to those recommended for your car. Looking at the length of the insulator nose will tell you comparatively little regarding heat range these days due to the many other variables in spark plug

design. If it's not the right number, don't use it. The exception being when it is a different brand that, therefore, has a different number, but is listed for your car by the spark plug manufacturer.

A final factor to be considered when changing plugs is gap style. There are two popular types used in cars today. The first, called *standard gap,* is the traditional plug design with its ceramic insulator nose wholly contained within the plug shell. The second type, called *projected nose,* is actually in wider use among car makers than standard gap plugs. Its insulator nose extends beyond the end of the threaded portion of the plug shell.

Both standard gap and projected nose plugs may be listed as alternatives for your car in the spark plug manufacturer's chart. If so, pick the projected nose type even if it costs a few cents more. They'll give better fouling resistance and increased power in most engines—although, in some cases, the spark may have to be retarded a few degrees to eliminate excessive "ping." Don't use projected nose plugs in engines for which they are not recommended—especially in flathead powerplants or those with highly domed pistons. There's a chance that the valves or piston crown will strike the plug nose. Plugs with platinum or other fine wire electrodes and surface gap plugs having no side electrode should not be used unless specified by the car manufacturer.

Used plugs that have been operating at the proper heat range and whose electrodes are not badly eroded or burned, can be filed and regapped after cleaning and will give added satisfactory mileage. The spark will jump from a sharp edge on the center electrode more easily than from a rounded, worn electrode. Put the spark plug shell in a vise, then bend the ground electrode out of the way and file the center electrode flat and sharp with a small file. Blow all the filings out, and set the gap with a round

wire gauge. If the insulator was previously sandblasted clean, you will now have new-plug performance from your old plugs. Always do the sandblasting before you file the electrode, because the sand will take away the sharp edge. Also, sandblasting or cleaning solvent are the only ways to clean plugs. Wire buffing wheels on a bench grinder are definitely out, because the wire wheel leaves metallic tracks on the porcelain that cause misfiring. Never adjust plug points by applying pressure to the center electrode, as damage to the insulator tip will result. Bend only the side or ground electrode when setting gap.

When installing new spark plugs, do not take their gap settings for granted. Sometimes the same plug will be used on different engines with different gap settings. So you must check the gaps to see if they are set for the engine you are working on.

Care should be taken when installing plugs, new or used. Be sure that the cylinder-head plug holes are cleaned and free of dirt or carbon particles both at the gasket seat and inside the threads. Plug threads should also be clean, undamaged, and lubricated.

Screw plugs in finger-tight against the gasket, then go an additional ¾-turn with a plug wrench. If you aren't sure of your ability to tighten plugs correctly, use a torque wrench. Folded gaskets, the type that screw on the plug threads, do not require a torque wrench, even when they are reused several times. Tapered seat plugs are another story. They don't use gaskets, and they can stick tighter than the government's grasp on a tax dollar if you tighten them too much. Check the tapered seats in the head, use a good torque wrench to tighten them, and by all means *believe* the wrench. You are not doing yourself a favor by going a few extra foot-pounds, as you will find out when you try to take them out a few thousand miles later.

On some Chrysler Corp. engines, the

Ignition System

plugs are mounted in long tubes and no plug gasket is used. The tube should be checked for burred edges and cracks in the plug mounting area. If any engine has an aluminum head, always inspect the plug threads with a jeweler's magnifying glass for any plug thread irregularities, and reject those with burred threads. A bad thread can quickly destroy the threads in an aluminum head and require that a Heli-Coil insert be installed to save expensive repairs or replacement.

RESISTOR PLUGS

Originally designed for the old flathead-6 Chryslers to allow wider gaps, which then gave a better idle, resistor plugs are now available for almost any car. If your engine has metallic wires, resistor plugs will help reduce gap growth.

Resistor plugs of 5000 ohms are standard equipment on late GM cars, which also use resistor wires. Before both resistor wires and plugs were used together, the resistance value of the plugs was 10,000 ohms. Champion makes both values: the 10,000-ohm with an R prefix, and the 5000-ohm with an X prefix. Theoretically, you should use the 5000-ohm plug with resistor wires, and the 10,000-ohm plug with metallic wires. But you can pair them up the opposite way, and it won't have any effect on engine operation. Other plug makers appear to have dropped their 10,000-ohm plug and are making only the 5000-ohm model.

SERIES GAP PLUGS

Series gap plugs, which have an internal air gap that the spark must jump before reaching the electrodes, are gaining wide acceptance among car owners. They have the ability to clean themselves quickly of fouling deposits accumulated in low-speed, stop-and-go driving when "opened up" on the freeway. It takes time for spark voltage to rise to the level required to jump a plug gap. If the plug is fouled, conductive deposits may drain off enough voltage before its peak is reached to cause a misfire. By forcing the spark current to jump an internal

1. When it comes to tightening plugs, the torque wrench is best, but if you don't have one, then tighten the plugs from ½ to ¾ of a turn after you get them finger-tight.

2. Wobbling the plug while cleaning is important. It allows sand to get into all parts of plug and remove carbon particles.

3. Air pressure test is interesting, but the only real test of a spark plug is its operation in an engine. Inspection with magnifier is good, too.

4. In a distributor with the weights below the plate, pins on the weights engage holes in the cam yoke. As the shaft increases its speed of rotation, the weights fly out against spring tension and the pins advance the cam's position on the shaft.

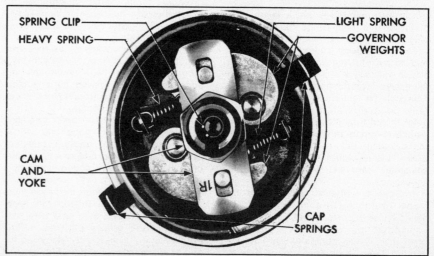

1. Installing Plugs

"WOBBLE" PLUG

2. Sandblasting Plug

3. Plug Pressure Test

SPRING CLIP — HEAVY SPRING — LIGHT SPRING — GOVERNOR WEIGHTS — CAM AND YOKE — CAP SPRINGS

4. Centrifugal Advance Weights

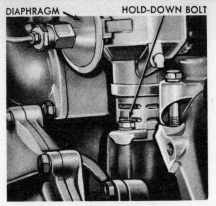

DIAPHRAGM   HOLD-DOWN BOLT

5. Distributor Hold-Down Bolt

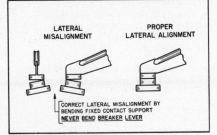

LATERAL MISALIGNMENT   PROPER LATERAL ALIGNMENT

CORRECT LATERAL MISALIGNMENT BY BENDING FIXED CONTACT SUPPORT. **NEVER BEND BREAKER LEVER**

6. Point Alignment

5. To actually remove the distributor, simply disconnect the vacuum advance line, take off the primary wire and distributor cap, and loosen the hold-down bolt. On most cars, the distributor can be lifted out after the bolt is removed.

6. Bad alignment shortens point life considerably, and the result in operation will be a poor spark because of insufficient point contact.

7. Chrysler Corp. has gone to the electronic (transistor) ignition system with its 1973 models. Available on some 1972 models, the EIS includes a pointless distributor for minimum maintenance.

gap first, it is certain to be at full voltage before ever arriving at the firing electrodes.

TESTING SPARK PLUGS

The best advice we can give you here is to forget it. There is no way to test spark plugs outside an engine, unless you own a million-dollar laboratory. The air pressure "plug tester" used in many garages is merely a way to pacify car owners who ask for a plug test. We like the plug tester, not for "testing" plugs, but for showing the action of the spark on a fouled plug, and for demonstrating spark action between the electrodes. Plug testers don't really test plugs because they are at room temperature, and the combustion chamber in the engine is at several thousand degrees. A visual inspection of plugs will tell you more than any tester. The inner porcelain should be clean, and the center electrode should be square and sharp, with the proper gap.

DISTRIBUTOR TYPES

There are three basic distributor systems in use on late-model American passenger cars: the conventional

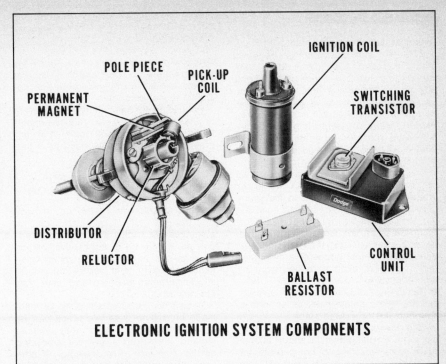

IGNITION COIL

POLE PIECE   PICK-UP COIL

PERMANENT MAGNET

SWITCHING TRANSISTOR

DISTRIBUTOR

RELUCTOR

BALLAST RESISTOR

CONTROL UNIT

ELECTRONIC IGNITION SYSTEM COMPONENTS

7. Chrysler Electronic Ignition

coil-condenser-contact point, the point-controlled transistor, and the pulse-controlled transistor. All are a combination of engine-driven rotor and electrical or mechanical switching, whose function is to deliver a usable spark.

CONVENTIONAL DISTRIBUTOR

Distributors, whether conventional or transistorized, are driven by a gear on the engine camshaft. The distributor shaft drives the breaker point cam and the rotor. Because the gearing of the distributor shaft is in time with the engine, care must be taken when replacing to see that it is in the correct position. The simplest way to do this—after disconnecting all wires, removing distributor cap, and loosening mounting clamp—is to mark outside of case for reference to a similar mark on engine block, then slowly withdraw distributor without turning it. As it is pulled out, the rotor will turn slightly as the helical gears disengage from the cam gear.

When it is completely disengaged, mark the rotor in reference to a similar mark inside distributor housing. Aligning these reference marks before reassembling will put the timing close enough that you should be able to fire up the engine, provided the engine crankshaft has not been turned while the assembly was out of the engine block.

The timing of the spark to the stroke of the pistons must be varied in relation to speed and load conditions. Timing is adjusted automatically by the distributor's internal spark advance system. Most distributors employ two forms of spark advance—a centrifugal mechanism that advances or retards the distributor cam in relation to the distributor drive shaft, and a vacuum diaphragm which advances or retards the position of the breaker point assembly relative to the distributor cam. Most Volkswagens and certain other economy cars use only the

vacuum controlled automatic advance mechanism.

Most cars being built today have dual chamber vacuum advance units to reduce exhaust emissions at low speeds. These can be identified by the two vacuum lines leading to the diaphragm chamber on the distributor. An important exception is to be seen on recent big engined Chrysler products. This distributor uses an electrical solenoid to retard the spark at idle or during certain types of low-speed driving. It can be identified by the plastic "box" on the side of the distributor which houses the retarding solenoid.

Ignition points are made of very hard, tough tungsten alloys but are subject to wear and spark erosion, and they require periodic replacement. They control both the low-voltage saturation of the coil when closed, and the release of the high voltage when they open. It is important that they are erosion free and mate as perfectly as possible to ensure total contact. The time the points are closed is called dwell or cam angle and will vary according to point gap.

Wide point gaps open slowly, causing excessive arcing and burning; and the wider the gap the shorter the dwell, which causes insufficient coil saturation and a missed spark (or maybe a whole bunch of missed sparks and an engine that won't run). If too close, the points are snapped open, and have a tendency to bounce. A close gap gives more dwell, but the points don't separate enough to give a clean collapse of the primary, and we have a misfire.

Point systems used on some cars have two sets of points connected so that the primary current flows when either set is closed. The points are staggered so that one set opens before the other, with the spark occurring when the second set opens. Because of the staggered position, the first set closes before the other, increasing the dwell for more spark in-

Ignition System

tensity at high rpm.

Another wear point is the rubbing block, a phenolic or plastic block that wears very well if there is a slight amount of lubricant in the form of light oil or a sparing smear of grease on the cam whenever points are checked or replaced. Many distributors have an oil-saturated wick for lubricating the rubbing block, and this should be changed, not re-oiled, when replacing points.

You can buy a "point file" in almost any auto parts house, but you would do yourself a favor by using it to file spark plugs, not points. If the points need filing, they should be replaced. Line up the point surfaces as we indicate in the tune-up chapter, and then set the gap either with a feeler gauge or a dwell meter. Don't ever attempt to gap worn or pitted points with a feeler gauge. A feeler gauge will not be accurate on a rough surface. Worn points must be set with a dial indicator or a dwell meter.

With new points, some mechanics recommend a setting that is about .003-in. wider than specified to compensate for the initial rubbing block wear. This is usually not necessary if the rubbing block lines up with the cam.

Make sure the rubbing block is resting exactly on the tip of the breaker point cam when you set point gap with a feeler gauge.

Tampering with the centrifugal or vacuum advance mechanisms without the proper test equipment may result in permanent damage to the engine from incorrect spark advance. There are specified advance curves for both of these functions for each make of car, and they are available to mechanics with test bench facilities for checking out and adjusting to manufacturers' specs.

Rebuilding for such things as bearing or shaft replacement also requires expert techniques and special tools; it is impractical for the occasional home mechanic to attempt.

POINT-CONTROLLED TRANSISTOR DISTRIBUTOR

Transistors—those mysterious "things" that have revolutionized electronics, miniaturized our radios and television sets, and are now used in automotive ignition systems—are accepted as a rather commonplace component, yet few people really know what they are and what they actually do in a circuit.

Transistors are a combination of man-made crystalline materials which can be likened in operation to a relay with no moving parts, or a current operated switch. They act as an insulator or non-conductor until small amounts of current are applied to the proper segment, then they become highly conductive and capable of carrying large amounts of current.

They are used as a master switch (instead of the points) to trigger the coil saturation and collapse; the points are used to control the very low voltage nec-

1. Delco's one-piece points/condenser unit was its 1972 improvement, but its replacement cost was challenged by government and Delco withdrew the unit from the market.

2. The unitary Delco points/condenser went into a standard window-type distributor. Now with replacement points/condenser units off the market, owners have to replace the distributor breaker plate to install standard condenser.

3. A reluctor (1) replaces the traditional cam in Chrysler's Electronic Ignition. The magnetic pickup assembly includes a pole piece and permanent magnet (2) and a pickup coil (3) and performs the functions of a set of contact points.

4. The control unit with switching transistor (1) is mounted on the firewall. Plug-in lead is secured by a screw (2).

5. Rear of control unit is sealed with epoxy-like material. Since no adjustments are possible on this item, the entire unit must be replaced if it gives trouble.

6. Normal ignition uses a single resistor; Chrysler EIS uses a dual ballast resistor mounted on the firewall and connected to the system by plug-in leads.

7. You can adjust the point gap on this Delco-Remy "window" distributor while the engine is running, either with or without a dwell meter.

1. Delco One-piece Unit

2. Distributor Breaker Plate

3. Chrysler Electronic Ignition

4. Control Unit

5. Sealed Control Unit

6. Dual Ballast Resistor

essary to make the transistor act as a higher voltage switch. As a result, the points are handling much smaller amounts of current than with a conventional system. Arcing, and the need for a condenser to reduce it are eliminated, increasing point life considerably.

Because of the very rapid flow of current, there is no appreciable time lag, and timing procedures and advance adjustments are the same as with conventional systems. Transistors are sensitive to heat and other electronic breakdowns and should be checked for shorting if the ignition fails to fire.

Heat sensitivity is partially controlled by mounting the transistors in a finned case or heat sink. This alone is not enough protection if the unit is placed where severe engine heat can reach it. On stock, factory-installed transistor systems, never change location of the heat sink. When installing optional transistor systems, mount in coolest part of the engine compartment.

Points do have to be checked but only to compensate for rubbing block wear, which, after the initial break-in, should stay stable for about 20,000 miles. Be very careful not to use an oily feeler gauge, since even the lightest film on the points can cause trouble with the low voltage carried by the contacts in a transistor system. Coils and transistorized ignition systems are slightly different in their primary windings from standard ones. It is recommended that only coils made for these systems be used, since adding only the transistorized switching unit with standard coil could shorten life of both parts, in addition to reducing the efficiency of the transistor operation.

PULSE-CONTROLLED TRANSISTOR DISTRIBUTOR

Used in some GM and all 1973 Chrysler products, the Electronic Ignition System is a highly sophisticated version of the point-controlled transistorized ignition in that all switching is done electronically. There is no rubbing block wear and no point gap to maintain, ensuring long and uniform operation. Both vacuum and centrifugal advance mechanisms are used to compensate for varying engine speeds and loads in much the same manner as conventional point distributors.

Internal construction consists of a rotating pole piece in place of the breaker point cam. This has the same number of equally spaced lobes as the number of engine cylinders. This rotates inside a magnetic pickup assembly which takes the place of the breaker plate/contact point assembly. This magnetic pickup is composed of a permanent magnet made of ceramic material, a pole piece, and a pickup coil. The stationary pole piece, like the rotating pole piece, has equally spaced internal lobes or teeth, one for each cylinder of the engine. This magnetic pickup, located in the lower section of the distributor housing, is moved by the vacuum diaphragm to control vacuum advance. The rotating pole piece is coupled to the centrifugal advance mechanism, providing spark control compensation for engine speed. A rotor tops the whole internal assembly and

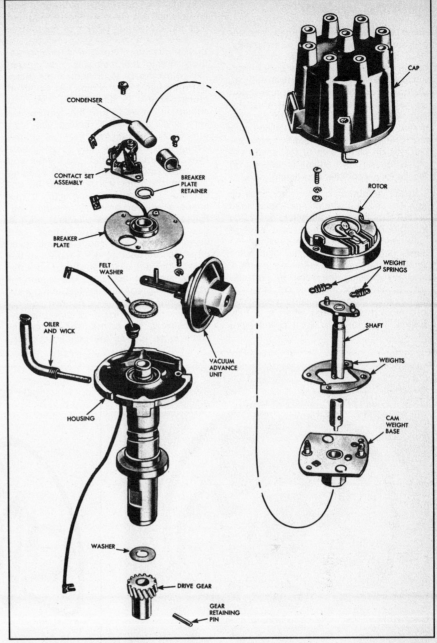

7. **Window-Type Distributor**

acts as the high-voltage distributor to the individual spark plugs.

As the distributor internal components rotate, the teeth in the rotating pole piece line up with the internal projections on the permanent magnet pole piece, causing an induced current in the pickup coil. This current is sufficient to trigger the transistors in the ignition pulse amplifier circuit, resulting in coil saturation, release of coil high voltage to the distributor, and proper distribution to the spark plugs. Because of the rather complicated circuitry in the pulse amplifier system, it is recommended that it be tested only with the proper equipment and by qualified ignition experts. A mistake in polarity, or high voltage reaching low-voltage segments of the circuits, can result in permanent damage to the transistorized circuit.

The pulse amplifier unit has no moving parts, and exclusive of the permanent lubricated bearings in the distributor, there are no rubbing or contacting parts that require adjusting to compensate for wear. A periodic check of both primary- and high-voltage wiring and both advance mechanisms should be all the maintenance required for the pulse-controlled transistor ignition system.

DISTRIBUTOR INSTALLATION

When installing a distributor that has been removed from the engine without being marked, it is important to establish an initial timing setting. For this operation it is necessary to line up the timing marks on the flywheel or vibration dampener in relation to the compression stroke of No. 1 cylinder.

Since modern auto engines are not equipped with provisions for handcranking, a remote starter switch or someone blipping the starter switch in the car will be necessary to get the timing marks coordinated with the compression stroke.

Remove spark plug from No. 1 cylinder. For deeply recessed plug access on

Ignition System

some Chrysler Corp. engines, a compression gauge is almost a necessity. Hold thumb over plug hole or observe gauge while blipping starter switch, noting pressure buildup which will indicate piston is coming up on compression stroke. Watch for timing mark which indicates the proper number of degrees before top dead center for ignition timing. Some vibration dampers have calibrations on either side of top dead center, so be sure the engine is stopped on the factory recommended timing mark.

Install distributor so that rotor lines up with the No. 1 cylinder spark plug lead on the cap. Ease the assembly down into the block mounting hole and engage lower gear with the one on camshaft. As these gears are helical, the distributor shaft will turn as the teeth are meshed, naturally causing the rotor to turn. Be sure to allow for this and set the rotor off just enough before inserting assembly into block hole so that when it is fully seated, the rotor is in No. 1 cylinder position.

Install the distributor mounting bolt and clamp, but leave it loose enough so that the distributor body can be turned. Turn the distributor body slowly opposite to the direction that the cam rotates. Stop turning the distributor the instant the points open, then tighten the hold-down bolt and your engine will be timed close enough to allow it to run. You should only have to turn the distributor a very small amount. If, before you start turning it, the rubbing block is on the wrong side of a cam lobe (closing side instead of opening side), then when you turn the distributor to the point opening position, the rotor will no longer be under No. 1 segment in the cap. If this happens, you are probably one tooth off. Remove the hold-down clamp, lift the distributor until the gears demesh, and move the shaft one tooth in whichever direction you need to go. Then move the distributor body to the position where the points are just opening. The important part of this procedure is determining exactly when the points open. You can do it with a piece of tissue or cigarette paper between the points. The paper will come loose just as the points separate.

A better way is to use a test light connected to the distributor primary terminal and ground. If your test light does not have a battery in it, turn the ignition switch on and the test light will be off while the points are closed. When the test light comes on, you will know the points have opened. If you have a battery-powered test light, then disconnect the primary wire from the distributor and connect the test light to the distributor primary terminal and ground. The light will be on when the points are closed and will go off the instant they separate. Remember that you turn the distributor body opposite to the direction that the cam rotates.

After tightening the hold-down clamp, check to be sure the points are just opening, and that the rotor tip is under the No. 1 segment in the cap. If, no matter what you do, the rotor and point timing won't check out, then you may have one of those rare cases of a distributor that is assembled wrong. There have been some cases where a cam that is pressed onto the shaft has slipped, making it impossible to set the point and rotor timing correctly. The engine may run,

1. Delco-Remy Distributor

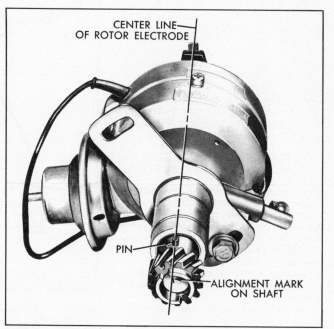

2. Chrysler Distributor

CENTER LINE OF ROTOR ELECTRODE

PIN

ALIGNMENT MARK ON SHAFT

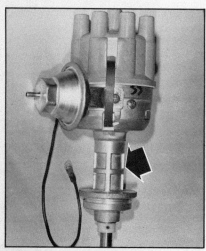

3. Chrysler Distributor Housing

4. Dual-point Distributor

1. Delco-Remy 4- and 6-cylinder distributors have greasy mesh to lubricate cam. Note arrow on top of shaft to indicate rotation.

2. Chrysler Corp. distributors are quite conventional and easy to repair. It is very important to reassemble the gear, shaft and rotor in their correct relationship for proper distributor positioning.

3. Chrysler Corporation distributors are quite conventional and easy to work on. The housing of Chrysler distributor is aluminum; waffle pattern gives housing added strength.

4. Dual-point Prestolite unit was used on Chrysler high-performance models. Housing is cast iron instead of aluminum. Some models of the dual-pointer came with tach drive, but fit only Chrysler engines.

but not very well because the rotor is between two segments and the spark sometimes goes to the proper cylinder and sometimes to the wrong one. Your chances of finding this condition are extremely rare.

Static timing should always be followed by a timing light check with the engine running. When using a timing light, the vacuum hose must be taken off the distributor and plugged. Remove and plug both hoses on cars with double chamber advance units. Chrysler products with solenoid controlled distributors should have both the vacuum hose and solenoid wire disconnected. Always remove the solenoid wire from the carburetor, not the distributor. This prevents accidental shorts and damaged wiring.

Before replacing cap, examine it as well as the rotor for cracks. Very often undetected damage at these points can cause trouble not apparent in circuit test procedures.

CAPACITOR-DISCHARGE IGNITION

Transistor ignitions came on the marketplace with a big splash. It seemed as if everybody was making one. It also seemed as if every garage had one lying in the corner somewhere that they had taken off because it didn't work right. Transistor ignitions were pretty much of a failure because the transistors were so delicate. All you had to do to blow the things was to pull the wire out of the coil and crank the engine. The tremendous buildup of voltage would back up and blow one or more of the transistors.

Capacitor-discharge ignitions are admittedly a type of transistor design but they are considerably better and a heck of a lot tougher. A transistor ignition uses the same old method of collapsing the coil field to create the secondary spark. The capacitor-discharge or C-D ignition uses an entirely different method. It charges up a capacitor which then is triggered by either points or a pulse control distributor so that the capacitor fires a charge through the coil primary. Because the capacitor kicks about 250 volts into the coil's primary windings instead of the 6 or 12 volts of a conventional ignition, the result is one heck of a spark that does the job a lot better than either transistor or conventional ignition systems.

One trouble with conventional ignitions

5. Seldom-seen feature of Presto-lite dual-point distributor is an adjustable cam. Timing can be altered without loosening the distributor body in block by loosening Allen screw in center of the shaft and moving cam. Engine must be dead if this method is used.

6. The rotor may turn as the distributor is withdrawn from the engine. Note its final position. When reinstalling the distributor, place the cam in this same position and it should turn back to its original position as the cam and distributor gears engage.

7. This is a typical Delco 6-cylinder distributor having both centrifugal and vacuum advance systems.

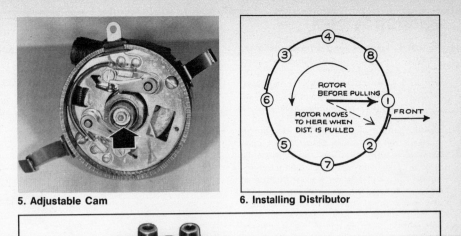

5. Adjustable Cam

6. Installing Distributor

7. Six-Cylinder Distributor

Ignition System

is that it takes a long time to build up enough voltage to jump the spark plug gap. During the time that it is building up voltage, the current can leak away across a dirty spark plug porcelain so that the plug never really does fire. In that case we have a fouled plug and a dead cylinder. The capacitor-discharge ignition will fire spark plugs that a conventional ignition could never hope to fire because the capacitor-discharge ignition does not rely on a slow buildup of voltage. It zaps the coil and the coil zaps the spark plug, right now, so that there is no chance for any leakdown of voltage that would cause a misfire. There are some good capacitor-discharge systems around but there are also some very bad ones, just as bad as some of the old transistor systems. If you spend a lot of money for a special ignition, make sure that you get a good one. The only way to be sure is to talk to somebody who has already been successfully running the same ignition you want to buy.

IGNITION BYPASS

It may seem strange, but the ignition coil does not receive full battery voltage during normal running of the engine. A primary resistor is inserted in the circuitry between the ignition switch and the battery terminal on the coil. Current from the battery flows through the ignition switch, through the resistor, then into the coil primary and on to the distributor points. The resistor cuts down on the amount of current flow in the circuit so that the spark is not as strong as it would be if the resistor were not there. Cutting down on the spark output might seem kind of stupid, but the system is designed that way for a particular purpose. It would be easy to design an ignition coil that would work on full battery voltage. But then the coil would only put out the same strength spark no matter what conditions were. We need an excessively strong spark during cranking to get the engine started, but during running we don't need as much. What the engineers have done is design a coil that works with a resistor to give a normal spark during running, but when the engine is being cranked there is a special circuit that bypasses the resistor so that the coil receives more voltage.

The coil was actually not designed to work under full battery voltage. When it is operated on full battery voltage it puts out a spark that will knock you right out of the engine compartment. However, it would be impossible to operate the coil on full battery voltage very long. It would burn up. So the coil receives full battery voltage only during engine cranking, and this is accomplished with a special bypass circuit.

All that the bypass amounts to is a connection that is made somewhere in the circuitry to go around the primary resistor and feed full battery voltage to the coil primary terminal. This bypassing can be accomplished at several different places, and it seems as if every manufacturer tries to put his bypass in a different location. In some cases it is in the

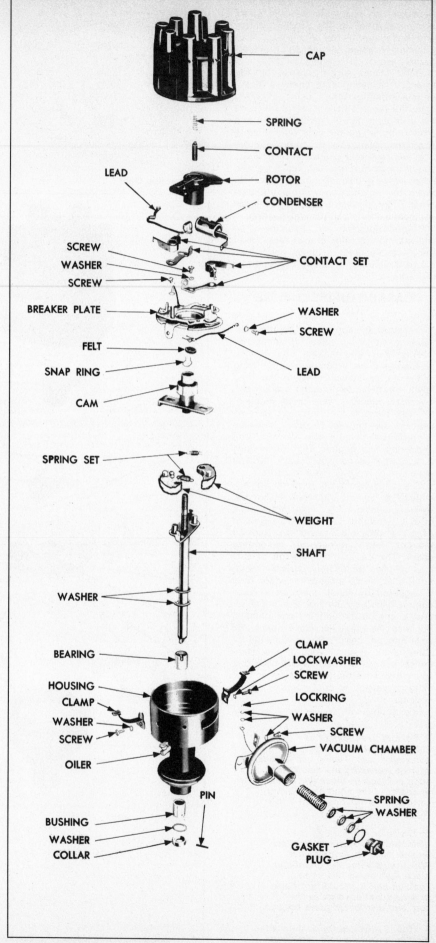

1. Prestolite Dual-Point Distributor

2. Hemi Dual Drive

3. Breakerless Distributor

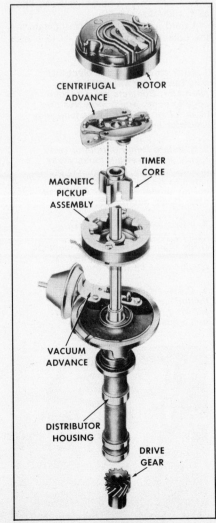

CENTRIFUGAL
ADVANCE — ROTOR

TIMER
CORE

MAGNETIC
PICKUP
ASSEMBLY

VACUUM
ADVANCE

DISTRIBUTOR
HOUSING

DRIVE
GEAR

4. Breakerless Advance System

1. Chrysler has used the Prestolite dual-point distributor on some of its high-performance models. This unit differs from the Ford dual-point unit in that it has both vacuum and centrifugal advance.

2. Looks like it doesn't know which way to go. Dual distributor drive, and safety rpm cutoff, are for Dodge Hemis with two plugs per cylinder.

3. Breakerless (no points) Delco-Remy distributor was option on some GM cars. It is used with a separate amplifier to fire the coil.

4. Breakerless distributor has same vacuum and mechanical advance parts as normal distributor. Magnetic pickup moves for vacuum advance.

ignition switch, with an extra pair of contacts that shunt full battery voltage to the coil. Of course this only happens when the key is in the start position. When the driver lets the key come back to the run position, the extra pair of contacts is disconnected and the coil receives its battery voltage through the primary resistor. Another place for bypassing is at the solenoid on the firewall. When the solenoid plunger moves to make contact for the large amount of current that flows direct from the battery to the starter, it also contacts a small finger that sends battery current to the ignition coil through a separate wire. On General Motors cars the ignition bypass is in the starter-mounted solenoid. A little finger in the solenoid makes contact and sends full battery voltage through a separate wire that connects with the coil primary terminal.

The resistance itself may be either in the form of a wire wound around a ceramic insulator and mounted on the firewall or near the coil or, in the case of Delco systems, a resistance wire between the ignition switch and coil. If the car starts but stalls as soon as the key is turned from the "start" to "run" position, it may be that this wire is burned out. Connect a jumper wire from the hot side of the battery to the small coil terminal that's not connected to the distributor. If the engine keeps running you'll know that the resistance wire is shot.

SPECIAL IGNITION ACCESSORIES

Beware of the carnival pitchman who demonstrates the marvel ignition intensifier. These gimmicks are by and large resistance-increasing bits of metal, air gaps, or coils that do produce a hotter spark. However, they are disgracefully over-priced. Series-gap or resistor plugs do the same job for only pennies more than standard plugs.

A stock ignition system, properly maintained and adjusted for the engine it is designed for, will give excellent service for a long time. As the requirements for more intensity occur, accessory components from reliable makers are valuable.

Spark cables with silicone rubber insulation should be used where unavoidable proximity to the exhaust headers requires extra heat protection. Solderless plug connectors such as the Rajah ter-

minal ends have been and still are the mark of well maintained ignition systems.

Spark plugs are no exception to the "something for nothing" pitch exploited by exaggerated advertising claims. Plugs from reliable manufacturers are the result of extensive and expensive research and development, and none will compensate for a poor ignition system or a worn-out engine. Special racing plugs are available for a wide variety of reach lengths and thread diameters, and because of their wire-type electrodes, require special tools for changing the gap. When buying such plugs, make sure that the proper gapping tools are included in the purchase.

MAGNETO IGNITIONS

Basically, a magneto is an engine-driven linear alternating current generator combined with a system of distributing the generated voltage to individual spark plugs at the proper time. Linear means that the faster it is driven, the more voltage it produces. This has a distinct advantage with high-speed engines but some disadvantages at low speeds. Provision for spark advance in early mags was strictly manual, and their use confined largely to racing cars that were push-started.

As automotive competition spread from pure racing cars with special engines built for the purpose, to drag and stock car events—and the hot rod enthusiast began extracting more and more performance from modified passenger car engines—the need for high-performance ignitions was obvious. Names like Joe Hunt, Harmon-Collins, Bendix, and Scintilla Vertex were added to the list of brand name speed equipment. Joe Hunt was making Offenhauser engine mags out of aircraft units before he devised a vertical magneto that replaced the standard automotive distributor. He still is a distributor for the Vertex, and sells more of those than anything else. He goes through each new Vertex, too, so he knows they are right when you get them. Harmon-Collins, now known as the Cirillo Super-Mag, developed a similar unit, and others are currently available from Mallory known as the Mini-Mag.

These vertical units are made to fit a variety of stock block engines, sliding into the regular distributor hole. Some use auxiliary coils or vibrators to provide the necessary starting voltage to the magneto, because mags do not provide their hottest spark at cranking rpm.

As stated earlier, high-performance distributors have largely filled the need for high engine performance on everything except the fuel-burning, supercharged race cars, but more than a few car owners still swear by the vertical magneto for their combination street-strip machines.

The modern magneto requires very much the same maintenance as a distributor. It has breaker points, mechanical centrifugal advance, and on some units, optional vacuum advance systems. In addition, these units are tailored more critically to engine requirements and are not just something one buys and sticks into the distributor hole of any old engine.

Charging System

Would you believe that you could generate electricity just by moving a coil of wire or even a single wire between the ends of a horseshoe magnet? We don't know why it happens, but really there's no need to. As long as we accept the fact that magnetism plus movement will create electricity, then all we have to do is learn how to use it. If moving the wire between the ends of the horseshoe magnet will create electricity in the wire, it seems logical that we might get more electricity if we use two wires. An automotive generator actually uses a lot of wires and gets a lot of electricity, enough to charge the battery and run the car's complete electrical system.

There's another peculiarity about this magnetism and electricity business. Granted: magnetism and movement will create electricity. But it also works the other way around; electricity will create magnetism.

GENERATOR SYSTEMS

Here's the way it works in an automotive generator. The frame of the generator has some coils attached to it called the field coils. In the middle of each field coil is a hunk of iron called the pole shoe. The pole shoes are a kind of weak magnet, probably not even as strong as the little magnets that you use on a magnetic bulletin board. But the magnetism that is in the pole shoes is enough to create electricity in any wire that moves through the magnetic field. The wire in which the electricity is created is in the armature. Of course, the armature has a lot of wires because we want a lot of electricity.

When the engine starts, the generator is turned by the fan belt and electricity is created in the armature because it is rotating in a magnetic field. If the weak magnetic field around the pole shoes was all we had, then we wouldn't get much electricity out of our generator. But a generator feeds itself. The electricity that is created from the armature is fed back into the field coils. This additional electricity strengthens the magnetic field around the pole shoes and causes a greater strength of electricity to be created in the armature.

Now that we have the thing going, electricity in the armature is available to charge the battery, run the lights, blow the horn, or anything else. The problem is getting the electricity out of the armature while it is moving. This is where the commutator and the brushes come in. One brush running on the armature picks up the electrical current and connects to a wire that runs the current out of the generator so that it can be used

to operate the car's electrical system. From the light bulb, radio, ignition system or whatever unit is being operated, the electricity returns along a ground path to the frame of the generator and then through the other brush back into the armature. In most cases the electricity must return to its source in a complete circle route. In fact, the word circuit means "circle."

A generator alone can be hooked up to the electrical system of the car and it will put out both current and voltage enough to do the job. But you will have no control over it. The faster the engine goes, the more the generator puts out until it reaches a point where it blows itself right out of the car from trying to put out more than it can stand. An uncontrolled generator will put out 30, 40 or 50 volts, even higher. The car's system is made to run in the area of 12 volts, so we must do something to control the output of the generator if we don't want to burn out all the light bulbs and blow up the radio.

Remember we said that a generator starts putting out electricity because of residual magnetism in the pole shoes. But any electricity above that very small amount depends upon a feedback of current from the armature into the field windings. If the current were not fed back into the field windings, generator voltage would never rise. It just wouldn't charge. To control the generator then, all we have to do is regulate the amount of current that flows through the field windings, and that is the function of the regulator.

Regulation in all modern generators is done with a vibrating regulator. The regulator is set up so that field current runs through a pair of points. Underneath the points there is an electromagnet operated by electricity from the generator. There are two of these electromagnetic regulating units in the regulator, each with its own pair of points. One of them keeps the voltage from going too high, and the other limits the current. If either voltage or

current rises above a safe value, the strength of the magnet increases so that the points are pulled apart. The instant the points separate, the generator goes dead because there is no field current. When the generator goes dead, this kills off the electricity it is feeding the electromagnet, and so the magnetism dies and a spring pulls the points back together. The instant that the points come together, the generator is back in business, and then the same thing happens all over again, separating the points.

Any time either current or voltage rises to the preset value, the voltage or current regulator points will start vibrating. Adjustment is by setting the tension on the spring that pulls the points closed. It amounts to a balancing of the two forces—the spring versus the magnetism that tries to pull the points apart. This, combined with the vibrating of the points, results in a system that can be set to current or voltage limits as close as 1/10th of a volt.

A third unit in all modern regulators is the cutout. If the generator is to charge

1. Look carefully at the electrical plug (arrow) on this 1972 Delco alternator. Contacts are arranged edge-to-edge, which indicates this is an integral charging system, with regulator inside alternator.

2. Standard Delco alternator (with regulator on firewall) looks pretty much the same, but contacts placed side-to-side are the tipoff. Service on this model is similar to that on older Delco alternators.

3. Inside integral Delco alternator, held by three Phillips-head screws, is the regulator. Diode arrangement is different, too, much easier to change than on older models.

4. These are typical generator mountings on late-model car, showing retaining brackets and belt adjustment provisions.

1. Delco Integral Charging System

2. Delco Standard Alternator

the battery, it must be electrically connected to the battery. If the engine is stopped and the generator is still connected to the battery, current can flow from the battery into the generator in an attempt to turn the generator into a motor. All that the cutout does is disconnect the generator from the electrical system whenever the generator is either not working or is operating at so slow a speed that current would flow from the battery to the generator. When the engine is at rest, the cutout points must be open. Any time the engine is running above idle and the charging system is operating correctly, the cutout points must be closed. If you are lucky enough to have a car with an ammeter that is sensitive to small fluctuations in current flow, you will notice that as you allow the engine to come down to a normal curb idle, the ammeter will go slightly to the discharge side of zero and then it will spring back to the zero position. What has happened is that the generator is turning too slowly to charge the battery, so the battery starts to feed current back into the generator. The minus reading that you see on the ammeter is that current flow back through the generator. But it doesn't show on the ammeter very long because that reverse current forces the cutout to open and then the ammeter returns to the zero position. If your car only has a red discharge light instead of an ammeter, then you can't watch all these fancy goings-on.

Normal and abnormal charging is far more easily spotted if the car has a dash-mounted ammeter. Usually, the ammeter will show a charge rate of about 7 to 10 amps at normal driving speeds soon after the engine is started. This may be as high as 20 amps following a very long, hard cranking session in cold weather. After the car has been driven for a short distance at highway speeds, the reading should drop to about 2 to 5 amps—depending on how many lights and accessories are in operation. At an idle, the ammeter should indicate no more than a 3-amp discharge, although this may fall to as much as a 15-amp discharge if several accessories are in use. Cars equipped with alternators should seldom show any discharge.

The ammeter needle should never follow engine speed from one extreme of the dial to the other. If it does, the headlights probably also grow very dim proportional to rpm. This condition—or a constant discharge reading, exceptionally high amperage at highway speeds, and conspicuous deviations from the "norms" outlined above—are all signs that the charging system needs work.

DIAGNOSIS AND CORRECTION

Low charging or *no charging* is undoubtedly the most common type of trouble. If the generator light has come on—and stays on—or the ammeter shows a constant and steady discharge, there is no charging taking place at all. If this is accompanied by rising cooling system temperatures, it is probably a broken fan belt, but if the belt is properly tensioned and in one piece, the charging system is the culprit.

A glowing generator light, or an ammeter reading slightly below zero when

3. Delco Integral Regulator

driving at highway speeds, means a low generator output. Once again, this may be only a sign that the fan belt is loose, but if it's not, the trouble is electrical.

Perhaps you're driving along and the ammeter dips suddenly into the discharge zone and then bounces back a few moments later to a point well up in the charge zone. This shows that the charging system is functioning only part of the time. An "idiot light" that winks on and off as you cruise, indicates the same type of trouble exists. If the light has a slight glow, look for a high-resistance connection at the starter solenoid or the ignition switch.

In some cars, the light will glow at cruising speed even though the entire charging system is in excellent condition. Why does this happen? Well, here's a simple explanation. In the first place, we know that the light is connected between the generator output and the battery, and when the generator is dead or at low rpm its voltage is less than the battery's, so current flows from the battery through the light to the generator. We also know that when the generator is charging, it raises the voltage throughout the electrical system of the car. And since the voltage on both sides of the light is the same, no current flows through it and the light stays off. However, in some cars—and here's our problem—the wire from the battery to the light is too long, and this results in more voltage on the generator side of the light. Because of the unequal voltage, current flows through the light and makes it glow.

You can eliminate the bothersome glow by running a wire directly from the battery terminal of the regulator to the battery side of the ignition switch. This will equalize the voltage and keep the light out. But if you are going to go to all that trouble (and if you're *that* sensitive about your generator), why not install an ammeter so you will really know what's going on? Instructions come with every new ammeter, and they're not hard to install if you follow directions carefully.

Anyway, with a light or a meter, you can still have charging system troubles; with the following series of steps you can diagnose and correct the problem.

Step 1—Examine the Battery. Test it with a hydrometer. If it is fully charged, discharge it by running the starter for a few moments. Then start the engine. If the ammeter shows a normal charge rate it may be that all is well, but probably

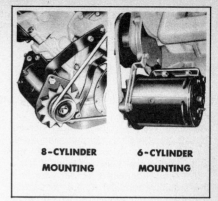

4. Generator Mountings

the low-charge, no-charge condition will still be present if the original indication of trouble was a discharge reading and not merely a zero reading. If hydrometer testing shows all of the battery cells to be uniformly discharged, there is a definite charging system problem.

Step 2—Clean the Connections. There is very little use in trying to test the charging system unless you're sure that all connections are making good electrical contact. Sometimes a bad connection can be located with the engine running by having someone watch the ammeter while you wiggle the various wires and terminals that are part of the charging circuit. The connections involved are those on *both* ends of the battery cables (if these are at fault the engine probably won't start anyway), the two terminals on the generator, all voltage regulator connections, and those on the back of the ammeter and ignition switch—as well as the primary (small) wires on the coil and distributor.

Battery cable terminals should be removed and cleaned with sandpaper or a wire brush. Corrosion should be washed away with a solution of baking soda, detergent, and water. Shims can be placed on the battery posts if the cables no longer fit tightly, and new cable terminals installed if necessary. After clamping the terminals in place, they should be lightly coated with vaseline to ward off renewed corrosion. Make absolutely certain that the ground connections are good electrically and, if there is a separate ground strap between the engine and frame, this must also be checked.

Other connections can simply be removed, both surfaces brightened with sandpaper or emery cloth, and the parts rejoined tightly.

Step 3—Eliminating the Regulator. When the battery and connections look good but the charging system still won't put out, the next step is to find out whether the trouble is in the generator or in the regulator. First, disconnect the field wire at the generator itself. You can usually tell which of the two wires connected to the generator goes to the field because it will be slightly smaller than the armature wire. The field terminal may have an "F" stamped next to it, or it may even have a paper ring around it underneath the wire warning that it is the field terminal. This warning, incidentally, is to keep you from connecting any radio condensers to the field terminal. They will really raise heck with the regu-

Charging System

lator. After disconnecting the field terminal at the generator, fold a piece of tape around it so that it won't ground out and ruin the regulator.

There are two types of circuits that supply the current to the generator fields. One is called the "A" circuit and the other the "B" circuit. Most General Motors cars are "A" circuit, and Fords are usually "B" circuits. In an "A" circuit, ground the field terminal. If it's a "B" circuit, connect a jumper wire from the armature terminal to the field terminal. If you can't remember which circuit your generator has, try grounding the field terminal first and then try it with the jumper between armature and field. With the correct field connector, run the engine to see if the generator will put out. Because you have an uncontrolled generator, you must not run the engine too fast or the generator will put out excessive current.

During the test, all accessories such as windshield wipers or radios should be off so that they won't be damaged. But it's a good idea to turn the headlights on because that tends to draw enough current from the generator so that the voltage will be down a little. You should have a voltmeter to make the test but you can do it by watching the brightness of the headlights if your battery is a little bit weak. On a voltmeter, an uncontrolled generator will show at least 15 volts and as high as 20 or 30 if you're crazy enough to run the engine that fast. If you are going to do it by watching the headlights, watch to see if they get brighter when you rev up the engine. If the generator puts out, and you are still having trouble, it's in the regulator.

Step 4—Generator Removal. Let's assume that electrifying the fields did nothing, and the generator's output remained lower than the hobnails on a coal miner's boot. This means that you must re-move the generator from the car for bench testing.

The first step in taking out a generator is to detach the wires from it. Label the wires in some way—perhaps wrapping one with a bit of tape—so that you'll be able to put them back in the same position they were originally.

The generator is supported on the engine by three bolts. You'll have to use a wrench on both ends—on the nut as well as on the bolt—to undo these, but fortunately, the car makers have used different hex sizes for the nuts than they have for the bolts, so you won't need two wrenches of the same size to do the job. Usually the bolts are 1/2-in. and the nuts 9/16-in.—common tool sizes.

Loosen the bolt that fastens the generator to the slotted belt-adjusting bracket first. This will allow you to slip the belt off and swing the generator to a position that makes removing the other two bolts easier. After you've taken the nuts and lock washers off the two mounting bolts, remove the belt-adjusting bolt completely and support the generator with one hand while taking out the mounting bolts with the other. The generator can then be lifted away from the engine.

Step 5—Generator Examination. Once the generator is out of the car, undo the two bolts that hold the brush end plate onto the generator body. These are at the end opposite the fan belt pulley. If the generator has an inspection band,

1. Generator Disassembly

1. Generators will reveal a lot about their condition if you just take them apart and look. In many cases, all that is needed is new brushes.

2. When you get the pulley off the armature, this is what the whole mess looks like. Don't try to slide the front bearing and plate off the armature shaft until you have removed the pulley and the Woodruff key.

3. Put too much oil in the cup next to the pulley and the only damage will be oil flying out all over the engine, but if you over-oil the rear cup, the excess may flood the commutator and knock out the generator.

4. Generator armature and field terminal points are usually marked, but not prominently. If you can't find any well defined marking, the one with the large-diameter wire should be the armature terminal.

5. After this little plate is removed, the bearing will fall right out into your hand.

2. Pulling Pulley from Armature

3. Generator Oil Cups

4. Terminal Markings

5. Removing Bearing Retainer

this may be removed instead. You should then be able to see the brushes and commutator end of the armature.

The brushes are two graphite-carbon blocks that are mounted in spring-loaded holders. They are pressed by the spring against the commutator—a shiny brass part on the end of the armature shaft.

Check the condition of the commutator while turning the generator shaft by hand. If any of the brass segments are pitted or burned, the armature probably has shorted or grounded circuits and should be removed for testing.

If the commutator is fairly clean, smooth and bright, lift out the brushes and examine them. Brushes that are worn down to a length of 5/16-in. or less are definitely in need of replacement. On the other hand, the brushes may appear to be in good condition. In this case check to see that they slide smoothly in their holders and that the springs are not broken or out of place.

If you've left the generator on the car and are making the examination through the inspection ports in the generator frame, it is often possible to pinpoint brush trouble by pressing down on the brushes with the tip of a screwdriver while the engine is running. If the generator begins charging, the brushes are not making good contact.

Step 6—Servicing Brushes. If the brushes are sticking in the holders, are worn down to minimum length, or the commutator and brushes are coated with grease or a brownish-green glaze, you've probably found your trouble— especially if the ammeter (or "idiot light") indicated a no-charge or only intermittent charging periods.

Greasy or glazed commutators and brushes can be serviced with the generator in the car—providing it has an inspection band. The commutator can be cleaned by inserting a strip of #00 or #000 sandpaper or crocus cloth between it and one of the brushes and rotating the generator by hand until the

brass segments are bright and shiny. The sandpaper is then turned over and pulled between the brush and the commutator to make a clean and properly contoured surface on the brush end contacting the commutator.

If the brushes are worn out, new ones must be installed—although an *emergency* on-the-road repair can sometimes be affected by placing a wadded piece of paper between the spring arm and the brush to increase the pressure. Clean the commutator and look closely at the spaces between the segments. If the insulating strips between the segments are flush with the surface of the commutator (or are projecting above it), the armature should be removed and taken to an automotive machine shop for servicing before new brushes are installed. At this time the armature will be checked to see if the commutator is round and concentric with the shaft. If it is not, it will be placed in a lathe and light cuts made across the face of the commutator until the wear is corrected. The insulating strips will then be undercut to a depth of about 1/32-in. using a special tool. You can do this commutator work yourself if a lathe is available and then carefully undercut the insulating strips using a section of hacksaw blade.

The brushes on all modern generators have wires attached to them. It's an easy job to unscrew the old wires from their terminals and fasten the new ones in their place. Give the holders a check to see that the brushes move freely and sand the new brushes to shape by drawing a strip of fine sandpaper under them after they are in position against the commutator. When you put the brush end plate back onto the generator body, be careful not to pinch any wires between it and the generator frame. One of the brushes is grounded to the end plate. The other one, the insulated brush, connects to the armature terminal on the generator. A pinched or grounded wire on the insulated brush or any of its

connections will keep the generator from charging and may cause permanent damage. The end plate on a generator usually has a rivet or other projection that fits in a notch on the field frame so that you can get the end plate back in the right position.

If brushes were causing your trouble, you should have it licked now—so put the generator back on the engine, tension the fan belt, and hook up the wires. You're all ready to go!

Step 7—Armature Bench Tests. Back in Step 5 we talked about inspecting the commutator for burned or pitted segments. Actually this is one of two or three possible indications of a shorted, grounded, or open-circuited armature. Loose or broken wires are sometimes visible, and in rare instances the armature may become so overheated that solder will melt from the commutator connections and be thrown onto the inspection band. If severe, either of these last two forms of damage should be cause for installing a new or rebuilt generator. If only one or two wires are loose, they can be resoldered, the commutator turned, and the armature tested for other damage. If none shows, the armature is fit for further use. However, it should be remembered that the damage is probably not due to trouble in the generator, but to a faulty voltage regulator. The regulator should therefore be tested and adjusted or replaced before putting in the generator or its replacement. Otherwise, another generator burnout will probably result. In all probability the original cause of the generator failure was overcharging. The no-charge condition occurred only after the windings had burned out.

If the armature is in really bad shape, there may also be trouble in the field coils. But, in the case of burned and pitted commutator segments, the damage is likely limited to the armature alone. The extent of the damage can be determined with accuracy only by testing both the

Charging System

armature and the field assembly. Should the trouble be restricted to the armature —or for that matter, to the frame—it may be possible to save a few dollars by replacing only the part needed. However, if the price in your locality turns out to be over half that of an entire rebuilt generator, it's probably best to settle for a complete replacement. When a used part or a used (not rebuilt) generator is to be installed, it should always be tested before being put into the car.

It may be desirable to "farm out" all charging system test work. The majority of automotive machine and supply shops have complete test facilities on hand for this. If you suspect internal generator or alternator defects, the unit can be taken to them for testing and, if it's repairable, you can buy the parts and put them in yourself. If not, they'll be more than happy to sell you another generator or voltage regulator for a reasonable price.

In checking the armature for open, grounded or short circuits, there are several tests that can be conducted:

1) *Open circuits* in the armature are the usual cause of burned segments on the commutator. The burning is produced by an electrical spark that arcs each time the segment connected to the open circuit passes under a brush. Further testing requires specialized equipment not normally available to the home mechanic. Burning is also occasionally caused by oil or grease on the commutator, in which case the generator will begin charging after the commutator has been lathe-turned, undercut, and the brushes sanded to fit.

2) *Grounded cirucits* can be detected with a voltmeter or a battery-powered test light. You can make your own tester using some dry cells, two wires, and a flashlight bulb. Grounded armature circuits are found by touching one test wire to the armature core and the other to the commutator. If the lamp lights, the armature is grounded and must be replaced before further tests.

3) *Shorted circuits* in the armature require a test device called a "growler" to locate them—and a bit of experience in its use. If you have this test made, and a short *is* found, you'll have to replace the armature or obtain a rebuilt generator.

In most cases, it's not necessary to take the fan belt pulley and front end plate off the armature while making the above tests. However, if a new armature is to be installed they must be taken off. To do this it is only necessary to undo the large nut at the center of the pulley. It may be impossible to get this nut loose without clamping the armature in a vise. If you do, use soft jaws or two pieces of wood to protect the armature core from damage. You should not attempt to remove the pulley nut by holding the pulley. If you do, the result will probably be a bent or mangled pulley. The only correct way to remove a one-piece pulley is to disassemble the generator so you can put the armature in a vise. The exception to this is the impact wrench method, used mainly by generator rebuilders. Because the armature is heavy, an impact

wrench can spin the pulley nut off or on with the generator fully assembled.

There is a Woodruff key located in a slot between the pulley hub and the generator shaft which you must be careful not to lose as the pulley is slipped off the shaft.

Step 8—Field Coil Bench Tests. Field coils rarely give any trouble. Maybe that's the reason why a lot of mechanics don't know how to test them properly. The field coil, being responsible for creating the full strength magnetic field in the generator, must not have any shorts, grounds or opens. Let's see now

what effect each one of these conditions would have on generator output.

1) *Short Circuits.* Field coils are designed with a certain length of wire wrapped around the pole shoes. This particular length of wire has limited resistance, and therefore it determines how much current will flow through the field coils. If somewhere in the field coil there is a bare wire touching another bare wire, then the distance that the electricity travels will be shortened and we have what is known as a short circuit. A short circuit eliminates some of the wire that the electricity travels through and therefore cuts down on

1. Brush Insulation

2. Comparing Commutators

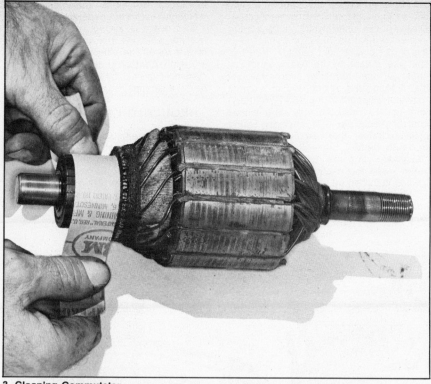

3. Cleaning Commutator

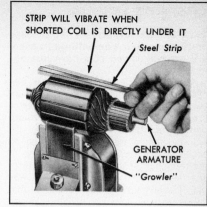

STRIP WILL VIBRATE WHEN SHORTED COIL IS DIRECTLY UNDER IT

Steel Strip

GENERATOR ARMATURE

"Growler"

4. Growler Test

some of the resistance in the circuit. Less resistance means that more current will flow in the field coils, which burns up the regulator. This situation is rare, but it is one instance where our field electrification test made earlier will get you in trouble. A generator will put out fine with shorted field coils, but the regulator has great difficulty controlling it and eventually burns up.

Shorted field coils cannot be checked with a test light or any other simple instrument. A field current draw test is required and to do it you must have an ammeter that will read accurately to a fraction of an amp. Field current draw on most 12-volt generators is only about 1½ amps. If you can find an automotive electrician who will make the field current draw test for you while you have the generator apart, it's a good idea. However, you must select your automotive electrician carefully. Most mechanics will think you're some kind of a nut if you ask them to make the test. The specifi-

1. Recognizing the insulated brush is easy. Just look for the strip of insulating material between the brush holder and the field frame.

2. The upper commutator has a normal amount of streaking from the brushes, but the lower one is black from excessive accumulation of carbon, which must be removed by sanding with sandpaper.

3. Many generators will not charge simply because the commutator has an excessive accumulation of carbon from the brushes. A little sandpaper will clean it up nicely.

4. The growler test will find many shorts in armatures, but not all of them. Some will only show up when the generator is running.

cations on field current draw are in the shop manual for your car.

We feel we should warn you about a common mistake made by generator rebuilders, especially with 12-volt Ford generators. It seems that there are a lot of parts floating around a generator rebuilding shop, whether it's big or small. If they aren't careful, they can easily get 6-volt field coils in a 12-volt generator. When you put it on your car, it will do all kinds of crazy things, like charging at idle, or making a buzzer out of the cutout above idle, with the red light flashing on and off. No adjustment of the regulator will cure the problem, but since the regulator is the part that is acting up, you will probably be sure there is something wrong with it. The problem is that the 6-volt fields are allowing twice as much current to go through the regulator control circuit. Get a generator with the right fields and you won't have any more trouble. You can also get some wild regulator gyrations if the wire that connects the two fields in a Ford generator is grounded out against the through-bolt. In either case, a check of generator field current on the assembled generator would locate the trouble.

2) *Open-Circuited Fields*. This is another rare one, but it's easy to check. All you have to do is trace the wiring in the fields until you find each end. One end will be connected to the field terminal on the generator frame and the other will either be connected to the insulated brush or to a ground somewhere in the generator. To check it, just use a battery-powered test light connected to each end of the field coils. If the light lights, you're in business. If it doesn't, you have a broken wire somewhere and a generator that will not charge.

3) *Grounded Fields*. This is another easy one to check. If the field circuit is grounded in the generator (a "B" cir-

cuit), then you will have to disconnect the grounded end in order to make the test. If the field is not grounded in the generator (an "A" circuit), then you don't have to disconnect anything, but be sure that the field lead is not touching the case. To make the test, just put one probe of your battery-powered test light on the field terminal and the other probe on the generator case. If the light lights, something is getting through where it shouldn't, so you'd better find the ground or get yourself another generator. The ground in the field circuit could produce either over- or undercharge, depending upon the design of the system and where the ground was. You can see that checking out the fields correctly is important unless you have so much money that anytime something goes wrong you can throw away the old regulator, generator, and wiring in favor of a complete new system. Admittedly, that is much faster than intelligent diagnosis, but it certainly is expensive.

VOLTAGE REGULATOR

Voltage regulators can be a pretty complicated business for the backyard mechanic to handle. In fact, the majority of automotive service garages do very little actual work on them. The faulty unit is simply exchanged for a new replacement regulator.

It would be more expensive for the average customer to have his old regulator tested and repaired than to simply have a new unit installed.

There are a number of safe and simple repairs and adjustments that you can make yourself, and in about 90% of the repairable kinds of regulator trouble, these uncomplicated fixes will cut the ice. If the regulator is so ancient that wear and old age have destroyed the last vestige of its original factory adjustments, the contacts are probably so burned that even the most professional test and repair work couldn't save it. If somebody else hasn't tinkered with them, most regulators will retain their adjustments quite accurately. If something has caused them to go out of balance electrically—such as burned-out resistances—they probably would need replacement, anyhow.

Although commonly called "voltage" regulators, regulating voltage is only one part of their function. After taking out the screws and removing the cover, you will

Charging System

see that there are actually two or three coil-like units inside—although some alternator-equipped cars have just one relay.

A closer inspection will reveal that each relay has at least one pair of electrical contacts. Many regulator problems are nothing more than dirt, corrosion, and burned faces on these points. It's not uncommon for moisture to find its way inside the cover and contribute to the formation of a white, powdery corrosion residue that eventually finds it way onto the contacts. In such cases all that needs to be done is a little "house cleaning."

After all foreign matter has been removed from the regulator, the points can be cleaned with a strip of crocus cloth. However, the wires leading to the voltage regulator should be disconnected before you attempt this or other point-polishing operations. If the contacts are conspicuously burned or pitted, you may have to do some smoothing with a point file or fine emery cloth before applying the final polish with crocus cloth. The more mirror-like you leave these surfaces, the less likely future burning is to occur. Following the "sandpaper treatment," the contacts should be cleaned with alcohol to remove any grease or dust that might initiate fresh erosion.

After resurfacing the contacts, the air-gap between them must be set to the correct width. A specification book or shop manual for your particular car will list this under "voltage regulator specifications." Most public libraries have shop manuals on their shelves that tell how to fix particular makes, and one of these may be borrowed to find the regulator specs for your own make and model.

The gap is adjusted with the movable contact held at its widest point. The stationary contact arm is then bent until a feeler gauge of the correct thickness will just slip into the opening. Care must also be taken to align the contact points so that they will meet squarely when closed.

If the contacts have only been cleaned, or polished lightly with crocus cloth, no further adjustment will probably be needed. If more than .002-in. or .003-in. was removed, the spring tension may require some adjustment, but even then only very slight deviations from the original specs are usually found.

Three or four means of effecting voltage regulator spring-tension adjustments are in current use. The most common form consists of a flat leaf spring on top of each unit which presses against an angled metal strip projecting from the frame of the relay assembly. Spring tension is adjusted by bending this piece of metal so that it produces more or less of a deflection in the leaf spring. Another frequently seen type of adjustment utilizes screws that are threaded into the relay frame. These can be turned in and out to change the degree to which the spring is flexed. The last common domestic type employs small coil springs to pull the contacts together. These are adjusted by bending the lower spring hook to increase or decrease the tension on the spring.

Before adjusting the regulator you should know the function of each relay. One of these units—which all generator system regulators have in common—is the circuit breaker or "cutout." You can spot the cutout by its heavy windings, larger (or dual) contacts, and by the fact that it is located at one end of a 3-unit regulator adjacent to the "BAT" (battery) terminal. It is also the only relay whose contact points are held *open* by spring pressure rather than closed. This relay prevents battery current from flowing "backward" into the regulator and generator when the engine is idling or the ignition is turned off.

The centermost relay is usually the current regulator. It too has a heavy winding, but less of it. The purpose of this unit is to limit the maximum flow of electricity out of the generator.

Also, there is the voltage regulator itself. Its windings consist of many turns of fine wire. The voltage regulator relay is a limiter, which protects the electrical system of the car by keeping the voltage below a set limit.

REGULATOR ADJUSTMENTS

One fault with voltage regulators is that they are too easy to get to. If the car makers would seal the voltage regulator in a fireproof, theftproof box so that nobody could fuss with the darn thing, there would be a lot less trouble with charging systems than there is today Because the regulator is so easily fiddled

1. Checking Armature for Ground

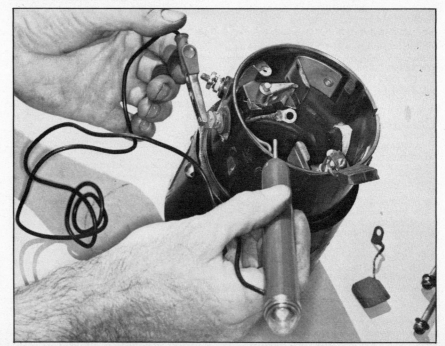

2. Checking Field for Ground

3. Checking Field Continuity

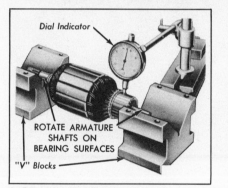

4. Checking Commutator Runout

Dial Indicator
ROTATE ARMATURE
SHAFTS ON
BEARING SURFACES
"V" Blocks

1. Checking the armature for ground. If the light comes on, then we know the armature is bad.

2. Checking the field windings for ground. Note that the field lead is disconnected from the insulated brush holder. If a ground shows up, we know that the holder itself is not causing the problem. The stud through the steel frame could also be disconnected to eliminate it as a possible source of a ground.

3. Checking the fields for continuity. The light should come on unless the field windings have a break somewhere.

4. Whenever brushes are changed, the commutator should be checked for runout and smoothness. Turn true in a lathe if necessary. In many cases, mica insulation must be undercut.

5. When new generator brushes have been installed, they should be sanded as shown to assure good initial contact and proper wear pattern.

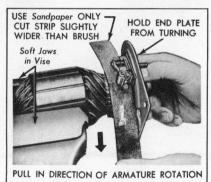

USE *Sandpaper* ONLY
CUT STRIP SLIGHTLY
WIDER THAN BRUSH
Soft Jaws in Vise
HOLD END PLATE FROM TURNING
PULL IN DIRECTION OF ARMATURE ROTATION

5. Seating Brushes

with, everybody who has a charging system malfunction immediately takes the cover off and starts playing with the thing.

In nine cases out of ten, it's the generator that wears out. Either the bearings go bad, the brushes wear out, the armature flies apart, or maybe even the belt is loose. But in spite of that, everybody goes directly to the regulator and starts playing with it. We want you to know how to make regulator adjustments, but you'll be a lot happier and better off if you will concentrate your efforts on the generator and be positively sure that it is OK before you start working on the regulator. Adjusting a regulator is not difficult, but you have to have a delicate touch—and an accurate voltmeter and ammeter. Let's take a look at the three units in the regulator, one at a time.

1) *Voltage Regulator.* The voltage unit is a limiting device. It doesn't do a thing until the voltage gets up to the point where it might damage the electrical system. Then the voltage regulator cuts in

and keeps the generator from burning out all of the light bulbs.

A generator does not put out full voltage all the time. One of the characteristics of an automotive generator is that it cannot put out maximum voltage and maximum amperage at the same time. When it is putting out maximum current or amperage, the voltage falls to a comparatively low level. When the generator is putting out maximum voltage, there is practically no current flow at all.

A generator is somewhat like a city water system. It supplies current and voltage to all of the electrical units in the car in the same way that the big water pump down at the city water works supplies water and pressure to all the homes in town. If everybody turns on the faucet at the same time, the pressure will drop but the flow of water will increase so that everybody gets an adequate amount. If only a few people have the faucet turned on, then the pressure builds up while the flow of water is considerably less.

The automotive generator works the same way. When you have a lot of accessories on—headlights, radio, air conditioner—then the voltage falls because the generator is supplying a lot of current. When you turn everything off except the ignition, then the generator voltage rises and charges the battery until the battery gets up to a full charge, at which time the generator voltage tries to rise above the fully charged battery but is prevented from doing so by the voltage regulator. This is the only time that the voltage regulator actually works— when the generator is operating at high voltage, as it would against a fully charged battery.

In order to test the voltage regulator, we either have to have a fully charged battery in the car or we have to fool the generator into thinking that there is a fully charged battery in the car. This fooling process is done simply by inserting a ¼-ohm resistor in the line between the generator and the battery. Some of the tune-up equipment companies make ¼-ohm resistors, and sell them for use with an ordinary voltmeter, but most of the generator testing in garages is done with a volt-amp tester, which has the resistance built into the unit. The resistor limits current flow the same way a fully charged battery would, and the generator voltage rises to the point where it is controlled by the voltage regulator. With a ¼-ohm resistor in the line and the engine operating at about 2000 rpm, all you do is take your voltage reading off the armature terminal either at the generator or at the regulator, whichever is most convenient. The reading you get will be the voltage as limited by the voltage regulator.

Some regulators have double contacts in the voltage relay. One pair of contacts is called the series set, and the other the shorting set. In Delco-Remy regulators, the series set is the lower one, and the shorting set is the upper one. In Chrysler and Ford regulators, the position of the two sets is reversed. When the regulator is limiting the voltage at low speed, and the generator output is low, the regulator vibrates against the series contacts. At

Charging System

high speed, and close to zero output, the regulator vibrates against the shorting contacts which results in about 1/10- to 1/2-volt less than when the series contacts are used. A 1/4-ohm resistor used with a double contact regulator will check the shorting contacts. To check the series contacts, about 10 to 15 amps must be allowed to flow which means you must remove the 1/4-ohm resistor and put a light load on the system. The process is admittedly tricky, but modern volt/amp testers will do it with just a few twists of a knob. However, the difference between operation on the series and shorting contacts is so small, that a quick check of the system voltages with the battery operating against a 1/4-ohm resistor (or a fully charged battery) is usually sufficient. The purpose of the double contacts is to ensure more precise control of voltage, and longer contact life. Changing the voltage setting is the same on either single or double contact units.

To increase the setting, you merely increase the spring tension that holds the points together on the voltage unit. If the voltage is too high, a little less spring tension will lower it. It takes a delicate touch because a very slight change in spring tension will give a big change to the voltage. It also takes certain precautions to keep from burning everything up. You should shut the engine off and disconnect the battery ground cable before you take the cover off the regulator, because if you accidentally move the cover sideways while you are taking it off you can easily ground out something and burn up the regulator.

After making each adjustment, the cover must be in place on the regulator because it holds in the heat and also has an effect on the magnetic field. When you fire up the engine, you can see on your voltmeter the change that you have made, but it's a good idea to allow the engine to go back down to idle so that the cutout opens. Then bring it up again and check to see if the reading is in the same place. Allowing the cutoff points to open like this is called "cycling the regulator," which gives it a little exercise and helps stabilize the reading you get.

2) *Current Regulator.* To check the current regulator we must have maximum current flow out of the generator to find out if the current regulator will limit the flow to a safe value. We don't want the ¼-ohm resistor in this case, but we do have to disconnect the battery wire at the regulator anyway in order to insert leads from the ammeter. A test ammeter is always connected so that all of the electricity flows through the ammeter or the shunt that is part of the ammeter. With the ammeter connected and the engine running, we turn on as many accessories as we can in order to get maximum current flow. If you don't have enough accessories to get a large current flow, then you can crank the engine a few times in order to run down the battery a little.

If you get enough load on the generator, the current flow will rise high enough that the current regulator unit will regulate it. Current regulation is necessary for only one reason—to keep from burning up the generator. The generator is peculiar in that the faster you turn it the more it will put out. It can easily burn itself up if it doesn't have the current regulator in the system to protect it. If your car does not have a lot of accessories and you always keep your battery in good condition, it's possible to drive for several years without ever needing your current regulator. The current regulator is adjusted the same way that the voltage regulator is—simply by increasing or decreasing the spring tension on the points.

3) *Cutout.* If we didn't have some way to disconnect the generator from the battery when the engine was idling or not running, the battery would discharge back through the generator and be dead in a few hours. Any time the engine is idling or not running, the cutout points are open, disconnecting the generator from the battery and the rest of the car. A generator is a self-generating device, so the minute it starts turning it puts out current and voltage. The current goes up through the wire to the voltage regulator, but it can't get any further because the cutout points are open. However, some of the current is taken from the wire through the cutout coil and directly to ground. The cutout coil thus acts as an electromagnet to close the cutout points. The electromagnet overcomes the spring that holds the cutout points open. We can adjust the spring tension so that the cutout will close at any voltage we de-

1. Belt Adjustment

2. Tightening Belt

3. Three-unit Regulator

4. Regulator Wiring

sire. Cutouts are usually set about 1 volt above normal battery voltage. Thus, a 12-volt system with normal battery voltage of 12.6 would have its cutout set at approximately 13.5 volts. As long as the generator is operating at a normal or high speed, the cutout points will remain closed because current flows at all times through the cutout coil. However, when the generator speed falls down to a slow idle or the engine is shut off, current immediately runs from the battery to the generator in a reverse direction through the cutout coil. Because the current is now running in a reverse direction through the coil, it reverses the magnetism in the cutout and forces the points open. The current that forces the points open is called the reverse current, and it can be measured with your ammeter in the circuit. Reverse current usually runs less than 5 amps. If it takes any more than that, the cutout points are probably sticking.

There is very little that can go wrong in any of the three units in a regulator. They are adjusted accurately at the factory, and ordinarily they will stay in adjustment through many years of use. The only weak element in a regulator is the points themselves. They pit and the point surfaces get so bad that they won't conduct electricity any more. If you get in there with a riffler file and really clean out the points well, you can reset the regulator and probably get another 5 years of service out of it. If you do file away a lot of metal to get the points

1. You may have to adjust the belt tension two or three times until you get it to where it's exactly what you want. New belts will stretch, so check them again after about a half hour of running time.

2. If generator must be pried against to adjust fan belt tension, use a piece of soft wood. Make sure belt has correct degree of side play as specified in owner's manual.

3. Typical 3-unit regulator, with voltage, current, and cutout relays. Point spring tension on this model is changed with screws.

4. Wire going to base of regulator is merely a ground to insure that the regulator points will work correctly. It's a good idea.

clean, it will be necessary to set the point gap and also the air gap between the armature and coil.

You can see that the adjustments on a regulator are somewhat complicated, and this is the reason that very few adjustments are ever made in commercial garages. It's much easier to throw the old regulator away and put on a new one. New regulators that are made by major companies are usually adjusted perfectly at the factory and do not require any checking or adjusting when they are installed. If you buy a rebuilt regulator, or one that is not a major brand, you had better check it carefully to see if it's in adjustment.

ALTERNATOR SYSTEMS

In order to be precise both generators and alternators produce alternating current, and therefore might properly be called alternators. Yet, their electrical circuitry and construction features make them as different as boys and girls. The brushes of a generator are arranged so that the current reaching the armature is always of the same polarity. This is really quite inefficient, since only a small part of the generator's armature windings are producing useful energy at any one time. The rest are just waiting their turn and placing a drag on the engine's horsepower. Having a relatively low output for its size, the generator is often unable to supply the current demands of modern cars equipped with many electrically operated accessories. This shows up especially in city driving where you'd best not try to use the heater, lights, wipers, and radio all at the same time, or you might not start up next morning.

Alternators will produce usable electricity from *all* of their windings *all* of the time. Thus, they can be smaller and lighter, yet still put out almost full voltage even with the engine at an idle. Alternators do this by using some ingenious little devices known as rectifiers. A rectifier is a small disc formed from a substance that has the highly unique property of allowing electricity to flow through it freely in *one* direction, but not in the other.

The rectifiers—there are six of them —are divided up into two groups of three each. One group allows a steady flow of positive-polarity electricity to pass

through while rejecting negative current. The other group permits the passage of negative current while rejecting the positive current.

The diodes—another name for the rectifiers used in alternators—can be burned out almost instantly if current of the wrong polarity is accidentally routed into them. One of the most common causes of "sudden death" among diodes is the incorrect use of jumper cables to start balky cars in winter time. Some cars have the positive pole of the battery grounded while others have a negative ground system. Frequently, someone will unthinkingly connect a booster cable from the positive side of his battery to the negative pole of the other car. Zap! —no more diodes.

A *no-charge* condition is, of course, the most frequently encountered charging system trouble. Your first action should always be to check for the obvious. Has the fan belt broken? Is it loose and slipping? A quick glance at the water temperature indicator may give you the answer. If a no-charge is shown by the glowing indicator light, but the battery is fully charged, there is probably just a bad connection in the indicator light circuit. A careful inspection under the hood, giving special attention to the battery cables, wiring and drive belts, should eliminate many of the possible causes of the failure. But if all proves to be in order, there are still other easily-checked items that can solve your problem—or at least point to the correct solution.

ELIMINATING THE REGULATOR

If the alternator system isn't working properly, the first thing to check is the battery. Be sure it's right before you go any further. When you are sure that the trouble stems from undercharging, overcharging, or no charge at all, it's time to determine whether the regulator or the alternator is at fault.

A generator creates its own field current, but an alternator receives its field current from the battery. There are several different circuits, but in most of them current flows from the battery, through the ignition switch, through the regulator, and into the alternator field. The regulator controls the alternator by

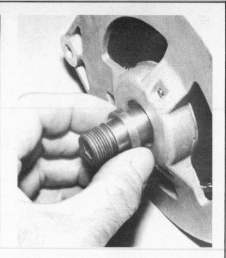

1. Always mark across housings before splitting halves. Assembly will be easier if the housings are put back together the same way they came apart.

2. Never clamp pulley in a vise. Use an Allen wrench in the end of the shaft, and the pulley nut can be removed with hardly a grunt or groan.

3. Spacer ring is important. It keeps pulley fan from scraping on housing. Rebuilt alternators may come without pulley or spacer, so save old ones.

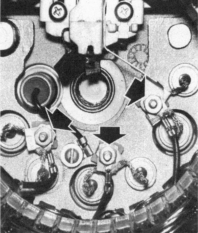

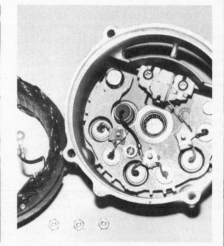

4. Surprise! There's another spacer inside. Three capscrews hold felt dust shield and keep bearing in housing. Bearing taps out of housing easily.

5. Take out four through-bolts, remove drive-end housing with rotor, and this is what you see. To remove stator, take off three nuts (arrows).

6. With the stator out of the way you can see the diodes, and with their leads disconnected, you can now easily test them with a battery test light.

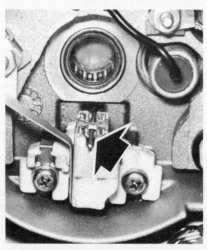

7. Positive diodes are pressed into the plate, and negative are pressed into the housing. Pressing diodes in or out requires special tools. Don't hammer!

8. To reassemble, brushes must be held down in holder with drill bit pushed in from outside housing. Do it carefully so you don't damage brushes.

9. Line up housing marks, put bolts back in, then pull drill bit out and brushes will go against rotor slip rings. Your alternator job is finished.

1. Three bolts hold the Ford-Autolite alternator together. Be sure you mark the housings before disassembly. Rotor comes off with drive-end housing.

2. Stator and diode plate are removed as a unit, but first you have to collect an endless number of nuts, steel washers, and insulating washers.

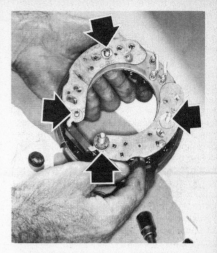

3. Arrows indicate the four posts that attach the diode plate to the housing. All posts and washers must be assembled exactly as removed, or it's no charge.

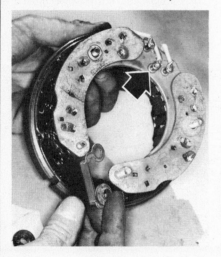

4. Little box is really a condenser. Arrow points to three stator leads that are soldered to diode plate. If any diodes are bad, entire plate is changed.

5. Removing diode plate reveals an extra lead. It is the Y connection between the three stator phases. It should be tucked away, insulated from ground.

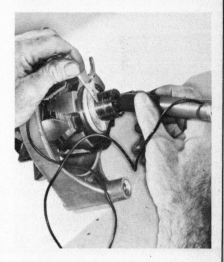

6. Testing rotor for continuity. Test bulb should light when probes are put on both slip rings. If no light, the rotor must be changed.

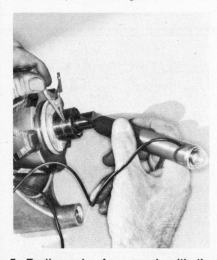

7. Testing rotor for ground, with the probes on shaft and one slip ring. If bulb lights, rotor is grounded, and must be changed.

8. To reassemble, load brushes into the holder with springs underneath, then slip drill bit in from outside housing. Work carefully, don't damage brushes.

9. After assembly, bit is pulled out to allow brushes to ride on slip rings. Note the five posts (arrows). Some are insulated, some not. Don't mix 'em.

Charging System

cutting down on the amount of current that goes to the field. Transistor regulators are different, and we suggest that you leave them to the experts, because it is very easy to blow a transistor if you hook testing leads in the wrong places.

To eliminate a mechanical regulator from the charging circuit, all you have to do is disconnect the field lead at the alternator and attach a hot lead directly from the battery. You will then have full field current. Make sure all the accessories in the car are off, then start the engine and take a reading of the voltage at the alternator output terminal with the engine idling. If the battery is fully charged, you will get 14 volts or more at idle. If the battery is low, you may have to increase the engine speed slightly above idle. Either way, if you get 14 or 15 volts out of the alternator, you can be pretty sure that it is OK, which means the trouble must be in the regulator. Revving the engine to produce more than 15 volts is unnecessary, and may blow some part of the electrical system. Never run an alternator with the output wire disconnected. They will put out 200, or even 300 volts, which is enough to fry the alternator and maybe a few other units as well. If the alternator does not put out 15 volts in this test, then there is something rotten inside it. The regulator may also be bad, but you can't check it out until you know the alternator is doing its job.

ALTERNATOR BRUSHES

Yes, Virginia, alternators *do* have brushes—and one of the nicest things *about* alternators is that many of them can have the brushes quickly removed and checked without taking the unit apart or removing it from the car. This is true of all Chrysler alternators, as well as the larger GM and Ford units. Sticking or worn-out brushes are a common source of trouble.

There are two brushes in an alternator. They are located in the alternator housing on the end opposite the V-belt pulley. On Chrysler Corporation units, one brush is mounted in an insulated plastic holder that has the alternator's field terminal attached to it. The ground brush is mounted separately in a metal holder that is screwed onto the alternator end housing. Taking off the field wire and removing the Phillips-head screws from the holders will get the brushes out and into your hands quicker than you could spend $10 on a spree in Tijuana.

GM's Delcotron alternators employ two systems of brush mounting. On the larger types, the brush holder—complete with the two brushes, the alternator terminals and a capacitor—can be taken out simply by removing all the wires and undoing two regular screws. The small 5½-in. Delcotron must have its four through-bolts removed and the end housing taken off before you can get at the brushes. The alternator should be removed from the car to do it, but some mechanics have found out that they can remove the end housing with the alterna-

tor still mounted on the engine. They don't even remove the belt. It's a neat trick if you're in a hurry.

The larger Ford alternators have two separate brush holder assemblies that are threaded so that they may be screwed directly into the alternator's end housing. These are easily removed using a wrench on the large hex at their outer ends. Like the small GM units, Ford's little ones must have the end housing taken off before you can work on the brushes.

On the Chrysler units it is sometimes possible to locate brush trouble by loosening the holders slightly and wiggling them while the engine is running. If the ammeter needle jerks up into the charge range, or the "idiot light" winks while you are doing this, you are on the right track. But remember one thing when working on the alternator or generator with the engine running. Those fan blades going around between the engine and the radiator may be invisible, but they're still plenty solid! Don't become so interested in what you're doing that you accidentally saw off a finger.

ROTOR TESTING

If you have a testing ammeter avail-

able, you can make a further check before disassembling the alternator that will show up trouble in the brushes and slip rings, or perhaps point to burned-out rotor windings. You can take the alternator out of the car for this test if you want to.

Disconnect both wires from the alternator's terminals. Connect the ammeter's positive lead to the battery's positive terminal. The battery must be fully charged. Attach the other ammeter lead to the alternator's field terminal. As mentioned earlier, this is on the insulated brush holder of Chrysler products. On most alternators it is marked "F" or "FLD." Connect a jumper wire from the battery's negative pole to the frame of the generator—although this is not necessary if the alternator has been left mounted on the engine. Turn the alternator shaft slowly by hand. The ammeter should indicate a field coil draw of between about 2.3 and 3.0 amps at 12 volts—depending on the make and model car. A lower reading indicates a high resistance in the circuit, which means poor electrical contact between the brushes and the slip rings, or maybe even a faulty field winding. Higher-than normal readings indicate that there's a possible ground or short in the rotor coil.

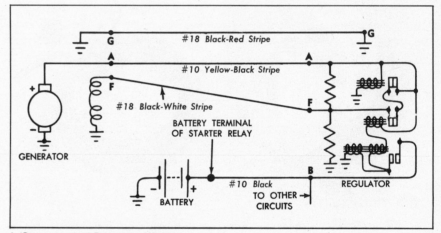

1. Generator and Regulator Wiring

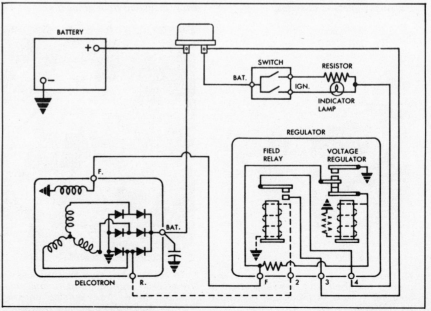

2. Alternator and Regulator Wiring

3. Screw-type Adjustments

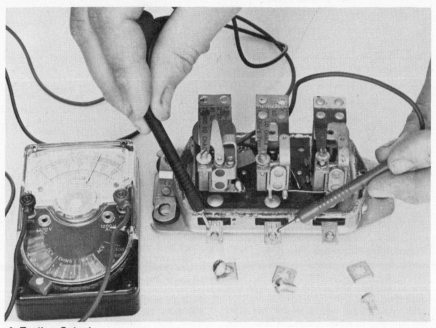

4. Testing Cutout

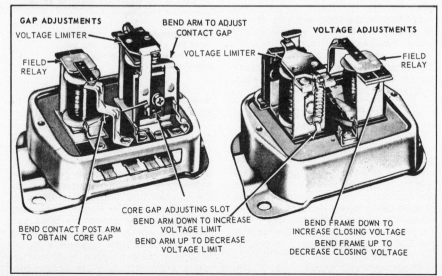

GAP ADJUSTMENTS

VOLTAGE LIMITER

FIELD RELAY

BEND ARM TO ADJUST CONTACT GAP

VOLTAGE LIMITER

VOLTAGE ADJUSTMENTS

FIELD RELAY

BEND CONTACT POST ARM TO OBTAIN CORE GAP

CORE GAP ADJUSTING SLOT
BEND ARM DOWN TO INCREASE VOLTAGE LIMIT
BEND ARM UP TO DECREASE VOLTAGE LIMIT

BEND FRAME DOWN TO INCREASE CLOSING VOLTAGE
BEND FRAME UP TO DECREASE CLOSING VOLTAGE

5. Regulator Adjustments

Most ammeters are not accurate enough to read to 1/10th of a volt. So it isn't practical to measure field current draw unless you have an accurate ammeter. If you do get an ammeter that will measure in tenths of a volt, be very careful when hooking it up. An accidental ground can burn out a low reading ammeter very quickly. It's a good idea to hook up your ammeter in series with an adjustable rheostat just in case current draw might be excessive.

If you haven't guessed it by now, the difference between a generator and an alternator is the location of the magnetic field and the wires in which the current is generated. In a generator we have a wire rotating in a magnetic field. An alternator is just the opposite, with a magnetic field which rotates inside of a coil of wire. When we measure field current in an alternator, we are measuring the amount of current that flows through the rotor coil which rotates in the center of the alternator. Brushes last a lot longer in an alternator because all they are required to carry is the small amount of field current, whereas in a generator they must carry all the current a generator produces.

Current in the alternator is produced in the stator, a heavy coil of wire that encircles the rotor. Because the stator has so many more loops in it than there are in a generator armature, the alternator will put out current at a much lower rpm than the generator. Alternators will charge at a normal curb idle. Some of them—the heavy-duty ones used on police cars—will even put out 100 amps at idle. And the alternator has another advantage in that it does not need a current regulator because it is self-limiting. You can spin it as fast as you want to and it will only put out so much current, so there's no danger of burning it up.

Alternators are a lot easier to work on than generators, once you get the hang of installing the brushes. Some alternators require that a small pin or drill be inserted to hold the brushes in place while the alternator end-frame is being put in position. Many alternators are designed to work with only a single unit regulator which controls voltage. A cur-

1. This diagram shows the relationship of the generator to the voltage regulator and battery in a Ford system, which has the field grounded at the generator, known as a "B" circuit.

2. General Motors has several wiring setups, all using the same alternator. This schematic is for an indicator lamp (idiot light) with field relay.

3. Cutout at right has normally open points. The others are normally closed. Note lock nuts on adjusting screws.

4. A shorted cutout can be found by testing between the "BAT" and "GEN" terminals. If an ohmmeter reading is obtained, the unit is faulty.

5. Field relay in Ford regulator rarely needs adjusting. A special bending tool is recommended, but pliers will work when adjusting regulators with bendable posts.

Charging System

rent regulator is not needed because the alternator is self-limiting in its current output. A cutout is not needed because the diodes themselves prevent any reverse current flow from the battery. There is a certain amount of drain through diodes because they are not perfect, but normally it would take several months before the diodes would discharge the battery completely, so the current drain is not enough to worry about. Besides the voltage units, some regulators have a relay which may be used to feed current to the field, to turn out the light on the dash, or to do both these functions.

REMOVING THE ALTERNATOR

On most cars, the alternator is an easy component to remove. It is often mounted high up on the engine and, unless buried under a maze of power accessories, even the low-mounted ones are easy to pull. After disconnecting all wires from the alternator and labeling them for future replacement, the bolt holding the alternator to the slotted belt-tensioning bracket can be readily loosened. Two wrenches—one for the nut and one for the bolt—must be used. Once the bolt is loose, swing the alternator into the position that makes reaching the other two bolts easiest. When the nuts and lock washers are off these, the adjustment bolt can be taken out and the alternator supported by hand while the remaining bolts are taken from mounting brackets.

ALTERNATOR TESTS AND REPAIRS

When disassembling the alternator, it is necessary to first remove the brushes and holders on those units which do not require dismantling to do so. The bolts or screws holding the end shields can then be removed and the housing pried apart gently with a screwdriver. You will then have complete access to the rotor, stator and diodes. With the help of a battery-powered ohmmeter or test light the following tests can easily be conducted:

1) *A grounded rotor* may be detected by touching one test lead to the rotor shaft and the other to each of the slip rings. If the ohmmeter reads low, or the lamp lights, the windings are obviously grounded and a new rotor is required.

2) *Open circuits* in the rotor are found by touching one test light lead to each slip ring. If it does not light, the windings are open and the rotor unit must be replaced.

3) *A shorted rotor* can be checked with an ohmmeter or a low reading ammeter. As most rotor specifications are given in current draw, the usual way of checking for a short is with the ammeter. The same technique and cautions apply as when checking field current draw on a generator, covered earlier in this chapter.

4) *Grounded stators* are tested for with the help of a *110-volt* test lamp, or an ohmmeter. Connect the test leads to the frame and to any of the stator leads. If

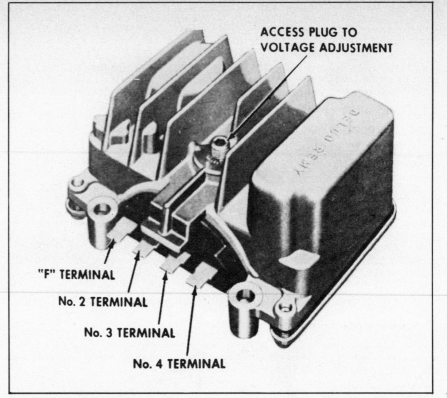

ACCESS PLUG TO VOLTAGE ADJUSTMENT

"F" TERMINAL

No. 2 TERMINAL

No. 3 TERMINAL

No. 4 TERMINAL

1. Transistorized Regulator

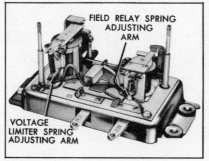

FIELD RELAY SPRING ADJUSTING ARM

VOLTAGE LIMITER SPRING ADJUSTING ARM

2. Regulator Adjustment Points

the lamp lights, or a low ohmmeter reading is shown, the stator windings are grounded.

5) *Open stator windings* will not light the test lamp when its leads are connected to successive parts of stator leads.

6) *Shorts* in the stator are very difficult to pinpoint—even with special equipment. However, if the rotor, stator, brushes, and diodes are all OK when tested for *other* flaws, and the alternator output *still* remains low, shorted windings are the probable cause.

DIODE TESTS AND REPLACEMENT

The diode can be tested either with a 3-volt battery-operated test light, or an ohmmeter powered by a 1.5-volt battery *and no more.* The test lead probes are first touched to the wire and to the case of each diode in one direction, and then reversed to test it in the opposite direction. A good diode will light the lamp or produce a high ohm reading in one direction, but not in the other. If both readings are about equally high or low, or if the light will or will not light in both

1. Terminals on most GM transistorized regulators are identical to those on conventional regulators and the various types are often used interchangeably on the same model.

2. Regulator relays with coil tension springs are sometimes adjusted by bending the hook—or spring adjusting arm—that holds the lower end of the spring in place.

3. Check diodes in transistorized regulators by unsoldering their lead wires and testing with an ohmmeter. A high resistance must be recorded in one direction, and a low resistance in the other.

4. Regulator that goes inside Delco alternator may be colored black or white, but pay attention only to the part number, not the color. Regulator at bottom has been cut away to show miniature circuitry.

5. Delcotron has not changed much over the years. Diodes are still pressed in. Note internal fan on alternator at right.

directions, the diode is considered to be bad.

For many years diodes were replaced by unbolting or unsoldering their leads and then using a special C-clamp tool to press them out of the alternator housings. Today, diodes cannot be replaced individually on many alternators. They are mounted in a circular plate that contains all six diodes. If one diode tests bad, you simply unbolt the plate and throw the whole thing away. In some cases, no soldering is required. If you do replace a diode or diode plate that requires soldering, there are certain precautions that you must take.

When soldering the diode's leads, a heat dam (a small metal clamp that drains off excess heat) should be attached to the wire between the solder joint and the diode itself during the soldering operation. Otherwise, you'll barbecue the diode. Delcotron positive diodes have red markings, the negative diodes are black.

REGULATOR CHECK AND REPAIRS

One of the first things to look for are burned-out fuse wires in Chrysler-built regulators. Two fusible wires are commonly soldered into these units to protect the system from damage due to shorts, excessive charging, and other electrical system overloads. The wires act as fuses, and whenever too much voltage passes through them, they simply overheat and melt. They are then no longer usable.

The fusible wires can be seen after removing the cover of the regulator unit. If they *have* burned out, a complete test of the regulator's operation should be made before soldering in new fusible wires and placing the regulator back in service.

To replace the fusible wires, it is first necessary to *cut* the remains of the old ones from their terminals. You should not try to unsolder these since by doing so you may damage the fine wire coming from the relay coil. Tin the end of the new fuse wires using rosin-core solder *only*. The tinned end of the wire is then inserted into the hollow rivet at the base of the regulator so that it is against the old piece of fuse wire that was left after cutting. Apply solder to the tip of the iron until a drop falls onto the joint being formed. When both wires are soldered at their lower ends, the opposite end may

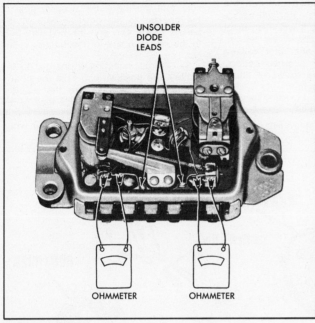

3. Testing Diodes

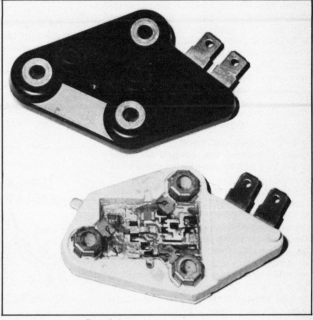

4. Delco Integral Regulator

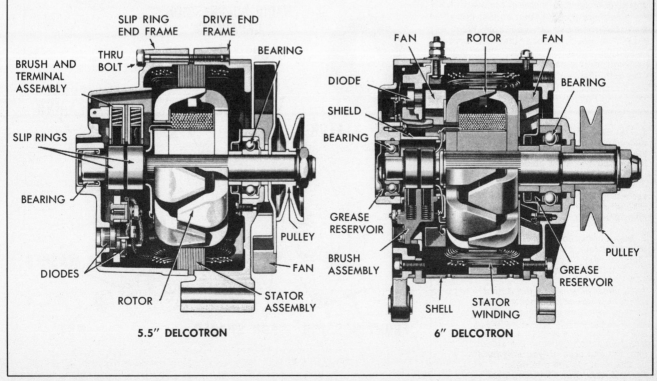

5.5" DELCOTRON

6" DELCOTRON

5. Delcotron Alternator

Charging System

be wrapped around the upper terminals and soldered—even though the original wires may only have been twisted into place.

The regulators used by Chrysler Corp. cars have just one relay unit. GM regulators have two relays and Ford even goes as high as three. Two GM-Delco types are in common use. One is a conventional load limit cutout and voltage regulating combination, and the other employs two transistors plus load and voltage relays.

The first thing to look for is dirt, corrosion residue, and burned areas on the contacts. The contacts can be cleaned with crocus cloth or a fine file. GM recommends filing with a riffler file only. Once the contacts are assured good condition, the point gaps and air gaps (the space between the relay coils and the movable point arm) should be checked and adjusted to the manufacturer's specifications.

Delco regulators have an adjusting screw to control the air gap on some units. This is a little 6-lobed knob on top of the voltage control relay. The point gaps are adjusted by bending the stationary contact mounts. On the transistorized unit the two screws holding the contact bracket are loosened and then the entire bracket moved until the correct point adjustment is attained. Single unit regulators such as those on Plymouths and other Chrysler products have their air gaps adjusted with the stationary contact bracket attaching screw fully tightened. The factory tolerance for regulator adjustments is usually around ±.002-in., which should give you a little leeway for point cleanups. Readjustment will therefore not usually be necessary unless considerable metal is removed. If the points are so badly burned that more than .004-in. must be filed from them, there's a good chance that the unit should be replaced, anyway. When you perform point cleaning and adjustment jobs with the regulator in the car, the wires connecting it to the battery should always be taken off and insulated.

1. You will rarely have to take an alternator apart this far, unless you buy a junked model for rebuilding, which may save some money.

2. Switching from a generator system to an alternator is not as difficult as you might think. The alternator will charge at idle.

3. Wire connections on this Ford alternator look complicated, but they are easy to get back on right if you mark the wires.

4. On most alternators, the output terminal is directly connected to the battery, which means it's hot all the time. If you accidentally place a pair of pliers or a wrench so there is a connection between the output terminal and ground, you may burn up the wiring to the alternator. So be careful when working near the output terminal.

REGULATOR ADJUSTMENTS

There is no cutout or current regulator in most alternator regulators, so all you have to make adjustments on is the voltage unit. It is adjusted in much the same way as a generator voltage unit, covered earlier in this chapter. But there is one big difference. If you use a ¼-ohm resistor to simulate a fully charged battery, you must be careful to keep the engine speed down. Run the engine only fast enough to make the alternator work against the regulator. You can easily see it on your voltmeter. When the regulator starts controlling the voltage, the meter needle will hold steady somewhere between 13 and 15 volts. If you run the engine too fast, the alternator will barbecue the ¼-ohm resistor. It will even do it on a piece of test equipment. We recommend that you check alternator voltage settings against a fully charged battery, so that you don't have to worry about burning up test equipment.

POLARITY

Whether the charging system in your car has an alternator or a generator, correct polarity is a very important consideration. Alternator systems can be seriously damaged by even momentary reversals of polarity, and the voltage regularity in any system is also highly vulnerable. The following precautions should always be observed when working on the charging system:

1) When putting in a battery, *always* make absolutely sure that the ground polarity of the battery, regulator, and generator or alternator is the same. Do not install regulators from negative ground systems in cars having positive ground.

2) If you have occasion to use a booster battery and jumper cables, be sure that you hook the positive pole of the booster to the positive pole of the battery in the car, and the negative pole to the negative side of the battery in the car.

3) When connecting a charger to the battery, the positive lead from the charger must be connected to the positive battery pole and the negative lead to the negative pole.

4) Never continue to drive a car when

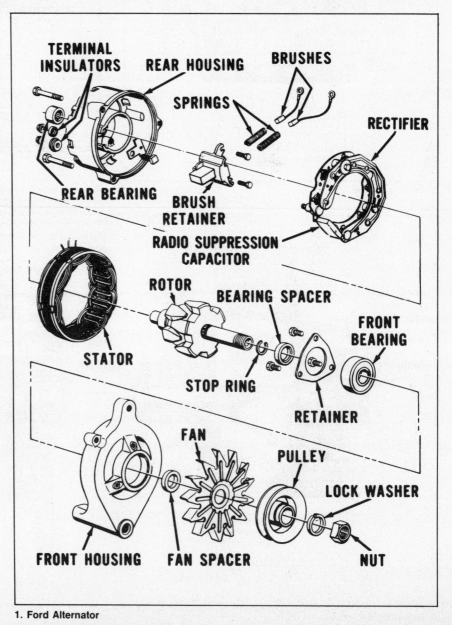

1. Ford Alternator

2. Alternator Installation

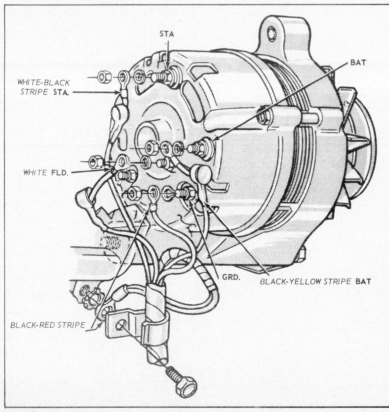

STA

BAT

WHITE-BLACK STRIPE STA.

WHITE FLD.

GRD.

BLACK-YELLOW STRIPE BAT

BLACK-RED STRIPE

3. Ford Wiring Harness

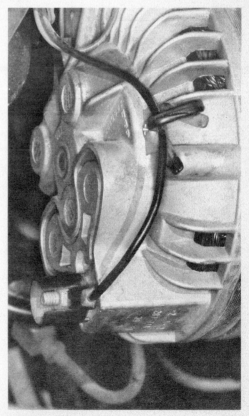

4. Output Terminal

Charging System

charging system trouble is evident. In the event of a loose connection that produces an open charging circuit, unregulated current of the wrong polarity may be allowed to enter the battery or alternator diodes.

5) Do not short across or ground any of the terminals on the regulator or the alternator *on alternator systems.*

When a new regulator or generator is installed, or when the old one is reinstalled after testing, the generator *must be polarized.* If this is not done, the generator—or regulator—will probably be burned out in a very short time. This is especially true on cars that have "Idiot lights." An ammeter will show a no-charge more reliably following installation of an unpolarized unit. Polarizing the generator and regulator is a step that is often overlooked when making engine swaps. If you're the hot rodder type, don't bypass this vital step before "firing 'er up" for the first time, or you'll have part of the rod-building job to do over again—plus the cost of a new generator and regulator, or both.

Polarizing the generator is necessary to restore the residual magnetism to the pole shoes. A generator that sits around on the bench for a long time, or one that has been dropped during handling, may lose its residual magnetism. The momentary surge of current through the field coils that you give when you polarize the generator is enough to restore the residual magnetism. Polarization amounts to electrifying the fields with a battery. But it must be done in the right direction. The generator and all wiring should be installed and ready to operate. With the engine dead and the ignition off, connect a jumper lead to the battery terminal of the regulator and touch the other end of the lead to the regulator armature terminal for just a fraction of a second. It

only takes just a touch and the job is done.

Polarization is not necessary on an alternator because it does not have a cutout. The alternator gets field current whenever the ignition switch is on, so there is no need to polarize it or make any jumper connections when installing a new alternator.

BEARINGS

Generator and alternator bearings have a particular notoriety for "going out" at the worst possible times. Even if they don't seize up half-way between service areas on the New York Thruway, they can still start making more noise than a worn-out cement mixer filled with empty beer cans—usually when you've just driven off on your first date with the prettiest girl in the whole world.

Most generators have one or two oil holes that are meant to be given a tall drink of engine oil when the car is greased. Unfortunately, these are frequently overlooked by filling station attendants, since some cars have them and others do not. The generator must be lubed according to schedule.

Most alternators, and an increasing number of generators, have "oil-less" bearings—which is to say, they have been prelubricated at the factory or are only packed upon installation. On the majority of alternators, the bearings must be replaced if they have lost their lubrication. Delcotron 6-in. and 6.2-in. units can have their bearings removed and relubricated with Delco No. 1948791 grease or its equivalent. The 5.5-in. Delcotron has ball bearings only at the drive end so that is the only end that can be repacked.

If bearings have gone bad in an alternator or generator you will, of course, need to replace them.

The bearings can be driven out of the end plates using short sections of pipe that have approximately the same diameter as the inner and outer ball bearing races. On most units, the brush-end bearing has a stamped metal grease retaining cap over its outer end. The bearing is driven from the "inside" so that this cap is forced out by the old bearing. A new cap is sometimes a part of the replacement kit. Check before destroying old one.

The drive-end bearing can be removed only after the V-belt pulley has been tak-

1. Wiring diagram with Ford alternator and transistorized regulator. Modern charging circuits like this require very little maintenance.

2. MoPar alternator is of same basic design as Ford alternator, except that until 1972 the rectifiers (diodes) mounted directly into the stator rather than a separate subframe, and could be replaced individually. From 1972 on, rectifiers are mounted in negative and positive heat sink units and entire assembly must be changed if one or more rectifiers are bad.

3. Ohmmeter hook-ups used to test diodes and field current. Test A: This is a check of the positive diodes. Note reading and reverse test leads. The meter should record a high reading in one direction and a low reading in the other. Test B: Perform same test as A. Similar readings in both directions mean faulty negative diodes. Test C: Meter should read a maximum of 7-10 ohms. Low reading means bad brushes.

4. The insulated brush can be removed separately from Chrysler Corp. alternators. Notice also the three diodes in their external heat sink adjacent to the terminal in the rear.

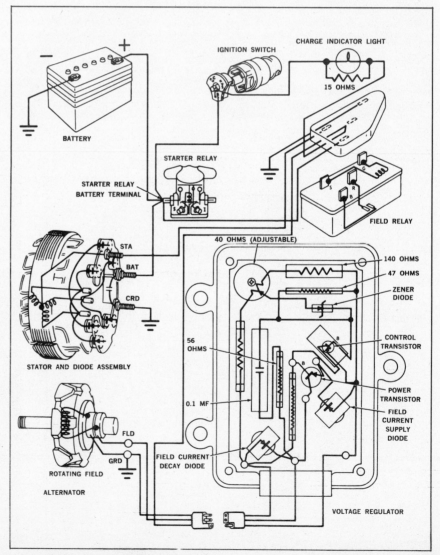

1. Alternator and Transistorized Regulator

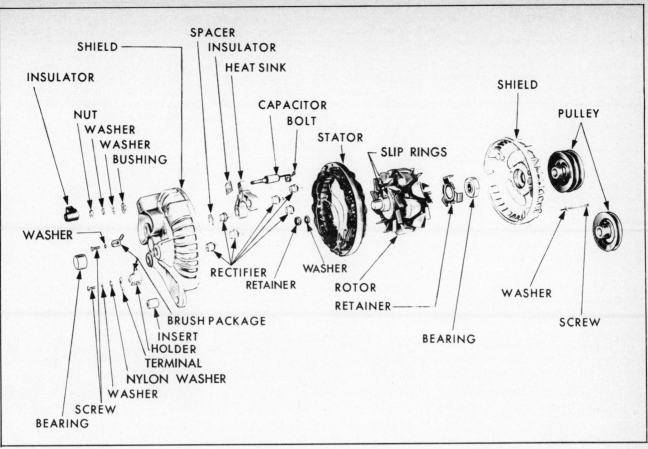

2. MoPar Alternator

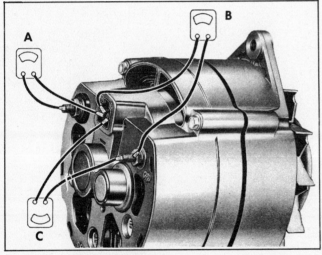

3. Delcotron Diode and Field Test

4. Insulated Brush Removal

en off the shaft. On Chrysler alternators this requires some special tools, since the pulley is an interference fit with the rotor shaft. In view of the fact that the tools cost more than having the bearing replaced in a shop, it's probably best to farm out the entire job. On other generators and alternators a nut is removed from the center of the pulley and the pulley slipped off the shaft. On Ford alternators a gear puller can be used without damaging the pulley. Delcotron alternators have a particularly nice feature for pulley removal. The end of the rotor shaft has a recess that will accept a 5/16-in. Allen wrench. The Allen wrench allows you to keep the rotor shaft from turning while undoing the 15/16-in. nut

with a box wrench. When reinstalling the pulley nuts, a torque of approximately 50 ft.-lbs. is adequate.

Pulleys themselves frequently go bad—especially on generators that have stamped metal pulleys made up of two spot-welded halves. The reason for their failure is not that the pulleys are of inferior quality, but that fan belts are often overtightened. A fan belt that does not have the correct degree of deflection, as it is specified in the car owner's manual, puts an extremely heavy strain on the generator pulley as well as on the generator and water pump bearings. The pulley, being weakest, is usually the first part to fail, but if the car's owner has been careless about oiling the generator

bearings, they are also quite likely to burn out.

When tensioning the fan belt, use only a soft piece of wood to exert pressure against the side of the generator. On V-8's with high-mounted alternators or generators it is usually possible to tension the belt correctly with only hand pressure. Incidentally, *never* pry against the side of an anti-smog pump to adjust belt tension. The housings are very thin and can be easily bent, which will interfere with the action of the air pump's rotor.

Once the pulley is off the shaft, the bearing can be driven out along with the rotor or armature by suitably supporting the end plate and tapping on a short

Charging System

length of pipe set against the *outer* bearing race. In some cases a bearing retainer must first be removed. Assuming that the bearing is no good, it can be clamped in a vise and the shaft driven out by placing a block of hard wood against it and striking it with a hammer. If you are trying to "save" the bearing, a special puller is needed in order to prevent damage.

The new bearing can be driven into the end housing using the same piece of pipe that was used to remove the old one. The bearing and end plate are then driven onto the shaft using a smaller diameter piece of pipe (⅞-in. or 1 in. works for most bearings) to drive against the *inner* race. Amply detailed instruction sheets often come with rebuild kits.

The brush-end bearing is frequently a simple bushing that can be removed and replaced with the use of a regular bushing driver tool or a piece of pipe or steel rod somewhat larger in diameter than the armature shaft. When driving in bushings and bearings, always lubricate the outside to help them slide into place more easily. Also, be very careful that they are started straight to avoid damage. Alloy end frames can be very easily deformed if excessive force is used in removing and installing bearings. Always support the bearing area as closely to the edges of the bearing assembly as possible to prevent this. Chrysler alternators should have the pulley pressed onto the shaft before the brush-end housing is installed on the alternator so that the force can be directed against the rotor shaft itself.

In conclusion, let it be said that charging systems, like many of the electromechanical components found on modern automobiles, *do* have some rather complicated aspects. But they also have some extremely simple qualities as well. At first you may feel yourself incapable of handling some of the electrical diagnosis and adjustment, and may wish to leave this to an "expert" while limiting your own part of the repair work to removing and installing the related components.

However, if your repairs include changing a regulator or an armature, keep the old part. Practice making your own tests, and take it apart if you wish to find out what makes it "tick." The next step is to conduct the tests used in making adjustments on the regulator in your car—without actually making the adjustments. Eventually, the electrical parts of the charging system will lose much of their mystery, and the first time your checkup actually finds something wrong, nine times out of ten you'll have lost your reluctance to make the necessary repairs and adjustments yourself. It may be only changing the generator brushes, or setting the regulator cutout, but it's a step in the right direction.

It has been said that familiarity breeds contempt. The old graybeard who authored that famous cliche neglected to mention that it is only fools who become contemptuous—on the other hand, the wise develop confidence.

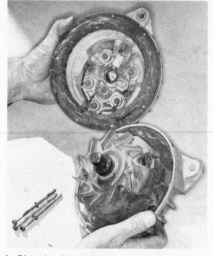

1. Chrysler Alternator

2. Motorola Alternator

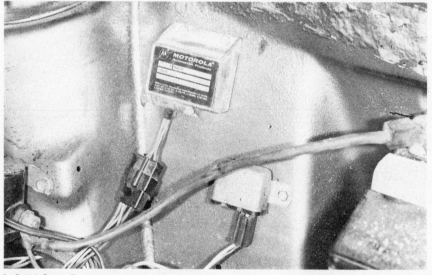

3. Solid-State Regulator

1. This is a Chrysler alternator separated into the two pieces by removing the through-bolts.

2. Low-mounted alternators like this Motorola are difficult to reach for belt tightening. When you remove this unit, take it out from the bottom.

3. Motorola solid-state regulator is a nonadjustable plug-in unit on the fenderwell—if it malfunctions, you have to replace it with a new one.

4. This is the solid-state diode rectified voltage regulator unit incorporated as an integral part of all 1973 Delcotron alternators. It's a replace-only unit if it goes bad.

5. Voltage regulator adjustment is made with screw (1). Incorrect adjustment on this unit caused the lower points (2) to arc continuously, burn out, and ruin regulator assembly.

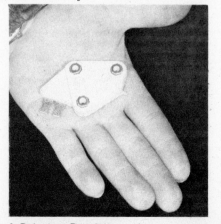

4. Delcotron Regulator

5. Voltage Regulator Adjustment

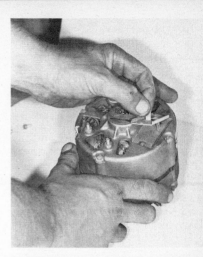

1. Disconnect plug at regulator (1) and at terminals (2,3). Run hot wire to (2). Engine at 2000 rpm should give 15 volts at output terminal (4).

2. To remove and replace the brushes, the first thing that you have to do is remove the two screws that hold the terminal plate in position.

3. The plate with ground terminal attached lifts right off once screws are removed, but you may have to jiggle plate a bit first time around.

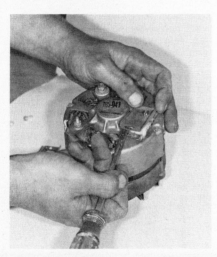

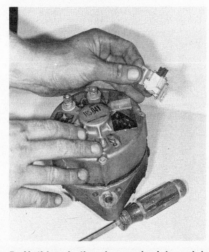

4. Underneath the terminal plate, you'll find an insulator. This is a very important piece; don't forget to replace it and don't lose it.

5. Nothing further is required to get to the brushes. Assembly lifts out with ease and replacement brushes are a relatively simple slip-in.

6. Removal of four through-bolts is necessary to split the housing. As with any alternator, mark position of housings for correct assembly.

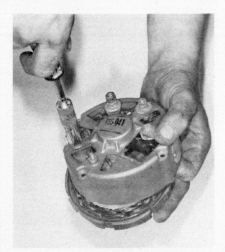

7. Disconnect terminals that come through the housing to remove diode plate. Lay out variety of washers in the order of removal to avoid mistakes.

8. Unless you want to unsolder diode leads, this is as far as you can go. If diodes or stator have to be changed, you'll have to unsolder leads.

9. American Motors uses a Motorola charging system. ID plate on side contains alternator rating and information needed for replacement parts.

Lights, Gauges, Wiring

This chapter is the do-it-yourselfer's paradise. Since the first automobiles came out, car owners have been carrying spare fuses, spare light bulbs, and maybe even doing a little bit of their own wiring when they want to add an accessory. If you're a little bit timid about working on some of the more complicated units of the car such as the starter, the generator or engine parts, the lighting system is a good place to get started and build up your confidence. It's also a good place to practice ahead of time so that when a headlight or even a fuse burns out in the middle of the night you have a pretty good idea of what you have to do to fix it. The wise driver will keep a roll of electrical tape, extra fuses, a spare sealed beam headlight unit, and some simple tools in the car at all times to cope with any highway emergencies that may come up.

FUSES AND CIRCUIT BREAKERS

A fuse is nothing more than a glass or ceramic insulator with metal contacts at the ends which are connected to one another electrically by fine wires or thin metal strips. The latter will melt like a chorus girl's heart at a millionaires' convention, if a precise electrical current load is exceeded. Short circuits that might otherwise transform your car's wiring into a Fourth-of-July display of flaming spaghetti are quickly "switched off" when the fusible wire burns apart.

Lately, car makers have been eliminating many fuses in favor of circuit breakers. The circuit breaker is basically an electro-mechanical device that functions as a fuse does, but has the added advantage of being able to restore the flow of electricity automatically once the

trouble is past. Headlights, wipers and other safety accessories are often controlled by circuit breakers to prevent their complete failure in the event of an intermittent short. After all, no one wants to have his lights go out while crossing the Nevada desert at 90 per—just because something went haywire with the cigarette lighter!

Circuit breakers are sealed assemblies and should one go bad (which seldom ever happens) the whole unit must be replaced. Just make certain that you install a new one of the identical type and amperage as the original. In many cases the circuit breaker is an integral part of the headlight switch, in which case that part must be replaced in its entirety. Late GM cars have a release button on the switch behind the dash which, when pushed, allows the light control knob and shaft to be pulled completely out of

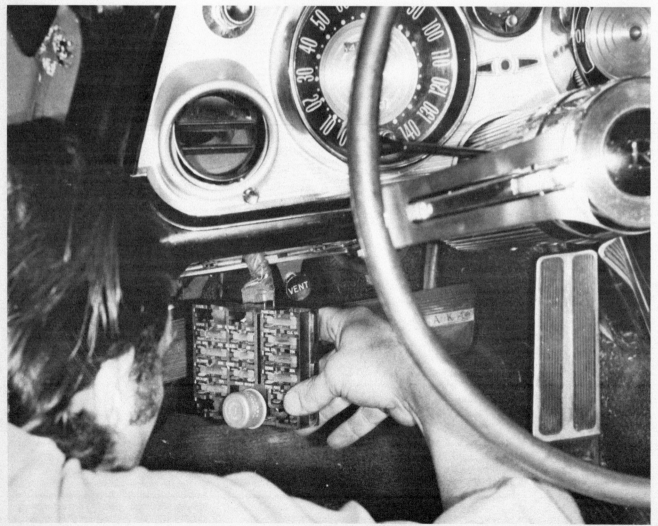

1. Fuse Block Under Dash

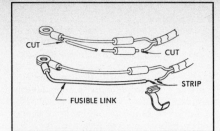

2. Fusible Link Repair

3. Headlight Connections

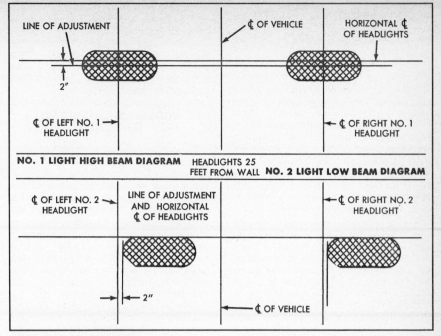

4. Headlight Aiming Chart

5. Twin-Filament Bulb

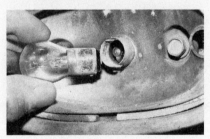

6. Corroded Socket

7. Auto Meter Tachometer

1. You're most likely to find the fuse block under the forward edge of the instrument panel. Carrying a few extra fuses can be a lifesaver in case of an emergency.

2. Repair damaged link by cutting as shown. Strip insulation back, splice wires with a splice clip and then solder. Be sure to tape splice with a double layer of electrical tape.

3. Most headlights have two or three prongs for connection. The third one on this sealed beam is for a ground. It's usually connected to the shell of the headlight, but can be switched to the car body for a better ground.

4. Draw this diagram on your garage door, and you can do your own light adjusting right in your driveway, as long as the pavement is level.

5. Note the two terminals on this typical twin-filament bulb. Sockets for these will have two wires; one may be for stoplight filament, the other for turn signal or taillight.

6. Most bulbs ground through socket. If the bulb doesn't work, check the filament first and if it's all right, then clean any corrosion from socket.

7. Probably the most popular gauge sold on the aftermarket is the tach. This Auto Meter unit features rubber in the mounting for anti-vibration.

the dashboard before removing the retainer ring that mounts the switch on the car.

The majority of American cars have their fuse panel located under the forward edge of the dashboard. On some models the fuse panel is located on the firewall just above the driver's feet. Most fuse panels have each fuse marked according to its function (radio, heater, etc.) and its amperage. Check the ampere rating for the fuses in your car and buy a few extras to slip into the glove compartment. This simple act could save you lots of trouble.

On many fuse blocks there isn't enough room to label all of the circuits that the fuse protects. Only the most prominent item, such as the radio or the wipers will be printed on the fuse block. If some electric unit on your car stops dead, but you can't find a label for that unit on the fuse block, check the wiring diagram in the factory shop manual. In some cases, the owner's manual will give a more complete description of the circuits protected by each fuse. There may also be fuses in some other location, nowhere near the main fuse block.

A fuse that blows—or a circuit breaker that cuts out—may indicate either a shorted circuit or one that is being overloaded. If the fuse blows again after it replaces the original, or if the circuit breaker cuts out repeatedly, it's time to plop on your Sherlock Holmes cap and start looking for the source of the trouble. However, if the second fuse doesn't blow, the first incident was possibly only the result of a momentary overload. This may occur on those rare occasions when several accessories sharing a common fuse are in operation simultaneously. Should one accessory begin drawing abnormally high current—as a windshield wiper may when pushing aside heavy snow—the fuse may be momentarily overloaded. A circuit breaker will simply cut the current for an instant and then things should return to their normal conditions.

Lights, Gauges, Wiring

FUSIBLE LINKS

A few years ago it wasn't unusual to hear of a car that had burned up from a short in the wiring. All it took was a bare wire against the frame or body, and the battery would pour out enough current to heat up the wire, set the insulation on fire, and turn your pride and joy into smoldering ashes. It is now extremely unlikely that car fires will occur from shorts or grounds in wiring. Every car today has one or more fusible links, that will burn in two if they are forced to carry any overload of current.

The fusible link is a piece of wire about 6 ins. long that is spliced into another wire. The link can be in many different locations in the engine compartment or behind the instrument panel. In some cases it is identified by a special color or a lettered tab. It may be looped so it stands out from other wiring, or it may blend in so you don't even know it's there. Some links can burn in two without any change in appearance, but the better links have a special insu-lation that bubbles and swells when the wire burns up. New links are available at parts stores and dealers. The old link should be cut out, and the new link spliced and soldered into position. If the new link comes as a piece of bulk wire, it should end up the same length as the old link after being spliced in.

WIRES—SHORTS AND GROUNDS

Shorted wires are the usual cause of blown fuses. Whenever a "hot" (as opposed to a "grounded") wire starts to suffer from worn or frayed insulation, there is a danger of this. Occasionally some Grade "A" boulder-brain will decide it's too much trouble to keep replacing fuses, so he deftly inserts a piece of a 10-penny nail into the fuse holders. It might be better to simply trace down the short, but never mind, that's even harder than changing fuses. This knot-headed trick burned up a car in New Jersey just a few years ago. Unfortunately, it was parked in the garage under the owner's new split-level house at the time. If you want to start fresh with a new house and car, plus all your belongings, that's one way to do it—but it's expensive.

The first places to check for worn or broken insulation are at metal clips or other wire supports. On some cars, wires may pass *under* the automobile. Here, exposed to weather and road splash, the wire's life expectancy is considerably reduced.

We were once driving with a friend whose lighting-system fuse kept blowing. After using several fuses, repeated taping and inspection of the wires, and much soul-rousing profanity, we finally noticed that the fuses only blew when the brakes had been applied for a few seconds. The trouble? Worn insulation on the one wire we didn't check—the stoplight switch wire. It was located under the car and its insulation had practically rotted away. When the brake pedal was depressed, the arm on the stoplight switch barely touched the wire, but it was enough to produce a shorted circuit. Three inches of plastic tape around the wire got us home, and a new wire took care of the problem.

Other wire trouble is frequently encountered at the terminals. Corrosion and vibration can eventually produce

1. Accessory Gauges

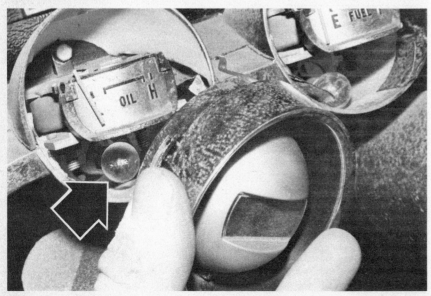

2. Access to Bulbs

1. When considering extra gauges to supplement factory instrumentation, oil pressure and ammeter gauges are the first ones to get, and are available in panels that mount below the dash.

2. On most cars, the bulbs that light the gauges are accessible only from behind the dash, but on this model removing the front half of the gauge exposes the bulb for replacement.

3. The control knob must be removed before replacing switches mounted through the instrument panel. This Buick knob comes out when button on switch body is depressed.

4. Fuse block has to be dropped to gain access under dash. After knob is removed, a retaining clip is popped off from behind, and the unit can then be removed.

5, 6. Bakelite connector has burned itself out. Faulty connection between this and the switch (6) allowed constant arcing that ruined both units and presented a definite safety hazard in terms of fire as well as lights that fluctuated while in use.

3. Control Knob Removal

4. Fuse Block Removal

5. Burned Bakelite Connector

6. Burned-out Switch

GUIDE TO FUSIBLE LINKS

MAKE	LOCATION	COLOR
AMC	Battery terminal of starter relay to main wire harness..................	RED
	Battery terminal of horn relay to main wire harness..................	PINK
	Accessory terminal of ignition switch to wire harness.................	BROWN
	Battery terminal of starter relay to heated rear window relay........	RED
	B-3 terminal of ignition switch to circuit breaker..........................	RED
	I-3 terminal of ignition* switch to circuit breaker..........................	YELLOW
	I-3 terminal of ignition* switch (single wire at the switch splits into two feed wires)...................	YELLOW
	I-3 terminal of ignition* switch to throttle stop solenoid..............	YELLOW

*Only one of these links is used on any one vehicle.

MAKE	LOCATION	COLOR
BUICK	Battery terminal of starter solenoid to lower end of main supply wires................................	BLACK
CADILLAC	Battery terminal of starter solenoid to main wire harness.	
CHEVROLET	Molded splice at solenoid battery terminal............................	BROWN
	Molded splice at horn relay.	BLACK
	Molded splice in voltage regulator #3 terminal wire...............	ORANGE
	Molded splice in ammeter circuit (both sides of meter).................	ORANGE
CHRYSLER	On battery terminal of starter solenoid................................	DARK BLUE
	Above bulkhead connector..........	DARK BLUE
	Between battery and terminal block.	DARK GREEN
FORD LINCOLN MERCURY	Between starter solenoid battery terminal and alternator (Mustang and Cougar only).	
	Looped outside wire harness between starter solenoid and alternator (T-Bird and Lincoln only), behind point at which harness is dipped to the right rocker cover (above starter).	
	Twin links between starter solenoid and alternator (1) and starter solenoid to vehicle equipment harness.	
OLDSMOBILE	At horn relay jet block (All except Omega)....................	BLACK
	Twin links at horn relay jet block (Omega only)....................	BLACK/ORANGE
	At starter solenoid battery terminal (Omega only).................	BROWN
PONTIAC	Positive battery cable pigtail lead (requires entire cable replacement)............................	BROWN
	At horn relay..............................	BLACK
	Molded splice in circuit at jet block and horn relay (some single and some twin)........................	ORANGE

Lights, Gauges, Wiring

poor contact. A regular check for terminal tightness, and a cleaning with abrasive cloth when trouble strikes, will usually prevent most of the bad contacts. Broken wires can be repaired in one of three ways. First—and best, if the insulation is in generally poor condition—is to replace the wire in its entirety. Wires can be spliced by simply twisting the ends together, soldering the joint if possible, and covering the area with electrical tape. A coating of liquid rubber over the taped joint will make a very permanent and weatherproof joint. In some cases it is possible to install a crimped-on splicing tube. These, however, require a special tool to compress them.

A very great variety of specialized wire terminals are available from automotive supply stores. These must be crimped into place with a special tool. Such terminals require no soldering, and their addition will always insure a flawless connection.

HEADLIGHTS

Replacing a burned-out sealed beam unit is perhaps the simplest of automotive repairs—next to changing fuses. Still, more "first time" home mechanics have botched this job than would ever care to admit it to even themselves.

Dual headlight installations employ two different types of sealed beam units. The high beam lamps which "go out" when the headlights are dimmed, have only two terminals on the back, and their lens is marked with a number "1." The other units operate on both high and low beam, and like the sealed beam lamps found on cars with single headlights, they have three terminals on the back. The lens of these is marked with a number "2." Before buying a new one, be sure you know if you're replacing the high/low #2 lamp or the high beam #1 lamp only. On cars with the dual lights arranged side by side, the outermost lamps are the 3-terminal high/low combination. On Pontiacs, Plymouths and other cars that have one light mounted above the other, the high/low #2 unit is the upper one.

The first step in making the actual replacement is to take off the decorative trim surrounding the headlight. On most cars with dual lights there are three or four screws used to do the job. Cars with single lights usually have only one screw directly at the bottom of the chrome ring. Once the trim is off, there will be several screws visible around the circumference of the headlight. Three of these will be removed to change the sealed beam unit. The other two must not be tampered with since they are for aiming the lights. These aiming screws are larger than the retaining screws and are therefore pretty easy to spot.

Once the retaining ring surrounding the light is off, the sealed beam unit can be pulled out and the plug withdrawn from its terminals. Putting in the new lamp is simply a reversal of the removal process, but be sure to position the lens so that the word "TOP" is at the top where it is supposed to be.

HEADLIGHT AIMING

Twenty years ago the highways were peppered with immature squirrels who deliberately aimed their car's headlights in a way calculated to blind other drivers. Quite a few even mounted spotlights for this very purpose. If your lights were brighter than the other guys, you were a bigger man. Or at least brighter.

Well, the police finally got tired of hauling dozens of these rabbit-brained anthropoids off to the cop shop every night, and state legislators passed laws in many locales that required car owners to either obtain a certificate to the effect that their headlight aiming had been carried out by a "professional," or to have the headlight aim checked annually by state-licensed inspectors.

If you live in one of these areas where the government is trying to save the populace from its own folly, there's not much you can do about aiming your own headlights unless only a state inspection is required. However, if there are no such legal requirements in your particular state, you can do your own headlight aiming with relative ease.

You'll need to find a place where your car will sit level, such as a paved driveway or parking lot. Or you can drive your car to such a place and lay a carpenter's spirit level on the front bumper and on one of the door sills (with the door open). Even on a level surface, the car may not sit absolutely level, or the bumper may be mounted in a slightly tilted position in relation to the car, so mark the location of the bubble in the level with a grease pencil. Rock the car from side to side and allow it to assume its normal attitude before making the tests with the spirit level.

The car can then be driven home to

1. Some switches are more difficult to get to. Radio has to be pulled to allow arm access behind dash for this light switch to be removed.

2. Rear view of the same dash panel shows how light switch (1) is placed. Wiper switch (2) and signal light (3) can be taken out without removing panel, but steering column must be dropped, and as you'll be working blind, expect bruised knuckles.

3. Late-model speedometers have a thumb latch for disconnecting the cable, instead of the old-fashioned type with a threaded ferrule.

4. Most gauges can't be taken apart for repairs, but this fuel gauge can be adjusted with a small screwdriver.

5. Here's an example of well-planned and well-executed wiring job on a custom dash with many gauges. Note the use of neat wire bundles and wiring terminal blocks.

1. Light Switch Removal

2. Rear View of Light Switch

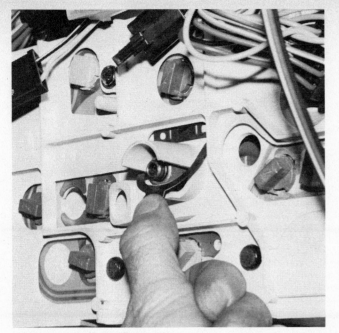

3. Speedometer Cable Connection

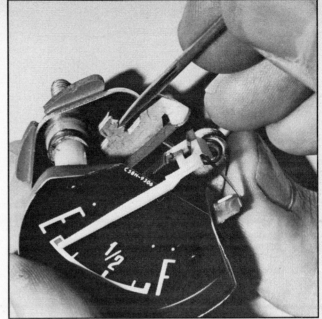

4. Adjusting Fuel Gauge

your own un-level driveway and a jack or two used to adjust the level of the car slightly to duplicate the bubble position obtained with the car on level ground.

The car should be positioned 25 ft. from a garage wall or an aiming screen improvised from a large piece of cardboard. The aiming screen should have one horizontal line and three vertical lines drawn upon it. The horizontal line can be laid out with the help of the carpenter's level and should be at the identical height above the ground as the center of the car's headlights. The center vertical line should be at the car's exact centerline. This can first be drawn at right angles to the horizontal line, if desired, and the aiming screen shifted from side to side until it is lined up with the center of the car's hood. You can "sight" through the rear window to do this. If there is no distinct center line in the hood, the center can be located with a tape measure, a small suction cup placed there for a "front sight" and a yardstick held straight up from the trunk lock for a "rear sight."

Two other vertical lines are then drawn which are the same distance apart as the centers of the car's headlights. These should be located equi-distant from the centerline, which will place them directly in front of the car's lights.

The adjustment on all Type-2 units is made with the headlights on low beam only. This will assure adequate illumination with the lights dimmed, and the built-in angle between the high and low beams will take care of the aiming for the "brights." Type-2 units, whether used on two- or four-headlight systems, have a "2" molded into the lens for identification. If the car has dual headlights, the high-beam-only #1 lights are adjusted separately. Three other prerequisites must be observed if you wish to do a good job: (1) Have the tires inflated to the correct pressures; (2) Have the car filled to capacity with gas, water, and oil—but no cargo or passengers; (3) Make sure all grille, fender, and headlight assembly bolts are tight.

5. Custom Wiring Job

AIMING TYPE-2 UNITS

On most cars you will have to remove the headlight trim ring to gain access to the adjusting screws. Some late-model cars, though, have access holes in the trim rings that allow you to stick a screwdriver through for adjustments.

Switch the lights on low beam. Cover the right headlight with your jacket, an old blanket, your mother-in-law, or anything else that's handy. Adjust the left light vertically until the top edge of its high-intensity zone is exactly on the horizontal line. The vertical adjustment screw is at the top of the sealed beam unit on most cars. When adjusting the aiming screws, move them first counterclockwise until the lights are definitely *out* of adjustment, and then gradually clockwise to bring them in. Otherwise the spring may not expand properly and

will later allow the lamps to change their aim.

After positioning the light vertically, use the same procedure to move the beam horizontally until the left edge of the high-intensity zone is 3 ins. (2 ins. in some states) to the right of the vertical line in front of that headlight. The light's horizontal adjusting screw is located to one side of the sealed beam mounting. By moving the covering from the right headlight to the left, it will be possible to make the same adjustments to the right side. This is the end of the job for cars with single lights. Dual headlight installations must still have their #1 lamps aimed.

AIMING TYPE-1 UNITS

The actual work is done exactly as it was in aiming the #2 lamps, but the

Lights, Gauges, Wiring

beam is positioned differently on the screen. Cover the three lights not being adjusted. Aim the exposed high beam until the center of its "hot spot" is 2 ins. lower than the intersection of the horizontal line and the vertical line in front of that light. On station wagons and softly-sprung sedans the hot spot should be centered further below the horizontal line to compensate for vehicle loading differences. This measurement depends on your state's particular motor vehicle requirements.

If you have a car with single headlights that is equipped with the old 5000 series sealed beam unit (without the #2 on the lens), then they should be adjusted while on high beam only, according to the instructions given above for aiming #1 units (those with a single filament high beam).

SOME OTHER LIGHTS

Burned-out taillights, instrument panel bulbs, and what have you, are usually fairly quick and easy to change. The average car has about 15 or 20 small lamps—not all of them the same size. When a small bulb stops functioning,

you should take it out and check to see that the lamp itself is really to blame. Quite often, parking light and turn signal units will suffer the ravages of weather, water and roadside mud until the wires or sockets themselves finally succumb to corrosion and rot. If the bulb turns out to be OK, insert the probes of a test light into the socket (with the switch controlling the light turned on) and see if current is actually reaching the lamp. If it is, the trouble is probably nothing more than a coating of crud on the socket or bulb contacts. Scraping the terminal contacts on both the bulb and socket should do the trick. Poor ground contact could also be a factor, so don't forget to polish up the lug pins on the lamp base, and also the slots in the socket that they fit into. Check the ground between the socket and its holder, between the holder and the fender, and between the fender and the body. The electricity has to get back to the ground terminal of the battery. It can be stopped at any one of those points. We have fixed many an old car that was hopelessly rusted up by running a ground wire from the bulb sockets to the frame of the car. It's a lot easier than trying to get a ground through all that rusty sheetmetal.

If no current is reaching the socket, a broken or shorted wire—or possibly a

faulty switch—is at the bottom of it all. However, most switches operate more than one bulb, or at least something else besides the bulb. If the other components in the circuit are functioning properly, the trouble is not likely to be in the switch.

Every bulb has a number printed on its base, and when buying a replacement you should try to find a lamp having the identical number. Often the parts store will have a chart or booklet listing the bulbs used for particular applications in various makes and models of cars. Tell them what kind of car you drive, and which lamp has burned out, and they'll probably be able to fix you up.

The lights on the outside of the car's body are pretty easy to work on, but some of those located behind the dashboard seem to have been put there by Houdini's ghost. Trying to get your hand up through the maze of wires and controls sometimes requires the agility of a serpent and the patience of a saint. These small instrument panel lamps are usually retained in sockets that can be taken out of the back of the instrument panel by turning them about ¼-turn counterclockwise and pulling them out. The sockets on a few cars simply press into holes in the back of the panel. Once the socket is out it can be pulled from

1. Ignition Switch Housing

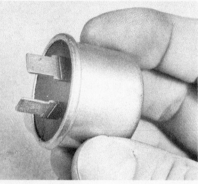

2. Flasher Unit

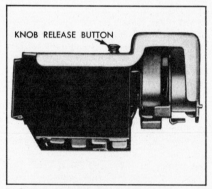

3. Switch Handle Release Button

KNOB RELEASE BUTTON

4. Dimmer Switch

5. Ignition Switch Terminals

1. *The switch end of ignition switch will accept your old lock, so you don't have to change keys if you replace the electrical part of switch.*

2. *Flashers for most late-model cars are simple plug-in type. They come in many different electrical values, according to the number of bulbs on the car that are in flashing circuit.*

3. *The knob and shaft on a headlight switch are removable by pushing this button (arrow) on the switch.*

4. *Late-model dimmer switches are 1-piece units with plug-on terminals for the wiring. They can't be taken apart for servicing.*

5. *Center post at back of ignition switch is for accessories. The other terminals are shielded to prevent shorts, or "hot wiring."*

6. *If you've wondered where that obnoxious noise comes from when you open the door of a late-model car without first removing the ignition key . . . here's the culprit. Buzzer is usually buried in the most inaccessible place behind the dash to discourage disconnecting or removal.*

6. Safety Buzzer

under the dash, the old bulb exchanged for a new one, and the socket reinstalled behind the instrument panel.

Taillights, backup lights, parking lights, and turn signals are generally serviced by removing the lens and trim ring. Most cars have from one to four screws holding the trim ring in place and, once these are taken out, the ring, lens, and gasket will come off to give access to the bulb. Actually, on some late-model cars—including nearly all Chevrolets—it is possible to replace the bulbs in the tail, stop, and backup lights from inside the trunk. These lights have sockets that can be pulled out in a way very similar to the bulb holders used on the back of the instrument panel—making the whole job easier.

Many of the bulbs used in rear-end lighting are "combination" types that have two filaments and serve as both a taillight and turn signal, or as a stoplight and taillight. For this reason it is imperative that the same type of bulb be used. Also, only by installing bulbs of the right specifications, can you be sure of getting the precise degree of brightness required for safety by the motor vehicle laws.

SWITCHES

If the bulbs are all OK, but your stoplights or backup lights *still* won't work, or dimming your headlights for an upcoming car sometimes makes them go *completely out* you've got switch troubles. Usually, the only cure is to put in a new switch.

In the case of light, heater, and windshield wiper switches that are mounted *through* the dash, it's necessary to take off the control knob before the faulty unit can be removed. In the majority of cases, a small set screw—often the "Allen" variety—must be taken from the underside of the knob before it will come off the shaft. Some controls may have

knobs that are threaded onto the shaft and can simply be unscrewed, while others employ spring retainers that are freed by inserting a small wire into a hole in the bottom of the knob. As mentioned earlier, the knob and control shaft on some GM cars is taken out as a unit by pulling the control to the "ON" position and depressing an under-dash button located on the switch body to free it.

The ferrule nut that holds the switch in the dash often takes some pretty exotic shapes. A few are easy to grip with fingers or with common tools, but others are intended to be taken off with a special tool. It's usually better to improvise such a tool from wood or wire than to try "brute force" (such as a pair of pliers), which will only lead to unsightly scratches on the ferrule nut and dashboard. Once the switch is out of the dash, the wires can be disconnected and a new switch installed.

Whenever you change a switch, it's a good idea to label all wires so that they can be reinstalled in the correct positions. However, most late-model cars have plug-in connectors that preclude any possibility that the wires may become confused. These plugs also make the job much quicker and easier. As a further precaution, the battery ground cable should always be disconnected during the switch changing operation to prevent accidental shorts that could blow fuses, start fires, or run the battery down.

While nearly all switches are serviced as complete units only, there are a few which may be returned to useful service by simply tightening, adjusting or lubricating the switch or its linkage. Stoplight switches that are operated mechanically off the brake pedal can cause two kinds of easily-fixed trouble. Those found on older cars with brake pedals that pass through the floorboards are located *under* the car, and are therefore frequent victims of dirt and corrosion.

These switches have a lever on them which contacts the brake pedal. The lever is spring loaded so that it will swing around in an arc as the brakes are applied and the pedal arm moves away from it. The switch lever is connected internally to a pair of electrical contacts which trigger the stoplights when they come together. If the switch lever's shaft becomes rusted or coated with dirt, it will no longer turn properly to follow the movement of the brake pedal arm. Result: no stoplights. In most cases a few drops of "Liquid Wrench," or a similar rust-dissolving oil, will free the frozen shaft. In bad cases the switch can be removed and washed in kerosene. After the Liquid Wrench or the kerosene bath, work the lever back and forth a few times and it should start to move freely once again. If it does not, the spring is probably broken and a new switch is required.

The stoplight switch used on late-model cars with "hanging" brake pedals is usually mounted under the dashboard just below the steering column on the brake pedal stop. Any trouble caused by these switches is more likely to result from vibration than corrosion. Should the retaining nut become loosened, it may allow the switch to move away from the pedal and the stoplights will remain permanently on. The switch must be remounted tightly in such a position that electrical contact is made when the brake pedal is depressed ⅜- to ⅝-in. from the fully released position, when the brake is "off."

Some stoplight switches are a friction fit in their bracket. To adjust them, push the switch toward the brake pedal with the pedal depressed. When the pedal is released, it will bottom the switch and push it back in the bracket to the right position.

The backup light switches fitted to most of the automatic and column-shift transmissions seldom cause trouble

Lights, Gauges, Wiring

since most are mounted on the steering column inside the car and out of the weather. If one goes bad, simply put the selector switch in neutral, disconnect the wires from the switch, unscrew the unit from the car, and install a new one. However, many cars with floor shifters have the backup light switch mounted on the side of the transmission *under* the car. These switches and their connections can take quite a beating from the weather, and may eventually cause trouble. Also, the small rod connecting the switch to the reverse gear bellcrank may become loose or rusty and fail to function at all.

To replace such a switch, the wiring is disconnected at an inline plug some distance from the switch itself. The cotter or wire clip is then removed at the point where the reverse lever rod is connected to the switch's control arm. Then you can remove the switch and its splash shield by taking out two screws. The bracket remains mounted on the transmission and should not be disturbed. After the new switch is in place, test its action by shifting the transmission in and out of reverse. The mounting holes on the switch are elongated, making it possible to adjust the switch's position for proper operation.

Like a well mannered rattlesnake, dimmer switches usually give some warning before they slip you the needle. You'd be well advised to investigate the cause of any malfunction at the first sign of trouble. Otherwise, you might suddenly find yourself driving 60 mph on a winding, tree-lined road without any headlights to show you the way.

Sometimes dimmer switch trouble is nothing more than a sticking plunger.

Dirt and snow from your shoes may work its way into the switch and cause it to jam. Remove the switch and blow out any debris that's under the pedal cap and inject a few drops of penetrating oil into it. If the switch now works normally, you're back in business.

If the headlights refuse to go on and you suspect trouble in the dimmer switch, you can check the circuit with a jumper wire. By connecting the center wire leading to the switch to one of the other two wires, you should be able to make the lights operate on either bright or dim. If the jumper wire gets results, the trouble is probably in the switch. But, before condemning the dimmer switch itself, be sure that the trouble isn't poor contact between the wires and the switch terminal connections.

Most dimmer switches can be removed by folding back the upper left corner of the front floor mat and removing the wires and mounting screws from the switch assembly. Most late-model cars have a multi-wire plug connector which is simply pulled from the terminals. Place the multi-plug connector on the terminals of the new switch and check the headlight operation. If everything works OK, bolt in the new switch, replace the floor mat, and the job's done.

If the neutral safety switch found on cars with automatic transmissions goes bad it can stop you deader than Sitting Bull stopped Custer or, if it permits the engine to be started with the gear selector in the "drive" or "reverse" range, it might even convert your car into a lethal battering ram. As part of the circuit controlling the starting system, its failure will definitely be more than a slight inconvenience.

One type of neutral safety switch is screwed directly into the transmission, and the other mounts with two or three

screws somewhere on the transmission selector linkage. It is commonly inside the console on cars with floor-mounted gear selectors, and somewhere on the steering column of others. Once the actual location is determined, the removal and replacement operation should be fairly obvious. In some cases the trouble is nothing more than dirty, burned, or grease-coated contacts. A little judicious cleaning will usually be all that's needed. But if there is obvious breakage, or signs of wear, get a new switch.

INSTRUMENTS

With the exception of the speedometer, and in a very few cases the water temperature and oil pressure gauges, all modern dashboard instruments are electrically operated. In recent years it has become common to limit standard instrument clusters to a speedometer and a fuel gauge with only indicator lights to warn the driver of flow oil pressure, engine overheating, and inadequate battery charging. Higher-priced cars and "sports" models usually hark back to the standard instrumentation of pre-1955 models and include an oil pressure gauge, temperature gauge, and ammeter. An electric tachometer and perhaps a clock may also be part of the instrument group.

The lamp bulbs of the indicators ("idiot lights") are replaced in exactly the same way as other dashboard lights. There is no regular maintenance that needs to be performed on any of these instruments.

CLUSTER REMOVAL

Many of the less elaborate instrument layouts can be serviced without taking the panel out of the car. However most

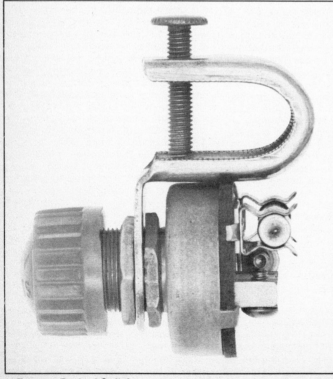

1. Fuse on Back of Switch

2. Bat Handle Switches

3. Keyless Switch

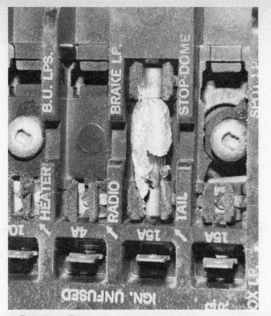

4. Tinfoil on Fuse

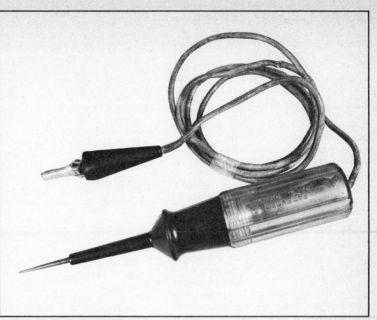

5. Non-Powered Test Light

1. Some switches have their own fuse right on the back, plus a mounting bracket for use under the edge of the instrument panel.

2. For accessory installations, bat handle toggle switches like these by Aris Sales Co. bolt easily under the dash and are available with one, two or three switches, with or without the indicator lights.

3. Keyless Key by Karset Co. not only helps prevent theft but may cut down on drunken driving, because a drunk can't work the combination.

4. Wrapping a blown fuse with foil to keep from blowing fuses is just asking for trouble, even fire. Better to track down what caused the first fuse to blow and correct it.

5. The old non-powered test light is extremely reliable. The light bulb is inside the handle and can easily be changed when it burns out. To use, ground the clip, then touch the point to any terminal to see if it's hot.

of the cars that have "extra" instruments installed as "options" must have the panel removed before you can get at the gauges. The battery ground cable must in every case be disconnected when the instrument cluster is being taken out to avoid electrical damage. On most cars it is also necessary to remove the steering column housing or in some instances to "drop" the column assembly from its dash mounts. Since in many cases the instrument cluster will slide along the steering column jacket as it is removed, the jacket should be wrapped with masking tape to protect it from scratches.

Before loosening the cluster from the dashboard, the retaining collar holding the speedometer cable must be unscrewed and the cable slipped out of its socket in the speedometer head. If there is an oil pressure line (as on many GM "sports" models), this must also be taken off. The screws holding the instrument cluster in place may then be removed. There are generally from four to

six of these located around the cluster, Phillips-type screws being commonly used to retain it.

Once the retaining screws are out, the cluster can be pulled out of the dashboard. When there is adequate working space between the cluster and the dash, the remaining wires can be unplugged or disconnected if it is desired that the instrument cluster be removed completely from the car. However, if the car has console-mounted instruments, it may be necessary to dismount the main instrument cluster before the front of the console can be lifted off.

Since many instrument panels are now being made of plastic, there may also be one or more ground straps to provide ground polarity to the instruments. When replacing the panel, be very sure to reinstall these properly to secure the best possible electrical contact and assure a good ground.

FUEL GAUGE AND VOLTAGE LIMITER

All modern fuel gauges are electrically operated and are actually nothing more than simple devices capable of measuring the amount of voltage transmitted from a sending unit located in the car's fuel tank. There is also a voltage-limiting relay in the circuit to prevent inaccurate readings due to voltage changes initiated outside the gas gauge's own wiring system. On some automobiles the voltage limiter is an integral part of the fuel gauge itself, but it may also be a separate behind-the-dash unit. In most cars equipped with electric oil pressure and water temperature gauges, these units are connected to the same voltage limiter as the fuel gauge. In rare cases, each gauge may have its own built-in limiting device.

A fuel gauge that shows a "full" tank whenever the ignition is switched on is probably not "stuck" as it may seem to be. There are three other far more likely electrical causes for this malfunction. The most common is an improperly grounded gauge or instrument cluster. If

the cluster is not grounded, all other electrical gauges will also be against the peg at the high end of their scale. The ammeter, however, will not be affected, and an electric tachometer that is not properly grounded will read a constant "zero." The only necessary repair in such cases is to restore good ground contact to the instruments or to the panel. In the case of a plastic panel, there is often only one ground connection or ground strap for all instruments. The individual units are then grounded to one another. This is why all gauges may be affected by a poor ground potential. If the car has a metal panel, however, the problem may affect only the fuel gauge.

You can test for faulty ground connections simply by connecting a jumper wire to some grounded point on the car and touching its opposite end to the back of the high-reading instrument (or zero-reading instrument in the case of the tachometer). If it then reads normally, you've found the trouble.

A faulty voltage limiter can also cause the gauge(s) to read high or low—either at one peg or the other, or at any "odd" place in between. If the needles occasionally make sudden "surges" to higher-than-normal readings, this is also the result of a faulty voltage limiter.

A quick check of the instrument voltage limiter can be made by connecting one lead of a test light to the temperature-sending unit on the engine and the other lead to ground. Leave the instrument wire attached to the sending unit also and have the ignition switch turned on. A flashing lamp indicates that the limiter is working. A voltmeter can also be used to make this test. The reading should fluctuate between 0 and 7 volts on a car with a 12-volt electrical system.

If the car has only a fuel gauge, the limiter can still be tested, but it will probably require that the instrument cluster be removed from the dashboard. The limiter is tested by connecting a jumper wire from the "hot" post of the car's battery to the input (battery) terminal on the limiter. (Or fuel gauge, if the limiter is an

Lights, Gauges, Wiring

integral part of it.) Another jumper is connected from the grounded battery post to the case of the limiter or gauge. A test light—or the correct polarity lead of a voltmeter—should also be connected to the battery's grounded pole, and the remaining voltmeter or test light lead touched to the limiter's input terminal. A full 12-volt reading should be shown or, in the case of a test light, the bulb should burn brightly. The test lead must then be moved from the input terminal to the terminal that leads to the gauges. There should be a fluctuating reading of from 0 to 7 volts, or a flashing test light. If not, the limiter (or gauge limiter combination) is defective. It should be replaced.

Another possible cause of a constant "full" reading is a short in the wire coming from the tank. If the wire proves to be OK, the gauge well grounded, and the voltage limiter operating properly, any trouble that exists must be in either the gauge mechanism itself or in the tank's sending unit.

The next item to check is the proper grounding of the sending unit. Clean away a small area on the fuel tank and another on the top of the sender. (Its location on the fuel tank can be determined by inspecting the tank to find the gauge wire's connecting point.) Attach a jumper wire to a good ground on the car's body and touch the other end to the clean spot on the fuel tank. If the gauge reads normally, the trouble is a poorly grounded tank. If the gauge still does not read accurately, touch the jumper to the clean spot on the sending unit. A normal reading here indicates poor ground contact between the tank and the sending unit. Should the reading still be "off," the trouble is either in the

gauge or in the sending unit mechanism.

The best way to make further tests is with the help of an extra sending unit. By doing this, you can avoid going to the trouble of needlessly removing the car's sending unit from the gas tank. The extra sending unit can be a junkyard cheapie and does not even have to be from the same model car as yours. It must, however, be in good working condition. Once you've obtained the extra sending unit you can wire it to the car's gauge by grounding it to the vehicle's body with a jumper wire and attaching the gauge's lead wire to the test unit's terminal rather than to the terminal on the sender in the car. Turn the ignition switch to "on" and move the float of the sending unit up and down. The needle on the instrument panel should traverse the full range from "empty" to "full." There should be no sticking or jerkiness in its movement. If the gauge does not work properly, it will have to be replaced. If it *does* work properly, it means you'll have to work on the sending unit in your car.

It may be necessary to take the tank out of the car on some makes, but it's usually possible to remove the sending unit with the tank still in the car. *However, be sure you disconnect the battery cables first.* One little spark is all it would take to turn you and your car into a king-size torch.

Clean all undercoating, dirt and corrosion from the area around the sending unit and take out the cap screws or locking ring holding it in place. Locking rings are designed to be removed with a special wrench, but we have found that a large screwdriver laid across the ring will get enough bite to remove it. Remove the sending unit from the tank, and clean away all dirt and corrosion from its electrical connections and components. Working a safe distance from

the open gas tank, connect the sending unit to the gauge wire and to ground as you did with the test sender. Use a couple of long jumper wires for this. If the sending unit now operates the gauge normally, your cleanup did the trick. If not, you'll need a new unit. Before putting the unit back, you should get a new gasket from your car dealer. Sealer or gasket cement is unnecessary. Just put it on dry.

TEMPERATURE AND OIL PRESSURE GAUGES

If your car should be equipped with electrically-operated temperature and oil pressure gauges, the tests used on the fuel gauge should work on these as well. If their needles move to the maximum reading when the ignition is switched on, the trouble is poor ground contact, a faulty voltage limiter, or a shorted lead wire. A "zero" reading means broken or dirty electrical connections, a faulty voltage limiter, or a defective sending unit or gauge. If the gauge can be made to go from "zero" to "maximum" by disconnecting the wire from the sending unit and grounding it, the trouble is in the sending unit, which must therefore be inspected and cleaned or replaced as an assembly.

Electric gauges commonly used in modern cars work on the thermal principle. That is, voltage differences produce temperature changes in the gauge's mechanism which in turn move the needle. If the instrument panel loses its ground contact, the needles on the fuel, temperature, and oil pressure gauges may be forced far above their normal maximum dial readings. This may result in the permanent destruction of their accuracy. When a good ground is restored, the gauges will operate normally once again but at somewhat higher lev-

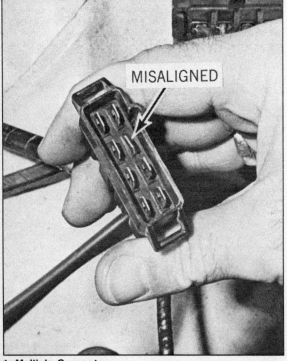

1. Multiple Connector

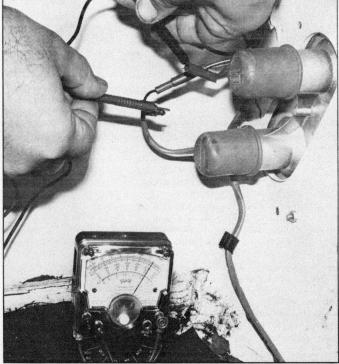

2. Testing Circuit

BELDEN AUTOMOTIVE PRIMARY WIRING SAFETY GUIDE

Total Approx. Circuit Amperes		Total Circuit Watts		Total Candle Power		Wire Gauge (For Length in Feet)											
6V	12V	6V	12V	6V	12V	3'	5'	7'	10'	15'	20'	25'	30'	40'	50'	75'	100'
0.5	1.0	3	12	3	6	18	18	18	18	18	18	18	18	18	18	18	18
0.75	1.5			5	10	18	18	18	18	18	18	18	18	18	18	18	18
1.0	2	6	24	8	16	18	18	18	18	18	18	18	18	18	18	16	16
1.5	3			12	24	18	18	18	18	18	18	18	18	18	18	14	14
2.0	4	12	48	15	30	18	18	18	18	18	18	18	18	16	16	12	12
2.5	5			20	40	18	18	18	18	18	18	18	18	16	14	12	12
3.0	6	18	72	25	50	18	18	18	18	18	18	16	16	16	14	12	10
3.5	7			30	60	18	18	18	18	18	18	16	16	14	14	10	10
4.0	8	24	96	35	70	.18	18	18	18	18	16	16	16	14	12	10	10
5.0	10	30	120	40	80	18	18	18	18	16	16	16	14	12	12	10	10
5.5	11			45	90	18	18	18	18	16	16	14	14	12	12	10	8
6.0	12	36	144	50	100	18	18	18	18	16	16	14	14	12	12	10	8
7.5	15			60	120	18	18	18	18	14	14	12	12	12	10	8	8
9.0	18	54	216	70	140	18	18	16	16	14	14	12	12	10	10	8	8
10	20	60	240	80	160	18	18	16	16	14	12	10	10	10	10	8	6
11	22	66	264	90	180	18	18	16	16	12	12	10	10	10	8	6	6
12	24	72	288	100	200	*18	18	16	16	12	12	10	10	10	8	6	6
15	30					18	16	16	14	10	10	10	10	10	6	4	4
20	40					18	16	14	12	10	10	8	8	6	6	4	2
25	50					16	14	12	12	10	10	8	8	6	6	2	0
50	100					12	12	10	10	6	6	4	4	4	2	1	0
75	150					10	10	8	8	4	4	2	2	2	1	00	00
100	200					10	8	8	6	4	4	2	2	2	1	0	4/0

*18 AWG indicated above this line could be 20 AWG electrically—18 AWG is recommended for mechanical strength.

3. Wiring Guide

1. Multiple connectors such as used on most cars today at the firewall are excellent places to make tests with a voltmeter in tracing wiring problems. The terminals themselves should be checked for any damage or corrosion as possible trouble-spots.

2. A voltmeter can be very useful for detection of any shorts or open circuits in the wiring. Test probes are inserted into a separate inline connecter here to see if the circuit is on or off, not to measure it.

3. This Belden wiring guide is a handy item to have when doing wiring and trying to figure out what gauge wire to use for a certain length.

els. If it's possible to "get inside" the individual gauges, you can usually restore their accuracy with a little judicious bending or—in the case of most imported cars—some careful fiddling with the calibration adjustments. If the gauges are "sealed units," then they'll have to be replaced.

Water temperature gauges that are connected by a long copper tube to a fitting in the engine's cylinder head are thermo-mechanical rather than electrical in operation. When the copper tube is broken, the gas or liquid it contains is lost and a new gauge—complete with tube and sensor—must be obtained. So long as their tube is not bent, dented or broken, these instruments are quite accurate and free of service problems.

Oil pressure gauges that actually have an oil line leading to them can eventually be rendered inoperative if the tube becomes plugged with sludge. It is usually possible to unplug these by simply disconnecting both ends of the line and blowing it out with compressed air.

AMMETERS

Ammeters are always made as sealed assemblies and cannot be repaired. Trouble—though seldom encountered on ammeters—is always shown by a constant zero reading. An operating ammeter will always show a discharge when the headlights are switched on and the engine is not running. Since ammeter failures are so rare, it is always advisable to check the wiring thoroughly before condemning or replacing the instrument itself.

SPEEDOMETER SERVICING

The speedometer head should be serviced only by an authorized agent. If you try to save a few bucks by working on it yourself, you'll probably end up paying twice the amount in fines for speeding. However, you can reduce the labor costs somewhat by removing and installing the unit yourself.

On some cars—including practically every import—the speedometer can be removed from the back of the dash. This is done by unscrewing the speedometer cable, disconnecting the illuminating light(s) and taking out the two screws holding the speedometer onto the rear of the panel. Most late-model American cars must have the instrument cluster taken out of the dash as described earlier, and the speedometer subsequently dismounted from the removed cluster.

With all the furor about the difficulty of repairing cars, many of the car makers are now designing speedometers and other instruments that come out the front of the dash, after a small piece of trim is removed. Look for these easy removal jobs before you start crawling under the instrument panel with a flashlight.

If the speedometer makes weird noises—particularly in winter—or if the needle jerks back and forth instead of producing a steady reading, the trouble is probably that the speedometer cable needs lubrication. A broken cable will prevent the speedometer (and odometer) from registering at all.

To remove the speedometer cable for lubrication or replacement, it is first disconnected from the back of the speedometer as outlined earlier. Once the retaining ring is unscrewed or unlatched from the speedometer it should be possible to pull the cable's flexible conduit from behind the instrument so that the cable itself may be withdrawn from it. If the cable is broken it may be necessary to remove the retaining ring that holds the conduit to the transmission housing and take the lower half of the cable out from that end. On some Oldsmobiles the speedometer is driven off the left front wheel. By removing the hub cap, the cable can be withdrawn from the center of the wheel spindle.

Use only an approved speedometer cable lubricant. Ordinary grease will become stiff in cold weather and liquify in summer. Apply the lubricant to only the first ¾ of the cable as you reinsert it into the conduit. Enough grease will rub off in the first part of the conduit to lubricate the remainder of the cable. When the cable reaches the transmission, it is

Lights, Gauges, Wiring

often necessary to rotate it several times before it engages the recess in the transmission's speedometer drive gear. Once the cable is in place the conduit should be reattached to the speedometer head and the car road tested to check its operation.

INDICATOR LIGHTS

When the ignition is switched to the "on" position, the oil, temperature, and generator lights should come on. If one fails to do so, the bulb and its connections should be checked to locate the trouble. If the generator light stays on after the engine is started, the charging system and the indicator light circuit should be checked.

A temperature indicator that continues to report a "cold" engine even after the car has been driven for several miles, or indicates a "hot" engine immediately after starting, probably has either a defective sending unit or a shorted wire between the sending unit and the indicator light.

Oil pressure indicators that come on and stay on while the engine is running should always be ample reason for turning off the engine and leaving it off until the trouble is pinpointed. Start by checking the oil level. If it's OK, the trouble may be only a dirty sending unit—or more serious, a defective lubrication system. Take the sending unit out and ex-

amine it. If the opening in the end is clogged with sludge, clean it and reinstall the unit on the engine. Start the engine briefly. If the light goes out, fine. If not, try a new sending unit. If it does not work, start checking the lubrication system.

Faulty sending units that fail to switch on the indicator light when the ignition is turned on can be spotted by taking the wire from their terminal and grounding it. If the lamp lights, try cleaning the sending unit. If it still does not function properly, replace it.

TACHOMETERS

Cable-driven tachometers are not used on American cars except Corvette and some Chevys that use Corvette distributors. In actual practice their cables are serviced and lubricated exactly as speedometer cables are, and again, as in the case of the speedometer, actual repair of the instrument itself should be trusted only to authorized service agencies. The "factory-option" tachometers commonly installed on U.S. cars are serviced only as complete units—which means if yours goes bad you'll have to buy a new one. However, those sold as add-on accessories—providing they are a well known and reputable brand—can usually be repaired by the maker. Their addresses can often be found by checking the ads in the better-known motoring magazines.

Probably the most common tachometer failures are those traceable to poor

connections. In some cases the tachometer's only ground contact is provided by a wire serving the instrument's dial-illuminating light. If its socket does not fit tightly, there may not be adequate contact. Poor ground potential is always the first thing to check for when an electric tachometer fails to operate. The actual test is made by touching a grounded jumper wire to the tachometer housing while the engine is running. If the tachometer proves to be properly grounded, its connections with the ignition switch, coil or distributor (depending on the car) should then be inspected for poor contact and repaired if found to be the problem.

CUSTOM GAUGES

Most custom gauge installations consist of an oil pressure and ammeter duo to replace the idiot lights. The oil pressure gauge is easy to hook up, with its plastic tube and brass fittings. The usual place for attaching the tube is at the sending unit for the idiot light. A surprising number of the ammeters in dual installations are never hooked up, because the wiring is difficult to figure out. The ammeter should be spliced or connected into the wire that conducts charging current to the battery. If the ammeter is going to read correctly, the electrical load of the car (everything electrical except the starter) must be connected to the same side of the ammeter that the generator connects. On a generator car, the connection can usually be made at the

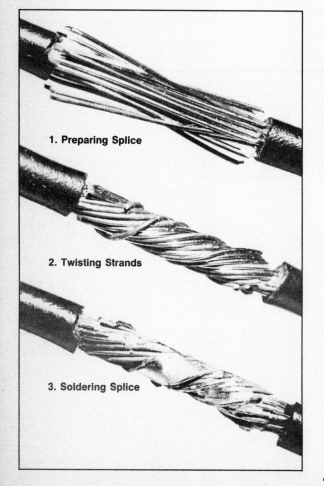

1. Preparing Splice

2. Twisting Strands

3. Soldering Splice

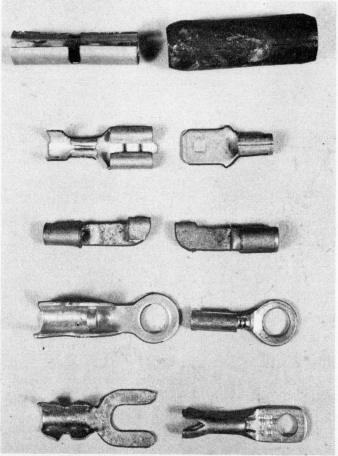

4. Solderless Terminals

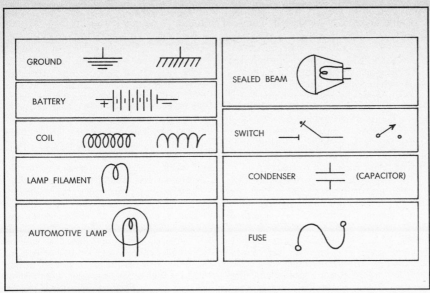

GROUND		SEALED BEAM	
BATTERY		SWITCH	
COIL		CONDENSER	(CAPACITOR)
LAMP FILAMENT		FUSE	
AUTOMOTIVE LAMP			

5. Wiring Diagram Symbols

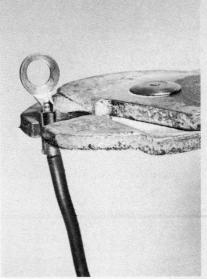

6. Crimping Solderless Terminal

1. Whether starting from scratch or just doing a repair, making good splices is important to trouble-free service. First step is to "skin" the wires. Then intersperse the strand tightly as shown here.

2. Second step in making a good splice is to twist the joined strands one or two complete turns.

3. Solder is applied from the tip of a hot iron so that it flows into twisted strands. Remove iron as soon as possible to avoid melting the insulation. Splice is then taped.

4. If you don't have access to a soldering gun or electrical outlet, then neat, simple solderless terminals like these are for you. They come in sizes for every gauge wire and type of connection desired.

5. These are some of the symbols used in wiring diagrams and what they stand for. Note the six cells in the battery, indicating it is a 12-volt. A 6-volt battery would have only three cells indicated.

6. Special pliers are used to crimp solderless terminals onto the wires.

starter solenoid. Alternators may require some extra wires to make the ammeter work right. Before buying an accessory ammeter, take the instructions out of the box and make sure you can understand the hookup. If the instructions are poorly written (as many are), then you'd better find a good automotive electrician.

Some of the more elaborate hot rod and custom car dashboards will sport such extras as a voltmeter, differential temperature, transmission temperature, head temperature and inside-outside air temperature gauges, an accelerometer and perhaps an altimeter. These should be installed and serviced according to the instructions and recommendations given by the instrument manufacturers.

TURN SIGNALS

The heart of any turn-signal system is the flasher with its regular beat. But it's a strange heart, because it stops working whenever a bulb burns out. Replace the bulb and the flasher will work again. The system is designed that way on purpose, so the driver will know he has a bulb burned out. The flasher depends on a certain amount of current flow to heat up a wire and cause the flasher points to separate. When the points separate, the circuit is broken, so the wire cools off and lets the points go together again. If a bulb is burned out, there will not be enough current flow to heat up the wire, so all the other bulbs on that side of the car will burn steadily, with no flasher action at all.

This type of flasher is designed with a specific load. It is made in different current-carrying capacities, according to the number of bulbs that need to be flashed on one side of the car. In the Tung-Sol brand, the first digit of the part number indicates the number of bulbs the flasher will operate on one side of the car (223 for two bulbs, or 322 for three bulbs). Signal-Stat doesn't have such an easy numbering system, but their specific-load flashers must still be selected for the number of bulbs on one side of the car.

Specific-load flashers can burn out easily, or their flashing rate will change if the wrong bulbs are installed in the turn signals. If you are having problems, check the flasher for the right part number, and look up the wattage of the bulbs you are using. Heavy-duty bulbs have a different current draw than standard bulbs, and that can goof up the flasher action, also. Heavy-duty, specific-load flashers are better made, but they still must be selected according to the number of bulbs.

Variable-load flashers, sometimes called heavy-duty, are wired differently so they will flash anywhere from one to six bulbs at the same flashing rate. Hazard warning flashers are the variable-load type and can be used on any car as long as the total number of bulbs on both sides of the car does not exceed the design capacity (usually six). Of course, you could put a hazard warning flasher in your turn signal circuit and it would work fine. But then you would never know when a bulb burned out, be-

cause the flasher would keep right on working.

Because the hazard warning system is a second source of electricity feeding the same bulbs, some strange feedback situations can occur, but they are nothing to worry about. In some cars you can have a lot of fun with your technically-minded friends by leaving the ignition switch off, turning on the radio and the hazard warning switch, then stepping on the brake pedal and listening to the radio play a song about Ralph Nader. Another peculiarity is that the hazard flashers won't work if you step on the brake. This also means that they won't work if the stoplight switch is maladjusted, so it is on all the time.

In the regular turn-signal system, the stoplights are tied in so that the stoplight on the side being flashed is disconnected by the turn-signal switch. The stoplight has to be turned off because the turn signal uses the same bulb. If it wasn't turned off, stepping on the brake would cancel the turn signal on the flashing side.

Older cars with a single turn-signal indicator light on the instrument panel use a 3-prong flasher. The third prong is connected to the indicator. Inside the flasher, a special relay feeds current to the indicator, flashing it just like the signal lights. The special relay has to be there to prevent a feedback that would flash all the lights instead of just those on one side, because the indicator light is grounded directly to the body of the car. The "P" terminal on 3-prong flashers is the one that goes to the indicator light.

Later cars with a single indicator light use a 2-prong flasher. They get away with it because the indicator light is grounded through the front turn-signal light on the opposite side from the one that is flashing. This produces the strange situation wherein you notice that the indicator light doesn't work when you signal to one side, and the signals don't flash at all when you signal to the other side, but the indicator light burns steadily. The problem is a burned out front bulb on the side that doesn't flash.

If your car has two indicator lights,

Lights, Gauges, Wiring

both right and left systems are separate, which eliminates all the strange symptoms mentioned above.

Many cars have the flasher on the fuse block. If you can't find it, turn the signals on and then start hunting for the noise. If your hand touches the flasher, you can feel the vibration of the relay. Luckily, most late-model cars have plug-in flashers, so you can unplug and replace the flasher behind the instrument panel strictly by feel, without ever seeing where it plugs in. Be sure to take your wristwatch off when you grope behind the instrument panel. A metal watch can cause a bad short, and you could even get a burned wrist for your trouble.

REWIRING

When building a hot rod, or when doing extensive rewiring on any car, all electrical components should be in place before you start stringing wire. This will allow you to cut all wires accurately to length and bind them into neat bundles with electrical tape.

The ends of all wires should be fitted with appropriate terminals and connectors. Merely wrapping the bare wire around the terminal screw is neither a neat nor a professional way to build a car. Furthermore, such haphazard connections will almost always produce trouble later on. A wide variety of automotive terminals and connectors are readily available from parts stores.

WIRING DIAGRAMS

It is almost impossible to do an intelligent job of tracing electrical malfunctions without a wiring diagram for the particular make and model car you are working on. In the past, wiring diagrams were often difficult even for most mechanics to read, since they included many symbols which—although meaningful to engineers and trained electricians—were practically incomprehensible to the average person who reads them. Nowadays, automotive wiring plans consist of more-or-less accurate pictures of the actual electrical components with lines drawn between them to indicate the interconnecting wires and circuits.

Chevrolet began a new system in their '72 shop manuals that does not have the lines drawn between units. Instead, each connection has a code number, with a corresponding number it is connected to another unit. Doing the wiring diagram this way eliminates the laborious process of drawing the lines (and also eliminates the foulups when the lines are drawn incorrectly). Maybe other manufacturers will adopt it, and the traditional wiring diagram with all the squiggly lines will disappear.

Each line or connection in most diagrams is labeled with a letter or number (or both) that indicates the color of the actual wire's insulation. If, for example, you wish to know which wire on the back of the ignition switch is connected to the ignition coil, you can quickly learn its color by checking on the diagram. If it indicates a *yellow* wire between these two units, you should be able to find it easily at the coil and on the ignition switch itself. Wires that are thought to have shorts or grounds can thus be located, disconnected at each end, and tested with a battery-operated test light or voltmeter to determine if trouble really exists.

Wiring diagrams also make it possible to determine what electrical components share common circuits. This makes it much easier to isolate trouble that is located in one component but is affecting other units as well. Wiring diagrams for your individual car can be obtained either from a factory shop manual or from one of the independently published books that deal with the repair of specific makes.

The best wiring diagrams we know of are put out by National Automotive Service, Dept. SP, P.O. Box 10465, San Diego, Calif. 92110. They take the factory diagrams and re-do them, correcting mistakes and rearranging the elements so that all units are in the same relative place in each diagram. They don't sell single diagrams, but they put out a repair manual each year that has all the diagrams for that year's cars, plus a lot of other info. Both Chilton and Motor also publish repair manuals, available at your local bookstore, but their wiring diagrams are in a separate book.

With the diagram's help—plus a few tools and some of the practical knowhow gained from this book—you should be able to keep your car's lights lit, horns tooting, and instruments registering accurately. What more could one ask for?

1. New type of wiring diagram used in '72 Chevrolet factory manuals has no lines between connections. Each connection can be identified with a number and letter. Take the horn, for instance (arrow). It is in circuit 29, which is the horn circuit. The number on its right shows: 12, the gauge of the wire; DG, dark green; and 16B, the location of the other end of the wire. Simple! This new system is designed to make it easier to read wiring diagrams.

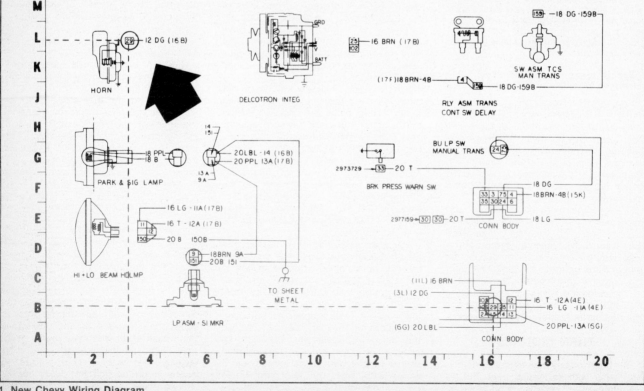

1. New Chevy Wiring Diagram

1. You'll have to pull the wheel if the directional signal cancellation mechanism doesn't work properly. Start by disconnecting the wiring harness.

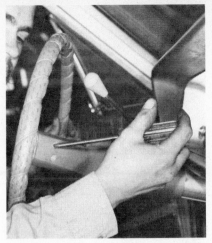

2. The horn actuator cap unit usually comes off when you remove the rear-mounted screws. Once these are free, the cap will just lift off.

3. A socket wrench and a bit of arm muscle are needed to remove nut before pulling wheel. This may be a bit hard if the wheel hasn't been off before.

4. With a wheel puller fitted in place, an ordinary open-end wrench makes the job of wheel removal a real snap; you can't get far without it.

5. After lifting the wheel off, carefully remove the tension spring on the horn contact, if there is one. You'll be sorry if you lose this little fellow.

6. Remove the large spring on the shaft and the switch actuator plate beneath it will just lift up and off, thus revealing the signal mechanism.

7. The underside of the actuator plate shows the switch canceling lobes. And the circular brass plate that you see is a contact ring for the horn.

8. Three screws hold the directional mechanism in place, but the screw that holds the signal operating lever must come out first.

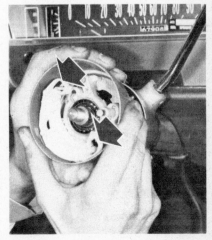

9. Mechanism now lifts out. Two screws separate it from horn assembly on right side. Plastic arms (arrows) operate with the actuator and often break.

Fuel System

It's unfortunate that the carburetor is up on top of the engine, because in that position it's too easy for everybody to fiddle with. Most so-called carburetion problems are caused by ignition timing, spark plugs, loss of compression, inadequate fuel delivery to the carburetor, or maybe even a clogged air cleaner element. The carburetor itself rarely gives much trouble in normal operation.

Spark plugs, coil, distributor, engine compression, engine vacuum, anf fuel delivery should all be checked before you tear into that carburetor. Not that carburetors can't cause trouble. It's just that carburetor trouble usually comes on slowly from an accumulation of dirt. Breakdowns and other malfunctions that occur suddenly like a thunderstorm in the middle of a big blue sky are not usually caused by the carburetor itself.

Carburetors have so few moving parts that there really isn't much in them that can wear out. The throttle shaft or the accelerating pump are probably the biggest offenders in the wear department. The throttle shaft wears from the pressure of the throttle return spring and lets air into the engine where it shouldn't be, or at least not very much of it. The accelerating pump plunger wears out and doesn't squirt as much as it should, causing a flat spot when the driver steps on the gas.

The rest of the carburetor doesn't have any significant wear points, but it has about a jillion points where it can get dirty. If you have trouble with your carburetor, the chances are about a hundred to one that it's caused by foreign matter reaching the carburetor through the air or through the fuel, or by gummy fuel deposits.

Did you ever drive a car that stalled at every signal? Maybe you've known of a car that lost power when it got up to cruising speed, or maybe you know somebody whose car billows black smoke out of the tailpipe as he drives down the street. Those things can be caused by dirt trapped in the carburetor.

The dirt or foreign matter may be rust particles that slough off the sides of the gas tank, or dust in the air that is inside the tank. When the dirt is carried up to the carburetor by the fuel, it means trouble. Airborne dirt gets lodged in the air bleeds and passages, upsetting the balance between air and fuel that the carburetor is made to control.

And even if you had a perfectly clean atmosphere for your engine to operate in, with hygienically clean gasoline and a scrubbed fuel system, you would still have a dirty carburetor in time because of the way gasoline evaporates. Not all the substances that make up gasoline will readily pass into the air and turn into smog. The heavier fractions of gasoline turn to a kind of gooey mess which eventually hardens about the same as a good brand of household glue.

So dirt is the primary enemy of the carburetor. A good tune-up man's carburetor work consists mostly of disassembly, cleaning, and reassembly, without making any adjustments at all. This is true even when he replaces parts, such as accelerating pumps and needle seats. The old and the new parts go back into the same positions, so that all he has to do is make careful checks of specifications.

However, there is one other cause of trouble in carburetors that has plagued good tune-up men since the first carburetor popped and sputtered into life. That cause is the inept workman. Call him backyard mechanic, peppertree mechanic, garage mechanic, tune-up expert, or just plain car owner. It doesn't matter what his title is or where he works. If the man working on the carburetor has

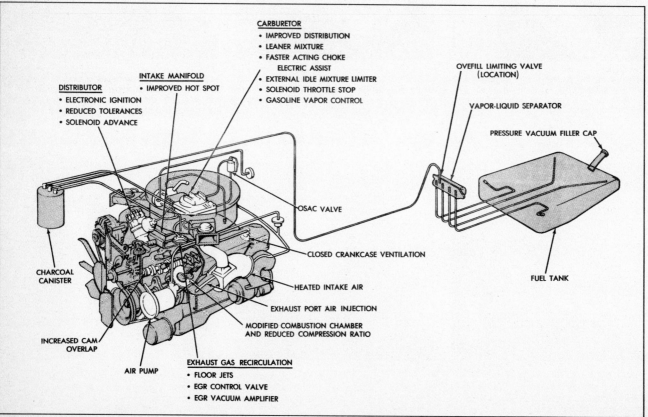

DISTRIBUTOR
- ELECTRONIC IGNITION
- REDUCED TOLERANCES
- SOLENOID ADVANCE

INTAKE MANIFOLD
- IMPROVED HOT SPOT

CARBURETOR
- IMPROVED DISTRIBUTION
- LEANER MIXTURE
- FASTER ACTING CHOKE ELECTRIC ASSIST
- EXTERNAL IDLE MIXTURE LIMITER
- SOLENOID THROTTLE STOP
- GASOLINE VAPOR CONTROL

OVEFILL LIMITING VALVE (LOCATION)

VAPOR-LIQUID SEPARATOR

PRESSURE VACUUM FILLER CAP

OSAC VALVE

CLOSED CRANKCASE VENTILATION

CHARCOAL CANISTER

HEATED INTAKE AIR

EXHAUST PORT AIR INJECTION

MODIFIED COMBUSTION CHAMBER AND REDUCED COMPRESSION RATIO

FUEL TANK

INCREASED CAM OVERLAP

AIR PUMP

EXHAUST GAS RECIRCULATION
- FLOOR JETS
- EGR CONTROL VALVE
- EGR VACUUM AMPLIFIER

1. Chrysler Emission Controls

not taken the time to learn a little bit about how it operates, then he is going to cause trouble not only for himself, but for every mechanic thereafter who tries to undo his well meaning but fumbling fingers.

Trying to correct malfunctions can take an awful lot of time if you don't know what you're doing. You could spend days taking a carburetor apart, putting it back together, running the car and then going back through the same procedure all over again, simply because when you get the carburetor apart you don't know what to look for.

Other malfunctions cannot be seen, but once you know how a carburetor works all you have to do is stop, look, and listen, because the carburetor is trying to tell you something if you have the knowledge to understand it.

Now let's take a look at what makes the carburetor the smoothly operating mechanism that it is, with quick descriptions of the six basic systems.

1. Emission Controls for 1973 are the most complicated yet. This is Chrysler Corporation's latest.

2. This little beauty is mounted on the intake manifold of '72-'73 Buicks. It lets exhaust gas recirculate into manifold at throttle openings above idle.

3. Six-cylinder GM engines have two electric gadgets for '72-'73. Upper one is familiar CEC valve. Its stem (1) is for CEC valve setting. Solenoid body (2) is turned to set curb idle.

4. There's no normal throttle cracking screw on '72-'73 GM 6-cylinder engines. "Solenoid off" idle speed is set with an allen wrench in end of solenoid.

5. Pushing on the needle for any reason is verboten. The rubber tip of the needle can easily be compressed out of shape.

6. Fuel flows into the bowl past the needle whenever the float drops enough to let the needle come off the seat.

2. Buick Exhaust Gas Recirculator

3. Rochester 6-Cyl. Carburetor

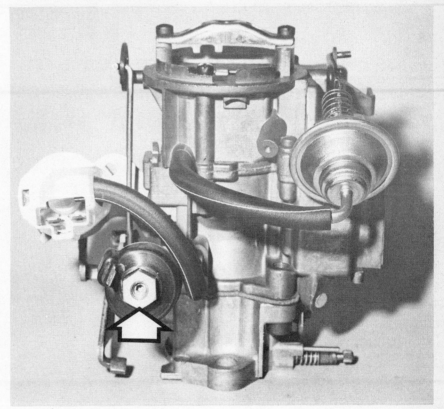
4. Low Speed Idle Adjustment

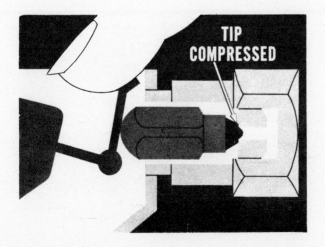
TIP COMPRESSED

5. Don't Do This

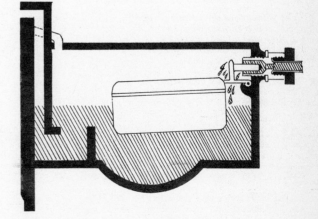
6. Float System With Needle Open

Fuel System

FLOAT SYSTEM

Fuel enters the carburetor through the inlet seat and fills the float bowl. The fuel rises in the bowl, lifting the float, which pushes the needle into the seat and regulates the flow of gasoline.

The object is to keep the fuel in the bowl at just the right level. Too much, and the engine will run rich. Too little fuel in the bowl and the engine will run lean, maybe even coughing back through the carburetor. Sometimes the coughing back results in a flame that's about 3 ft. long shooting from the air horn. You only have to see that once to have a lot of respect for a carburetor that's being run without an air cleaner. At the very least you will make sure it's not pointed in your direction.

To adjust the fuel lever, you bend an arm on the float or bend a little tab that is attached to the arm and pushes on the needle. The "float level" specification is a measurement from some part of the carburetor casting to the float, when the float is resting on a closed needle. If the float is attached to the bowl cover then the measurement is taken between the float and cover, with the cover inverted so that the weight of the float closes the needle.

If the float is attached to the bowl itself then the measurement is taken from the top of the float to the top edge of the bowl, with the float and needle in the closed position, of course. To get the needle and float into the closed position on this type of float system, you might

1. Float system with a horizontal needle. A vertical needle works better. The tube at upper left is an internal bowl vent which raises pressure above the fuel when the engine is running at speed.

2. Float level is the only internal adjustment on a Holley. The measurement is made at the location shown, but it differs with other models of carburetors, so you should check your shop manual for correct specifications.

3. Float adjustment on a Holley 4-bbl. is made with a screwdriver. The entire seat assembly is threaded, and can be screwed up or down to change position of the float.

4. On some carbs you can actually check the wet fuel level, as on this Holley 1-bbl. Economizer diaphragm is removed to provide a hole for scale.

5. Main metering system has several functions. Note that end of main nozzle is in middle of narrowest part of venturi, where the suction is greatest. This is single-venturi carb.

6. Main nozzle is sometimes called main discharge tube. Holes in tube bleed air into fuel to help atomize it.

7. Suction in the venturi pulls fuel out of the nozzle. Actually, it's the pressure on the fuel in the bowl that pushes the fuel out of the nozzle.

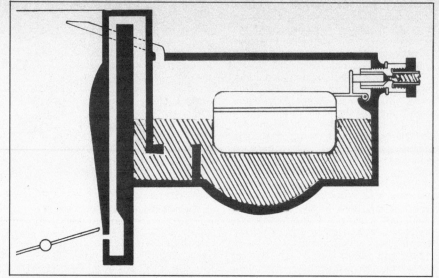
1. Float System With Needle Closed

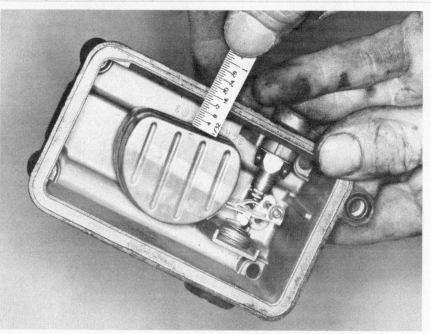
2. Checking Float Level

3. Adjusting Holley Float Level

push the float and needle closed with your finger—but don't

That was OK in the old days when we had steel needles, but now there are teflon-tipped needles, neoprene-tipped needles, and teflon or neoprene inlet seats. These needles and seats will last a long time with only the pressure of the float against them, but the pressure of your finger pushing on the needle may be too much, and you will end up with a groove in the neoprene. The neoprene will slowly come back to shape, eliminating the groove so that a few hours later the float level has changed from where you set it. If the neoprene or teflon does not come back to shape, the groove may cause flooding because it provides a place for particles of dirt to lodge.

To get the float and needle into the closed position on a carburetor with the float attached to the bowl, invert the carburetor and take the measurement. With the carburetor on the car, the easiest way to do it is to pour some gasoline into the bowl until the float rises to its maximum height, then take the measurement. There is usually a tolerance on float adjustments and a good mechanic will adjust to one end or the other of the tolerance because he knows a particular carburetor will run best with that setting.

It's important that you don't confuse fuel level and float level. Float level is a measurement from the float to some part of the carburetor bowl or the cover. Fuel level is an actual wet measurement of how far the fuel is from the top of the bowl. If the float needle and seat are

attached to the bowl, then the actual fuel level can be measured with a scale. If the float needle and seat are attached to the bowl cover, then the fuel level cannot be measured in most cases unless the carburetor manufacturer has provided sight holes in the end of the bowl. The fuel level specification, if given, is really nothing more than a double check to be sure you have set the float level correctly and accurately.

When the engine uses fuel and the float drops, it is possible on some carburetors that the needle could fall out of the seat. If this happened the carburetor would receive just a little more gas than it needs. The engine would be flooded, not only on the inside but probably on the outside.

To keep all of that from happening there is a little tab on the back side of the float that limits the drop. The float drop measurement is taken with the bowl cover off the carburetor. Hold the cover in the normal position and measure from the underside of the bowl cover to the float.

If the float is attached to the bowl itself, there usually is no float drop measurement. The float in that case may be designed so that at maximum drop it rests on the bottom of the bowl.

If by some chance the little tab that limits float drop has become bent, then the float may not drop enough. In this case the needle will not pull away from the seat far enough, and you might have fuel starvation at wide open throttle.

Dirt, as mentioned, is a big enemy of

the float system. If it weren't for dirt there probably wouldn't be any need for all the fancy filters that we have on cars nowadays. The needle and seat are so sensitive to dirt that the smallest particle can cause flooding. This is the reason for using teflon or neoprene seats and needles. The theory is that teflon or neoprene has enough give to it that it will conform to the shape of the speck of dirt and seat around it. Sometimes it does, sometimes it doesn't.

If a particle of foreign matter should cause the needle valve to leak, then enough fuel can be pumped into the engine to kill it, and make restarting almost impossible until the excess fuel evaporates. If you ever see a carburetor that is all beat up around the needle and seat area, it's a good bet that the driver was standing there beating on the carburetor trying to jar a piece of dirt out of the seat so the flooding would stop.

You can see that keeping the fuel at the right level is very important. We'll find out why when we go into the main metering system.

MAIN METERING SYSTEM

Now that we have the float bowl full of gasoline, the next step is to get this gas mixed with air and feed it into the engine. The base of every carburetor is really nothing more than an air valve with throttle plates hung on a shaft controlled by your foot. Wide open throttle means just that. When you step on the gas you are opening the throttle valve so that the

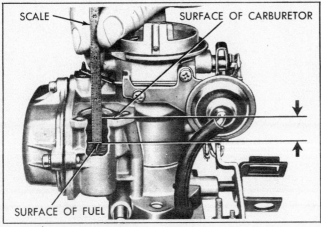

4. Checking Wet Fuel Level

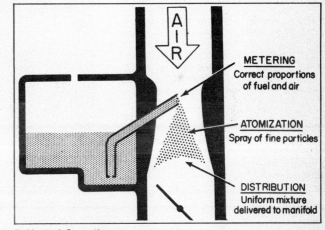

5. Venturi Operation

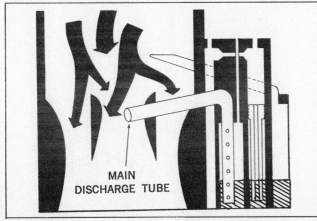

6. Main Nozzle

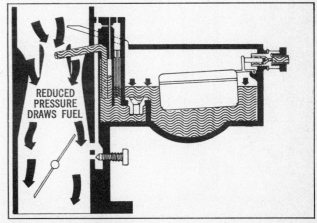

7. Main Metering System

Fuel System

maximum amount of air can enter the engine. But in order for the engine to run, this air has to have gasoline mixed with it in the right proportion. This is done by running a tube from the float bowl ending in the middle of the air stream where it goes through the carburetor. The end of the tube, called the main nozzle, is positioned so that it is in the center of the venturi, a narrow section of the air passage through the carburetor. Because this section is narrow, it causes reduced pressure at the end of the tube, and this reduced pressure or suction draws fuel from the float bowl where it mixes with the air, then goes past the throttle valve and on to the combustion chamber. The tube begins in a well at the bottom of the float bowl called the main well. Fuel enters the main well through a calibrated hole called the main jet, which is located at the bottom of the float bowl so that during all types of engine operation it will always be submerged and able to draw fuel.

The main metering system has had many refinements since the first simple carburetor was made. There may be air bleeds or little baffles in the main nozzle and there may be vacuum or mechanically operated metering rods in the main jet. The object of all the refinements is to be sure that the engine receives more fuel when it needs it and less fuel when it doesn't.

Metering rods are designed so that they stay in the main jet when the engine is running at low power. But when the engine is running at maximum power, the rods will lift out of the jet so that the engine gets the fuel that it needs. At any point between closed throttle and maximum power, the rods will be partially in or partially out of the jet, according to how much fuel the engine needs at the time.

Mechanically operated rods are lifted by a lever hooked to the throttle. Vacuum-operated rods are pushed out of the jet by a spring and pulled down into the jet by engine vacuum acting on a piston hooked to the top of the rod. A passageway from the intake manifold

runs up through the carburetor so the engine vacuum can act on the piston.

Without engine vacuum the carburetor wouldn't work. This vacuum exists below the throttle valves when the engine is running, and at idle on a good engine is about 18-21 ins. As the throttle is opened, engine vacuum drops off until there is zero vacuum at wide open.

It's rare to have a main metering system plug up completely unless it was done deliberately for a test of mechanics, such as the Plymouth Trouble-Shooting Contest. If the main nozzle was plugged, but the main jet still open, the carburetor would idle perfectly, but gasp and die completely the second the throttle was opened. However, if the driver got his foot out of it quick enough, the idle system would take over again and the car would come down to idle perfectly.

We have to have an idle system, because at idle the throttle valves are almost completely closed and there is not enough flow of air through the venturi to draw fuel out of the main nozzle. Now let's see how the idle system does its job.

THE IDLE SYSTEM

At idle the engine is drawing air around the throttle plate, which is just barely open, but this air has no fuel in it. The fuel is coming through the idle port hole in the throttle body below the throttle plate. An idle mixture needle screws into the outside of the throttle body and is used to regulate the amount of fuel flowing through the port and into the engine.

Fuel enters the idle system through a tube which is mounted in the carburetor,

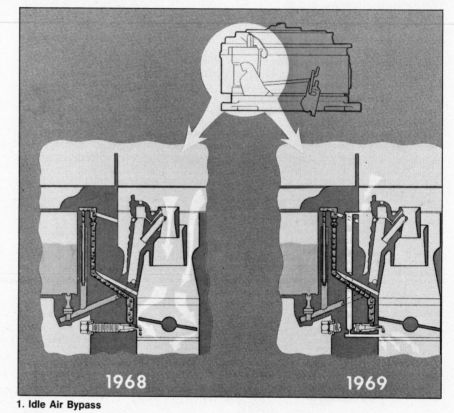

1968   **1969**

1. Idle Air Bypass

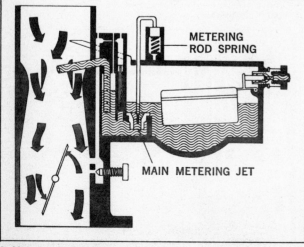

METERING
ROD SPRING

MAIN METERING JET

2. Metering Rod System

IDLE AIR BY-PASS
ADJ. SCREW

LOW
SPEED
PASSAGE

PICK-UP
PORT

IDLE
PORT

DISCHARGE
PORT

BODY CAVITY

3. Adjustable Idle Air Bypass

usually between the float bowl and the carburetor throat. The end of the tube is a calibrated hole, called the idle jet. Fuel comes up through this tube, makes a U-turn, picks up some air through air bleed holes, then goes through a long passage to exit underneath the throttle plate. Some idle tubes can be changed merely by unscrewing them, but others are part of the metering cluster and the whole cluster must be changed in that case.

As the throttle is opened, the high vacuum beneath the throttle plates starts to fall off and fuel flow lessens through the idle port. To keep the engine from faltering at this crucial moment, another hole called the idle transfer is uncovered which feeds more fuel to keep the engine going. By this time enough air is coming through the venturi that the main metering system will start to take over. However, in most carburetors the idle system will continue to feed even up to as high as 70 mph.

It's important to keep clear in your mind that the engine idles on air from two sources and fuel from one. Air goes into the engine around the partially opened throttle plate, and a fuel and air mixture enters through the idle port, controlled by an idle mixture screw. The screw is spring-loaded, and you control the idle mixture by setting the screw.

Engine idle speed is something else. You control that with a spring-loaded screw on the throttle shaft. When the

1. In 1968, Oldsmobile used a Quadrajet that cracked the throttle plate for idle air. In 1969, they allowed the throttle plate to close completely, and idle air came through an adjustable bypass.

2. Metering rod is hooked to a piston and spring, with engine vacuum acting on the piston. Any fuel that flows out the main nozzle has to go through the main jet first.

3. If idle air is supplied through a bypass, the throttle plates can be allowed to close almost completely at idle. This helps to prevent carbon formation in the throttle bores, which causes erratic idling.

4. Note how the idle tube picks up fuel from within the main well. Some late-model carburetors designed for emission control have the idle tube outside the main well.

5. In this type of spring-operated accelerating pump, it doesn't matter how fast you step on the gas—the spring itself is what pushes the pump plunger down.

6. The "duration spring" is actually an override spring that prevents everything from bending if the driver shoves his foot down too fast. The discharge check ball usually has a spring or a weight to help prevent fuel from being drawn into the venturi at high speed.

7. Little lever opens the bowl vent whenever the throttle linkage is at the idle position. Bowl vent is really not part of idle system, but it prevents rich running at idle (and hard starting) by venting fumes.

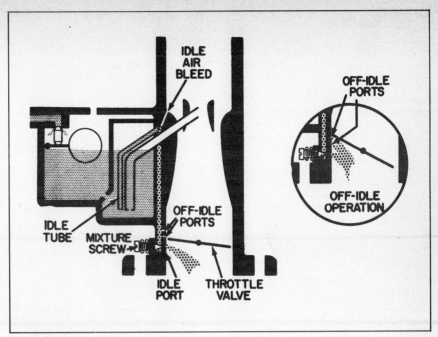
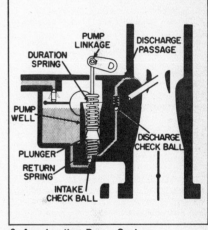

4. Idle System

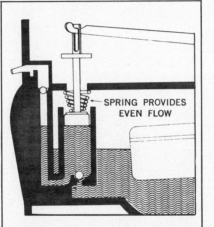

5. Accelerating Pump Duration Spring

6. Accelerating Pump System

7. Bowl Vent Lever

Fuel System

driver takes his foot off the gas, the throttle will close down to the setting you have made with the idle speed screw. If you have made the wrong setting and the throttle closes too much, the engine will die. If the screw holds the throttle open too far, then the driver is going to have to put both feet on the brake to keep the car from driving down the street at a 40-mph idle speed.

So far, we have a carburetor that will cruise and idle, but what happens when we really step on the gas? It will fall flat on its face. To cure the problem we need an accelerating pump.

ACCELERATING PUMP SYSTEM

If we open the throttle suddenly on an engine, the air reacts instantly and rushes past the throttle blades, but the

1. Accelerating pump on the AFB is adjusted for more or less stroke by bending the pump link.

2. Only one screw holds the Holley accelerating pump cam, but it can be put in two different positions to control the length of the stroke. Cam is hidden behind throttle lever.

3. Holley accelerating pump outlet check is under the pump nozzle. Many carbs have a removable nozzle with a needle or ball check under it.

4. When manifold vacuum is high and during closed or partly closed throttle, the power valve piston is held up off the valve.

5. As the throttle is opened, vacuum drops and the spring opens the power valve to allow extra fuel into the main well.

6. Here the power valve and power piston are separate. In the power valve the top hole that the plunger sticks through is merely the entrance for the fuel. The calibrated holes are the ones on the side just above the threads.

fuel coming out of the main nozzle takes a little while before it catches up. During this period the engine will run lean and stumble. The problem is solved by using an accelerating pump. It's nothing more than a piston hooked to the throttle linkage and operating in a cylinder so that every time we step on the gas a squirt of fuel goes into each throat on the carburetor. The pump only squirts when the throttle is moved. At all other times it does not feed any gas but just sits there

waiting until the time when you put your foot down.

The pump system includes an inlet check valve and an outlet check valve so that it can suck fuel into its cylinder from the bowl on the upstroke and then squirt this fuel into the carburetor throat on the downstroke.

Some pumps are not directly operated by the throttle linkage but *allowed* to operate by the linkage. They have a duration spring that actually pushes the

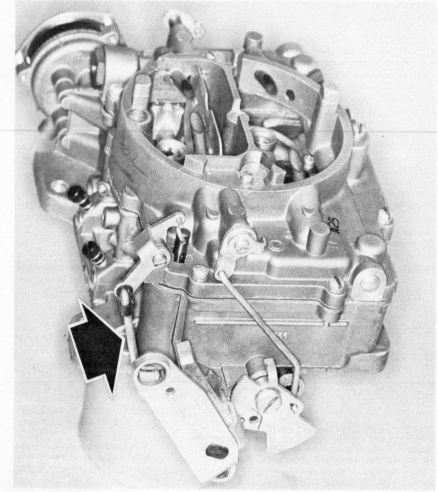

1. Pump Arm Adjustment

2. Holley Pump Cam Adjustment

3. Holley Pump Check Valve

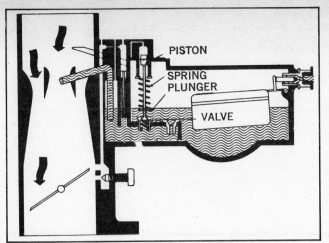

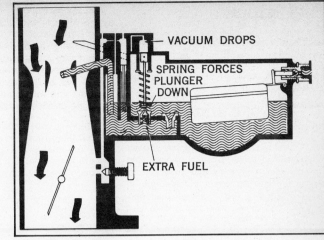

4. Power Valve Closed

5. Power Valve Open

pump down. This is done so that the length of time that the pump is operating is always the same, no matter how fast the driver opens the throttle.

The well known "flat spot" on acceleration is usually caused by something wrong in the accelerating pump. Most of the time it is a pump piston that doesn't fit well in its cylinder, either because the piston is worn out or because it is made of leather and the lip of the leather curled up when the piston was installed. Or it could be maladjusted linkage, so that the pump stroke is too long or too short.

The jet that controls the amount of squirt on an accelerating pump is usually built into the pump nozzle, mounted above the venturi. In an extreme case, that defies the best efforts to correct the trouble, it is possible to drill out the pump jet for a little more squirt, so you won't have that sickening feeling of nothing happening when you mash your foot down to the floor.

With the system so far described, our carburetor will work fine, until we get up to wide open throttle. Then the engine needs more fuel than is admitted by the main jet. To let this fuel in we must have what is called the power system.

POWER SYSTEM

Main metering jets with or without metering rods work fine above idle at almost any cruising speed but when the engine is really called to put out, with the throttle wide open, the main jet just doesn't let enough fuel in. In order to admit more fuel, there is another passage into the main well and up into the main nozzle. This passage is closed at all times except when the throttle is opened enough to allow engine vacuum to fall below about 10 ins. At that point a spring opens the power valve and additional fuel is allowed to enter the main well, go through the main nozzle and into the venturi.

Power valves can be vacuum or mechanically controlled. Some Stromberg carburetors have the power valve at the bottom of the accelerating pump cylinder so that when the throttle is open wide and the accelerating pump bottoms, it tips a little plunger opening the power

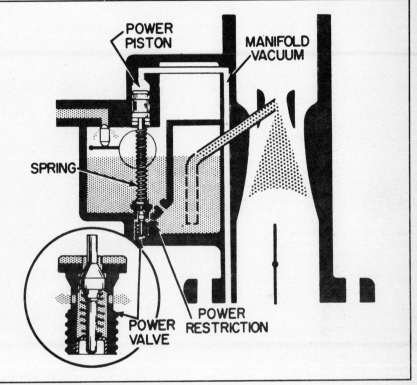

6. Power System

valve. Other power valves operate off engine vacuum opposed by a spring, and they can be either a piston operating in a cylinder or a diaphragm.

The unfortunate thing about a power valve is that you may not know if it is bad until it is too late. If a power valve should fail in the closed position, the engine would not get the fuel it needs at wide-open throttle, and it might even run lean enough to burn a hole in a piston, depending on how long you ran the engine wide open.

Luckily, vacuum-operated power valves are held closed by engine vacuum, and opened by a spring. So if they fail, they usually fail open, allowing a lot of fuel to go into the engine at all speeds above idle, and in some designs even allowing fuel to dribble out onto the top of the engine, which is good if the driver pays attention to the smell of gasoline. Of course it's not so good if somebody starts lighting matches in your engine compartment.

HIGH SPEED PULLOVER

Main jets must be lean on late models to cut down on emissions. Unfortunately, the main system is so lean that there isn't enough fuel supplied under a high-rpm, part-throttle condition. At part throttle, the metering rod hasn't lifted to the high speed step because engine vacuum hasn't dropped low enough. But the engine needs more fuel because of the high rpm. Rochester carburetors provide this extra fuel with a pullover system, which consists of a passageway from the float bowl up to the air horn, exiting above the choke valve. There is usually one hole for each carburetor throat. Because of their position, these holes are sensitive to air velocity. Any time there is high air velocity through the carburetor, as at high rpm, the pullover holes feed additional fuel into the airstream. Pullover starts at about 50 mph on part throttle. Pullover is also called High Speed Fuel Feed, or Auxiliary Fuel Feed.

Fuel System

Now with all of the systems we have described so far we have a carburetor that will really run. There is only one thing wrong, it won't start. For this we have to have a choke system.

CHOKE SYSTEM

If an engine could be heated up to operating temperature before you started it, you would never need a choke. This is one reason why people who live in California with its warm climate can in many cases take the choke off their carburetors and never have any trouble. But if they had to live in the Midwest or in the East through one winter, they would find out just what a choke is for.

A cold engine is just that. It is so cold that the fuel condenses out of the mixture onto the intake manifold passageways and the walls of the combustion chamber.

Fuel alone will not burn. It has to be mixed with air. The only way we can get a mixture on a cold engine is to feed more fuel into the engine than we need to make up for the fuel that condenses. The choke is an air valve placed above the main nozzle, so that it can shut off all the air going to the engine. This allows the full force of engine suction to operate on the main nozzle so the engine gets the fuel it needs.

The problem with chokes is not in making them work but in getting them to shut off (open) at the right time. The choke is closed by a thermostatic spring and opened by this same spring when heat from the exhaust manifold allows it to relax. However, the spring control alone is not enough. To get a more positive control there is a vacuum piston that opposes the strength of the spring, and the choke valve itself is offset so

that the air entering the carburetor tends to push it open. When it all works right we have what is called an automatic choke, instead of the old fashioned manual choke that the driver had to remember to open himself. When it doesn't work we have a big problem, and the engine will lope and blow black smoke out the tailpipe.

Sticking chokes have been so much of a problem that now some carburetor manufacturers are coating their choke shafts with teflon. It seems to work, although the adjustment of a choke will

probably continue to be a touchy problem for some time.

UNLOADER

Nobody should ever go to wide open throttle on an engine while it is cold, but some drivers will. Other drivers will very absentmindedly pump the throttle when trying to start the engine, thus flooding it. Both of these conditions are taken care of by the choke unloader. It's a little tang that opens the choke enough to clean out the engine when the throttle is pushed to wide open position.

1. High-speed pullover holes in '72 Rochester 2-bbl. are shown with carb top inverted, but they can easily be seen on car by removing air cleaner.

2. Rochester 2-bbl. carbs used on Vega in '71 and later had a different power valve: gravity operated; no springs, just a weighted needle. Early models had metering passage built into carb.

3. Late Vega 2-bbls. use power valve with metering at inlet orifice. Shake valve and you can hear weight rattle.

4. The choke system is a balancing of forces. The offset choke valve, the vacuum piston, and the heat from the stove all tend to open the choke, while the thermostatic coil spring is attempting to close it.

5. Well-type chokes do have an adjustment, but it is usually only a setting made at the factory.

6. Exposed spring on Rochester carbs is choke closing assist spring. It ensures full closing of the choke.

7. Choke springs are getting extremely sophisticated. Hidden under this cap (arrow) is a bucking spring (2-bbl. GM models) that works against choke coil spring for precise choke opening.

1. High-Speed Pullover Holes

2. Gravity Power Valve.

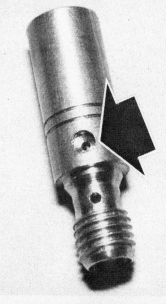

3. Power Valve Metering Hole

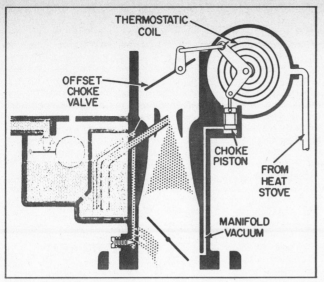

4. Choke System

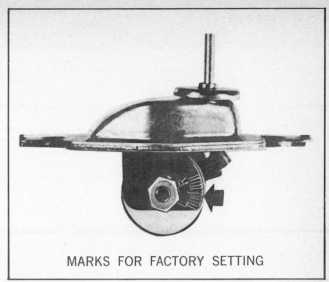

MARKS FOR FACTORY SETTING

5. Well-Type Choke

FAST IDLE

While the choke is operating, the engine can't use the extremely rich mixture unless it is run at a faster than normal idle. To accomplish this we have a fast idle cam and linkage that works in conjunction with the choke to raise the idle speed any time the choke is operating.

MULTIPLE BARREL CARBS

All of the systems described so far have pertained to a carburetor in its simplest form, but we haven't said anything about the number of barrels or throats on the carburetor.

Most engines from one cylinder up to six cylinders have a carburetor with only one throat. In that case there is only one of each carburetor system. Some 6-cylinder and some V-8 engines come with a 2-throat carburetor. In that case, the main metering system and the idle system are duplicated for the second throat.

The float system does not have to be duplicated because the bowl has enough fuel capacity to serve two main jets with ease. The same reasoning applies in the accelerating pump system. One pump is used, but it has two nozzles, one for each throat.

The power system also stays basically the same as in a 1-bbl. carb, except that it feeds two main metering systems instead of one. In the choke department there isn't much change either; they just make the choke valve big enough to cover both carburetor throats.

When we go beyond two barrels, however, there are some real differences. In a 4-bbl. carburetor the two barrels that the engine runs on normally are called the primaries. The extra two barrels only operate at high engine speed, when most needed.

As mentioned before, the carburetor is really nothing more than an air valve. At idle the air valve or throttle is closed because the engine doesn't need much air. As the engine goes faster it needs more air, or we might say that if the engine gets more air it will go faster.

At low speeds around town only a small throttle opening is needed to make

6. Rochester Choke Assist Spring

7. Rochester Bucking Spring

Fuel System

the engine do its job. When we get out on the highway we open the throttle and we go faster, up to the point of wide open throttle. But the engine won't go as fast as it is capable of running because it isn't getting enough air.

It's like the nozzle on the end of a garden hose. You open it up all the way, but you still don't get enough water. The only solution is to get a bigger nozzle.

To solve this problem the 4-bbl. carburetor was invented. The engine runs around town at low speeds on the primary barrels, but when we get out on the highway and really want to go, all we have to do is step on the gas and the secondary barrels open up. Then we have all the air the engine needs and away we go.

Admittedly, the job could have been done with a larger carburetor, eliminating all the complicated vacuum and mechanical controls that operate secondaries, but in that case there is a problem with driver education. An engine needs just the right amount of air to do its job. With a large carburetor the driver has to have an educated foot, and open the throttle just the right amount so that the engine doesn't get so much air that it gasps and wheezes. A 4-bbl. with primaries and secondaries is the only an-

swer, because it gives the driver more positive control of his car.

There is no general rule about what systems feed the secondary barrels. Of course there is a main metering system, but there may be a power system or even an idle system. It all depends on what problems faced the designer and how he went about solving them.

Secondaries can be either vacuum or mechanically controlled, with maybe a velocity valve to boot. Mechanically controlled secondaries start to open when the primaries reach about ¾ throttle. The secondaries open at a faster rate, so that all four barrels reach wide open at the same time.

It is possible, on mechanically controlled secondaries, for the driver to open the throttle wide at a low speed when the engine doesn't need all that air. To correct this mistake, there is usually an air valve or velocity valve in the secondary barrels above the throttle

valve. The air valve does not open until there is a sufficient rush of air past it to raise a weight or compress a spring. Of course the only time we have sufficient airflow is when the engine is going fast, which is the only time we need the secondaries anyway.

Vacuum-controlled secondaries do not have this problem. They are controlled by either manifold vacuum or venturi vacuum, so they open only when the engine needs the extra air, regardless of what the driver does or what he wants the car to do.

Now we have a carburetor that will work under just about any engine condition but there are other features that have been added to make it work a little bit better.

CARBURETOR HEAT

If you do a lot of driving around town, you need a heated intake manifold to im-

1. With the engine at normal operating temperature and curb idle, the cam is placed in this position to set the fast idle speed to the specified rpm. Specifications and adjusting techniques vary on every carburetor, so be sure you work from the right instruction sheet.

2. Holley 4-bbl. fast idle is adjusted by bending this little arm that rests on the fast idle cam.

3. Screw at arrow on the 4300 is for fast idle adjustment only.

4. On this Rochester BV, as on some other carburetors, there is no separate fast idle screw. If the idle speed screw is set correctly, then the fast idle cam will determine the fast idle speed, providing the choke rod has been set to specifications. The choke rod is shortened or legthened by bending.

5. The famous (or infamous) link and slot on the Holley 4-barrel. It's a safety feature, designed to positively close the vacuum-operated secondaries if they should stick open. Accessory manufacturers have made all kinds of gadgets to link the primaries and secondaries together, using this slot and removing the vacuum diaphragm (or creating a leak so it doesn't work). Some of the gadgets don't work very well.

6. Holley 4150 has a thick metering block between the bowl and the main body on each side of the carb. This model has fully mechanical secondaries, with a separate accelerating pump for both primary and secondary.

7. This slotted machine screw goes in this position only, when replacing the bowl cover on the 4300.

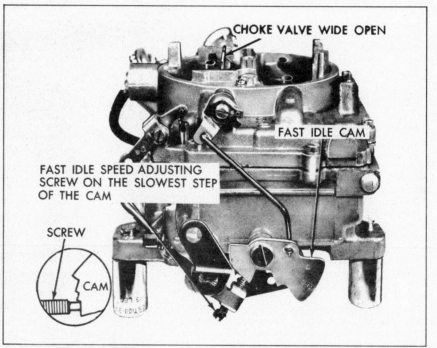

1. AFB Fast Idle Adjustment

2. Holley Fast Idle Adjustment

3. Autolite Fast Idle Screw

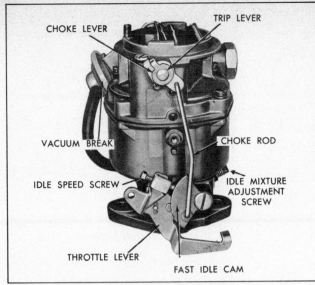

4. Rochester BV Fast Idle

5. Holley Secondary Link

6. Holley 4150

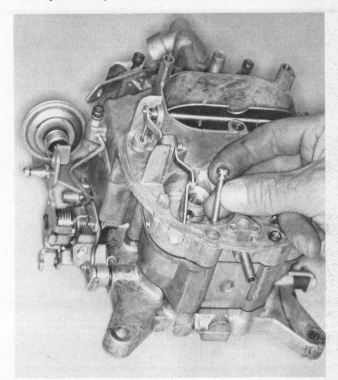

7. Autolite Special Bowl Screw

prove the low-end response. At a low speed the fuel mixture is moving slowly through the intake passages, and droplets of fuel have a tendency to fall out of the airstream. A heated manifold helps to keep the fuel vaporized. Heat comes from the exhaust gases which are usually channeled in some way so that they go up under the base of the carburetor to heat the intake passages. However, we do not want the fuel in the carburetor bowl to become heated, just the intake passages themselves. So you may find carburetors that are installed on their manifolds with a large insulating block or extra thick gasket.

ANTI-STALL DASHPOT

If you step on the throttle hard to go across an intersection, and all of a sudden you decide, because of the sudden appearance of a large object such as an 18-wheel truck, that it would be a good idea to stop, your engine may die when you take your foot off the throttle, unless it has an anti-stall dashpot, also known as a slow-closing throttle dashpot. The engine dies because you have already started a big load of fuel on the way to the cylinders but when you take your foot off the throttle, you shut off the air supply. The large load of fuel then floods the cylinders and kills the engine. An anti-stall dashpot stops this by holding the throttle open for a few seconds and allowing it to come down to idle slowly, which gives enough time for the engine to burn off the rich mixture.

By now you should have a pretty good idea of how the carburetor works. So let's go into a little troubleshooting and some of the repair procedures that you may have to perform.

IDLE MIXTURE ADJUSTMENT

One of the oldest tests in the world for finding out if a carburetor is operating correctly, is to make an attempt to adjust the idle mixture needles. If possible, mixture needles should always be adjusted with the fingers. If it is necessary to use a screwdriver because you can't get to the needles with your fingers, be very careful that you do not screw the needles in so far that you force them into the idle port hole. If you do this you will either put a ridge on the needle or may even break off the end of it.

Idle mixture is adjusted by screwing the needles in for a leaner mixture or out for a richer mixture. The usual setting at which almost any pre-smog engine will idle is 1½ to 2 turns unscrewed from the completely closed position. Late-model emission control carburetors

Fuel System

may require 3 turns before they will keep running. When you adjust idle mixture, the engine must be at operating temperature. The choke must be off and the fast idle cam must not be holding the throttle open.

Many other things must be checked before you actually set the idle. In some cars the headlights must be on so that the alternator puts a load on the engine. Some cars are adjusted in drive, some in neutral. Get the correct specifications for the car you are working on and be sure that you follow them to the letter. When the engine conditions are the way they should be, then It's OK to go ahead with the actual idle speed and mixture adjustment.

Screw one idle needle in slowly and you should notice a point where the mixture becomes so lean that the engine starts to falter. This is called the lean roll point or sometimes the lean fall-off point.

Unscrew the needle and you should notice a point where the mixture becomes so rich that the engine starts to roll; this is called the rich fall-off point.

Late models run so lean that these points can be very hard to detect. On pre-smog carburetors, the usual setting for an idle needle is midway between the two points, or a little bit toward the lean side for better mileage. On emission control carbs we deliberately adjust for a poor idle, screwing the needles in (leaner) until the rpm drops by a specified amount. This is the only way that a late-model car will pass the idle emission test. However, if done exactly according to your factory shop manual, the idle will not be bad enough to bother you, and the air will be a heck of a lot cleaner. An exception to the rpm-drop method is

1. Business End of Holley 4500

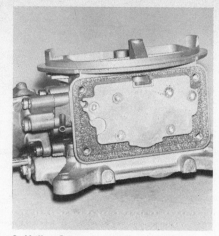

2. Holley Secondary Metering Plate

3. Rochester 4MV Idle Screw

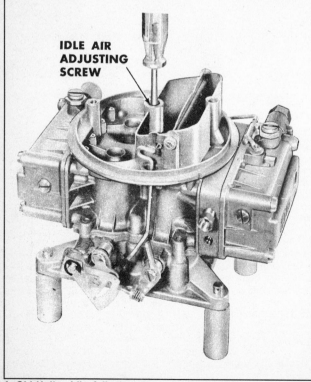

IDLE AIR ADJUSTING SCREW

4. Old Holley Idle Adjustment

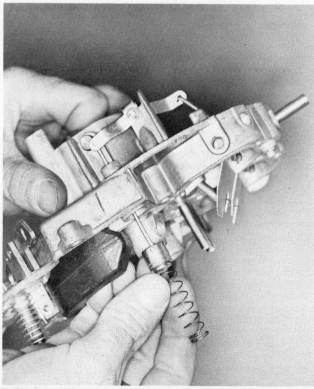

5. Air Valve Piston

those engines with air injection pumps (smog pumps). These engines must have a richer exhaust to burn up the hydrocarbons, so the mixture needles are usually adjusted ¼-turn out (richer) from the lean roll point.

AIR/FUEL RATIO

Air/fuel ratio is a fancy term that you won't hear much. What you will hear is talk about a carburetor running rich or running lean. Running rich means that the engine is getting too much fuel; running lean means just the opposite. Sometimes running rich provides an obvious symptom such as black smoke coming out of the tailpipe, but most of the time if the mixture is off it will show up either as poor gas mileage or a lack of power.

If you want power, it takes gasoline to produce it, so you can usually assume that the engine is running too lean if it doesn't seem to have much push. If the gas mileage is so poor that you can't even make a short trip without stopping at three gas stations, then you can be pretty sure that the mixture is too rich.

Carburetor men measure the air/fuel ratio with an exhaust gas analyzer. The analyzer takes a sample of the gas from the tailpipe, and a meter gives the ratio of air to fuel by weight. An engine will run from about 11-to-1 up through 15-to-1. Carburetor men have always felt that mixtures leaner than 16-to-1 wouldn't even run an engine, but with refinements in emission controls, the carburetor makers are now talking about mixtures in the area of 20-to-1. The ordi-

nary exhaust gas analyzer is useless with such lean mixtures. The needle will reverse, going off scale to the rich side. So most shops are now getting hydrocarbon meters, which are expensive.

Some carburetor men don't use an exhaust gas analyzer. But the ones who do have found that the small amount of time it takes to hook the analyzer up will save them a lot of trouble in the long run because it gives them an immediate check on how well the carburetor is running, both before and after they have worked on it.

It is not necessary for you to go out and buy an exhaust gas analyzer. A good one is expensive, a bad one is worse than none at all. And there are some bad ones on the market. The point is that when working on a carburetor you are mainly concerned with mixture control. Power, performance, and smoothness are all dependent upon having the right amount of gasoline in the

air to match the needs of the engine.

Of course the greatest enemy of mixture control is dirt. If the idle mixture needles will not adjust or you keep having problems with rough idle and stalling, just look at the outside of the carburetor. If it's all encrusted with fuel residue and dirt, you can be pretty sure it's almost as dirty on the inside. So the first thing you have to do is get it clean.

CARBURETOR CLEANING

Removing a carburetor is more or less an obvious procedure. It is held on at the base by studs and nuts. Remove the nuts, the throttle linkage, the hot air tube to the choke housing (if there is one), and any wires to such things as the transmission kick-down switches or air-conditioning idle speed-up switches. Remove the carburetor and take it to the bench for disassembly procedure.

Exploded views of carburetors usually show the parts as if they were disinte-

1. Secondary linkage on Holley 4500 is concealed in a cavity between the throats. Linkage is rugged.

2. On the Holley 4160, the secondary metering block is a thin plate with no replaceable jets.

3. Secondary linkage on Rochester 4-bbl. is a rod that can be adjusted by bending. Screw (arrow) is for curb idle adjustment.

4. The idle air screw is a means of supplying air to run the engine when the design of the carb allows the throttle plates to close completely at idle. You'll never find this one if you don't know it's there, because the air cleaner stud screws in on top of it. A disadvantage is that idle adjustments must be made with air cleaner off.

5. Air valve piston on the 4300 has small spring underneath that returns the air valve to the closed position.

6. Power piston stem on 4300 is just visible between halves of float. It opens the power valve, which is in the bottom of the bowl.

7. When the Rochester 4-bbl. choke is on, this little tab prevents the secondary air valve from opening. That's so you can't get on it when the engine is cold.

8. Carter AFB primary main jets are in the little niches (arrows). Secondary main jets are in the end of the bowl.

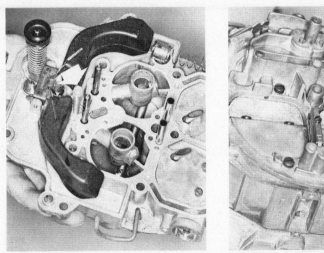

6. Power Piston

7. Rochester Choke Lock-Out Tang

8. AFB Main Jets

Fuel System

grated by a bomb. Never under any circumstances take a carburetor apart this far for cleaning. A good rule to follow is that anything with a gasket should be removed so that the gasket can be renewed. Also any jet that is screwed in should be removed so that the cleaning fluid can get up into the passages behind the jet. Choke vacuum pistons should be removed if they are of the type that is built into the carburetor.

Never under any circumstances should throttle shafts or choke shafts be removed for ordinary cleaning. If you do you'll just be making a lot of extra work and you won't be accomplishing anything because the cleaning solution easily finds its way alongside the throttle and choke shafts without their being removed. If power valves are the screw-in type, they can be removed. If they are pressed or staked in, they should be left alone.

After the carburetor is disassembled, the large parts should be put in a basket and the small parts in a closed screened container which will allow cleaning solution to enter but keep the small parts from being lost. A good holder for small parts is a tea ball, ordinarily used for making tea, available at any store with a housewares counter.

The basket for the large parts comes with either a 3- or 5-gal. bucket of commercial carburetor cleaner. However, if you are only doing one or two carburetors a year, you can buy the carburetor cleaner in pint cans to do the cleaning. Use a coat hanger to fish the parts out. The cleaner is a very powerful chemical—you should never put your fingers in it and be very careful not to splash it in your eyes.

Some cleaners will clean a carburetor in 20 mins. Others won't do a very good job. You will have to find out by experimenting with what is available in your area. Any cleaner will ruin rubber or neoprene parts, so if there are any parts like this in your carburetor be absolutely certain they are removed before the carburetor is dunked.

After the carburetor has remained in the cleaning solution long enough, the whole basket should be removed and allowed to drain. Then all the parts can be submerged in cleaning solvent or kerosene. If the carburetor cleaner did its job right, the solvent is only to wash out the cleaner, but in some cases you may have to use a brush with the solvent in order to loosen and remove some of the more stubborn deposits.

Swish the carburetor around in the solvent so that all the cleaner is washed out of it. Then remove the carburetor piece by piece and blow all the passages with compressed air. If you don't have an air compressor then blow the passages out with a tire pump. At least be sure that you blow the carburetor with something so that you will remove any remaining pieces of dirt.

After the carburetor is clean, it's simply a matter of reassembling it with new gaskets and new parts where necessary and checking the various adjustments on the carburetor. You should never put a

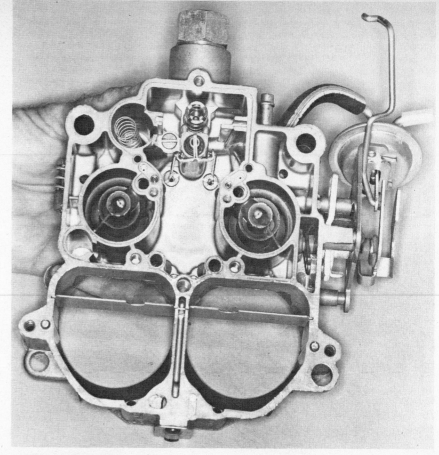

1. Inside The Float Bowl

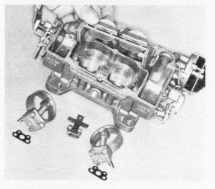

2. AFB Air Valve

carburetor back together with the old gaskets unless it's an emergency. At least buy a gasket set or have one on hand before you start the job.

The next step up from a gasket set is a zip kit or pep kit. This includes gaskets plus a few of the parts that wear out, such as needle and seat and accelerating pump. If the carburetor is really in bad shape, then you will need an overhaul kit which includes just about every part on the carburetor that could wear out except the shafts. If even an overhaul kit won't restore the carb, then your only recourse is to buy the parts that you need. However, it is usually cheaper to buy a new carburetor than it is to go that far.

While assembling the carburetor you will set the float leve, but that is ordinarily the only internal adjustment. After the carburetor is assembled there are all kinds of external adjustments that make it operate correctly.

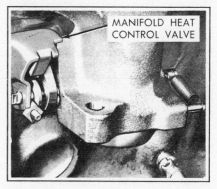

3. Heat Riser Valve

When you buy a repair kit for your carburetor there will usually be a sheet included that will show all the adjustments and specifications. If not, there are auto repair manuals available at bookstores that will give you this information. Also the factory shop manual put out by the manufacturer of your car has all this data.

If after you get the carburetor back on your car, it still doesn't run right, you may have to change the jets. This is usually not necessary. In fact, in some cases it will increase exhaust emissions and is therefore illegal. But changing jets is a procedure that you must know to make a carburetor work correctly.

IDLE JET

After the fuel enters the idle jet it picks up air as it moves through the idle passage in the carburetor. When it reaches the idle port below the throttle

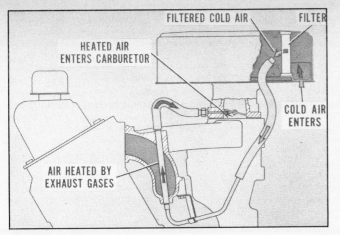

4. Anti-Icing System

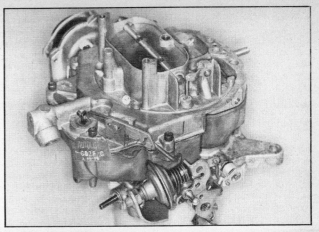

5. Anti-Stall Dashpot

6. Rochester 4MV

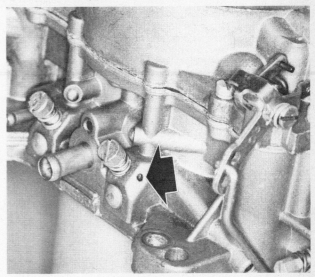

7. Mixture Screw Retaining Pin

1. Lift the Rochester 4-bbl. bowl cover off and this is the sight that will greet you. We have also removed the float, needle and baffle.

2. Remove the secondary clusters on an AFB and then the secondary air valve will come out.

3. This may not look like part of carburetion, but it is. If the heat control valve is stuck shut, forcing too much heat up under the carburetor, it can cause uneven running.

4. Some cars have trouble with throttle plate icing, which causes the engine to die or results in extremely rough running. This system on a Chrysler Slant-6 channels heated air to underside of throttle plate and prevents icing.

5. Anti-stall dashpot on autolite 4300 is not connected to engine vacuum. It works on a bleed-down principle.

6. Ever hear of a Chevy burning up? Sometimes this plug falls out, which gives the engine a gasoline bath.

7. To prevent over-rich adjustments, the idle needles on some carbs are limited with a pin in the body of the carburetor.

8. Go easy when using a screwdriver on idle mixture needles. They can easily be ruined if they are screwed in tight against the throttle bore.

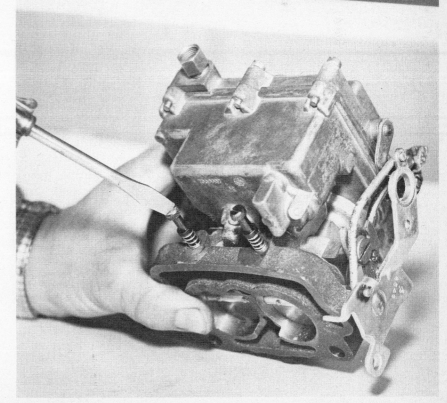

8. Adjusting Mixture Screws

Fuel System

plate, it is in reality a mixture of fuel and air, and it is the amount of this mixture that you control with the idle mixture screw. However, the idle mixture screw does not control the fuel that comes from the idle transfer port. That fuel mixture is controlled by the size of the idle jet and the idle air bleeds.

If the idle jets are screwed in it's a simple matter to change them. However, if they are pressed into a metering cluster, the only way to change idle jet size is by drilling or buying a different cluster, if one is available—and it usually isn't.

MAIN JET

Main jets are usually screwed in and easily changed. However, main jets for the secondary side of a 4-bbl. carburetor may be just orifices which are not removable. When removing main jets be sure to use a screwdriver that fits the slot in the jet. If you don't, it's very easy for the screwdriver to slip part way out of the jet and chew up the soft brass. On a carburetor that uses metering rods, the usual procedure is to change the rods.

POWER JET

If you want a richer mixture at wide open throttle, but wish to retain the mix-

ture you already have at cruising speed, then the power jet is the one to change. A lot of ingenuity has been used in the design and placement of power jets and sometimes you have to use almost an equal amount of ingenuity to find them. Some of them cannot be changed because they are nothing but a restriction in a passageway. Others can be changed or drilled in order to enrich or lean the wide-open throttle mixture. In most carburetion tuning on stock automobiles, the power jet is seldom changed. The best reason for this is because the only way you can check the mixture to find what you have is to put the engine on a dynamometer—and there aren't many dynamometers that are readily available.

ACCELERATING PUMP JET

Accelerating pump jets can also be a restriction in a passageway that is impossible to change or even drill. Sometimes the restriction is in a removable pump nozzle that is screwed into the carburetor throat. If so, the nozzle sometimes has a number stamped on it which indicates the size of the accelerating pump restriction.

Drilling or changing of accelerating pump jets is usually done to eliminate a flat spot on acceleration that cannot be cured by lengthening the stroke of the pump.

It is possible to have 99 identical carburetors that will run well, but on the 100th one the accelerating pump might be just a trifle lean, causing a flat spot when you step on the gas. In that case a larger pump jet or pump restriction does wonders to cure the problem. This procedure should only be attempted by a carburetor expert because ordinarily you can set the pump linkage for a longer stroke to overcome any flat spot.

FLOAT LEVEL

It's easy to think of the fuel level as the measurement of how high the gasoline is in the float bowl, but this is not the part that's important. The critical point is the main nozzle and whether the gasoline is right at the tip of it ready to spill into the venturi or way down inside where the venturi suction will have to build up considerably before any gas will come out.

Fuel level can be so high with a maladjusted float that gasoline actually drips out of the nozzle when the engine is shut off, or fuel level can be so low that venturi suction cannot pull the gasoline out of the nozzle and the engine will gasp and wheeze instead of cruising along.

A high fuel level can cause dying on turns or dying on sudden stops, and a low fuel level can cause poor response

1. Replacement mixture screw caps come in all sizes to fit various carbs. These are Rochester.

2. Mixture needle on left has 15 degree taper, providing finer (less sensitive) adjustment on '72 Buick 2-bbl. Needle at right is old style, with sharp taper.

3. Idle mixture screws have limiter caps, to prevent over-rich adjustment by tuners.

4. Electrical connection on this Carter AVS is for the solenoid retard on the distributor. It retards the spark at closed throttle. Idle speed screw is above terminal

1. Mixture Screw Limiter Caps   2. Idle Needle Taper

3. Idle Mixture Screw Caps

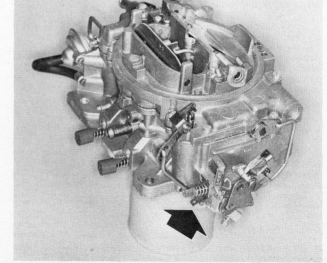

4. AVS 4-Barrel

when the main metering system attempts to take over from the idle system. With experience you will be able to recognize high fuel level or low fuel level because of the way the engine acts.

Suppose you have a car that runs very good at high speed but extremely rich at idle so that the engine rolls. You adjust the idle mixture screws but it doesn't help, so the logical thing to suspect is the fuel level. There are many problems that are obvious if you just give them a little thought and analysis.

CRANKCASE VENTILATION VALVES

The so-called smog valve can cause mixture problems too because it is allowing crankcase vapors to enter the engine. These crankcase vapors are mostly

5. Many cars use anti-dieseling solenoids. Normal curb idle is controlled by the adjustment screw in the solenoid itself. If the solenoid has a wire only going to it, then it is a true anti-dieseling solenoid. But if there is also a vacuum line to the solenoid, then it is a CEC valve, which is never used to set curb idle.

6. Rochester 4-bbl. with anti-dieseling solenoid. Curb idle is set with the solenoid adjustment.

7. The Combination Emission Control Valve (CEC) is used mostly on Chevy cars, but also appears on some other GM makes. Curb idle is set with the normal throttle cracking screw, not the CEC plunger screw. There is a specification in rpm for the plunger screw, but setting it is not necessary unless you disturb the original setting. CEC valve rpm setting varies as much as 300 rpm above normal curb idle. If you set curb idle with the CEC valve plunger by mistake, engine braking on deceleration will be greatly reduced, which can be dangerous.

unburned gasoline or just air, on an engine in good shape. On an engine in bad shape there is a lot of oil smoke mixed in with them.

The only thing you can do with smog valves is to make sure that the hoses connecting them do not have any leaks and that the valve itself is clean. If the valve is an orifice type, a visual inspection is good enough. If the valve is a plunger type you should use both a visual inspection and shake the valve to be sure that the plunger is completely free inside.

Smog valves can be cleaned in carburetor cleaner, although many car makers recommend replacement instead of cleaning. Since the smog valve is allowing unburned gasoline or air to enter the engine, if you pinch the hose or if you put your finger over the end of the valve, the engine will actually idle slower because you are taking some of the air and gas away from the idle mixture. If the engine does not idle slower then you can be pretty sure that the valve is plugged or restricted.

AIR CLEANERS

Nothing will make an engine run rich quicker than a clogged or restricted air cleaner. If the element in your cleaner is made of foam or steel mesh, it should be cleaned in solvent or kerosene, shaken or squeezed dry and lightly re-oiled. Foam-type elements must be handled with care because they are fragile and frequently split at the seam where they are glued. If you have this trouble, instead of repairing them or getting another foam element, there are paper elements available that will take the place of the foam.

If you have a paper element, you can gently tap it or blow it to clean it. But the best idea is to throw it away and put on a new one. The best test ever devised for a paper element is to hold it over a bare light bulb. A new element will look bright and clean while a dirty one is obviously plugged up.

When cleaning air cleaners of any kind, the housing should be cleaned with solvent, but do not submerge it in a solvent tank. There are inner chambers that can become full of solvent and it's impossible to pour it out. Also be very careful not to cut your fingers when you are wiping out the inside of an air cleaner. The cleaner is made of sheetmetal,

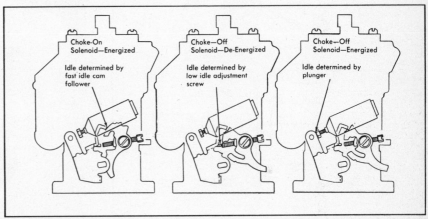

5. Anti-Dieseling Solenoid

6. Anti-Dieseling Solenoid on Rochester

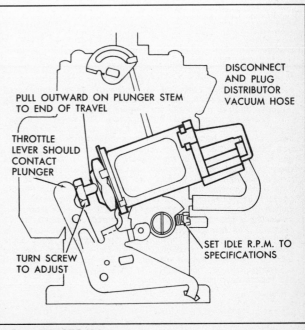

7. Chevrolet CEC Valve

Fuel System

and there are sharp edges that can really cut.

FUEL DELIVERY TESTING

If possible, you should not think in terms of testing a fuel pump no matter how much you read elsewhere about testing procedures. If you will think only of testing fuel delivery at the carburetor, you will be a long way toward solving whatever the problem is.

To test fuel delivery take the line loose at the carburetor, slip a tight fitting rubber hose over this line and let the hose dangle over the fender into a bucket. Then start the engine and let it idle just on the fuel that is in the carburetor bowl. You will get a series of squirts into the bucket as the fuel pump operates. An experienced mechanic can just look at the size and length of the squirts and tell if the pump is in good condition or not, but you should actually measure the amount of fuel that you get in half a minute. Ordinarily this would be about a pint if the pump is in good condition.

We had a peculiar experience with a new fuel pump that illustrates the fuel delivery problem. The car would starve for fuel on full throttle acceleration, especially on long, uphill, freeway on-ramps. The original fuel pump on the car was a Carter, but instead of buying another Carter we bought a brand new pump made by another company. With the new pump installed, the fuel starvation was still there, even though the new pump put out a pint of fuel in less than 30 secs. Everybody we talked to said there couldn't be anything wrong with a fuel pump that would put out like that. But we stuck to our guns, hunted up a Carter dealer, and bought an original equipment Carter pump. After installing it, the car ran beautifully, without a trace of fuel starvation. Then, to satisfy our curiosity, we tested the new Carter pump, and found out it would put out a pint in 18 secs. That's a heck of a lot of fuel, but evidently the engine needed it, and Carter's original equipment pump was designed to put it out. The other manufacturer's new pump was evidently a universal design that would fit anything, but it wasn't good enough for our engine.

If you have good fuel delivery then you are pretty sure there is nothing wrong from that point all the way back to the tank, but you still haven't tested the passageway from the carburetor inlet fitting into the float bowl. This passageway frequently contains a bronze filter. The easiest way to test it is to dip it into a bucket of gas and see if it will hold the gasoline. If it does, throw it away and put on a new one, because that means that the pores in the bronze are filled with dirt.

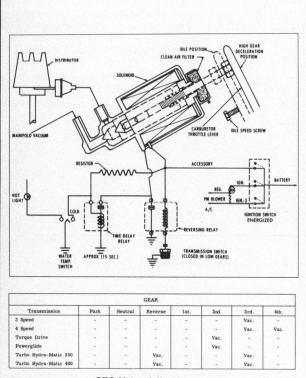

GEAR							
Transmission	Park	Neutral	Reverse	1st.	2nd.	3rd.	4th.
3 Speed	-	-	-	-	-	Vac.	-
4 Speed	-	-	-	-	-	Vac.	Vac.
Torque Drive	-	-	-	Vac.	-	-	-
Powerglide	-	-	-	-	Vac.	-	-
Turbo Hydra-Matic 350	-	-	Vac.	-	-	Vac.	-
Turbo Hydra-Matic 400	-	-	Vac.	-	-	Vac.	-

CEC Valve Adjustment

CEC (Combustion Emission Control) valve is a complicated arrangement because it does so many different things. Using a combination of electricity and engine vacuum, the valve controls spark advance and throttle opening. The valve is normally closed, which shuts off vacuum to the distributor and eliminates all spark advance. When the transmission is in a position labeled "Vac" on the chart, the transmission switch opens, which operates the reversing relay to energize the valve. This opens the vacuum line to the distributor, giving normal vacuum advance, and also extends the plunger to the high gear deceleration position which gives a larger throttle opening on deceleration for fewer emissions. The water temp switch is in the circuit so that the CEC valve is energized below 82°. The time delay relay energizes the valve for 15 seconds after the ignition switch is turned on, to improve cold running. But we're not through yet. An additional solid state device turns on the air conditioner for three seconds after the ignition switch is turned off, to stop the engine and prevent dieseling. This is '71 model. The '72's have slightly different hookup, to keep you on your toes.

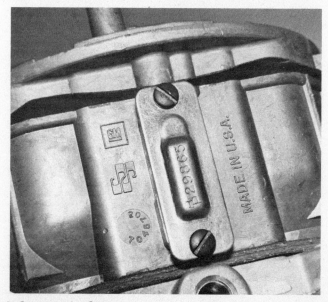

1. Hot Idle Compensator

2. Compensator Cover

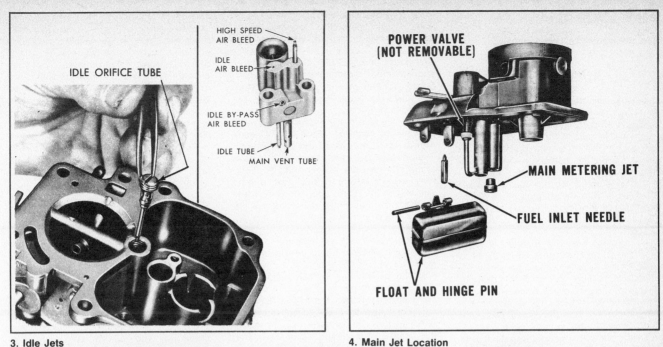

3. Idle Jets

4. Main Jet Location

5. Chrysler Retard Solenoid Contact

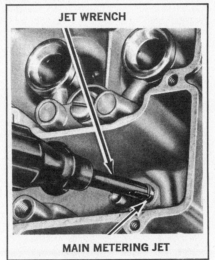

6. Removing Main Jet

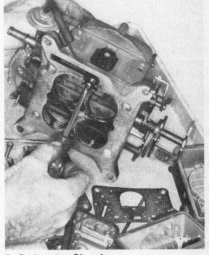

7. Carburetor Cleaning

1. Remove the cover on this carb and there is a hot idle compensator. Note gasket, important to prevent leaks.

2. Under this cover on a Rochester may be a hot idle compensator or nothing at all.

3. Idle tube is another name for the idle jet. The calibrated restriction is at the lower end of the tube where it appears pinched together.

4. Autolite 1101 upper body. You might also hear this called the air horn or the bowl cover.

5. Terminal on Chrysler product Carter retards spark at idle. If contact is not made, idle will be too fast, since spark will remain advanced.

6. Main jet on this Ford-Autolite 2100 carb is on the floor of the bowl.

7. Carburetors should be disassembled thoroughly for cleaning, but only by removing screws or clips. It isn't necessary to remove any rivets or lead plugs that are pressed in.

If you don't have good fuel delivery at the carburetor, then start checking each component all the way back to the tank. This may include a fuel filter mounted on the engine, a fuel filter on the tank side of the fuel pump, a filter in the line between the pump and the tank and maybe even a filter on the pickup tube inside the tank.

Any of those filters could be restricted because of dirt or water. If they are, change the element or if it's a throwaway filter, change the whole filter. If you find nothing wrong with the filter, then it's time to start checking for a kinked line. This can happen because somebody jacked up the car where a line runs outside the frame. Or it could have been caused by a mild collision that kinked a hose. Take nothing for granted when you work on a fuel system. Just because a rubber hose looks good on the outside doesn't mean that the inside isn't all swelled up so that it won't pass any fuel.

A complete fuel delivery test also involves testing the pressure at the carburetor. Do this by inserting a T in the

line and checking fuel pressure with the engine idling, or pressure can be checked statically. Disconnect the line from the carburetor and hook it directly to a pressure gauge, then idle the engine and check the pressure.

Correct pressure can be anywhere from 1½ lbs. to 6 lbs. at idle. On older cars, part of the pressure test was to shut the engine off and see if the pressure would hold, or at least only fall very slowly. This test is not valid on late-model cars, because they have a bleed-back feature in the pumps or in the fuel filter that allows fuel pressure to drop to zero whenever the engine is shut off.

Did you ever park a car in the hot sun on a day when the mercury was up at the top of the thermometer? Fuel pressure can go high enough to override the float and fill the bowl to over-flowing so that fuel runs into the engine. Then when you come back to your car you have several minutes cranking ahead of you before you finally get your flooded engine cleaned out. The bleed-back feature on late-model cars eliminates this problem. When the engine is shut off,

Fuel System

fuel pressure drops immediately to zero and, therefore, prevents flooding.

FUEL PUMPS

Finding the fuel pump is not too difficult, but removing it can really be a job because in many cases it is in the most inaccessible part of the engine compartment. Fuel pumps usually operate off an eccentric on the camshaft with an arm and some linkage to move the diaphragm up and down. An inlet and outlet valve work with the diaphragm, creating suction on the line from the tank and pressure to push the fuel up to the carburetor.

Fuel pumps are very dependable. Usually their malfunctions consist of a cracked or broken diaphragm which allows fuel to leak out onto the ground. They can have problems too with worn linkage which reduces the stroke on the diaphragm so that the pump can't put out the way it should.

Older pumps were put together with screws and could be disassembled. The diaphragms and valves were replaceable and it was possible to rebuild the pump like new. But rebuilt exchange pumps were inexpensive so it really didn't pay to put in a new diaphragm and valves yourself. The result was that most parts stores quit handling replacement parts for pumps and only sold rebuilt exchanges or new pumps. In a few years there won't be any more rebuilt pumps, because the late-model cars all use a pump with a crimped edge instead of screws. Those pumps cannot be taken apart. They must be thrown away when they go bad. The most practical thing to do in any case when a fuel pump is bad is to throw it away and put on either a good rebuilt or a new one.

FUEL PUMP REMOVAL

To remove the pump, simply disconnect the lines, take off the two capscrews holding the pump on the engine block and remove the pump. There are usually two fittings where a line enters a pump. If you put a wrench on the outer fitting and start turning it to take the line loose, the chances are good that you're going to ruin something, because the inner fitting will turn also. Whenever you take a line loose, always use two wrenches, one to hold the inner fitting and the other wrench to turn the outer fitting. Ideally you should use tubing wrenches to keep from rounding off those brass fittings.

After the lines are disconnected and the pump is removed, there will be some fittings still screwed into the pump. These must be transferred to the new pump. If they are directional be sure they are installed in the new pump, pointing in the same direction they were on the old pump. That will make it a lot easier when you put the new pump on the car.

Before you install the new pump compare it with the old pump from every angle. The mounting flange and the arm must be exactly the same configuration as on the old pump. There is nothing more sickening than the sound of hearing your camshaft break in half the second you turn your engine over because the pump arm was jammed between the cam and the block. Many pumps have the same body and flange, the only difference being in the arm. So be very careful.

If there is a pushrod that operates the pump, be sure the pushrod is not worn. If in doubt, replace it. A worn pushrod will not give full stroke.

Some pumps are dual, with one half pumping fuel and the other half creating vacuum to act as a booster for the windshield wipers. Of course you only find those pumps on a car with vacuum wipers, and most cars nowadays use electric wipers. But if you do have a car with a double pump that's giving trouble, it's a good idea to check the camshaft eccentric. Those double pumps put an awful lot of pressure on the cam eccentric and can wear it down to where it's just a little bit of a nub. In case the eccentric is worn, the easiest way to fix it is to put on an electric pump. Otherwise, you'll have to tear the engine down and put in a new cam.

ELECTRIC FUEL PUMP

Foreign cars have used electric fuel pumps for years but they have never caught on for domestic vehicles. Probably the reason is that electric fuel pumps can cause operating difficulties if the driver is not aware he has an electric pump. The electric pump is operating any time the ignition is on. If a piece of dirt gets under the needle valve in the carburetor and the engine floods and dies, the driver may leave the ignition switch on. Of course the electric pump is still operating, so it'll pump the complete contents of the gas tank into the carburetor and out over the top of the engine and onto the ground, which is a bit inconvenient.

There are ways around that by installing an oil pressure switch so that the electric pump will not operate until the

1. Holley Secondary Main Jet

2. Economizer Valve

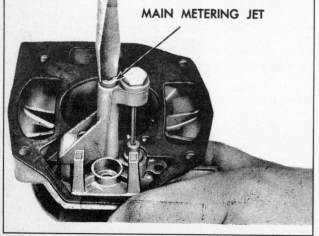

MAIN METERING JET

3. Main And Power Jets

BEND ARM TO ADJUST

BEND TANG TO ADJUST

4. Adjusting Float Level

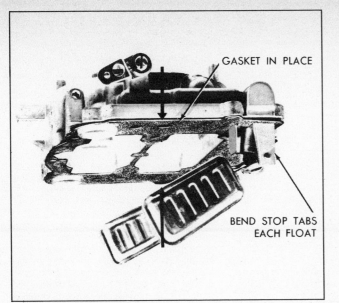

GASKET IN PLACE

BEND STOP TABS EACH FLOAT

5. Checking Float Drop

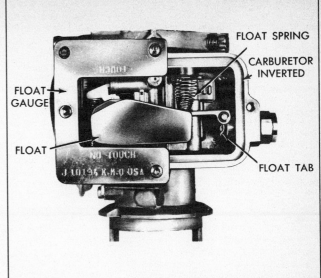

FLOAT SPRING

CARBURETOR INVERTED

FLOAT GAUGE

FLOAT

FLOAT TAB

6. Float Level Gauge

1. With the Holley secondary metering body removed, you can see the little holes on the bottom of it that are the secondary main jets. They are not removable.

2. Holley calls this little screw-in part an economizer valve, but it's really a power valve, or power jet.

3. Rochester model B 1-bbl. has power jet under cap next to main metering jet. Check power jet to be sure spring is not broken. Broken spring makes engine run rich all the time.

4. Float level adjustment is usually achieved through bending a float arm or tang. This 4-bbl. carburetor features both methods. On the left is the bending point for setting the level, and on the right is the adjustment for float drop.

5. Float drop is not as precise a measurement as float level. In many cases there is no precise point on the float from which float drop is measured.

6. This single-barrel Holley carburetor is representative of many 2- and 4-bbl. units in that float adjustment is done by bending the float tab rather than the float arm.

7. On Holley 4500, accelerating pump discharge check is under the pump nozzle on top of the carb. Holes in nozzle meter the fuel.

8. Here, when the float is adjusted correctly, gasoline should just wet the bottom of the threads in the sight plug hole. Note the float-adjusting nut and lockscrew atop the bowl of this 4-bbl. Holley. If you have already set the float with a gauge and the fuel level doesn't reach the bottom of the sight plug hole, you should reset the float with the lockscrew and nut until the wet fuel level is correct. Best results are achieved with the adjustment being made while the engine is running at a normal idling speed on level ground.

9. Four long screws hold the Holley 4-bbl. bowl in place. This is center-pivot float bowl, for racing.

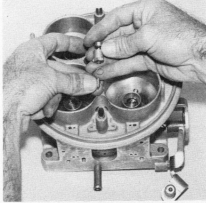

7. Holley 4500 Accelerating Pump

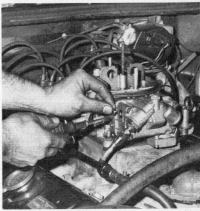

8. Holley Sight Plug

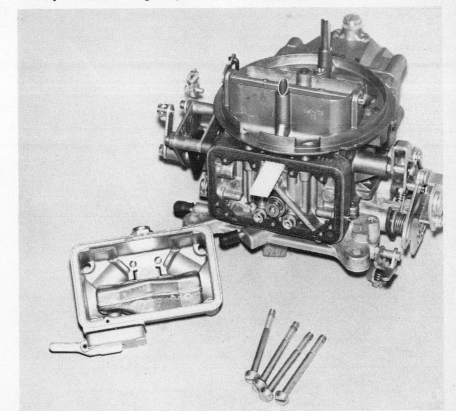

9. Removing Holley Bowl

Fuel System

oil pressure comes up. But then you have the problem of getting fuel to the bowl after the car has been sitting awhile. This means that the driver must hold down a push-button bypass when starting. It can also be done the other way around with a switch to turn the pump off in case of carburetor flooding so that the engine can be cranked to clean it out without getting fuel. Some installations on new cars use an oil pressure switch in conjunction with a starting motor bypass. The pump operates only when there is oil pressure, or when the starter is operating. So don't be surprised if you turn the ignition switch on with the engine dead and the pump doesn't work. It's not supposed to.

There are many types of electric pumps around. They are designed mainly as pusher pumps so they must be mounted as close to the gas tank as possible and as low as possible so that they don't have to suck the gas uphill from the tank.

If you do decide to install an electric pump on your car, check the specifications of the pump carefully. Some of them do not have enough capacity and you will find your engine running out of fuel when it needs it the most. When installing an electric pump, it is best to bypass the mechanical pump that is on your car. If you don't bypass it then you will have to worry about two pumps because even though the mechanical pump is not doing any pumping, it still has a diaphragm that can rupture and leak gasoline. After installing an electric pump always test the pressure and volume compared to the old pump to be sure it is adequate.

FUEL FILTERS

Fuel filters or screens can be in some surprising places on an automobile. As long as they work right you don't care where they are, but when they plug up and your car can only run a block without stuttering and stumbling, you have to find those filters in a hurry to clean them out. Regular cleaning and maintenance on filters will eliminate the trouble.

Some filters have an element that can be cleaned, such as a ceramic or metal screen, and others use a paper or fiberglass element that must be replaced. With a little experience you can tell by looking at an element whether it should be cleaned or replaced. If in doubt, check the specifications for your car in the factory shop manual.

Many carburetors have a filter made out of bronze at the fuel inlet. You would think that this filter could be cleaned, but for some reason or other when the dirt settles in the pores of the bronze it stays there, and there really isn't much you can do except change it. How do you know when to change it? Well, the hard way to find out is to be going up a long hill at wide open throttle with a heavy load on your car and momentarily run out of gas. The easy way is to take the filter out, dip it in a bucket of solvent or gasoline and see if the solvent runs through it. If the solvent stays in the filter just like you had a cup of coffee in your hand, then you'd better throw it away and get a new one.

The next place you may find a filter is on the engine a few inches from the carburetor. If it's a glass bowl type, it will probably have a replacement element in it. The element however, could be made out of ceramic material. In that case, all you have to do is clean it and put it back in. The inline or can-type filter will also be found mounted on the engine between the carburetor and the fuel pump. This filter may be made of metal or plastic so that you can look into it to see if it's dirty. The best way to change these (whether they are transparent or not) is on a strict mileage basis, again, referring to the factory shop manual.

Some of the can-type filters are made specially for air-conditioned cars, with a bleed hole that bleeds fuel back to the tank. This is done to help prevent vapor lock which is caused by fuel vaporizing in the fuel lines before it reaches the carburetor. Vaporizing fuel, of course, will go right out through the bowl vent, thus leaving the engine with no fuel to run on. The fuel is actually boiling in the line, vaporizing at a rate faster than the

1. Cadillac Smog Valve

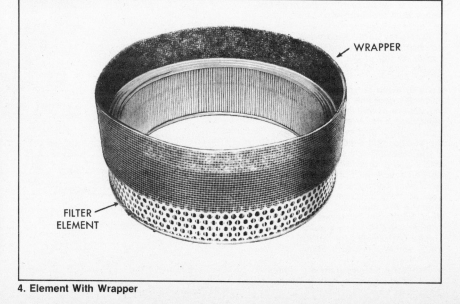

2. Paper Air Cleaner

3. Foam-Type Element

4. Element With Wrapper

fuel pump can pump it. So the carburetor is receiving nothing at all except vapors—and it's kind of hard to run an engine that way.

That usually happens on a hot day in the middle of summer, on a long hill in heavy traffic. The only thing to do is get out and get some kind of liquid on the fuel pump and on the fuel lines even if you have to pour Coca-Cola on it. The liquid will cool the lines and the pump so that they will work again.

Fuel filters can also be found on the pump, either on the pressure side or the vacuum side. If they are part of the pump itself they are usually a glass bowl with maybe a changeable element or maybe not. With no element, the glass bowl merely acts as a sediment trap.

In the line from the fuel pump back to the tank there may also be a filter mounted somewhere on the frame-rail, and in the tank itself on the end of the pickup tube there is a filter made of fiberglass on every late-model car. These fiberglass filters on the pickup tube are designed to plug up in case any water gets in the tank, and they really do a good filtering job.

If you've ever seen a carburetor with fuel pump can pump it. So the carburetor is receiving nothing at all except vapors—and it's kind of hard to run an engine that way.

5. Fuel Delivery Testing

1. *If the engine doesn't idle right, don't be quick to blame the carburetor. Maybe the smog valve needs cleaning. On a Cadillac it's plugged into the right rocker cover.*

2. *Typical air cleaner used on General Motors cars. The gasket at the bottom goes between the cleaner and the carburetor, to prevent dirty air from getting in. In some cases, the bottom gasket is permanently held onto the air cleaner by metal tabs. Many air cleaners have additional filters inside them to trap oil that may come in through breather hoses. Don't forget to clean them, too.*

3. *In addition to wrapping snugly and evenly over the inner supporting element, a foam-type filter element must fit correctly within the metal air cleaner cover. If the foam is ripped or misshapen—or shows a tendency to crumble from age—it cannot filter effectively and should be replaced.*

4. *Some dry-type elements are encased in an outside wrapper usually made of a screened material. This wrapper is designed to keep the oil fumes from ruining the relatively fragile dry paper element. When removed from around the inner element, the outer wrapper may be washed, dried and replaced. One should never attempt to wash a paper element.*

5. *Accurate fuel delivery testing requires a stopwatch, a graduated container, and a long hose. Let the engine idle, and note time it takes to put out one pint. Compare results with specs or with other cars.*

6. *Typical heated air entry used on all late-model cars. System usually takes place of heat riser valve that was formerly found in exhaust.*

7. *This typical diaphragm-type AC fuel pump uses vacuum—as in an internal combustion engine—to alternately pull gas from the tank, then push it into the carburetor. The vacuum-producing motion of the diaphragm is provided by an eccentric attached to and driven off the camshaft. Note crimped cover, making rebuilding extremely difficult.*

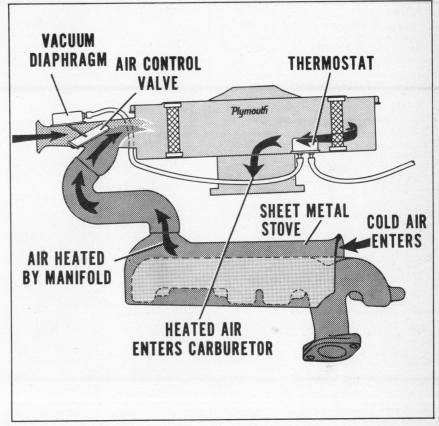

6. Heated-air Air Cleaner

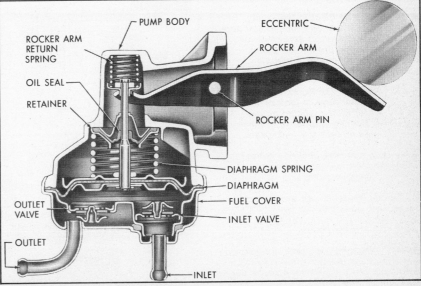

7. Crimped Cover Fuel Pump

Fuel System

If you've ever seen a carburetor with water in it you won't forget it. A white residue forms created by a reaction between the water and the metal of the carburetor. It plugs up everything, and there's just nothing you can do except throw the carburetor away if the reaction has gone on for very long.

Filters are really important because of all the foreign matter that gets into the gas tank and comes from the tank itself. It's impossible to keep a gas tank full at all times. When it isn't full, water vapor can condense out of the air onto the sides of the tank causing rust. These rust particles will come through the fuel line and cause all kinds of trouble in the carburetor.

If you do get water in the fuel tank, you will have to remove the tank to clean it out. So let's take a look at how we do that next.

FUEL TANKS

If you take fuel out of the tank, you have to let air in—so there has to be a vent somehwere on the tank, usually in the cap. If all caps were vented there wouldn't be any problem, but some tanks have a separate vent with a sealed cap. Put a sealed cap on a tank that is supposed to have a vented cap and you're going to have trouble. Your fuel pump might be strong enough to suck so hard that the walls of the tank actually col-

1. Old-style fuel pumps could be taken apart and fixed with a kit that had new valves and a diaphragm.

2. Typical vapor-diverter filter used on General Motors cars.

3. When Chrysler put the smog pump on its '72 Calif. Imperials, they found out there was no room left for the fuel pump, so they used an electric. It's the old familiar Bendix.

4. A bronze filter—at the carb's inlet side—is usually a spring loaded device that seats the W-shaped filter against a small gasket. When plugged, it can cause agony.

5. Vegas use an electric fuel pump, combined with the tank pickup unit and gauge. Note fiberglass screen (arrow). It's necessary to protect the pump, but it can be a source of fuel starvation if it gets clogged.

6. Inlet fitting on '72 Rochester carbs is different; you have to look closely to see it. Old fittings seated on a shoulder, but new one seats at inner end to keep threads dry and clean.

7. Modern fuel tank package houses a combination fuel pickup, filter and gas gauge sending unit.

8. Special wrenches are available to get tank units out, but two screwdrivers will work just about as well if you are careful.

9. Most new cars have pressure-vacuum fuel tank caps that are supposed to keep vapors inside the tank so we don't have to breathe 'em.

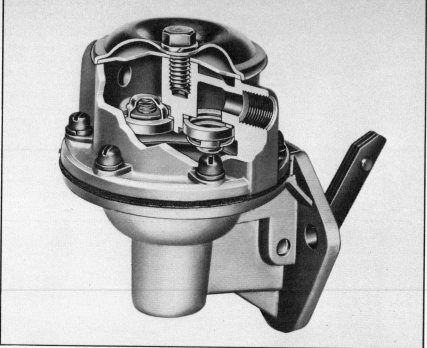

1. Old-Style Fuel Pump

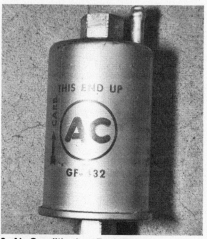

2. Air-Conditioning/Fuel Filter

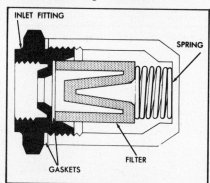

4. Bronze Carburetor Filter

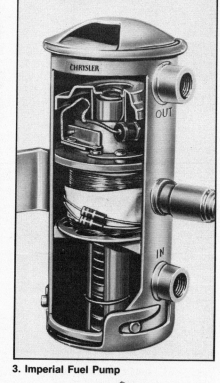

3. Imperial Fuel Pump

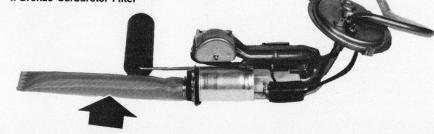

5. Vega Fuel Pump

lapse. But probably long before that happens the engine would run out of gas from fuel starvation. About that time somebody will take the cap off the tank to see if there's any gas and of course that let's the air in. Then the fuel pump will pump until it reaches the point where there is a vacuum in the tank again.

If you are in doubt about the kind of cap your tank is supposed to have, crawl under the car and see if there is an actual vent coming off the tank somewhere. If you see a vent tube then you can be pretty sure that the tank is supposed to have a sealed cap. Also if you ever take a cap off a tank and hear a rush of air into the tank, you can be pretty sure it has a sealed cap on it but it should have a vented cap.

If you have been unlucky enough to get water in the gas tank, it will plug up the fiberglass filter that is used on the end of the pickup tube on late-model cars. Ordinarily this means removing the tank because there is no tank drain on most cars manufactured nowadays.

Always siphon a tank completely dry before attempting to remove it, then remove all lines, wires and filler neck braces, and put some blocks up under the tank to hold it while you remove the two long straps that hold it against the car. Then remove the blocks and lower the tank.

You can clean the tank out by pouring solvent in through the filler neck opening and through the opening for the tank gauge unit. Tank gauge units usually use a locking ring which takes a special wrench, but with a little ingenuity and some careful prying you can usually get the gauge unit out. Don't pry on the pickup tube under any circumstances because it's very fragile. Tank gauge units should always be handled with extreme care so as not to bend the gauge arm or break any of the soldering loose.

LINES AND FITTINGS

It used to be customary to have a steel line running from the tank up to a point on the frame near the fuel pump, then a flexible hose went across to the pump and another steel line went from the pump to the carburetor. Some later cars made the steel line jump off the frame and go through a long arc and attach directly to the fuel pump so that the flexible line was unnecessary. Still later models use a combination of neoprene rubber and steel lines. Copper line should never be used in a fuel system because it sometimes can have a reaction with the gasoline.

Any flexible fuel line should be inspected from time to time to be sure it is not cracking; other than that, there is no maintenance required on fuel lines. Whenever you replace a line be sure that the fitting is matched. Just because two fittings will screw together does not mean that they are going to make a good seal. Several different types of brass fittings are in common use on automobiles today. If you have to replace a fitting be sure that the new one is exactly the same both inside and out.

6. New Rochester Fitting

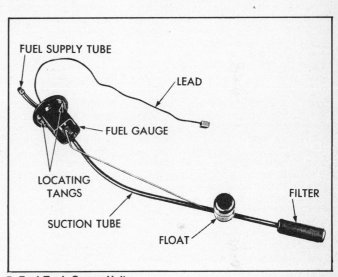

7. Fuel Tank Gauge Unit

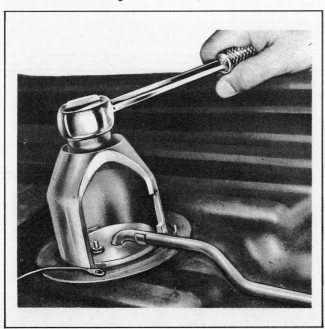

8. Removing Tank Unit

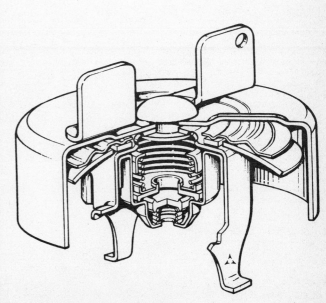

9. Pressure-Vacuum Tank Cap

Overhauling Your Engine

Many young people who would like to work on cars feel that a carburetor, distributor, or even a light switch is much too complicated for them to attempt taking it apart. The engine block is something else. Everybody seems to feel that no matter how little he knows about the car, he can unscrew nuts and bolts with the best of them. Many budding mechanics get their first taste of wrench twisting when they take a cylinder head or an oil pan off an old engine. It's unfortunate that young men who want to become mechanics should consider engine work as being easy or something that they can do without having to study up on. In reality, engine work cannot be done well by someone whose only qualification is grease under his fingernails and a lot of nicks and cuts on his hands.

Overhauling an engine is not simply a matter of taking it apart and throwing it back together. A man who rebuilds engines can truthfully be called an automotive machinist. He has to be able to work accurately to tolerances of less than 1000th of an inch. It is true that he does not have to have as delicate a touch as someone who works on carburetors or distributors, but his sensitivity with a micrometer is the equal of anybody who sets the gap on a pair of distributor points to the exact thickness of a feeler gauge.

An engine overhaul done correctly will result in the same amount of life that was obtained from the original engine.

Done incorrectly, an engine overhaul will result in burned valves, high oil consumption, knocking bearings, and a car owner who firmly believes that engine rebuilders are a bunch of clods and that the only way to go is with a new car. Actually, an engine can be rebuilt just as good as new if proper techniques are followed.

DISASSEMBLY

Repair of a specific portion of the engine, such as a valve or piston, may be performed in most cases with the engine still in the chassis; but an extensive overhaul necessitates that the engine be removed from the car. This is one place the amateur can create many problems for himself. All the engine wiring must be disconnected, exhaust pipe and fuel line must be removed, throttle linkage detached, and the radiator hoses loosened.

Unless the mechanic has worked on a specific car several times, he usually finds it helpful to tag each electrical wire with a piece of masking tape, making note on the tag exactly where the wire connects (generator field, coil, oil pressure, etc.). The fuel line is taken loose at the fuel pump and plugged (otherwise the gas may siphon out and create a fire hazard), then the line is tucked out of the way. The exhaust headpipe(s) is often difficult to remove due to rusted nuts. A generous application of rust penetrant will cure this problem quickly.

Before the bolts holding transmission

and engine together are removed, the engine weight must be supported by either a hoist or a jack beneath the oil pan. The front motor mounts can usually be loosened at any time. While all the various accessories can be removed while the engine is still in the car, it is simpler to leave them in place for the time being. However, always remove the carburetor before lifting the engine from the chassis, or you'll stand a good chance of breaking the alloy casting. If the hoist chain is adjacent to the distributor, the latter should also be removed.

An engine stand is one of those luxury items never essential but always helpful to mechanics. Quite often a spare stand can be borrowed from a friend, and stand fabrication kits are available through parts supply houses. As an alternative, some kind of portable engine dolly will suffice. Never work on an engine on a dirt surface! Always have a clean floor and keep any dust to an absolute minimum.

Once the entire engine package is removed from the vehicle, direct disassembly may begin. At this time it must be pointed out that whatever comes off the engine first will usually be the last for reassembly. That is, the exhaust manifolds-heads, etc., come off first and go on last.

Unless he is careful, the mechanic can misplace a simple, but vital, bolt or nut or bracket. Jars and boxes should be labeled and parts from each particular

1. Awaiting Rebuilding

2. Steam Cleaning

3. Boring the Cylinder Block

4. Crosshatch Patterns

5. Honing the Cylinders

1. Engines—engines—engines—all awaiting rebuilding at Tomadur Engine Company in California's City of Industry. The only factory-authorized Ford rebuilder on the West Coast and the only factory-authorized Chevrolet rebuilder in the U.S., Tomadur rebuilds up to 1500 monthly and maintains ground vehicles of all major airlines at the L.A. airport.

2. We're going to follow a Ford 390-cu.-in. block through Tomadur's rebuilding procedure to give you an idea of how a professional rebuilder does it. A thorough steam cleaning follows disassembly to the bare block.

3. All cylinders are rebored two at a time using this Rottler Boring Bar. Once machine is set to specs for the type of engine on the line, the rest is automatic.

4. This is the proper crosshatch pattern in a cylinder bore. If angle is too shallow, rings will not seat during early stages; oil consumption and compression will also be poor.

5. After reboring, cylinders are finish honed. This produces the desired 45° crosshatch pattern on each cylinder wall, insuring maximum ring life and minimum oil consumption.

area placed in separate containers; *i.e.,* generator and bracket, head bolts, etc.

It is absolutely essential that the amateur carefully study each piece during disassembly. Note the sizes and number of bolts involved, the position of the piece, and any other peculiarity. Blindly tearing an engine apart is a good way to a future basket case that will have to be turned over to an unhappy professional.

As each major component, or group of parts, is taken from the engine, those caked with grease or oil should be set in a bucket of solvent and cleaned. Always work with a group of parts, such as connecting rods and pistons, to avoid misplaced pieces. The order of disassembly is not terribly important, but as a matter of convenience, the heads are usually removed first. What is found beneath the valve covers will be a direct indication of engine condition—thick sludge is normally a sure sign of a heavily worn engine.

The intake manifold must be removed, followed by the valley cover. Next all head bolts may be removed and, in the case of an overhead valve engine, the rocker arm shaft assembly taken off as a unit. Heads on any engine are usually quite heavy, so remove with caution. OHV heads are no problem, but flathead engines often use studs rather than capscrews to position the heads. If this is the case, the head may seem firmly rooted in place. While there are special cutters that slip over the stud and simplify removal, the more common method is to gently tap around the head circumference with a mallet. Once the head is loosened slightly, screwdrivers may be inserted at each end; then pry lightly and tap until the head is off. Obviously, once is enough with this problem, so the studs may be replaced with capscrews if desired. Set the heads aside and continue with the engine disassembly.

In the absence of a good engine stand, the engine may be set vertically on the bellhousing and the water pump/timing chain housing removed. The oil pan follows, with the oil residue at the pan sump bottom telling more of the engine condition story. Any kind of bearing or excessive metallic wear will be apparent as a thick or thin coating on the sump floor. Sludge buildup on the oil pump

pickup screen will be common if the engine has not been cared for, and will mean excessive wear at all lubricated surfaces. Remove the oil pump and set aside. Do not disassemble the major components at this time. It is easier to take them apart when ready to work on them, and this cuts down on the small pieces lying about the work area.

Use a center punch or number stamp to mark the connecting rod caps, then remove them. Very gently tap the loosened piston assembly out the top of the cylinder. Use the handle of a hammer for this job, not an object likely to damage the rod bolt threads or the crankshaft bearing surface. It is especially critical to be careful of the crank journals. The rod bolts can scratch a journal easily, and the condition of a journal may not require repair unless it is damaged in disassembly. Before the piston assembly is removed, however, it is necessary to check the top of the cylinder bore for an excessive ridge. Run the fingernail up the shiny part of the bore. If the dull, discolored ridge at the top of the bore is more than a few thousandths smaller than the bore, the fingernail will hang up solidly on the ledge. In this case, the lip may have to be removed with a ridge reamer before the pistons are knocked out of the block. Otherwise it is possible to break the rings, and while new replacement rings are probable, the piston (which might be reusable) may be severely damaged by the broken ring and have to be discarded.

One of the greatest mistakes the mechanic can make is to reassemble the engine with mismatched connecting rods and rod caps. To preclude this, most engines have the rods marked on one side near the bolt to match the caps. There might be a number, or dots, or lines. In the event there are no matching ID's, make your own before removing the assembly. After the rods are removed, replace the cap in the proper manner.

The main bearing caps are held in place by large-diameter bolts which usually need a little extra effort to be broken loose. In addition, some engine designs have the main caps recessed slightly in the block web to ensure maximum strength. A slight tap will unseat these

Overhauling Engine

caps. The crankshaft is then free for removal.

While it's best to replace camshaft bearings, they may be retained as an absolute budget measure. Although this is not recommended, the bearings can escape injury during disassembly if the camshaft is very, very carefully removed through the front of the block. However, before a camshaft may be removed each valve lifter must be taken out, and the location of each lifter should be carefully observed. Oversize lifters, especially hydraulic types, are not uncommon and may have been used.

With all the major parts groups thus removed, the engine is ready for careful inspection, cleaning, repair and finally reassembly.

CLEANING

While it may seem extra work, no part can be thoroughly inspected while dirty or oily. Obvious broken parts don't require cleaning to verify the need for discarding, but failures are generally small and hard to see. The initial cleansing may be nothing more than wiping an oily part dry, but it is important.

There are a number of different cleaning compounds, but under no circumstances should a highly volatile fluid be used, such as gasoline or benzene. Kerosene or a commercial cleaning compound available at the parts store is the best, and inexpensive. Stiff bristle brushes from the dime store are usually sufficient for most cleaning needs, while small-diameter, round steel brushes (such as used for cleaning gun barrels) are a necessity.

Initial cleaning may be limited to a group of parts. That is, the connecting rod and piston may be cleaned while still assembled, as may the head, distributor, etc. This is merely the first phase of cleanup. Although a thorough cleaning of the cylinder block may be deferred for a while, the crankshaft must receive an intensive cleaning at this time. Using the small round wire brush, clean the oil passages in the crank, and use the solvent liberally.

While most mechanics agree that "boiling out" the block and cylinder heads is a good initial cleaning process, many racing engine builders prefer to merely steam clean the block. Their reasoning is that the chemicals used for the hot boiling bath tend to enter the iron casting pores and remain there until the engine is again heated during actual operation. Then the compounds enter the oil. This is minor concern for a general overhaul, however, and is mentioned merely to point out that steam cleaning can be effective.

This is the initial cleanup only, and will be followed by a more comprehensive cleaning before the engine is finally reassembled.

INSPECTING THE PARTS

It is not difficult to recognize an unusually worn engine part, particularly those parts generally accustomed to fail-

1. Grinding a Crankshaft

2. Chamfered Oil Holes

3. Checking Crankshaft Straightness

ure, such as bearings, rings, and valves. Obviously, a broken connecting rod will be easy to spot. Virtually impossible to see, however, is the rod almost ready to break. Continual work loads imposed upon any mechanical assembly will eventually lead to a failure of some degree. Finding that potential failure early is the key to successful engine rebuilding, and it's the main reason professional mechanics subject suspected bad parts and vital components to Magnaflux inspection.

This type of inspection has become widespread during the past decade and is now available to the smallest communities, through either the auto parts stores or the heavy-duty/farming equipment dealers. Any engine rebuild should include a Magnaflux of the crankshaft, connecting rods and rod caps, connecting rod bolts and main bearing bolts. If the engine has been run for a long time, it is also wise to include the rocker arms and rocker arm shafts. Often such an inspection will reveal the smallest trace of a fatigue crack starting at some critical point, such as the radius of a crankshaft rod journal. If caught soon enough, such a potential danger spot can be re-

paired inexpensively by a machine shop. If a connecting rod bolt is ready to break, but appears normal to the eye, the rebuild is likely to be short-lived!

Anyplace there is metal-to-metal contact, suspect wear. This is the job of lubrication, surely, but wear is bound to occur to some degree in any mechanical apparatus. Look at the oil pump as a prime example. Here is a unit continually soaked in oil, but the pump end plate will wear nevertheless, due to the constant contact of the pump gears. Slight wear of any such area will appear as a polished surface. If the surface has not been receiving enough lubrication, the area will turn blue from excessive heat. Grooves worn in the surface are an immediate indication that the part should be replaced. As a general guide, replace a worn part if there is the slightest doubt of condition. Take that oil pump end plate, for instance. It could be resurfaced, of course, but the cost of this repair would be more than a new part.

Just looking at a part may or may not disclose wear. A crankshaft journal should be shiny all the time, and unless there is discoloration due to overheat or gouges worn in the surface, the journal

4. Miking a Crank Journal

5. Checking Journal Surface Finish

6. Grinding Camshaft

1. While the block is in the works, another line works on the crankshaft. After being checked for straightness, the crank is reground, and the journals are polished for the correct surface finish and clearance.

2. After a shaft has been ground, the edges of the oil holes are beveled to prevent shaving the bearing while the engine undergoes the break-in period.

3. Quality control inspector then checks crank with dial indicator to make sure that it's straight.

4. He also checks the size of the crank journals with a micrometer.

5. A magnetic pickup unit is connected to the measuring gauge and tells inspector if journal smoothness is correct. Too smooth a surface is as bad as one too coarse, as it passes oil too quickly.

6. While crankshafts are prepared, similar treatment is given to camshaft. Lobes must be perfectly shaped if engine is to run correctly.

may appear perfectly normal. The mechanic then relies on measuring instruments to detect undue wear.

There are three basic types of measuring tools a mechanic will use: the inside and outside micrometer, the feeler (thickness) gauge, and the dial indicator. The last is not an absolute necessity for the casual mechanic, but the first two are and should be used whenever necessary.

A micrometer, or "mike," is designed for linear measurement with accuracy of .001-in. or better. This means it will detect a measurement well within the range that concerns most mechanics. The inside mike is used for measuring the distance between two parallel surfaces, and is commonly used to measure the cylinder bore (taper, size, etc.), connecting rod big end, and block main bearing bore. The outside mike is used to measure the outside diameter of cylindrical forms and material thickness.

When using an outside mike, always measure several different points on the cylindrical object. For instance, a crankshaft journal may be flat in one spot only, and sloppy mike use would not show that spot. Even if the person could not read the mike, he could use it as a comparison instrument and rapidly find a problem area.

The inside micrometer is a bit harder to use, because the instrument must be absolutely perpendicular to the surfaces measured. As can be seen, if the outside diameter of a crankshaft rod journal is measured, and a similar measurement taken of the inside diameter of a coupled connecting rod big end, the difference in measurements should be the exact clearance involved (taking into account the bearing thickness, if the bearing is not included).

A measuring device of sorts is Plastigage, a soft thread-like pliable material. Plastigage comes in specified diameters, and when flattened out to predetermined widths will equal some specified clearance. Common use of this material is to check clearance between crankshaft and main/rod bearings. A short length of material is laid crossways in the bearing, then the main/rod caps torqued to the correct reading. The crankshaft must not

be rotated. The caps are then removed and the flattened piece of material measured to determine clearance.

Feeler gauges are an absolute necessity in any mechanic's toolbox, and may range through a variety of sizes and shapes. For engine overhaul, the feeler gauge will come into play often, measuring piston ring end clearance, valve lash, ignition point spacing, spark plug gap, rod side-play, crankshaft thrust play, and other critical clearances.

REPAIRING CRACKS AND THREADS

Although the amateur will find repairing cracks in the cylinder block or heads a touchy subject, he can do much for total block and head preparation without calling on a professional service.

The first thing to check for is warpage of the head(s) or block. Because cylinder blocks are relatively strong structures to begin with, any warping will usually be minimal in the case of cast iron. Alloy blocks (aluminum) will and do distort considerably, so they must be checked especially well. The critical areas of block warpage are head and crankshaft mating surfaces. The former may be corrected by grinding or milling if it is not too severe (seldom), and the crankshaft bore can be line-bored (common). The head(s) can be milled or ground true, but only if distortion is minimal (check with the machine shop for this minimum measurement; it varies with engine and operating condition).

To check for distortion, lay a perfectly straight edge of some sort across the surface and then try to slide a feeler gauge between the surfaces. Do this lengthwise, crosswise, and diagonally. As a guide, anything more than .020-in. is excessive warpage and requires machine shop correction.

Although corrosion is not a crack, it can cause irreparable damage, and must be expected if the engine is very old or of alloy construction. This problem will exist principally in the water circulation passages, and will be pronounced around the mating surface openings, as between head and block or water pump and block. If dissimilar metals are used

Overhauling Engine

on the engine—such as an alloy block with steel cylinder liners, or alloy heads, or alloy water pump housing—an electrolytic action can occur. Clean the affected area thoroughly, grinding away any pieces that could become dislodged and work into the water system, and definitely determine if the sealing surface has been adversely affected. To counteract corrosion, always use a soluble oil or antifreeze mixed with the coolant.

A cracked cylinder block will show up right away if it is external, and may be welded by an expert professional. Under no circumstance should the amateur try crack repairs without qualified instruction. However, repairs are common when new replacement parts are difficult to find or expensive, such as in the case of an antique engine. External cracks are usually the result of water freezing in the block. The problem cracks are those occurring inside the engine.

Overhead valve engines are not prone to having cracked cylinder blocks (internal), but flathead (valve in block) engines are. This problem usually occurs between the valve seat and the cylinder bore, aggravated by poor water circulation and engine overheat.

Cracks between valve ports can be repaired by peening the fracture carefully (small cracks), or by welding. Large cracks that extend well into the cylinder bore make the block unusable.

Sometimes cracks in blocks or heads are repaired by drilling holes at either end of the crack and inserting threaded studs. These are cut off at the surface and another hole drilled adjacent to the first, half in the cracked surface and half in the stud insert. This is continued until the crack is filled. But as can be seen, crack repair of any kind is tedious and time consuming, and necessarily, expensive. Replacement of the part is usually less expensive.

Threaded holes in the block and head(s) can easily become damaged, especially on older engines. The solution is to run the proper size tap into all threaded holes, cleaning away rust and refuse metal or dirt in the process. If the threads have been damaged beyond return to normal size, the simplest method of repair is to drill the hole oversize and use a thread insert, such as Heli-Coil. Use of such thread inserts is especially advisable in alloy blocks or heads.

Slight distortion is a standard part of fastening two metal surfaces, and is engineered into both the bolt and the pieces being bolted together. However, in the case of threaded holes in the block or head, this distortion may often be too much, and will cause the threads to ''slip.'' The resulting lip around the threaded hole will then make subsequent mating less than ideal. The cure is to countersink each threaded hole very slightly.

REPAIRING THE CYLINDER BLOCK

Wear in an engine is usually greatest in the cylinder bore, followed by the crankshaft bearing areas, the valve

1. Checking Camshaft

2. Polishing Camshaft

3. Sandblasting Cylinder Heads

guides, valve seats, etc. Thus, much attention to basic cylinder block reconditioning is necessary in practically any engine overhaul.

During disassembly the ridge at the top of the cylinders was removed. This was, in itself, a definite indication of cylinder bore wear. However, a cylinder will not wear the same at top and bottom; rather, the top will wear more than the bottom. The result is a taper to the bore, and this is the culprit that causes most overbore requirements. When bore taper, or the difference in size between top and bottom, exceeds .010- .012-in., the block needs boring. A very slight taper can be cleaned up by a hone, as can minor scratches on the cylinder wall, but such easily corrected conditions are unlikely to exist in any engine with 50,000 or more miles.

While pistons may sometimes be resized if the cylinders are only slightly enlarged by honing, the typical rebuild will require a reasonable overbore and new oversize pistons. These pistons should always be bought before the block is bored, then the block matched to the pistons. Sometimes, the piston manufacturer will include the operating clearance in the piston size, sometimes not, so make sure what size you're working with and you won't experience trouble.

Because most older engines are not nearly as powerful as their modern counterparts, increasing the displacement via an impressive overbore is a direct route to greater power. However, this is possible only on engines made before the thinwall casting process came into widespread use in the late 1950's: a process designed to reduce engine block weight drastically. Therefore, older engines can usually take up to .125-in. overbore, while thinwall engines can seldom take more than .030-in. In essence, this

means that the modern engine can seldom take more than one rebuild where boring is required.

If the piston pin has slipped in the piston, it can cause extensive damage to a cylinder wall, sometimes beyond repair with an overbore. In such a case, the cylinder can be bored to accept a sleeve, but the cost is high. If the cylinder has been scored due to broken rings or seizing pistons, an overbore will probably also be necessary. However, if aluminum pistons have only deposited excess alloy material on the cylinder wall, a minor honing will usually solve the problem.

Using a boring bar is not difficult, but such equipment is not likely to be in the amateur's toolbox. Instead, work such as this is best farmed out to a machine shop specializing in such things, and will cost from $2 to $4 per cylinder. Nevertheless, it behooves the mechanic to understand how the boring bar is used.

Boring bars may locate off either the head surface or the crankshaft bore, but in each case the idea is to get a bore exactly perpendicular to the crankshaft centerline. Therefore, the block must be securely mounted to the cutting equipment. Seldom is the entire cut made at one time, rather the bar may need a few passes through the hole to get the preliminary sizing. Most bars are automatic, in that they will shut off when a predetermined depth has been reached, but all must be attached to the block carefully to insure accurate boring for each cylinder.

Following the boring operation, each cylinder must be carefully honed, a procedure usually included to give the final sizing. The correct surface for a cylinder wall is not glass-smooth. New rings will not seat when the walls are perfectly smooth, and oil control or com-

4. Magnafluxing a Cylinder Head

5. Cleaning a Cylinder Head

1. After grinding, camshaft is also inspected for correct dimensions before polishing of journal surfaces.

2. After journals are given the final polishing, all exposed camshaft surfaces will be wrapped with tape to prevent damage while awaiting installation.

3. Heads are sandblasted as first step in their rebuild. A circular stage carries heads through process and returns them to operator.

4. Each head is then magnafluxed before further work is carried out. Rejection rate here can run as high as one out of four.

5. After head is checked for cracks, it's placed inside these constantly revolving tires and tumbled to free whatever sandblasting debris might remain in the passages, then it's completely cleaned with compressed air.

pression blow-by is sure to be a problem. At the same time, a too smooth cylinder may score from lack of lubrication.

While the honing operation is usually included with any bore job, the mechanic may sometimes be required to do the job himself. In this case, he must remember that the scratches are so tiny they can be measured only in microinches (that's one millionth of an inch!). However, he will force the revolving

hone down the cylinder at a smooth pace, then pull it back up so a cross-hatch pattern is formed on the cylinder walls. This cross-hatch will have intersecting lines from 45° to 60°.

The amount of clearance involved in piston-to-cylinder wall fit will vary considerably due to engine operation. However, since most modern replacement pistons take into account the wide operational requirements of automotive engines, it can be assumed that .001-in. per inch of piston diameter is a safe guide. This means a 4-in. piston will get .0035 to .004-in. wall clearance. In all cases, the piston manufacturer will have a recommended clearance and this should be followed explicitly. It may be as little as .0005. Of course, engines that will be operated at rpm's greater than stock, such as racing engines, will require greater piston clearances.

After the cylinder walls have been honed, each piston should be slipped into a cylinder and the clearance checked with a long feeler gauge.

Following the reboring job, the top lip of the bores may be slightly chamfered to make it easier to get the rings into the bore. The block is line-bored if necessary. Again, this is a job normally left to a machine shop, because they have the equipment. What is involved is a safety check of the crankshaft bore, since it can get out of alignment due to distor-

tion. For line-boring, the main bearing caps are torqued in place, then the bore is trued. The camshaft bore may also be line-bored, but this is not common.

The lifter bores should always be checked, and if the clearance is greater than .005-in., new lifters will be required (oversize). In this instance, the lifter bores are also honed out.

After all the block machine work has been accomplished, the soft plugs (freeze plugs) should be removed and replaced with new ones. These plugs often corrode on the inside, and although they look OK, may soon fail.

The final block cleaning is now at hand. The block can be given the hot or cold tank cleaning treatment (soaked), or it can again be steam cleaned. In either case, after this cleaning, the newly machined surfaces should be thoroughly washed with ordinary soap and warm water. All oil passages in the block should be cleaned out with the small wire brush, and blown clear with compressed air. This operation is vital, since any small particles of metal or dirt trapped in an oil gallery can cause immediate engine failure. After this cleaning, all machined surfaces should be coated with a light oil to inhibit rusting.

The engine may be painted with some kind of heat-resistant paint, preferably that from a spray can rather than by brush, as a thick coat of paint will tend to flake off later on. All the inside surfaces of the block that are not machined may be painted with a very light coat of Rust-Oleum. This will tend to keep sludge from finding a foothold on the rough casting; the practice is common in race engine building. To keep dust from collecting on the oiled block, cover it with a plastic bag like those available from the dry cleaner.

THE CRANKSHAFT

A brand-new crankshaft is seldom necessary to an engine overhaul, unless a journal has been severely damaged. However, it is not common to grind a crankshaft more than .030-in. undersize.

Wear to a crankshaft may come from several different causes. Forces on a rotating crankshaft are much heavier at some points of the journal than at others. As an example, the explosion force is much stronger than the compression stroke force, which will tend to cause a "flat spot" on the journal at that point. A bent or misaligned connecting rod will rotate in a cocked fashion on the crankpin journal, and this will cause the bearing surface to wear in a taper. The engine block may twist during operation, and in the case of engines with only three or four main bearing journals, the crankshaft can distort during rotation. All this will tend to wear the main journals in either a tapered or warped fashion and regrinding is necessary.

Individual bearing journals will not have the same amount of wear, because of oil supply to specific journals, abrasives entering the oil, misaligned rods, etc. Therefore, some kind of crankshaft reconditioning should be expected with any overhaul.

Very carefully inspect the crankshaft journals, both main and connecting rod,

Overhauling Engine

as tiny cracks may develop here long before a failure occurs. If these cracks are visible to the eye, replacement of the crankshaft is a necessity. At the same time, a Magnaflux inspection will reveal unseen cracks. Repair of a crankshaft may include regrinding the journals to an undersize, or welding and regrinding. If the journal must be repaired in any way, it is advisable to have the edges of each journal radiused slightly. A sharp junction between journal and check will encourage stress concentration and metal fracture.

To determine the condition of the crankshaft, measure with an outside micrometer, checking both sides of the journal. Two measurements should be taken at each point, 90° to each other

(top and bottom, and sideways). Because of the operating pressures creating a flat spot on the top of the crank, this measurement will usually be slightly smaller than the sideways measurement, and is normal. However, if this reading shows a difference of more than .002-in., the crankshaft must be reconditioned.

Bearings come in a number of undersizes (the bearing is really oversize, to compensate for the worn crankpin), from .001 on up to above .030-in. If the crankshaft is in good shape except for a minor undersize, a replacement bearing may be all that's necessary. If the shaft needs regrinding, it may be taken down .010, .020, or .030-in. When a shaft is reground, it is usually taken down to a standard undersize to make bearing selection easy.

It is not unusual for a crankshaft to be bent, that is, warped through the center-

line. When a machine shop repairs a crankshaft, they always check for this warped condition by using a dial indicator along each main bearing journal. Only minor hydraulic pressure or taps with a sledge are required to straighten the shaft. Even if the shaft proves reusable without journal regrinding, it should be checked for straightness, anyway.

Never install a reconditioned crankshaft as received from the machine shop! It may not be clean. Anytime a crankshaft is removed from the engine, thoroughly clean each and every oil delivery gallery with a wire brush (preferably a stainless steel wire). Wash the crank with both clean solvent and warm soap and water, then blow it dry with compressed air. The tiniest bit of carbon or foreign material in the oil passages can lead to a sudden demise of an otherwise excellent engine.

1. Resurfacing Cylinder Head

2. Installing New Valve Guides

3. Grinding Valve Seats

4. Facing Valves

1. Head is resurfaced where necessary to assure uniform fit when replaced on block. Automatic machine moves head back and forth under a steady stream of oil.

2. On heads that lack integral valve guides, old ones are machined out, replaced with new ones, and honed. This insures that valves will all work in a straight line.

3. Cutting a valve seat increases the width of the seat. Final stone used has a 60° angle to face seat and return it to correct width.

4. Each valve is then checked for straightness and refaced.

5. Valve spring assemblies are not complicated; note the little seal on the intake valve stem. It's there to keep oil from running down the valve stem and getting into the combustion chamber. If additional seals were used on ends of guides, they'd have to go inside the inner spring, but there might not be room for such seals on this double spring setup.

After the crankshaft is clean, coat the machined surfaces with a light oil and prepare to install it in the block.

BEARINGS

Rod and main bearings are the most abused parts of an internal combustion engine. They must operate under the most difficult conditions, yet remain faithful for thousands of miles. And even when they do fail, they are not expected to cause excessive damage to their closest ally, the crankshaft. Because of such high requirements, bearing designs and construction have received special attention for as long as automobiles have run.

There is no single bearing metal that can meet the requirements of an engine, at least in the pure state. Such a material would have to have a melting point consistent with manufacturing processes, the proper malleability (softness), low coefficient of friction, high fatigue resistance, resistance to high engine temperatures, resistance to corrosion, ability to adhere to steel or bronze backs (shells), and ready availability at reasonable cost. Since no specific material fits all these requirements, bearings are therefore made of alloys.

These alloys include tin-base babbitt, lead-base babbitt, copper, aluminum, and multi-layer copper and aluminum. Most bearings in use today are of the thin-shell type, which consists of a thin layer of bearing alloy supported by a steel backing. For heavy-duty service, such as racing engines encounter, the multi-layer bearing is more reliable.

Unless the engine is being rebuilt with heavy-duty operation in mind, it is best to follow the original manufacturer's recommendation as to bearing type. If the original bearing had a certain type of oil hole and no grooves, then the replacement bearing should be similar (unless otherwise specified). Under all circumstances, the oil hole in the bearing must align with the delivery hole in the block or connecting rod.

Most modern engines keep the bearing

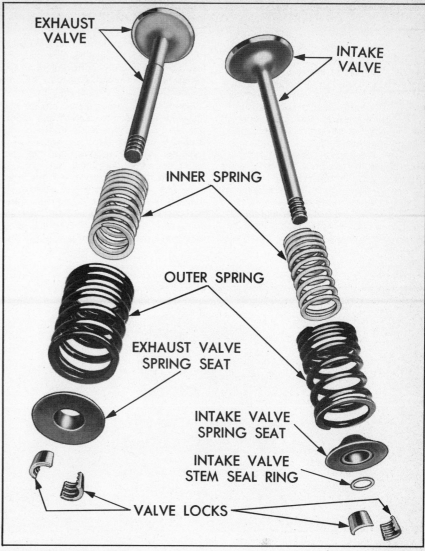

5. Valve Spring Assembly

inserts in place by a locating lug stamped in the bearing shell and a corresponding slot in the housing to prevent rotation.

Bearing manufacturers also make each bearing half slightly greater than 180° This allows a slight bit of bearing to stick up beyond the intended housing. When the other half of the bearing assembly is installed and torqued into place, this "crush" area will cause the bearing to positively seat in the housing. Never file the edges of a bearing because it seems too big, and make sure there is no foreign material between the mating edges of bearing halves. In either case, the proper crush would be disturbed.

CONNECTING RODS

Although the engine may have been running reasonably well before disassembly, with no apparent connecting rod trouble, each and every rod should nevertheless be checked and reconditioned if necessary. Such service is simple: recondition the big and little bores, and straighten if needed.

However, reconditioning of the rod is only a recent requirement, necessary because of the changes in both rod and bearing design. When engines were sel-

dom producing more than 200 horsepower, and internal loads were much less than the modern engine, rods could—and would—seemingly last forever. While the primary function of the rod is to transmit combustion forces to the crankshaft, it has the secondary responsibility of lubricating other parts of the engine. The condition of the rod big end (saddle bore) must therefore be as near perfect as possible. If the rod bearing fit is improper, it can cause scored cylinder walls, pistons, and rings, or excessive oil pumping.

While insert bearings have undergone excellent design changes during recent years, connecting rod design has kept pace, with heavy-duty and high-performance requirements creating a full line of top-quality rods for practically any engine. If an engine is going to be subjected to greater than normal loads, better rods should be installed. As an example, a Chevrolet V-8 engine (283-cu.-in. small-block version) can have as much as 5 tons of explosive pressure exerted on the piston. In addition to this tremendous force, at 4500 rpm the rod reverses direction 150 times per second. That's hauling, and the rod is doing a tremendous job under strenuous conditions.

New rods are expensive, so rebuilt rods are commonly used. In this case,

Overhauling Engine

the normal approach is to remove a slight amount of metal from the mating surfaces of the cap. This reduces the internal diameter of the rod, thus allowing the saddle bore to be honed to original size. This kind of rework must be done with the greatest possible accuracy, therefore it is a machine shop operation and should be left to professionals with proper tools.

Should the rod be bent, it can be straightened in a press. If the rod is bent edgewise, such as might occur from seizure, or if bent sideways, the alignment will be improper and cause wear at the bearing. After the rod is straightened, the rod center-to-center length must be accurately measured, and the rod may be checked against a flat surface to make sure all bends or twists are removed.

The small end of the rod must likewise receive attention. If the piston pin bushings are only slightly worn, they may be honed and oversized pins can be installed.

However, if new pistons are to be installed—and this is likely if the block has been bored—the new piston pins will probably be standard. Therefore new bushings will be required for the rod small end. Installing new bushings is easy, and it may be done with an ordinary vise. Care must be exercised so that the bushings enter straight and are not cocked. At the same time, any oil holes must be aligned. Thin-wall bronze bushings must be pressed tightly into the small end rod bore, and then honed to fit the piston pin.

There are two different ways that the piston pin bushing may be clearanced: by expanding hones, or diamond boring. A diamond boring machine is useful when a large amount of material has to be removed, but the best pin fitting is done with a honing machine. It can provide exact pin fits as close as .0001-in.

If a reamer is used, the bushing surface will not be smooth; therefore the pin must do the final fitting during initial operation. Because of this rough surface, a reamer pin fit is called either thumb or palm, meaning the amount of pressure required. A thumb fit requires less pressure than the palm, etc. Far better is the honed or bored bushing, where the fit is determined by clearances in ten-thousandths of an inch. As a rule, a pin will fall through a dry bushing of its own weight when the hole diameter is just right, but will drag somewhat when lubricated. If manufacturer clearances are not available, a rule of thumb is to use .0004-.0006-in. per inch of pin diameter. These clearances may vary according to type of pin action (full-floating, bushed, setscrew, etc.), so checking the engine manufacturer's charts is vital.

The full-floating piston pin design is finding great favor in modern engines, but the pin fit must be very close to perfect. As a rule, a bushed pin hole may use a slip fit of .0002-in. cold. Under normal engine operating conditions this clearance will increase to .0004-in., which is still acceptable for normal engine life.

PISTONS

If the cylinder bores are not worn

1. Using a Spring Compressor

2. Grinding Rocker Arm Face

3. Pressing Out Rocker Arm Bushing

excessively, it is possible to reuse the same pistons with new rings. There is a limit to this economical repair, however, and if the engine has many thousands of miles on it, don't consider this.

There are times, however, when nothing more than minor piston work is necessary. Sometimes, inferior rings are used in an engine, causing the rings to wear out too soon, and in this case a replacement is all that's needed. However, the wear of the rings in the piston grooves may require special piston reconditioning. Because the ring is trying to drag on the cylinder wall, it will work up and down in the piston groove until this groove is opened up, or widened. Excessive widening is normally restricted to the top groove, but if the lower two or three grooves open up, the piston must be replaced. If the top groove is widened, the opening will taper toward the outside. By cutting the groove with a special grooving tool this edge can be straightened out, and special spacers installed above the top ring. This is to keep the compression ring from traveling a fraction of an inch too high in the cylinder bore and striking any ring ledge.

If cylinder rebore is not necessary, but new rings must be installed, it may be necessary to also expand the piston skirts.

The most common method of expanding a worn skirt is by knurling. With this process, the skirt of the piston is given a waffle-groove effect. A tool forced against the skirt causes some material to displace, or squirt outward, effectively increasing the skirt diameter. Such a process can increase diameter as much as .008-in., often just enough to keep the piston from rocking in the bore and wearing the rings oval-shape.

There will be a difference in various piston designs. Some will be perfectly round and others will be cam ground; that is, there may be a difference in measurement across the thrust face of the piston versus the piston pin face.

Such a feature will keep the piston quieter when cold, and allow expansion room when the piston reaches operating temperature. The amateur will seldom be faced with this as a basic rebuilding problem, inasmuch as the machine shop or original supplier will grind the pistons to size if necessary.

Whether the pistons are new or used, they should be carefully inspected for cracks, especially around the pin bore and the ring lands. Used pistons should

4. Pressing New Bushing Into Rocker Arm

5. Reassembly of Rocker Arm Shaft

1. An air-operated C-type valve spring compressor is used to hold the spring and seat down while locks are installed. For the tool fancier, this one's elegant.

2. Rocker arm radiused tip is just lightly touched to grinding stone. This trues up the face that operates on the valve stem.

3. New bushings are then pressed into rocker arms for a precision fit.

4. New rocker arm bushing is reamed to factory specifications and then installed on new rocker arm shaft.

5. Reassembly of the rocker and shaft assembly is done with new shafts, springs, etc. as these parts are usually too worn to be trusted. Quality control at Tomadur keeps rejection/return rate to a minimum.

6. A slight amount of metal is removed from the mating surfaces of the connecting rod cap, reducing the internal diameter of the rod and allowing the bore to be honed to its original size.

6. Grinding Rod Cap

Overhauling Engine

have the grooves cleaned and all oil holes unplugged.

Assembly of the rod and piston is a precision affair only in that care must be taken to get them together in proper relationship. Individual shop manuals must be consulted in this respect, since different manufacturers use different types of identification. However, if there is a necessity, the piston is identified in some way as to which is the front side and which should be toward the rear of the block. This is another reason disassembly should be thoughtful and careful. In general, the front top edge of the piston will be marked by a notch.

If the piston pin is retained by some sort of lock, make absolutely certain this lock is in place. Small nicks or burrs in the lock groove may cause it to seat improperly and cause serious damage later. When inserting the lock, squeeze it together only enough to slide into the pin hole. If it is compressed too much, it may take a set and not spring outward in the groove sufficiently. Always use new lock rings.

How well the engine performs after the rebuild will depend on how good a ring job the mechanic does. The modern automobile engine works under such severe conditions that every vital part must do its job correctly, and nothing is more vital than proper ring action. To achieve this with a rebuild, the correct replacement rings are mandatory. A brand-new engine works under considerably different conditions than a rebuilt engine. Rust and scale have built up on the coolant side of the bores until a different type of temperature range is occasioned; distortion will change with a rebore, etc. Therefore, it has been found that modern high-speed engines need something different in the way of rings than factory originals. As an example, any rebuild will generally include expander-type oil rings to control the oil under these different-than-new conditions.

Rings are of three basic types: compression, scraper, and oil control. Another division separates the iron rings from spring-type expander designs, in that the expander rings are placed behind regular rings to force the latter more firmly against the cylinder wall and thereby aid sealing.

The compression ring has the prime responsibility of keeping the burning combustion chamber gases from reaching the lubricated part of the cylinder wall (this is called leaking down, or blow-by). The modern engine uses a tapered-face compression ring which will tend to slide over the oiled cylinder wall on the upstroke (thereby not pumping much oil into the combustion chamber), but will scrape excess oil off the wall on the downstroke. Such rings always have the top so marked, and this side must always be positioned up.

The second ring, or scraper, is used to help the compression ring. It scrapes oil on the downstroke and is a secondary seal against blow-by. There are several different designs of scraper rings, and in all cases the manufacturer's recommendations must be followed explicitly. The

1. Honing Rod Ends

2. Press-Fitting Pins

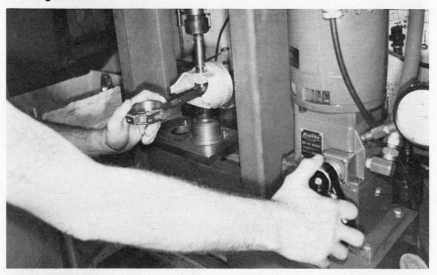

3. Installing Floating Pin

1. Honing restores bore to stock specs. Small end of rod is then bored, bushed, and honed to retain the stock center-to-center measurement.

2. Connecting rods in many stock engines are fitted with pressed-in wrist pins. Pin is a press-fit in rod but a slip fit in the piston.

3. Floating wrist pins are tapped in place with a mallet.

4. Lock rings or pin retaining clips are inserted at ends of wrist pin.

5. Actual block assembly begins with the installation of oil galley plugs.

6. Freeze plugs are seated by gently tapping in place as shown.

4. Installing Pin Retaining Clip

5. Installing Oil Gallery Plugs

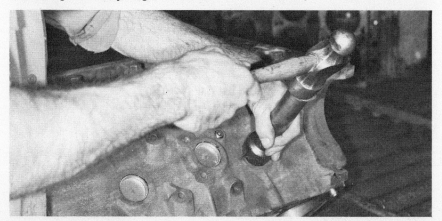

6. Installing Freeze Plugs

oil control ring is designed to keep oil from entering the combustion chamber and varies in design depending upon the amount of oil control necessary. These rings are vented so excess oil can be sloughed through the piston and back to the supply point.

Installation of piston rings is a careful, methodical procedure, where sloppy work cannot be tolerated. Never assume that any new part is "just right" for the engine—always measure to make sure. With the piston, the ring groove should always be measured and compared with the requirements of the replacement rings as set forth by the ring manufacturer. Rings are produced to fit factory pistons perfectly, but replacement pistons may vary. Gauges for checking ring groove depth and width are available wherever rings are sold, and should be used. If the piston does have deeper than normal grooves, special expanders are available for the rings in a variety of sizes to counteract the difference. If the grooves are too shallow, it is best to re-groove them more deeply.

Side clearance of the ring is absolutely imperative, and each ring should be checked along with each ring groove. On old pistons the ring groove will usually have worn until excessive clearance is the norm. New pistons, though, can have insufficient ring groove side clearance, which should be .002-in. for the top or compression ring, and .0015-in. for the remaining rings. To check this, slide a feeler gauge alongside the ring to the full depth of the groove. If the rings are slightly large, they can be reduced in thickness by rubbing them against a perfectly flat piece of emery cloth, then polishing with crocus cloth. Sand the top of the compression and scraper rings and the bottom of the oil ring.

Perhaps the most overlooked part of amateur engine overhauls is piston ring end-gap. This should always be checked, and each individual ring must be inserted in the cylinder bore during the procedure. Ring end-gap is normally .004-in. per inch of cylinder diameter for the compression ring, and .013-in. for the remaining rings. For a 4-in. bore, this would mean a .016-in. gap for the top ring, and .052-in. for the remaining rings.

This is a minimum clearance, and having too much is not a problem. Too little will allow the ring gap to squeeze closed, and broken rings and/or lands are the result. If the cylinders have not been rebored, always check this gap at the smallest portion of the bore, or the bottom of the piston travel. If the engine block has been rebored, the fit will be identical everywhere.

To check a ring, insert it about 1 in. down the bore and square it with the wall by tapping lightly with a piston. Measure the gap with a feeler gauge. If it is too little, remove the ring and run an end across a file. Be careful of the tiny parts, as the ends may break. As the rings are gapped, leave them in the cylinder bore until time to assemble to a piston, and mark that piston correspondingly. This will ensure the right rings per bore.

Placing the rings on the piston is a simple operation, but the novice may

Overhauling Engine

break one or two in the process. Slide one lip down at a time if a regular ring expansion plier is not available, and work slowly. Installed, the ring gaps should be rotated 90° or more from one another, otherwise a straight-through gap is left for combustion gases. Multi-piece oil rings must also be treated specially during installation. Place the steel expander gap over a piston pin hole; place one steel segment with its gap 90° off, followed by the spacer or cast iron center section with a gap over the opposite pin hole; then place the final steel segment 180° to the first.

SHORT BLOCK ASSEMBLY

With the piston/rod assembly completed, the basic short block may now be assembled. There are various assembly lubricants on the market, and all work well. Remember that for the first few minutes a rebuilt engine is running, lubrication is super critical. Even when the oil pump has been prerun, oil will take a moment to reach the proper parts. An assembly lube will counteract this early starvation problem and should be used.

With the block upside down on a stand or dolly, wipe the main bearing saddles clean. A tiny piece of dirt behind the bearing will cause all kinds of bearing problems. Install the correct bearing half-shell in both the block and main cap, then install the proper cap to each block web. Lubricate the main bearing bolts with a good anti-seize compound, then torque each cap to the prescribed setting. Do not put assembly lube on the bearings at this time.

With an inside micrometer, check the inside diameter of each and every bearing bore, measuring both up and down and sideways. If everything has been correct up to this point, the measurement obtained should be the diameter of the crankshaft journal plus the prescribed oil clearance. This clearance will vary according to the individual engine, but the manufacturer's specifications should always be followed. In the case of main bearings, the clearance will be somewhere between .0015 and .0025-in. For rod bearings it will be from .002 to .003-in. If the engine will be used in high-performance or heavy-duty applications, oil clearance should be increased slightly, or run at the upper limit. Always consult a qualified mechanic or authoritative publication, such as *Hot Rod*

magazine, for performance specifications.

The connecting rods should be assembled and checked in the same way. However, as mentioned previously, Plastigage may be used to check clearance, and if the mechanic is not sure of his mike-reading ability, this "actual condition" type measurement is recommended for best results.

After main bearing clearance has been checked, the caps are removed and the bearing faces coated with assembly lube. The crankshaft is carefully laid in the block and the caps reassembled and again torqued to specifications.

The crankshaft should spin freely in the bore, without the slightest uneven drag. If it doesn't, something is wrong and work should not proceed until the trouble is found and corrected. Here is one place where the bent crankshaft and/or distorted block will show up immediately. Finally, check the crankshaft end-play, or the amount the crank can slide back and forth in the bearings.

End-play is checked between the crankshaft journal thrust collar and the main bearing thrust flange, using a feeler gauge to measure the distance. Pry the crankshaft away from the bearing surface. High-performance engines will

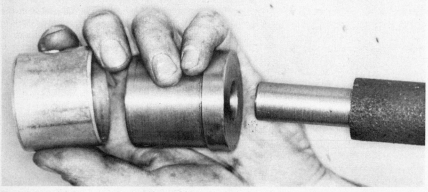

1. Cam Bushing Installation Tool

1. *Use camshaft bushing installer to install bushings properly. Tool fits all the way inside cam bushing.*

2. *Bushings are installed from rear to front. Oil passage holes must line up with feed hole in the block or bearings will seize from lack of oil when engine is operated.*

3. *Once cam bearings are installed, new welch plug is fitted to back of cam bore. Plug's O.D. is coated with nonhardening sealer before fitting.*

4. *After removing the protective tape from the cam surfaces, it's carefully installed by hand to avoid marring the bearing surfaces.*

5. *Cam is seated completely by tapping into place. Note use of bolt screwed into cam face. This centers force of impact, as an off-center blow could mar the bearing surfaces as cam moves backward. Bolt is removed when cam is seated.*

6. *Camshaft retaining plate is secured in place and tightened with an impact air wrench.*

2. Installing Cam Bushings

3. Installing Cam Plug

4. Installing the Camshaft

5. Seating Camshaft

6. Installing Cam Retaining Plate

have more clearance than stock engines, but as a guide, crankshaft journals from 2 to 3 ins. need .005-in. Journals of 3 to 3½ ins. need .008-in., and journals over 3½ ins. need .010-in.

Assembly of the pistons comes next. The pistons should be liberally coated with assembly lube, or dipped in oil, then a ring squeezer tightened to compress the rings. With the piston in proper position to the block, the piston crown is gently tapped with a hammer handle to force the assembly into the bore. It is vital that the rings be fully compressed into their grooves, or they will hang up on the entrance to the bore and may be broken. Revolve the crankshaft until the respective journal is at the bottom of its travel for each piston insertion, thus gaining working room for the connecting rod. After the last ring has cleared the ring compressor, the piston may be tapped through the bore until the connecting rod seats on the proper crankshaft journal.

For protection to the crankshaft, slip small pieces of rubber tubing over the rod bolts, and carefully guide each rod onto the journal. Once in place, the tubing is removed and the proper cap is installed. After all rods are in place, the caps are torqued to the correct specifications and individual journal side play is checked. This will not have changed normally, but if different rods or crankshaft from the original are involved, this should be checked during crankshaft preparation. This end-play is important to lubrication, and may be checked by inserting a feeler gauge between one rod side and the crankshaft cheek. If it is between .004 and .010-in., this is sufficient for stock engines. High-performance engines will need additional clearance.

Often overlooked by novice mechanics is the fact that oil on a bearing acts as a coolant as well as a lubricant. Oil enters the bearing through a delivery hole, is forced across the entire bearing surface,

and exits through the clearance at each bearing side. As engine temperatures increase, the metal will expand. If the side clearance has been insufficient to begin with, the oil flow across the bearing is impaired until heat buildup is increased, failure is near. Too much side clearance is just as bad as not enough, since oil squirting out the side of rod bearings is used to oil cylinder walls, camshaft, and other components.

With the pistons assembled in the block, the crankshaft should still rotate without an uneven drag, although it will take more effort.

THE CAMSHAFT

The camshaft can be a real pain for the novice mechanic. It is one of those parts that wear in a most uneven manner, and unless carefully inspected will contribute to much head-scratching later on. A camshaft may have only one lobe slightly worn, and this will be enough to make the engine run slightly bad. The mechanic may suspect any number of causes before finding the culprit. The cam can twist, which will change the valve timing between front and rear cylinders. It is, therefore, to be suspect from the start of any engine overhaul.

Reconditioned camshafts are available through larger engine rebuilding shops, since they will never return an old cam to an engine. These cams are reground, and often rehardened if necessary, much as a crankshaft is repaired. Whether a new or reconditioned cam is used, the mechanic must be satisfied with spending a few dollars. This is one place it doesn't pay to be skimpy; simply reusing the old camshaft is merely asking for subsequent trouble from the entire valve train.

The camshaft rotates at half total engine speed, yet the very high loads imposed by the lifters make cam lobe wear a foregone conclusion. If an engine is

Overhauling Engine

running rough for no apparent reason, the ultimate cause may be traced to a single camshaft lobe that has worn round, thereby letting one valve loaf on the job. This is not at all uncommon on engines with many miles, and is particularly true of medium-to-high-performance engines.

The selection of the proper camshaft has a direct effect upon how the finished engine will perform. If the engine is to remain stock, then a stock replacement should be utilized. However, it is possible to install a camshaft with different valve timing (the relationship of valve opening/closing to piston location in the cylinder). This does not automatically mean installing a high-lift racing camshaft. There are several different factory-type camshaft patterns available for the small-block Chevrolet engine, for instance (265 through 350-cu.-in. design), and each can actually be called a normal design. However, one will give better low-end torque, while another is better for higher speed operation.

Another example is the pre-1964 Oldsmobile V-8. The 1964 camshaft is an excellent all-around pattern, having been developed for a reasonably large displacement engine that must have both low-end torque and good cruising rpm. This cam can be fitted to any of the earlier Olds V-8's (lifters must also be used), and is superior to any of the earlier cam designs. It costs no more than any of the previous camshafts. As a guide, pick an engine of the same type as that being rebuilt, then investigate the factory parts manual for camshaft specifications. If a 283 Chevrolet V-8 is being overhauled, it is entirely possible to use a camshaft from one of the milder performing Corvettes, and in one simple operation to update the older engine performance.

When the engine block was being cleaned, the camshaft bearings were removed, either by a drift punch or a special puller. If the engine was placed in a caustic immersion bath, the bearings would have been eaten away and useless anyway.

New bearings can be put in at any time, but care must be taken to get the bearings installed properly. Coat the outside of the bearing with engine oil to help installation, and make sure the oil supply holes in the bearing are aligned with those in the block. And make certain the right bearings are being used! Most mechanics install cam bearings with drift punches, firmly tapping each one into place, but the tapping is done on a steel plug that fits inside the bearing, with a shoulder that pushes on the bearing shell. The edge of the bearing must not extend beyond the bearing bore, or it may come into contact with a rotating cam lobe.

After the bearings are in place, coat the inside diameter with assembly lubricant, and very, very carefully slide the new camshaft into position. There are from three to six bearing journals on a camshaft. After each one has passed through a bearing, there is nothing but the mechanic to keep the sharp lobe

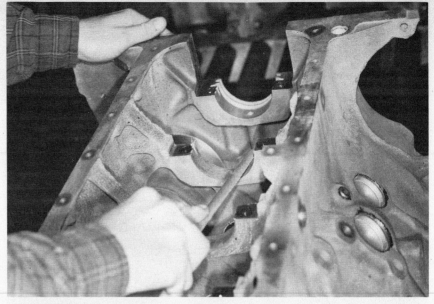

1. Deburring Main Bearing Seats

2. Installing Main Seal

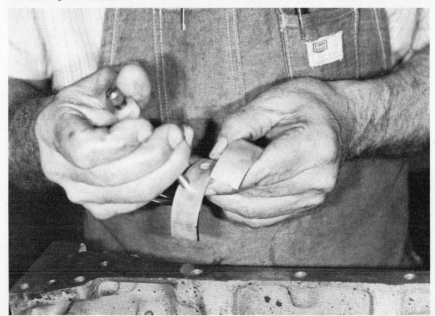

3. Miking Main Bearing Shell

1. Crankcase bearing seats are light-ly filed to remove any burring that might affect bearing performance.

2. Crankshaft bearings are inserted from the rear, beginning with the rear main bearing oil seal.

3. All bearing shells are miked before installation. While this should not really be necessary, even the factory occasionally fouls up.

4. Plenty of lubricant is in order to protect the bearings and crank surfaces until oil is pumped through block when engine is first fired up.

5. The clean crankshaft is lowered into the bearings with care, then turned to make sure that it's free. Little friction should be felt, as crank is not secured.

4. Lubing Engine Bearings

5. Installing Crankshaft

edges from tearing up the bearing sur-faces. Go slow and easy.

A camshaft will try to wind out of the bore—that is, move forward during run-ning; therefore, some kind of thrust re-tainer will be involved. It may be a plate that bolts to the block, or simply a rub surface on the timing gear cover. What-ever is used, must be used. Camshafts have end-play specifications just as crankshafts, and should be checked in the very same manner.

If the original camshaft timing gear is in good shape, it may be reused, and is held in place by a Woodruff key. Some-times a bolt is also included. There will be a timing mark on the front of the tim-ing gear, near one of the teeth, and a similar mark on the crankshaft gear. In some cases correct valve timing is achieved by placing these marks directly opposite each other, and in others there are a specified number of teeth between the sprocket marks.

To set the timing in the first type (called timing marks on center), merely rotate both crankshaft and cam until the respective marks are closest to each other and on a direct line. In the second method of timing, turn the crankshaft un-til two timing marks are toward the left side of the engine; then adjust the timing chain so that the correct number of sprocket links are in the chain between the crankshaft gear mark and the cam-shaft gear mark. The timing chain can-not be installed if both gears are already in place, therefore the camshaft timing gear (the big one) is positioned to the correct timing location within the chain (the chain already being positioned on the crankshaft gear), then the timing gear is slipped onto the camshaft regis-ter and secured.

Timing of an engine has a tremendous effect upon final performance, and being off one or two teeth will be enough to keep the engine from ever running as it should. However, this is one of the basic precepts of hot rodding and is utilized by all the racing engine builders. Do not at-tempt any timing modifications to a stock engine without consulting an expert!

Whether or not the timing chain cover is installed at this point depends upon how it mates with the oil pan. In some cases the timing cover must be in place before the oil pan is installed, but most

American cars have independent timing covers and oil pans.

OIL PUMP AND PAN

While the camshaft may be correctly termed the heart of an engine's perform-ance, the oil pump and lubrication sys-tem may aptly be called the center of mechanical longevity. Just how long an engine will run depends entirely on lu-brication, and the oil pump starts the en-tire cycle. In this respect it is a cast iron heart pumping a petroleum blood stream.

Location of the oil pump may vary from one engine design to another, but the average system has the pump driven by the camshaft, or at half the engine rpm. This is accomplished by placing the actual pump somewhere in the pan cavi-ty (or low on the outside of the cylinder block), and providing the drive through an extension of the distributor driveshaft. The driving gear which meshes with the camshaft may be on either the oil pump or the distributor.

Two types of pumps are in normal passenger car use: the rotor type com-mon to Chrysler products, and the gear type on Fords. Both obviously do the job, and the only real difference is in the op-erating clearances. Since they are literal-ly bathed in oil most of the time, me-chanical wear is less likely than with oth-er engine parts; still the shaft and end plate must be carefully checked and re-paired or replaced if needed.

Wear is most common to the end plate, and if this exceeds .001-in. (wear or warp), the plate must be replaced or machined smooth. Anything under .001-in. wear can be dressed out with emery cloth. To check the clearances of a gear-type pump, place a straightedge across the housing and gears, then slide a feeler gauge between both surfaces. If the distance is greater than .003-in. either the gears or housing must be re-placed (whichever is worn). The gears should clear the pump body by a max-imum of .005-in. Such tight tolerances are imperative if the pump is to operate correctly.

Overhauling Engine

The rotor pump looks much different from the gear type, having a 4-lobed cam working inside a 5-cavity secondary rotor, but the end plate clearance must also be .003-in. or less. One of the primary rotor lobes must be pushed into a secondary rotor cavity as far as it will go, then the clearance of the lobe exactly opposite must not exceed .010-in. as measured between the primary lobe and a high spot on the secondary rotor. The outer, or secondary rotor is perfectly round, but since it also rotates, clearance between it and the stationary housing should be a maximum of .012-in.

There are no special assembly instructions for oil pumps other than those contained in repair kits, which may include special clearance gaskets for the end plate (necessary for proper end float of the gears/rotors). However, there should be between .003 and .009-in. end-play between the drive gear or shaft retainer and the stationary housing neck.

Use a gasket between the pump and the cylinder block; do not use any kind of sealing compound. The pump may be primed with oil before it is attached to the engine, but more on preliminary lubrication later. It is absolutely vital that the oil pump pickup tube and screen be perfectly clean before reassembly. If the tube or screen rotates in any way, it must be free to do so without binding, and there should be no air leaks in the pickup tubing. Incidentally, the size of the pickup tube has been engineered for a particular engine, so any interchange of tubes may be a detriment unless the inside diameter is the same.

Oil pans as supplied on any engine are designed to do a specific job. The only consideration that might be given to a different, or modified, pan would be to increasing the capacity or including additional baffles. Added capacity will be helpful if the engine tends to run hot (remember oil is a coolant), and baffles will keep the oil from sloshing away from the pickup screen on hard acceleration, deceleration, or violent turns. Such modified pans are common to race cars of every type but not necessary on ordinary passenger cars.

Unless the pan has been damaged by rocks, it will bolt back to the block with no trouble. Gaskets must be included along each rail and at each end, usually attached with a good sealing compound. Do not overtorque the pan bolts, as the light sheetmetal will easily distort and won't seal well.

After the pan is installed, the harmonic balancer or the crankshaft pulley, or both, may be bolted to the crank snout. These pulleys are often cracked or bent, so replacement should always be considered if the unit proves to be bad. The oil filter finishes work to the bottom of the engine, which may be turned over now to complete work on the top portion.

HEADS

Overhaul of automotive heads is almost a special repair project unto itself, since heads play such a vital part in an engine's performance characteristics.

1. Seating Crankshaft Seal

2. Torquing Main Caps

3. Installing Woodruff Key

1. The rear crank flange is gently tapped with a rubber mallet to seat the rear seal. If this is not done, the crank may not rotate once the bearings are installed tightly.

2. Bearing inserts are put into main caps and oiled, then caps are fitted in place and torqued down to factory specs.

3. Tapping Woodruff key in at front of crank finishes installation.

4. Pin pressed into camshaft timing sprocket will fit into cam, assuring that sprocket turns with cam.

5. As crankshaft sprocket is seated in position, timing sprocket is fitted to face of cam.

While the cylinder block, crankshaft and piston assemblies are responsible for changing energy of the burning fuel into mechanical advantage, the cylinder heads are directly involved in the creation of that initial energy. Whereas the other parts mentioned (known as the basic block, or lower end) experience mechanical wear for the most part, the heads are subject to tremendous forces associated with combustion: intense heat, high pressure loads, rapid changes in temperature, etc. At the same time, overhead valve head components experience mechanical wear that is difficult to control. It is a significant tribute to the automobile engineer that problems as this have been successfully solved.

Basic head repair is of a distinct mechanical nature, with emphasis given to valve seats, cracks, distortion, and valve guides. Obviously, these are problems attendant to the overhead valve engine only, since the flathead has the valve mechanism in the block.

A cracked cylinder head may be caused by several factors, such as water freezing (expansion), combustion (pressure), distortion (bolt torque), or running without water (expansion again). Of these, combustion and excessive heat (running without water or detonation) are the common villains. For this reason, head cracks are generally confined to the immediate combustion chamber/valve seat area, and are difficult to repair. Although there is a set procedure for such repair, this is one job that should definitely be left to the professional, as he will have both the experienced skill and the tools to do a good job. As long as the crack is within the valve seat area—that is, normally well into the port and partially in the combustion chamber—the repair is not too difficult. However, a severe crack in the top of the combustion chamber caused by excessive pressures or a mechanical malfunction (dropped valve, etc.) will usually mean a new head.

Discounting cracks, the amateur can do as good a head overhaul as the professional, providing he takes time and works thoroughly. After the rocker arm assembly has been removed during initial disassembly, the only moving parts left on a head are the valves and springs. To remove them requires a special compression C-clamp, one end holding the valve head and the other pressing down on the valve spring. In this way, the valve spring may be depressed enough to remove the split keeper retainers. It's simple with the right tools.

As each individual valve/spring retainer assembly is removed, it should be kept together, particularly the valves. Mechanics use a yardstick drilled full of holes as a handy valve organizer. If the valves are in reasonably good shape, and the valve guides in the head are not worn excessively, each valve should return to its original location—all because each valve/guide combination will not have the same amount of wear as the others. Under such a condition, average repair calls only for valve and valve seat refacing.

With the valve assemblies removed and the spark plugs taken out, there is nothing left in the head that can come out, with the exception of the valve seats and possibly the guides. Both will require attention in a general overhaul of an engine with many thousands of miles.

Before work is started on either of these areas, the head should be thoroughly cleaned. This consists of chipping away all carbon deposits in the combustion chambers and ports, either with a sharp instrument (putty knife, screwdriver) or a rotary wire brush. This is a time-consuming job at best, but should not be overlooked. Oil passages should be cleaned with the small wire brush, and blown clear—a procedure that should be duplicated before reassembling the head.

If valve guides are worn, the valve can hardly be expected to do a good job. Wear is caused by the standard rubbing of metal against metal, a factor aggravated by difficult lubrication requirements. The intake valve stem is constantly being washed by the fuel mixture, and the exhaust valve stem is subjected to intense heat. Add to this the fact that a guide is just that—it must guide the valve in a straight line while the force moving the valve is working through an arc. The tip of the valve stem in contact with the rocker arm is being pushed up-and-down as well as back-and-forth, therefore guide wear is likely to occur in a slotted fashion in line with the force exerted by the rocker arm.

Before guides are replaced, the originals should be measured to see how far each protrudes into the intake or exhaust port. These special shaped bushings can be pressed out, or driven out by hammer if a special punch is available. Replacement guides are available in a number of different metals, depending upon the punishment they must take.

Contemporary engine designs are leaning toward the integral head/guide system, wherein the head metal is also the guide. This kind of approach has several advantages, one being reduced valve temperature as heat is whisked from the valve stem more easily, and another is lower production cost. However, when an integral guide wears, it

4. Installing Camshaft Sprocket Pin

5. Installing Crankshaft Sprocket

Overhauling Engine

cannot be replaced. Instead, valve stems are made in oversizes, such as .003, .005, .015, and .030-in. In this way, the worn integral guide is reamed to the next applicable size, allowing for clearance. This takes special tools, however, and is usually left to the machine shop.

Another type of guide repair, or modification, that has been finding favor with high-performance engine builders is guide knurling. Just as knurling the skirt of a piston will effectively increase the diameter of the piston, so will knurling the inside diameter of a guide decrease the I.D. The guide may be reamed to a larger true size, then knurled back to stock clearances. An advantage of this procedure is the creation of hundreds of small oil traps in the guide wall, which will give better stem lubrication. This, too, is a machine shop operation.

Clearance is a very special problem with guides, and the specified measurement for a particular engine should be adhered to exactly. Excessive clearance around an intake valve is a sure way to encourage high oil consumption. A good insurance against oil sucking into the combustion chamber is the valve stem seal, a nylon insert that fits around the valve stem on the rocker side of the head. These are reasonably priced and easy to install.

No engine overhaul should be attempted without at least refacing the valve and valve seat. It may be nothing more than a touch with the grinding stone, but it is essential to a successful job. While some engines seat the valves directly against the head or block metal, most designs call for specially hardened valve seat inserts shrunk into the head.

These inserts must be carefully checked, as they crack, and may be loose in the block/head. A loose insert, or one that is cracked or burned beyond repair must be replaced. They can be punched out from the back side (through the port), or pried out with a curved bar. They are brittle and the small pieces fly in every direction when they break, so place a rag over the pry bar and wear protective goggles.

The insert does not fit a perfect hole in the head. Instead, the machined depression is an interference fit, from .005 to .008-in. smaller than the diameter of the insert. From this it is obvious the head must be perfectly clean or the little insert won't insert so well. On the other hand, a loose insert will allow carbon to build up around the edge. Although this is such a tiny bit of insulation, it is sufficient to keep the exhaust valve from transferring heat to the head rapidly enough. A burned exhaust valve is next on the list.

If the original insert hole in the head is the proper size, a new insert can be set in place "as is." Otherwise, the hole must be machined to the next insert oversize. To make insert installation simple, place the unit in a freezer. This will shrink the metal more than enough and it will drop right in place. When the insert warms to room temperature it will be tightly wedged in the block or head.

Valve seats must be ground by a tap-

1. Aligning Timing Marks

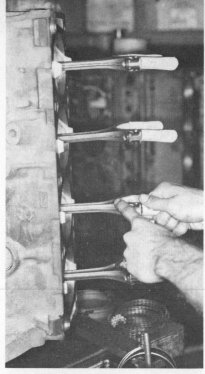

2. Protecting Rod Bolts

3. Installing Pistons

4. Installing Piston Rings

ered stone. It is absolutely essential that the pilot shaft fit the guide snugly. Too loose a fit allows the stone to wander; this is one reason the guides are reconditioned or replaced before the seats are fixed.

It is possible to rent seat grinders, but since accuracy is essential, such a grinder may not be the best. Fortunately, machine shops and professional mechanics are well equipped for valve work. So this job is a snap for them, and if the head or block is disassembled, the cost is quite low.

Valve seat grinders usually come in a case, complete with a full range of stones of varying angles. The most common angle is 45°, with some 30° designs still in existence. It is imperative that the stone be dressed before use, to insure maximum accuracy (seats should not exceed .002-in. off-center, and can be checked by a dial indicator).

A soft touch is required when you're using a seat grinder. Do not press down. In fact, you should support the weight of the driving motor with your hands. To do a good job, raise and lower the grinder

5. Oiling Piston and Rings

6. Using Ring Compressor

1. Timing chain completes crank/cam assembly and block moves to next station for piston installation.

2. Pistons are inserted wrong way in cylinders while rubber "fingers" are fitted over rod bolts. This protects crankshaft when pistons are inserted properly.

3. Pistons are then reversed to proper position in preparation for ring installation.

4. Working from bottom toward top of pistons, rings are positioned on each one. End-gaps are alternated 90° to lessen chances of blowby.

5. Plenty of lubricant is applied before seating the pistons in bore.

6. With the piston set in block and facing the right direction, the compressor is held tight against block and piston tapped lightly. If not held tight, the rings will pop out of the compressor before they are in the cylinders and are likely to break on the block.

about twice every second. This will let the stone revolve at high rpms, and the cut will be made rapidly. It only takes a few seconds to true up a valve seat (Stellite is different—it takes several minutes because it is so hard to cut with a stone).

A coarse stone is used for the initial grinding, then a fine stone to finish the seat. Because any grinding of the seat face will also widen it, a third stone with a greater angle is used to face the inside or outside diameter of the seat and return it to the correct width. This width is

quite important and should not be overlooked. Exhaust valve seats should measure between .090 and .100-in., while intakes are .070 to .090-in. The exhaust valve has more heat and, therefore, it has more contact area to transfer heat better.

Final head work includes grinding away any sharp edges inside the combustion chamber. The threads of the spark plug holes are an example of this, and although not absolutely essential, this just makes a good job better. The head must be checked with a feeler gauge and straightedge for warpage.

VALVES

The automobile engine is a bag of serious compromises, and the engineers have been able to perform seeming miracles over the years in making an internal combustion engine as efficient as it now is. Part of the problem stems from getting the right amount of fuel mixture into the combustion chamber at precisely the correct time, then effectively sealing that chamber for subsequent fuel burning and expansion. It all boils down to some kind of valve in a 4-stroke engine.

Inventors have spent hundreds of thousands of hours trying to develop a better or more efficient valve, with the list including sleeve valves, rotary valves, poppet valves, slide valves—and still the search continues. In the interim, the standard poppet valve as we know it continues to be developed to ever greater degrees as engine performance requirements continue to increase.

Operating conditions for a poppet valve are brutal, to say the least. Unlike

the other parts of the engine, a valve is exposed to intense combustion temperatures with almost no chance to cool off. While the head of a piston is also exposed to these high readings, it can pass off heat through the skirt and the rod, as well as the surrounding water-cooled cylinder block—the valve should be so lucky! Instead, it must have a large-diameter head (to give maximum breathing capacity for best performance) and a small stem. Heat can therefore be passed along only through the tiny stem and during the very few moments of each revolution when the valve face is in contact with the valve seat. Considering that explosion temperatures inside a combustion chamber may reach 5000° F. for a split second, the task would seem impossible. Furthermore, the poor old exhaust valve must open at the most inopportune time and pass the hot gases out the exhaust port. This is why valve jobs are so common to an engine that is in otherwise excellent running condition, and why keeping the valves adjusted is so vitally important.

Temperatures of a valve head may reach 1000° F. or more under these conditions, and certainly higher for racing engines (racing engines use exotic valve materials). It is easier to understand just how difficult a job the valve has when you consider how short a time the valve is seated. If the engine is turning 3000 rpm, or the average cruising speed of most cars, it means that one of the several cylinders will have ignition 1500 times per minute, and that means the valves are off the seat the same number of times. Not very much time for a valve to cool off.

While the seating surface area of the

Overhauling Engine

valve head may only reach 1000°, the center will be 200-400° hotter and the stem just below the head slightly below the 1000° F. This is red hot in any language. If the valve does not seat against the insert exactly right, due to a bent stem or a piece of foreign material, the edge will burn immediately. Once decay starts it spreads rapidly. The intake valve does not have these great temperature problems, because it is seated when the heat is being passed out, and the incoming fuel mixture is at or below atmospheric temperature.

Because of the extreme temperatures involved, exhaust valves are normally made of heat-resistant alloy steel. Sometimes the stems are made hollow and filled with mineral salts such as sodium, which is a fast heat conductor. All the exhaust valve's operating problems are further aggravated by operational changes in the engine. The engine may be in perfect condition cold, but when it warms up to running temperatures, some kind of distortion is likely to occur. This in turn may cause localized hot spots near the valve, with attendant heat problems transferred to the valve. The metal may distort enough to slightly misalign the valve between guide and seat, causing an improper heat transfer, and so on. All this just goes to prove that valves are one of the most important areas of engine overhaul, and must be treated with care and precision.

Of course, if the deposits on the upper part of the valve stem (just below the head) could be minimized, this would in turn cut down on the chances of a valve sticking slightly open—and most of the valve problems would be over. One way to reduce the effect of such deposits (caused by the combustion particles sticking to the exhaust valve as they flow out) is to have the valve rotate slightly each time it is lifted. There are two types of rotating valve designs currently popular, one called the free-type wherein the valve rotates at no particular rate, and the other (called a Rotocap system) where the valve rotates an exact number of degrees each time it is opened.

The amateur mechanic is faced with a basic problem when it comes time to do the valves. If they look to be in good shape before disassembly, then it would seem reasonable to reuse them with no refacing. This is just asking for trouble. It's like putting on three new tires, and leaving a fourth one bad. A valve job should be part of any engine overhaul.

Valves may be lapped if precision grinding equipment is not available, but this is not the best procedure. To lap a valve, special grinding compound is placed on the seat and the valve is rapidly rotated back and forth against the seat. The required tool is a rounded handle with a small suction cup that sticks to the valve head in order to turn it.

There are two kinds of compound available: coarse and fine (the fine is preferred). They come in either oil or water mixtures (use water to remove excess of one, solvent for the other). When lapping a valve, use a very small amount

1. Installing Connecting Rod Bearings

3. Rotating Crankshaft

under the valve head, as it can work down around the clean stem and be just as effective at opening up the guide clearance. Inspect the valve face often, and when a small, even, gray ring appears the full circumference of the face (the width of the seat) the job is finished. Of course, there must be no pits or nicks in the mating surfaces.

Lapping is inferior to precision grinding in every circumstance, and never should a precision-ground valve be mated to a lapped seat, and vice versa. As a guide, restrict valve lapping to conditions where precision grinders are not available, or the valves are in nearly perfect condition to start with.

Ordinary passenger car valves have reasonably thick heads, making it possible to reuse burned valves. When the grinding equipment refaces the valve, it also trues the head and usually very little must be taken from the face to remove minor pits and burn traces. If the valve has burned badly, however, it must be replaced. Normally, there will not be more than one or two badly burned valves involved, since the car will run so poorly with just one bad valve.

2. Torquing Connecting Rods

4. Checking Rod Bearings

After the valves have been ground, they must be cleaned of any stem deposits. The heads are also cleaned, and it is time to assemble the valves in the head.

ROCKER ARMS

As with valves, rocker arms also can and do wear rapidly. They should be carefully inspected for wear at three points: where the valve tip touches the face, the shaft bushing, and the pushrod stud. The stud ball tip may be worn away, or the adjusting threads may be bad. Repair to all these areas may be made by the mechanic, but a cracked or bent rocker arm should be replaced.

If the rocker face is pitted, it may be dressed flat. While such a unit could be retained and the valve lash adjusted with a dial indicator, this would not solve a basic wear problem. If the face pitting seems excessive, it is possible the rocker arm material is faulty.

It is not uncommon for the adjusting stud threads to break or gall in the rocker, so these should be run through with a screwdriver several times as a check.

5. Installing Hydraulic Valve Lifter

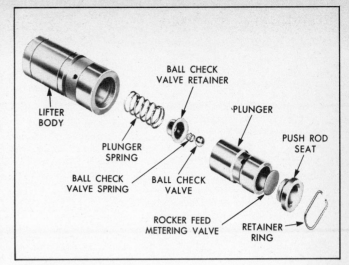

6. Exploded View of Lifter

LIFTER BODY

PLUNGER SPRING

BALL CHECK VALVE SPRING

BALL CHECK VALVE RETAINER

BALL CHECK VALVE

PLUNGER

PUSH ROD SEAT

ROCKER FEED METERING VALVE

RETAINER RING

7. Spraying Head Gasket

1. *New connecting rod bearings are fitted to caps before installation.*

2. *Caps are torqued to factory specs. New lock nuts are used here.*

3. *Crank is turned to work pistons, once piston/rod assemblies are in.*

4. *Each rod cap is removed and bearing surface checked after crank has been turned several times.*

5. *New lifter assemblies are installed. While lifters can be disassembled and tested for their leakdown rate, new ones are really inexpensive in a rebuild situation.*

6. *The plunger spring in hydraulic lifter keeps the plunger and pushrod seat up against the pushrod. When lifter body is raised by cam lobe, oil trapped underneath ball check valve lifts plunger and opens valve.*

7. *New head gasket set is sprayed with a gasket adhesive sealer just prior to installation.*

The slightest bind means some kind of trouble. If the lubrication has been poor, the stud ball end may have become pitted, and in extreme cases will even wear away in the pushrod socket.

Because both the valve spring and the pushrod are always forcing the rocker upward, all wear of the rocker bushing and the rocker shaft will be on the bottom side. Such wear is readily apparent and common to engines with many miles. To inspect for the wear, force the rocker to the side with a bar. If the shaft is worn, it will show as a ridge of metal riding in the bushing oil groove. Worn shafts should always be replaced, and used with new rocker arms.

When reassembling the rocker and shaft assembly, it is often difficult to get the rockers in the correct place, since exhaust and intake rockers may be of different lengths or shapes, or both. To circumvent this, leave one shaft assembled while working on the other. This is a good guide as to how things are supposed to be put together.

Don't overlook the rocker shaft supports, as they often break from excessive bolt torque.

PUSHRODS AND LIFTERS

Cam-in-block overhead valve engines use pushrods to connect the camshaft/lifter assembly and the rocker arm. Overhead cam and flathead engine designs do not have the pushrods. A pushrod should be inspected for wear or warpage and discarded if either is found. Wear will be found where the rod enters the lifter, or at the upper end that contacts the rocker adjustment (some engines do not have an adjustment if the lifters are hydraulic). A slight pit in the lower ball or the upper socket is a sign of trouble, so replacement is suggested.

Lifters come in two versions, solid (mechanical) and hydraulic. The solid lifter is nothing more than a cam lobe follower, but it has been precision engineered for that purpose. The hydraulic lifter is a different breed of horse.

The hydraulic valve lifter is designed to keep a zero-lash clearance—that is, to reduce engine noise there is no clearance between the cam and ultimate valve stem. If this were the case with

solid lifters, the expansion of the metals would cause the valves to remain slightly open during running temperatures. With the hydraulic lifter, any lash in the system is compensated for by hydraulic (oil) action. A hydraulic lifter has three basic parts: the body (housing), plunger, and valve.

Oil from the main oil gallery passes through the lifter check valve, forcing the plunger up from the bottom and into contact with the pushrod, and ultimately the valve stem. This oil is under pressure determined by metering holes in the lifter and the oil gallery.

As the lifter is raised by the camshaft action, there is a further pressure on the trapped oil inside the lifter. This closes the check valve and the lifter then becomes a solid lifter for all practical purposes. A tiny amount of oil is allowed to leak from between the plunger and the housing during this open valve phase so that when the cam rotates to the closed position, the valve will not be kept slightly open by an over-full lifter. This lost oil is replaced again by oil from the gallery. When an engine with hydraulic lifters is first started, a clattering sound from the lifters indicates that one or more have leaked completely dry and will take a while to pump up again.

It is possible to wear out lifters of this type, although the plunger movement is very small during operation. Dirt, varnish, carbon and similar foreign materials can get into the lifter and cause the check valve to stick. Keeping the engine oil clean and free from either physical or chemical contamination will make you and the lifter great friends.

Economics of engine rebuilding being what they are, novice mechanics often try to "get by" with the old tappets when a new cam or complete overhaul is involved. Good luck. Most modern engines have been designed to include revolving lifters, and this means that lifter-to-camshaft lobe contact points must be absolutely correct. Most cam problems stem from incorrect lifter contact (the contact point should be slightly off center to the "high" side of the lobe).

Camshaft lobes taper from one side to the other, usually between .002 and .004-in. The face of the lifter is ground slightly rounded, or about .002-in., and

Overhauling Engine

by placing the lifter bores slightly to the higher side of the cam lobes, each revolution of the camshaft will cause the lifter to rotate a few degrees. If either the cam lobe or the lifter face are not ground correctly, or have flattened during use, this rotation is nullified and rapid wear in one spot will result.

VALVE SPRINGS

Valve springs are especially susceptible to life-span problems. Spring steel being what it is, operating under even ideal conditions, will not ensure perfect spring life. Therefore valve springs can be expected to fail from time to time since they must operate in unfavorable conditions.

Each and every valve spring should be checked for tension on a special reading scale. The spring must be measured for free (unloaded) height. If this is in the limits prescribed for the particular engine (line them all up together and a comparison check will show minute differences in height), then the spring is compressed a certain distance. At this distance the coils should be exerting a certain amount of pressure. If not, shims may be required between spring and head, or spring and retainer, to get the prescribed pressures.

At the same time, the coils of the spring must not bind against each other, or the spring will break during use. If the springs will not come up to proper pressure with minimum shims, they must be replaced.

HEAD ASSEMBLY

Now everything is ready for assembly of the head. The valves are replaced in their respective guides one by one. The oil seal is inserted over each stem, followed by the spring and shims if necessary. With the big C-clamp, the spring is again depressed and the retainer washer and keepers are reinstalled. The head(s) are then ready to be installed on the cylinder block.

FINAL ASSEMBLY

Unless the camshaft has been changed to a high-lift version, or the piston head design is different, there is usually no need to check piston-to-valve clearance. However, if such a change has been made, this check is imperative, for flathead as well as ohv engines.

To check this clearance, lay thin strips of modeling clay atop the piston for ohv engines, and over the valves for flathead engines. Bolt on the head, using the old headgasket, and torque it to the correct specification. All the valve mechanism must be included. Rotate the engine several times, then remove the head(s). If the clay measures less than .060-in. where it has been pressed between valve and piston or valve and head, more clearance will be necessary. In case of the overhead engine, the clearance must be flycut into the piston or the valve set deeper in the seat (which is

not recommended). For the flathead engine, the head chamber above the valves must be flycut the necessary amount.

If the camshaft or piston design has not been modified, there will be no need for this clearance check, provided all stock replacement parts have been used. The head gasket should be installed as marked, with the indicated top and front portion so placed, if necessary. Sealing compound or aluminum paint may be used on both gasket surfaces, and the gasket prescribed for the engine should absolutely be used. In case a thin high-compression replacement gasket is involved, then the valve-to-head or valve-to-piston clearance will need to be checked.

All headbolts should be inspected before reuse, and any slight distortion means the bolt should be replaced. Coat the threads with an anti-seize compound, then torque the bolts to the prescribed pounds and in the torque pattern established by the engine manufacturer. This pattern usually starts in the middle of the head and works toward either end. It is imperative that the proper torque pattern and pound limits be followed to minimize block and head distortion!

The lifters may be placed in the respective bores before the head is installed (remember, they go back to the same hole they came from), and so may the pushrods. However, the pushrods must be in the rocker arm pivots before any of the headbolts are tightened in place.

The valley cover may be replaced now. Since this is separate from the intake manifold on most modern V-8's, it should have sealing compound included on both sides of the gasket. Also, if small rubber seals are involved around the central hold-down bolt(s), new seals should be included. Nothing is more discouraging than to have an oil leak around these bolt seals after the engine is assembled and back in the car.

MANIFOLDS, INTAKE AND EXHAUST

When the head was being checked for a warped condition, one of the surfaces involved was the manifold flat, for both intake and exhaust manifolds. Naturally,

1. Pre-assembled head is bolted in place and torqued to factory specs.

2. Rocker arm shaft assembly and new pushrods are installed, then head bolts are tightened.

3. Clearance in the hydraulic lifter is checked. If clearance is not sufficient, a shorter pushrod is used; if clearance is too much, a longer one is substituted.

4. Engine is positioned on a run-in stand and coupled to an electric motor that turns the engine over at a constant speed.

5. Compression testing of each cylinder and check of oil pressure completes rebuild. Engine is now ready for painting and sealing in plastic prior to delivery.

1. Torquing Cylinder Head

2. Installing Rocker Arms

3. Checking Hydraulic Lifter

this same check must be given the manifolds, and they must be trued up by grinding, if necessary.

There is not much that can go wrong with the manifold, but if it is cracked the break must be repaired. This can be done by welding or brazing, the latter most common, and is acceptable on both intake and exhaust systems. After welding, the manifold should be heated to relieve any stress concentrations, and the mating surfaces machined true.

The manifolds must be cleaned of any carbon buildup, then assembled to the engine with torque specifications observed. A sealing compound may be desirable around the intake gaskets. The spark plugs are then torqued to the heads, and exhaust/intake opening taped shut. This will prevent any loose "goodie" from falling inside and undoing all the hard work you've just completed.

Valve covers may be installed at this time, but no sealing compound will be necessary as they utilize thick, soft gaskets. Make sure all the block plugs and fittings are in place and the assembly should be complete. All that remains is to hang on the accessories, and you may want to do that after the engine is in the car, to prevent damage to them during the installation.

PREVENTING DRY STARTS

An engine can wear more in the first 30 secs. after it is started up than in the next 6 months if it has a prolonged dry start. Special lubes are available for coating the camshaft lobes to prevent galling. Every other part in the engine should have been assembled with liberal amounts of engine oil. It's good practice to pack the oil pump with Vaseline when it is assembled. A pump primed with Vaseline will start circulating oil almost instantly, whereas one that has to start dry may take several seconds before it can suck oil up from the pan and distribute it through the engine oiling system.

Some engine builders prime the oil pump by driving a dummy distributor with a drill motor. The distributor must

have the gear removed so that it does not try to turn the camshaft. The drill motor is chucked onto the top of the distributor shaft, and the tang at the bottom end of the shaft will drive the oil pump just as if the distributor were being run in the engine. It only takes a few seconds of drill motor operation to get complete oil pressure even to the point where it starts squirting out of the rocker arms. Drill motors rotate clockwise, so this technique can only be used on those engines with distributors that also rotate clockwise. If you turn the dummy distributor and the oil pump in the wrong direction, you won't hurt anything but you won't be pumping any oil either. You'll just be blowing bubbles down into the oil in the pan.

A reversible drill motor will work on any engine, but all of the problems with figuring out how to do this can be avoided in the first place simply by packing the oil pump with Vaseline. As soon as the engine oil gets warm the Vaseline melts, and then dilutes to the point where it never congeals thereafter.

ENGINE TIMING

Setting valve lash and timing the distributor are where many amateur mechanics fall down. They may have assembled a very good engine, only to have things unravel in either or both of these categories.

To time an engine, rotate the crankshaft until the No. 1 piston is on top dead center (TDC) of the compression stroke. Move the crank back and forth a few degrees either way and watch the No. 1 rocker arms. If they move, the engine is on the exhaust stroke and must be rotated again. With the piston on TDC of the compression stroke, the timing marks on the crankshaft pulley should be aligned with the timing pointer attached to the timing cover.

Now install the distributor with the rotor pointing directly to the No. 1 distributor cap terminal (the secondary, or ignition wires were taped, remember?). Adjust the distributor by turning it in the direction of rotation until the distributor

points just barely begin to open. In this way, a very slight lead is involved and the engine will start. Final distributor adjustment is then made with the use of a timing light.

It is common for amateurs to get the ignition installed to fire on the exhaust stroke, and this leads to all kinds of frustration. If the engine does not start right away, recheck to see that the distributor is not out of phase with the cylinders.

Setting valve lash is not difficult, but is often accomplished in a most rough-shod manner. Hydraulic lifters require no lash adjustment per se, but some engines call for one turn adjustment from zero lash. This places the lifter plunger in the center of the housing travel. To make this kind of adjustment, loosen the rocker adjustment stud until the valve clatters, then tighten it to zero-lash, or when the valve is quiet (this is a close point, so listen carefully). Now tighten the adjustment screw by one additional full turn; make the adjustment ¼-turn at a time to allow the lifter to bleed down. Some engines have different length pushrods for adjustment.

Adjustment of the solid lifter is made with a feeler gauge and requires nothing more special than patience. The lifter must be on the heel of the cam for this adjustment; that is, the valves must be fully closed. Turn the adjusting screw in the rocker until the feeler is a snug but removable fit, and tighten the locknut. Until proficient in adjusting mechanical lifters, the mechanic should recheck the initial cold settings after the engine has warmed up (the settings are different and are called out in the shop manuals).

ENGINE BREAK-IN

How an overhauled engine is broken in will determine how well it runs. As soon as it is started, it should be set at an rpm equivalent to 20-30 mph, or slightly over 1000 rpm. This allows the oil to circulate through the engine galleries well, and throws oil onto the cylinder walls.

As a rule, don't let the engine idle, and don't operate it with cold water running through the block. So that takes care of the idea of letting the engine break-in with a garden hose stuck in the radiator. The engine must reach operating temperature for the rings to seat, and the closer to the boiling point the better, although it shouldn't be allowed to boil.

After the engine has run awhile, drive it around to get everything loosened up. This will be but a few miles. Then retorque the head and manifold bolts and reset the valve adjustment with solid lifters. The ignition timing should be rechecked, and the carburetor adjusted for correct idle speed.

To seat the rings, accelerate the car at full throttle briefly from 30 mph. This will load the rings and cause the slight wear necessary. Hard rings will take slightly longer to seat. Drive the car under 50 mph for the first 250 miles, and at no sustained high speeds for the first 1000 miles. Drain the oil and change the filter at 1000 miles and then observe regular lubrication maintenance.

4. Engine on Run-in Stand

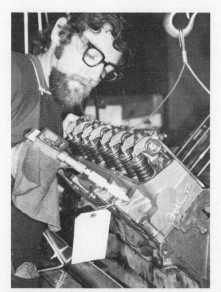

5. Final Test Before Painting

Engine Oiling

Diagnosing an engine oiling problem, such as excessive wear from lack of oil, or excessive oil consumption from too much oil, requires a lot more savvy than just knowing where the dipstick and the oil filler tube are. The engine oiling circuit diagrams that are in the shop manuals and also in the Petersen *Complete Book of Engines* are not there just to satisfy an engineering curiosity. Those diagrams will point out how the oil gets where it is supposed to be and may give you a clue as to why you are getting either too much or not enough oil.

To fully understand the oiling system of an automobile engine, it is first necessary to understand something about oil itself. In an engine, oil is called on to reduce the friction between moving parts. This will reduce the destructive heat caused by excessive friction, conserve power, and reduce wear of contacting metal surfaces. Oil acts as a seal between the piston ring and cylinder to prevent combustion leaking down into the crankcase; it washes away abrasive metals worn from friction surfaces, and by flowing continually over heated surfaces keeps operating temperatures down. It must do all these things even if the weather should be desert hot or arctic cold.

Under ideal conditions, oil will form a thin film between two surfaces so that these surfaces never touch. Therefore, no metal wear would ever occur. Unfortunately, this ideal condition seldom exists. When ambient temperature is low, oil viscosity is such that the oil does not flow well during engine warm-up. When the temperature is hot, or high, the oil may thin too much and the lubricating film is easily broken. To be of maximum effectiveness, the oil must flow well at cold temperatures but maintain body at high temperatures. During this time, it must also keep an unbroken film between the metal parts.

OIL PANS

Automotive engines use either a wet or dry sump oil reservoir. In the first, the oil is maintained at the proper quantity by a sump in the oil pan. In other words, all the oil is carried within the confines of the oil pan, but must be isolated from the revolving crankshaft by a baffled sump. In the dry sump system, which is something of a misnomer, the main oil supply is kept in a tank outside the engine. The engine oil pump draws the oil from the tank, then another pump scavenges it from the flat pan back to the tank. This type of system is common to aircraft, motorcycles, and racing engines. It is more positive and allows extra cooling because of greater oil capacity, but is also more expensive.

While the transmission and rear-end gears splash the oil around and thus lubricate themselves, the engine needs a more sophisticated approach. Every

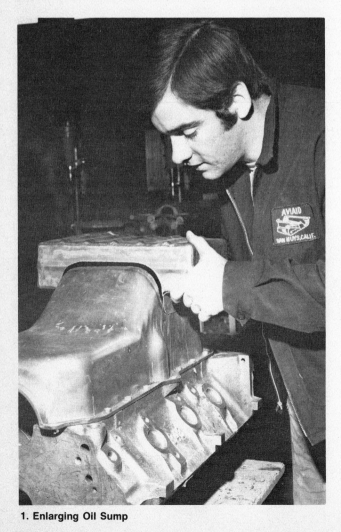

1. Enlarging Oil Sump

2. Sludge in Oil Pan

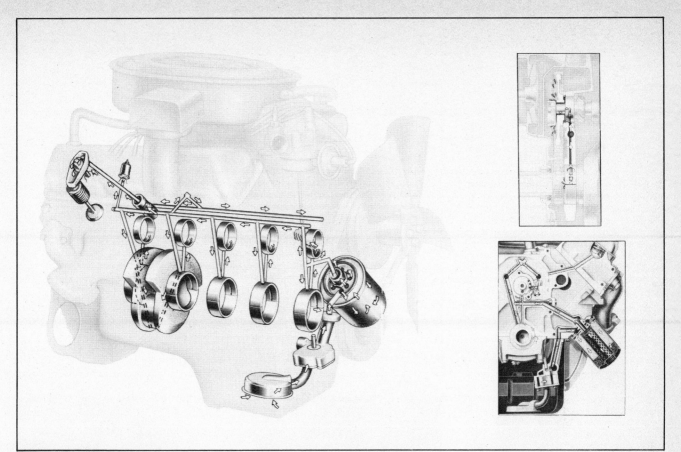

3. Ford Lubrication System

1. During high-speed operation, most of the oil normally in a stock pan is "in suspension," therefore little is ever found in the pan. By enlarging the oil sump of the pan, as seen here, more oil can be carried, thereby allowing any given quantity more time to cool before being circulated again, thus protecting the engine.

2. Ever try to lubricate an engine with molasses? In this instance molasses would probably be as effective as the oily sludge found in this pan. Such a condition indicates infrequent oil and filter changes, which will result in a marked decrease in engine life.

3. These illustrations show how oil is picked up in the pan, delivered through the filter, and carried through the galleries of the Ford 429 engine to lubricate the crank, cam, lifters, rockers and timing chain.

4. Oil pickups are covered with a filter screen to prevent the pump from sucking up any large foreign matter that may find its way into the pan sump. This pickup is stationary, whereas some can swing in an arc about the pan, following oil movement and thereby preventing oil starvation.

5. For best oil flow, considering the ambient temperatures, use an oil of recommended viscosity rating.

4. Pickup Filter Screen

OIL VISCOSITY CHART

Lowest Temperature Expected	SAE Viscosity Number
Above +32°F.	SAE 30 SAE 20W-40 SAE 10W-30
+32°F. to +10°F.	SAE 20W SAE 10W-30
+10°F. to −10°F.	SAE 10W SAE 10W-30 SAE 5W-20
Below −10°F.	SAE 5W-20

5

moving part inside an engine must be oiled, from the crankshaft bearings to the valves. Splash is not the answer now, although it was common to the low performance engines of years past. It would not work today.

There are three basic types of oiling systems in engines: splash, modified splash and full pressure. In the first, the crankshaft splashed oil around inside the engine and gravity caused it to drain back to the pan. The modified splash design had little troughs across the oil pan. When the connecting rod revolved at the bottom of the stroke, oil was scooped up by dippers on the rod cap. An improvement of this was the addition of oil nozzle pipes that shot a stream of oil into the approaching dipper. Neither the splash nor modified splash are ideal. Most modern engines use full pressure lubrication, whereas an oil pump packs

Engine Oiling

the oil into a main delivery gallery and from there to the points of the engine that are in need of lubrication.

OIL PUMPS

These pumps are engine driven and draw oil through a screen on the pickup tube immersed in the pan sump. Depending upon the individual pump design, the oil is under a specific pressure and goes first to the oil filter (usually), then to the main oil gallery (gallery or header). From the main gallery (which is usually drilled in the cylinder block), the oil goes through secondary galleries to the crankshaft main bearings, camshaft bearings, timing drive mechanism, rocker arms, and lifters.

All this initial oiling route is usually within the confines of the cylinder block and in the case of overhead valves, the heads. Since these passages can, and do, get plugged, that is the reason for emphasis on cleaning during overhaul.

The oil pump is detachable from the cylinder block, and may be located in a number of different places. In some designs, such as Chevrolet and flathead Ford, the pump is actually immersed in oil near the sump; in others, the pump may be outside the block with an internal pickup leading to the sump.

Because different parts of the engine need a diffreent amount of oil, some kind of limitation must be placed in the delivery system. This is normally taken care of by the size of secondary delivery passages between the part and the main gallery, but often a further control is included in the bearing and/or bearing clearance. For instance, in some engines the various main bearings may require different amounts of oil, usually discovered during trial-and-error engineering by the factory. Restrictions in the passages take care of these requirements effectively.

However, anytime an engine is modipartially or the full circumference, to aid oil flow. Part of the oil thus delivered to the bearing will flow across the surface and out the sides to drop back into the oil pan. A greater majority will flow into a hole in the crankshaft journal that connects to the rod journals.

At the connecting rod bearings, the oil will flow across the bearing surface and out the sides to fall into the pan. In some engine designs, the connecting rods are drilled from the big end to the fied for higher performance, the oil pump pressure is usually increased to around 80 lbs. to insure maximum pressure at critical bearing points. When this happens, it is possible to give too much pressure to a particular bearing, and a further restriction in the secondary passage may be necessary. This is often taken care of via drilled jets. Because this is a highly specialized practice, the amateur should never do it without expert direction.

At each crankshaft main bearing, the oil enters the bearing through a hole. Sometimes either the bearing surface or the crankshaft journal is grooved, either piston pin bore. If this is the case, the oil

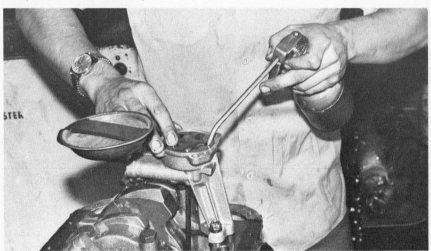

1. Exploded View of Oil Pump

2. Priming an Oil Pump

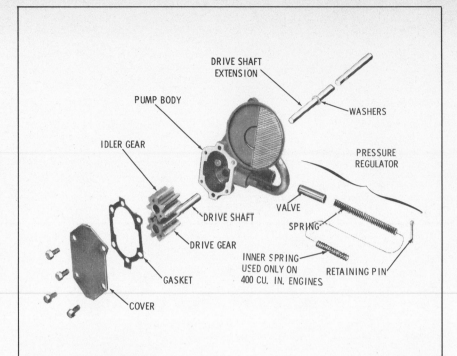

3. Burned Engine Bearings

1. This exploded view of a 1968 Oldsmobile oil pump illustrates the various components that go to make up such an assembly.

2. It's always wise to prime an oil pump when assembling an engine to avoid scouring the cam, lifters, bearings, etc. One method is to remove the oil pump cover plate and prime the cavity as the engine is being assembled.

3. Insufficient lubrication was responsible for these wiped-out bearings. Not only were the bearings burned up, but the rods and crank suffered irreparable damage.

4. Block of typical V-8 shows oil passages. Note oil supply to rocker arms goes through gasket surface into head. Passage should be cleaned whenever head is removed.

5. Cutaway of filter element used in full-flow applications. The different material at left end of element is sisal, used to increase flow characteristics. This "sisal doughnut" was developed to allow depth-flow oil filters to pass the amount of oil needed in a full-flow oil system. The other element material is Vac-Cel, a mixture of cotton linters and rice hulls.

6. This is the type of element used on most new cars. Note that the oil is only required to pass through one thickness of the paper. This filter will last longer than the cotton type, but it does not filter as effectively.

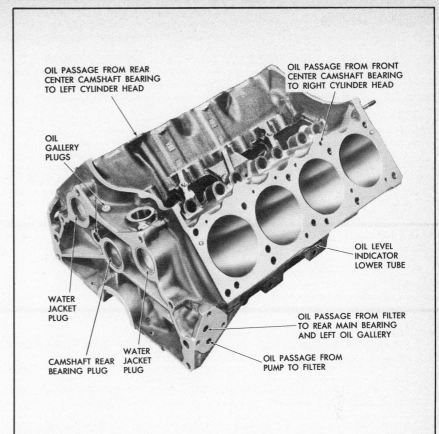

4. Engine Oil Passages

5. Full-Flow Filter

6. Paper Filter Element

then continues up the rod and flows across the pin bushing before falling back to the pan.

Clearance of any and all bearings thus has a direct effect on total oil pressure within the full pressure system. If all the connecting rods have .0025-in. clearance, but one of the main bearings is worn and has excessive clearance, oil pressure will force more than normal oil through this bearing. Therefore, other bearings will tend to run at reduced oil flow.

While direct cylinder oiling has been tried by continuing the oil from the piston pin to a hole in the piston, the most common type of bore oiling is direct

splash. When the crankshaft is rotating in the crankcase, it churns up considerable oil spray, which gets on everything in sight, including the cylinder walls. At the same time, as the rod journal goes through the top portion of rotation, oil being squeezed out the bearing surface is thrown on the walls.

At the front of the engine, some kind of oiling for the timing gears and/or chain is necessary. This may be either a direct or remote delivery, but the common system is from the front camshaft bearing. This oil is then thrown on the gears and chain and drains back into the block through a hole at the bottom of the chamber.

Oil to the valve system in overhead valve engines may be via internal or external passages, with the internal passage most common. An oil passage in the block mates with one in the head. The head passage passes the oil directly to a rocker shaft support and then out the shaft to the individual rocker arms. This supply is usually of low volume, but increases in direct consequence of engine rpm. As the oil squeezes out the sides of rocker and support bearings, it splashes onto the valve stem, and thus lubricates the valve guides. Getting the correct amount of oil to the rocker system is a definite problem on some older ohv engines, such as Ford design. In

Engine Oiling

these cases, an extra outside lube line may be installed (kits are available through most parts supply houses).

Many engines now use stud-mounted rocker arms which receive their oil flow through hollow pushrods. The same oil that operates the hydraulic lifter runs up through the pushrod and through a hole in the pushrod seat at the end of the rocker arm. The oil then runs down into the middle of the rocker arm and lubricates the pivot point at the rocker ball. After a few seconds of operation the rocker arms fill with oil, and then the oil spills over the rocker arm lip at the opposite end of the pushrod and runs down on the valve spring and the valve system. Too much oil on the valve system will flood the guide, and the the high vacuum in the combustion chamber will suck the oil into the engine. The amount of oil that is allowed to go through the guide into the engine is controlled by some kind of seal, which can be a simple O-ring underneath the valve keeper, a rubber umbrella that shields the end of the guide, or even a teflon seal that is a positive fit on the guide. At high rpm the oil that comes through the pushrod can squirt out and hit the rocker cover so that it runs down the inside of the cover without ever getting down in the rocker. The result can be burned rocker balls and very quick rocker arm

failure. Many engines now have little tabs welded to the underside of the rocker covers to catch the oil at high rpm and let it drip back into the middle of the rocker for proper lubrication.

Because wear of all the working surfaces is normal, thus increasing bearing clearances and lowering final point oil pressures, most engines are equipped with pumps of large capacity. To control the oil pressure, then, a special bypass valve is installed, normally in the pump housing. When a predetermined oil pressure is reached, this spring-loaded valve is opened and the excess oil is bled back to the pan. As bearing wear increases, requiring slightly more oil pressure at the pump to compensate for a loss of pressure at the bearing, the relief valve is used less and less. It is possible to shim the pressure relief spring, carefully following engine manufacturer instructions, but under no condition should the spring be stretched in an attempt to increase the oil pressure.

OIL FILTERS

Oil filters may be of full or partial flow design, and the included elements may be of cloth, paper, felt, or combinations thereof. In all cases, their prime job is to remove physical contaminants that get into the oil.

The full-flow filter passes all of the engine oil through the filter before it can reach the various bearing surfaces, while

the partial-flow filter cleans only a portion of the circulating oil at any particular period. The advantages of the full-flow system are apparent, in that nothing harmful should reach the bearings. However, the full-flow filter does not filter constantly. Whenever the oil is cold or the filter is plugged with dirt, a bypass valve opens so that the engine can continue to get oil. Some engine designs have this bypass valve built into the engine block. In others it is in the filter can itself.

Some full-flow elements have a valve built into the element itself to prevent drainback into the pan. If the filter emptied every time the engine was shut off for a few hours, every start would be without lubrication. Because of this extra valve that works with the bypass valve in the engine, it is important that the correct filter element be used. Just because the element fits onto the mounting pad doesn't mean it will work correctly. The wrong element can ruin an otherwise good engine.

There are two types of engine oil filters available today: the depth type and the paper type. In the paper type a special paper is used that will stand up under the detergents, high temperature and pressure in an oil system. The paper-type elements are all designed to trap particles only. The better paper filters will trap particles that can be measured in millionths of an inch. The best paper filter we have heard of is the AC, which

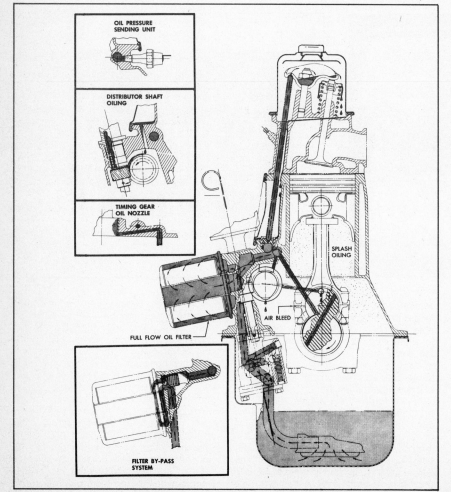

1. Six-Cylinder Lubrication System

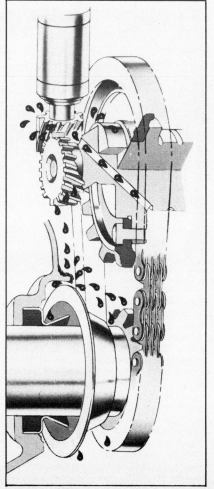

2. Camshaft Drive Lubrication

3. Filter Adapter

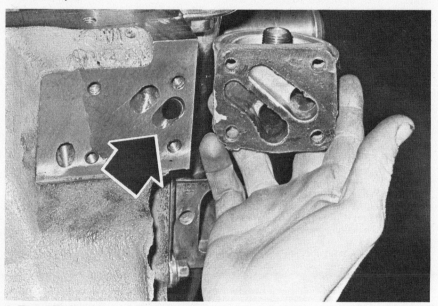

4. Flared Oil Passage

1. In the oil's journey from the pan up to the rockers, it is pumped through a filter. If the filter is plugged with impurities, a bypass system will reroute the oil, as on this Chevy 6-cylinder.

2. A small oil gallery feeds oil directly to distributor gears, while splash takes care of the timing chain and its sprockets on this Buick design.

3. A number of companies have oil filter adapter kits for Chevy V-8 engines, '56 through '67, allowing use of modern disposable filters rather than the cartridges. This one is by AC, of General Motors.

4. It is wise to flare the oil passage on cylinder blocks, like this Ford, where the filter hooks up. Likewise, the same operation can be accomplished on Chevrolets where the pump rides on the rear main cap. All of these "tricks" are designed to improve oiling.

will trap particles as small as 30 microns, a micron being one thousandth of a millimeter.

Engineers who believe in the paper filter design say that it isn't necessary to refine the oil as you filter it. If you remove the solid particles—the grit and the dirt that do the damage to the rubbing surfaces in the engine—then it doesn't make any difference whether the engine oil is as clean as when it was first put in. A good paper filter will stop all of the solid matter but will pass any of the detergent or anything that is actually dissolved in the detergent.

Those who back the depth-type of filter, and this includes Ford Motor Co. because all of their engines are factory equipped with depth-type filters, feel that simple filtration of the solid particles in the oil is not enough. The depth-type filter not only removes solid particles but it attempts to remove water and other liquid contaminants that are actually dissolved in the oil. In a depth-type filter the oil has to pass through several

inches of filtering medium. Oil will stay clear a lot longer with a depth-type filter, but one of the reasons it stays clear is that a certain amount of the detergent in the oil is being removed.

For many years, depth-type filters were not used on full-flow systems, because the extreme thickness of the depth-type filter would not pass cold oil. The result was a filter that only did half a job, because the bypass valve was open during a good part of engine operation.

The Baldwin Manufacturing Co. pioneered the use of a sisal doughnut in one end of the full-flow filter. The doughnut passed oil freely, but with very little filtering effect. The result was a filter with bypass action (filtering only part of the oil) on a full-flow system. A controversy still exists between the various filter companies over which is best for a full-flow oiling system—paper or depth type. Baldwin Manufacturing Co. stays out of the controversy by manufacturing and selling both types, for almost every car. Therefore you can pick whichever you think is the better.

What about toilet paper filters, the accessory gadgets that you buy and change yourself because very few service stations will have anything to do with them? Toilet paper filters are the depth-type but the trouble with them is they are too efficient. They not only remove the contaminants but they have a tendency to remove most of the detergent also. That's why a toilet paper filter will keep the oil as clear as if it had just been put in. Keeping the oil that clear is defeating the purpose of the detergent that we put in it in the first place. Those detergents have to circulate to do their job.

Toilet paper filters, in our opinion, must be changed at the recommended intervals in order to avoid shredding of the paper from the high temperature and pressure of the oil. There is a screen in the toilet paper filter can, but it is about the same mesh as ordinary window screen, and we feel it will not stop small particles of paper that could be shredded if the toilet paper were left in for long periods of time. We have personally disassembled an engine that had the crankshaft passages plugged with shredded toilet paper, but in all fairness to the toilet paper filter makers we feel that the engine had been run with the same roll of toilet paper a heck of a lot longer than the recommended period.

We do not like the look of dirty oil on the dipstick any more than anybody else does, but we must face the fact that oil in today's engines is designed to get dirty. It gets dirty because it's cleaning the engine, and it should be changed whenever it has become so loaded with contaminants that it can't do an effective cleaning job any longer.

If you keep a new car only a few months, it is doubtful that changing the filter or the oil will give you any benefit, other than keeping your warranty in effect. But if you keep your car, new or used, for several years, then filter elements and oil are cheap. The best of each will keep your engine running longer, with less trouble, if they are changed often.

Cooling System

Although we often describe automotive engines as being either air-cooled or liquid-cooled, all are cooled by air in the final analysis. The use of a circulating coolant fluid is nothing more than an added step that transfers excess heat caused by combustion to a point outside the engine where it can be dissipated. So why use this secondary step? Why not just design all auto engines to be air-cooled? Good question—it's true that air-cooled engines are efficient and dependable; they warm up more quickly than the liquid-cooled variety and run at a slightly higher temperature.

But when you consider today's engine requirements, air cooling is impractical for most, and impossible for many. Such a system requires deep cooling fins on the block and head to draw the heat from the combustion chambers, and a fan to force cool air across the finned area. To a large extent, this necessity tends to dictate engine design and so becomes self-restricting. Air-cooled engines currently in use (most notably the VW and Corvair) are referred to as pancake designs, as cylinders are horizontal and semi-independent instead of being grouped in a vertical block.

Enclosing the basic engine in a container or water jacket filled with a fluid (usually water) that will absorb the excess heat is the most common type of automotive engine cooling. This is done by casting passages into the engine block allowing the water to circulate around cylinder walls, valve seats, valve guides, the combustion chamber top and wherever else heat must be removed. As some spots in an engine may run hotter than others, it's common practice to include deflection guides in the passages and distribution tubes or water nozzles to direct water to potential dead or hot spots.

There's a limit to how much heat water can absorb before it begins to boil away, and so it has to be circulated constantly. As the water in the jacket is heated, it must be moved outside the engine to a place where it can cool. In a liquid-cooled system, that place is the radiator and there are two methods of moving the water—natural and forced circulation.

Natural circulation, or thermosiphon, is no longer commonly used—today's engines are too large and run too hot to depend upon water expansion for circulation. Briefly, it works like this: As the water surrounding the cylinders heats up, it expands. Like hot air, hot water is lighter; as it rises, the heavier and cooler water from the bottom of the radiator displaces it. The hot water goes through a hose to the radiator where it becomes heavier again as it cools and sinks to the radiator bottom, exerting pressure on the hot water presently surrounding the cylinders. This action is a continuous cycle and the hotter the engine, the faster the water circulates, maintaining fairly constant cylinder wall temperatures, as long as the engine is a low-output, low-compression design. In a modern engine with increased horsepower output, thermosiphon won't do the job.

Forced circulation, a much more dependable method, uses a belt-driven pump mounted at the front of the cylinder block. The pump is simply a housing with an inlet and outlet for water travel and an impeller, or flat plate with a number of blades or vanes, mounted on the pump shaft. As the pump impeller rotates, it pushes cool water into the cylinder block that forces the hotter water out. The faster the engine runs, the faster the water pump works.

RADIATOR DESIGN

The hot water is pumped into the radiator, a tank-like device used to bring a large amount of hot water in contact with a large amount of cool air to let the heat transfer from water to air. Forced into the radiator's upper tank, the hot water cools as it filters down through tiny copper tubes in the core (copper is an excellent conductor of heat) and into the lower tank where it returns to the engine block. Most radiators are made of copper and brass, but some models of Corvette have an aluminum radiator. While there are five basic types of core construction, tube-fin and ribbon-cellular are most often used today.

Obviously, the greater the distance between the upper and lower tank, the

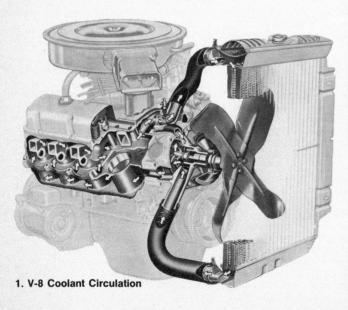

1. V-8 Coolant Circulation

2. Oldsmobile Fan Shroud

3. Vega Coolant Siphon

Cooling System Capacity in Quarts	"Prestone" Brand Anti-Freeze Coolant Required (in Quarts)											
	2	3	4	5	6	7	8	9	10	11	12	13
5	−12°	−62°										
6	0°	−34°										
7	6°	−17°	−54°									
8	10°	−7°	−34°	−69°								
9		0°	−21°	−50°								
10		4°	−12°	−34°	−62°							
11		8°	−6°	−23°	−47°							
12		10°	0°	−15°	−34°	−57°						
13			3°	−9°	−25°	−45°	−66°					
14			6°	−5°	−17°	−34°	−54°					
15			8°	0°	−12°	−26°	−43°	−62°				
16			10°	2°	−7°	−19°	−34°	−52°				
17				5°	−4°	−14°	−27°	−42°	−58°			
18				7°	0°	−10°	−21°	−34°	−50°	−65°		
19				9°	2°	−7°	−16°	−28°	−42°	−56°		
20				10°	4°	−3°	−12°	−22°	−34°	−48°	−62°	
21					6°	0°	−9°	−17°	−28°	−41°	−54°	−68°
22					8°	2°	−6°	−14°	−23°	−34°	−47°	−59°
23					9°	4°	−3°	−10°	−19°	−29°	−40°	−52°
24					10°	5°	0°	−7°	−15°	−24°	−34°	−46°

4. Coolant Chart

greater the cooling effect that takes place in the core. But the low-silhouette designs of recent years required that the vertical core be redesigned and so today, the crossflow or transverse core is popular. This amounts to tipping the radiator on its side, with the top and bottom tanks becoming side tanks and water flowing horizontally instead of vertically. In many transverse designs, the water pump pumps into the "bottom" tank (the one without the radiator cap). The result is reduced pressure against the cap, allowing the temperature to rise higher before the cap blows. "Blowing the cap" on a vertical tube radiator is common whenever the tubes get clogged with rust or scale. The water can't get down through the tubes, so it goes out through the cap. Changing the cap won't help, because there's nothing wrong with it. The only remedy is to clean out, boil out, or rod out the tubes, depending on how bad they are.

In a transverse core radiator, plugged tubes will slow down the circulation and

1. Coolant circulation is a simple but essential system to proper operation of an engine. Any blockage in the path of the arrows will cause overheating, possible damage.

2. Fan shrouds come and fan shrouds go, but Oldsmobile's Venturi Ring is the most sophisticated yet. The ring only clears the tips of the fan blades by 2/10-in., which makes the fan more efficient. In order to maintain the blade tip clearance, the venturi ring is mounted on the engine, with a flexible rubber seal between the ring and the radiator shroud.

3. In case you hadn't noticed, the Chevy Vegas coming out now do not have any coolant drains. The only way to change the coolant is to siphon it out. Easiest way is with Thexton's new Syphone-Aire, which uses air or mouth pressure to start the siphoning action.

4. Cooling system capacity can be found in your owner's manual, and then with this chart you can add antifreeze to protect to the lowest expected temperature.

5. The same cars often have different fan assemblies. Make sure you replace with fan of your model.

may cause overheating, but they will not cause the cap to blow and lose water because the water pump is exerting pressure on the "bottom" tank. There have even been some vertical designs that pumped into the bottom tank (notably Pontiac), but they aren't common.

FAN DESIGN

To increase the radiator's cooling action, a fan mounted on the water pump shaft and driven by the same belt draws air through the radiator core. There are several types in use: the fixed fan that rotates constantly with the pump shaft; a thermostatic fan that slows down when cooling is not needed; a centrifugal fan that reduces its speed at high engine rpm; a fluid coupling fan that adjusts its speed to driving conditions; a flexible blade fan that reduces pitch at higher speeds for easier turning, etc. As any fan requires engine power to rotate, these latter types reduce drag on the engine and so increase available horsepower. If radiator placement is too far from the fan, a sheetmetal shroud is used to prevent recirculation of the same air, thereby increasing the fan's efficiency. Blade number and arrangement differ depending upon requirements.

CAPS AND PRESSURE

Pressurizing a radiator system improves its cooling efficiency and prevents evaporation and surge losses. The pressure cap increases air pressure in the system by several pounds per square inch, allowing water to be circulated at higher temperatures without boiling. With the greater difference between the water and outside air, heat passes from the water faster. A pressure cap contains a blowoff valve and a vacuum valve and seats tightly over both the filler mouth and its edges. A calibrated spring in the blowoff valve holds the valve closed, producing pressure in the system. If the pressure exceeds the amount for which the system was designed, the valve blows off its seat, relieving the excess. When the engine has been shut off and cools down, a vacuum might form, dropping the inside pressure sufficiently to let outside air pressure collapse it. If a vacuum does start to form, the vacuum

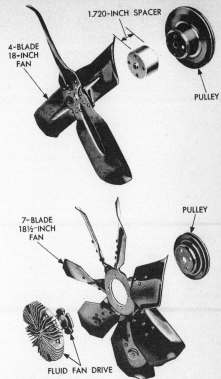

5. Fan Assemblies

valve opens to let air into the system before damage is done.

Many cooling systems now use a coolant recovery system in conjunction with the radiator. This small additional tank provides room for its expansion. It eliminates loss of coolant when the engine is turned off and "boils over." The pressure cap used on a radiator with a recovery system must have a gravity-operated vacuum valve. If the vacuum valve is spring-loaded, it must hang open or it will prevent the flowback of coolant to the radiator.

ANTIFREEZE

Up to this point, we've referred to coolant and water as one and the same, but ordinary water is no longer recommended and seldom used today except in emergencies. Antifreeze solutions with an ethylene glycol base have replaced the use of plain water. When mixed proportionally with water, they provide protection from freezing temperatures and prevent a cracked engine block. They also contain additives to combat corrosion and neutralize rust formed in the engine block before it can plug the radiator core.

For best corrosion resistance and rust prevention, a 50% solution of antifreeze and water should be used. This will raise the boiling point at sea level to 227° F.; 15° higher than plain water. And a 50% solution will lower the freezing point to -34° F. That is much lower than most areas need, but the 50% solution should be maintained even in hot climates because of its corrosion protection.

Glycol is more expensive initially, but it doesn't boil away, and it's a good water pump lubricant. However, if you have a leaking head gasket, a cracked block or cylinder head, the glycol will pass into the oil, and contaminate it very quickly.

Cooling System

If it's not caught in time, this can lead to a locked-up engine, since glycol will congeal when it mixes with oil and in doing so, completely plug oil pump screens, oil filters and oil passages. A white discoloration on the dipstick is the danger signal, and the most convenient check point is the oil filter. If the filter sludge looks like curdled milk and molasses, you've got troubles, but it's worth attempting an oil flush before bracing yourself for a complete engine teardown to clean up the mess.

Hustle down to your local paint supply store or wholesale dealer and purchase a quantity of butyl "Cellosolve." A retardant used to slow the action of solvent, butyl "Cellosolve" is packaged on a regional basis according to frequency of use; in warm climates, it's available in 5-gal. or larger containers, but those who live in colder areas can find it in 1-qt. cans. How much you'll need depends upon your crankcase capacity. Figure adding two parts butyl "Cellosolve" to one part SAE 10 oil.

Drain the engine oil while it's warm. If your engine uses a disposable oil filter, leave it in place; if it has a cartridge filter, remove the filter and replace the empty can. Fill the engine with the mixture then start it up and run at fast idle, watching the oil pressure and operating temperature carefully during this time. The oil pressure should read normal and operating temperature must remain above 150° F.

Stop the engine after approximately 45 mins. to 1 hr. and drain the crankcase. If the contamination was really severe, it may be necessary to repeat the operation more than once to completely dissolve the sludge. After you're satisfied that the sludge is gone, refill the engine with a flushing oil or fresh 10W oil and run at fast idle for another 10-15 mins. Drain the flush oil and then replace the disposable oil filter with a new one, or insert a clean cartridge into the can, and refill the crankcase with the oil you'd normally use. Having saved the engine from total disaster, all you have to do now is find the leak and correct it before driving the car again.

It may be possible to free a "seized" engine by circulating hot water of at least 140° F. through the cooling system. Attach a hose from a hot water source to a nipple installed in a core plug hole, then allow the water to flow through the engine and out through the radiator fill neck. If the engine will turn over on the starter, follow the steps outlined above with butyl "Cellosolve."

If the engine doesn't turn over, remove the spark plugs and pour undiluted butyl "Cellosolve" through each hole until the pistons are covered. Wait about 15 mins., then jump on the starter again. Let it spin until the mixture has been pumped out through the plug holes. Now, replace the plugs and, again, follow the steps indicated above with butyl "Cellosolve."

Anti-leak antifreezes have been on the market since about 1969. Some people

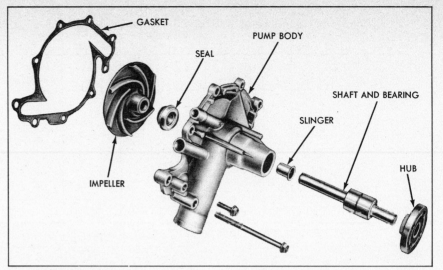

1. Pump Components

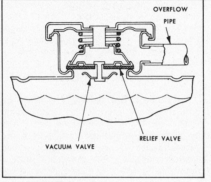

2. Vacuum Valve

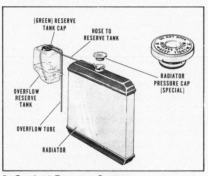

3. Coolant Reserve System

feel that there is a danger of plugging up the cooling system, that perhaps anti-leak really means anti-flow. Such fears are groundless. In the few cases where plugging has occurred, the cooling system was on its last legs, with rust-clogged passages that probably would have plugged up anyway the first time the car hit a good bump and shifted the sediment around. The cooling system should never be drained and new antifreeze dumped in unless you flush it out. And it's a good idea to use flushing chemicals, too.

In 1972, Prestone announced a new antifreeze called Prestone II. It has a new formulation for better engine protection and without any anti-leak properties. So those of you who didn't feel quite comfortable with the anti-leak formulas can now head for your nearest Prestone dealer. If you like anti-leak, look for du-Pont or Dow brands.

1. Water pumps should be replaced as a unit, but an understanding of how they are constructed can help when you try to diagnose problems

2. This type of cap is open to the atmosphere until the rush of air or coolant trying to escape closes the vacuum valve. A cap like this is easier on the radiator because the system is only under pressure part of the time. Other types have a spring on the vacuum valve, which does not allow any pressure to escape. Spring-type vacuum valves will not work with a coolant recovery system. Use the open type.

3. Coolant reserve systems, such as this '73 Dodge version, prevent the loss of radiator coolant. Special pressure cap allows coolant to overflow into plastic reserve tank. When engine cools, pressure differences between tank and radiator cause coolant to flow back into radiator.

4. This pressure tester will determine if there are internal leaks in the cooling system.

5. Add an adapter and you can also test the cap. This one's a dud.

6. Three types of intercoolers. Fitted into the radiator's bottom tank, they allow automatic transmission fluid to circulate for cooling, preventing transmission overheating.

7. Service stations usually have a Bloc-Chek kit. This simple test for exhaust gas leakage involves a change of fluid color if gas is present.

RUNNING PURE WATER

In older cars, you could run pure water with a rust inhibitor and not hurt a thing. Don't try this on a late-model car, because your hot indicator warning light will not work with pure water. Here's why. New cars recently came from the factory in most cases with a 33% antifreeze solution and a 14-lb. pressure cap. With this combination, the coolant will boil at approximately 256° F. Temperatures in the 250° range may seem awfully hot, but they won't hurt the engine as long as the coolant doesn't boil.

4. Pressure Testing

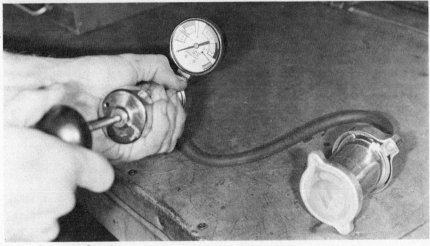

5. Cap Pressure Check

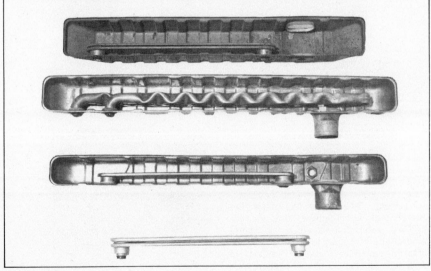

6. Intercoolers

7. Exhaust Gas Check

With no danger present at the lower temperatures, the engineers designed the warning light to come on at about 256° F. If you run pure water, it will boil at 247° with the factory 14-lb. cap. Thus, with pure water your engine could be boiling, sustaining a lot of damage from uneven cooling, and the hot warning light would never come on. For proper warning light operation, you must run at least a 33% antifreeze solution, and 50% is even better. New cars are now coming off the end of the assembly line with 44-55% antifreeze. Your owner's manual will tell you how much you should have. If not, stick with the 50% solution.

COOLANT ADDITIVES

There are many chemical compounds and additives on the market designed to give last-minute hope to the unfortunate soul facing a major radiator repair job. These chemicals range from pellets to be dropped in the radiator to fluids designed to dissolve rust or stop radiator leaks. Use of these products inevitably guarantees that the repair will have to be done anyway, but buying a $3.00 can appeals to the innocent who is otherwise faced with a large repair bill, and he figures it's worth the gamble. Radiator shops will tell you that stop-leak prod-

ucts are really one of their most dependable business builders, followed closely by the anti-rust solutions. However, many new cars come from the factory with some kind of anti-leak chemical in the cooling system. The difference is that the factory knows exactly how much to put in. They don't just dump a lot of goop in that will plug everything up.

If the leak is a minor one, the stop-leak solution may work temporarily, but most drivers then put off the inevitable repair and that's where they make their mistake. Remember, the radiator is made of brass and copper and these metals don't rust—they corrode. Corrosion is a chemical process that is self-accelerating in nature and once it starts, the affected area must be completely cleaned to stop it.

Any rust found in the coolant comes from the engine's water jacket and can settle in the tiny radiator tube passages, blocking coolant flow. So you're actually faced with two different problems that using chemicals to solve will only aggravate. Anti-rust solutions will actually free rust that has accumulated in the water jacket passages and let it circulate into the radiator; stop-leak solutions will plug minor holes that corrosion continues to enlarge.

But if you have one of the 1973 Hornets without air conditioning, it's probably fitted with an aluminum fin radiator; check before you add anything to the cooling system. These are identified by two decals containing warning and repair information. Hot water or steam are the only cleaning agents to use, as anything caustic will eat holes in it faster than moths in a wool factory. Repairs should be done only with Alcoa Flux #64, 30/70 or 40/60 tin-lead solder and a minimum of heat.

So what's the answer? Simple—change the coolant at regular intervals. All major brands of antifreeze contain additives to

...on and the for-... block, but these ...ng before the anti-... the coolant once a ...urself a lot of head-a... old-fashioned and still insis... ...g water during the summer mo... ...be sure to use anti-corrosion and rust inhibitor additives with it or you'll defeat everything that antifreeze has done for your cooling system.

The new super cooling additives are another controversy. They are supposed to transfer heat better than any antifreeze, and thereby keep the engine cooler. Prestone engineers tell us that they have never found a chemical on the market that will increase the heat transfer any better than antifreeze. And in some cases the super cooling additives will affect the anti-foaming properties of the antifreeze, thus giving less efficient cooling.

FINDING LEAKS

One source of damaging corrosion comes from exhaust gas leaking into the cooling system. The strong acids in the gas combine with the water in the coolant and eat away at the radiator tubes.

You can also check exhaust gas leakage by using a block check kit. Insert the block check tool into the radiator filler neck and hold just above the coolant level. Squeeze the bulb and fill with air. If the tool fluid changes from its normal blue to a transparent yellow, exhaust gas is present. By running the engine with the spark plugs grounded on one bank at a time, you can determine which head gasket is at fault on a V-8 engine. An equally simple way is to disconnect the upper hose, drain the radiator until the coolant is just above the cylinder head and remove both thermostat and fan belt. Start the engine and accelerate rapidly a few times. If exhaust gas is leaking, the coolant level should rise considerably, and bubbles will appear.

Water leaks in the cooling system will cause a loss of pressure and can lead to serious problems. To check for a water leak, top up the radiator to about ½-in. of the filler neck and run the engine until it's at operating temperature. Then attach a pressure tester in place of the cap and apply 15 psi pressure. If it holds steady, there's no leak, but a pressure drop tells you to check the hose connections, water pump, radiator and engine expansion plugs for an external leak. If the pressure tester needle fluctuates, you've got an exhaust gas leak that should be checked out. Pressure caps can also fail and should be checked with the same tester. If your cap won't hold the rated pressure, replace it with a new one of the proper rating.

Some radiators contain special tubing in the bottom tank that acts as an intercooler or heat exchanger. Automatic transmission fluid flows through this intercooler and prevents the transmission from overheating. An intercooler leak not only affects your cooling system's performance but can spell transmission problems if it's not taken care of.

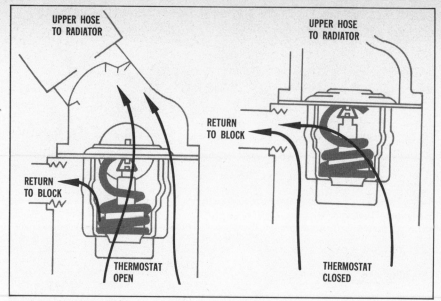

1. Thermostat Operation

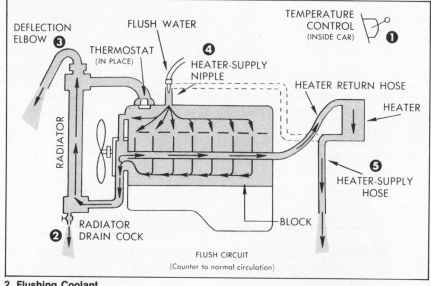

2. Flushing Coolant

THERMOSTATS

Check the thermostat when you change the coolant. This simple temperature-sensitive valve tends to fail gradually, either from corrosion or foreign matter. Thermostat failure (or the use of none at all) means that the engine will not reach its proper operating temperature because the coolant circulates through both it and the radiator at all times. Operation below proper temperatures results in premature engine wear. The heater also works very inefficiently, if at all, a condition easily noticed during cold winter months, but not necessarily in the summer. Unscrewing the cap screws holding its housing lets you reach the thermostat easily. The housing is usually found at the point where the outlet hose is attached to the engine. Avoid a mess by draining the coolant below the housing level before loosening the bolts.

Thermostats are marked with their designated opening point (usually 180° through 205° F.) and you should always use the exact one specified for your engine. To test your old thermostat or even

3. Stuck Thermostat

a new one (brand new is no guarantee that it will work), rig up a simple apparatus and borrow the kitchen stove. You'll need a water container, preferably Pyrex or equivalent so you can see better, a household cooking thermometer that reads up to 250° or so, a wire hook to suspend the thermostat, a feeler gauge and a piece of string. Insert the feeler gauge between the valve and its seat and attach the string to the gauge.

You'll need the temperature figures for both the initial and fully opened positions. These are available from your dealer or wherever you buy the new

4. Bolt-in Core Plugs

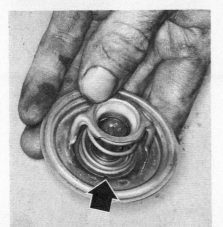

6. Thermostat Bleed Hole

1. *Replacement is the only cure for a faulty thermostat. Always check the specs for your engine, since the old unit may have failed because it was the wrong one.*

2. *Prestone recommends this method of flushing the cooling system. Note accessory deflector in radiator neck.*

3. *This thermostat is stuck open—but instead of causing cold running, it actually caused overheating, because it was stuck half-way open and didn't allow enough coolant to pass through the system.*

4. *Bolt-in core plugs are a cinch to install, and to remove if necessary. Some types of block heating elements are inserted in these holes.*

5. *This design of thermostat, made by Robertshaw, has given excellent performance in our cars, because it closes tightly when cold. You can identify a thermostat's opening temperature by the stamp on its bottom.*

6. *A thermostat must seal tightly if it is going to give a quick engine warm-up. We have found samples of this particular design of thermostat that allowed enough of a gap when they were closed to give the engine an inordinately long warm-up time. All thermostats have bleed holes to enable air trapped in the block to escape (arrow).*

7. *Sometimes it's a tricky job to remove spring-type radiator hose clamps. These special pliers make clamp removal a simple, easy chore.*

5. Robertshaw Thermostat

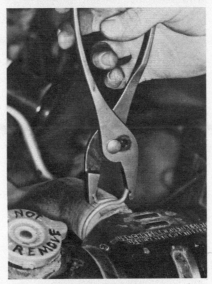

7. Spring-Type Hose Clamp

thermostat. It must not touch any surface while being heated and the water should be stirred gently to ensure even distribution of the heat. A typical set of specs for a 195° thermostat is that a .003-in. gauge should slip free within +3° of the rating and the valve should be fully open at 218° F. To replace the thermostat, let it rest in position with the longer or valve end toward the engine, then refasten the housing. You'll need a new housing gasket which can be purchased ready-cut from a dealership or made at home from ordinary cork gasket stock. The mating surfaces should be clean and the gasket coated with cooling system sealant. The hose is reattached using a screw-type attaching clamp.

FLUSHING PROCEDURES

The average car owner's idea of flushing consists of opening the petcock on the radiator bottom and maybe the two on each side of the engine block (the Vega has none and must be siphoned), sticking a garden hose in the radiator and letting the water flow. Unfortunately, this accomplishes very little. Outside faucets are normally connected only to cold water, so sticking the hose into the radiator filler opening and waiting until the water from the drain cock appears to be clear flushes only the radiator. The cold water keeps the thermostat leading to the engine cooling passages closed and even if the engine drains are open in this procedure, there's incomplete circulation, with residue from old dirty coolant remaining in the engine. The following

step-by-step procedure is basic to an effective annual coolant change.

1) Set heater temperature control to "high." If your car is equipped with a vacuum-operated heater valve (check with your dealer—this is found mainly on newer cars with factory air conditioning), run the engine at idle during all flushing procedures described, as a vacuum valve will only stay open with the engine running. Keep a close watch on the engine temperature gauge.

2) Open radiator drain cock and let radiator drain. Do not open engine drain cocks.

3) Remove radiator cap and put a deflection elbow in the filler neck to prevent excessive splash into the engine compartment.

4) Remove hose from heater supply nipple at the engine block. Point this hose downward for drain.

5) Connect water supply to the heater supply nipple at the engine block. This does not have to be a positive connection; an ordinary garden hose will do as long as most of the water can be directed into the engine.

6) Turn on the water, make sure it is cold and flush for 3 to 5 mins. without the engine running, unless you have a vacuum valve. Squeeze the outlet or upper radiator hose during the last minute of flushing to remove any trapped liquid.

7) Turn off water and close radiator petcock. Reconnect heater supply hose to its nipple and remove deflection elbow from radiator. Be sure the system is normally full of coolant.

CORE PLUGS

Every engine has at least seven "freeze" or core plugs—three on each side of the block and one in the back. These are filled with metal, but it's softer and thinner than the block material. If the coolant freezes, the expanding fluid pushes out the plugs, sometimes preventing block damage but not always. Core plugs are subject to corrosion and can develop small leaks. Most are a simple press fit and can be removed if faulty by drilling a hole in the center and prying out with a screwdriver. Drain the block before starting work and take care not to let pieces of the plug fall into the coolant passage. The same press-in replacement type can be used but bolt-in plugs are easier to seat and remove. These use a toggle bolt that slips into the water jacket, with the plug bolting up with a gasket or O-ring between itself and the block.

HOSE REPLACEMENT

You can sometimes tell how good a hose is by its appearance and feel, but many hoses have a spiral wire reinforcement inside, and this can rust and disintegrate without affecting the outside appearance. Squeeze the hose at midpoint and you should be able to feel the wire; if not, replace the hose. Unfasten the hose clamp, then twist as you pull the hose off. Stubborn hoses may have to be cut off with a knife. Apply a dab of sealing compound around the connecting nipple and fit the new hose over it.

Cooling System

Use screw-type clamps for replacement, as spring-type clamps may leak.

FAN BELTS

Fan belt tension should be checked periodically. Low tension means belt slippage, which will wear out the belt, let the battery run down and cause the engine to overheat. Too much tension overloads the water pump and wears it out prematurely. Adjust by loosening the alternator mounting bolt and moving it toward or away from the engine block before retightening. If you don't have access to a belt tension tool, you can set it by this rule of thumb—belt deflection with your thumb pushing on it, should be about ¼ in. at the midpoint of its longest unsupported section. A loose belt wears out fast, but a tight belt wears out the bushing (or bearing) in the water pump. So, if you don't have a tension gauge, keep that belt a little loose. Belts are much cheaper to replace than pumps.

HOT RODDING THE COOLING SYSTEM

Remember, the manufacturer put no more radiator into your car when it was built than was considered adequate to handle the original engine under normal driving conditions. So if you do anything to significantly add horsepower or change to a larger engine, you should change radiators too. If you have a 1960 model or later, it's likely that there's a heavy-duty package available for it. This package will include the automatic transmission cooler, fan, and water pump with the radiator. But if you stuff a Hemi in a Plymouth Belvedere that came factory-equipped with a Slant-6, you'll have to add a radiator which the factory designed for use with the Hemi. Depending upon your car, this may or may not bolt right in, but there should be no great problem in the installation. Just secure it at the four corners, make sure the fan has proper clearance and connect a pair of universal hoses. Be sure to change the thermostat and pressure cap to conform to Hemi specs.

If the old radiator adequately protects against overheating, there's no point in putting in a larger one. And don't think of radiator "bigness" in terms of coolant capacity; the Model A Ford had a radiator twice the capacity of a current Mustang equipped with a 289-cu.-in. V-8. The differences are the improvement in pump efficiency and the pressurized system, not to mention that the fins are in a better cooling arrangement than the A's old cellular structure.

Eliminating the fan should be approached with caution. You can sometimes improve the engine efficiency if your driving doesn't involve much city traffic. In cases of marginal overheating caused by hopping up the engine, the shrouds used with air-conditioned cars will usually clip right into their non-air-conditioned counterparts. For more extreme modifications, where the shape of

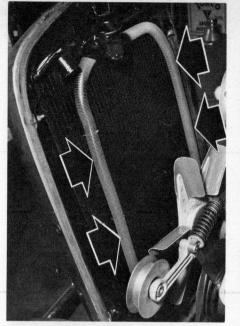

1. Auxiliary Flex-O-Kool

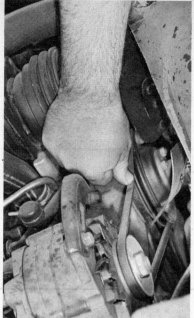

2. Belt Deflection

3. Types of Clamps

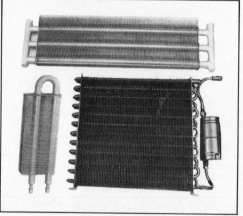

4. Accessory Oil Coolers

the radiator is important to achieve a desired styling effect, any competent radiator specialty shop can adapt almost any radiator to your needs, but this is expensive.

Take care when you buy a chrome-plated pressure cap; it must be designed to operate at the same pressure as the original. Radiator covers, which can be as simple as a window-shade-like arrangement pulled by a string from the dashboard, help warmup in extremely cold climates. Visual indicators for the coolant level are quite helpful in discouraging the service station attendant from opening the pressure cap. Filters are sold for cooling systems, but if they contain chemicals, they may not be compatible with the brand of antifreeze you use.

Radiators through the years have been made in different basic designs. The cellular is somewhat inefficient because it won't pass the water fast enough. Tubular is better, but the comparatively recent tube-fin design, in which the fins are made in accordion pleats between the tubes, is a tremendous improvement over the plain tubular core. Changing to a tube-fin core might even solve a hot rod

cooling problem for you if you were trying to run a big engine in a small car that won't accommodate a large size radiator.

That's about all there is to a cooling system. Now if you can just stop service station attendants from removing your radiator cap when your engine is hot and allowing all of your antifreeze to burble out on the ground, you've got it made.

1. Easiest oil cooler to install is the Flex-O-Kool. Bend it to desired shape and wire it to radiator. We installed a Flex-O-Kool on a flathead Ford, it reduced temperatures, and decreased oil consumption. It's available from Car Care Parts, 6900 Valjean Ave., Van Nuys, Calif. 91406.

2. Set belt tension by rule of thumb. Quarter-inch deflection at midpoint saves belt as well as bushings.

3. The wire-type clamp on the left is often used by the factory, but does not seal very well when it gets old. Throw it away and use screw-type.

4. Accessory oil coolers come in all shapes and sizes. If placed where fan causes air blast, they will definitely keep temperature down.

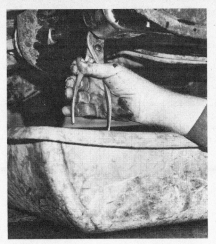

1. Removing a radiator is one of the easiest things you can do in your own backyard. Place a container beneath the drain cock to catch the coolant.

2. Remove the radiator cap so air can displace coolant, then open drain and let fluid out. When radiator is empty, loosen upper connecting hose clamp.

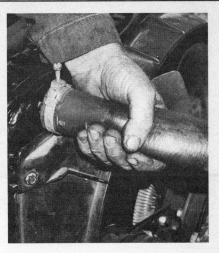

3. Grasp the hose and twist it as you pull it off. It may require twisting back and forth several times to break the hose loose from radiator inlet.

4. The lower hose is usually hard to reach from above. Use an extra long screwdriver to avoid scraped knuckles, or you may have to reach it from below.

5. The automatic transmission cooling lines are best disconnected from below using an open-end wrench. Jacking car up may make access to lines easier.

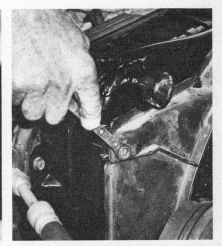

6. Now, remove the capscrews that hold the radiator shield in place. A box wrench is best to avoid rounding off the heads of the capscrews.

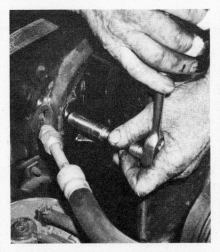

7. A socket wrench will come in handy when you take out the bolts holding the radiator. There are usually four, one in each corner of the frame.

8. Lift the radiator up and out, angling it if necessary. Be careful to not scrape fin surface. On some cars removal of the fan may be necessary.

9. Either hang the shield back behind the fan pulley or remove it. Now you are ready for a trip to the radiator shop for repair or cleaning.

HOW-TO: Removing Water Pump

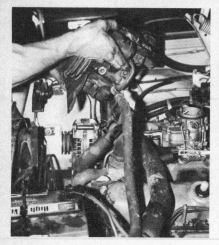

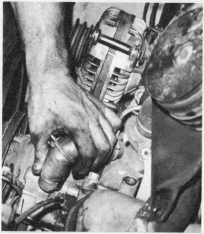

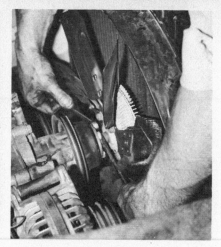

1. Before pulling the water pump, it will be necessary to remove everything blocking access. Here we've unbolted the air-conditioning pump.

2. Once we've got clear access to the water pump, all connecting hoses are detached. Drain radiator to prevent a mess and to save coolant fluid.

3. The fan usually has to come off to provide clearance for pump removal. Be careful not to gouge the radiator fins. Finally, remove the drive belt.

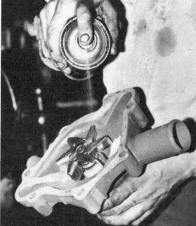

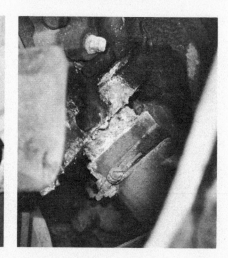

4. After all the pump retaining bolts have been removed, a sharp blow with a mallet will break the pump loose. Some may require only wiggling.

5. Before replacing new water pump, use a dab or spray of adhesive to set the gasket In place. It's no fun to get pump on, then find a gasket leak.

6. Other problems may arise when you dig into the water pump area. Extreme corrosion as shown here means that the radiator hose has to be replaced.

7. In days past, water pumps were relatively simple affairs. It took only the removal of six bolts to remove the pump from a Kaiser-Frazer engine.

8. The pumps used on the 6-cylinder Ramblers were a snap to remove, too. Taking off one V-belt and five bolts put the whole thing right in your hand.

9. But now, the average V-8 engine pump is more complex. You'll have to pull the fan, a pair of belts and three hoses to get this one off a Buick.

10. Other side of the same Buick shows alternator and three hoses which must be removed for pump access. Be sure new hoses are available, just in case.

11. The F-85 uses a shield to protect the distributor in case of water pump failure. It will come off when you remove the water pump unit.

12. Similar to the Galaxie, this Fairlane pump has the alternator bracket attached. It has to be removed before the water pump can be taken off.

13. On the Galaxie 500, the pump has a bracket on either side. Both of them have to come off, making the job just that much more difficult.

14. Other side of the Galaxie looks clean, but that's because the fan and the radiator have been removed. This allows more wrench-swinging space.

15. The Bel Air pump has a bracket and two hoses that have to come off. This will be a greasy, grimy job on older cars with a lot of mileage piled up.

16. Once everything is stripped off, as on this Catalina, there should be no difficulty in getting at the water pump itself. Again, it's a dirty job.

17. Although it may be funny looking when you get right down to it, your Dart or GT won't run very long if the pump fails. This one's easy to pull.

18. Check the thickness and the number of gaskets on the pump. Some pumps may require two gaskets so the impeller doesn't hit block inside pump cavity.

Exhaust System

Many people consider a car's exhaust system in the same light as a sewer pipe. It's necessary, but it isn't something that is very interesting or pleasant to work on. But an exhaust system is not just a bunch of tubes to get rid of waste gases. It can result in your engine running good or bad because of a little gadget in the exhaust called the exhaust manifold heat valve. Many engines have this valve, whether they are 4's, 6's or V-8's. Its purpose is to block the direct exit of the exhaust gases from the manifold and force them along a path that leads through the intake manifold under the carburetor. The exhaust gases heat up the passages in the intake manifold and thereby aid in more complete vaporization of the gasoline. Good vaporization is necessary to prevent a stumble when you step on the throttle. Believe us, the exhaust heat valve really does its job. We have seen engines that could be warmed up until they were just about as hot as you could get them and they would still stumble when you step on the throttle just because the heat valve was frozen in an open position. Free up the valve so that it worked properly and the car would run like it was just off the showroom floor. Cars that do not have the heat valve in their exhaust system usually circulate coolant from the engine block through a passageway in the intake manifold just under the carburetor. Some late model cars have been able to do away with the heat valve because they have a hot air inlet on the air cleaner for the carburetor.

Exhaust heat valves are usually held in the closed position by both a weight and a spring. The spring relaxes as the exhaust heats up because not as much heat is needed under the carburetor when the engine is warm. The weight is offset so that it has a tendency to hold the valve in the closed position, but the valve itself is also offset on a shaft so that any excess rush of exhaust gases will have a tendency to open it. A combination of these factors results in an exhaust heat valve that forces the right amount of exhaust gas through the heating passages in the intake manifold so that the engine operates without any stumble and has sufficient vaporization of the gas to get good gas mileage.

HEAT VALVE PROBLEMS

The valve, regardless of type, can cause a lot of trouble under certain conditions. If the car is driven only short distances at a time and never completely warmed up, the conditions are present in the heavy condensation of moisture while the engine is cold plus the extra carbon caused by the engine running "rich" on a partial choke setting. The moisture and carbon don't need much time to "freeze" the shaft on the butterfly valve in the closed position. Once rust and carbon have a good grip on these exhaust thermostat valves, all the high-speed driving in the world won't free them. All exhaust gases from the cylinders on the side with the "frozen" heat valve must therefore pass through the heat riser passages of the intake manifold. Not only does this make four cylinders practically useless but it also insures an over-supply of heat to the base of the carburetor, making "vapor-lock" a cause of distress in many cases.

If the car is factory equipped with a dual exhaust system, a butterfly-type heat valve will be located between one of the exhaust manifolds and the exhaust headpipe which leads to the muffler. If this valve should become "frozen" due to the above conditions (excessive oil consumption will also help "freeze" the heat valves), the exhaust must still pass through the intake manifold risers and into the opposite exhaust manifold.

If your car uses the obsolete, internal "duck bill" heat valve, the crosspipe between manifolds has to be taken off to make sure that the valve is not choked shut. The other type with an external spring and weight can be checked while

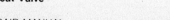

1. Exhaust Manifold Heat Valve

2. Replacing Muffler

3. Cutting Valve Shaft

cool to make sure that the shaft through
the collar holding the butterfly valve will
move freely. If frozen, it can sometimes
be loosened by moving back and forth
by hand until the rust is broken loose,
then lubricating with special manifold
heat valve lubricant. If this doesn't do
the job, then a new valve should be installed in its place.

TYPES OF MUFFLERS

Most stock mufflers are designed to
lower noise to a minimum and contain a
series of baffles and noise-deadening
chambers through which the gases must
pass. These stock mufflers have a restrictive effect on the exhaust gases but
this restriction is not too great at low
engine speeds. As the engine speed increases and more gases are crammed
through the muffler, the back pressure in
the system increases and engine efficiency is lowered. This well known fact
has been the big reason for the popularity of dual exhaust systems for many
years among the hot rodders, and it is
also the reason that most of the higher
powered stock cars use dual exhaust
systems.

By using a dual system, the automotive
manufacturer has cut in half the volume
of gases to be muffled by a stock muffler
but he has also increased noise. The

*1. The exhaust manifold heat valve,
at the end of the exhaust manifold,
tends to have deposits build up on
the baffle shaft, causing the valve
to stick and the engine to either
vapor lock or stumble on takeoff.*

*2. Chances of fixing an exhausted
exhaust system are next to nil. Most
become so corroded by salt or sulphur
that the repair job becomes strictly
"remove and replace."*

*3. When carbon and rust "freeze" the
exhaust heat valve, best bet is to
replace it. Here the valve shaft is
cut with a torch; you can use a hacksaw to do the same thing.*

*4. New shaft and weight assembly is
inserted through butterfly heat valve
in exhaust headpipe.*

*5. Spring is fitted on shaft with end
of spring against headpipe stud.*

*6. Retaining spring fits over end of
heat valve shaft and headpipe stud.
Spring and weight hold valve in
closed position.*

4. Inserting Weight & Shaft Assembly

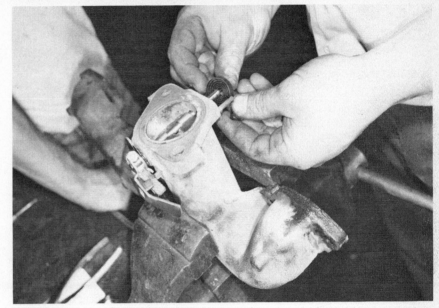

5. Fitting Spring on Shaft

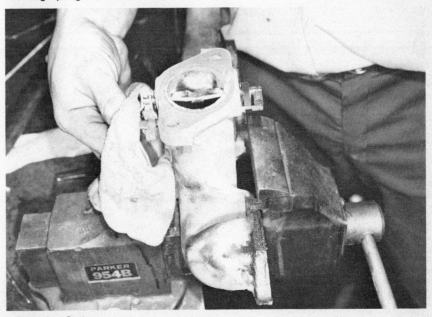

6. Retaining Spring

Exhaust System

fewer cylinders per muffler, the more the noise. In other words, a stock muffler for each 4-cylinder bank of a V-8 engine will produce more noise than if one of the same mufflers is used for all eight cylinders. To keep this noise down, the number of baffles and chambers has been increased, with the end effect that the newly found horsepower due to the dual system is lost, especially at high engine speeds, due to the increased restriction and back pressure in the muffler.

Straight-through type mufflers are, as the name implies, straight-through with no restrictive baffles or chambers. The center pipe can either be slotted, drilled, louvered, saw cut or even a large twisted spring type. The area between the center pipes and the muffler shell is then packed with steel shavings or fiberglass to absorb the exhaust noise that passes through the openings in the center pipe. While very efficient in exhausting the burned gases, the straight-through type does not always lower the exhaust noise to the desirable minimum. If the noise level is too high after the installation of the straight-through mufflers, a resonator muffler can be added.

The resonator muffler is actually in most cases just a short-length, straight-through muffler, either glass or steel packed, that is installed in the exhaust system to provide extra sound muffling to the exhaust. These resonators can sometimes be placed in the tailpipe behind the regular muffler to provide maximum quietness. Exhaust gases cool off as they near the rear of the car, which causes the volume of gas to be lessened. When resonators are installed near the end of the exhaust system, the cooler gases are more easily muffled due to the decrease in their volume.

While the heat valve is, as mentioned, one of the main causes of grief in the exhaust system, the prime enemy of the entire system is the moisture content of the exhaust gases. This moisture is by no means pure water but contains all sorts of corrosives, the main one being sulfuric acid from the sulfur content of the gasoline and oil. In a car that is being operated mainly for short trips, such as going to the store or school, this acid-laden moisture can collect in all sorts of places where it eats away at the thin-metal exhaust pipes and muffler shell until these pieces look as if moths with tungsten carbide teeth have been at them. Particular trouble spots are dips in the tailpipes ahead of the rear axle, the section just behind the axle, the rear end of the headpipe and the bottom of the muffler shell.

Other areas prone to attack are, unfortunately, the joints where the various pipes are attached to each other, which can make things a bit tough to pull apart. However, there is one good thing about it: This is the one area of repair where you can vent your feelings with a hammer and chisel and epithets.

MUFFLER REPLACEMENT

There is no such thing as "repairing" or "fixing" a deteriorated exhaust system; all you can do is replace it. Conse-

1. Welding Valve

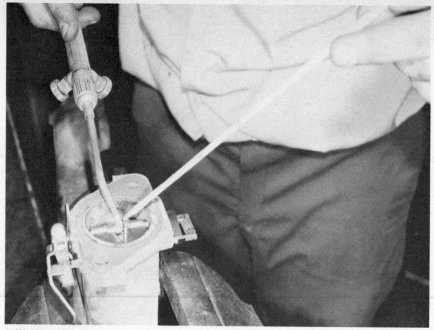

2. Cutaway of a Typical Muffler

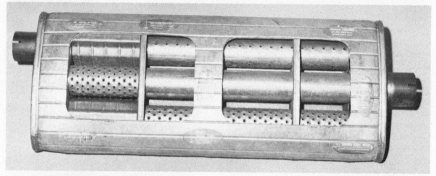

3. Exhaust Flow Through a Muffler

4. Bracket and Clamp Support

quently, as long as you confine your attentions to the pipework and muffler, you can bang away to your heart's content. If you have access to a torch and know how to use it, you can flame-cut the corroded joints—which is how the professionals do it—but it isn't absolutely necessary. All that is needed is a hammer, a round-nose or diamond point chisel, a hacksaw and a set of open- or box-end wrenches. Exhaust system work is neither the cleanest nor the messiest form of auto repair work but it is pretty much the simplest and, for the home or amateur mechanic, generally the starting point after plug-changing and simple tune-ups to bolster his confidence.

The first step in any exhaust work, unless you're a midget or claim kinship to the worm family, is to get the car up off the ground. If you can gain access to the use of a hoist or greasepit, so much the better but it isn't necessary. What is necessary is a safe method of supporting the car. By "safe" we don't mean a couple of bumper jacks or packing crates. If you can possibly afford it, purchase four adjustable jack stands from any parts house, Sears, Montgomery Ward or one of the automotive chain outfits such as

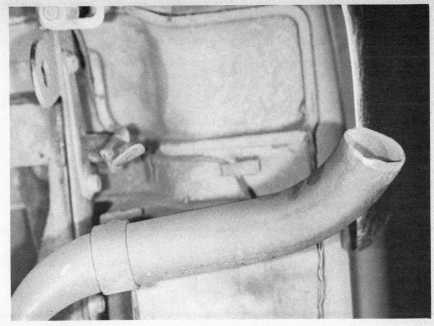

5. Bent Tailpipe

1. As butterfly valve revolves freely on shaft, the two are welded with the valve in the closed position. Screw seen here was wedged in against valve to hold it correctly for welding and is removed once job is finished.

2. The quiet stock mufflers, with their many pipes, chambers and baffles, tend to corrode faster than the straight-throughs because they trap and retain exhaust condensation, which is loaded with sulphuric acid.

3. The restrictive nature of common mufflers will seriously affect the high-speed operation of an internal combustion engine. More efficient dual exhaust systems, featuring either smaller mufflers or straight-throughs, can be purchased and installed for less than $100.

4. U-clamps must be securely fastened with enough clearance for the bracket to stop any rattle problem.

5. This station wagon was backed too closely against a parking lot wall, causing a severe bend in the tailpipe that restricts exhaust passage. As you may not realize this happens, it's a good idea to periodically check the pipe.

6. These are the basic tools the pros use to make the job an easier one. Shown top row, from left: vise grip-type welding clamps, air-operated impact wrench; middle row, from left: hacksaw, pipe cutter; bottom row, from left: sheetmetal shears, ratchet-type box-end wrench, and a tube or pipe expander.

7. Even though the high sulphuric acid content of the exhaust gas condensation causes rapid deterioration of the muffler, some tightwads try to extend the life of their noise suppressors by covering the rust holes with pieces of sheetmetal.

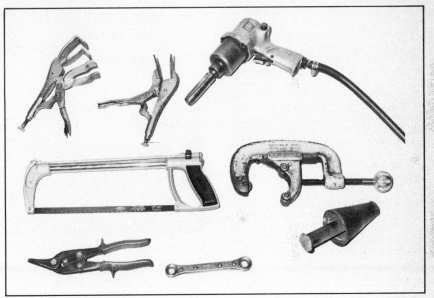

6. Exhaust System Tools

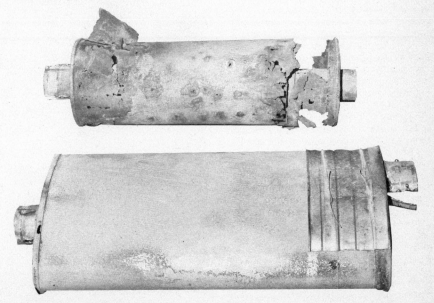

7. Rusted Out Mufflers

Exhaust System

Pep Boys or Western Auto. If you can't see your way to such a purchase, borrow the stands or at the very least go down to the lumber yard and get enough solid 4-by-8 blocks to hold the car securely suspended once it has been jacked up. Never trust a jack to hold the car while working other than changing a tire. Bumper jacks can slip and even hydraulic jacks can be inadvertently bumped and lose pressure in an instant.

Once you have the car up and blocked, get under and look at the exhaust system. If the tailpipe shows signs of rot or corrosion, the muffler is almost sure to be the same inside although it doesn't show on the outside. In virtually every case you'll find that if the muffler needs replacing, the tailpipe will also need replacing, and vice versa. Not so, necessarily, in the case of the headpipe—the pipe that leads from the manifold to the muffler. It's made of sterner stuff than the rest of the system and, being subject to hotter gases, tends to stay dry. But if it is corroded, it's a sure bet the whole system will need replacing.

When you have determined just what needs to be replaced, get out the appropriate wrenches, generally 1/2, 9/16 or 5/8-inch, and loosen all the clamps from the piping. Knock the ones that aren't attached to the frame back along the pipe to make sure they are loose and out of the way of the joint. Unbolt any that are attached and knock them loose too. At this time check the attaching straps to see if they are brittle or broken, or in the case of the rubber-insulated ones, if the rubber block is loose or deteriorated. If they are faulty, they'll have to be replaced, too. The unattached clamps—and those attached clamps in good shape—will be reusable.

When removing exhaust parts, always work from the rear to the front. The tailpipe is removed first, then the muffler, and then the exhaust pipe (headpipe). If you can't break the joints loose with liquid wrench, and you don't have a torch to do it like a muffler man does, then you will have to cut a slot in the pipe or muffler with a chisel. Of course, that ruins the pipe or muffler, but, hopefully, that will be the part you want to replace anyway. Don't expect to do muffler work with a butane torch or blowtorch. Breaking rusty joints loose requires an oxyacetylene torch.

Tap the headpipe along its length with a hammer. If it rings true, it's probably in good shape; if it doesn't, it's either cracked or corroded through and should be removed and replaced, a simple wrench job. Do the same thing with the crossover pipe in a single system or, if you are changing to duals, remove it entirely to make way for the new left-bank headpipe.

When purchasing the new components, be sure you state not only the make and model but whether the car is equipped with automatic shift or power steering as these items sometimes require different pipe routing from those models not so equipped. With the new equipment in hand, installation is a

1. Damaged Tailpipe

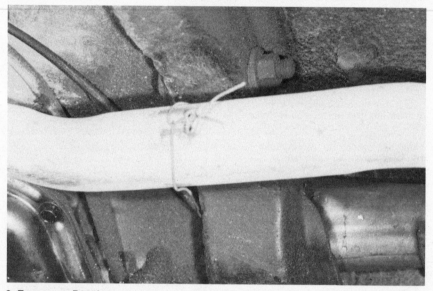

2. Temporary Repair

3. Rusted Out Tailpipe

breeze but a certain amount of care should be taken. Headpipe ends should be thoroughly cleaned with a wire brush and coarse sandpaper if you are retaining the original units. If they are also being replaced, use a wire brush or a knife to scrape the manifold outlet flange surfaces, making sure that there are no pieces of the original gasket material left which can cause a leak when the new gasket and pipe are installed. Put all the clamps involved near their proper places along the pipe, leaving them loose enough to move freely back and forth. Lift the muffler and slide it on the headpipe, again leaving all clamps loose. Then slide the tailpipe over the rear axle and join it to the muffler. You may have to use a jack on the car frame to raise the frame and body high enough for clearance to get the tailpipe in position. If so, put stands or blocks under the frame in case the jack should fail. Loosely bolt all the clamps that attach to the frame to their attachment points. Now the system is in place but loose enough to move about within restricted space limits.

The next step is to align all the components so that none of the piping rubs against the frame, fuel lines or brake lines—in other words, so that the whole system is completely isolated from other chassis components except where the various insulated clamps and straps attach to the frame. After a complete recheck, tighten all bolts and clamps so that you have a completely solid system. If you are replacing or installing duals, repeat the procedure on the opposite side of the car.

Now you can fire up the engine. Set it on a fast idle and listen carefully for any hissing, intermittent spitting sounds or

1. Occasionally, you can extend the life of a manifold or tailpipe by welding the damaged area, but it's only temporary, since the exhaust gases continue to eat the pipe away. Remove and replace—this is certainly the best and safest bet.

2. Here's a combination to avoid— a welded pipe held by a makeshift wire hanger. This is OK for a temporary repair, but such have a way of becoming permanent, and as long as it "works" the driver does nothing about correcting the basic problem.

3. Tailpipes rot where the exhaust gases condense. Rule of thumb here is the closer you get to the engine, the less the chance of heavy corrosion. Heat eliminates condensation.

4. In the not-so-tight-situations, most pros heat the two pipes to a cherry red condition, then work the pipes free with a set of interlocking joint gripping pliers.

5. The new muffler or resonator is then slid over the tailpipe, using a twisting motion. Even though they're made out of galvanized stock, resonators are usually the first portion of the exhaust system to go because of condensation buildup.

6. The flat end of the ball peen hammer can be used to force the old tailpipe onto the new muffler end.

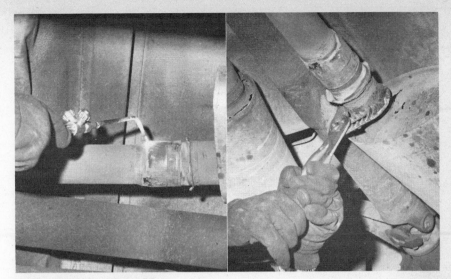

4. Heating Muffler; Using Pliers

5. Sliding Muffler on Tailpipe

6. Forcing Tailpipe over Muffler

Exhaust System

droning of metal-to-metal contact that might be telegraphed through the frame. If you have done the preparation and installation carefully, there should not be any such noises. If there are, leave the engine running and locate the source. It is much easier to correct any faults at this point than later when carbon and beginning rust will make moving the pipes either extremely difficult or downright impossible.

Once completed, that should about do the job. However, for the first few days of driving, listen for any odd noises and, if they occur, find and cure them as soon as possible.

There is one thing to remember: You cannot "repair" a faulty exhaust system. Any "michael mouse" attempts at plugging holes or making temporary repairs could create a fire hazard or cost you your life, either from carbon monoxide inhalation or from the drowsiness it can cause at the wheel. Replace worn-out components and visually check the system from time to time while the car is being serviced. And watch that heat valve; if you keep it free, your exhaust system will last twice as long—to say nothing about how much better the car will run.

EXHAUST GAS RECIRCULATION

In theory at least, exhaust systems on 1973 cars should have a longer life because of the reduction of nitrogen oxides in the exhaust brought about by the introduction of the Exhaust Gas Recirculation system. EGR, as it's known, first appeared on 1972 Buicks, and variations of the system are now in use on all domestic '73 cars. As high combustion temperatures cause nitrogen and oxygen to combine, nitrogen oxides form and pass through the system into the air as a pollutant. EGR simply recirculates exhaust gases through the engine intake manifold and into the cylinders where they combine with the air/fuel mixture for combustion. Since exhaust gases are relatively inert and burn at a considerably lower temperature than the air/fuel mixture in the cylinder at the moment of peak combustion, they dilute the combustion chamber charge, slowing the process of combustion and so reducing the combustion temperature to a level where formation of nitrogen oxides is inhibited. EGR compliments the AIR system that's been used for several years now to reduce the hydrocarbon and CO_1 content of exhaust gases, and as the smoggy state of the art now exists, Detroit's gone about as far as it can go until the catalytic muffler is perfected.

A vacuum-operated recirculation control valve generally mounted at the rear of the engine manifold and connected to an inline temperature control valve is the heart of the EGR system. Vacuum supplied by the carburetor is blocked by the temperature control valve whenever underhood temperatures are below 55° F. When the throttle valves are opened beyond the idle position, vacuum is applied against the EGR valve actuating

diaphragm. As the diaphragm moves up against spring pressure, it opens the exhaust gas intake valve, allowing exhaust gases from the manifold exhaust crossover channels to be drawn back into the engine intake. The valve remains closed during idle and deceleration, when excessive exhaust gases added to the

air/fuel mixture would cause rough engine idling.

You can't disassemble or service the EGR valve or its companion temperature control valve, but both can and should be checked periodically for correct operation. This is done by opening the throttle to 1500 rpm; at this point, the valve

1. Tightening C-Clamp

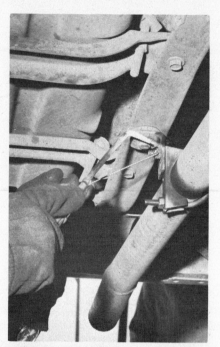

2. Tacking Nut to Stud

3. "Custom" Exhaust

stem should move downward when the vacuum line is disconnected, and upward when it's connected. If it doesn't move at all, replace the unit. While this movement can be felt by putting your hand under the rear of the valve, this is rather tricky as you're likely to get a good burn from either the hot valve or the engine manifold. It's much smarter to hold a pocket mirror behind the valve where you can watch its operation as you remove and replace the vacuum line. Check the temperature control valve when the engine is cold; this assures that the underhood temperature will be under 55° F. Start the engine and open the throttle to 1500 rpm. If the EGR valve stem moves as you increase the engine idle to this speed, the control valve should be replaced.

Maintenance of the valve is important, especially as the car gets older. If the valve sticks closed, you won't be able to tell from the engine's performance whether or not the system is functioning properly. And if it sticks in the open position, you'll have a great deal of difficulty in starting the car and keeping it going at lower engine rpm's—such is the price of progress. ♛

1. You can use a ½-in. socket and short extension attached to a ratchet to cinch down the nut on the end of the U-clamp. Make sure the nut is securely tightened so it won't work loose and cause a rattle.

2. The pros make sure the nut will never back out by tacking it to the stud. However, it's hacksaw time when an "R 'n R" is necessary.

3. You don't often see an exhaust tip like this—and we can all be thankful for that. It looks like a water pipe with a "T" in the end that squirts in both directions at once.

4. E.G.R. valve (1) is mounted on right rear of '73 Buick engine manifold; exhaust gas intake port connects to intake manifold exhaust crossover channel where it picks up exhaust gases. Valve is operated by vacuum from the carburetor and is controlled by the inline temperature control valve (2).

5. Cross-sectional view of Buick E.G.R. valve shows how the system works. If valve sticks in open position, starting the car becomes a major problem.

6. A.I.R. diverter valve attaches to rear of air pump and opens during sudden deceleration to pass air from pump outside the system. Bolts on this '73 Buick pump are torqued to 120-160 in.—lbs., but vibration causes them to work loose, so tighten bolts every few thousand miles.

7. The venturi vacuum control system used on Chrysler, Dodge and Plymouth cars differs from the ported control system such as Buick's in that an amplifier (1) is necessary to increase carburetor-provided vacuum to operate the E.G.R. valve (2). Temperature control valve is firewall-mounted (3) and connected to amplifier unit. E.G.R. valve is on left side of engine in various locations, depending upon engine size.

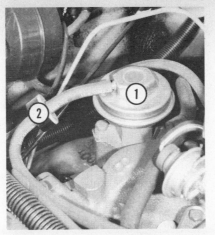
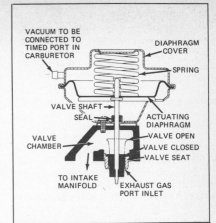

4. E.G.R. and Temperature Control

5. Cross—section of E.G.R.

VACUUM TO BE CONNECTED TO TIMED PORT IN CARBURETOR

DIAPHRAGM COVER

SPRING

VALVE SHAFT
SEAL

ACTUATING DIAPHRAGM

VALVE CHAMBER

VALVE OPEN
VALVE CLOSED
VALVE SEAT

TO INTAKE MANIFOLD

EXHAUST GAS PORT INLET

6. A.I.R. Diverter Valve

7. Venturi Vacuum Control System

Clutch & Flywheel

The clutch is a weak link, not because of any manufacturing oversight or lack of engineering but because it is designed that way. The car makers have tactfully admitted this by their refusal to warranty the clutch under any circumstances. They will guarantee that it was manufactured right and installed correctly, and after that you are on your own. Actually a clutch is designed to wear out; how fast it wears out depends on you, the driver.

A clutch is nothing more than a rotary coupling device between the engine and transmission that can slip while it's gradually picking up the load of moving a car—and then hook up "solid" when the car gets rolling. Also, we need a way to disconnect the engine from the rear wheels to smoothly shift gears, allowing the car to be stopped without putting the transmission into neutral. The clutch does this.

The clutch mechanism is quite simple. You have a friction disc that is splined to the transmission input shaft. This disc is squeezed between the engine flywheel and a heavy "pressure plate" inside a clutch cover or housing which is bolted to the flywheel.

The pressure plate is pressed forward by some type of spring arrangement—either a series of small coil springs or a circular diaphragm spring.

When the clutch disc is squeezed between the pressure plate and the engine

flywheel (engaged position), torque is then transmitted to the rear wheels. To disengage the pressure plate (against the spring pressure), we have several release levers that pivot in the clutch cover. These, in turn, are moved by a throwout bearing that rides on a collar extending about halfway up the transmission input shaft, or clutch driveshaft, and is moved by the clutch release fork that is pivoted on the bellhousing.

The release fork can be actuated in one of two ways: by a fully mechanical linkage of levers and rods which extends to the clutch pedal in your car, or by what is called a "hydraulic" clutch, which has a master cylinder (similar to the brake master cylinder) which is connected by linkage to the clutch pedal. The clutch master cylinder operates a "slave cylinder" connected to the clutch release fork with a short adjustable rod. When pressure is applied to the slave cylinder, it in turn operates the fork.

ADJUSTING LINKAGE

It should be understood that you should *expect* to have to adjust the linkage between the clutch pedal and throwout arm now and then—just to compensate for wear of the friction disc facings. Obviously as the facings wear down and get thinner, the clutch pedal will have to move farther and farther to fully engage

the clutch. Eventually you reach a point where the linkage is against the outer stop before the clutch is engaged, and then you will have definite slip.

The adjustment procedure is so simple that you can figure it out yourself. Get under the car and trace down the linkage from the pedal to the clutch release fork on the engine bellhousing. Your adjustment(s) are generally on threaded rod(s) going directly to the clutch release fork—usually there are jam nuts that must be loosened before you turn the rod one way or the other to adjust the pedal freeplay.

You can determine if the linkage is at fault by checking the amount of "play" (free pedal travel) at the clutch pedal. Using your fingers and holding a ruler next to the clutch pedal, depress the pedal. It should move very easily inward for only about 1 in. This is designated "freeplay." After that it will seem to strike something and you will have to push much harder. The hard point was where the throwout bearing and the clutch release levers contacted. A mechanically operated linkage will have one or possibly two points at which the rods can be adjusted. The threaded adjustment rod(s) usually have locking nuts (or jam nuts) which must be loosened before the rod length may be adjusted. Make two turns on the free travel adjustment, reconnect the clutch rod, and check pedal travel. Repeat this process

1. Reinstalling Pressure Plates

2. Checking for Warpage

3. Miking for Wear

4. Steel Safety Housing

5. Organic Lined Disc

6. Aluminum Flywheel

7. Cutaway Clutch Assembly

1. To avoid clutch chatter, be sure to keep greasy fingers off the flywheel or pressure plate facing during reassembly and reinstallation.

2. If the pressure plate ring on your clutch is badly checkered from heat, or grooved, replace entire unit. You can check ring for warpage by measuring it at all bolt flanges, comparing depth readings of mike.

3. To check overall wear on a clutch disc, use a micrometer. Clamp Marcel-type discs in a vise, gently, so they will compress. Bonded discs can be checked in hand. As lining wears, clutch pressure is reduced accordingly.

4. This hydro-formed steel housing is a product of Lakewood Industries. It is stronger and safer than stock housings and can be used on the street as well as strip. A and B surfaces are parallel machined.

5. This is a Weber Series clutch disc, for street or strip. Organic lining is backed by a .020-in.-thick aluminum heat shield. Springs about hub absorb shock of engagement.

6. A sintered iron replaceable face is used by Hays on their billet aluminum flywheel, which is designed for both street and strip purposes.

7. This cutaway of a clutch and flywheel assembly illustrates how they function. As pressure is placed on fingers, pressure plate moves away from disc, allowing it to float free or become disengaged from flywheel. Thereby power transmission from engine through clutch is stopped.

until you have about 1 in. of pedal travel.

The adjustment of a hydraulic clutch is the same process, with the adjusting link between the slave cylinder and the clutch fork. However, before adjusting a hydraulic clutch, check to see if the fluid is full and "bleed" the line to remove any air. Air in the system will prevent the clutch from operating correctly and smoothly. A hydraulic clutch is bled the same way as a brake system—have someone pump up pressure and hold until you allow fluid to escape and retighten the fitting. You should do this three or four times, or until all air has been let out of the system. Keep the master cylinder full during bleeding so that new air does not enter the system, and fill to the recommended level when bleeding is complete. Also check fittings for leaks.

REMOVING THE CLUTCH

More serious clutch troubles will require taking the clutch assembly out of the car. This is a big job—but not impractical or impossible for the beginner or home mechanic who is willing to work.

Clutch removal by pulling the transmission is the shortest and easiest way for an experienced mechanic, but you'll never believe it if you do it yourself because of the many parts that must be disconnected.

On a car with an open driveline, start by disconnecting the universal joint(s) on the driveshaft and removing it. Use a plastic sandwich bag to cover the end of the transmission housing and secure it tightly with a large rubber band. This is to prevent the transmission oil from leak-

ing out as well as to keep dirt from getting in. Disconnect the speedometer cable and transmission shift levers. If the car is equipped with overdrive, disconnect all wires. *Note: Do not attempt to disconnect the overdrive unit from the transmission.* It doesn't come apart this way and *must* be removed as a complete unit. Disconnect the parking brake cable, remove the rear transmission mounting bolts and support the rear of the engine with a jack or blocks. Now remove the bolts that attach the transmission to the flywheel housing. At this point you're ready to remove the transmission, but be careful—some transmissions weigh over 100 lbs., so it's best to have a friend help you lift it out. The transmission must come straight back until the input shaft clears the clutch splines. With the high weight leverage it's easy to have the splines bind in the disc, making removal difficult and possibly bending the disc.

On some cars it will be possible to remove the bellhousing to completely expose the flywheel and clutch unit, or the bellhousing may be part of the transmission case. On others, you will have to be content with the removal of a lower half only or an inspection cover. The lower-half type makes for slower work because you have to rotate the flywheel to expose each set of clutch mounting bolts. Then, when the last bolts are removed, the clutch must be slipped out the bottom and you must be careful so as not to mash your fingers. It's heavy when you only have a small place to hold on to, so don't let it drop on the floor.

Before removing the bellhousing, check to see if there are any brake or clutch linkage brackets that need to be disconnected. If you have a factory manual it will tell you exactly what needs to be disconnected. Also at this time, disconnect the clutch release fork. It's held in place only with a spring or snap-spring clip.

With the clutch and flywheel exposed, take a center punch and make a mark at the edge of the pressure plate cover. Make another mark directly opposite on the edge of the flywheel. This must be done so that the pressure plate and flywheel will be assembled in exactly the same position—because they may have been balanced as a unit. If you don't do this, you won't know where to remount the pressure plate and your engine might be out of balance. It might be well to note here that if you can see that the pressure plate must be replaced entirely, then marking is not necessary.

it has been balanced. In many cases the only thing to do is install the unit and keep your fingers crossed. Luckily, out-of-balance clutches are seldom a problem.

Now, to remove the clutch: There are two ways to do it correctly. The first way, and probably the best, is to use a steel bar (jack handle, etc.) to pry down each clutch release finger, one at a time. As you do this, insert a large nut about ¼-in. in height between the release arm and the cover. This releases all the pressure from the pressure plate, and all the cover bolts may be removed quickly and easily, in any order.

The second way, and this goes for all diaphragm-type clutches as well as the finger type, is to back off each clutch cover bolt in order around the cover about one turn at a time. You must loosen the bolts evenly so as not to warp the pressure plate. At first they'll turn hard because of the spring pressure, but when they're about halfway out, the release fingers will contact the cover and relieve the pressure. At this point you can just run the bolts right out.

Now that the clutch is out, start inspecting all the components. If the disc is oil soaked, has cracked or broken friction lining, warped or loose rivets at the hub or is worn down to the rivet heads (bonded lining less than 1/32-in. thick on either side), then the disc must be replaced. Also check for broken springs. Springs loose enough to rattle will not cause noise when car is operating. If the pressure plate was at fault, but if the lining is half worn, replacement is recommended to get a new, full life span of the complete unit.

Check the pressure plate for scoring, burn marks (blue color spots) or ridges. Generally, pressure plate resurfacing is not recommended. However, "minor" burn marks and scratches can be removed with crocus cloth.

Examine the flywheel for scoring, burn marks or deep ridges. If any of these problems exist, or if the surface is highly polished, then the flywheel must be resurfaced. Taking a light cut off the face will insure you like-new performance—and it's not that expensive. However, be sure to do this before rebalancing.

The clutch release bearing is prelubricated and *should not* be cleaned in solvent. Instead, wipe it clean and hold the bearing inner race and rotate the outer race while applying pressure to it. If the bearing rotation is rough or noisy, replace the bearing.

Most release bearing failures are caused by improper clutch pedal adjustments. If the clutch linkage does not have enough free travel, the release bearing will constantly touch the release fingers and will spin whenever the engine is running. Riding the clutch is also a cause for bearing failure. This constant turning heats up the bearing and burns out the lubrication—shortly thereafter you have a bearing failure. Since this bearing is an inexpensive part, it should be replaced. This goes for the pilot shaft bearing (ball bearing or bushing) too. You should check it for wear or roughness, but it's far easier and safer to replace it and forget it.

If the flywheel is off the engine, there is no problem knocking the pilot bearing out. But if the flywheel is still in place on the crankshaft, then the pilot bearing must be removed with a special puller. There are a number of ways to do this, but usually a slide-hammer puller is used which has a hook on the end of it. The hook is inserted in the hole in the pilot

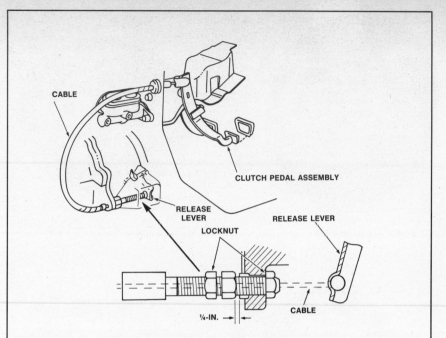

PINTO CLUTCH ADJUSTMENT

Only one adjustment is required, and it is made where the cable goes through the bellhousing. Early models have a locknut on the rear face of the housing, as shown in our illustration. Late models have done away with the locknut, but the adjustment is the same. A quick check on late models can be made by pulling the cable housing toward the front of the car just enough to put the throwout bearing up against the clutch fingers. In that position, the adjustment nut should have ¼-in. clearance from the boss in the bellhousing, as shown. On early models you can't make this check until you loosen the rear locknut. To adjust the clutch, loosen the locknut(s), and turn the adjusting nut until the gap is ¼-in., with the cable pulled forward by hand. When tightening the locknut(s), be sure you don't move the adjusting nut. Ford does not give a pedal free-play specification for Pinto. This ¼-in. cable adjustment is the only specification, and will result in the right amount of pedal free-play.

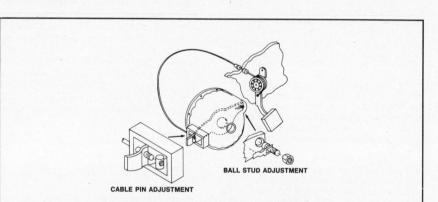

VEGA CLUTCH ADJUSTMENT

Two adjusting points make the Vega clutch adjustment a little tricky. Ordinarily, the ball stud does not have to be adjusted unless the clutch is changed, but it's possible somebody has turned the stud and gotten everything out of kilter. To adjust the ball stud, you must have a Chevy gauge No. J-23644. It is nothing more than a hook that positions the clutch arm while you adjust the ball stud. You can easily take the measurements off it at your local dealer, and then make your own gauge. In use, the gauge hooks over the front face of the bellhousing and over the clutch fork. While the gauge is holding the clutch arm, the ball stud nut is loosened and the stud screwed in (forward) until the throwout bearing touches the clutch fingers. Tightening the nut locks the stud in position on the bellhousing. Final adjustment for clutch pedal free-play is made with the cable pin. Just screw it up against the clutch fork, making sure that the cable is all the way to the rear, with the pedal up against the rubber bumper. After the pin hits the clutch fork, screw it in about an additional ¼-turn so it drops into the groove in the fork. This will give you about 1-in. free-play.

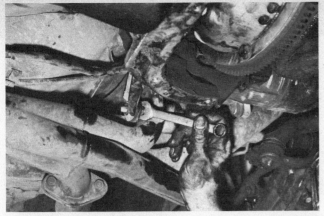

1. Plymouth Linkage Adjustment

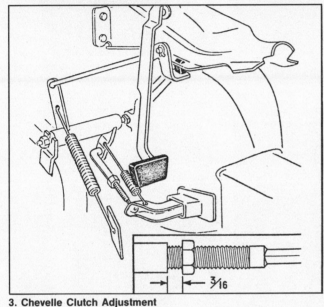

3. Chevelle Clutch Adjustment

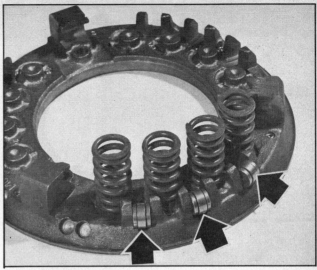

2. Clutch for Automatics

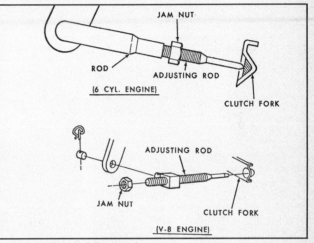

4. Firebird Clutch Adjustment

1. When you install a new clutch in a car or your old clutch has been in service for awhile, you should readjust the linkage. After adjusting clutch linkage, make sure jam nut is tightened. Free play should be around 1 in. on most automobiles. The linkage shown here is Plymouth.

2. Weber developed this 9-roller pressure plate for use with Borg & Beck clutches intended for use with clutch-operated TorqueFlite and Turbo-Hydro transmission. Extra rollers boost clutch pressure without upping spring and pedal pressure. Unit is offered for stick boxes, but features fewer rollers.

3. The clutch adjustment rod on Chevelles is very similar to that on all GM cars. After disconnecting the spring between the cross shaft lever and clutch fork, loosen the push rod locknut. Hold the clutch fork rearward until the throwout is lightly against the clutch release fingers, then adjust rod length until rod just touches its seat in the fork. Now back rod into sleeve 3/16-in., tighten lock nut, and check pedal free play. It should be between ¾-in. and 1 ⅛-in.

4. The clutch adjusting rods on Firebirds are typical of most cars. Spring is removed, jam nut loosened, then rod adjusted until proper free play is achieved at clutch pedal.

bearing on one side of the bearing, and the slide hammer is used to knock the bearing out.

Clutch release bearings, sometimes called throwout bearings, are usually pressed onto the bearing hub. The old bearing can be easily knocked off the hub and a new bearing tapped on with a hammer. However, many mechanics do not bother to do this. They buy the bearing and hub already assembled. It's a little more expensive that way but it saves time and trouble.

Inspect the release bearing hub for burns or scratches. The release bearing should slide freely. If you're in doubt or you feel a scratch, polish it out with crocus cloth. Coat the release bearing hub with a thin coat of oil before assembling release bearing and hub assembly.

With your new disc in hand, check it out on the splines of the input shaft. It must slide smoothly. If it doesn't, see what's wrong. Crocus cloth can and should be used to polish up the spline to a smooth finish.

If your clutch disc was ruined because of an oil leak, you must determine the cause—engine or transmission—and get the leak repaired before assembly. If you don't, your new parts will last only a short time.

Now you are about ready for reassembly. Be sure your hands are free of grease for the initial assembly. A greasy

fingerprint on the flywheel or pressure plate facing or clutch disc can ruin a good clutch job. It can cause chatter. Clean the flywheel and pressure plate faces just before assembly.

The assembly process is the reverse of the removal operation. Start by installing the flywheel and putting a thin coat of bearing lubricant inside the pilot bushing or bearing race.

To align the disc you're going to need some kind of pilot shaft. You can't do it "by eye." There are special tools for this, but the most inexpensive way is to cut an input shaft off a junk transmission to use as a guide.

Now hold the pressure plate and disc in close location and push the alignment shaft through the disc spline and into the pilot bearing. Line up your centerpunch marks and start bolting up the pressure plate, using the same procedure you followed during removal.

It should be noted here that both the flywheel and the clutch bolts must be torqued to factory specifications. Once the pressure plate is torqued down, remove the spacers and pull out the alignment shaft.

Lubricate the clutch release fork at the pivot points and then complete the assembly. Remember, you'll need help installing the transmission, and you must be extra careful not to bend the disc and ruin your clutch job.

1. First operation involved in pulling a transmission so you can replace the clutch is to remove the driveshaft. Start at rear U-joint.

2. On most cars with floor shifts, you'll have to drop the shifter as a unit, for the simple fact that it is bolted to the side of the transmission.

3. On transmissions with removable pan on bellhousing, pull the pan. This saves you the trouble of having to remove the entire housing.

4. Raise rear of engine slightly with jack to take pressure off crossmember, then remove crossmember. Be sure engine is supported firmly and safely.

5. Once the crossmember is out and speedometer cable and all linkage is disconnected, you can proceed with removing transmission itself.

6. After removal of all linkage, rear crossmember, shifter, etc., it is possible to remove a manual trans by hand. Just don't drop it though.

7. If your starter bolts to your bellhousing instead of the engine, you'll have to remove the starter before you can take off the bellhousing.

8. Next operation involves removing linkage at clutch throwout arm. At this point, clutch and/or housing is ready to be pulled from car.

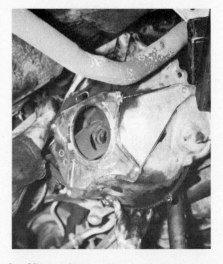

9. After using a long extension and maybe a flex-socket to get upper bolts at rear of engine, you can remove the bellhousing (heavy!).

10. A special ratcheting tool is used to rotate flywheel around so pressure plate bolts can be pulled. A screwdriver will work here, too.

11. This clutch assembly came out of a MoPar and was slipping badly at 28,000 miles. Pressure plate face is really worn. All parts replaced.

12. Sandpaper can be used to remove the glaze from the flywheel facing, but if the surface is irregular, you should get the flywheel face ground.

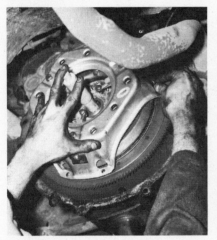

13. Either the front shaft of an old transmission or wooden pilot is used to line up the disc while you start the bolts in around clutch.

14. When all the bolts are started and lightly run down, they should be torqued to keep the pressure even around the circumference of clutch.

15. On cars that permit you to leave the bellhousing in place, install the new throwout bearing in the throwout arm as shown in this photo.

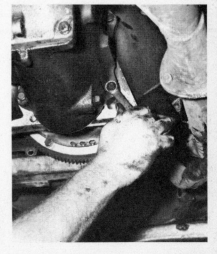

16. When the bellhousing is all one piece you have to remove everything to get at bearing, so it's wise to replace it too when you R 'n' R clutch.

17. Greasing front of splined shaft makes installation of trans easier. You should also grease the surface that the throwout bearing rides on.

18. Once transmission is back in the car, cinch it down and replace shifter and linkage. Be sure to readjust the clutch linkage, too.

Manual Transmission

If Bill Lear had succeeded in producing a steam engine to replace the smog makers we now use, we might have seen the end of all transmissions as we know them today. But Bill Lear didn't quite make it, and it doesn't look like anybody else will, either. So we are stuck with some kind of a transmission to multiply torque so that we can drive our cars.

Obviously, any vehicle with a typical internal combustion engine will need some kind of power-changing device between engine and rear wheels, simply because contemporary engines cannot operate over the very wide rpm range an automobile requires. To start a 3000-lb. car rolling requires more power than is required to keep it rolling. The gasoline engine develops the least amount of torque at low rpm's; consequently, the transmission must multiply what force is available at low engine speeds. In this respect all transmissions are alike, both standard and automatic.

The transmission, then, is nothing more than a mechanical torque multiplier. If you want to move that big rock over there, get a longer lever or move the fulcrum closer to the rock. Now consider the teeth of meshing gears as the fulcrum. The gear with the smaller diameter has the advantage of rotational leverage, and since it will turn faster than the big gear, the engine can run at a higher rpm where greater torque is developed.

Gearing, therefore, of both the transmission and final drive assembly becomes directly responsible for vehicle performance. To this end, the truck may have a very high numerical transmission and rear end combination, the better to move heavy loads. The racing car may have lower numerical gear ratios, since the engine is kept running near maximum power range at all times. To clear up a bit of confusion, low numerical numbers (those numbers closer to 1) are generally referred to as being high gearing. High numerical numbers mean low gear ratios. The lower the gear ratio, therefore, the greater the torque multiplication between crankshaft rpm and driveshaft or axle rpm.

A Frenchman named Levassor is credited with inventing the sliding gear transmission, although gear or rotational torque multiplication has been around for many decades. Until the automobile created such a wide-spread demand for special gearboxes, however, the sliding gear-type multiplier was of little necessity. The changes in the very few years since cars became common are readily apparent—the Model A and a modern Ford are proof of that advancement.

Before any kind of detailed work can be accomplished on a manual transmission, it is advantageous to understand just how the pieces function—at least briefly.

There is nothing secret about how a transmission works, and that's why repairs are so easy to handle. However, before tearing into the gearbox, be advised that there are certain tools which are essential to efficient work. First of all, a good set of expander pliers will undoubtedly be needed to remove the several snap rings. Bearing pullers or graduated diameter punches are essential, and even a dial indicator will come in

1. Working on a manual transmission like this Super T-10 is really quite easy; all you have to do is remember the sequence in which you took the parts out, and put them back in same order.

2. Your two basic types of manual transmissions are called selective and progressive. The selective type features neutral in the center or middle of the shift pattern. From neutral, in a selective, you can select any gear you desire. The progressive design, on the other hand, is the type of torque multiplier found on most motorcycles. Neutral is at the bottom of the shift pattern and you must progressively upshift or downshift to reach the particular gear you want.

3. Gear changing on a fully synchronized, constant mesh (including reverse), 3-speed manual transmission is accomplished by shifting forks that have the job of sliding dog clutches over synchros.

4. GM's medium-duty Saginaw 4-speed trans is used on its intermediate cars when a 4-speed is ordered with a 6-cylinder engine. All four gears are fully synchronized. The unit can be distinguished from the Muncie by the fact that the reverse lever is mounted on the side cover rather than in the extension housing.

5. Like the manual 3-speed trannys, modern four-on-the-floors feature a constant mesh principle except when reverse is grabbed. Then a special fork on the linkage meshes the free-wheeling reverse gear to the reverse idler gear on countershaft.

6. Muncie 4-speed transmission is used on most GM high-performance options. The gearbox itself contains the four forward gears, while the tail section houses the reverse gear assembly; trans is quite strong.

1. Super T-10 Transmission

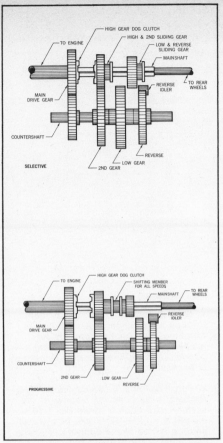

2. Selective and Progressive Transmissions

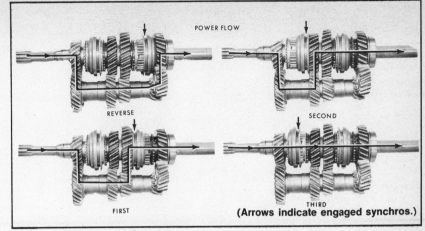

3. Fully Synchronized 3-Speed

(Arrows indicate engaged synchros.)

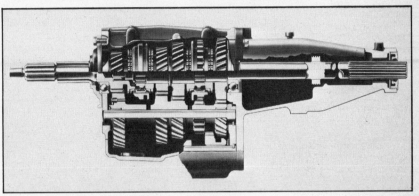

4. Saginaw Medium-Duty 4-Speed

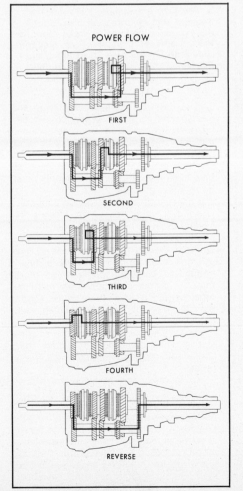

POWER FLOW

FIRST

SECOND

THIRD

FOURTH

REVERSE

5. Modern 4-Speed Floorshift

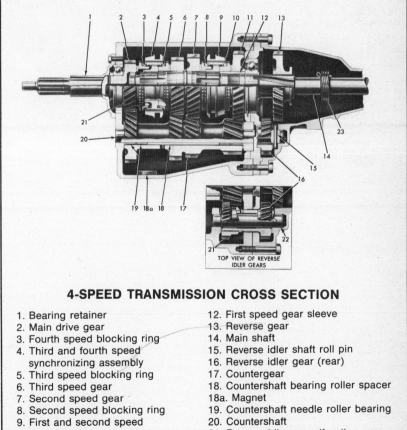

TOP VIEW OF REVERSE IDLER GEARS

4-SPEED TRANSMISSION CROSS SECTION

1. Bearing retainer
2. Main drive gear
3. Fourth speed blocking ring
4. Third and fourth speed synchronizing assembly
5. Third speed blocking ring
6. Third speed gear
7. Second speed gear
8. Second speed blocking ring
9. First and second speed synchronizing assembly
10. First speed blocking ring
11. First speed gear
12. First speed gear sleeve
13. Reverse gear
14. Main shaft
15. Reverse idler shaft roll pin
16. Reverse idler gear (rear)
17. Countergear
18. Countershaft bearing roller spacer
18a. Magnet
19. Countershaft needle roller bearing
20. Countershaft
21. Reverse idler gear (front)
22. Reverse idler shaft
23. Speedometer drive gear

6. Muncie 4-Speed

Manual Transmission

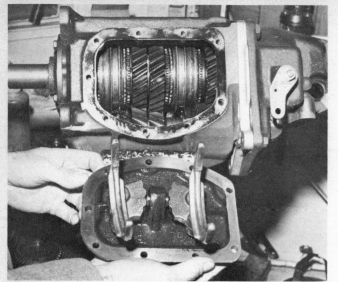

1. Shifting Forks

2. Comparison of T-10 and Super T-10

3. Warner T-10 Parts

1. Shifting forks can be worn or bent through hard usage. Inspect both the fork faces and connection pins for excess play if your trans is shifting poorly. Then replace the pins if the slop is excessive.

2. Borg-Warner's T-10 and Super T-10 (bottom) have been the favorite of the performance addicts since the T-10's inception on the '57 'Vette. Its ease of shifting is due to the lightweight gears. The Super T-10 features heavier, stronger gears.

3. The T-10 is basically a Warner T-85 3-speed with reverse gear moved into the extension housing to make room for the 4th gearset. Chrysler, Ford, GM and American Motors have used this first of the four-on-the-floors in many of their muscle cars.

handy. All these may be purchased, of course, or rented.

INSPECTION

Because the transmission gears are literally immersed in lubricant, the early part of the repair will of necessity be dirty. Working in a large drip pan or some kind of shallow tub will confine the oil and make subsequent clean-up much easier. Do not drain the transmission lubricant before initial disassembly, because much may be learned from it.

During initial inspection, remove the top cover plate, if the gearbox is so equipped, or the shifting lever cover. Do not jostle the transmission too much as it is being removed from the vehicle,

since small particles of metal, such as chips from broken gears, will wash around and become lodged in bearings, etc. After the cover plate is removed, feel in the bottom of the case for these pieces of metal. They are not uncommon, and will give some clue as to transmission failure—whether the gear tooth was broken by fatigue or from hard shifting, and so forth. The synchronizer clutches are sure to wear, resulting in fine particles of brass in the case sump.

All the lubricant may then be dumped in the pan, and the gearbox given a cursory cleaning if desired. Disassembly of the component parts comes next, but careful inspection at this point can save much labor. While broken gears are not uncommon within a standard transmis-

sion, excessively worn synchronizers are perhaps the greatest enemy to smooth transmission operation. Because of them, the transmission will not stay in 2nd gear, nor will it shift smoothly without clashing gears, etc. Now is the time to determine just how far disassembly must go to effect a repair.

If gear teeth are involved, very carefully go over each gear. It is possible for several teeth to be broken on the output shaft, but no damage on the counter shaft. If this is true, and none of the counter shaft gear teeth have been gouged or chipped, then nothing more than the output shaft assembly need be repaired. If, however, there is the slightest indication of harm to counter shaft gears, replacement is in order.

Because the synchronizers are constantly being subjected to friction, they should be replaced in practically every repair job.

The hardest part of fixing any transmission is getting it apart and back together. If you can get it apart without having to resort to a hacksaw and a cutting torch, then getting it back together is merely a matter of remembering where all the pieces go. To help your memory along, on the following pages you'll find step-by-step photos covering assembly and disassembly procedures on four popular manual transmissions. ☗

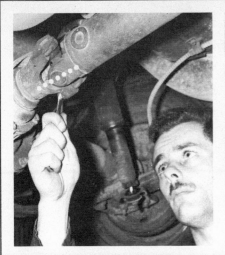

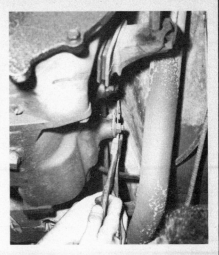

1. Before you drop your trans, find drain plug and remove oil. Then mark chalk across U-joint's face for reassembly in original position.

2. Four nuts, two U-bolts will free assembly from rear yoke. Inspect U-joint for wear at this time; replace or rebuild it if necessary.

3. Remove exhaust system if it is an obstruction to disengaging of shifter linkage or lifting of trans. Now pull linkage cotter keys.

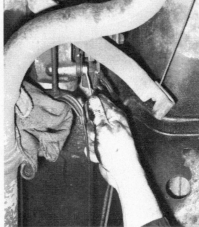

4. Speedometer cable can be disconnected by taking off Phillips cap screw. If location of pipe hampers work, use shorter tool.

5. Disconnect shift linkage at transmission. If linkage is for a floor shifter, you may be able to lift entire assembly from inside car.

6. Middle crossmember, holding tailshaft, is now unbolted from frame. If handbrake cable is in the way, it too will have to be removed.

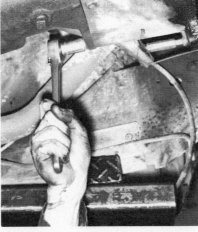

7. As arrow indicates, you must support rear of engine when you take off transmission support. If you fail to do so, engine will fall out.

8. You needn't support trans. Main shaft and bearing sleeve on bellhousing will keep gearbox in place as you loosen bolts with a ratchet.

9. "Get all the goodies out of the way!" Exhaust head pipes, linkage and hand brake cables will make a hard job harder if they aren't removed.

HOW-TO: Disassembling a Chevy 3-Speed

1. Before disassembling/reassembling Chevy's old 3-speed trans, drain lubricant and; remove both side cover assembly, tailshaft housing assembly.

2. Now slide reverse, first gear from clutch sleeve; remove them from case. Remove pilot bearing, retainer screws before tapping out countershaft.

3. Lower countergear to bottom of case before removing clutch gear, bearing. Otherwise bearing will strike countergear. Now pull snap ring.

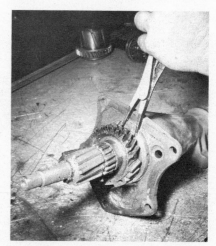

4. Tap end of shaft with a soft mallet to move gear and bearing assembly into front of case. Then total assembly is pulled from rear of case.

5. Now tap out reverse idler gear, thrust washer, thrust bearing and bearing washer after driving out plug located ahead of idler shaft.

6. To take mainshaft off extension, expand bearing snap ring; tap rear of shaft with a soft hammer to free the shaft, speedo drive, and second gear.

7. Place clutch gear in a vise and remove bearing retainer nut and oil slinger with some water pump pliers. Bearings must be pressed off shaft.

8. Replace gears if they show unusual wear; check first, reverse, be sure they slide easily on clutch sleeve. Do same on clutch sleeve-to-mainshaft bit.

9. To remove synchronizer ring from clutch sleeve, turn ring until its ends can be seen through slot. Slide retainer out of groove with snap rings.

10. Cluster is a prime point of hard wear; its bearings should be renewed. Note number of thrust washers on each end of gear; reassemble with same.

11. Before installing assembly, use heavy grease to hold needle bearings in cluster. Fit gear into case; install cluster countershaft.

12. Position reverse idler assembly in case so thrust bearing faces rear. Install idler shaft, make sure flat spot is down so extension will fit.

13. Use cup grease to hold mainshaft pilot roller bearings in clutch gear. Make sure no bearing escapes. Insert clutch gear assembly from inside case.

14. Next insert synchronizers, low/reverse slide gear in case. Install rear housing with main shaft to front of case, finish off with main drive gear.

15. Install clutch gear bearing retainer and make sure oil slot in retainer lines up with the oil slot that's in the front face of the transmission.

16. Now slide reverse/low gear into neutral (center) position on 2nd and 3rd-speed clutch before you bolt side cover plate to trans case.

17. Inspect shifter forks for wear (replace if necessary). Preset forks for neutral. Hump on first, reverse must face toward rear of trans.

18. Use new gasket; coat the capscrews with Permatex No. 2. Cinch up with torque wrench or impact gun. Recommended torque is 15-18 ft.-lbs.

HOW-TO: Assembling a Muncie 4-Speed

1. Drain lube from trans; remove side cover, clutch retainer housing, rear extension housing, countergear, main drive gear units; clean and inspect.

2. Begin assembly by checking bearings for undue wear, then lubricate with light engine oil. Check gears for wear, clutch sleeves for sliding.

3. After inspecting all moving parts, insert rear bearing in rear bearing retainer; release snap ring, position correctly in retainer groove.

4. Once 1st and 2nd gears (with their synchros, clutch sleeves, etc.) have been installed on mainshaft, tap rear bearing retainer onto shaft.

5. Spread snap ring with pliers, then allow ring to align with groove in end of mainshaft to help retain rear bearing. Install reverse, anti-rattle springs.

6. Install 3rd and 4th gears (hub to front of trans), synchronizers and 3rd, 4th gear clutch assemblies with both sleeves to front of trans case.

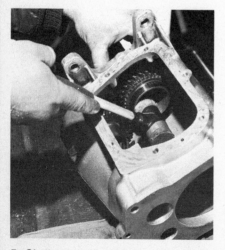

7. Cluster goes in bottom of case with all bearings held in place by dowel. Then tap main drive gear and bearing into hole in case; work from inside.

8. Position reverse idler gear thrust washer on machined face of ear cast in case of reverse idler shaft. Hold assembly in case with heavy lube coating.

9. Shove reverse idler gear next to thrust washer, with the hub facing to rear of case. Install flat thrust washer on reverse idler gear.

10. Stick cage and its 17 roller bearings into main drive gear; use heavy grease to hold bearings in place. Put oil slinger (concave forward) on gear.

11. Now you can lower mainshaft assembly into case. Be sure notches on 4th gear synchro ring correspond to the keys on the clutch assembly.

12. Align countergear with shaft in rear and hole in front of case, press counter-shaft in case, push assembly dowel out until shaft is flush with case.

13. Cut on rear of countershaft must be aligned so it will mate to similar cut in rear extension housing to keep shaft from spinning in trans case.

14. Install reverse idler shaft roll pin (pin should be in vertical position), and thrust washer into gear, front boss of case; pick up front-tanged washer.

15. Rear extension housing is turned to reveal shifter fork for reverse gear. Arrow shows slot that reverse idler shaft roll pin aligns with.

16. Pull reverse shifter shaft to left side of extension, rotate shaft to bring reverse shift fork into extension housing (reverse detent position).

17. Start rear extension housing onto trans case, while slowly pushing it on the shifter shaft to engage the shift fork with the reverse shift collar.

18. Pilot reverse idler shaft into extension; slide onto case, attach bolts. Line up shaft with holes in boss and inset lock pin. Install shifter, side cover.

HOW-TO: Disassembling a Warner T-10

1. Drain out lubricant from Warner T-10 4-speed; shift it into 2nd, remove side cover bolts. Pull cover assembly and gasket off case.

2. Remove front bearing (or clutch gear bearing) retainer bolts from transmission case; slide both retainer and gasket off main drive gear.

3. Take off backup light switch, plunger from trans. Drive lock pin from reverse shifter lever boss, pull shifter out slightly to free fork from reverse.

4. Inspect shifting forks, fork faces, connection pins for abnormal wear or shape. Shifting forks should be replaced to eliminate any excess play.

5. Remove rear extension retaining bolts. Tap housing with soft mallet to loosen it. Slide off housing and gasket. Remove reverse idler from case.

6. Shift transmission into 3rd to keep mainshaft from turning. Slide off snap ring from rear splines on mainshaft; remove speedo, reverse gear.

7. Free self-locking bolt attaching rear bearing retainer to trans case. Remove case-to-retainer pin with channel locks or vise grips.

8. Pull clutch gear snap ring so entire assembly can be removed. You may find it necessary to lightly tap shaft and bearing with a soft-headed mallet.

9. To further inspect mainshaft assembly for wear, remove front snap ring, then slide 3rd, 4th clutch assemblies, synchro rings from shaft.

1. Before reassembling bearings and spacers in countergear, inspect teeth closely for excessive wear, chips or cracks; replace it if worn, damaged.

2. While you're at it, check spacers, countergear roller bearings for wear. Inspect countershaft, reverse idler; replace them if necessary.

3. Use a dowel pin or shaft to retain bearings, spacers; slip solvent-cleaned bearings and washers into countergear. Dip in lube so they'll stay in place.

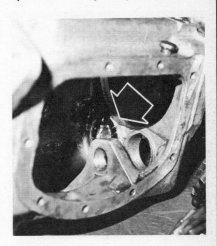

4. The 40 rollers inside countergear are in 4 rows of 10 each, separated by two narrow spaces, one long spacer. Pin is removed as rollers go in.

5. Liberal application of lube on cluster gear thrust washers helps hold them in place when countergear is inserted into transmission case.

6. Rest transmission on its side, with side cover opening toward assembler. Put countergear thrust washer in place; hold with a coat of heavy grease.

7. Set countergear in place at bottom of case; be sure the tanged thrust washers have not been moved or dowel pin has not slipped away from rollers.

8. Shaft must be removed or it will interfere with assembly of mainshaft and clutch gear. Leave thrust washer in place, countergear at case bottom.

9. Reinstall the 14 roller bearings inside main drive gear; use heavy-duty grease to hold bearings in position while assembly is inserted.

HOW-TO: Assembling a Warner T-10

10. When assembling the front reverse idler gear, make sure the teeth are pointed forward with hub facing to rear of the transmission case.

11. The 1st, 2nd and 3rd gears, with synchro rings, are assembled on mainshaft. Hub of 3rd, notches on synchro ring should always face forward.

12. Install 3rd, 4th gear clutch assembly with taper to front. Be sure keys in hub match notches in 3rd gear synchro ring. Insert main drive gear.

13. Before assembly is put in case, put new selective snap rings (that'll fit in groove) on mainshaft in front of 3rd-, 4th-speed gear clutch unit.

14. Rear bearing retainer can be slid over end of mainshaft. Spread snap ring in pliers so it will drop around rear bearing when aligned with groove.

15. First insert reverse idler shaft into housing, then slide flat thrust washer in place. Tang on thrust washer should face thrust portion of case.

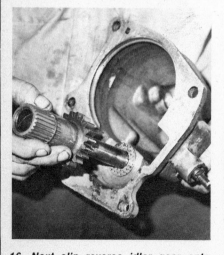

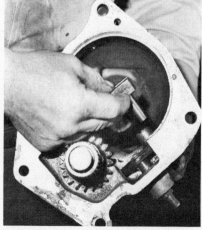

16. Next slip reverse idler gear onto shaft, engaging splines with portion of gear within case. Place new gasket on rear bearing retainer's face.

17. Pull reverse shift shaft partially out of extension; rotate shaft to get reverse shift fork as far forward in rear extension housing as possible.

18. Now, you can start the extension onto the mainshaft while pushing in on shifter shaft to engage shift fork with reverse gear shift collar.

19. When fork engages shift fork, rotate shifter shaft to move reverse gear rearward, permitting extension to mate to transmission case.

20. With pin in shifter lever boss, torque rear extension housing bolts to 40 ft.-lbs.; install rear extension-to-bearing retainer bolts, 25 ft.-lbs. maximum.

21. With hammer and punch, tap clutch bearing in place. Be sure bearing is clean, lubricated, checked for roughness (by turning race in hand).

22. Use snap ring pliers to slide selective fit snap rings, spacer washer, bearing snap ring over maindrive gear and into proper places.

23. Be sure to use a new gasket that's slightly moist with lube, before you bolt bearing retainer to front of T-10 transmission case.

24. New front bearing retainer gasket should be firmly in place and the retainer snug on case. Use good sealer, torque capscrews to 18 ft.-lbs.

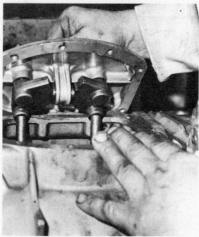

25. Shift forks must fit snugly in grooves on 3rd, 4th-speed clutch sliding sleeve and 1st and 2nd-speed clutch sliding sleeve, as shown.

26. Shift trans into 2nd, position side cover, attach new gasket, engage shift forks in collars; install side cover, seal and torque capscrews.

27. After trans is filled and shifter linkage is attached, your just-like-new Warner T-10 transmission is all ready to tackle the streets again.

HOW-TO: Assembling a Ford 4-Speed

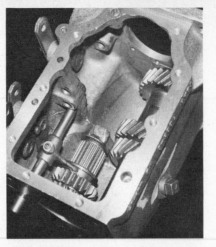

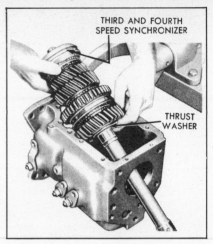

1. Assembly is started by putting the cluster and reverse goodies in position, but the cluster is lying on the bottom of the case without any shaft.

2. The reverse shifter shaft is now in and secured. A set screw holds the shifter fork to the rail. Note the holes for two more shifter shafts.

3. Support thrust washer and low gear to prevent them from sliding off end of shaft; then carefully lower output shaft assembly into case.

4. Place front synchronizer into 3rd gear position; install set screw in 3rd and 4th gear shift fork. Move synchronizer to neutral.

5. The mainshaft, with all the gears already on it, goes in through the top of the case. Then the shift forks and the shafts are put into their positions.

6. Tightening the set screw in the shift fork that helps secure it to the rail. All of the steps are described in detail in genuine Ford shop manual.

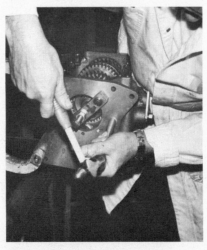

7. The detent on the bottom shift rail screws in from the side of the case. Note dummy aluminum bearing temporarily holding mainshaft in position.

8. Another shift rail is tapped in from the front. Bar across the front of the trans holds the front of mainshaft in position while doing the good work.

9. Not many people have this press, but it's the right way to put the rear bearing into the case—with no beating. Hammer mechanics, please take note.

10. After the bearing is in position, the snap ring slips on easily—if you have snap ring pliers. Another snap ring goes on the shaft against bearing.

11. After the main drive gear and its bearings are slipped into position, the front bearing retainer, with a new seal inside, is bolted on the case.

12. Standing the box on end makes it easier to move the gear cluster into position so the shaft can be inserted. Lower hand is catching dummy shaft.

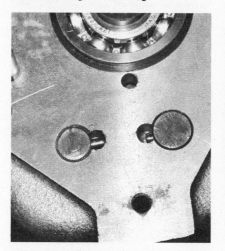

13. The cluster gear shaft and reverse idler shaft are kept from turning by roll pins that must enter these recesses in the case to be held securely.

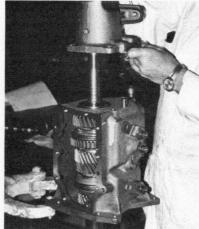

14. First a gasket, and then the tailshaft housing is slid into position. A new seal should be installed in the end of the housing, to stop the drip.

15. Extension housing bolts should be torqued to specs, but you'll not see many mechanics who do it. Tightening by feel might turn out inaccurate.

16. Detent for the top shift rail is dropped into the hole, and held in place by the cover. Note breather on top of housing, to relieve pressure.

17. The bolts are well greased so that the torque readings will be consistent, but no sealer is used on the cover gasket. Fluid leaks are not a problem.

18. That's right, even the cover is torqued. If you're going to be superaccurate, why not go all the way? Reminder: Don't forget to put in lube.

Automatic Transmission

There is no reason to be afraid to work on an automatic transmission. Once the thing is out of the car and you have a nice big bench or clean floor to work on, it's simply a matter of undoing some bolts and nuts, prying out a few snap rings, and surprising yourself that it comes apart so easily. The hardest part about automatic transmission work is getting the darn thing out of the car. It is so big, clumsy, and heavy that you aren't about to lift it out of there without some help, either in the form of some husky friends or an automatic transmission jack. Dropping the transmission would be a disaster, maybe to your foot but surely to the transmission itself because many of the cases are made of aluminum.

Before tackling your automatic you should get a manual that gives detailed explanations and pictures of the disassembly procedure. The manuals are usually available through your local auto parts store or car dealer. Each one of the manuals will be almost as thick as this book and well worth the several dollars that you will have to pay for it. Without the specialized manual you will be faced with a hit-or-miss proposition, and almost surely your transmission will not go back together the way it should.

Overhaul and repair of any automatic transmission is well within the realm of an amateur mechanic's skill, since it is primarily a remove-and-replace procedure (much the same as manual transmissions). However, the average mechanic faces an automatic transmission repair with some trepidation, simply because he does not fully understand the inner workings of the magic box. Whether the model is an early Hydro, a 2-speed, a Dynaflow, or the modern 3-speed, the same basic design principles are involved.

AUTOMATIC TRANSMISSION DESIGN

In essence, all automatics currently popular include one or more sets of planetary gears, one or more fluid couplings or a torque converter, and control valves to direct hydraulic fluid. The control systems may vary considerably, since an automatic transmission may be controlled manually by the driver (shifting lever), hydraulically by throttle movement, by the engine vacuum, by speed-sensitive governors, or by an electrical device. Additionally, two or three of these types of controls might be included on any one transmission.

The biggest difference between automatics is the type of connection between engine and transmission. The Hydra-Matic of earlier days used a fluid coupling, while the later transmissions rely on the torque converter. The advantage of a torque converter is simple; through ingenious routing of the fluid, considerable torque multiplication can be gained when a car needs it most—at standstill and during the first few moments of movement.

Within either the simple fluid coupling or the torque converter, a pump located near the center of the revolving wheels distributes oil outward through vanes. As the engine rpm drops below a certain point near idle, this hydraulic pressure is not enough to overcome the static weight of the vehicle. However, as engine rpm increases, the hydraulic pressure also goes up. The oil thrown across reaction vanes then begins to turn the transmission smoothly, with a certain amount of slippage. At high engine and hydraulic pump rpm, the driving and driven members of the coupling or converter are operating at a near 1:1 lock-up ratio.

From the driven member of the converter or coupling, power is transferred through a shaft to clutch/drum assemblies inside the transmission housing. These clutches are similar to the single large clutch common to the standard transmission in that they function solely on the principle of friction. Planetary gearsets are connected to the clutch packs, producing the final gear ratios that exit through the transmission output shaft. Of all the workings inside an automatic transmission, the amateur would have most difficulty with the valve control body. For this reason, it is advisable to purchase a new valve body should one be damaged. There is very little choice with the torque converter, as repair of such must be left to the professional shop equipped with specialized tools.

It is virtually impossible to present detailed illustrations on how to assemble and/or repair all automatic transmissions in current use, for this would require the entire length of this book. Rather, we are presenting studies of two popular transmissions that will satisfy a great many readers: the Chevrolet Turbo Hydra-Matic 400 and the Ford C-4 Cruise-O-Matic.

1. Automatic transmissions look scary to the beginner, but there's no reason why any amateur mechanic can't handle the job once he understands the basic principles involved.

2. The illustration shown here is of a 2-speed Ford-O-Matic. Callouts are invaluable because they name all of the components.

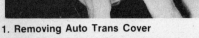

1. Removing Auto Trans Cover

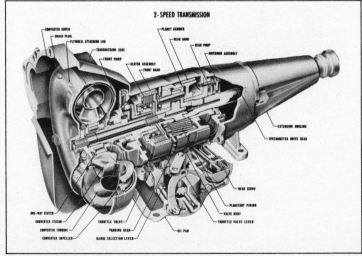

2. Ford-O-Matic Cutaway

1. Harold Shafer, R&R man at Steve's Transmission Service, 9012 Sepulveda Blvd., Sepulveda, Calif., installs a C-4 Cruise-O-Matic in a customer's car. Transmission jack is vital.

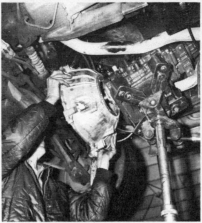

2. The bellhousing is a separate piece on the C-4, so trans is jacked up under car by itself, then housing is fitted in place. Jack adjustments allow trans movement.

3. Bellhousing is attached to trans with bolts. While it is possible to build your own trans on a bench, a car hoist and jack are necessary for installing the transmission in the car.

4. A new converter is installed in car along with rebuilt trans. If you have pulled or installed an automatic trans on your back, you'll appreciate use of a hoist and jack.

5. After the converter is wiggled into place, Shafer bolts an end wrench along one side of the bellhousing. This holds the converter in place until trans is raised up.

6. Converter is now attached to the starter ring, or flywheel, if you prefer. Four nuts secure ring to the converter which features built-in studs. Unit is rotated.

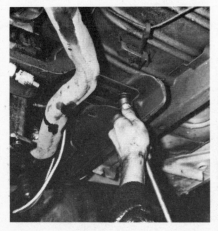

7. Removable crossmember is attached to the tail housing of the C-4 trans, then member is aligned with bolt attachment holes of chassis. Crossmember is now bolted secure.

8. Remaining operations involve installing oil lines that run to the radiator cooler (to cool the oil) and return, and connecting the speedometer cable and transmission shifting linkage.

9. A liberal amount of trans fluid is doused on forward driveshaft yoke which is then slid into tail of the trans. Rear U-joint is hooked, then trans is filled with fluid.

Automatic Transmission
Ford C-4

Of all the components in a modern automobile, probably none scare the average occasional mechanic more than the thought of tearing into an automatic transmission. Let's face it! Most of us know we shift OK by themselves for maybe 50,000 miles, and the fluid should be changed every 20,000 miles or so, along with the filter, before a teardown is necessary. But few of us really know how they operate, or how they come down and go back together. That's why we rely on shops such as Steve's Transmission Service to rebuild our automatic trans for us on those rare occasions when it is necessary. They are specialists, and know what they're doing. We don't. Right? Well, yes and "know."

They are specialists, and they do know

what's happening. But that's no reason we can't learn to do the same things, like going through a transmission. Take the C-4 Ford Cruise-O-Matic and the Chevy Turbo Hydra-Matic boxes on the following pages. They are commonly used units, found in tens of thousands of cars. Maybe one is in your car, and it needs repairs. You know it does because it slips, or hesitates between gear shifts, etc. Now you're asking us, what next?

OK. By using this manual, and maybe a factory shop manual which will cost you another few bucks, you can easily pull your trans down with a minimum of hand tools. Parts cleaner can be used to wash all of the components, followed by solvent and an air hose to blow the parts and passages clean. New seals, O-rings, gaskets, bands and clutches are available over the counter at your local dealership, parts house, or trans repair service. Perhaps a good buddy will assist you, or at least give moral support. But if you are careful and take your time, there

is little reason you can't rebuild your own automatic trans.

The hardest job comes in pulling and replacing the trans itself. Like the rest of us, you have a few sturdy jack stands that will hold the car a couple of feet off the garage floor, but you don't have a transmission jack handy. It's almost impossible to lift one of these boxes, or lower it, safely without a jack. The answer lies in going to a nearby tool rental agency to rent a small floor-type transmission jack. This is the only way to go to make the job easier and safer.

As we said, take your time, use this manual, and you can do it.

1. Detail drawing of C-4 gear train, showing clutches, band and drum.

2. C-4 intermediate band surrounds reverse-high clutch drum; it is adjusted by an external screw via struts. Low-reverse servo and band action is controlled by applied and released pressure on servo piston.

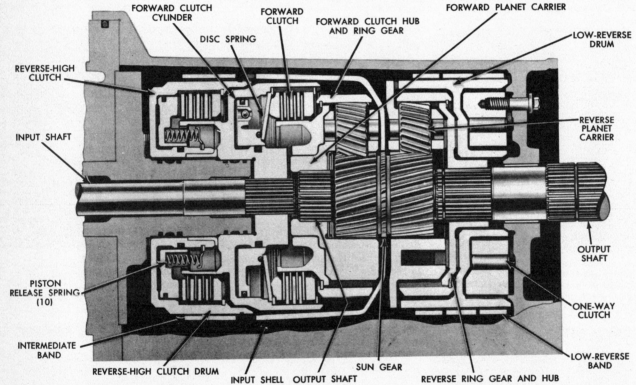

1. C-4 Gear Train, Clutches and Bands

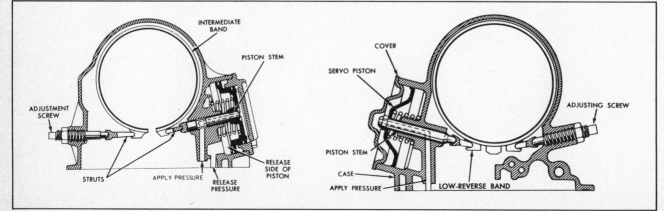

2. Intermediate and Low-Reverse Servo and Band

1. After thoroughly cleaning all components of the C-4 transmission, apply a little grease to the rear of the No. 9 thrust washer and then insert it in rear of trans case.

2. Following the installation of the thrust washer, insert the spring retainer cage that will support both rollers and springs of the one-way clutch. Inner race will follow.

3. The outer race is already in the aluminum transmission case, so now we can install the inner race as shown; 12 springs and 12 rollers are used in the C-4 one-way clutch.

4. Now the 12 springs and 12 rollers can be installed in the one-way clutch. The two components are alternated between races, as shown, and provide low gear for the Ford C-4 trans.

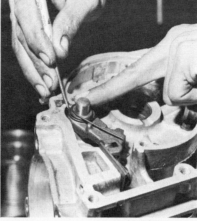

5. The parking pawl retaining pin is installed in the transmission case, then the pawl and pawl return spring are installed over the pin as demonstrated in this photo.

6. Thrust washer No. 10 is then attached to the parking pawl gear with the aid of a dab of grease. Reason for use of grease is to prevent washers from falling away.

7. The parking pawl gear with thrust washer attached beneath it is now positioned on back face of case. Once transmission is put to use, the grease will mix with trans fluid.

8. The governor distributor sleeve with oil delivery tubes is carefully installed on case. Tap sleeve down snug with a plastic-faced hammer; install bolts with torque wrench.

9. With the secondary governor bolted to the governor distributor, unit (arrow) is slipped over the transmission output shaft. Next, install snap ring to retain governor.

HOW-TO: Assembling a C-4

10. Steve Bustamente, an assembler at Steve's Transmission Service, Sepulveda, Calif., is installing the output shaft with the governor through the rear of the trans case.

11. The rear, or low and reverse, band is installed through the front of the C-4 Cruise-O-Matic case. End of band for the small strut must face toward low-reverse servo.

12. The two band struts (arrows) must be installed as shown, securing the low-reverse band in place in case. Struts lock in tangs on band and ride against aluminum case.

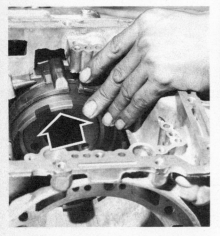

13. After a No. 8 thrust washer has been slipped into low-reverse drum (held firm with grease), the drum (arrow) is slipped through case and into the low-reverse band.

14. Reverse ring gear and the hub are then fitted (arrow) into the low-reverse drum and secured with a snap ring on the output shaft. Snap ring pliers are a must, here.

15. A No. 7 thrust washer is then installed on the rear of the reverse planet carrier (small end), held with grease. No. 6 washer (shown) is applied to front of carrier.

16. Now the reverse planet carrier can be installed in the reverse ring gear. Tabs of the carrier should be engaged with slots in the low-reverse drum, already in case.

17. Lining-covered clutch plates are stacked alternately with steel plates in both clutch packs. These plates wear out, as do the bands, and must be replaced at overhaul.

18. After the outer edge seal is clipped on to the reverse and high clutch cylinder piston, the piston seal is liberally coated with an STP-type of lubricant before installing.

19. An inner seal is installed in clutch cylinder, then reverse and high piston is installed. Now the 10 piston return springs are set in place. They return piston to normal.

20. The spring retainer is held in place with a snap ring, then the clutch is placed in a press, so the springs can be compressed and snap ring installed in proper groove.

21. After the first driven plate is installed in reverse-high clutch, each alternate friction plate is dipped in automatic trans fluid. A clutch pack snap ring holds them.

22. The inner piston seal of the forward clutch cylinder can now be installed. Next, the outer clutch drum seal is installed on the piston and the unit lubed completely.

23. At this juncture, the piston is installed into the forward clutch cylinder, rim outward. One must use caution to make sure that all of the O-ring seals are installed and lubed.

24. The steel ring shown is then installed on top of clutch piston. Make sure clutch piston and cylinder are free of scoring or burrs. Use crocus cloth to remove imperfections.

25. The disc, or diaphragm, spring is now installed in the clutch cylinder, concave side up, followed by installation of the snap ring, which will hold the disc in place.

26. The lower pressure plate is installed first, followed by alternating drive and driven plates, and finally the upper pressure plate and then the snap ring which holds the assembly together.

27. A No. 3 thrust washer is placed atop the forward clutch, then unit is stacked on reverse-high clutch drum, followed by assembly of the forward clutch hub and ring gear.

HOW-TO: Assembling a C-4

28. A No. 4 thrust washer is placed in back of front planet carrier, which is set on clutch assemblies. Now install input shell, shown, with sun gear and No. 5 thrust washer.

29. After installing a new front pump bushing in that unit, drop the front pump drive and driven gears in place. Use caution, and do not scratch or damage the pump gears.

30. Install the four seal rings (arrows) on the stator support, then install stator into front pump. After attaching stator to front pump, check for free gear movement.

31. Install the selective thrust washer (arrow) on rear of stator, followed by installation of smaller selective thrust washer on end of stator shaft, being held by lube.

32. A large O-ring must be installed (arrow), then front pump gasket. A converter anti-ballooning valve is inserted in hole leading to converter. Dab of grease will hold it in place.

33. The complete clutch pack can now be installed through the front of the C-4 transmission case, with the input shell being fed in first. Unit is now nearing completion.

34. This operation is followed by installation of the intermediate band over the reverse-high drum. It would be wise to purchase a shop manual for more detailed instruction.

35. Stator and pump are installed in front case. Pump is held in place temporarily by two bolts until it is put in car. The input shaft is next slipped into the hollow stator.

36. Air hose is held against inlet (large arrow) and trans is tested at 40 psi air pressure to check for any leaks in clutch packs. Intermediate band struts are installed first.

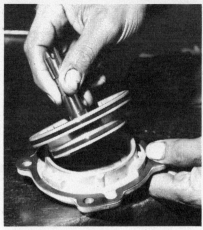

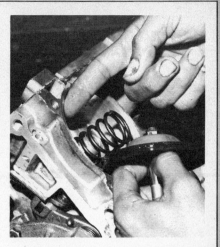

37. Two seals (see arrows) must be installed on the intermediate servo piston, then lubed with STP-type lubricant before installation. These lubing operations are very important.

38. After lubrication, the intermediate servo piston can be inserted into its cover. All brand new seals and gaskets are used at Steve's when any automatic trans is rebuilt.

39. After installing the low-reverse servo piston return spring, lube the cavity with an STP-type lubricant. The piston seal is also lubed before it is installed in the case.

40. After lubing the walls of the servo cavity and installation of the servo piston return spring, install the servo piston and cover, with new gasket. Press cover down and bolt it.

41. The reverse band can now be adjusted. The adjusting screw is then torqued to 10 in.-lbs., then the screw is backed off three full turns to arrive at proper final setting.

42. A new manual arm seal must be installed in the case after it has been disassembled. After this step, the manual arm for selecting reverse and forward gears can be connected.

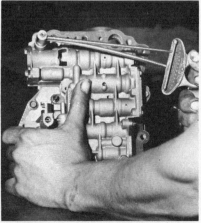

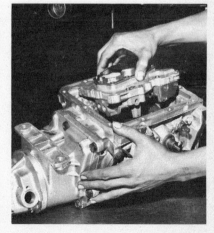

43. The inner downshift lever can now be installed, followed by tightening of the nut on the manual arm shaft inside case. O-ring seal is installed on the outside portion of the case.

44. After assembling the valve body, the bolts should be torqued to 20-35-in.-lbs. The valve body filter should be torqued to 80-120 in.-lbs. of pressure. Follow these specs.

45. A new rear extension housing bushing should be driven into place, housing installed, followed by valve body installation. The final operation is that of installing the oil pan.

Turbo 400

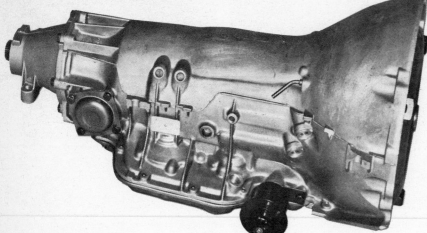

Due to the great number of Turbo Hydra-Matic 400 automatic transmissions in service today, it was only appropriate that we should feature a transmission build-up article on this popular unit. The Turbo 400 is found in many of General Motors automobiles, and because many of these vehicles are now approaching 50,000-60,000 miles, the gearboxes are undoubtedly in need of rebuilding.

A visit to Steve's Transmission Service, 9012 Sepulveda Blvd., Sepulveda, California—a large, reputable automatic transmission establishment—permitted us to obtain these step-by-step assembly photos of a 400 going together. Use of this article in conjunction with a factory-prepared manual will permit anyone with a limited number of hand tools to assemble (and disassemble, by reversing the operations) his own Turbo 400 transmission. Scanning through the transmission section of our own shop manual revealed dozens of specialized tools recommended for use in installing seals, etc. Yet, we found during our picture taking session that very few special tools were actually required to complete this transmission.

An inch-pound torque wrench, sockets, a few end wrenches, snap ring pliers and screwdrivers were about all that were really needed, along with a bit of caution and care when it came to installing the seals and O-rings.

Most of us know someone who is a full-time mechanic, and if he isn't a transmission specialist he surely knows someone who is. These people may be able to help you out during assembly when it comes time to install the intermediate clutch piston snap ring, the direct clutch snap ring, or the forward clutch spring retaining snap ring, for example. They may not charge you a cent, thinking you're pretty trick if you have decided to tackle this transmission by yourself. If not, the damage to your wallet won't be that bad.

Too many people are afraid to tackle a job that appears as difficult or challenging as rebuilding an automatic transmission, but if you follow directions carefully, you can't go wrong. So, if you're mechanically inclined at all, and have the time and tools—along with the desire to do it yourself and save some bucks—then just follow the bouncing ball. ☙

1. Turbo Hydra-Matic Trans

2. Disassembled Turbo Trans

3. Turbo Drivetrain

1. General Motors Turbo Hydra-Matic transmission is one of the best of the automatics available. A strong unit, it's also adaptable to racing.

2. There are many components in the Turbo 400, but with a little care, the right tools and following the directions, you can assemble one. Across the top we find the tail housing, main case, and valve body. Through the center are the many clutch housings and shafts with the front pump. At bottom are the pan, bands and clutches, converter.

3. Assembled, the Turbo gear train looks like this. The converter is at right. Drive clutches are hidden inside the clutch drums, with the bands outside. Front pump is located directly behind converter.

1. Assembler Steve Bustamente installs rear internal gear to sun gear thrust bearing and two races on rear internal gear mainshaft.

2. After dropping the rear internal gear mainshaft into output carrier, install the output shaft assembly into the output carrier, as shown.

3. The output-shaft-to-carrier snap ring can now be installed. A steel speedometer gear has already been put in place on the output shaft.

4. Before installing the output shaft to the case thrust washer, Steve adds a dab of grease to hold it. Retaining tabs are locked in pockets.

5. A composition ring (arrow) is slipped about output carrier to hold noise down. Another thrust washer is added prior to the reaction carrier.

6. With the sun gear in place, the roller clutch cage and rollers are installed in the reaction carrier, which is then placed on output unit.

7. The intermediate clutch piston inner and outer seals are put in place, then the unit is set into the main center support assembly.

8. The intermediate clutch release springs are installed, then the intermediate clutch spring retainer is installed, held by a snap ring.

9. Center support assembly is turned over, and its thrust washer is then set in place. Clutch piston should be air checked with compressed air.

HOW-TO: Assembling a Turbo 400

10. Grease is dabbed on the needle bearing and thrust washer before it's installed on end of center support. Support to case spacer is now added.

11. The center support assembly is next installed into the roller clutch in the reaction carrier. Be sure to check rotation of center support.

12. Install the rear unit selective washer into slots provided inside rear of trans case. Proper washer was determined by end-play check.

13. Install rear band assembly so that the two lugs index with the two anchor pins. Check to make sure that band is seated on the lugs.

14. Install proper rear selective washer into slots provided inside rear of case, then install complete gear unit assembly into the case.

15. Steve aligns application hole on center support with case application hole. Then he installed a screw for the intermediate clutch apply.

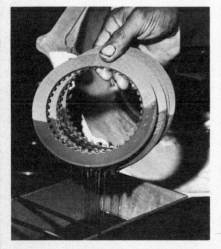

16. Center support to case spacer and snap ring are installed, then intermediate clutches are soaked in ATF before being installed in case.

17. After installation of the three steel and three composition clutch discs, alternated, the intermediate backing plate is installed next.

18. The direct clutch piston outer seal is already installed, and now inner seal is being inserted in the piston. Seals are both lubed.

19. Direct clutch piston is placed into the forward clutch housing, then 16 clutch release springs are set into pockets about the piston.

20. Steve's uses spring compressor to compress the clutch release springs after a retainer plate is installed. Now install a snap ring.

21. The direct clutch backing plate can now be installed in the direct clutch housing, preceded by wavy steel, flat steel and clutch plates.

22. The backing plate snap ring can now be installed in the direct clutch housing. Small screwdriver will assist in getting it in groove.

23. Moving back to the transmission, install the front band with anchor hole placed over band anchor pin and apply lug facing servo hole.

24. The direct clutch drum is now installed in turbo case without the clutch plates (being installed in photos 21, 22); it's easier empty.

25. Steve rotates forward clutch piston as he installs it in the forward clutch housing. A .006-in. feeler gauge helps slide seal down.

26. Sixteen clutch release springs (green) are installed in pockets of forward clutch piston. Always lube seals during assembly; use caution.

27. Place forward clutch assembly in press, install retainer ring and snap ring. Job can be performed without a big spring compressor.

28. Waved steel plate, then the composition and flat steel plates, alternated, are dipped in fluid then installed in forward clutch housing.

29. Forward clutch hub and thrust washers are installed, followed by direct clutch hub and snap ring. Turbine shaft is on clutch housing.

30. Grasp turbine shaft and slide forward clutch drum assembly into direct clutch drum. Direct clutch hub will move right into the drum.

31. Front pump body with driven gear is ready for drive gear. Oil teeth before installing gear. Make sure tangs are installed on the top side.

32. Pump cover can now be installed onto pump body. Hole in bench top accepts shafts of different parts, making work on trans quite easy.

33. A pair of ballpoint pens may be used to index bolt holes; then it's easier to install fasteners. Tighten pump cover bolts to 15 ft.-lbs.

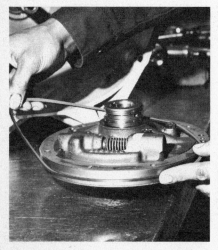

34. Install front pump gasket, then the O-ring seal. Lube seal with STP-type lube; carefully install front pump assembly on trans case.

35. Front pump is secured to case, then end-play is checked with dial indicator. Should be from .003-in. to .024-in. Install new pump seal.

36. At this juncture, the case to center support bolt is installed. Hollow bolt is used as oil passage for intermediate clutch apply.

37. New O-ring is installed on rear servo piston, which is lubed. Then rear accumulator spring is dropped in place, followed by the piston.

38. Metal rear servo gasket is next installed, then rear servo cover is bolted down. Torque all the attaching screws to 15-20 ft.-lbs.

39. The front servo piston can now be installed in case, adjacent to rear servo. Care should be taken to make sure components are clean.

40. Arrows depict six check balls that must be installed in pockets. Now install valve body spacer plate and gasket; gasket next to trans.

41. Valve body can now be installed. Make sure manual valve is properly indexed with pin on manual detent lever and governor pipes are in.

42. Guide pins or screwdriver may be used to align valve body so that screws can be installed. Now install manual detent roller spring assembly.

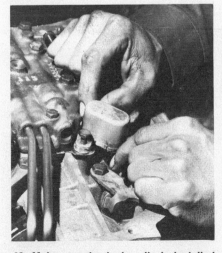

43. Make sure lead wire clip is installed (except P model), then tighten solenoid, valve body bolts. Install filter intake pipe, O-ring.

44. Use new filter, make sure it's properly installed on intake pipe. Never wash old filter, but replace it. Install new bottom pan gasket.

45. Install bottom pan, torque pan bolts to 15 ft.-lbs. Then, finally, install governor assembly and rear tail housing onto trans case.

Driveshaft & U-Joints

If you've ever wondered why your car has to have a driveshaft, the answer is it doesn't. Most of the motorcycles around use chains to accomplish the same purpose, and their owners wonder why anybody uses a driveshaft.

Chain drive on automobiles went out with button shoes, which must have been an awfully long time ago. Most American passenger cars use a single-piece driveshaft with a U-joint at each end. U-joints allow power to be transmitted through the various angles that the rear end causes as it goes up and down and travels over the road. Working in conjunction with the U-joints is a slip-joint on the back of the transmission, which allows the driveshaft to move in and out. This is necessary because the movement of the rear end actually shortens and lengthens the distance between the rear end and the transmission whenever the rear end goes over a bump.

That's about all there is to a driveline. Ordinarily nothing would ever go wrong here except for possible replacement of the U-joints. Some cars have grease fittings, and you're supposed to lubricate the U-joints when you lube the chassis. In the course of hard driving you occasionally hear of someone breaking a driveshaft or U-joint, but normally U-joints just wear out. You can tell when they're worn and loose by a "clunk" sound when you put the car in gear. Improper rear-end gear lash can also make this type of sound so you'll need to put the car on a lift to check it out.

We have two general types of drive systems on American passenger cars. One is the "torque-tube" drive. Here, the driveshaft is enclosed inside a large tube that bolts solidly to the rear axle. The tube pivots on a large ball joint on the back of the transmission, and there is a

U-joint inside this ball. There is no joint at the back of the driveshaft. The large outside torque tube absorbs torque and drive forces on the rear axle, with radius rods of some kind to keep the axle in line. Cars using torque-tube drive include early Ford products up through 1948, Chevrolets through '54, and Ramblers and big Buicks up to the early 1960's. Torque-tube drive has fallen out of popularity on late cars because the tube telegraphs too much road vibration to the passenger compartment of the car.

All other cars use an open driveshaft with U-joints at each end and a slip joint at the front. The shaft has to transmit only engine power, not take rear axle forces and twisting. These forces are taken either by long leaf springs, as on late Chrysler products, or by trailing suspension arms on late GM and Ford lines that use coil springs.

The principle in coil or leaf spring designs, is really the same. The driveline only has to transmit power, and rear-end drive forces are absorbed either by leaf springs or suspension arms and cross links.

It should be mentioned here that a number of General Motors cars (including Chevrolet) used 2-piece driveshafts with X-type frames in the late 1950's and early 1960's. These had a support bearing near the center of the shaft, in the center of the X-frame, with a short section of driveshaft in front and behind the center bearing. There were three U-joints. Servicing this type of driveline is a little more work, but the operations are essentially the same as for various other designs.

SETTING UP THE DRIVESHAFT

Driveshaft vibration is a chief cause of

roughness and rumble in passenger cars, and companies spend a lot of effort in engineering and testing to get rid of it. They also carefully balance driveshafts on all cars on the assembly line, and adjust U-joint angles and phasing, to control the problem in production, and *you* can mess everything up in a few minutes when you start tearing into a driveshaft and U-joints—if you do not know what you're doing.

In the first place, when removing the driveshaft you should make sure that you will get all elements back in the same position or "phasing" they originally held. U-joint yokes, for instance, should be in the same rotational position on the shaft as they were. This can be easily done by merely marking the shaft and yoke before disassembly. (Usually, there are phasing marks from the factory, but these are sometimes hard to find.) Note that most shafts have their U-joints phased so yokes at the front and rear of the shaft are at 90° to each other. If you should forget to mark, or can't find the factory marks, do it this way as a rule of thumb. But the safest thing is just to remember to mark the shaft and joints when they are removed, and then they can be bolted right back together in that relationship.

Driveshaft or U-joint *angles* are also critical. A little thought will show why. When a U-joint is transmitting power through an angle, the yokes have to flex back and forth at high speed as the shaft turns. The rotational motion they deliver is not an even rotation, but a kind of pulsing motion that speeds up and slows down twice each revolution. The greater the angle through which the power is transmitted, the more uneven this pulsing delivery and the more vibration. The easiest answer is just to see

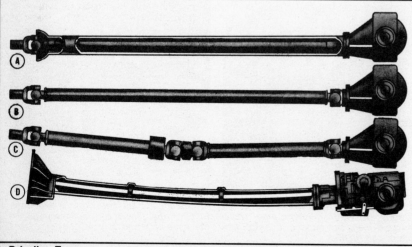

1. Driveline Types

2. Torque Tube Drive

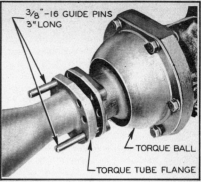

4. Buick Torque Ball

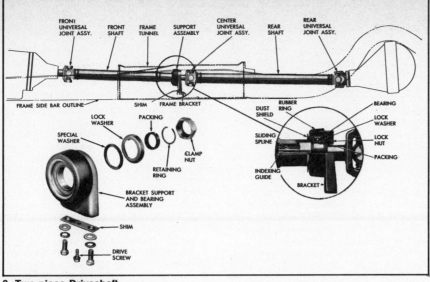

3. Two-piece Driveshaft

1. *The basic driveline types: (A) Torque tube, (B) One-piece open driveshaft, (C) Two-piece open driveshaft, (D) One-piece curved driveshaft without universal joints.*

2. *Torque tube drive was formerly used on several makes of cars. The tube containing the driveshaft is rigidly attached to the differential housing and absorbs driveline reaction torque.*

3. *Two-piece driveshafts were used at one time on several U.S. cars, including Chevrolets. Shorter unsupported driveshaft length added complexity, reduced vibration.*

4. *At the front of a torque tube drive is the "torque ball," an enclosed housing containing the universal joint.*

that the driveshaft angles are kept as straight as possible, so the U-joints don't have to flex very much as they turn. The ideal driveline would have zero angles in the U-joints. But, of course, this is impossible with the rear axle bouncing up and down.

Each different car maker has certain recommendations for maximum and minimum U-joint angles. Space won't permit covering all of these, but you can find them in the shop manual for that model at your car dealer. As a rule of thumb, just keep the angles very small with a normal load in the car—like 1° or 2°, and with 3° to 4° as maximum. This is the angle between the axis (centerline) of the driveshaft and the axis of the U-joint yoke at the front and rear end. About the only way you can measure it accurately is with a bubble protractor. This has a long flat flange on one side, to lay against the shaft or yoke housing, with a rotating bubble wheel in the center that will show angles very accurately. One of these instruments is expensive, but a garage may have one.

In most cases, the factory recommendation for setting driveshaft angle involves changing the angle of the rear joint so it exactly matches up with whatever angle the front joint has. When both angles are the same on a 1-piece driveshaft, the U-joints work together instead of fighting each other. When there are

leaf springs supporting the rear axle, the rear U-joint angle—sometimes called the pinion angle—can be easily changed by putting wedge-shaped shims between the spring and its seat on the housing.

On Ford and GM models using coil springs and trailing suspension arms it's usually necessary to shim either at the front pivot of the suspension arm or where the rear axle pivots on the arm. Your shop manual will tell all about it. All you're doing, in effect, is to tip the rear axle nose a little to change the angle between the rear U-joint yoke and the driveshaft.

REMOVING THE DRIVESHAFT

Most cars have a plain open driveshaft with a U-joint at each end and slip joint at the front, either ahead of or behind the front U-joint. Study the design of a typical U-joint and you will see that there are two Y-shaped yokes with a cross-arm piece that connects them, usually with needle bearings where the cross-arm revolves in the yokes. (The cross piece is called the "trunnion.") Most cars use this type of trunnion-type joint.

In this case, the rear U-joint on the driveshaft will be made so the bearing bosses on the rear yoke are split, enabling the joint to be quickly taken apart. The trunnion bearings will be secured to the yoke by simple U-bolts or some kind of little casting with cap screws, or maybe just a strap of steel with clamps or bolts. This design is necessary in order to get the driveshaft out of the car. In other words, you just split the rear yoke bearing retainer (whatever the design), and the U-joint will come right apart and the driveshaft will drop down at the rear. Be careful that you don't drop the trunnion and needle bearings and damage them. The needle bearings should be taped to protect them in storage, until reassembly. Note that the rear half of the split rear yoke is attached directly to the rear axle input shaft. This is called the "companion flange." You won't be doing anything with this in normal U-joint service, unless it's broken.

After the rear U-joint is split and the back of the driveshaft is dropped, the

shaft can be removed by merely pulling it back until the splines in the front slip joint slide apart. This distance might be 2 or 3 ins.

Getting the driveshaft out of a torque-tube car is more of a job. On Fords and Buicks, for instance, you have to loosen the whole rear axle assembly and move it back a little in order to get the ball joint at the front of the torque tube apart. It's simple to unbolt the ball retainer from the rear of the transmission. When taking the ball assembly apart, be careful not to lose the seals and O-rings that retain the lubricant (though these should be replaced with new parts before reassembly). It's much simpler on a pre-'55 Chevrolet with torque-tube drive. Here you just unhook the hand brake brackets and cables from the drive tube, remove the cap screws that hold the ball-retainer collar to the back of the transmission and slide it back on the driveshaft housing (or torque tube). Next remove the cap screws that hold the trunnion bearings to the front yoke. Place a jack under the driveshaft to keep it from dropping, and carefully remove the two front-yoke trunnion bearings. Then the driveshaft torque-tube assembly can be lowered—and the rear yoke of the U-joint will slide right off the shaft splines.

Keep in mind that you rarely have to remove the complete driveshaft from a torque-tube-drive car. Usually, if there's anything wrong, it's the front U-joint or ball joint around it (there isn't any U-joint in the back). So your driveshaft removal job is usually just a matter of removing the front ball-joint retainer from the back of the transmission, and dropping the shaft down to get to the U-joint.

Installing a driveshaft is pretty much the reverse of the above. The toughest part is holding the shaft up while you connect the U-joint. When reinstalling a torque-tube drive, especially where you have replaced the oil seals and O-rings, the ball joint might be too tight in its socket for easy movement of the axle up and down. On pre-'55 Chevrolets this adjustment of the ball tension is made by adding or subtracting shims under the cap screws that hold the ball-retainer to the transmission. With the screws tightened you should be able to move the ball with hand pressure on the tube. If too tight, add shims and check again.

SERVICING U-JOINTS

In late years, the car manufacturers haven't been recommending any regular

Driveshaft & U-Joints

service work on U-joints other than periodic lubrication through a grease fitting. But a few years ago they used to suggest taking them apart, cleaning, and lubricating every 2 years. If you might want to do this on your car, you will need some information on assembly and disassembly.

On a conventional trunnion-type joint, as we mentioned, you have needle bearings on each end of the trunnion where it pivots in the two yokes. It's a bit of a trick to get these bearings out and the joint apart. You will note that the bearing cups are retained in the outer ends of the yokes by C-shaped clip rings in a groove. On many models the clips are on the inside of the yoke, so you will have to tap them out with a punch and hammer. Then there are the designs without any clips at all. The cups are held in place by plastic injected through a hole in the yoke. You can disassemble these joints, because the plastic will shear when you hammer or press the cups out. But you can't use the same cups and trunnion again. You must get a replacement kit that comes with the clips and grooved cups.

After you are sure that there are no clips, or have removed the clips, set the joint up in a vise or on a support of some kind that will be open below the bearing hole in one end of the yoke (there are four of these ends in all). Then take a punch and gently tap the *opposite* bearing cup *inward* with a hammer. This will push the trunnion through the yoke far enough so the bearing cup will drop out of the other end. You have to repeat this the other way, then on the two bearings on the other yoke.

Another approach is to use a punch and tap on the center of the trunnion (at the cross) until the bearings drop out. Just tap easy, not too hard. Be careful not to damage the bearing bores in the yokes or the surface on the trunnion. And it's a good idea to cover the bearing cups with tape to prevent damaging them until reassembly is completed.

Servicing this conventional trunnion-yoke joint is very simple. First clean everything carefully with solvent, including the grooves for seals and rings, then inspect everything. There shouldn't be any excessive wear in the yoke bores or on the bearing surfaces on the ends of the trunnion arms. The needle bearings should look good, with no looseness in their cups and no obvious wear, galling, or broken needles.

After everything is clean and ready for reassembly, put a small amount of chassis grease in the bearing cup. This will be retained by the seal and retainer, and you should have adequate lubrication for at least 2 years; or, as they say, "for the life of the car," on late models.

1. Assembly of bearings to the trunnion. Examine each bearing and bushing carefully, replace if required. Keep it clean!

2. The normal "one-piece" driveshaft, showing two U-joints and slip joint.

Now you're ready to reassemble. This procedure is pretty much the reverse of what you've done. Modern U-joints have seal and retainer rings on the inner ends of the bearing cups, that go between the cup and a shoulder on the trunnion arm. These will have to be assembled before the bearing cup. A standard procedure is just to put the seal and retainer rings on the trunnion, then tap the bearing cups into the yoke bores part way, alternating each end so the trunnion journal can be slipped up inside the bearing. You can readily see the easiest way with your particular joint design. Just be very careful when tapping these bearings into place that nothing gets damaged. It's a ticklish job. Also be sure the little C-shaped clip rings are snug in their grooves. If one of these were to break or slip out you'd have big trouble.

The U-joints in the front end of torque-tube drives are generally of this trunnion-type, with minor variations, so the servicing procedure would be about the same as above.

The unique "ball-and-trunnion" joints used on one or both ends of most Chrysler products of the 1950's (Plymouth, Dodge, etc.) are another deal entirely. These are designed to combine the flexing of a conventional U-joint with the in-and-out motion of the slip joint. There is a round boss on the front end of the driveshaft with a hole in it and a pin pressed through it. Needle bearings and balls are on the outer ends of the pin, and these ride in round slots in a large collar that bolts to the transmission output shaft. In this way we get the necessary flexing and plunging motion by the balls rolling in the slots.

Servicing is quite simple. The drive-

1. Trunnion Assembly

shaft is dropped by splitting the rear conventional U-joint. To withdraw the driveshaft from the front, you have to detach the ring clips that hold the rubber boot, and then the shaft will pull right out of the collar (or body) with the pin and rollers intact. Inspect all parts for wear and clean everything carefully (including the inside of the collar and slots) with solvent. Do not press the pin out of the driveshaft boss unless it is loose. This pin has to be pressed in very accurately, within .006-in. on each side, or you're apt to get driveline vibration. It's rarely necessary to replace a pin. If the rollers, needles or centering buttons are worn they can easily be replaced. When assembling, repack the body or collar with 1¼ oz. of chassis grease, and put the joint back together, following the disassembly procedure in reverse.

A word about servicing the U-joints on Chevrolets of the 1960 era that had the 2-piece driveshaft: To remove the complete driveshaft, you need to remove the bolts that hold the center support bearing to the X-frame, then split the rear U-joint in the usual way to drop the back of the driveshaft. Then the whole shaft assembly can be withdrawn from the front slip joint. The center bearing and support remains on the front shaft.

To remove the center U-joint, take out the large bolt that holds the joint yoke to the front driveshaft; then disassemble the joints in the usual way, as they are of the conventional trunnion-yoke type. It's recommended that you *do not* try to remove the support bearing or bracket. It rarely needs attention, and it's very easy to damage either the bearing or the shaft in pressing it off. Special tools are needed to remove it. Take this job to a Chevrolet garage.

Some cars have constant-velocity joints. They look like a double U-joint with a heavy connecting double yoke. Before disassembly, mark all three yokes with aligned punch marks. They come apart about the same as a regular joint, except that there's a bunch of parts hidden behind the center yoke (a ball and socket arrangement) that keeps the two parts of the joint in line. Watch carefully when you disassemble it so you can get the pieces back together right. During reassembly, line up the punch marks you made before so the joint will keep its original phasing.

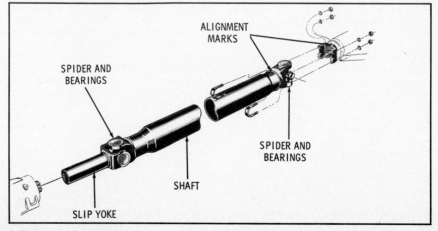

ALIGNMENT MARKS

SPIDER AND BEARINGS

SPIDER AND BEARINGS

SHAFT

SLIP YOKE

2. One-piece Driveshaft

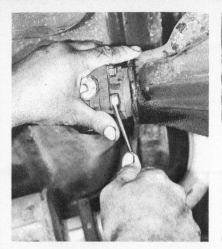

1. To repack U-joints that do not have grease fittings, unbolt both sides of the U-joint from the companion flange on the differential.

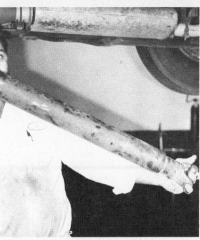

2. Drop the end of the driveshaft from the companion flange. Lower it as shown then pull it rearward until slip yoke comes free of transmission.

3. Clamp the shaft securely in a vise and with a pair of pliers, remove each of the retaining clips. Needle-nose pliers work best on these spring clips.

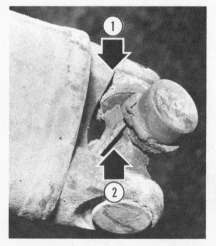

4. Some types of U-joints have retaining clips on the inside (1). Note the strap (2) that holds cups in place when removing shaft from the car.

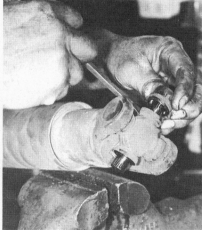

5. Use a screwdriver to carefully pry the two free bearing cups before removing the U-joint cross from the shaft. They could fall off and be damaged.

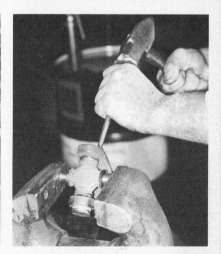

6. There are special tools for this job, but a hammer and a punch will do it just as well. Apply enough force on the flange to free the cross.

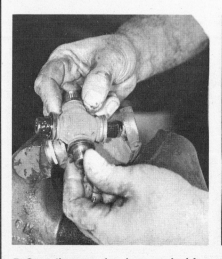

7. Once the cross has been worked free, remove the other two bearing cups. Pry them loose with a screwdriver as you did the first pair.

8. Wipe the inside of each cup with a clean cloth. Inspect for signs of wear on needle bearings. Work carefully to avoid disturbing the bearings.

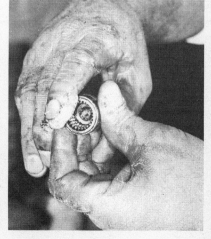

9. Wipe a dab of grease in each bearing cup and replace it. Press the cross back into the shaft, snap in retaining rings, and replace shaft on car.

Rear Axle

With a little luck you could wear out the engines in a half dozen automobiles and never have any trouble with the rear axle. The days are gone when wheel bearings and rear axle gears used to give out with regularity. In fact, it is sometimes a wonder why car makers put so much meat in their axles and rear ends. These units don't really need to be that tough, but we can be thankful they *are*.

A rear axle is basically a simple thing. Its essential purpose is to convert the driveshaft torque into thrust at the two rear wheels by using a form of bevel gear to turn the rotation through 90°. This is the "ring and pinion" gearset in the large center housing. The pinion is the small gear driven directly from the driveshaft, just behind the rear U-joint. This turns a large ring gear that turns the rear wheels. We also need a "differential" here so that one rear wheel can turn faster than the other when going around a corner. This is a small bevel planetary gearset inside the ring gear. The ring gear is bolted to the differential outer housing, and the axle shafts to the two rear wheels are splined into side gears, in turn connected to the ring through bevel pinions. This allows one wheel to overspeed the other and still feed torque to both of them.

There's one serious disadvantage to a conventional differential. It exactly splits the total driveshaft torque between the two rear wheels. This means that if one wheel gets on ice or mud, there's no bite; the other wheel can't transmit any more torque—so the car sits there and spins one wheel while the other is doing nothing, even though it may be on dry ground. You've all seen this effect. This is also a problem on the drag strip, where driveshaft torque reaction tries to lift the right rear wheel and let it spin. Then the other wheel just doesn't do anything.

This is where your "limited-slip" (Posi-Traction, Equa-Lock, etc.) differentials come in. These have special clutches between the side gears and differential case to lock up the assembly when one wheel starts to spin. Some clutches are applied by springs, others have cams that increase clutch pressure as axle torque increases. Either way offers a big advantage on ice or on the drag strip. We suggest ordering a limited-slip differential (about $40 extra) on any high-performance car. Or you can get kits and install them on older cars.

DIAGNOSING AXLE TROUBLES

Most rear axle trouble shows up in the form of some unusual noise from the axle, usually either gear noise in the ring and pinion (seldom the differential) or bearing noise in the outer ends of the axle housing.

Gear noise is a rather high-pitched whine that tends to "cycle"—it gets louder and softer, sometimes higher and lower, in a definite rhythmic pattern. The

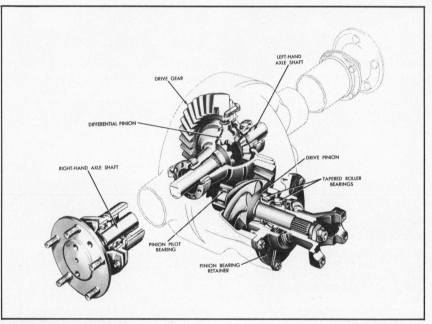

1. Standard Rear End and Axles

2. Removing Axle

3. Rear End Parts

noise is much more pronounced at certain car speeds than others. In fact it might also disappear at some speeds. You have to drive the car up and down the speed range on a smooth road to find it, checking under "pull" and "coast" conditions.

Bearing noise is entirely different. It has a lower-pitched whine or growl that remains quite steady, and tends to be louder when accelerating under load than when coasting. Most often the trouble will be in the wheel bearings at the outer ends of the axle (usually just one of them). It usually can be pinpointed by driving the car down the road and suddenly swerving to one side, then the other. This throws additional side load on the wheel bearings—and the growl should get louder. The best way to tell *which* bearing it is with this test (as a bearing can make noise with thrust in either direction or both): have someone ride in the trunk or rear seat to listen on both sides for the noise while you drive.

There's a chance the bad bearing could be one of the differential side bearings or the pinion bearing in the nose of the axle center section. In this case the whine would be higher pitched (because of the higher shaft speed) but would tend to remain steady. Also it would be louder under power, but would not change when you swerve the car on the road. Bearing trouble in the axle center section is much less likely than in the wheel bearings.

There are other possible axle troubles. A broken axle shaft is clear enough. The car won't move with a conventional differential, though it will move slightly under half-power with a limited-slip. A bad grease seal is clear enough—oil all over everything. Main grease seals are at the nose of the center section (just behind the rear U-joint), and at the wheel bearings at the outer ends. Usually it's the wheel bearing seals, as they are subjected to more stress forces under driving loads. Broken gear teeth in the differential are not common, but easy enough to detect. There will be a clunking feel each revolution. And a good fullpower run with teeth out will usually shuck out what's left—so the trouble won't be hidden for long!

1. The carrier side bearings are adjusted by means of a threaded ring in this design. Adjustment can only be done properly while the carrier is out of the axle housing.

2. The axle comes out with the bearing, after the bearing retainer has been unbolted from the backing plate.

3. Here are the component parts of a typical differential. While rugged and trouble-free, a differential is a piece of precision machinery that requires expert assembly.

4. Typical modern rear axle unit has inner retainers, straight roller bearings operating directly on the rear axle shafts themselves.

5. This type of differential and rear axle assembly disassembles from the front. It's probably best to let a specialist repair shop handle major rear end jobs.

MINOR AXLE SERVICE

With a little experience, you can safely tackle some rear axle service, but not too much. It's too easy to mess things up. The simplest job is to pull the axle shafts and wheel bearings—either to replace a broken shaft, wheel bearing or outer grease seal. Even this will take some special tools, and you may have to have the bearing replaced at a garage. But you can pull the shafts, bearings, and seals on most late-model American cars with just a slide-hammer type axle puller and ordinary hand tools, which can be rented, borrowed or bought at a reasonable price.

AXLES WITH RETAINERS AT WHEELS

Jack up the rear end and remove the wheel lug nuts and the wheel. The brake drum is retained by these same nuts, and you can pull this off after the wheel. (It fits on there more snugly, so it will take some yanking—and a gasket may come with it.) When the drum is off, it will expose a broad flange on the end of the axle shaft (forged as part of the axle) that has studs spaced around it for the lug nuts. This is what you pull out of the

axle housing; the shaft, bearings, and seals will come with it. But before it will come out you have to go behind the flange and remove the small bolts that hold on the axle bearing retainer plate and brake backing plate (which holds the shoes and cylinders). Remove these bolts and remove the retainer plate. But then put a couple of them back on to hold the brake in place, as this doesn't need to come off when changing axle shafts. Just tighten a couple of them up finger-tight and they will hold the brake.

Now you're ready for the axle-puller. This is a device that has a bracket on one end that attaches to the studs on your axle flange. There's a weight that slides back and forth on a rod attached to the bracket, and you can hammer this against the stop to pull the axle shaft and bearing out of the axle housing. Don't bang it too hard. Take it easy, and work the shaft out slowly so the jarring won't damage the ball bearings. You can buy one of these axle-pullers for your particular car at your car dealer, or universal types are available at any auto parts house. It's a good tool to have.

After the axle shaft and bearing are out, inspect them for wear, corrosion, and cracks. You can tell a bad bearing very easily. It will feel sloppy or rough—

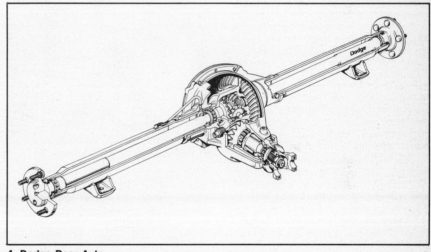

4. Dodge Rear Axle

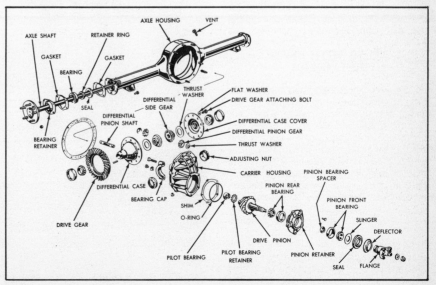

5. Rear Axle Assembly

Rear Axle

that is, the outer race will be loose on the balls. Sometimes the balls are pitted and galled, and the central ball cage may be loose. Replace the bearing if you have any doubts at all, as they aren't expensive. However it does take a special tool and sometimes a press to remove the bearing and replace it, so you'll probably need to have this done at a shop. And this would also have to be done if you broke an axle shaft.

But if you're just replacing an outer grease seal, this can be done quite easily without removing the bearing from the shaft. There are different types and designs of seals, and sometimes there are two or three on both sides of the inner race of the bearing and a ring around the outside. Usually these rubber seals can be pried off with a screwdriver. This would damage them beyond repair, but you will always be replacing them anyway when you pull an axle shaft. Sometimes seals can be put back without special tools, or with a makeshift drift or collar. Just be careful not to damage the seal surface putting it back on the bearing. And always replace the seal with the open edge or flange facing the lubricant. If you put it on backwards, it won't work.

After everything is cleaned and lightly lubricated with chassis grease, you're ready to put the axle shaft back in. The first thing you have to do here is to run the shaft clear into the housing until you can feel it strike the differential side gear bearing or shaft. This will have splines that must fit the splines on the end of the axle shaft. You just have to feel around with the shaft in there until the end slides into the splines. You can't see anything. Just work it around until it slips in. Nothing to it.

From here you drive the bearing into the outer axle housing with the axle-puller, working in reverse as a drive hammer. (Or you could do it with a heavy hammer on the face of the axle flange.) When the bearing is seated in the axle housing, you just replace the bearing retainer plate (after removing the finger-tight bolts holding on the brake). Tighten these up good and snug. Then back go the brake drum and gasket, and finally the wheel and lug nuts.

AXLES WITH INNER RETAINERS

Chevrolet since 1965, and many other cars, do not have the retainer at the wheel behind the axle flange. After pulling the wheel and the brake drum, you will notice that there are no bolts in the area behind the axle flange that have anything to do with retaining either the axle or the bearing. This type of axle is held in place by a C-washer at the extreme inner end of the axle shaft. To remove the axle, you must remove the rear cover on the rear end housing, which of course lets all the oil run out. Then you have to remove a long screw that holds the differential pinion shaft in position so that the shaft can be pulled out of the differential carrier. Once the shaft is out of the way, the axle shaft

can be pushed inward enough to free the C-washer, which will then fall out into your hand. Once the C-washer is out, you can slide the axle out of the housing. The bearing and seal are pressed into the end of the housing and must be removed with a slide hammer puller that will reach in and pull from behind the bearing.

THE CENTER SECTION

There are two general types of rear axle center-section designs on modern American cars. The most common is where the main axle and differential housing is like a large banjo in the center, with tubes tapering off on each side for the axle shafts and to hold the wheels. The banjo is closed at the back. Then the gears and differential are carried in a cast iron "carrier" that bolts to the front of the banjo. You can get to the gears by merely unbolting the carrier and pulling it out.

In the other layout, the carrier housing is much larger and contains the entire differential. The side axle tube housings are pressed into this carrier casting, and it's closed at the back by a stamped cover that bolts on. This design is used for the late Chevrolet axle and the small Chrysler models, etc. It has the advantage of keeping all parts in a bit more rigid alignment, but it's harder to work on the gears and seals. In both cases, of course, when removing the carrier, you must disconnect the rear U-joint, drop the driveshaft, and pull out the axle shafts from the outer ends of the axle housing (as outlined earlier).

Obviously any center-section service work will be quite a bit easier on axles with a removable carrier. Here you just unbolt the carrier from the banjo housing and pull it out (after you remove the axles). All gear adjustments can be made right on the carrier assembly. And you can put the assembly up on a bench to work on it. With the "integral"-type axle (late Chevrolets, etc.) you either have to pull the entire axle out of the car to work on it, or put the car up on a hoist and work from underneath.

Rear end gear adjustments are critical for low axle noise, especially with these "stiff" 4.11 and 4.56 ratios. For instance,

2. Removing Differential Cover

1. Unbolting Sway Bar Shackles

3. Removing Pinion Shaft Lock Screw

gear "lash" (the distance a tooth on the ring or pinion can be moved back and forth before contacting the next tooth) must be held generally between .004 and .008-in. That's pretty tight. Lash is adjusted by shim spacers on the pinion stem and at the differential side bearings. (These adjustments move the pinion gear back and forth and the ring gear from side to side, respectively.) Needless to say, making these adjustments is complicated work. Not only do you need special tools to get at the adjusting shims, but you need a pretty sophisticated dial indicator rig just to *check* lash. So this is best left to pros.

But you can save plenty of money by removing your own replaceable carrier assembly (on 90% of cars) and taking it into the shop for work. Then you won't pay labor for removing this from the axle. You can fairly well tell whether your gears need adjustment by gear whine on the road—which you can interpret from instructions earlier in this chapter. Also a quick inspection of the ring and pinion gear teeth can tell a lot about gear lash. If adjustment is right, the wear pattern (where it is shiny and smooth) should be right in the middle of the tooth face. This is both across the tooth and up and down on the tooth. Right in the middle. If there is a wear spot at one end of one tooth and at the other end of the mating tooth, or if the wear spots are high up on the tooth or low down, or if they are egg-shaped and slightly off center or slightly tilted...you can be sure your gear adjustment needs attention.

One more word about center-section work: If you break an axle shaft on your car, you will need to pull both the axle shaft and the carrier section. This is because the broken end of the shaft can't come out with the main part of the shaft—as they usually break near the splines at the center section. So you would need to pull the carrier to fish the broken end out. However, if an axle breaks beyond the spline, you might be able to bend up a tool out of a coat hanger to "fish" out the broken end without removal of the center section.

DETERMINING AXLE RATIO

Rear axle gear ratio has a huge effect on the acceleration performance of a car, as most of you know. This ratio determines how fast the engine turns in relation to rear wheel rotation, or the car speed. With a 3.55:1 ratio, for instance, the driveshaft would turn 3.55 times for each 1 full turn of the rear wheels. (This would be in high gear; but if the transmission is in low or second, the engine would be turning more than 3.55 turns per 1 turn of the wheels.) In general, the faster the engine turns in relation to car speed, the snappier the acceleration. There have been cases where just changing the axle ratio from 3.55 to 4.11 has knocked a full second off the elapsed time (e.t.) at the drag strip! This is quite a hop-up weapon.

So it's important for you to know the axle gear ratio that's in your car. In most cases you will have a pretty good idea by the standard ratio that is supposed to be in that model, from the factory catalog. If you bought the car new, there may be a listing of the ratio on the invoice or price sticker. Also on assembly-line cars there is always a mark or number stamped on the differential housing that indicates the ratio that was put in that axle at the factory (and whether it's a standard differential or limited-slip). Unfortunately each company uses its own code of numbers or letters to indicate these ratios. There would be no way you could interpret them without consulting the shop manual for your model. Space won't permit any detailed list here, but any car dealer will help you.

Gear ratios do get switched around from time to time—and you may still not be sure of the ratio that's in your car. This will require actually measuring it. It's simple! Make a chalk mark horizontally at some point on the driveshaft and a vertical mark on the outside edge of the tire. Block the front wheels, jack up the rear end and put the transmission in neutral. Now turn the driveshaft around slowly (accurately counting the revolutions) and have someone tell you when the rear tire has made exactly one full revolution.

4. Using Magnetized Rod

5. Removing the C-Lock

6. Pulling Shaft From Housing

1. If your car uses a rear anti-sway bar like this Pontiac Trans-Am, you'll have to unbolt the shackles and swing the bar out of the way.

2. Place a container beneath the differential before removing the cover. This comes under the heading of good housekeeping.

3. After the differential has been drained, wipe exposed parts dry and remove the lock screw holding the pinion shaft in place.

4. You'll have to push each wheel in toward the differential in order to remove the C-lock from button end of axle shaft. A magnetized rod makes removal easy.

5. The C-lock is the key to differential reassembly, so for heaven's sake don't lose it. Pull it out and put it where you can find it again later.

6. Remove the axle shaft from the housing by pulling outward. Be careful not to damage the oil seal in the differential when pulling axle out.

Rear Axle

You can't get an exact measure of the ratio this way, because it's hard to pinpoint accurately the degrees of rotation of the driveshaft when the wheel has made its full turn. But you can tell the difference between the various ratios that are available for your model in the catalog. Let's say the catalog lists optional ratios of 3.08, 3.36, 3.55 and 3.70 for your car model. You could tell the difference between these. The 3.08 ratio would be just a shade more than 3 turns of the driveshaft. The 3.36 gears would be about 3⅓; the 3.55's, 3½; and the 3.70 gears would see the shaft turn roughly 3¾ times for one turn of the wheels.

HOPPING-UP WITH GEARS

As we have said, putting stiffer axle gears in your car—gears with a numerically higher ratio—is one of the simplest and cheapest ways to hop-up the acceleration performance. And, fortunately, you can now get a wide range of gear ratios for almost any late-model car, either through a factory parts warehouse or from one of the specialty suppliers like Getz Products or Precision Gear.

These available ratios run from as low as 2.56 to 6.17 or more. Something here to fit every need. And the prices are not impossible. Usually from a low of around $40 for a set of factory gears to $75 to $100 for special-cut performance and racing gears. Get a catalog and do some shopping.

Space won't permit any deep discussion of optimum gear ratios for various performance requirements. But it's not hard to come up with some suggestions that won't be far off the mark, since the science of gear selection has become very refined in the hot rod field in the last five years—especially as more ratios become available for various car models. For instance, we know that a ratio somewhere around 3.5 is best for top speed on most cars. This ratio is also a pretty good compromise for the street and highway. (You'll note that many high-performance factory cars have standard ratios in this range.) If you do most of your driving on the open highway, we would suggest a ratio closer to 3.0:1. On the other hand, if you do most of your driving at moderate speeds around town, and want a lot of pep on the street, try gears around 3.9. Actually 4.11 would be even stronger. For the drag strip, most full-bodied stock and modified stock cars

(even Super/Stocks) like ratios of 4.56 or 4.88. These allow the engine to just peak going across the finish line. Your 5.12 and 5.37 gears are for small-engine Gas Coupes that want to wind up 7000 to 8000 rpm at trap speeds of 100 to 120 mph. Ratios from here on up are pretty much for track racing on short ¼- and ½-mile ovals, where your car speed might be only 60 to 80 mph and you want an engine speed of 5000 to 6500 rpm. It's either run these wild ratios or run in 2nd gear all the time!

In conclusion, a word about installing these special gears. Here again it's a job for a professional. In fact, high ratios from 4.11 on up seem to take extra precaution on gear lash to get away from whine on the road. Gear noise is definitely more of a problem with high-ratio performance gears. So we would suggest that you just pull out your axle carrier section, take it and the new set of gears down to an experienced mechanic, and let him make the change and adjustment. The job requires pulling the pinion stem, the differential case and side bearings—and it requires a lot of special tools. Don't try to do it unless you have the help and advice of somebody with experience—*plus* the proper tools. 🛠

1. Differential Side and Pinion Gears

1. Comparison of two limited-slip differential spiders. Design at left requires four pinion gears between the side gears for high torque capability in small size.

2. Assembly of limited-slip differential. Amount of preload is critical; too little and an unloaded wheel will spin uselessly, too much and the differential will act like a locked rear end when negotiating a corner.

3. This type of limited-slip differential uses cone clutches in place of plate clutch packs. Advantages are fewer parts, simpler design, better lubrication, and longer life.

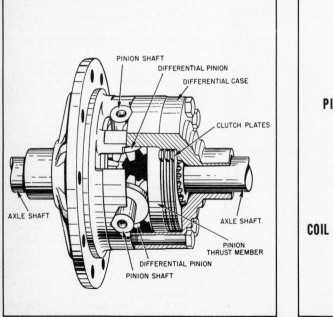

2. Chrysler Limited-Slip Differential

PINION SHAFT
DIFFERENTIAL PINION
DIFFERENTIAL CASE
CLUTCH PLATES
AXLE SHAFT
AXLE SHAFT
PINION THRUST MEMBER
DIFFERENTIAL PINION
PINION SHAFT

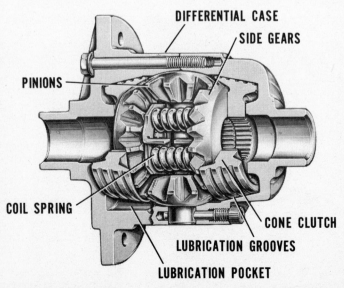

3. Cone-Clutch Limited-Slip

DIFFERENTIAL CASE
SIDE GEARS
PINIONS
COIL SPRING
CONE CLUTCH
LUBRICATION GROOVES
LUBRICATION POCKET

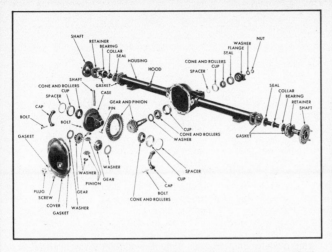

1. In this Dodge axle assembly the carrier is integral with the axle housings. First the cover plate must be removed, then differential case can be pulled by taking off two caps. Adjustment of the side bearings is done inside the housing.

2. On many cars the rear axle must be allowed to hang down all the way on the springs to provide fender clearance for removal of rear wheels. If you have access to a chassis hoist, job will be easier, but it can be done without one.

3. Give those drums a chance to cool before grabbing hold; they get hot. Drum can be slid off the lug bolts, or it may have to be unbolted. The bolts are visible if your car has them. Make sure to release emergency brake to remove drum.

4. Turn axle until you can fit the proper socket through access hole in the flange and remove the nuts holding the bearing retainer in place. On some cars, the nuts will be on the back side. A heavy screwdriver will give leverage.

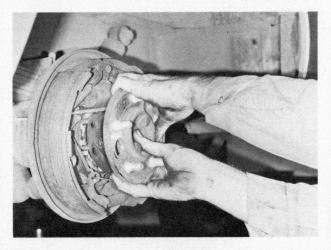

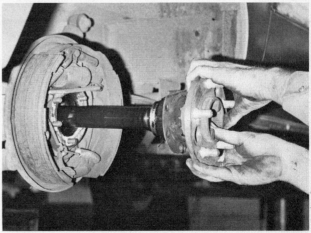

5. You may be able to pull the axle out this way. If not, put the drum back on the lug bolts backwards, and use it to pull out the axle. If the axle is really frozen (not uncommon), you may have to resort to using a slide hammer.

6. Once you've broken the axle free, draw it slowly out of the housing. Notice that wheel bearing will come out with the axle. Be careful as axle comes free that you don't hit yourself in the face with it! Now, third member will come out.

Brakes-Drum & Disc

Brakes don't ordinarily go bad all at once. It just seems that way. You might drive for many thousands of miles and never have a bit of trouble with your brakes. Then one day you have to make a panic stop and you discover that you would probably get to a halt quicker if you dragged your foot through a hole in the floorboards. The seemingly instant decay of brakes is caused by their over-capacity in most ordinary situations. If you drive like a normal human being, you just don't need much brake. So it's possible to have the brakes worn to a dangerously low level and not know anything about it until it's too late.

The only way to prevent this unfortunate situation is to inspect the brakes regularly. Every 12,000 miles or each year, whichever occurs first, is a good interval for pulling at least one drum and taking a look at what's going on. Pulling all four drums is much better. Whichever you do, you have to know what to look for. So let's start at the beginning and go through the brake system completely.

HYDRAULIC DESIGN

Hydraulics are quite simple and easy to understand, and are based on the simple principle that fluids cannot be compressed like gases. It is therefore possible to move a column of liquid (hydraulic brake fluid) from the actuator or master cylinder, through a pipeline system, to the slave or wheel cylinders, whose movement causes the friction material (brake lining) to come in contact with the wheel driven drum or disc and force it to slow or stop.

The master cylinder is filled with fluid and has a piston at what might be termed bottom dead center, with the connecting rod linked to the brake pedal itself. Hydraulic lines connect this cylinder with the slave units at the wheels. These are best described as a cylinder with a piston at each end. As the pedal is pressed, the master cylinder piston pushes the fluid through the lines to each wheel cylinder, causing the wheel cylinder pistons to push outward, forcing the brake shoes against the drum. Since this pressure is equal to all wheel cylinders, effective braking pressure cannot be applied to any one wheel until all the shoes on the wheels are in contact with their respective drums, providing a self-equalizing effect.

Drum brake systems are designed so that there is always a little pressure in the line when the brakes are not being used. This pressure is maintained by the check valve, sometimes called a residual pressure valve. The large spring in the master cylinder makes it work, and

keeps slight pressure in the lines to hold the wheel cylinder pistons out against the shoe tabs. Without the residual pressure, the pistons might vibrate away from the shoes, which would cause low pedal and lack of brakes. Disc brakes do not use the check valve because their seals fit much tighter, keeping the pistons from vibrating away from the disc. With a disc/drum system, it is necessary to have a check valve in the line to the drum brakes, but not to the disc brakes. In disc/drum systems that have a dual master cylinder, the check valves are in the master cylinder outlet, right where the drum brake line screws on. With a single master cylinder, the check valve has to be further downstream, in the line that feeds the drum brakes.

As we said before, liquids cannot be compressed, but gases such as air can be, so it is very important that such a hydraulic system be free of any bubbles of air. Removal of such extraneous air is done by bleeding, an important part of the servicing procedure. To insure that the system is always air free, cup-like seals of rubber or neoprene are used on all master and wheel cylinders, and a fluid supply reservoir is incorporated into the master cylinder. The fluid itself is compounded especially for automotive hydraulic brake systems and should never be mixed with or contaminated by solvents. It will withstand very low temperatures without freezing and very high tem-

peratures without boiling away; it gets sticky on exposure to air and will ruin paint or brake lining material.

In addition to the self-equalizing feature, and the elimination of mechanical linkage from brake pedal to wheels, hydraulic systems can be used to create multiplication of force or leverage. In mechanical leverage, where the length of the lever determines the increase in force (such as the brake pedal itself), the area of the actuating (master cylinder) piston in relation to that of the slave (wheel cylinder) piston determines the amount of hydraulic leverage. In addition to being used to apply the necessary force of shoes against drums, it is also used to compensate for a change of weight distribution under rapid stopping conditions. Here the front wheels are subjected to as high as 75% of the vehicle's weight and, therefore, must exert more braking force without locking the rear wheels. This is done by making the front wheel cylinders slightly larger in piston diameter than the rear cylinder pistons.

There are tremendous hydraulic pressures involved in the braking system, which is why it's important to be sure that the plumbing and cylinders are free from leaks and bits of dirt or other foreign particles that might disturb the seals, and that the lines themselves are not cracked or fractured in such a way that a sudden surge of pressure will

1. Slider Type Disc Brake

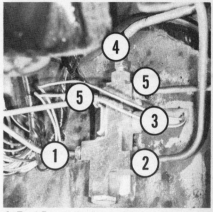

3. Chrysler Proportioning Valve

4. Ford Proportioning Valve

2. GM Proportioning Valve

1. Newest design in disc brakes is Chrysler Corporation's slider type—a single-piston floating caliper that slides on the two machined outer surfaces of the disc during application. A 3rd-generation Chrysler disc design, it offers better performance with simpler construction and is standard equipment on all 1973 V-8 models.

2-4. Combination brake warning switch/ proportioning valves differ in appearance from car to car, but all have same function: (1) Outlet to rear brakes, (2) from "R" outlet of master cylinder, (3) switch assembly, (4) from "F" outlet of master cylinder, and (5) outlet to front brakes.

5. All late model cars now use a tandem master cylinder to prevent 4-wheel brake failures. You'll find a double hydraulic cylinder.

cause them to break. With a pedal force of 100 lbs.—which is not hard to exert under panic stop conditions—hydraulic line pressure will be anywhere from 800 to 1300 psi (pounds per square inch), depending on mechanical pedal linkage and hydraulic leverage between master and wheel pistons. Power-assisted brakes require less foot pressure but exert the same amount of line pressure.

A part of the hydraulic system on late-model cars with dual master cylinders is the brake failure warning light switch, sometimes called the differential pressure switch. The switch consists of a piston inside a bore with one end connected to the front hydraulic line and the other end connected to the rear line. Normally the piston doesn't move, be-

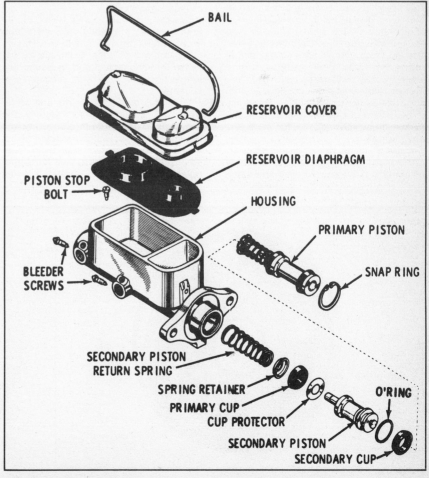

BAIL
RESERVOIR COVER
RESERVOIR DIAPHRAGM
PISTON STOP BOLT
HOUSING
PRIMARY PISTON
SNAP RING
BLEEDER SCREWS
SECONDARY PISTON RETURN SPRING
SPRING RETAINER
PRIMARY CUP
CUP PROTECTOR
O'RING
SECONDARY PISTON
SECONDARY CUP

5. Tandem Master Cylinder

Brakes--Drum & Disc

cause hydraulic pressure is equal throughout the system. But if there is a leak in one half of the system, pressure will drop in that half, and the normal pressure in the other half of the system will move the piston in the bore and turn on the light. Some of the switches turn the light on only while your foot is on the brake, while others leave the light on. Late-model switches are made in one piece with the metering valve and proportioning valve. Connecting passages in the one-piece casting eliminate the many lines that looked like a bowl of spaghetti when there were three separate units.

BRAKE DESIGN

All friction-type braking systems are essentially heat systems. Bringing the average-sized car to a maximum effort stop (just short of locking the wheels) from highway cruising speeds generates enough heat in the linings and drums to melt them if it were not dissipated properly. The lining material is very important but it must also be compatible with the drum material, maintaining its coefficient of friction throughout the braking cycle without excessive wear to either lining or drum. Any oil, water, or hydraulic fluid that comes between lining and drum effectively destroys this correct coefficient of friction.

Cooling a conventional drum brake assembly is difficult, and the number of successive high-speed stops is limited to the ability of the brake cooling design to stay ahead of the heat build-up. Cast iron drums, the most commonly used, depend mostly on air passing by them in the rather restricted confines of the wheel recess. Engineers have been improving this airflow by ducting air into the wheel/drum cavity, finning the drums and combining cast iron liners with aluminum drum housings. All for more efficient brakes.

Modern linings also assist in transferring some of the heat, but the necessity of a backing plate makes internal cooling without ducting difficult. In addition

to holding the necessary shoe assemblies, the backing plate is designed to minimize entrance of water and abrasive dirt into the critical space between shoe and drum. While moderately effective in keeping small quantities of dust and water out, large doses get through and are retained by the very same shield. The adverse effect of dust and water (especially the latter) on braking efficiency has been virtually eliminated by the caliper disc systems available on the late model cars.

The efficiency of a braking system, in addition to properly conditioned hydraulics, depends on proper lining material of adequate thickness, internally smooth and round drums, maximum contact between lining area and drum surface, and cooling. In addition to the force exerted on the shoes by the mechanical and hydraulic leverage, additional pressure between shoes and drum is achieved by self-energizing where the actual contact of the shoe with the drum is used to apply additional force to the drum. As the brakes are applied, the friction between lining and drum wants to force the shoes around in the direction of drum rotation. The location of the shoe pivot point determines whether the shoe is forced against the drum (self-energizing) or away from the drum by the rotation of the drum itself. Most designs today get additional power by linking the two shoes together so that not only are both shoes self-energizing, but the primary shoe exerts pressure on the secondary shoe, pushing the secondary shoe into the drums that much harder. This is called "servo" action.

Despite the rather long travel of the brake pedal, the wheel cylinders and brake shoes do not move very far to make contact with the drum, mainly because the mechanical and hydraulic leverage necessary for the pressure requirements.

To compensate for lining and drum wear, an adjustment for setting the shoes closer to the drum is incorporated into the brake assembly. In recent years, a self-adjusting feature has been standardized to eliminate the need for a periodic "setting up the shoes" service procedure. In simple terms, self-adjusting

linkage uses the rotating shoe action in reverse to operate a lever that picks up an extra notch on the star wheel adjuster nut, if wear allows the shoes to move far enough for the lever to engage. Self-adjusters work only when the brakes are applied while the vehicle is moving backwards. They do not compensate for drum expansion caused by heat. If you back up when your brakes are hot, the automatic adjustment can cause the rear shoes to drag when the drums cool off.

ROAD TEST ANALYSIS

Before beginning any type of brake service or overhaul, it is best to determine by actual road test just what might be required. Select a smooth, paved, dry section of street or road free of traffic or other obstacles. At a speed of 20 mph, apply the brakes firmly for as rapid a stop as possible without locking the wheels. If the pedal depresses to within 2 ins. or less of the floorboard, the linings are badly worn, brake fluid level is low, or the shoes need adjusting. A spongy feeling to the pedal indicates air in the system (except on some disc brakes, which are designed that way). With the car at rest, press brake pedal as hard as possible, holding it down firmly to note whether it continues to move slowly downward. Any such movement indicates poor sealing master or wheel cylinders or a leak somewhere in the plumbing system.

Should the car pull to one side or the other, or if one wheel grabs, it is an indication of several possible problems: improper adjustment, grease or hydraulic fluid on the linings, loose backing plate, reversed primary and secondary shoes, brake shoes not properly arced to drum resulting in partial contact, plugged master cylinder relief valve, poor pedal linkage adjustment, or an out-of-round drum. While conducting these rolling brake tests, listen for grinding or rubbing noises with brakes off and applied. Rubbing sounds without brake application indicates improper initial adjustment, faulty or broken return spring, binding wheel cylinder or shoe guides.

Grinding or squeaks when the brakes are applied can mean brake linings worn

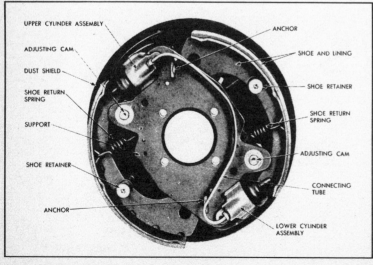

1. Leading-Shoe Brake

2. Cracked Brake Rotor

1. *There is no servo-action in a leading-shoe brake, but each brake shoe is self-energizing. Late model cars favor the servo-action design.*

2. *Chalk-marked area has crack in brake disc, rendering it unsafe for use. Discs should be checked for such failures every time pads are changed.*

3. *Velvetouch Metalik brake linings are latest wrinkle for the performance-minded. Since linings were almost as good as new two years after installation, there's something here for the economy-minded also.*

4. *There are pros and cons on arcing new brake shoes before installing them, but many brake specialists wouldn't think of a brake job without this.*

5. *Velvetouch Metalik disc linings should be chamfered at each end before use. As lining material is soft metal, there's a certain amount of residue caused by braking action, and this creates a place for it to go.*

6. *Metalik brake installation is very similar to that of ordinary organic lining, except that starwheel adjuster is not connected to self-adjusting lever. By themselves, there's very little wear; adjustment every 6-9 months will do. Self-adjusters will cause constant drag on linings and wear them down fast. Use heavy-duty shoe return and hold-down springs, too.*

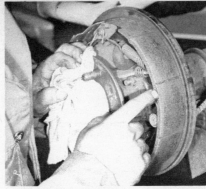

3. Metalik Brake Lining

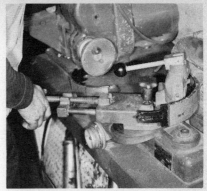

4. Arcing New Brake Shoes

5. Chamfered Brake Linings

6. Installing Brake Adjuster

to rivets or shoes, dust in rivet holes, improper lining material, oil or grease on linings, or warped backing plates. Faulty front wheel bearings can also affect braking efficiency and cause a lot of unnecessary searching for defect in the brake assembly if they are not checked during the overhaul. Don't get carried away setting up the mechanical linkage for the parking brake, as drag here can ruin a set of rear brake assemblies.

For cars equipped with power assists—either the booster type used on Ford and Chrysler products, or the combined unit featured on GM cars—there is a simple drive test to determine faults in this area that may save unnecessary tearing into the entire system.

With the engine off and the transmission in neutral, press the brake pedal several times which will bleed off the vacuum reserve in the reservoir. Apply a light pressure to the pedal, depressing it just beyond taking up any slack in the linkage, and hold it there lightly while starting the engine. As the engine starts, the pedal will feel like it is dropping away underfoot, requiring less pressure and indicating that the assist system is working. If there is no action, the fault can be assumed to be in the power assist unit.

Again with the engine off, deplete the vacuum reserve as before, then start the engine, run at fast idle for a few moments, then stop engine with throttle closed. Wait for about 2 mins. and try the brake again. There should be enough vacuum reserve in the system for several assisted braking efforts. If there is no such reaction, the cause can be isolated to a faulty vacuum check valve.

RELINING

It is not likely that the home repair enthusiast will have all the equipment necessary for machining drums, relining shoes, or arcing them to conform to the drum diameter. Therefore, the car should be jacked and placed on suitable stands so that all four wheel assemblies can be removed at the same time.

Select a level surface for this jacking operation, preferably a paved one to insure sturdy jack stand foundation and to reduce the possibility of extraneous dirt entering the system. The ideal equipment for this operation is a regular hydraulic floor jack and four jack stands. Remove wheel covers, loosen wheel stud nuts, and with the rear wheels blocked, raise the front end just enough for the tires to clear the ground by jacking in the center of the front crossmember. Place a jack stand under each lower suspension arm as close as possible to the inside of wheel and tire but not interfering with their removal, then lower jack slowly so front end is resting securely on stands. Raise the rear wheels by jacking at the differential, placing jack stands under axle housing carefully so as not to endanger any hydraulic lines that may be strung along this housing.

In lieu of such professional jacking equipment, a bumper jack and a quantity of short pieces of lumber, preferably 2 × 4's about 12 ins. long, can be used very well to raise and hold the car safely off its wheels for brake servicing. With the rear wheels well blocked to prevent rolling, begin by bumper jacking each front wheel separately, just as you would to change a tire. Using the short pieces of lumber, build a stand under the front suspension by placing the wood pieces

log cabin style to the required height. Lower the car and repeat for each wheel. Don't use rotted lumber or skinny pieces on end and expect it to safely support your car. Avoid orange crates or boxes which can collapse and not only injure you, but also damage the car.

A friend with access to a frame-type grease lift in a garage or service station, who is willing to allow it to be tied up long enough to do all of the wheel work in connection with a brake line/drum grind operation, can be a great asset and solve all of the jacking and jack stand problems.

REMOVING WHEELS AND DRUMS

Whatever jacking system is used, the next step is to remove the wheels and then the drums. Begin with the front ones, as in most cases except later model GM cars, the wheel hub is part of the brake drum, and front drum bearings, seals and lubricant. Once the cotter pin is freed of the axle nut, carefully remove nut and washers. The brake shoes may have to be backed off at this point to allow the drum to be wiggled off. The star wheel, similar to a coarse-toothed gear, is located at the bottom of the shoe assembly and is accessible through a slot in the drum.

Some cars like early Lincoln and Mercury have the slot in the backing plate covered by a pop-out plate. If the car has self-adjusting brakes, the adjusting lever must be held out of the way while the star wheel is turned. This means inserting two tools—a thin screwdriver to hold the lever up, and a brake adjusting tool—into the slot at the same time. Follow the same procedure for backing off

Brakes--Drum & Disc

on rear shoes prior to drum removal, if necessary.

It is a good idea to mark the drums and shoes so that each complete assembly can be returned after servicing to the original wheel position. Keeping them in paired sets will save a lot of reassembly time. The marking should include identity for forward and reverse shoes on each wheel. Scratching with a sharp instrument or center punching with a series of coded dots is a good method.

Remove drums, taking care to protect front wheel bearings and seals from dust and dirt. Examine backing plate for presence of wheel cylinder stop plate. Late-model cars have these stops to prevent wheel cylinders from popping out when shoes are removed, as there is always a slight static hydraulic pressure in a well working brake system. If there is no stop plate, a wheel cylinder clamp will be required to hold the cylinders in position while shoes are removed. Under no conditions should the brake pedal be depressed while the drums are removed.

Before proceeding further, study the indicated illustrations to be sure of the identity and functions of the internal brake parts. The brake shoes can now be removed by detaching the shoe hold-down discs, springs and pins, and then the return springs from the anchor pin. In shop practice, this latter operation is done with a special tool but can be accomplished by grasping the long shank of the spring firmly with vise-grip pliers, stretching the spring sufficiently to remove it from the anchor pin. On rear brakes where the parking brake operates on the rear shoe only, disconnect the parking brake cable and remove parking brake strut and lever. Final removal of the shoes front and rear on single anchor brakes, is done by spreading them to clear the wheel cylinder connecting links, whereupon both shoes will come off as a unit, still held together by the adjustment screw and spring.

Total-contact brakes, used on earlier Chrysler products, have a slightly different hold-down and return-spring arrangement, and a special tool is required to prevent damage to the shoes. With guide springs, retainers and return springs removed, further dismantling is the same as with conventional assemblies.

CLEANING AND INSPECTION

Now is the time to clean and inspect the brakes, and while they are removed, the front wheel bearings. If air pressure is available, use it to clean drum dust from all parts, being careful not to blow it into wheel bearing assembly. A stiff brush is a good substitute for compressed air. If very dirty, wash drum, backing plate, and metal part of shoes in clean solvent and dry thoroughly. Be careful to keep the solvent away from cylinder boots and brake lining. Check for pits or dark spots on the bearing races and plan to replace before reassembly if bearing wear is indicated. Check for oil leaks around the rear wheel bearings and replace seal if in-

dicated; seepage here can spoil a good brake job very quickly.

Check all wheel cylinders for piston leaks by carefully lifting each boot to note if interior is wet with brake fluid. If so, the wheel cylinders must be overhauled or replaced (this procedure is discussed later in this chapter).

Examine the linings and drums for wear and grooving, to see if braking problems might be caused by other than normal wear. The lining should show evidence of uniform wear both along its contact arc and across it. Thin spots in the center of the shoes are normal with oversize drums, because the shoe radius and drum radius are not the same. Thinner edges side-to-side show that the

shoes have been canted by bent backing plates or anchor pins.

DRUM TURNING

Most drums, after periods of normal use, become out-of-round and almost always grooved from the abrasive action of dust and dirt between linings and drum. Drums can be restored by machining or grinding on special drum lathes, and it is safe to remove as much as .030-in. of material to bring them back to normal roundness and smoothness. This means that the internal drum diameter will be increased by .060-in. and the relined shoes must be altered to conform to the new diameter. This is done by use

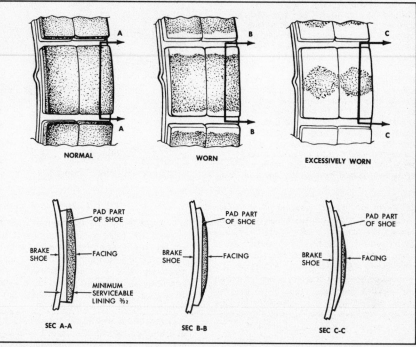

1. Lining Wear

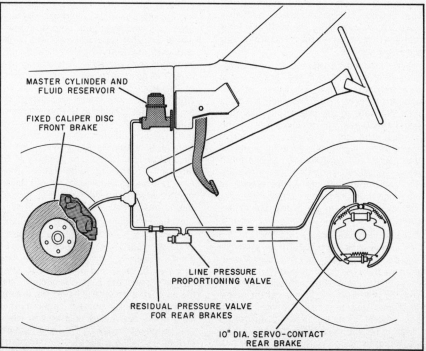

2. Hydraulic Schematic

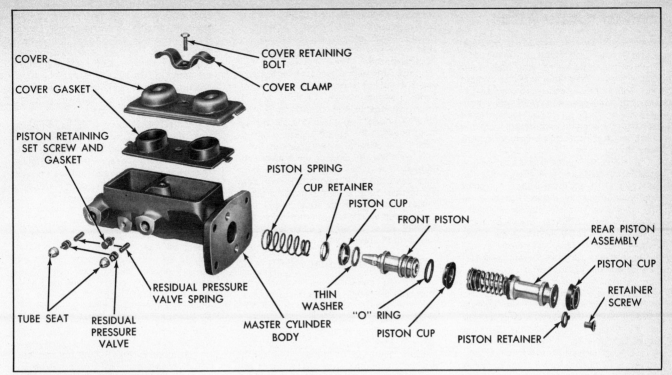

COVER

COVER GASKET

PISTON RETAINING
SET SCREW AND
GASKET

COVER RETAINING
BOLT

COVER CLAMP

PISTON SPRING

CUP RETAINER

PISTON CUP

FRONT PISTON

REAR PISTON
ASSEMBLY

PISTON CUP

RETAINER
SCREW

TUBE SEAT

RESIDUAL
PRESSURE
VALVE

RESIDUAL PRESSURE
VALVE SPRING

MASTER CYLINDER
BODY

THIN
WASHER

"O" RING

PISTON CUP

PISTON RETAINER

3. Disassembled Master Cylinder

1. These illustrations show brake linings in different stages of wear. Once the linings get down near the steel brake shoe or pad, it's time to replace the linings. If they aren't changed, then your drums will be ruined, costing you more money, maybe your life if they fail.

2. The proportioning valve limits the pressure to the rear brakes to prevent them from locking up. Also in most disc brake systems, but not shown here, is a metering valve which delays the application of the front brakes until the rear brake shoes have had a chance to expand against the drum, thus helping to equalize brake action.

3. If this master cylinder were on a car with disc brakes, the outlet to the disc brakes would not have a check valve, but it would have a tube seat insert.

of oversize lining or shimming standard lining, then arc grinding to conform to the new drum diameter.

LINING MATERIALS

Modern brake lining materials—that used generally for the past 10 to 15 years—is molded, then bonded or riveted to the shoes to insure positive contact and maintenance of constant curve and to prevent shifting or coming off the shoe. Equipment for relining, drum grinding, and shoe-to-drum matching is not only expensive, but requires training for proper use. These factors alone make it impractical for an amateur mechanic to own things as drum grinders, arcing jigs, and a stock of lining material, rivets, and bonding ovens.

Brake lining can be purchased in several ways. Professional brake servicing companies use rolls of material that must be cut to size, drilled and countersunk

for rivets, beveled, and fitted to the shoes. Precut and drilled linings are available to fit specific car models, and replacement shoes, completely lined and ready to install, can be purchased from brake supply houses and new-car service departments. All forms are available in oversize thickness to compensate for drum grinding, as is shim stock for use under standard lining material, although oversize lining is the usual method. Premium lining materials, such as sintered metallic and a wide variety of various degrees of hardness for specific purposes, are available as replacements for standard material. Brake supply houses which handle name-brand items will have specifications for just about any car made, and following their recommendations will provide the right lining for the indicated purpose.

As with riveted linings, bonded materials require special skills and equipment to replace. Old linings must be chiseled or burned off the shoes, which are then carefully sanded in preparation for the liquid cement or special tape adhesive. Cemented shoe assemblies are then clamped in a special jig that applies high, even pressure and heat over the entire contact surface to insure adequate bond. It is obvious that the home brake repairman who purchases relined shoes properly arced to his professionally ground drums is getting a better and lower cost job than he could possibly do himself.

REINSTALLING SHOES AND DRUMS

Installing the relined shoes and matching drums must be done with great care and cleanliness. Avoid touching linings or drums with greasy hands, and allow no hydraulic fluid to come in contact with the lining material. If the shoes and drums have been kept separated in

matching sets as previously suggested, prepare to assemble each to its matching wheel.

While it is readily accessible, the adjusting screw assembly should be dismantled, cleaned in solvent, dried, and lubricated before reassembly. The inboard side of the backing plate should also be cleaned of road grime; this will ease locating the cylinder bleeder valve and anchor pin adjustment, if there is one.

Proper lubrication of all brake friction points is necessary for long trouble-free operation. For this purpose, a special compound brake grease is used. It has properties just for this application that prevent it from running or vaporizing under the heat of severe brake application so that it may be safely used without fear of getting into the drum/lining contact area. However, it should be used sparingly when the adjusting screw mechanism is assembled and at all mechanical contact points between shoes and backing plate. On rear brakes be sure to lubricate the parking brake cable assembly.

If the system has a self-adjusting mechanism, this should be assembled and lubricated prior to the installation of shoes. In any case, the star wheel adjusting nut must be centered over the backing plate slot (if this type of accessibility is provided) or centered to afford proper adjusting movement (if this is done through an opening in the drum itself). As these adjusting assemblies are not interchangeable with the opposite wheels, care must be taken to keep the parts for each wheel exclusively for that wheel.

Place shoes on backing plate, engaging them with the anchor pin and the wheel cylinder connecting links. Be sure the shoes are in proper relative position. Usually the forward has the short lining, but not always. The shoes should be

Brakes--Drum & Disc

marked forward or reverse. If not, and you can't tell by looking at them, ask a professional mechanic who has used that kind of brake lining. Some companies make both forward and reverse linings interchangeable. Others make both linings identical as far as appearance but the composition is different, and the lining will not work properly if shoes are reversed.

Don't feel self-conscious about asking a professional brake man which way the shoes go. It is a problem that has bothered mechanics for years. But be sure the mechanic you ask has had experience with the particular brand of lining or he may not know, either. If the counterman where you buy your parts is really hip, he may be able to help out. But don't necessarily count on it.

If the brakes are of the self-adjusting type, take care when assembling the self-adjuster mechanism. These are not interchangeable from one side of the car to the other and to interchange them will cause the adjuster to retract the shoes rather than advance them when the brakes are applied as the car is rolling backwards. Remember, make sure the parts are not binding on their anchor pin and that both shoe return springs are installed over the adjuster anchor fitting.

Adjusting screws for self-adjusting brakes are assembled with the thread screwed all the way in and then backed off about one turn. The star wheel is positioned toward the rear or secondary shoe, and the self-adjusting actuating lever is spring-linked to the primary shoe and cable- or rod-linked to top anchor pin. Before proceeding further, check operation of self-adjuster by pulling on cable or link toward secondary shoe just

enough to lift lever past a tooth in adjusting screw star wheel. The lever should snap into position behind the next tooth and return to original position when released.

Follow the same greasing procedure when replacing shoes on Chrysler total-contact brakes. Insert the long end of return springs in the shoe web (before placing shoes into position) by sliding them between the support plates and engaging the ends of wheel cylinder pushrods with the toe end of each shoe. Attach short end of return springs to their respective links by prying against them with proper tool. A long-handled Phillips screwdriver is a good substitute. Install guides and retainers making sure that the little lip or guide is positioned in the hole in the support plate.

ADJUSTING ANCHORS

With the exception of the Chrysler total-contact brakes, shoes must be centered in relation to the axle center-line when they are replaced. Professional mechanics use a grinder pivoting on the axle or axle flange for removing small precise amounts of lining material to provide exact and true centering of lining diameters in relation to the drum. Another method is to use a gauge bar pivoting on the axle to determine just how far off center the shoes are and in what direction. Early Chrysler brakes have eccentric anchors at the bottom which allow the shoes to be shifted to the proper position, and the gauge is necessary for this operation. By setting the gauge bar to the drum diameter and the indicated calibrations for proper clearance, the eccentrics are adjusted while checking with the gauge bar.

Early Bendix-type brakes employ two types of anchor pin adjustments for shoe

centering, making it possible to center without grinding or using gauge bars if the refurbished shoes and drums have been properly arced. Some anchor pins have eccentric threaded ends and others are mounted through a slotted hole, allowing them to shift when the nut is loosened. In either case, shoe centering procedures are the same.

Back off adjustment so drums fit easily onto mounting flanges or axles. In the case of front wheels with bearings integral with drum, be sure that bearing assembly is complete and lubricated, and that wheel bearing nut is snug enough to prevent any play in the bearing.

Turn the brake shoe adjusting nut until maximum effort is required to turn the drum with both hands. Mounting the wheel will ease this effort, but two hands should be needed to turn the wheel. Loosen anchor pin nut not over ¾-turn (with eccentric pin type it will be necessary to hold pin with square end tool while loosening nut). Turn eccentric pin to shift shoes. With slotted anchor pin mount, loosen nut and rap backing plate smartly with hammer to ease shifting of pin in slotted hole. Tighten nut and check brake drag by turning drum by hand, noticing any difference in drag from the initial setting. If drag is the same, the shoes are properly centered. If drag decreases, it indicates the anchor pin has shifted. Repeat by again setting brake adjusted nut to hard two-handed drag and effecting further shoe shifting by either turning eccentric or loosening anchor pin nut and then tapping the backing plate with a hammer.

Some cars use a nonadjustable anchor and if the lining and drums are standard it works fine, but when you go into oversizes there is a problem in getting the shoes centered. Some exchange shoes

1. Wheel Cylinder Boots

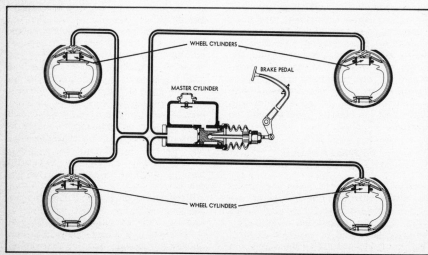

2. Wheel Cylinder Cutaway

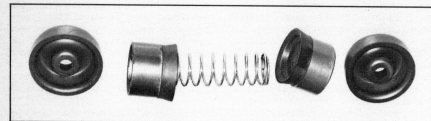

3. Hydraulic System Schematic

1. The end components here are press-on boots that cover the ends of wheel cylinders. Next are the metal pistons, which actuate the pushrods, thence the shoes. On the inside, separated by the coil spring, are the piston cups. The hydraulic fluid in the wheel cylinder is in this area, between the cups.

2. This cutaway cylinder reveals the boots on the ends, the pistons and pushrods (held in hand), the piston cups and spring. Fluid enters the cylinder via threaded opening, forcing the cups and pistons out, actuating the brakes.

3. Equal hydraulic pressure does not guarantee equal braking effort on each wheel. If the type of lining or metal in one drum differs from others, brakes may pull to one side.

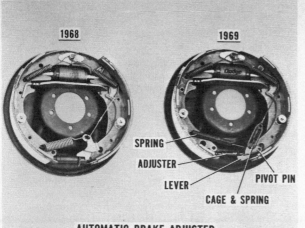

AUTOMATIC BRAKE ADJUSTER

1968   1969

SPRING
ADJUSTER
LEVER   PIVOT PIN
CAGE & SPRING

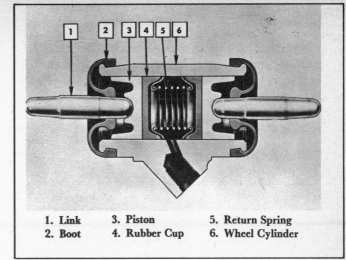

1. Link   3. Piston   5. Return Spring
2. Boot   4. Rubber Cup   6. Wheel Cylinder

4. Automatic Brake Adjuster

4. The automatic brake adjuster on '69 Dodges reduces possibility of over-adjustment, takes place when backing, with brakes applied.

5. This illustration shows the components of a wheel cylinder.

have the anchor hole relocated so that they fit properly. Otherwise the lining must be arced off center in a special jig that fits on the shoe grinder.

ADJUSTING SHOES

Whether late-model, self-adjusting brakes or older manual models are relined, an initial adjustment is required for proper operation. After the shoe centering operation on new brakes, or to correct for normal lining wear and to raise effective brake pedal, a minor brake adjustment is necessary to provide proper clearance between lining and drum. For brakes without self-adjusters, this is best done with all four wheels off the ground. Using a suitable tool through the backing plate or drum slot provided, turn adjusting wheel so there is a slight drag as the wheel is turned. Repeat with each wheel, trying for the same amount of drag. Then, back off an equal number of notches on the adjuster at each wheel—12 to 15 notches are average—making sure that there is no drag. If any is detected, back off an additional one or two notches on that wheel. Apply brake pedal firmly several times and check for drag again.

Bleed the hydraulic system (see details below) and make several slow speed stops to check equal braking. With self-adjusting brakes, centering procedures are the same and setting shoe-to-drum clearance is not as critical. Just be sure that the shoe adjusting screw for each wheel is backed off enough to clear shoes from any detectable drag, then achieve final adjustment by applying brakes while car is moving in reverse which will activate the self-adjuster and bring the shoes to proper clearance.

BLEEDING THE HYDRAULIC SYSTEM

Following any brake reline job, it is

5. Wheel Cylinder Parts

just good business to bleed the system, eliminating any air that may have entered. The idea behind bleeding is to drive any air out of the master cylinder, lines and wheel cylinders, out through special bleeding valves on each wheel cylinder. These are small fittings that look very much like Zerk grease nipples and are located on the backing plate directly behind the wheel cylinder. Unscrewing them slightly opens their passage into the wheel cylinder; it works like a small faucet with a ball-like end on it. As these bleeder valves are usually covered with road grime, they should be cleaned thoroughly for easy access and operation.

Make sure that the master cylinder reservoir is filled and that a supply of new, clean, hydraulic fluid of the proper specification is available to top this level off as the fluid level drops, depending on the amount of bleeding necessary. Pressure bleeding, used by professional brake mechanics, involves the use of a large reservoir of pressurized hydraulic fluid coupled to the system at the master cylinder, and supplying a flow of fluid through all the lines while each wheel cylinder bleeder valve is opened. However, bleeding can be done without this aid by having two people do the job—one to operate the foot pedal, the other to bleed each wheel cylinder.

For bleeding by the two-man method, a bleeding tube and a glass jar or bottle are required. The tube can be procured at any auto supply store and should be long enough to reach from the bleeder ball end to the bottom of the glass jar when it is setting on the ground. Put about 1 in. of clean hydraulic fluid into the jar, slip one end of the bleeder tube onto the bleeder valve, the other into the jar so that it is submerged in the fluid. Open the bleeder valve about ¾-turn and at the same time have the assistant press the brake pedal slowly a full stroke. Close bleeder valve just before brake pedal hits bottom and allow pedal to return slowly to full-out position. Repeat until expelled fluid flows in a solid stream with no presence of air bubbles. Tighten bleeder valve and remove hose. Be sure to constanly check fluid level in master cylinder and top up with new clean fluid only.

With careful work it is possible for one man to bleed brakes with the bleeder hose method. Just be sure the end of the hose is below the surface of the fluid in the jar. Open the bleeder fitting, then go to the pedal and stroke it easily once or twice using about ¾ of the full stroke. Replenish the fluid in the master cylinder, then go to the wheel and close the bleeder fitting. Repeat at each wheel. If the lines are empty it may be necessary to run as much as a cupful of fluid through each cylinder to get all the air out. This would require several strokes of the pedal for each cylinder.

The best procedure is to follow a wheel-to-wheel sequence beginning with the one closest to the master cylinder. This applies to caliper disc units and to later model cars with dual master cylinders. Begin with the left front, then do the right front, left rear, and right rear. This procedure minimizes the possibility of trapped air entering lines already bled. Under no conditions must the master cylinder be emptied during the bleeding process as this pumps air into the system.

WARNING LIGHT SWITCH BLEEDING PROBLEMS

The warning light switch is designed to turn the light on whenever there is a leak. This includes the "leak" you create when you open a bleeder fitting. If the switch is the type that only turns the light on when your foot is on the brake, then no special procedure is required. But if the light stays on after you take your foot off the brake, it means you have the type of switch that must be centered after bleeding. The design of the switch allows pressure from the non-leaking system to move the piston toward the leaking system. If the light is on, you must create a leak by opening a bleeder fitting on the other system. Then you step on the brake pedal gently until the light goes out; close the bleeder fitting and you're done. That's the way the book says to do it, and we wish it was that easy. When you step on the pedal, the light will go out, but the piston keeps moving toward the other side, and puts the light on again. Then you have to close the bleeder fitting, open the fitting

Brakes--Drum & Disc

on the other system (front or rear) and try again. After about a dozen trys you will get just the right amount of pressure on the pedal to get the light off. To eliminate all this monkey motion, you can buy a little threaded stud that screws into the switch in place of the electrical connection and holds the piston in the centered position during bleeding.

OVERHAULING THE HYDRAULIC SYSTEM

Hydraulic brake fluid has a distinct, sharp, alcohol-like odor in its fresh fluid state and becomes sticky upon prolonged exposure to air, making it pretty easy to identify should leaks develop in lines, master or wheel cylinders. Check all lines from master cylinder to each individual wheel, examining any grime-coated wet spots for evidence of hydraulic fluid. Should any lines need replacing, do not attempt to save any of the fluid for re-use as it may become contaminated and cause damage to the system. Use only steel brake line tubing, properly flared for the fittings. The flexible lines from tubing terminus to wheels are armored for maximum protection and should be replaced only with stock replacement parts for optimum service and safety.

WHEEL CYLINDER OVERHAUL

With the drums removed, examine wheel cylinders for leaks by carefully lifting boots from cylinder housing. Evidence of hydraulic fluid under the boot indicates a bad wheel cylinder, and shoes must be removed before attempting to work on that cylinder. Note: Hydraulic fluid will ruin automotive paint finishes and lining material. All parts of the system activated by hydraulic fluid should be cleaned only with alcohol or special fluids compounded for this purpose and available at automotive parts supply houses.

To remove the wheel cylinder, loosen flex line where it connects to cylinder at backing plate. Remove cylinder mounting screws, detach cylinder from backing plate, then finish uncoupling of flex line by rotating cylinder. Some hydraulic fluid can be saved by placing a well-fitting wooden plug into the end of the flex line. This should be tappered slightly but not driven in hard enough to distort line and cause a problem when reassembling is done.

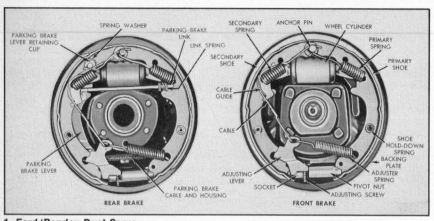

1. Ford/Bendex Dual Servo

3. Riveted Metallic Linings

2. '68 Chevelle Front Drum

1. A servo-action brake is one in which one shoe pushes on the other, giving the greatest braking action to the second shoe.

2. Front brake drums on '68 Chevelle are finned for improved cooling.

3. This NASCAR stocker features a super-size set of brakes. Riveted metallic linings are segmented so they dissipate heat more quickly.

4. Increased use of disc brakes on American-built cars is a boon to safety enthusiasts. Cars with discs stop faster and suffer less fade.

5. This power disc brake system is found on the Marlin, a former AMC car. Four pistons provide plenty of surface area for the linings.

4. Typical Disc Brake

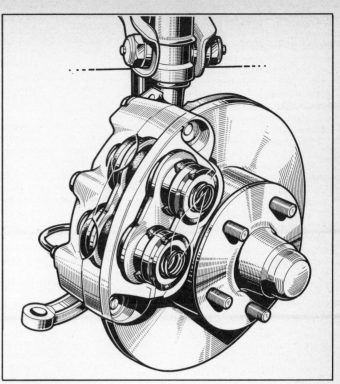

5. Power Disc Brake

Remove boots, springs, pistons and cups from cylinder and place in alcohol or brake parts cleaning fluid. Clean cylinder casting inside and out, but do not let it soak in fluid. Examine bore for scoring and pitting, and cups for swelling. Scored cylinders can be honed to restore the desired mirror finish but no more than .005-in. may be removed. If more is required, the entire cylinder must be replaced. Replacement kits containing all necessary parts for rebuilding wheel cylinders are readily available from parts houses, and all parts should be replaced while the cylinder is apart; a minor attempt at saving here might result in more expensive repairs later.

If the cups are swollen or mushy, it is an indication that the hydraulic fluid has become contaminated with oil, kerosene, or gasoline. Should this condition be evident, the entire system must be flushed and all wheel and master cylinder cups (and in severe cases, the rubber flex lines), must be replaced. Flushing procedures are covered later in this chapter.

Assembly of wheel cylinders must be carried out under clean conditions, free from possible contamination by dirt, oil, water and solvents, or even dirty or greasy hands. With the finger, coat inside of wheel cylinder wall, as well as piston and cups, with clean hydraulic fluid. Assemble carefully in proper sequence for each side, ending with the boots on the ends. Clean end fitting of flex line and screw cylinder onto line by rotating cylinder until snug. Place cylinder in position on backing plate. Secure cylinder to backing plate with mounting screws and complete tightening of flex line. Repeat for each wheel.

MASTER CYLINDER OVERHAUL

Master cylinders fail and require rebuilding for the same reasons as wheel cylinders. Normal wear, contaminated fluid, and dust and dirt entering the system will eventually spoil the sealing and pumping action. Single master cylinders have a piston and sealing cup actuated by the pedal linkage, a boot to protect pedal rod extension, a check valve, a spring and two small holes in the cylinder wall—a compensating port and a breather—connected to the integral fluid reservoir.

When the pedal is pressed, the piston forces hydraulic fluid through the lines, actuating the wheel cylinders. When the pedal is released, it takes a little longer for the fluid to catch up with the piston, creating a pressure differential between piston and primary cup. Fluid from the integral reservoir flows into the cylinder chamber behind the piston and rushes past the primary piston cup to equal the pressure in front of it. As the return stroke is completed, the piston cup, acting as a slide valve, uncovers the compensating port and any excess fluid is returned through it to the reservoir.

A check valve in the output end of the master cylinder maintains 5 to 8 lbs. of static pressure inside the lines, which serves to keep the lips of the wheel cylinder cups tight against the cylinder walls to prevent loss of fluid and entrance of air into the system.

The dual master cylinder, first used in 1962 by Cadillac and American Motors' Rambler and now mandatory on all new cars, has two outlets, two complete piston/cup/spring and check valve assemblies, and two separate reservoirs for fluid supply.

The pistons operate in tandem in a continuous cylinder barrel, and are operated by a single pushrod linked to the brake pedal. One of the outlets is connected to the front wheel cylinders, the other to the rear ones. Failure in one system still gives braking operation to the other. Newest safety version of the dual system is a warning light that indicates failure of either side of the hydraulic system. Failure can also be felt in the pedal itself as the piston of the failing circuit will bottom before the other exerts the required pressure. Pedal travel will therefore be longer.

Replacement parts for either single or double systems, with oversize pistons and cups, are available should cylinder require honing, but the maximum that can be removed is .005-in. Should this honing depth fail to remove scores or pits, the master cylinder will have to be replaced.

When overhauling master cylinders, always use all the parts in the replacement kit to insure long rebuilt life. Use care in reassembly and cleanliness throughout to avoid any grease or dirt entering the system. Clean all parts in alcohol or special cleaning compound for hydraulic systems, and lubricate cups and pistons with hydraulic fluid when assembling.

Dual master cylinders, with their tandem piston assemblies, require a little more care when the cups and pistons are slid into the cylinder barrel, since the outlets are usually at the sides along the cylinder walls. Observe the cups as they are pushed past these holes to see that they do not turn back the edge and destroy their sealing effect. A piece of small-diameter rod, rounded and smooth on the end, can be used through the outlet hole to ease the cups past the openings. Liberal use of hydraulic fluid as a lubricant will help keep the assemblies sliding through the barrel.

Follow carefully the instructions packed with dual master cylinder kits. Some of the kits have an adjustable piston which must be set for your car. If it isn't set correctly, the brakes won't work.

To fill the hydraulic system after rebuilding wheel and master cylinders, fill

Brakes--Drum & Disc

the master reservoirs and proceed as with bleeding the system, only open the bleeder valves fully and keep master reservoir filled as the foot pedal is used to pump fresh fluid into the entire system. Then bleed the system as previously described, after bleeding the master cylinder first.

Some master cylinders are equipped with bleeder valves which operate much like the wheel cylinder bleeders. To operate these, press the brake pedal slowly, and open the bleeder valve near the bottom of the stroke, then close the valve before pedal is released. Repeat, making sure that master reservoir is full, until fluid flows in a steady stream without bubbles. For bleeding without a valve, loosen fitting to brake line and force air and fluid out by pressing brake pedal. Air in system can be heard as it squirts out through fitting. Tighten and proceed with bleeding wheel cylinders. On dual masters, loosen both outlet fittings and proceed as described for single cylinders.

FLUSHING HYDRAULIC SYSTEMS

When preliminary examination of wheel or master cylinder indicates swollen or mushy piston cups, there is evidence that the fluid is contaminated by oil, kerosene, or foreign liquid that de-

stroys the rubber cups. All wheel cylinders and the master should be rebuilt with new parts, but only after the system is flushed. About a quart of brake fluid is required. Follow the same procedure as bleeding but open bleeder valves a full 1½ turns to speed up passage of old fluid being pushed through by the flushing liquid.

After flushing, proceed with wheel and master cylinder overhaul. Upon reassembly, bleed system completely with new hydraulic fluid.

Flushing fluid, an alcohol base solvent available at parts stores, can be used for flushing the brake lines. However, many carmakers warn against its use because of the difficulty in getting it all out of the lines so it won't contaminate the brake fluid. They recommend that any flushing be done with new brake fluid only.

PARKING BRAKES

Parking brakes fall into three types: the cable-operated rear brake shoes, the cable-operated external driveshaft brake, and the cable-operated internal expanding driveshaft type. A need for parking brake cable adjustment is indicated when the parking brake pedal or lever must be activated to the limit of its stroke in order to properly hold the car when parked. A minor brake adjustment on systems without self-adjusters should be performed before adjusting cable-operated, rear-drum-type parking brakes. When this is done, check slack in rear cables to brakes. If more than 2 ins. of slack is apparent, adjust by loosening lock nut on cable usually located in the forward or single cable part of the cable system. Hold cable to prevent it from turning while adjuster is pulled up to the required 2 ins. of slack with parking brake off, then tighten adjusting lock nut. Check for drag by jacking rear wheels

off the ground and turning for any indication that the parking cable is too tight.

The external driveshaft brake used on early Chrysler cars has two adjustments. Before any adjusting is done, jack rear wheels off ground and check for drag. Operate parking brake mechanism while watching external brake to determine if cable has stretched and is not closing band tightly on driveshaft drum. If there is too much slack here, tighten cable tension and check to see if band closes tightly. Should this prove ineffective, the band itself can be set closer to the drum by a band adjusting nut. Under no conditions should the clearance between band lining and drum be less than .015 to .020-in., measured by feeler guage at the band anchor point. Check by turning rear wheels by hand to detect any drag increase after adjustment has been made.

Chrysler cars were also equipped with a driveshaft brake that is just a mechanical version of the ordinary wheel brake. The first check for adjustment should be in the cable. If this does not prove effective, there is a star wheel adjuster for setting out the shoes just as on the wheel brakes. With the rear wheels jacked off the ground, set adjuster nut up until a slight drag is felt, then back off until the drag is eliminated. Do not overadjust either internal- or external-type driveshaft brakes, because sustained friction during driving can cause severe burning of all friction parts in the braking system.

POWER-ASSISTED BRAKES

The power-assisted brake systems generally used on passenger cars do not shorten the stopping distance of the automobile. They are designed to assist in applying pedal pressure to the hydraulic system, thereby reducing the pedal force

1. Cutaway of Worn Drum

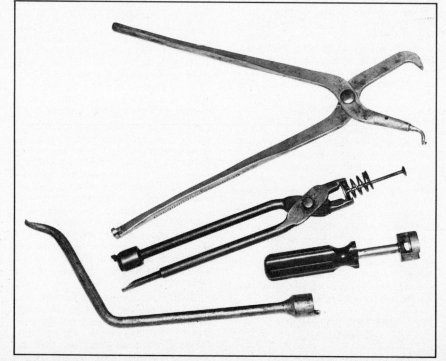

2. Brake Tools

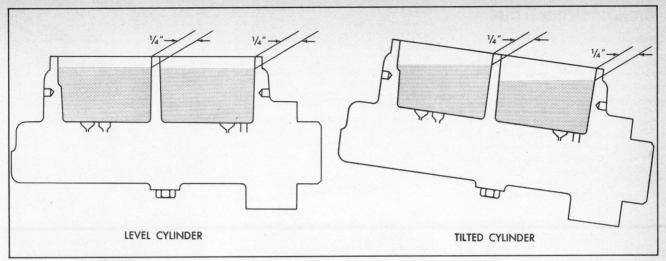

LEVEL CYLINDER   TILTED CYLINDER

3. Master Cylinder Reservoirs

1. This drum was so badly worn that it was necessary to completely back off the shoe adjustment in order to remove the drum from the car. Note ridge on the edge of the drum. Each make drum has maximum that it can safely be turned before it must be replaced with a new one. If turned too much, unit will overheat, warp, etc. Then you'll be in deep, deep trouble when your brakes fail at need.

2. Special brake tools make any such job a lot easier and quicker. These are a few of the tools used.

3. This illustration reveals the reservoirs in a pair of master cylinders, both filled to within ¼-in. of the top. Note the one that is tipped, or mounted at an angle, actually holds less brake fluid.

4. If the drums on a car show much wear at all they are probably grooved, therefore should be cut.

5. After being surfaced with a cutting tool, it is wise to have the surface ground with a grinding stone to remove traces of the cutting.

6. Special wrenches, such as brake bleeder wrenches, make this job easy. Angles are such that you can get to the fitting and loosen it.

7. When doing a brake job, make it complete by inspecting lines, too. This flexible line is cracked badly, and may burst under pressure and cause a severe accident.

4. Cutting a Drum

5. Grinding Cutting Marks

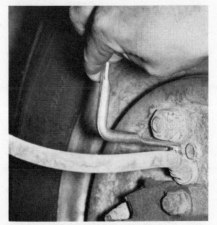

6. Brake Bleeder Tool

7. Inspecting Brake Line

normally required in a non-assisted system. Two basic types are used on passenger cars: 1) the Bendix/Moraine composite units composed of a vacuum-actuated power unit combined with a hydraulic master cylinder, and 2) the type used by Ford and Chrysler which uses a vacuum-operated power unit that applies assisting force to the brake pedal linked to the master cylinder. Both systems use engine intake manifold vacuum to operate them, but will operate with increased pedal pressure should the system fail or braking be necessary with the engine not running.

Power units are composed of three basic elements, all of which must function

to achieve assisted braking effort. These are: 1) vacuum chamber which provides the power as long as manifold vacuum is available; 2) the hydraulic master cylinder, necessary to transmit hydraulic force to the wheel cylinders; and 3) the control valve, which is operated by mechanical linkage to the brake pedal and triggers the vacuum force in proportion to the brake pedal pressure and travel distance.

Whether of the composite or isolated type, power units require much the same replacement of parts as do hydraulic systems in that every phase of their operation depends on good sealing and proper operation of the valves.

As outlined in the beginning of this chapter, follow the drive test procedure to determine if braking faults are in the hydraulic system or the power assist unit. Repairs of either the composite Bendix/Moraine or the auxiliary assist units are complicated and require a thorough knowledge of specialized repair procedures. It is best to effect repairs to power assists under the supervision of an expert, or replace the entire unit with a new or rebuilt one. However, before removing for repair, check all vacuum lines from engine manifold to the diaphragm housing, as any breaks or poor connections will hamper proper vacuum to atmospheric pressure balance and the

Brakes--Drum & Disc

unit will not operate as it should.

Pedal adjustment is also critical, especially if the proper ¼ to ⅜-in. freeplay in the pedal action has been reduced and the vacuum valving is not properly releasing. Pedal adjustments are incorporated in the linkage to the power units and are accessible from inside the car on suspended pedal systems. Before adjusting any pedal clearance, make sure the return spring is operating with sufficient force to return the pedal unassisted to its full-out position. If there is no return spring, be sure the pedal is free on its pivot.

CALIPER DISC BRAKES

These have been in growing use on American passenger cars for only the past few years, but race cars and many European passenger vehicles have used them as standard equipment for some time. In general, they are used only on the front wheels of American cars in conjunction with regular drum/shoes in the rear. The Corvette employs discs on all four wheels, and solves the parking brake problem by combining the rear disc with an internal expanding, mechanically operated shoe and drum system.

The operating principle is simple. Imagine a spinning iron disc taking the place of the conventional drum. An assembly known as a caliper, mounted to the wheel spindle and containing a system of hydraulic pistons opposing each other, pushes against the preshaped lining material known as pads or pucks. With the disc in between the opposing pads, stopping is effected much like squeezing the disc between thumb and finger, but with a great deal more pressure and area. Hydraulic pressure at the wheel pistons of caliper disc brakes is almost double that of conventional drum/shoe brakes. When used with drum-type rear brakes, a proportioning valve is installed in the rear hydraulic system to prevent rear wheel lock under braking conditions by allowing more hydraulic pressure on the front, and less on the rear.

Another unit used on disc brake systems is the metering valve. It is in the line to the front brakes. It holds back the hydraulic pressure on the front brakes until the pressure builds up a little, then it trips open and allows the front brakes to come on. The delayed application of the front brakes gives the rear shoes a chance to move out against the drums. The end result is that both front and rear brakes come on at the same time.

Check valves (for maintaining residual pressure in the system) are not used on disc brakes, only on drum brakes. With a disc/drum system, there will be a check valve in the line to the rear brakes (usually in the master cylinder outlet) but no check valve in the line to the front brakes.

Self-adjusting, and with visible indication of lining wear, caliper discs are rela-

tively easy to reline but require care and precision to rebuild. Unaffected by water, dust and dirt—since the close fitting pucks wipe as they are applied and water cannot be trapped on the spinning disc—they are sensitive to oil or hydraulic fluid the same as drum brakes. Passenger car disc systems do have a splash shield to divert dust-laden air and water as much as possible in an effort to reduce disc and lining wear caused by abrasives that might filter in between them.

RELINING DISC BRAKES

Before proceeding with lining replacement, siphon about ⅔ of the fluid from the master cylinder to prevent its overflowing as the caliper pistons are pushed back by the new thicker linings. Early GM 4-piston calipers can have their lining renewed without removing the caliper.

When inserting new linings, note the directional arrow on the steel backing of each one which indicates wheel rotation direction and provides for lining up the grain of the material in proper relation to the disc direction. The caliper pistons will have to be pushed back slightly with a thin smooth tool such as a putty knife to accommodate the new linings.

Budd caliper discs used on earlier Chrysler cars must be removed to replace the linings. This can be done without detaching the hydraulic line by removing the mounting bolts to the wheel spindle. A special tool is required that slides in between lining pads and piston insulator to hold them in position during removal. Then carefully slide the assembly off the disc, invert and remove the shoes one at a time. Replace with new linings, slide the assembly back on the disc, install the retainer and anti-rattle springs, tighten the mounting bolts and remove the special retaining clips. Apply medium pedal pressure while finishing the final tightening of caliper mounting bolts.

The Kelsey-Hayes discs, also used on earlier Chrysler Corp. and Ford Motor Co. cars, can be relined without removing the caliper assembly. They can be identified by an external hydraulic line that connects opposing piston assemblies. The lining material has a metal backing with tabs at each end and two small tell-tale detents. These detents create a scraping metal-to-metal noise against the disc, indicating that the linings need replacing. To replace, the splash shield and anti-rattle spring must be removed and the pistons pressed back into the cylinders by prying against the old lining with a thin smooth tool. It is a good idea to check the level of master cylinder fluid to guard against its overflowing during this operation.

With two pairs of pliers, grasp the tabs at each end of the lining pad and withdraw. Slide new pads into position with lining material facing the disc and the tabs seated firmly on the caliper. Replace splash shield and anti-rattle spring, then pump the pedal hard several times to advance the pistons and properly seat

1. Loose Lug Bolt

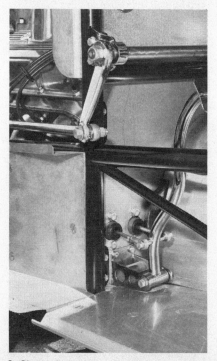

2. Stripped Wheel Nuts

3. Single Pedal, Dual Cylinders

linings. Check the master fluid level and bleed the system if the pedal is spongy.

CHECKING THE DISC

Most late-model cars have a single-piston floating caliper. The caliper can slide back and forth to center itself over the disc, which gives much better braking. In the old fixed caliper brakes, the slightest irregularity in the disc would knock the pistons back in their bores. When you stepped on the brake, you had to pump the pedal to get the pistons back out against the disc. With the floating caliper, it doesn't matter how wobbly the disc is. The caliper rides with the punch and gives a much better brake. All single-piston designs have to be removed from the mounting bracket in order to replace the lining.

The brake disc itself is machined to very precise dimensions and finish. Disc

1. Check the lug bolts in the hubs and axles. Loose bolts or ones with stripped threads can cause trouble by ruining your wheel.

2. Here's an example of how loose lug nuts can destroy a wheel. Latter wobbled badly, grinding away at the nuts. Wheels have come off many times due to loose nuts.

3. Another single pedal, dual master cylinder combination. This one is a floor-mount pedal, not swing-mount, but works the same.

4. If your car doesn't have the self-adjusting feature, then you must make future adjustments as the brakes wear, through the drum or through the backing plate.

5. This wheel cylinder broke on a car that was not involved in an accident, and driver narrowly avoiding becoming a statistic himself. Note that anchor pin stud broke first (this pin holds brake shoe springs), later causing wheel cylinder to separate.

6. This Safe Gage set features gages in 1/32-in. increments. They are .005-in. oversize; if any go into a bore of the size they are designed for, this means that bore is oversize by .005-in. or more and is therefore unsafe.

thickness is critical to proper lining clearance and piston travel, and the finish to proper coefficient of friction between pads and disc. Accuracy too, as to run-out or wobble, must be maintained as the calipers are solidly mounted to the spindle and must not be twisted by a warped disc. Run-out can be checked by removing the lining pads and clamping a dial indicator to the caliper. Tighten wheel bearing nut to remove all play from hub. Pick a smooth spot about 1 in. from the outer edge of disc for the indicator ball and turn it slowly. A total run out of .004-in. is maximum, and the disc must be replaced if it exceeds this because machining is not recommended.

Disc wear as to thickness also has limits and this can be checked with a micrometer. Overall wear that reduces the new thickness .035-in. for 1-in. discs, or .010-in. for 1¼-in. Corvette discs, indicates the need for disc replacement. Once a normal wear pattern has developed through use, minor scores in the disc surface have negligible effect on braking efficiency. As most discs are riveted to the hub assembly, replacement involves removing entire hub, drilling out rivets, and installing new disc. They do not have to be reriveted on GM cars as the wheel mounting studs provide necessary alignment. Be sure to secure with the wheel lug nuts when checking new disc for run-out.

CALIPER OVERHAUL

When relining caliper disc brakes, inspect inner cavity with pads removed. Any indication of moisture in the form of hydraulic fluid means that seals, pistons, or both, need replacing. To rebuild caliper piston assemblies, the entire caliper assembly must be removed.

Jack front wheels and secure with stands for safety. Remove and plug each main hydraulic line to save fluid. Remove pads, loosen caliper to spindle mounting nuts and bolts, remove and slide caliper off disc. Note location of any shims used to locate caliper.

Calipers are made in two halves, with the mating surfaces carefully machined for perfect fit. Before proceeding with any further disassembly, wash caliper thoroughly in alcohol or special brake

cleaning fluid prescribed for regular drum-brake wheel-cylinder service. Dry thoroughly and separate caliper halves by removing large cross-bolts. Note that the fluid passages where they cross from one side of caliper to the other are sealed with small O-rings. Remove these carefully and keep with other parts so that they are not forgotten on reassembly. Early Kelsey-Hayes calipers do not use internal crossovers, and the external tube must be removed before separating caliper halves. Do not bend excessively or reassembly will turn out to be quite difficult.

Removal of dust boots and seals is easier if the pistons are pushed back into their caliper half as far as they will go. Carefully pry off boot with thin screwdriver, remove pistons, seals and springs, and clean them all in alcohol or special fluid. Clean out bores and all fluid passages and dry before examining them for scoring or pits. Be careful with any tools when they are used to assist removal of any parts of the piston assembly to avoid puncturing seals and boots, or scratching cylinder walls or piston.

While all rubber parts should be cleaned and examined to determine the specific cause of piston leakage, it is a good idea to replace them all from the standard rebuilding kits available. Pistons and bores should be free of scores and pits. Minor ones can be removed by honing but not more than .020-in. can be removed for cleanup. Beyond that the caliper must be replaced. Bores that show very light scratches or corrosion can be cleaned with crocus cloth, a light abrasive material similar to jeweler's rouge.

With the caliper half clamped in well padded vise jaws to avoid exterior damage, begin assembly of springs, pistons, seals, and boots. Most of the assembly can be done by hand; use hydraulic fluid liberally to lubricate all parts. GM brakes require a special tool to compress piston seal and another for installing boot seal. Use of any other tools for this purpose will result in damage to rubber parts.

Kelsey-Hayes and Budd units, if held securely in a vise, can be hand-assembled with a small smooth screwdriver used carefully to work the lip of the boot into the groove provided around the bore diameter. Use no lubricant other than

4. Brake Adjustment

5. Broken Wheel Cylinder

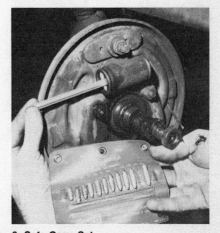

6. Safe Gage Set

Brakes--Drum & Disc

specification brake fluid as any solvent, grease or oil with a mineral base will damage the rubber parts and void all the work of the overhaul. Make sure that pistons and seals slide easily into cylinder bores, then place O-rings in cavities around fluid crossover passages and fit the caliper halves together. Make sure the mating surfaces are clean and free from nicks before installing cross-bolts and hex nuts. To insure proper pressure between caliper halves, a torque wrench is recommended for tightening assembly nuts. About 55 ft.lbs. for 7/16-in. bolts, and 155 ft.-lbs. for ½-in. will effect mating of caliper halves without damage or distortion. On caliper assemblies with external crossover, check the tube for cleanliness and freedom of fractures before carefully screwing coupling nuts to fittings.

Replace caliper assembly using a putty knife to keep pistons and boots from hanging up in edge of disc. Line up caliper to spindle mounting holes and secure with proper bolts and shims, if any. Check hydraulic line fitting for cleanliness and thread condition. Some systems use a small copper gasket in the male end of this connection which should be replaced to insure a good seal at this critical point. Install lining pads, retaining pins, anti-rattle springs, and splash shield.

Overhauling single-piston floating calipers is a lot easier than overhauling the older multiple piston jobs. To remove the caliper on AMC, Chrysler Corp., or GM cars, disconnect the brake hose, unscrew the two large guide pins, and the caliper will come right off. Ford has a similar construction, except that they use an anchor plate which comes off with the caliper. Don't forget to plug the brake hose after you disconnect it. If you don't, all your fluid will run out on the ground. Also, note the position of various clips, cotter keys, and springs on the caliper so you can get them back in the right places. Once you get the caliper off the car, the shoes will come out easily. The problem is in getting the piston out so you can install a new seal. Air pressure applied to the hole where you removed the brake line will take the piston out fast, so fast that you will probably break your hand if you are holding it in the wrong place. Auto parts stores have a tool made to grip the inside diameter of the piston and remove it, which is much safer than using air pressure. When installing the caliper, follow the instructions in the shop manual for your make and year of car. Some car makers recommend lubricating the bolts with silicone, but others say to have everything clean and use clear water as an assembly fluid. The object is to enable the caliper to slide on the guide pins so it can center itself over the disc. If you lose a mounting bolt or guide pin, get another one from your dealer. The use of ordinary bolts or pins is dangerous. It takes special hardware to withstand the tremendous forces applied to the caliper during braking.

DISC BRAKE BLEEDING

As with conventional drum brakes, the system must be bled if the hydraulic lines are disconnected or the wheel cylinders removed. Most service manuals recommend tightening the caliper to wheel spindle mounting bolts with brakes applied in order to center them properly. Before bleeding, make sure the mounting bolts line up with the holes and then tighten snugly only for bleeding procedure. After final bleeding, apply firm pedal pressure, back off mounting bolt nuts slightly, then torque to final tightness.

Road test at low speed with several good strong brake applications to seat the pads properly before taking the car out for normal driving. Be sure you have brakes before you take the car out.

Keep one thing in mind when working on brakes: They are probably the most important single factor in good vehicle control. Brakes seldom fail, but they can if you don't inspect them periodically for wear or leakage.

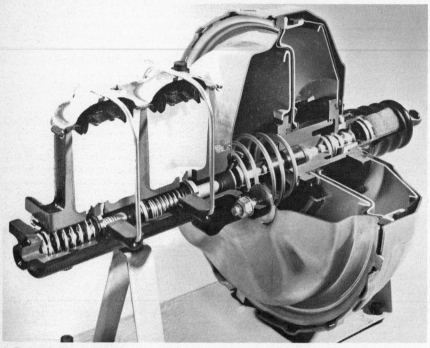

1. Power Brake Cutaway

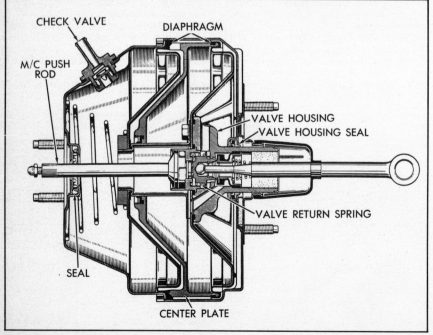

2. Power Unit Schematic

1. This example of the modern power brake unit is from a 1970 Olds. In cutaway form, revealed are the internal valves and dual cylinders.

2. While the pushrod on a non-power master cylinder can angle as it contacts piston, both pushrods in most power units must remain in straight line. Nut on the end of the master cylinder pushrod is for adjustments.

1. After removing the master cylinder from your car, pop the wire retaining spring loose (or remove fastener) so it can be drained.

2. All brake fluid should be drained out and disposed of. Never reuse any fluid once it has gone through lines or cylinders as it will be dirty.

3. Clamp cylinder in vise and remove retaining clip that holds primary piston and pushrod in place. Pull them and secondary piston out.

4. Note the sludge that had formed in master cylinder and gathered on secondary piston and return spring; this can cause brake failure.

5. If sludge collection has not damaged cylinder bore, it can be honed lightly to remove glaze and a master cylinder rebuild kit used.

6. Rinse cylinder with alcohol and check to make sure all passages are open and alcohol pours through freely, as illustrated in this view.

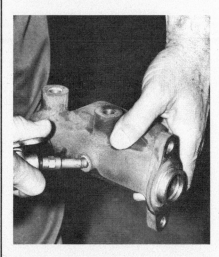

7. Use a high pressure air hose to remove all traces of alcohol from the cylinder and passages, along with any sediment that is still there.

8. Clamp cylinder in vise after pistons are installed. Fill with fluid and pump up by hand to bleed unit. Fluid should pour right out.

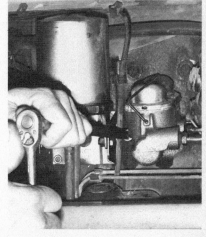

9. Now reinstall unit and hook up lines. Vanowen Brake, 11576 Vanowen St., No. Hollywood, Calif., performed operations shown on this page.

HOW-TO: Disc Brake Seal & Boot Replacement

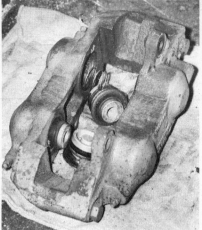

1. After removing cotter pin, then pull retaining pin from the caliper halves. Follow up by removing the brake shoes from the caliper assembly.

2. An air hose placed against the brake line entrance should pop the pistons free. Two came free here. If not, pry them with a screwdriver.

3. Caliper bolts, or retaining bolts, can be removed next. This will allow you to separate the two halves to get at the bores.

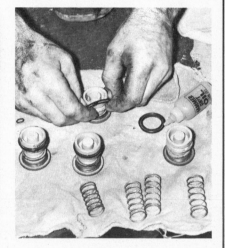

4. Clean, denatured alcohol is used to wash brake components. The bores are cleaned up with a super-fine hone within specifications.

5. Pull old seals and boots from the pistons, wash them carefully. Vanowen Brake & Wheel, North Hollywood, Calif., did this job.

6. Assemble boots on pistons, metal side out, seals with wiping edge (side that is cupped or grooved) out. Use plenty of assembly lube.

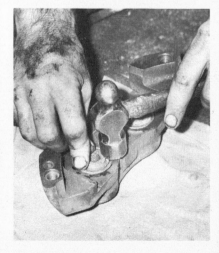

7. After washing in alcohol, parts are washed in water, then air dried. Bores are lubed, as are the seals and boots, then parts assembled.

8. If you haven't a seal installer, ease the wiping edge of the seals into the bore with a tiny screwdriver, moving it about the edge.

9. A small hammer is used to tap about the metal edge of boot, seating it in the bore. Now install shoes, retaining pin, cotter pin.

1. To reline disc brakes on a 1500 VW wagon, depress cross spring clip, drive upper pin loose with a punch, then remove same by hand.

2. Pin comes out easily. Note that one end of the pin is split. When reinserting the pins, be sure that the split end faces toward car.

3. Depress the cross spring clip again, then angle the clip up and over the bottom pin and out. The first may be hard, others easy.

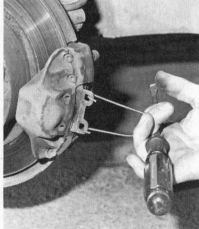

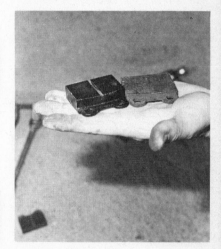

4. Now drive the lower pin free with a punch the same as the upper, and remove same. They are tight enough that you can't use a pair of pliers.

5. Make up a pad remover from a coat hanger. Make sure you don't remove the piston shield which has same kind of ends, but the pad itself.

6. The pad on the right has 45,000 miles on it and really shows the wear. For a few bucks and a few minutes, you'll have new brakes.

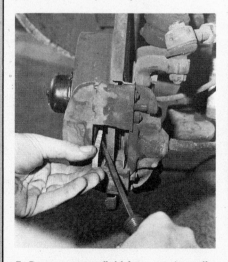

7. Remove some fluid from master cylinder, then use a piece of aluminum to return self-adjust piston back to original position. Install pads.

8. Once the self-adjust pistons are moved back, insert the new brake pads into the caliper, pushing them all the way into the housing.

9. Angle the new cross spring clip into position, install upper pin. Rotate disc to make sure it's free, then go ahead and install the lower pin.

HOW-TO: Wheel Cylinder Overhaul and Shoe Replacement

1. Remove outer wheel bearing, then replace nut so it can be used to pull seal from drum without damage. This step will work with roller bearings, but will ruin seal with ball bearings.

2. With the brake drum removed, the first operation towards rebuilding the brakes entails removing the secondary (rear) brake shoe return spring with brake tool.

3. Brake spring pliers are used at the bottom to remove brake shoe adjusting spring. Vanowen Brake, 11576 Vanowen St., No. Hollywood, Calif., performed these operations.

4. The primary (front) brake shoe spring and self-adjuster cable are removed, then the secondary shoe hold-down spring. Now the shoes can be removed from backing plate.

5. Remove wheel cylinder hold-down bolts. Bracket shown (arrow) keeps cylinder from coming apart should some part fail during operation. Car being repaired is a late Dodge.

6. Dust boots at each end of the wheel cylinder are removed, along with push rods and pistons. Now the wheel cylinder cups and cup expansion spring can be removed.

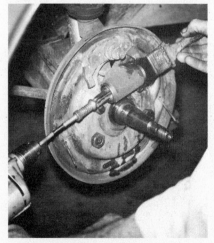

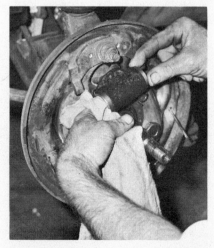

7. Physical evidence of sludge accumulation in one wheel cylinder after only 30,000 miles. Each wheel cylinder, the lines, and master cylinder are also contaminated.

8. Denatured alcohol is used with a fine hone in refinishing cylinders. Mike cylinder bores. Maximum overbore allowable is .003-in. After that, new wheel cylinders must be used.

9. The cylinder bore is wiped clean with a lintless cloth after honing and washing with alcohol. Alcohol cuts brake fluid, doesn't leave a residue, and doesn't harm the boots.

10. All internal cylinder parts are coated with an assembly lube, not brake fluid. Assembly lube will not mix with brake fluid, and will protect parts from any undue wear.

11. Assemble wheel cylinder pieces, then lube brake shoe backing plate platforms and the star adjuster screw with some Lubriplate. This is to reduce wear, help in adjusting.

12. The drum grinder used at Vanowen features both a cutting tool and fine grinding wheel. After removing .008-in. from this drum, note groove and low spot, illustrating drum wear.

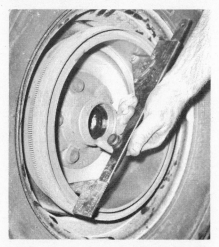

13. So, a second pass on the drum lathe was performed, removing all low spots and grooves. A drum gauge is used to mike inside of drum. If it measures too big, it must be replaced.

14. After cutting a groove in these new Bendix linings, to aid in cooling, shoes are arc ground so their radius coincides with that of the brake drum radius that has just been cut.

15. After blowing off all dust, the new rear shoe is slipped behind the wheel cylinder push rod and the shoe hold-down spring and clip are engaged in the brake backing plate.

16. The primary shoe and shoe-to-anchor spring is attached, then the secondary spring, cable guide and star adjusting wheel are replaced. Brake re-build job is nearly done.

17. Using your special brake spring pliers, install the lever return spring and hook the self-adjusting cable lever up with the secondary brake shoe. These pliers are a must.

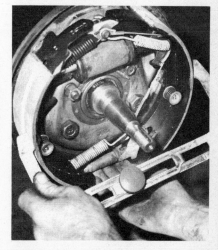

18. The brake adjustment gauge is first used to measure the drum I.D., then fit about shoes until they touch the gauge. Star adjuster is backed off three or four notches.

Suspension & Alignment

After so many years of automobile development it seems that by this time the suspension system should have reached a point where one basic design is admittedly the best, and everyone uses it. There is a certain amount of similarity in that most cars use independently suspended front wheels and a solid rear axle, but that's about the only statement you can make that applies to all American suspensions. The little engineering differences that separate one suspension from another are enough to change not only the ride and handling characteristics of the car, but also the way in which alignment is maintained.

Most of us, when considering alignment, think of tire wear, because this is the place where incorrect alignment shows up first. A unicycle doesn't have any problem with wheel alignment or tire wear because one wheel can go anywhere it wants to, but when you get four wheels tied together on an automobile, then they all have to work together. If not, one or more of them is going to be pushed slightly sideways as it rolls down the road, which scuffs rubber off the tread and can make a baldy out of a nobby in a few thousand miles. Alignment also affects the steering and handling of the car. If the wheels are not going down the road in a straight line, it's reasonable to assume that the car is not going to be as responsive as it should be when the driver tries to make it go where he points it.

ALIGNMENT BASICS

Factors involved in front-end alignment (and in some cases, rear-end alignment) are toe-in or toe-out, caster, camber and kingpin angle. Another factor in front-end alignment is known as "Ackermann," from the term Ackermann Principle in which the inside wheel of a car in a turn cuts a sharper angle so that each wheel follows the circumference of a correct circle, the inside wheel scribing a smaller circle than the outside wheel. This is a built-in effect and is a function of the relationship of the steering arms and drag link or the tie-rod and is not normally adjustable on any car.

Toe-in or toe-out describes the relationship of the front wheels to each other when the steering is in a straight-ahead position. In the average car there is a slight toe-in; in other words the front edges of the front wheels are closer together than the rear edges by roughly ⅛-in. It isn't much, but the effect is to keep all the steering linkage in tension, keeping any slop out of it in the straight-ahead driving position where no cornering forces are present to keep things

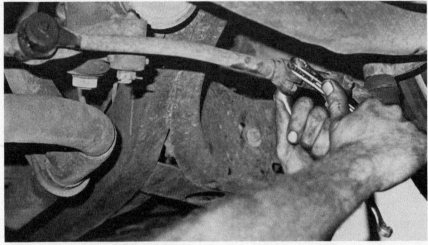

1. Wheel Alignment and Adjustment

taut. Toe-out is the opposite effect and is found, other than in a faulty system in the straight-ahead position, only in certain front-wheel-drive cars. Naturally, due to Ackermann effect, there is a toe-out in the turn position.

Caster is the effect formed by the inclination of the top of the kingpin or upper ball joint to the rear which imparts an action similar to a furniture caster in keeping the wheels headed in a straight line. You'll see this condition grossly exaggerated in a dragster or Bonneville-type straightaway record car. In the average passenger car this angle is 1° to 3° off a vertical line. On earlier cars with solid axles it is as much as 7°.

Camber, which is referred to as either negative or positive, is the inclination of the wheels inward or outward at the top; in other words, leaning into or away from the car. Earlier cars, meant for use on high-crowned roads, had quite a bit of positive camber (leaning out) to bring the tires perpendicular to the road surface. More recent cars have little or none, and some of the later high-performance cars have from 1° to 2° of negative camber to aid in cornering by offsetting the tendency of a tire to roll under in a turning situation.

Kingpin angle or kingpin inclination is now known as steering axis inclination because modern cars do not have kingpins. The steering axis is an imaginary line that intersects the centers of the ball joints. The angle that this imaginary line makes with the vertical is called the steering axis inclination. If kingpins were used, the steering axis would coincide with the axis of the kingpin itself. A theoretically perfect axis inclination would intersect with the road surface exactly at the center point of the tire's contact with the road. In that theoretically perfect condition the tire would merely

1. Most drivers pay little attention to wheel alignment until their tires are badly worn. Periodic adjustment checks are inexpensive when you compare them to the cost of premature tire wear.

2. Independent front suspensions are responsible for the demise of early drag link steering designs like No. 6. Note that with all the split tie-rod systems, toe adjustments must be made equally on each side to keep the steering wheel centered.

3. Without kingpin inclination, we have the condition on top which will pull the steering wheel right out of the driver's hands when he steps on the brakes. Note that when kingpin inclination line and tire and wheel center do not intersect at the road, the measurement they are apart is called the scrub radius.

4. Positive camber exists when top of tire is tilted away from the car, negative camber when the tire is tilted toward the car. Early-day cars had considerable camber to compensate for the high-crowned roads of the day.

5. The inside wheel has to turn more than the outside. If the wheelbase were longer, you would have to turn the front wheels more to get the same turning radius. The size of wheels and tires and the width of the frame limit how much the wheels can turn.

6. Most modern cars with independent front suspension use A-arms. Shims are used at the A-arm mounts to set front end alignment.

7. Removing the shim from one side of the upper control arm will give more positive caster.

8. Starting out with four shims on each side, we want to change the camber without changing caster.

STEERING CONTROL LINKAGE

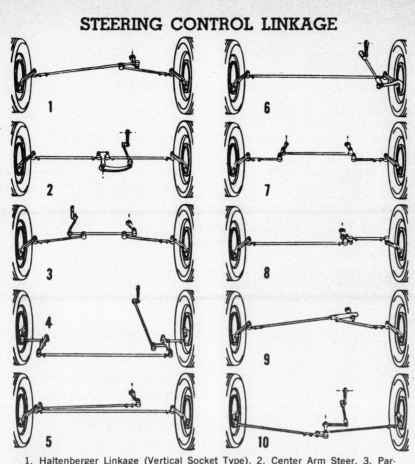

1. Haltenberger Linkage (Vertical Socket Type). 2. Center Arm Steer. 3. Parallelogram Linkage (Solid Center Link). 4. Parallelogram Linkage (Center Link Ahead of Axle). 5. Cross Steer. 6. Fore-Aft and Cross Steer. 7. Parallelogram Steer. 8. Long-Short Arm Linkage. 9. Haltenberger Linkage. 10. Haltenberger Linkage (Ahead of Axle).

2. Types of Steering Linkage

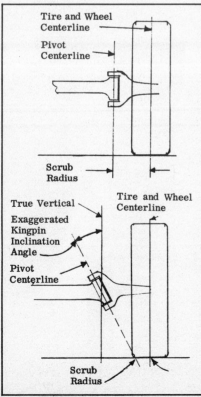

3. Scrub Radius

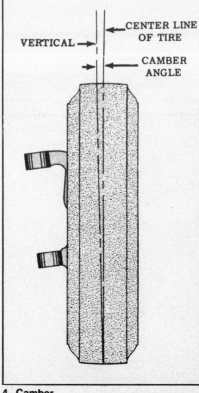

4. Camber

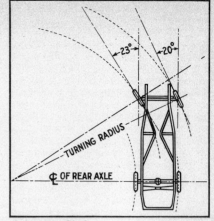

5. Turning Circle

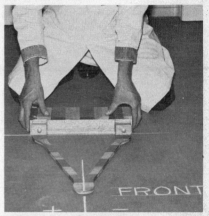

6. A-Arm Front Suspension

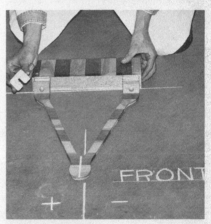

7. Positive Caster

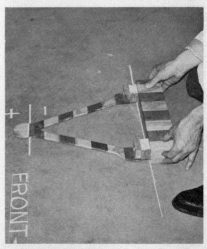

8. Changing Camber

Suspension & Alignment

pivot in place when the steering wheel was turned. In most cars the actual steering axis inclination is not that much. The imaginary line may intersect the road surface at the inner edge of the tire, or it may contact the road so far to the inside that it does not coincide with the tire's road contact area at all. If the steering axis were straight up and down, then the steering axis inclination would be zero and the wheel would be forced to rotate slightly every time that the steering wheel was turned. Front ends today are designed as a compromise between the theoretically perfect steering axis inclination and the perfectly vertical steering axis.

The actual measurement between the center of the tire's contact patch and the point where the steering axis hits the road surface is called the "scrub radius." An attempt is made to keep the scrub radius as small as possible when designing front ends so that steering and handling will not be affected too much.

Wheel offset has a big effect on how a car steers and handles because it changes the location of the tire's contact patch. If a wheel is offset to the inside more than stock, it moves the tire's contact patch to the inside so that it coincides with the steering axis. This would probably make it easier to steer the car when parking. If a wheel is installed that has less offset—moving the tire contact patch to the outside of the car for more scrub radius—steering effort would probably be increased. All of these things are figured out very carefully by the manufacturer when he designs the front end. When buying a wheel in a wrecking yard, you should not only look at the bolt circle and the fit on the hub, but also measure the offset. Just because the wheel will bolt onto the hub doesn't mean that it's the right one for the car.

TIRES TELL THE TALE

The first place to check for faulty suspension or alignment is the rubber on the front wheels. Discounting oddball wear that comes from under- or overinflation, check to see if the tires or one tire is worn more on one side than the other; if so, then toe-in of one or both is off. If it is only one that is off, it will show in steering on the road with a definite pull to one side or the other. If both are out of adjustment, tire wear and hard steering in either direction will occur. Tire cupping—an undulating, scalloped wear pattern—can be the result of poor shock absorbers, one wheel out of alignment, a bent spindle, or, what is more likely, a combination of these possibly complicated by loose-tie rod ends which can be caused by misalignment. As a matter of fact, misalignment can, in time, trigger a whole series of ailments and rapid wear. A car that is kept in alignment—with proper tires, good shock absorbers and periodic lubrication—is practically wearproof; but neglect one item and a chain reaction is inevitable.

CHECKING WORN PARTS

Before making any alignment checks

or adjustments other than the visual checks and road behavior tests noted above, a preliminary physical inspection must be made. It is absolutely of no use whatever to do any aligning on a system with worn or bent parts or with faulty or unequal-pressure tires.

Jack the front of the car up, one wheel at a time, so that the ball joints are under tension. If at all possible, use a jack stand in conjunction with the jack; even garage-type floor jacks can slip or lose pressure. Grab the upper and lower surfaces of the tire and shake, first vigorously and then gently. The first will give a clue as to whether there is play, and the second will help pinpoint it or show bearing play. A slight movement is all right, but any movement over about a 1/64-in. is too much. Watch or have someone watch to see if there is any

movement and where it is. The trouble may be in the bearing. In this case, remove the wheel and hub and check the bearing—it may be that a simple grease pack and retightening will do the job. If the race is burned or seems gravelly, replace it with a new one, and if you do it to one wheel, do it to both, since the other one will probably be about ready anyway.

Continue the inspection before doing any replacing or adjusting. Now, grasp the wheels and *gently* shake them from side to side to see if there is excessive play in the various linkages and rod ends. Clean and go over each of these as well as all steering linkages.

After you have checked all parts for wear or damage, replace those items that have been found to be functioning improperly.

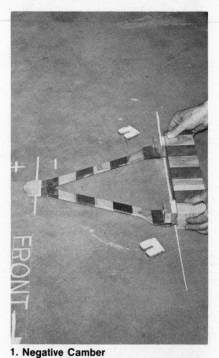

1. Negative Camber

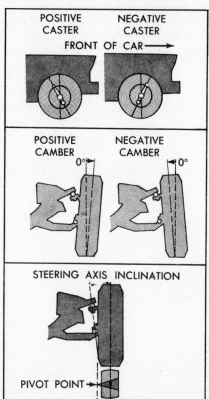

2. Eccentric Bolt

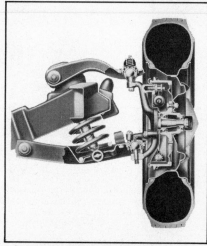

3. Independent Front Suspension

4. Wheel Alignment Factors

BEARINGS

Seldom, if ever, will you find a bearing that will make noise or give any indication that it is bad when you turn the wheel by hand with the car jacked up. A bad bearing will make noise when you're driving the car, but it can be very difficult to tell from which corner of the car the noise is coming. It all boils down to the dirty, time-consuming job of removing the bearings, cleaning them in solvent, and inspecting each ball or roller for pits or roughness. Just one rough roller or ball can sound like a square wheel, so you have to find it, unless you are rich enough to replace all the wheel bearings at once. A clue might be slightly increased play on one front wheel, but don't count on it.

Incidentally, to avoid confusing bearing play with ball joint wear, the car should be jacked up in the opposite way from that for checking the ball joints. In other words, if the spring is above the upper A-arm—as on Ford Motor Co. compacts, intermediates, and Thunderbird, American Motors products, and the Chevy II—the jack should be placed under the lower suspension arm. On those which have the spring *between* the suspension arms, or on cars with torsion bars, the jack should be placed under the crossmember. This keeps the ball joints in tension and allows only the movement at the bearing.

BALL JOINTS

For the next checks, reverse the jacking procedure outlined above; i.e., for cars with springs above the upper arms, jack from the frame or crossmember, and for those with springs between the arms, jack from the lower control arm. In each case use jack stands, since you are going to be doing some vigorous shaking and spending some time underneath the car.

With the car properly jacked for the type of springs involved, two checks are to be made, one for up-and-down play and another for side play. Up and down play, also known as axial or vertical play, should be checked with a long prybar under the wheel and against the ground so you can lift the wheel. Doing the job without a prybar requires a lot of muscle, which most of us don't have. You will find specifications in your factory shop manual for your car. If the specs aren't available, a general rule, suggested by Moog Industries, makers of ball joints and suspension parts, is that any vertical play over .050-in. is too much. However, this is a conservative estimate.

1. With four shims removed, there is a change in camber to the negative.

2. This Ford Maverick lower control arm uses an eccentric to align wheel. Just jack up the car, loosen the nut on the other end of the bolt, attach a socket and breaker bar, and the wheel will move laterally in and out as you turn the eccentric bolt.

3. This is the typical, Detroit-type independent front suspension setup. Two pivoting control arms, of unequal length, support the spindle and use a spring-over-shock between the lower A-arm and the frame rail to help in dampening the vertical travel.

4. You can see from these drawings how the factors in wheel alignment will affect handling and tire wear.

5. Condition of car, especially the springs, has a big effect on wheel alignment. When a car is lowered or raised, it throws alignment off.

6. Control arms are adjusted for front end alignment either by shims or mounting with eccentric bolts.

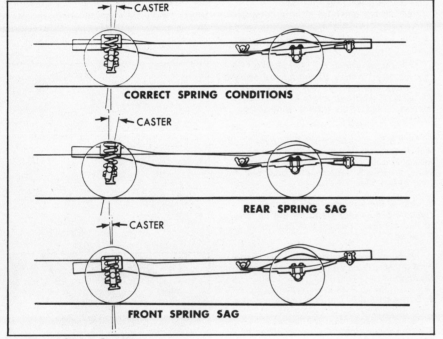

CASTER

CORRECT SPRING CONDITIONS

CASTER

REAR SPRING SAG

CASTER

FRONT SPRING SAG

5. Effect of Spring Condition

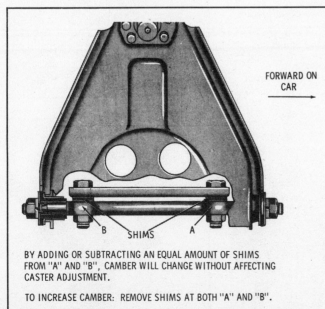

FORWARD ON CAR →

B   SHIMS   A

BY ADDING OR SUBTRACTING AN EQUAL AMOUNT OF SHIMS FROM "A" AND "B", CAMBER WILL CHANGE WITHOUT AFFECTING CASTER ADJUSTMENT.

TO INCREASE CAMBER: REMOVE SHIMS AT BOTH "A" AND "B".

TO DECREASE CAMBER: ADD SHIMS AT BOTH "A" AND "B".

TO DECREASE POSITIVE CASTER: ADD SHIM AT "A".

TO DECREASE NEGATIVE CASTER: REMOVE SHIM AT "A".

6. Shimming for Alignment

Suspension & Alignment

In some cases a brand new car will have more than the suggested maximum of .050-in.

In all cases, the joint to check is the load-carrying joint. If the spring or torsion bar pushes against the lower arm, then the lower joint is the one that carries the car weight. If the spring is on the upper arm, then the upper joint carries the load. The other joint just follows along and keeps the wheel pointed in the same direction as the car. Follower joints seldom wear out, but it's a good idea to change them whenever the load-carrying joint is changed.

Some manuals give a specification for side play, but it's difficult to check accurately. Side play, with much vigorous shaking, is what the con man shows you when he wants to sell you a set of unneeded ball joints. If your manual gives a side play spec, then by all means check it. Be sure you aren't picking up play in the follower joint or the steering linkage.

Specifics on replacing ball joints on every car are beyond the scope of this book, since the methods both of removal and of attachment vary considerably from car to car, even in a single manufacturer's line. However, certain general remarks are in order. A great number of cars have ball joints that are held to the control arm by a combination of rivets and bolts in varying combinations. When replacement becomes necessary, the bolts are removed in the normal way, and the rivets must be chiseled off. It is easier if the rivets are drilled first but avoid drilling through and enlarging the holes. The replacement unit will have special bolts included to take the place of the rivets and these, not ordinary bolts, must be used. On some Ford products and some GM cars the ball joints are pressed in, and it is inadvisable for these to be replaced anywhere but in a shop equipped with an arbor press to do the job. Some mechanics are real artists with a rivet gun, used as an impact hammer to force the joint into place when the weight of the car is on it. On Chrysler products the joints are threaded into the control arms, and you will need a special ¾-in. drive socket with at least a 3-ft. handle and lots of muscle. On all cars, getting the tapered ball joint stud out of the hole can really be a bear. Smacking the outside of the hole with a hammer may help, but only if you have tension on the stud. Wedges or screw-type pullers are available at some tool stores. If you can look over the shoulder of a local mechanic while he does a ball joint job, you'll be way ahead.

TIE-RODS AND DRAG LINKS

With the ball joints and bearings checked and found within tolerances or replaced, the next place to check is the tie-rods and links and their ends. Checking consists of visual inspection and manual moving of the linkage. It is best to have another person move the steering wheel while you hold a wheel against it, watching the action of the various links and ends. Some play is inevitable

and even desirable, but look for excessive slop that denotes obvious wear. Remember that this play is cumulative; a ¼-in. here and ⅛ there can add up to an impressive total that no amount of aligning will help—in fact aligning is downright futile with a front end that contains more than a minimum amount of excess play. It is also an excellent idea to wash down the linkage with solvent and dry it before trying to make your inspection of grime. It can hide defects and actually give a false "feel" at the various joints. Replace any worn rod ends, checking also for wobble or wear in the tapered holes into which they fit.

ALIGNMENT

Now that everything in the linkage and control departments has been checked and OK'd or repaired, the actual alignment process can be done, with a chance that it will stay that way.

First and foremost, let it be understood that except in dire need, caster and camber settings should not be attempted

1. This wedge-ended tool is called a "pickle fork," and is useful for removing ball joints and tie-rod ends. Sometimes it's difficult with ball joints to get a solid blow because of the rubber boot at top of ball joint.

2. "If it moves, grease it." This might well be your motto, for without proper lubrication at the ball joints and tie-rod ends, these components can wear out long before their time.

3. One of the best methods for the removal of ball joints and tie rod ends is to use a puller such as this tool made by Snap-On.

4. These control arm bushings are made by the JAMCO company and never need lubrication.

5. Some cars still use leaf springs at the rear. Tired springs can often be restored by separating the leaves, sanding them clean and using strips of grease-impregnated cheesecloth between the leaves of the spring. A recent trick is using strips of thin teflon between the leaves.

6. This schematic drawing shows the jack locations, maximum and minimum tolerances recommended by McQuay-Norris for most ball joint front ends.

without a front-end rack. Toe-in settings, on the other hand, are easily done with a minimum of equipment—and that can be homemade.

The first check for misalignment is whether or not the steering wheel is in the straight-ahead position when the car is moving straight ahead. If it is cocked to one side or the other, there is an excellent chance that toe-in is off. Assuming that the wheel has been properly installed in the first place (splined hub only; a keyed hub cannot be installed off-center), the off-center condition will probably be corrected in the alignment process.

By this time, if you have read the foregoing section, you will have noted the construction of the tie-rods and drag links. In most instances the systems will be of two types. In one system, the drag link from the pitman connects with an idler in the center from which relatively long steering links run to the steering arms at the front hub carriers. In the other, the pitman arm attaches to a center link and is matched by an idler arm on

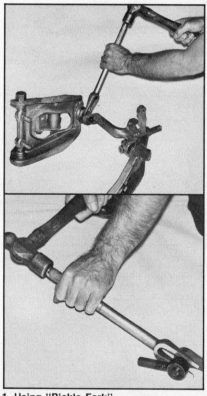

1. Using "Pickle Fork"

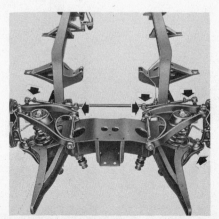

2. Front-End Lube Points

3. Snap-On Puller

the opposite (right) side of the same dimensions as the pitman arm. The center link connects these two arms, and from these arms run short links to each front steering arm on the hub carriers. A variation of this has a drag link from the pitman arm to a point on a heavy center link that connects a pair of idler arms, one at each side, each of which connects to the wheels via short links, as in the second system just described.

What is of importance here are the links that run from the steering arms *at the wheels*. It makes little or no difference whether their inboard ends attach to a center idler arm, to the pitman and matching idler, or to a pair of idlers. These links have ends that are threaded right-hand on one end and left-handed on the other so that once the clamps are loosened, they can be turned or twisted. This either lengthens or shortens them, depending on which way they are twisted, which in turn increases or decreases the toe-in relative to the centerline of the car at the wheel that is involved.

To find out how much or how little toe-in you have, raise the car and place axle stands under the lower A-arms as close to the wheels as possible. When you let the car down on the axle stands, the suspension must compress to its natural position, as if the wheels were on the ground, or as close to it as you can get. Next, use a piece of chalk to whiten

the center of the tread all around each tire. Then hold a nail firmly against a solid support such as a concrete block, and "scribe" a line in the chalk by spinning the wheel. Now, with the wheels in the straight ahead position, all you have to do is measure how far the lines are apart at the front and rear of the tires. Suppose you got 50 ins. at the front and 50⅛ ins. at the back. You have ⅛-in. toe-in, because the scribed lines are ⅛-in. closer at the front. To be more accurate, the measurements between the lines should be taken halfway between

the top and bottom of the tire. This is no problem in front, but when you move your tape measure in back, the frame gets in the way. What you need is a trammel bar. Get a piece of wood long enough to reach across both front tires, then make short extension pieces with a nail sticking out of each one so that the nail points can be put against each scribed line at the midpoint of the tire. By shifting the trammel bar from front to rear, you can easily see if the scribed lines are closer together at the front by the specified amount of toe-in. If they

4. JAMCO Bushings

5. Leaf Springs

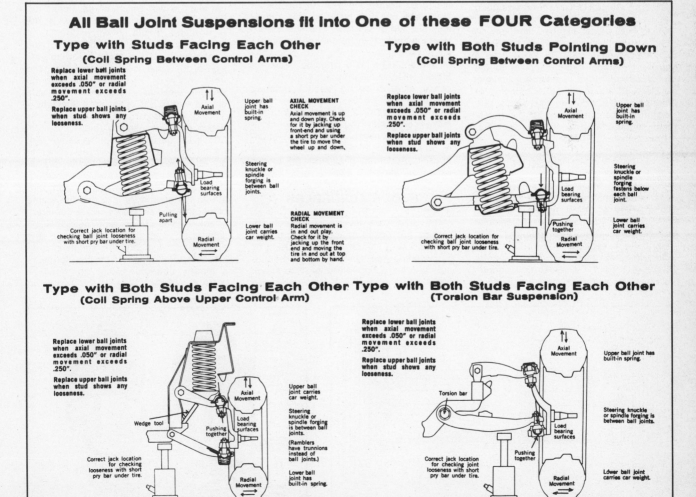

All Ball Joint Suspensions fit into One of these FOUR Categories

Type with Studs Facing Each Other
(Coil Spring Between Control Arms)

Replace lower ball joints when axial movement exceeds .050" or radial movement exceeds .250".

Replace upper ball joints when stud shows any looseness.

Axial Movement

Radial Movement

Upper ball joint has built-in spring.

AXIAL MOVEMENT CHECK
Axial movement is up and down play. Check for it by jacking up front-end and using a short pry bar under the tire to move the wheel up and down,

Steering knuckle or spindle forging is between ball joints.

Lower ball joint carries car weight.

RADIAL MOVEMENT CHECK
Radial movement is in and out play. Check for it by jacking up the front end and moving the tire in and out at top and bottom by hand.

Pulling apart

Correct jack location for checking ball joint looseness with short pry bar under tire.

Type with Both Studs Pointing Down
(Coil Spring Between Control Arms)

Replace lower ball joints when axial movement exceeds .050" or radial movement exceeds .250".

Replace upper ball joints when stud shows any looseness.

Axial Movement

Radial Movement

Upper ball joint has built-in spring.

Steering knuckle or spindle forging fastens below each ball joint.

Lower ball joint carries car weight.

Pushing together

Correct jack location for checking ball joint looseness with short pry bar under tire.

Type with Both Studs Facing Each Other
(Coil Spring Above Upper Control Arm)

Replace lower ball joints when axial movement exceeds .050" or radial movement exceeds .250".

Replace upper ball joints when stud shows any looseness.

Axial Movement

Radial Movement

Wedge tool

Pushing together

Load bearing surfaces

Upper ball joint carries car weight.

Steering knuckle or spindle forging is between ball joints.

(Ramblers have trunnions instead of ball joints.)

Lower ball joint has built-in spring.

Correct jack location for checking looseness with short pry bar under tire.

Type with Both Studs Facing Each Other
(Torsion Bar Suspension)

Replace lower ball joints when axial movement exceeds .050" or radial movement exceeds .250".

Replace upper ball joints when stud shows any looseness.

Torsion bar

Load bearing surfaces

Axial Movement

Radial Movement

Pushing together

Upper ball joint has built-in spring.

Steering knuckle or spindle forging is between ball joints.

Lower ball joint carries car weight.

Correct jack location for checking joint looseness with short pry bar under tire.

6. Ball Joint Suspensions

Suspension & Alignment

aren't, shorten or lengthen the rods until they are.

Now check the position of the steering wheel. If it is centered, you're in business and you can tighten the clamps. If not, lengthen one rod and shorten the other exactly the same amount until the wheel is centered at the straight-ahead position, which is to say the "high spot" in the pitman arm travel.

As mentioned, camber and caster setting are really jobs for shops equipped with front-end racks and the necessary special tools—items that aren't likely to be found in gas stations or neighborhood garages. However, it is worth the time to mention how these values are set into various front ends. Perhaps the most common method is by means of stacks of shims of several standard thicknesses placed in some instances between the cross-shaft of the upper control arm and its frame support.

In other cases, these shims are placed between the pivot bracket of the lower arm and the frame or bracket in the lower underbody. In certain Ford products such as early Fairlanes, '64 and later Fords and Lincolns, the whole upper control arm assembly is moved in or out in slotted holes to which the cross-shaft is bolted. This last requires a special tool and should not be attempted without it. In all recent Chrysler products, the upper arm attaching bolts are equipped with eccentric washers. Turning both equally will adjust camber, and turning one or the other will affect caster. Some late Chevys and early Ramblers have a similar eccentric system applied to the *lower* control arms. Caster adjustments to Corvairs are made by lengthening or shortening the front end tie struts running from the suspension to the frame, changing the tension on the lower end of the spindle.

REAR SUSPENSION

Systems on American cars have pretty well been stabilized in terms of design since the early 1950's. In fact, the basic layout is nearly as old as the automobile in one form. Generally speaking, with only three exceptions, they break down into two types: Longitudinal leaf springs with live ("solid") axle, or coil springs and live axle with appropriate locators.

The exceptions are the Corvette Stingray, '61-'63 Pontiac Tempest, and the Corvair, which have various forms of independent rear suspension systems. The Stingray system uses a transverse leaf spring, a lower control arm with forward locator links, and axle half-shafts with universal joints at each end. Early Corvairs use diagonal control arms with swing axles universally jointed at the inner ends only. Late models use a coil spring modification on the Stingray theme with fully independent axles U-jointed at both inner and outer ends. The third exception, the Pontiac system, is quite similar to that of the early Corvair. It was discontinued primarily due to the inability of the transaxle, which went with it, to take the torque of the various engines with which it came. Due to this transmission frailty, comparatively few of these cars are in current service on the road.

Taking the most common type of rear suspension first—the longitudinal leaf and live axle—prime points of wear, other than inside the axle itself, are few. They are almost all due to neglect, extended hard usage, or impact damage. So simple is the system that, properly assembled, there is very little that can go wrong in terms of alignment. In essence, the basic layout consists of two leaf springs, usually stacks of progressively shorter leaves and a master leaf (occasionally one single broad leaf), solidly anchored toward the front of the car at the frame rail and fastened via a movable shackle at the rear. The shackle allows longitudinal movement of the spring as it bends, but is rigid to sideways movement. The axle housing rests on blocks placed slightly forward of the center of each spring, each end being fastened solidly to, and above, the spring. In case of a multiple spring, the leaves are held together by what is known as a center bolt but which actually runs through directly under the axle housing. Additional clips keep the longer secondary leaves in line.

SHOCK ABSORBERS

On earlier cars, lever action shock absorbers are bolted to the frame rail and attached by a link to the axle housing or its mounting pad. On virtually all modern cars a direct-acting telescope-type shock absorber runs between the mounting pad

and either a bracket on the frame rail or the rear crossmember.

The main points of wear are generally the shock absorbers, the shackles and their bushings and pins, the front bushing and pin, and finally the leaves themselves on a car that has been neglected or overloaded so as either to bend the spring permanently, wear the ends of the leaves, or break one or more leaves.

Shock absorber wear is easy to detect and easy to fix in case of the tubular type. Press down vigorously on the corner of the car over the particular shock and then release quickly. If the car eases up to just above normal height and then returns gently to normal, the shock is working. If it continues to oscillate you have found a bad one and should replace it. Tubular shock absorbers are not refillable or repairable in service and must be replaced. To replace a shock absorber on the type of suspension under discussion is simply a matter of jacking the car up at the axle and unbolting the shock at the bottom stud or hanger and at the top and then removing it. Replacement is just as simple. Put the new unit in just as the old one was removed, being careful to use the new rubber bushings where noted.

REAR AXLE ALIGNMENT

Misalignment caused by axle displacement is easily detected by running the car over a wet patch of pavement followed by a dry section. The tracks of the rear wheels should be either directly on top or equidistantly inside those of the front wheels. If the track is off to one side or the other, or if a properly aligned front end must be turned slightly to go straight, the rear axle is off to one side or one end of it is misaligned respectively. Jack up the car and look at the lower spring clip plate directly under the axle. Check to see that the spring center bolt (or tie bolt) is in place in the center of the clip plate. If it is not, loosen the U-bolts and, with the spring supported, move the axle until the center bolt centers in the hole in the clip and the spring block. If the clips and bolts are centered, check to see if the axle is displaced sideways. This can be checked any number of ways but the simplest is to measure the distance from the spring to a clearly definable point on the axle housing on each side. If the two mea-

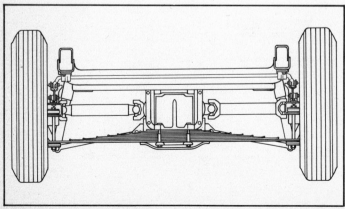

1. Corvette Rear Suspension

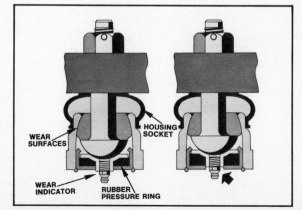

2. Ball Joint Wear Indicator

3. Moog Ball Joints

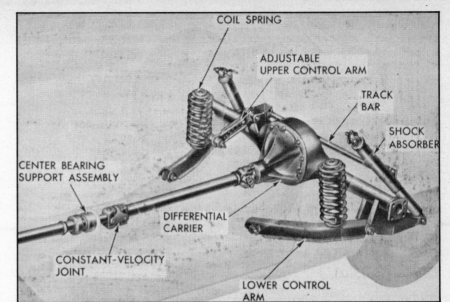

4. Typical Rear Suspension

COIL SPRING
ADJUSTABLE UPPER CONTROL ARM
TRACK BAR
SHOCK ABSORBER
CENTER BEARING SUPPORT ASSEMBLY
DIFFERENTIAL CARRIER
CONSTANT-VELOCITY JOINT
LOWER CONTROL ARM

5. Locking Turntables

6. Steering Wheel Clamp

7. Torquing Wheel Bearings

1. The '63 and later Corvette with independent rear suspension uses a transverse leaf spring reminiscent of the early (pre '49) Fords.

2. Oldsmobile ball joints are designed with a built-in wear indicator for 1973 models. As the joint wears in the housing socket, a rubber pressure ring expands and causes the wear indicator to recede into the housing. Replacement should be made when wear indicator has receded .050-in.

3. Some replacement ball joints, like this Moog unit, are adjustable to compensate for wear. If your old ball joint was held in by rivets, the replacement kit will have special bolts to replace the rivets.

4. Coil-sprung rear suspensions use upper and lower control arms to keep the rear end located and aligned. A track or sway bar is sometimes used.

5. When you pull into a front-end shop for an alignment, the first step the mechanic will take is to lock the turntables in place to protect the swivel bearings while you drive your car onto the rack.

6. The steering wheel (and often the brake pedal) is locked with a clamp like this to keep wheels from moving.

7. One of the first steps in a good alignment job should be adjustment of the front wheel bearings. Use of a torque wrench is not common, but it's the most accurate way to do the job.

surements are not equal, loosen the U-bolts on either end and bump the axle back into place—then tighten up the bolts.

To service shackles, bushing pins, and the spring itself, it is best to remove the spring entirely from the car. It is, strictly speaking, a relatively simple operation but one that requires care. A spring under tension is like a bomb with a lit fuse. If let loose under these conditions it can do a lot of damage, primarily to you.

LEAF SPRING SERVICE

To remove a leaf spring, raise the car and support it with axle stands under the frame, so that the axle hangs free. Then put your jack under the axle and raise it just enough to take the weight off the shackles. If you get the axle positioned just right, you should be able to unbolt the shackle studs and slide the shackles out easily. On some cars the shocks will not extend far enough to let the axle drop to where you want it. In other words, the shocks hold the axle up so that the springs are still under compression. It's easy to disconnect the shocks so you can let the axle down, but be careful of the flexible brake line. With the shocks disconnected you can easily let the axle down far enough to stretch the brake line, pull fittings loose, and generally ruin your brake system. If you have to, disconnect the line, and plan on

bleeding the brakes after you connect it up again.

With the shackles off, it's easy to take the nuts off the U-bolts and drag the spring out from under the car. Leave the axle right where it is, and you will find it a lot easier to get the spring back in.

Using a C-clamp or vise, hold the spring stack together near the center bolt and loosen the bolt, then slowly loosen the clamp or vise until the leaves are loose. Now you can check for broken or cracked leaves, worn anti-squeak inserts, and worn or distorted clips, shackle bolts, and bushings and replace where necessary. To reinstall, simply reverse the above procedure.

While on the subject of leaf springs, it might be wise to bring up the pre-1949 Ford products since there are still a goodly number of these in service either in standard or modified form—i.e., hot rods. In case you hadn't noticed, the pre-1949 Ford is suspended by means of one inverted semi-elliptic transverse spring at either end. The upper part of the spring bears against the front or rear crossmember and the ends ride on shackles at the outer ends of each axle. You don't just jack this one up at the spring and the frame, and lower the jack. If you try that, the doctor will be repairing you, instead of you repairing the car.

The sanitary way to remove a cross-spring is by means of a spring spreader. On these springs, the eyes at the ends

Suspension & Alignment

are rolled downward. A spring spreader is a device that is half thick-walled tube and half threader bar. A large nut rides on the threaded bar which slides into the tube. The ends of each half are beveled like blunt chisels. The nut is run down the bar to the tube, forcing the two halves apart. After inserting the chisel points into the rolled spring eyes, turn the nut which bears on the tube portion and forces the spring ends apart; this relieves the tension on the shackles which can then be removed safely. A less sanitary but effective way is to take a piece of heavy-wall pipe or tubing just a fraction of an inch longer than the distance between the spring eyes, and flatten the ends with the aid of a torch and hammer. By increasing the normal load on the spring as in a bump condition, you can force this bar into the eyes. When the load is removed the bar contains the tension. This is good only if all you want to do is get at the shackle bushings or remove the axle. Once you get out of the car with this system, the spring and bar had best stay together until the load has been replaced.

And don't do the job the way we saw it done by one young man who is alive today only because he's very lucky. He had the spring spreader in position and was trying to hammer the shackles off the end of the shackle studs without any support for the car itself. You must support the car frame firmly on stands. Then jack up the rear end to a point just before the jack starts to lift the frame of the car off the stands. Then you should put the spring spreader into position and put wooden blocks under the tires to support the rear end before removing the shackles. Any work under a car can be dangerous if you don't know what you're doing. When you're not sure, get some confident advice from somebody who has done the job before.

COIL SPRING REAR ENDS

Coil spring rear suspension systems have been used on Buicks literally since the year dot. Variations on this system were adopted by the General Motors compacts in 1961 for the small Buick, Olds, and Pontiac; the latter used an independent system for three years and then fell back into line with the others and used a live axle with locators.

The larger Buicks and the small Buick-Olds-Pontiac compacts differ significantly in detail in terms of the kind of locators used. Where the leaf spring rear suspension is self-locating due to the rigid fore-and-aft, side-to-side mounting action of the springs, coil springs by their very nature can be moved in any direction. Therefore a coil-mounted suspension system must be rigidly held in any direction but that in which it is supposed to move—i.e., up and down.

In the original Buick system, fore-and-aft location was by means of a torque tube, a large-diameter tube that surrounded the driveshaft and was solidly mounted to the differential housing. At the front it was attached by a large, hollow ball joint at the transmission; the ball housed the U-joint at that point. Side-to-side location was by a bar—attached to the axle housing at the right end and running to the frame on the left side—known variously as a track bar, Panhard

rod, and sway bar. This bar is still used on the large Buicks, but the torque tube is no longer with us. In place of the torque tube for longitudinal or fore-and-aft location, two diagonal lower control arms that also carry the springs are used in conjunction with a single upper control arm, adjustable for length and running from just to the right of the differential case to one of the transverse cross-members.

On the small B-O-P cars (except Tempest '61-'63) the action is somewhat simplified. Two larger control arms are pivoted from the frame ahead of the axle and connect to the lower side of the axle housing at the outer ends. These do the twofold duty of preventing "wrap up" and locating the axle along the longitudinal line.

The upper control arms provide both lateral and additional longitudinal support, and further control axle-twist. They run from the top of each side of the differential case forward and outward diagonally to the top of the rear crossmember. On both the large Buick and the B-O-P cars sealed, tubular, shock absorbers run from the outside rear of the axle housing diagonally inboard and forward to attaching points on the frame.

In no case do the service manuals give alignment or adjustment instructions on these rear ends. With all the locators properly in place the rear end is in align-

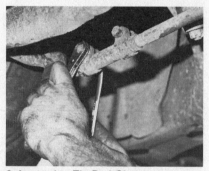

1. Hunter Alignment Arm   2. Loosening Tie Rod Clamp

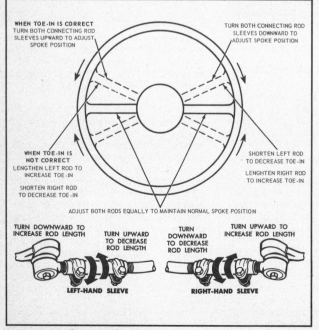

WHEN TOE-IN IS CORRECT
TURN BOTH CONNECTING ROD SLEEVES UPWARD TO ADJUST SPOKE POSITION

TURN BOTH CONNECTING ROD SLEEVES DOWNWARD TO ADJUST SPOKE POSITION

WHEN TOE-IN IS NOT CORRECT
LENGTHEN LEFT ROD TO INCREASE TOE-IN

SHORTEN RIGHT ROD TO DECREASE TOE-IN

SHORTEN LEFT ROD TO DECREASE TOE-IN

LENGHTEN RIGHT ROD TO INCREASE TOE-IN

ADJUST BOTH RODS EQUALLY TO MAINTAIN NORMAL SPOKE POSITION

TURN DOWNWARD TO INCREASE ROD LENGTH

TURN UPWARD TO DECREASE ROD LENGTH

TURN DOWNWARD TO DECREASE ROD LENGTH

TURN UPWARD TO INCREASE ROD LENGTH

LEFT-HAND SLEEVE   RIGHT-HAND SLEEVE

3. Centering Steering Wheel   4. Making Toe Adjustments

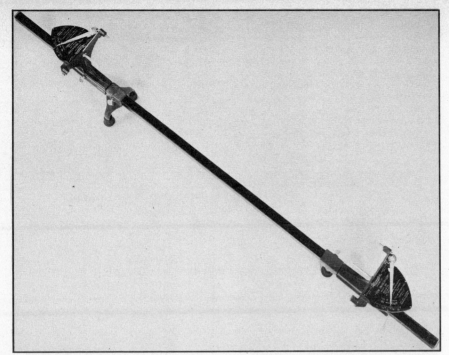

5. Bender Toe Indicator

1. There are several types and makes of alignment equipment, but a good job depends mainly on the way it's done rather than the equipment type. In most systems, an alignment arm is attached to the spindle. This is the alignment arm used in Hunter system.

2. Clamps on the tie-rods must be loosened to make toe adjustments. If you live in a very wet climate or if your front end hasn't been aligned in a long time, you may have to soak the tie-rod threads in penetrating oil for a few days and then go back to the shop for alignment.

3. When a car has two tie-rods, you can adjust either one, but this will also change your steering wheel's position. Check this guide for the way to correct placement of wheel.

4. Some alignment systems have wires running from the alignment arms on the wheels to a control panel with a monitor that shows the wheel alignment. This way is quicker and allows mechanic (who is watching monitor) to turn both tie-rods at once so as not to affect steering wheel position.

5. In the Bender system, this bar is used for setting the toe-in or toe-out. You can make toe adjustments at home by making a simple measuring bar and checking specs in a manual.

6. Large Ford products present a special problem when making camber changes. These tools make the task a great deal easier.

7. The tools are placed over the upper control arm shaft so that when the bolts that hold shaft in position are loosened, the control arm shaft will not slide around.

8. If it's necessary to change the camber on this Mustang, we go to a cam at the inner end of the lower control arm. Holding one side with a wrench while turning the other will make the camber change.

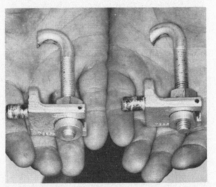

6. Special Ford Tools

7. Adjusting Ford Front End

8. Setting Camber on Mustang

ment and that's that. If it isn't in alignment, then one or more of these components has been bent or damaged and must be replaced.

On the B-O-P cars, virtually any or all of the various locators can be removed and replaced without removing the axle. All that need be done is to raise the frame to the point where the wheels are off the ground, then raise the axle housing until all strain is off either upper locator, at which point the various fastenings can be undone and the damaged unit removed. The lower locators require that the springs be removed, but here again the job is relatively easy if done with care. Raise and support the chassis so that the wheels are in the air, then raise the axle. Provide slack in the parking brake cable so that it will not be damaged and disconnect the shock absorbers at their lower ends. Remove the bolt and clamp that holds each spring at the lower end and then lower the axle. In replacing the springs, position the springs so that the larger end, which is also ground flat, is at the top of the upper spring seat. Raise the axle and connect the spring to it with the clamp and bolt. If you have found spring sag, there are several remedies: 1) Purchase new springs rated for your model; 2) There are shims available at B-O-P dealers; and 3) If you are looking for stiffer handling or plan on carrying heavy loads, there are special 200- and 500-lb. overload springs available for your car.

A word on coil springs and their removal in general is not out of place at this point. As with any kind of spring under tension, treat them as though they were live grenades. As outlined above, coil spring rear ends do not require any special tools or procedures, just care in assembly and disassembly so that they don't leap out under partial load when you're halfway into the job. Front end springs are a different breed of cat. First, in virtually all instances, the shock absorber rides inside the spring. Removing this leaves access from top to bottom through holes in either end or both, and while some manuals don't specifically recommend using special tools, a simple screw-type coil spring compressor is an especially useful object to have and to use both for simplicity and your own peace of mind. On cars with springs between the control arms it isn't necessary but is handy; on cars with the springs above the upper control arm it is a necessity. Among these are all the Ford products that use the system and certain of the American Motors products.

LATE CORVAIR OR CORVETTE

There are two types of rear end suspensions we haven't touched on as yet—the fully independent units of the '64 and later Corvair, and the Stingray Corvettes. Both are referred to as "4-link" systems using longitudinal torque arms, transverse strut rods and the axle half-shafts themselves. The torque arms also act as hub carriers. The major difference between these two is that the Corvette uses a single transverse leaf spring-stack mounted under the rear of the stationary center section, and the Corvair uses

Suspension & Alignment

coils mounted between the frame and the hub carrier ends of the torque arms.

These rear ends are hardly self-aligning, and both have definite camber and toe-in requirements. In no case is this a home garage or backyard type of job. About the only job that should be done on these cars outside of a properly equipped shop, as far as the rear end goes, is shock absorber replacement, which is done as on any other car. Springs also may be removed for renewal where there is a hydraulic floor jack and jack stand available.

In the case of the Corvette, the procedure is as follows: Raise the rear of the car and support it on jack stands placed just forward of the torque arm pivot points. Place the floor jack underneath the outer end of the spring at the link bolt. (Note: the Corvette spring, unlike the early Ford, does *not* have spring eyes. A link bolt through the torque arm holds it.) Raise the jack until the spring is nearly flat. Now wrap a chain of at least 1/4 or 5/16 size around the spring and the suspension crossmember above it, and secure it with a safe grab hook. *Do not use cable, rope or anything else for this purpose.* Cinch down a C-clamp inboard of the chain to keep it from slipping. Now lower the jack and remove the link bolt with the chain holding the spring. Raise the jack again and remove the chain and then slowly let off the jack and allow the spring to release fully. Repeat this process on the other end, and when both are released, remove the four bolts and spring pad under the differential case, then slide the spring out sideways. *Do not take any shortcuts!*

On the Corvair, things are a bit simpler. Raise the rear of the car and place on jack stands as with the Corvette, the stands placed at the pads forward of the torque arms. Place the jack under the torque arm at the hub carrier and raise it up to curb height. Release the rear strut rod at its differential carrier end and release the shock absorber at the bottom end where it attaches to the torque arm. Now slowly lower the jack, allowing the spring to extend to its full length. Remove the spring, spring retainer, and cushion from the frame. To replace it, reverse the above procedure, making sure that the spring is properly indexed into the cushion and seat.

ADJUSTABLE SHOCKS

There are three makes of shocks, or rather types within makes, that can be adjusted, rebuilt, or both. These are all, as far as the American market is concerned, replacement items.

Foremost among these is the justly famous Koni, made in Holland but marketed worldwide. Perhaps its first claim to fame is total, uncompromising quality. Every unit is matched internally to exact tolerances and all the valving and sealing is metallic; there is no plastic, leather or rubber on the piston whatever. Quality aside, what made it really well-known is the fact that it can be infinitely adjusted from just the soft side of firm to nearly rock hard when new. Except for com-

petition, very few are set hard to begin with. Tailored individually for the car involved in terms of control ratio, they are generally installed in their softer setting or just on the firm side and then as time goes on, they can be gradually adjusted to take up for wear or other conditions. Combined with the quality control, this feature makes them good for the lifetime of the car, which more than justifies their initially higher cost. Setting is accomplished on the Koni by disconnecting it

and collapsing the shock all the way, then turning the lower half gently until a slight click is felt. Turning one way hardens it and the other way softens it. The adjustment is done inside by a nut that progressively shuts off orifices in the central valving. Another point with the Koni is that it can be rebuilt and even tailored in action by any of the several distribution centers around the country.

Another of the adjustables is the Armstrong, which can be had in both lever

1. Adjusting Strut for Caster

2. Tubular Shock Absorber

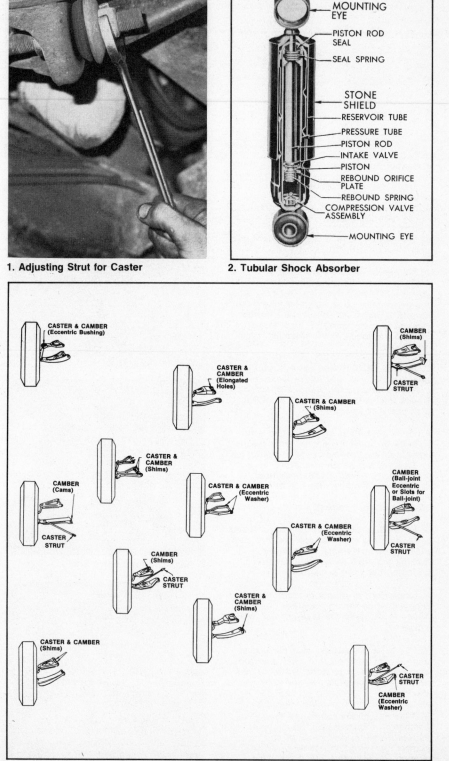

3. Front End Alignment Points

4. Positive Caster on Race Car

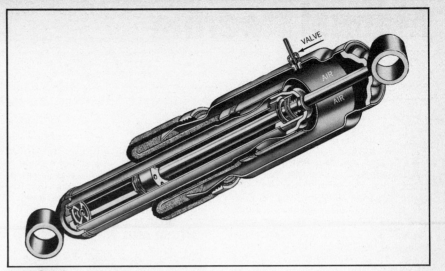

5. Air Shock

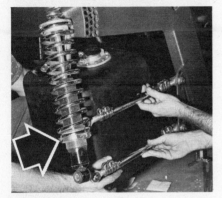

6. Coil/Shock

1. On cars with strut suspension, like this Mustang, the caster can be changed by lengthening or shortening the strut. Loosening one nut and then tightening the other will change the length of the strut.

2. The condition of your shocks has an effect on your handling. There's no sense in spending money for an alignment job if the shocks are shot. Most tubular shocks are of the design shown. Oil, moving through orifices, provides the dampening action.

3. This chart shows the various types of front ends and methods of alignment used on late model cars.

4. Drag racing cars are set up with several times the positive caster of a normal passenger car. By almost "forcing" the front wheels to go in a straight line, this makes the car handle better in straightline racing.

5. Air shocks are popular accessories today for vehicles that carry heavy loads, like campers and trucks. This cutaway shows how pumped-in air fills "bag" around top of shock, to either raise rear of car or provide extra load-carrying capacity.

6. Combination coil springs/shocks are used in many types of racing and street machines. This type features an adjustment (arrow) for changing the amount of spring tension.

7. Very popular with the street rod set are the independent rear ends like the Jaguar and Corvette. Note cam bolt used to set rear wheel alignment.

7. Street Rod Suspension

and tubular form. In the latter form, combined with an integral coil spring, it is used by most of the finest racing cars in the world. Its great advantage is that it can be adjusted from the outside while mounted on the car, a feature also available on a few models of Koni. There are two forms. One adjusts through 10 positions by means of a knob on the side of the shock tube or in the case of a shock meant to ride inside a front spring, by means of a slotted head in the same place that can be turned with a screwdriver. Another form adjusts from the dash through four positions by means of a remote control unit within the car.

A third adjustable is the Gabriel Adjust-O-Matic which is set, like the Koni, by detaching and collapsing the shock to engage a pawl inside the unit. The Gabriel, however, does not have the infinite adjustment of the Dutch shock but has three positions: soft, medium, and hard. Again the prime purpose is to take up for wear and age, but it can be used to make the car suitable for different road surfaces or high speeds. It is much more widely available than the other two and less expensive, which offsets its lesser range of capability.

There is also a so-called adjustable type of shock, the air-filled unit made by Delco for GM cars. This unit is optional as an overload item on most GM cars, especially station wagons and the El Camino pickup. Adjustment is by bleeding air off for softer settings and adding it from a filling station hose for harder settings. However, this is not a true shock

adjustment, but rather a helper spring, since the air does nothing to dampen the action, operating only on bumps.

CHASSIS MODIFICATIONS

The best advice we can give on chassis modifications is that if you don't really know what the modification is for and what it will actually do other than look different—then DON'T.

The chassis setting as it comes from the factory is a compromise meant to give the best ride with the best handling and ease of operation for everyday driving. A little of the ideal is given up in each area to produce a good balance. However, modifications can be and are made to produce a given effect for a given use—but there will always be a sacrifice in one or another area to produce the effect most desired.

A car modified for straight-line acceleration with soft shocks on the front, hard ones on the rear and the suspension raised to provide strong weight transfer to the rear wheels for traction will handle poorly on the street and will be unmanageable in highway cruising.

Conversely, a car set up to handle on a road course for sedan racing with its lowered suspension, stiff shocks front and rear set to a 50-50 or 60-40 ratio, and quick steering, will entail sacrifices in a harsh ride and stiff control at low speeds. Some high-performance factory cars are balanced in this direction for better road handling, however, and if you don't mind a slightly harsher ride they can feel very safe indeed. Low driveways and rutted country roads can be a pain, though.

In other words, don't depart from the factory chassis specs unless you know exactly what you want and can get the advice of an expert on what the effect of any given change will be. This even applies to the widespread practice of switching tires and wheels around either to get the wide look or for more traction. Done right, it's fine, but done without regard to the basic chassis geometry it can result in some funny steering conditions at least and very possibly ruined wheel bearings and even broken spindles. If you want to modify, do it—please do it right.

Manual Steering

Think back, if you can, to your first hot rod, not your first car, but the "soap box" racer you built from scrap wood and some "borrowed" baby carriage wheels. Steering was no problem. Right? You just made the 2 × 4 front axle pivot on a bolt at the front of the "frame" and steering was only a matter of putting your feet on the ends of the axles; or if you wanted to keep your feet in, you shortened your mother's clothesline and used the rope to steer. It seemed logical enough at the time; after all, didn't all those wagons in the cowboy movies steer something like that? Thankfully, steering gear design has progressed steadily since those wagons went out of favor and "the horseless contraption" was invented.

Faster cars required better handling for those poor roads. And when "balloon" tires and front-wheel brakes were introduced, steering became even harder, and led to the development of the steering box. Essentially, the driver steered a wheel at one end of a shaft, at the other end of which was a set of gears that transferred the motion, through arms and rods, to the wheels.

WORM AND SECTOR, WORM AND WHEEL DESIGN

The worm gear was, and still is, almost universal in its use on the steering column shaft. In the worm and wheel design, as the name implies, a toothed wheel meshed with the teeth on the worm, and a shaft connected this wheel with the pitman arm. The worm and sector was simply the same system, but instead of using a wheel, just a piece-of-pie portion of the wheel was used, since within the turning limits of the front wheels most of the wheel-gear could not be utilized.

Friction proved to be the common enemy of all steering designs, and these early types were no exceptions. Most of the loads in the box were concentrated on the gears at their mesh points, and constant lubrication was a necessary drawback. They also required frequent adjustment, and proper alignment became difficult at the mesh point because it was found that the gears wore unevenly. That is, they most often wore out in the straight-ahead position, where they received the most use.

Once the gears were worn, you could adjust them only so much before the gears would bind. The worm and wheel type did at least have the advantage that the wheel could be removed and reinstalled with fresh teeth at the mesh point.

ROSS STEERING

The introduction in 1923 of the Ross cam and lever steering gear was a solid step forward in terms of reduced friction

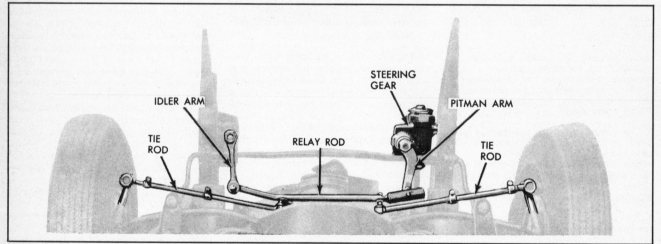

1. Modern Steering Linkage

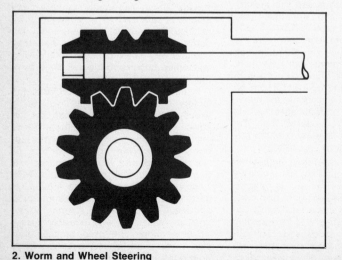

2. Worm and Wheel Steering

3. Worm and Sector Steering

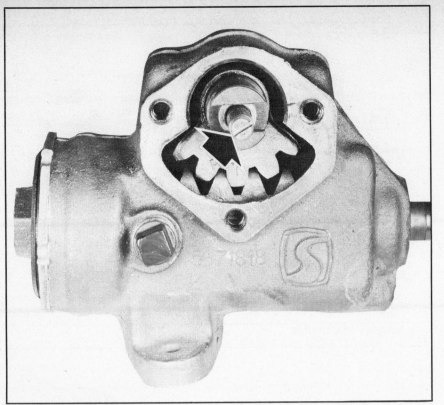

4. Saginaw Steering Box

1. For the last 20 years, American cars have used steering gear with split tie-rods rather than the older drag link system because of less lost motion and better geometry.

2. The worm and wheel was one of the first automotive steering designs. It proved to be inefficient, because all the friction was concentrated in the mesh area of the gears.

3. A variation of the worm and wheel was the worm and sector, which was cheaper and could be built as a more compact unit than its predecessor.

4. Here's a Saginaw worm and sector box with the side cover removed to expose the gears. Note the adjusting slot (arrow) for mesh load.

and wear. One long groove (the cam) spiralled around the end of the steering shaft and a lever on the pitman shaft had a peg on it that fit this groove. As the steering wheel was turned, the peg was forced to ride up or down the shaft in the groove, and this action turned the pitman shaft and arm.

The Ross steering was a very good compromise; it was *almost* irreversible. It was difficult for motion to be passed from the wheels back up through the steering wheel, but enough was felt at the wheel to give the driver that important "feel of the road" which gives him confidence in his control.

WORM AND ROLLER

Friction was still a factor to be reckoned with, though, as cars got heavier, tires got bigger and tire pressures became lower for a better ride. It wasn't just that it was becoming harder to steer the car, but friction and wear within the

gearbox was increasing again with these greater loads. So the people over at the Saginaw Steering Division of General Motors started making worm and roller steering in 1926 for the heavy Cadillacs. Basically, the worm on the steering shaft was hourglass-shaped; it was thicker at the ends than in the middle. Instead of a curved sector meshing with it, there was a roller, like a single large gear tooth, which was perpendicular to the steering shaft. It was mounted in roller bearings in a yoke that was part of the pitman arm shaft. These bearings took much of the load and the big roller distributed the wear more evenly. The design was so efficient that it is still used today.

RECIRCULATING-BALL STEERING GEAR

By far the most widely used steering gear today is the recirculating-ball type, introduced on the 1940 Cadillac. Another development by Saginaw, it was basically an improvement of the screw-and-nut design that had been around for many years. A long worm gear was on the bottom of the steering shaft, on which a large, coarse-threaded nut was fitted. The nut was inside a collar or sleeve that could slide back and forth inside the box, and this sleeve had teeth on one side that meshed with a sector gear on the pitman shaft. As the steering shaft was turned, the nut moved up and down the worm gear threads and pushed the sleeve up and down with it, so that the teeth on the sleeve moved the sector and turned the pitman arm.

Actually, it was a lot less complicated than it sounds, and had a number of features that have appealed to later engineers. One of the best features was its irreversibility; only enough road feel

came back through the steering for good control. And it considerably reduced the driver effort involved in steering even such "boat anchors" as the 16-cylinder Cadillacs on which it was used.

That old specter of friction is the area modern engineers have so improved in this basically good design, which is where the recirculating balls come in. The grooves in the worm and inside the nut were machined for ball bearings, so that, in a sense, the balls performed the function of threads and absorbed the steering gear loads and friction. As the car was steered to the right, the balls would circulate in one direction, and in the opposite direction during a left-hand turn. Two tubes connected four holes in the nut/sleeve unit so that the balls could circulate over and over again and distribute the wear evenly among all of them.

Friction was reduced so much that steering was made much easier without having to slow down the gear ratio, which as we have said results in more lock-to-lock turns for the driver. Except for power steering, this represents the furthest advancement of steering gear design thus far, at least on domestic cars.

RACK AND PINION STEERING

Across the Atlantic "river," car manufacturers through the years have utilized some of the same steering systems as we have, though the light weight and smaller size of their cars have permitted the use of generally faster steering ratios. Perhaps the most interesting and different design is the rack and pinion type, seldom found on American cars, but common on most foreign cars and many different kinds of race cars.

In this case the gear on the steering column is similar to the pinion gear in a differential—cut on an angle, and meshed with a steer bar (the rack) toothed on one side. The rack is mounted parallel to the front axle, and as the steering wheel is turned, it operates directly on the steering linkage without the use of a pitman arm or draglink. It's fast, simple to work on, and lightweight because it eliminates some of the usual linkage, which are the reasons it has been such a favorite on race cars and sports cars. Its one drawback is that it has very little inherent reversibility, but in a racing machine the driver isn't worried about comfort or parking ability and is usually interested in more feedback or road feel than the average driver. Rack and pinion steering is thus a natural. Its quick action has made it the standard system on most imported sports cars, which are small and light, and now that Detroit is moving back into the small car business, it's turning to rack and pinion for Pinto-size cars.

For passenger car installations, a compromise is often made by using a shock absorber-type damper on the linkage to reduce the reversibility. Since the damper's action is proportional to the amount of force put on it, small road shocks (desirable road feel) can be felt throughout the steering, but fast, hard, driver-jerking bumps are dampened.

Manual Steering

Currently, however, manual steering gears are made in three basic types. The Gemmer Worm and Roller Gear was used on Chrysler Corp. cars until the end of 1961, and on American Ramblers to date. General Motors passenger cars and Rambler, except American, use the Saginaw Recirculating-Ball type. Chrysler Corp. cars, 1962 and up, also have a recirculating-ball type, and so do Ford products. A seldom-used type is the Ross Cam and Lever, used on Jeep and pre-'61 Studebakers.

MAINTENANCE

In most cases, you won't have too many complaints about the steering gear on your car, mainly because modern steering systems are well designed and relatively trouble-free, and besides, you'll probably be spending all of your attention on good stuff like the engine and suspension. Taking care of your steering amounts to no more than checking periodically, keeping it full of grease or 90W oil, and making adjustments when necessary. Rarely will you ever want to *rebuild* a steering box. It would prove to be a pain in the bippy. Most guys are content to visit their friendly/unfriendly neighborhood junkyard for a replacement unit if something goes seriously wrong with it. You could buy a good used steering box and column for what it would cost to replace even one of the gears in your present box with a new factory unit. But, as with anything you buy used or from a wrecking yard, you have to be careful or you'll wind up spending good bucks for an item that later reveals itself to be pure mung.

If you do buy steering in a junkyard, check it over as carefully as you would select a used transmission, even to taking off the box cover and washing it with solvent so you can inspect the teeth on the gears. Inspect the box for defects, cracks, welds, etc., and if it's still in a car, try it out to see if it binds or has any play in it. If you're getting one from another model or year than your own car, see how many turns it is from lock to lock so you can determine if it has the ratio you want.

Before you start thinking about throwing out your steering and replacing it, check into it thoroughly, and even before attacking your steering box, try to determine first if it isn't something else which

1. The recirculating-ball steering mechanism was first used in 1940. It offered extremely low friction and is the most common type of manual box being used today by Detroit.

2. One of the most popular foreign car steering designs is the rack and pinion. Lacking irreversibility, it is often used with a steering damper. This is steering gear from Ford Pinto, one of few U.S. cars using it.

3. Part of the simplicity of the rack and pinion design is that it is connected directly to the tie-rods, so there is no need for idler arms or relay rods. This is Cricket.

1. Recirculating Ball Steering

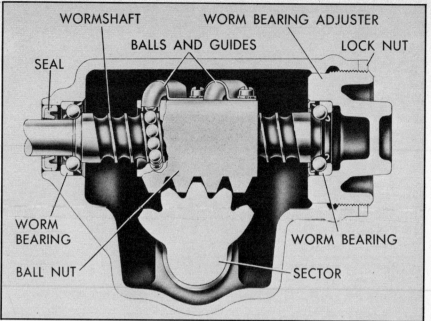

2. Pinto Rack and Pinion

3. Plymouth Cricket Steering

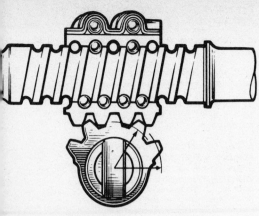

4. Variable-Ratio Steering gear

may be affecting the handling or steering. Things like poor shocks, unbalanced wheels, a misaligned front end, bad wheel bearings, or improper tire pressure can produce the same symptoms as defective steering gear.

If everything else checks out, then inspect your tie-rod ends and idler arms. As trouble-free and long lasting as these parts are, they wear out long before your steering box. Jack up the front end or put the car on a hoist and push up and down on the idler arm. If it's loose, pull it off and inspect it. Usually there is a bushing in the end that should be replaced. Tie-rod maintenance involves pushing up and down on the end of the tie-rod, checking for play just as with the idler arm. To remove them you may have to borrow a mechanic's "tuning fork" or

"pickle fork," which is a heavy steel bar forked at the end. It's machined at an angle, like a wedge, so that you can put the fork between the tie-rod end and the steering arm. Hitting the end of the bar with a hammer forces the stud of the tie-rod end out of its socket in the steering arm. Above all, the most important thing to remember when doing any work on the front suspension or steering is to *never* leave out the cotter pins. The life you save definitely will be your own.

GEMMER WORM AND ROLLER

The worm is an integral part of the steering shaft, being hourglass shape, or concave in the middle. It is supported at both ends by tapered roller bearings. The cross-shaft has a triple roller (instead of a sector gear) which fits into the teeth of the worm. An adjustment screw in the cover permits cross-shaft end-play adjustment which determines play between roller and worm. The pitman arm is fastened with a master spline

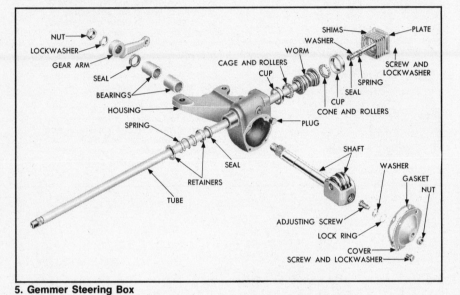

5. Gemmer Steering Box

4. The Dodge Colt, another mini-car using quick steering, has a variable ratio (15.58-18.18) achieved by a specially contoured worm gear. It uses recirculating balls to attain low friction during operation.

5. This exploded view of Gemmer box shows use of shims to adjust worm gear in the housing. You'll find a box like this on many older cars, but most had only bushings, no needle bearings, on cross-shaft.

6. The Gemmer worm and roller design was used by Chrysler for many years. Cutaway drawing shows construction of box, mast jacket and shift tube.

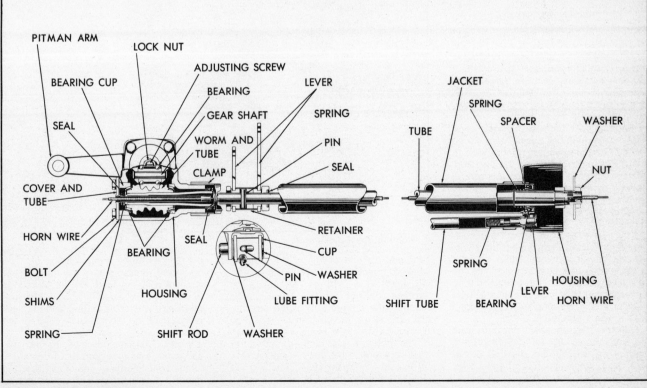

6. Chrysler Worm and Roller

Manual Steering

to the roller shaft by means of a large end nut.

Worm bearing adjustment: If adjustment is necessary, first disconnect the steering linkage from the pitman arm. To eliminate end-play in the steering shaft, loosen the four end cover plate screws, then loosen the cover plate and separate the shims with a knife (be careful not to damage the shims). Remove one shim at a time, retighten the screws, and check for end-play by turning the steering wheel full right and left. Repeat this procedure until there is no end-play and no noticeable tightness in the wheel movement to full right and left. Retighten all four screws. Then check bearing pre-load with a spring scale on the rim of the steering wheel. If the pull is less than 1½ lbs., remove another shim and repeat operation. If the pull is more than 1½ lbs., add shims to decrease pre-load until satisfactory. Be sure all screws are tight when testing with the spring scale.

Cross-shaft adjustment: Loosen the cross-shaft adjusting screw locknut in the cover. With the steering wheel in center position, tighten the adjustment screw slightly. Check amount of end-play by grasping the pitman arm. When end-play has been removed, use spring scale again on the steering wheel rim; if there is more than a 1-lb. pull above the first scale reading, loosen the adjustment screw slightly. **Caution:** *Do not overtighten.* The steering wheel should turn freely from one extreme to the other without binding or stiffness. When satisfied, tighten lock nut on adjusting screw. Recheck with scale.

Then fill the steering wheel box with proper lubricant. Reconnect the pitman arm to steering linkage, and recheck front wheel toe-in; adjust if necessary.

RECIRCULATING-BALL ADJUSTMENTS

For the late-model crowd, here's the "skinny" on adjusting the recirculating-ball steering. Here you have only two adjustments to make for end-play on each of the shafts. You won't have to worry about worm/nut mesh because the use of the steel balls between the teeth eliminates wear in most cases. Jacking up the car and disconnecting the pitman arm from the linkage is still the first step. Remember, when working on this type of steering system when the linkage is off, don't turn the steering wheel *hard* over to either extreme or you may damage the steel balls. If you suspect that the car may have been in a front-end collision at one time, then loosen the steering column support mount that is under or behind the dashboard to eliminate the possibility of a misaligned shaft during the adjustments. If your car has flexible U-joints in the steering shaft, you don't have to worry about this.

With the steering about one turn from the full left or full right, back off the locknut on the pitman shaft (opposite side of box from pitman arm) and loosen the adjuster a few turns counterclockwise to take the mesh load off the gears.

1. Removing Steering Wheel

2. Using Puller on Pitman Arm

1. The horn button ring can usually be removed by taking a few screws from the backside of the steering wheel. Then a puller like this is used to remove the wheel once the large shaft nut is taken off.

2. A gear puller is required to get Pitman arm off splined shaft of the steering box. The same type of tool is also useful for pulling tie-rod ends from spindle arms with no damage to the tie-rod ends.

3. The typical late-model steering box has a filler plug and only two adjustments, for bearing preload and end-play. Wormshaft bearing nuts may be at the top or bottom of the box, depending on the make of car.

4. On some late-model boxes, there are two different holes for filling and checking the lubricant level. A shop manual will tell you which is which on your car and also what type of lubrication should be used.

5. If you remove the steering box from the frame, make some alignment marks on the box and shaft so they can be reinstalled properly later.

6. You won't have a large enough wrench to loosen the worm bearing adjuster locknut, but a drift pin and a few hammer taps will do it. This job is a lot easier in a vise than on the car in cramped quarters.

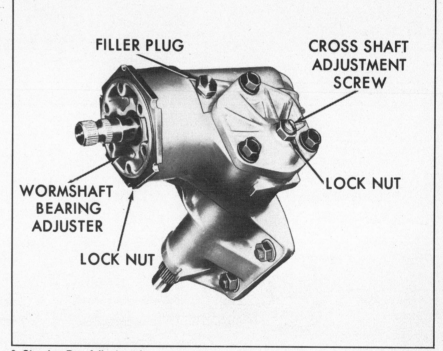

FILLER PLUG

CROSS SHAFT ADJUSTMENT SCREW

LOCK NUT

WORMSHAFT BEARING ADJUSTER

LOCK NUT

3. Steering Box Adjustments

Now pull up and down on the steering wheel to check for end-play in the steering shaft. Play can be taken out by another locknut/adjuster combination found at the bottom end of the steering box. The large locknut can be loosened by tapping it with a hammer and punch in the notches provided, if you don't have a wrench that big. Always check for lost motion again after tightening the locknut following an adjustment.

Now you can adjust the end-play in

the pitman shaft and at the same time take care of lash where the sector gear meshes with the teeth on the underside of the ball-nut mechanism. Since the gears are cut at an angle, end-play adjustment of the pitman shaft controls the mesh between them, too. Turning the adjuster *clockwise* will take up the lash, but make sure you don't overtighten it. These adjustments of late-model steering gears will only rarely be needed, but by all rights they should be made with the use of a pounds-pressure gauge on the steering wheel to measure drag or bind. Assuming that you don't have such a gauge, though, you can do it yourself as outlined above, or have it done at your dealer's garage.

Lubrication for the steering box (about SAE 90W) can be purchased at most parts stores or you can have it put in at a garage, since you don't need very much. Some steering boxes use chassis grease. If there is no filler plug on the box, or if it has a grease-gun-type lube fitting, it probably should have chassis grease. Using 90W in a box designed for chassis grease will result in a big mess because the 90W will probably leak out profusely.

STEERING WHEEL REMOVAL

The removal of the horn sounding ring or button can sometimes be more difficult and perplexing than the removal of the steering wheel. One of the cardinal rules of the good mechanic is: *Never use force to remove units or parts, unless you know how*. Forcing in the wrong place can lead to damage or breakage, and can cost embarrassment, time, and money.

To remove the horn switch or steering wheel, first disconnect the battery to prevent the horn from sounding. *In all cases a wheel puller should be used to remove the steering wheel*. Before removing the wheel, make a scribe mark on the end of the steering wheel shaft and on the wheel hub, so the wheel can be reinstalled correctly. Some cars have a blind spline for this purpose.

REMOVING THE STEERING BOX AND COLUMN

If all of the above adjustments have failed to correct any problems you suspect are coming from the box, then you haven't much choice but to replace the unit. It may look like it's going to be a beast of a job (it really isn't), but keep telling yourself that you need the exercise, or consider it as a challenge. Naturally, you first have to take that steering wheel off, and for this you're going to need a steering wheel puller or gear puller because it's on there pretty tight. You'll need it to pull the pitman arm from its shaft for the same reason.

Before starting, determine if the gear and column can be removed from the top—by raising it up through the dash over the driver's seat—or by dropping it down through the floor or dash, beside the engine and out from below the car. If necessary to drop it out through the bottom, arrangements must be made to jack up the front end of the car to permit the removal of the gear and also the column assembly.

Once the removal route has been determined, here are the steps you should follow:

1. Place protective cover over the front seat.
2. Disconnect battery cables.
3. Disconnect wires at bottom of the steering column, one at a time and tag each wire carefully.
4. Disconnect steering linkage from pitman arm.
5. Remove jacket tube clamps at steering gear housing (if any).
6. Disengage steering shaft flange from flexible housing. Note: Some late cars have a flex connection between gear shaft and steering wheel shaft. This will make it unnecessary to disturb the steering column and wheel.
7. Remove support clamp at instrument panel.
8. Remove horn and signal wires from steering column below instrument panel.
9. Remove horn ring and steering wheel—a wheel puller is needed.
10. Remove dust shield at firewall.
11. Remove floor opening panel (if any exist).
12. If car has manual shift lever on steering column, disconnect gear shift rods that are at the bottom of the steering column.
13. Disconnect neutral safety switch wire at bottom of column and tag it.
14. Unfasten steering gear from the frame (attached with three or four bolts).
15. If car has automatic transmission, disconnect gear indicator from the dash dial.

After disconnecting the electrical and shift linkage connections from the mast jacket—which is the column or tube covering the steering shaft—you can unbolt the box from the frame, the mast jacket from the dash bracket, and pull the mast jacket into the inside of the car and off. The shift arms on it can be worked through the flexible sealing around the steering column at the firewall. Now the box itself and the steering shaft can be removed from the frame.

Because safety is so important, the collapsible steering column has become a standard item on new cars. Some have a steel mesh section in the middle that folds up in a crash, while later versions utilize two sections held together with plastic pins that shear under impact, telescoping the two sections. When working with such a column, be careful not to collapse it by accident (no pun intended). Don't yank on it too hard, and don't use a hammer on the shaft to loosen steering wheel when removing it. ◆

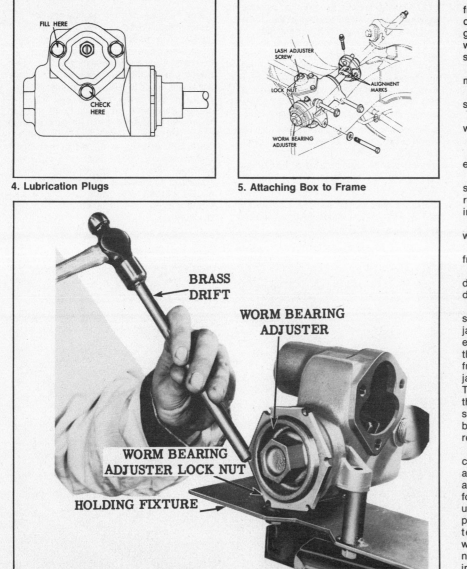

4. Lubrication Plugs

5. Attaching Box to Frame

6. Loosening Adjuster Locknut

Power Steering

As the modern automobile has grown longer, heavier and more complex, it has also become more and more difficult to maneuver in and out of city traffic. Even high-speed freeway driving can quickly become tiring. To reduce driver fatigue, make parking more manageable, and attract the lady of the house to their particular products, auto manufacturers have increasingly equipped their cars with power steering, either as standard equipment or as an optional (and often advisable) extra.

Power steering includes two basic units: the hydraulic oil pump and the steering unit. Mounted at the front, the hydraulic pump is belt driven by the engine and supplies oil pressure as needed to the steering unit. On some earlier models of the mid-1950 period, and the current Ford-Lincoln-Mercury line, the power steering unit is an "assist" or linkage type and can be replaced without removing the entire steering assembly. On others the unit is coaxial (Chrysler) or otherwise an integral part of the gearbox.

POWER STEERING HYDRAULIC PUMPS

All power steering pumps are constant-displacement type, delivering from 650 to 1300 lbs. pressure, depending upon the type and make of the system and the car. Special power steering fluid or Type "A" automatic transmission fluid is used. This fluid is stored in a reservoir attached to the pump with a filter in the reservoir to prevent foreign matter from entering the system. The pressure relief valve located in the pump prevents the fluid pressure from exceeding the predetermined maximum pressure of the system. Flexible hoses carry the fluid to the control valve of the steering unit. The smallest or high-pressure hose carries the fluid to the control valve of the steering unit. The larger of the two hoses is the return, or low-pressure hose. A flow control valve is combined with the pressure relief valve located inside the pump.

When the fluid circulation reaches about 2 gals. per minute, the flow control valve is forced to open a passage between the inlet and outlet sides of the pump, and all excess oil is sent back to the intake side of the pump and recirculates through the pump. When oil pressure exceeds the fixed pressure limit, the relief valve opens and allows fluid to flow back to the inlet side and recirculate in the pump without raising the pressure in the rest of the system.

There are five types of pumps in use: vane, rotor, roller, sleeve, and slipper. Detailed information for the pump concerned can be found in the shop service manual of the particular car make and model.

Before any major service operations are started, the following items should be checked and corrected.

FLUID LEVEL

Check level at regular intervals. Wipe the cover before opening to prevent dirt getting into the system. If there is no other specific filling instruction indicated, maintain fluid level 1 in. below the top. If fluid is very low, check system for leaks. If only a small amount of fluid is needed, automatic transmission fluid can be used. When using larger amounts or changing fluid it is advisable to use special power steering fluid. Oil should be at operating temperature, wheels in a straight-ahead position, and the engine stopped when you check or add power steering fluid.

BELT TENSION

Belt tension should be maintained to factory specifications with a belt-tension gauge. The specifications vary, so you must check the specs in your manual. A belt that is too loose will result in reduced pump output, while one that is too tight will wear out the bearings in the pump. If you don't have a belt tension gauge, and can't get one, a good rule of thumb is to tighten the belt just to the point where it doesn't slip and squeal when the steering is turned to full lock. Don't ever try this with a worn-out belt, however. Such a belt would probably squeal at full lock no matter how tight it is. Be careful with your pry bar when tightening the belt. It is easy to damage the pump.

Check the belt for evidence of age

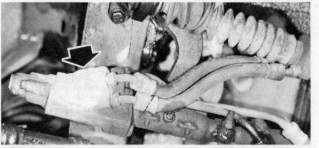

2. Ford Linkage Power Steering

1. Eaton Power Steering Pump

3. Integral Power Steering

1. *Several American Motors cars use an Eaton pump. This is what it looks like with the reservoir, pulley, and brackets removed. It can be purchased in this form for about $65, which is more than a stiff jolt in the wallet.*

2. *Ford uses linkage-type power steering. The housing indicated by the arrow has several seals inside that are usually the cause of most leaks. The hoses all screw in and can be replaced easily.*

3. *Most makes (other than Ford) use a power steering unit that is built into the gearbox. The hoses connect directly to the box.*

4. *Before removing the power steering pump V-belt, detach all connections.*

5. *You'll need an open-end wrench for this one. When replacing the pump, be sure all fittings are on the snug side.*

6. *Loosen the pump bracket and slip the V-belt off the pulley. Some mechanics prefer to remove the bracket attached to the pump; others prefer to leave it in place, removing the pump only.*

7. *Place the pump against a solid object like this vise and break cover seal by tapping with a mallet.*

8. *With the pump secured in the vise, remove and replace the O-ring seal. If this doesn't stop a pump leak, you'll probably have to buy another unit for best results.*

and wear. Frayed edges, separation of the layers of the fabric (look at the side of the belt), and cracks on the inside of the belt indicate age and brittleness. The application of a good belt dressing will reduce slipping and noise.

POWER STEERING CHECKS

The steering gear, linkage, and front end should be serviced, lubricated, and alignment checked before any major work is attempted on the pump. Check tires for correct air pressure. Steering effort can be checked with a spring scale, with engine idling and front wheels on a smooth floor or driveway. Attach a spring scale to the rim of the steering wheel; as you turn the wheels from one extreme to the other, the pull should not exceed 10 lbs. at any point.

You can check the oil flow and relief valves by turning steering wheel full right or left, with the engine idling. If these valves are working, a slight buzzing noise can be heard. **Caution:** Do not hold the wheel in this extreme position for more than 2 or 3 secs. If the relief valve is not working, the high pressure might damage the system. If no buzzing noise can be heard, a sticking or malfunctioning valve is suspected.

POWER STEERING REPAIR

Because the modern power steering unit is a precise piece of engineering,

and due to the requirement of a number of special tools, we cannot recommend that the beginning mechanic tackle this job outside of a completely equipped shop with the help of qualified professionals. If any of the faults mentioned above occur and the indicated repair consists of more than linkage replacement, belt tightening, or the use of an additive, take the vehicle to a qualified professional. Do not attempt to do it yourself. On the other hand, if you've got a reasonably well equipped tool kit and some savvy accumulated by working under the hood of your car, there's no reason why you shouldn't be able to disassemble and clean your own pump and steering box, taking care of a leak or two in the process. We've put together photo stories on a rotary vane pump and Saginaw steering gearbox, and should you have the misfortune to have sand poured maliciously into your pump (as did the owner of the Cutlass we photographed), it isn't going to steer very long. With a bit of care, some common sense and the right tools (a service manual is nice if you can borrow one), you should be able to save the $100 + that this type of cleaning job will cost you at the local repair shop. Buy a repair kit for your particular unit and set to work, but don't try to disassemble any of the internal components further than we've shown. That's really a job for the professional mechanic, no matter what the circumstances are.

CHRYSLER PUMP O-RING REPLACEMENT

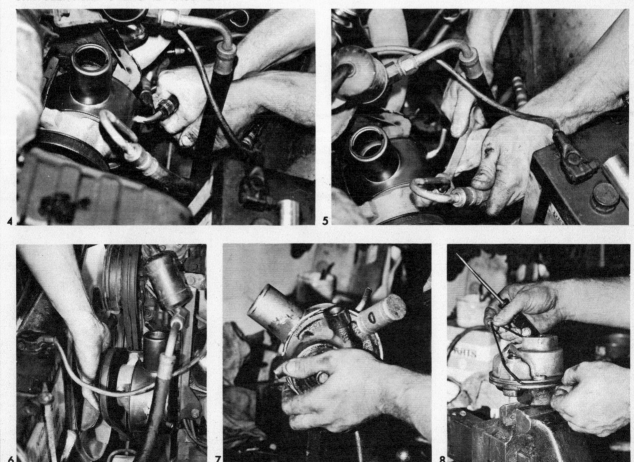

HOW-TO: Saginaw Power Steering Gearbox Overhaul

1. After disconnecting the steering column flex-coupling, a puller is handy for removing the Pitman arm. Unbolt and angle gearbox out of position.

2. Remove the two hose connectors from the oil pressure and oil return ports. Cap a finger over the connector to prevent creating a mess.

3. Pry the end cover retaining ring from the housing. This will allow you to remove the end cover and also the O-ring which is immediately inside it.

4. Vandals were responsible for the sand in this gearbox. While the majority of it came to rest against the end cover, the entire box must be cleaned.

5. The gearbox side cover is unbolted for removal. As the side cover comes off, the Pitman shaft will come off with it. Next, clean these parts in solvent.

6. Once you've pried the flex-coupling from the adjuster plug end, you'll find a spanner wrench is necessary in order to remove the adjuster plug.

7. As soon as the adjuster plug has been unscrewed, you'll be able to unscrew the valve body and worm shaft and take them out of gearbox housing.

8. After the valve body and worm shaft have been removed, take out the rack piston from the other end. Clean all of these components with solvent.

9. The next step is to pry out the retaining ring, the two back-up washers, the two oil seals, and the needle bearing from the Pitman shaft exit.

10. All these parts should be carefully inspected for wear and replaced if necessary. Replace the seven O-rings located on the valve body and shaft.

11. After you've cleaned all components thoroughly with solvent and a brush, replace the rack piston O-ring. This unit is the one you should reinstall first.

12. Hold the rack piston in place with one hand and screw the valve body and worm shaft in from the other end. This, you'll find, takes a bit of patience.

13. Next, remove the adjuster plug lock ring. Pull out the seal and the needle bearing and replace them with a new set; don't try to reuse the old ones.

14. Use a bearing installation tool to seat the new seal and needle bearing properly. Replace the adjuster plug and tighten it with the spanner wrench.

15. Now slip the new O-ring and gasket over the Pitman shaft. Position them carefully against the gearbox side cover and fit them precisely into place.

16. Then replace the Pitman shaft and rebolt the side cover. Make sure that the gasket is correctly positioned before torquing it to 30 ft.-lbs.

17. Torque rack piston plug to 75 ft.-lbs., fit end cover and retaining ring, and reseat flex-coupling in flex shaft. Seat it completely before tightening.

18. Install new needle bearing and oil seals around the Pitman shaft. Once you seat them in position, you're all ready to remount the gearbox on the car.

HOW-TO: Saginaw Power Steering Pump Overhaul

1. Begin removing the pump by unbolting it from its bracket. Unhook the two fluid connecting hoses. Now the drive pulley can be pried off its shaft.

2. With the pulley out of the way, the pump can easily be removed from the bracket without need for removing the bracket from the engine.

3. Use a plug in each hose connector to keep the fluid from spilling all over the place. The fluid is messy and it's also expensive.

4. Let the fluid drain out of the pump thoroughly. Pour it into a waste container if you're doing a complete overhaul. You'll need new fluid.

5. Now remove the union and the control valve by unscrewing the hose fittings on the reservoir. Let additional hydraulic fluid drain out.

6. After the mounting studs have been removed, a few mallet taps around the edge will free the reservoir itself from the pump housing.

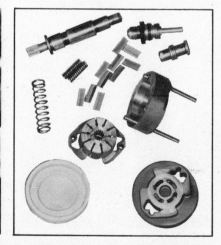

7. Pry out the end plate locking ring. Since the end plate is under spring pressure, this step may take a lot of careful prying.

8. Now the pump shaft assembly can be pulled out. Separate all the component parts and clean them carefully in a pan of solvent.

9. Remove the shaft, discard the retaining ring, and clean with solvent. Here are the separated internal parts ready to be reassembled.

10. Pry the shaft seal from the pump housing, then throw the used seal away. Clean the housing thoroughly with solvent and install a new seal.

11. Inside the pump housing you will find two O-ring seals. Take them out and deep-six them, then replace two new ones carefully in their grooves.

12. Reinstall the pump shaft then reassemble the rotor and vanes on the thrust plate. Keep parts clean and work away from dirt and grime.

13. Proceeding carefully and in proper sequence, insert the rotor/vane assembly. Next, the pump ring can be set in place in the housing.

14. Next the pressure plate and the plate spring can be replaced. Next comes the end plate which is secured with its locking ring.

15. Drop the control valve assembly and the spring down into pump housing. Clamping housing in a vise makes the job much easier and frees both hands.

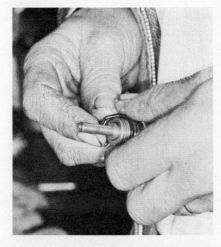

16. The O-ring must be placed on the union before screwing it in place. The union holds the control valve assembly in its proper position.

17. Remove the large O-ring on the pump housing and replace it with a new one. A damaged O-ring here is often the cause of a leaking pump.

18. Now it's time to replace the reservoir. Tap it firmly in place and replace the mounting studs. The pump is now ready for reinstallation.

Wheels & Tires

Tires, to put it very bluntly, are somewhat of a pain in the neck. It seems like they are always wearing out, going flat, or getting dirty, and no matter how well you take care of them, they never seem to look as good as they did the first day they were put on. You can wash them, scrub them, or paint them with tire paint that looks like something out of a tar pit, but they still never seem to regain the cool wet look of a brand new tire. We have been trying something recently that you may want to experiment with. We have found that spray can silicone will coat the tires with a moist film that does not soak in. But if you drive in dusty areas, you may have difficulty with it picking up a lot of dust.

TIRE CARE

The most important as well as the easiest single step in tire care is maintaining proper inflation. Pressures specified by Detroit in owners' manuals, ranging usually from 24 to 28 psi for normal driving, tend to favor comfort and quiet over tire life. A trained, conscientious tire salesman will more likely recommend 30 psi at all 4 wheels for maximum tire life. A certain amount of air seepage is normal, which is why tire pressures should be checked at least once a month and before any long trip.

These figures are for a "cold" tire and take into account the normal pressure buildup from the heat generated by the car in motion. A 3-mile drive to the neighborhood service station is enough to raise a cold pressure of 30 psi to a "false" reading of 33 psi. A stop after a long hot turnpike run can result in normal readings of 36 to 40 psi. Under no circumstances should this seemingly excess pressure figure be bled off.

Characteristic wear patterns will result from incorrect inflation. In the case of underinflation the center of the tread area bows upwards and hardly contacts the road surface, causing the outer tread areas to wear excessively. With overinflation this pattern is reversed and the center of the tread wears out first. With proper inflation there is a certain normal irregularity in the wear between tread ribs but this occurs early and does not proportionately increase once established. Treadwear indicators that tell you when a normally worn tire should be replaced are now required in all tires installed on new cars.

There are recommended 5- and 4-tire rotation patterns and car makers do not agree as to which, if any, is best. Simple mathematics prove that if all five tires are rotated every 6000 miles the car can be driven 30,000 miles with each tire in

1. Checking Inflation Pressure

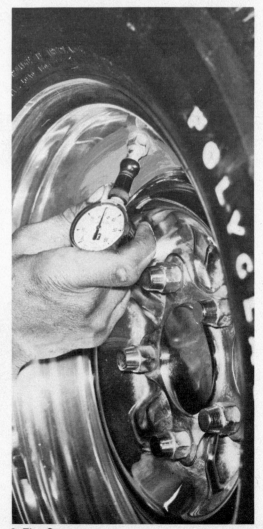

2. Tire Gauge

use for only 24,000 of this total. It also is likely that an unused spare will tend to deteriorate just sitting in the trunk.

On the other hand, you may have to rebalance after each rotation and the cost of this can at least equal the savings obtained from rotation. If it can be accomplished without rebalancing, 5-tire rotation at regular intervals will probably save you money. The problem is that while each tire and wheel may separately be in static and dynamic balance with its original brake drum (which rotates with it), changing the combinations can upset these happy relationships.

DETECTING TIRE DAMAGE

Tires should be inspected regularly for external evidence of cuts, cracking and separation of the rubber from the carcass. Small tread and sidewall cuts or cracks are of serious concern only when they penetrate far enough to expose the cord material. Assuming the cord is undamaged, exposure is not too much of a problem in a nylon or polyester tire, but rayon cord will absorb water and may be structurally weakened.

Irreparable damage will occur if the tire is run for any distance in a seriously underinflated or flat condition. This could be just that distance required to get from the fast lane to the emergency repair area of a freeway. Ply and tread separation can also be caused by underinflation, overload, or extreme speed—or combinations of these conditions. Tread separation will usually give a warning in the form of a loud slapping noise. In most cases the above types of failure will be covered under the tire builder's warranty which reimburses you for the unused mileage as gauged by tread depth remaining.

TIRE TROUBLESHOOTING

Tire problems caused by other than loss of pressure or chronic over- or underinflation can be due either to an inherent defect in the tire, or improper balancing. Tire problems could also indicate misaligned front wheels. Let's deal with the last item first as it is the most common and destructive.

Improper caster or camber will cause

1. Even though some of the new "wide weenie"-type tires feature softer, less durable compounding, you can still squeeze their maximum mileage if you're conscientious about maintaining their factory-recommended inflation pressures. For maximum ride comfort, figure on about 24-28 psi max. For maximum life, gas mileage, bump pressure to 30-32 psi.

2. Tire pressure gauge is handy for those who keep after their tires' health, or for those whose car's suspension is drastically affected by incorrect tire inflation.

3. Tire rotation has been practiced for years in this "schematic" manner. The idea is to put an equal amount of wear on spare, thus prolonging the life of the other four. Chances are, though, you'll end up having to balance the spare and two rears.

premature wear on one side of each front tire. Camber is the measurement in degrees of the lean of the wheels. A wheel whose top leans in toward the car has negative camber. If the wheel leans out, it has positive camber. Caster is a measurement in degrees of the inclination of steering axis at each front wheel. Suspensions of modern design frequently use zero camber. In other words, the two front wheels run in positions very nearly vertical and parallel to each other. Toe-in and toe-out define another possible misalignment plane of the front wheels. If any of these adjustments are incorrect, tires may wear out twice as fast as the normal rate.

Another form of accelerated wear results from driver habits. Rapid front tire wear can be caused by habitual fast cornering. The correction for this is, of course, entirely up to you. If you mend your ways, a tire such as this can be restored to a normal wear pattern by moving it to one of the rear wheels.

The practice of "laying a patch" wears the rear tires excessively as can be imagined, but also unevenly for reasons that are not quite so apparent. Maximum acceleration actually bends the rear axle housings temporarily, causing the tires to wear faster on the inner edges. An identical wear pattern will also be observed in a car that is habitually operated with a maximum passenger and luggage load.

WHEEL BALANCING

Although it is not always necessary, tires may require two types of balancing. Static balancing is a procedure to correct a situation where a tire, wheeel, or brake drum—or a combination of these items—is "heavy" at a single point. Although this may amount to only an ounce or so, the effect is greatly magnified by centrifugal force when the wheel assembly is turning at speed. The symptom is a pronounced vibration in the vertical plane at any one or all of the wheels. You can feel it and also see it

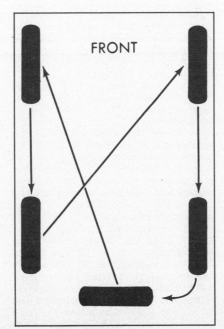

3. Proper Tire Rotation

because the vibration is transmitted to the body structure nearby, such as the fender. Service stations and garages have machines, and hopefully personnel competent to operate them, that tell how heavy a corrective weight should be used and where it should be placed.

Static balancing could probably best be described as a process by which a tire is put in balance so that there is no heavy spot anywhere that will force the tire to rotate when it is hanging free. For example, if a tire and wheel with a heavy spot is mounted on a precision spindle so that even the slightest amount of weight will rotate the tire until the weight is at the bottom, then we are checking static balance. The time-honored way of adjusting static balance is with the old-fashioned bubble balancer that enables the mechanic to get the tire in balance without spinning it. There are also machines that balance the tire on the car while it is spinning under power from an electric motor. Many people claim that such balancing, whether it is done by the operator's feeling for an unbalanced vibration or whether the imbalance is picked up by a stroboscopic light, is dynamic balancing. We feel that this is not dynamic balancing but merely a faster way to balance statically. When a tire is in dynamic balance, all of its weight is distributed equally from side to side so that there is no tendency for the tire to try to wobble as it rotates.

Suppose we had a tire that was 12 ft. wide, as an example. We could have a 100-lb. weight at one end of the tire and another 100-lb. weight at the other end. As long as the 100-lb. weights are diametrically opposite, the tire would be in perfect static balance and it would not have a heavy spot. But when you rotated this monster tire of ours, it would leap clear off the ground because when one 100-lb. weight is at the top of the tire, the other is at the bottom. One side of the tire is going to try to leap off the ground while the other side is trying to push itself into the pavement. You can see that the tire, although it is in static balance, is so far out of dynamic balance as to be useless.

Now, of course, our tires are not 12 ft. wide, but they are 4, or 6, or 8 ins. wide, and in that distance it is possible to have a heavy spot on one side of a tire so that it is in perfect balance statically but not dynamically. We feel that dynamic balancing can only be done on the type of machine that balances the wheel off the car while spinning it on a special arbor. Ordinarily this arbor is made to fit where the wheel bearings go into the drum so it balances the drum along with the wheel and tire. This is a convenient way of balancing, but it is not necessary to balance the drum because its diameter is too small to have much effect. The wheel and tire are the real culprits.

Now the question arises whether it makes any difference which way you have your tires balanced—on the car, or off the car. You can answer this yourself at a local garage after the tires are balanced, simply by having the car jacked up and the wheels spun in place. If spinning the wheels makes the car vibrate, then they are out of balance. It's as sim-

Wheels & Tires

ple as that. It doesn't make any difference whether you have them balanced on the car or off the car as long as they end up so that you can spin the wheels on the car without any vibration.

If the wheels do not vibrate when spun, but the car bounces all over the road when being driven, then there is nothing wrong with the wheel balance but you probably have a flat spot on a tire or an out-of-round wheel.

Checking tire and wheel radial and lateral runout is another method of determining if a chronic state of imbalance is caused by wheel damage, an improperly mounted tire, or a tire with manufacturing defects. To check radial runout of the tire, a dial indicator graduated to a thousandth of an inch is mounted on a convenient fixed surface and zeroed on the center rib of the tire. Rotate the assembly slowly. The combined runout of the wheel and tire should not exceed .050-in. Lateral runout of the assembly is checked by zeroing the dial indicator on the inside buff (curb protection) rib. It should not exceed .125-in.

To find out whether it is the tire or wheel causing the problem, check the radial runout of the wheel. This should not exceed .035-in. If the wheel is true, the tire is at fault. But before condemning it, deflate and rotate the tire a quarter- or half-circumference and check for runout again. This will correct a possible misalignment incurred in mounting.

If both wheel and tire show runout, check to see if all of the lugbolts are properly seated. An improper torquing sequence (to be described later) can cause binding and poor seating of one or more lugs. A tire with excessive radial runout due to a defect in construction should be replaced or the tread may be ground down on a special machine to where it is even. This procedure is not used so much for correction (an out-of-round tire is covered by warranty) as it is to obtain a maximum degree of trueness for high-performance purposes. Excessive lateral runout is almost invariably caused by damage to the wheel itself.

A new Tire Problem Detector is now being used by some new car dealers. In use, the car's normal weight pushes the tire against a roller while it is rotated. At the same time a pen draws a "picture" of the tire's circumference on a piece of paper. If there are too many lumps, or the tire is out of round, it will show up in the drawing. Of course, this does nothing to fix the tire, but it allows the dealer to point an accusing finger at the tire manufacturer, who then has to give you another tire (you hope).

TUBELESS TIRE REPAIRS

The advent of the tubeless tire, standard on all U.S. passenger cars since 1955—combined with the so-called "safety rim"—has made it difficult for do-it-yourselfers because expensive special equipment is required. This is not just for convenience but to avoid damage to the tire when it is mounted or

1. Tread Depth Gauge

2. Checking for Foreign Material

dismounted. A tubeless tire cannot be changed with the old-fashioned rubber mallet and hand iron without risking permanent damage. A basic tool needed is a tire mounting band and you really also should have an even more expensive item, called a bead breaker, to break the bead loose from the rim without damaging either in the process.

When using a tire machine, such as found in a service station, the narrow bead ledge of the rim should be up at all times although this is not necessarily the edge nearest the valve hole. Both the rim edges and tire beads should be lubricated liberally with a thick solution of water and vegetable oil soap (Palmolive or equivalent), and whether mounting or dismounting a tire, the beads should be "inched" into position rather than forced at a single spot.

With tubeless tires, it is good insurance to use a new valve whenever a tire is removed from its rim. Be sure the replacement matches the old one exactly as valves vary in length and stem diameter. Replacement valves are of the snap-in type and have been prelubricated with silicon for an easy, permanent fit. You'll find an identifying "TR" number molded into the valve base which is common to

1. Tread depth indicators are useful for measuring how much rubber is left between the top of the tire and the bottom of the groove. Anything less than 1/16-in. means new hides.

2. The next time you've got your car up in the air, check the tires for any foreign material working its way into the surface. Make a chalk mark as a start/finish line, then eyeball the tire very carefully.

3. Two and 4-ply tires and cord angle are part of modern tire design. The more plies the greater inherent strength . . . but at the expense of heat buildup by the plies rubbing against themselves. Today's technology has improved the strength of the cord so much as to make good 2-plies the equivalent of 4-plies, 4-plies as strong as 8-plies. Cord angle (cords angle across the tire from bead-to-bead) on a standard passenger tire is about 35°.

4. Most tires are statically balanced, that is they are so balanced as to not rotate if left hanging free. Tires can either be statically balanced by rotating them or placing them on a bubble balancer. Special lead weights are then added to offset the heavy side.

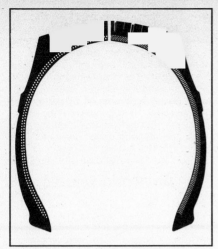

3. Two-, Four-ply Cross Section

all brands and is cross-indexed in the catalogs of the individual manufacturers for easy reference.

Caution: Temporary inflation pressures up to 40 psi—but no more—may be used to seat the beads on the rim. Many persons have been killed or seriously injured during this step in tire repairs. If the bead is not properly seated, pressures greater than 40 psi may cause it to break with explosive force. As a further safety measure, specialized tire shops use a clamp-on extension chuck on the air line to permit the operator to stand clear of the tire while inflating it.

Repairing small leaks in tubeless tires may be accomplished by any of four basic methods, and two of them do not require removing the tire from the rim or car. The first is to enlarge the puncture slightly if necessary, coat the hole with a suitable rubber cement and insert a rubber repair plug of the proper size. A repair of this nature should be looked upon as temporary.

The second and very recently developed method also uses a plug that may be applied with the tire on the car but it involves more permanency because the plug chemically vulcanizes itself to the tire. However, a $14 kit of special tools is required as well as compressed air to actuate the insertion gun.

Fully permanent repairs involve vulcanization with special dielectric patches applied inside the tire and special tools to supply current and pressure to the patch. This expense is practical only for those engaged in the tire repair business and, of course, the tire must be removed from the wheel to do the work.

Claimed to be permanent is an adaptation of the chemical vulcanizing procedure. After a certain amount of preparation, a special patch (Dill Sure-Cure or equivalent) may be applied much like a Band-Aid to the inside of either a tube-type or tubeless tire. The area around the cut or puncture must be buffed thoroughly with #3 sandpaper after first treating the area with a buffing solution (Dill B-4 or equivalent). The area is then treated with a self-curing vulcanizing fluid (Dill G-2 or equivalent) and the patch applied. The final step is to "stitch" around the edge of the patch with an inexpensive special tool (Dill Part No. 13 or equivalent). This looks and functions much like a cookie cutter except that it

4. Static Balancing

doesn't cut; it indents the patch to the surface for better adhesion. The above procedure, too, requires removal of the tire from the rim.

The careless—and expensive to the consumer—practice of "repairing" a tubeless tire by merely installing an inner tube is to be avoided except in an emergency. Tubeless tires are of a different cross section than tires designed for tubes and a tube installed in them will very likely chafe and fail. As we mentioned, tubeless tires have been standard equipment on all U.S. cars and most imports since 1955, and the wheels provided by the car maker of necessity are air-tight. The only exceptions are wire wheels that had a spurt of popularity as a factory option in the mid-'50's (and are still offered on many of the sportier imports) and certain very early aftermarket "dress-up" wheels of the so-called "mag" variety. Tubeless tires may lose air if used on some early model cars because the rims were not designed to totally resist bead separation during severe cornering. Rare instances of a leak in a modern rim may be repaired by sealants available at specialized tire shops. It is not practical, however, to attempt to seal the many spoke sockets in a wire wheel.

INNER TUBE REPAIRS

A permanent repair to an inner tube is best accomplished by vulcanization with dielectric equipment similar to that described above. Even a replacement valve may be installed in this manner. It also should be remembered that if the damage involves the tire as well as the tube, the tire too should be patched. When installing a tube, both it and the tire should be lubricated with a soap solution. A tube-type tire should be inflated slowly while you hold the valve firmly against its hole in the rim. As a final step, deflate completely and reinflate to insure proper positioning of the tube within the tire.

ROLLER WHEEL BEARINGS

Since the advent of tapered roller bearings for front wheels, car makers now recommend that the bearings and spindle be lubricated only at the time of brake lining change or when the wheel and drum are removed for any reason.

The important points to remember in lubrication and assembly are that the inner bearing races are designed to creep

Wheels & Tires

slightly around the spindle and therefore the latter should be smooth and lightly coated with lubricant to insure a slip fit. The second point is that the tapered bearings cannot function satisfactorily if any pressure is exerted upon them by the locking nut; yet, the locking nut must prevent excessive end-play.

Installation with a torque wrench is desirable, but if you don't have access to the tool or the torque figures specified by each car maker, the following procedure may be safely followed: Tighten the lock nut with an 8- or 10-in. wrench, using enough arm length leverage to ensure that all parts are properly seated while the wheel is spinning. Back off the lock nut finger-loose, then tighten finger-tight. If the hole in the spindle lines up with a slot in the nut install the cotter pin. If not, *back off* to the next slot and install the pin. Finally, clinch the cotter pin and cut off the excess length to ensure that the ends do not interfere with the dust cap or static collector. In some designs a tab-type lock washer is substituted, but the cotter pin is the most common type.

For lubrication, use nothing but an extreme pressure (EP), lithium-based grease compound made especially for this purpose. Special packing tools are available for greasing the bearings, but a suitable substitute is to put a quantity of grease in the palm of one hand and work it into the bearing with a rotating motion of the other hand. Prior to lubrication, all parts should be cleaned in kerosene.

If you have access to an air gun, then air pressure may be used to help clean out the old grease, if you do not spin the bearing. Never under any circumstances spin a bearing with air pressure or any other means. Not only is that hard on the bearings, but dangerous, because pieces could fly off the bearing and injure you. On top of that, spinning is completely unnecessary for proper cleaning.

New lubricant should not be added to the old, and whenever these parts are lubricated, a new oil seal should be installed. This seal can be seated by hammering gently on a block of wood placed on the seal.

On cars equipped with drum-type brakes, it may be necessary to loosen the brake adjustment before the wheel and drum can be removed as a unit. On cars with disc-type front brakes the caliper must be removed. The only caution to observe is to not let the caliper assembly dangle on its hoses. Hang it on the nearest convenient piece of steering linkage. On front-wheel-drive cars such as the Toronado and Eldorado the rear-wheel bearings may be removed, lubricated, and replaced in a manner quite similar to that described above.

BALL WHEEL BEARINGS

Procedures for removal and greasing of ball front wheel bearings are the same as for tapered rollers. However, the installation of the bearings is slightly different. Ball bearings must be installed with a slight preload so that the balls and races are brought into proper contact. All kinds of directions have been devised for adjusting ball front wheel bearings, most of them difficult to understand. Most castellated nuts have only six positions for the cotter key, so even after you get the nut exactly where you want it, you may have to turn it tighter or looser to insert the key.

The main thing to remember on ball front wheel bearings is that they must never be adjusted loose. This doesn't mean to put a 3-ft. breaker bar on the nut to tighten it. It does mean that you should have zero play, with a slight amount of preload.

Ball front wheel bearings were a great source of trouble on the cars that used them. Today all cars use tapered rollers, which have eliminated the front wheel bearing problems. There is no tapered roller that will interchange with the old ball bearings, but there is a trick that can be used to prolong their life.

The secret is to use a grease in the wheel bearings that is almost runny.

Some chassis lubes are soft and will work fine. If the grease is one of the newer "black" greases with moly in it, so much the better. Never use the old long fiber wheel bearing greases that were so stiff. The grease has to be loose enough so that it will run back onto the balls after it is thrown off by the rotation of the wheel. Hard greases will fly off the first time the car gets up to speed, and then the bearing runs dry until it is packed again. Invariably damage will occur to the bearing, and possibly hub.

MOUNTING WHEELS

When changing a wheel, start the lug nuts loose before jacking. The nuts rotate normally to the left to loosen except on older Chrysler Corp. products where the nuts attaching the left wheels require right-hand rotation to loosen. When installing a wheel, first tighten the uppermost nut firmly but not securely and then tighten the one opposite on the bottom. Continue to tighten opposing pairs just enough so that the nuts are firmly seated. When all have been tightened, rotate the wheel and check for an out-of-round condition that means the nuts haven't seated properly. Then lower the car from the jack and final-tighten the nuts in the same sequence as above. Remember that after a 100 or so miles of driving, the nuts should be rechecked for tightness. Car makers specify torque figures (usually 70 ft.-lbs.) for the lug nuts, but the lug wrench provided with the car is of a size that makes it impossible for a person of normal strength to over-tighten wheel lug nuts.

1. This is the only practical way to separate today's tubeless tires from their rims without damage.

2. Wheel bearings should be greased every 12 months or 12,000 miles, whichever comes first. Garages use a tool which forces fresh grease into bearing. Most backyarders can do the same by cupping one's hand, filling depression with grease, squeezing grease through by sliding bearing across palm in a wiping motion.

1. Removing Tubeless Tires from Rims

2. Wheel Bearing Packing

1. Want to know right way to mount mag wheels? An expert at Motor Wheel Corp., Lansing, Mich. 48914, shows how without scratching the wheels.

2. Drop wheel on changer, make sure flange is up. If rim is deep, mount face down to protect finish. Secure wheel by specific lug hole hold-down.

3. Many "mags" can be damaged when center-hold-down-method is used. Forget this technique if center can be damaged. Shop cloth protects finish.

4. Before putting valve stem through the stem hole, carefully inspect rim for leak-producing dirt, grit, etc., remove any labels, then clean 'em up.

5. Before placing tire on wheel, lubricate both of the beads with household variety soap. It dries quickly, stickly, won't harm rubber rim.

6. Take time and watch out for the finish, start installing by working top bead over the rim. Once done the first bead should fall in center well.

7. Like top bead, the lower bead can be worked over wheel in a similar manner so it drops into center well. Work slowly, don't try to force bead.

8. After you've inserted valve core, air up tire to a maximum of 40 psi. If the beads aren't sealing properly use bead sealing mag, relubricate tire.

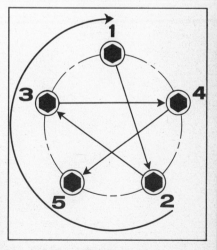

9. When installing assembly on car, make sure stresses are equally divided and torqued to 80-90 ft.-lbs. Shown is recommended tightening sequence.

Body & Paint

Body and paint is a fascinating subject, with much more science to it than you would think from watching a body man swing his big hammer. Bodywork is fascinating because there aren't any two body men who would repair a car in the same way. It may be termed scientific because the body man who is fast can do the job in an incredibly short time, whereas another body man may take much longer and as a result be making a lot less money.

More than any other types of automotive repair, bodywork and painting should be carefully observed before they are attempted. Most body shops will welcome the amateur who wants to sit quietly by and watch how work is accomplished, and the body men will often pass along pointers as they proceed. The important thing to consider when watching a body man work is how he approaches each and every bent panel.

How a vehicle has been struck—that is, the point of impact—will determine how the repair should be made. This cannot be overemphasized. A really good body repair specialist may sit looking at a wrecked car for an hour before ever touching a panel. He is trying to determine exactly where the initial contact was (usually simple), the angle of the blow, severity, secondary impact points, etc. Once he has figured out exactly where the initial blow was, he may be able to save many hours of needless work.

If a fender has been struck head-on near the headlight, there will be damage far removed from that impact point. Chances are the fender will buckle at one or two places above the wheel opening, a slight buckle may appear in the large area behind the wheel opening, and the panel may have been shoved back against the door. This is where the unskilled workman can get into trouble very quickly.

If some kind of panel-pulling equipment is available, it will be possible to pull much of the damage from the fender without striking a hammer blow. However, if the point of initial contact is hammered out *first,* the remainder of the damage will be exceptionally difficult to remove.

Again referring to the bent fender, if something can be hooked to the headlamp opening area and a pulling pressure exerted, the initial impact force is being reversed. The immediate crumpled area around the front of the fender will distort during this phase, but the force will tend to pull most of the buckles from the rest of the fender. This is imperative, and a part of almost every repair job.

Large body and fender shops will usually have a big pulling rig available. This is nothing more than a large I-beam that runs beneath the car and chains to the undamaged chassis in several points. The pulling apparatus is attached to the front and thus pulls against itself (the body attachments). Finding this kind of equipment for backyard repair is unlikely, so a push may be substituted for a pull. Body shops also have specially designed hydraulic jacks, usually referred to by the trade name of Porto-Power. With the bent fender, such a slim jack may be placed toward the rear of the fender on a strong frame point and the fender pushed back into rough shape. The jack is easier to use, but care must be taken to push the fender back in the same *direction of impact.* If the fender

were struck at a front angle, pushing straight forward may do more damage than good. Work a little bit at a time with hydraulic jacks and you'll always come out OK. Of course, an ordinary bumper jack may be utilized where hydraulic jacks are unavailable. Which brings up the question of the tools that may be needed.

TOOLS

Obviously the amateur body man does not need a $1000 tool chest to fix up a dented fender, but there are several tools that are prerequisite. At the same time, many of the specialized body tools will find constant use in all aspects of automotive repair, and should therefore be considered as desirable. Following is a list of tools common to bodywork. An asterisk denotes those tools absolutely essential to the simplest repair job.

Wedge dolly
Combination spoon/dolly
Toe dolly
Anvil dolly (or "railroad" dolly)
*Tear drop dolly
*Scratch awl or ice pick
*File holder (adjustable type)
*Cheese grater (for epoxy fillers)
*Single-blade spoon
Double-blade spoon
Cross-mill shrinking hammer
Double-end flat face hammer
*Pick hammer
*2-lb. sledge hammer
Vise grips (pliers)
Large water pump pliers
*Pry bar
*Hacksaw
*Tin snips
Hydraulic jack
*Electric drill

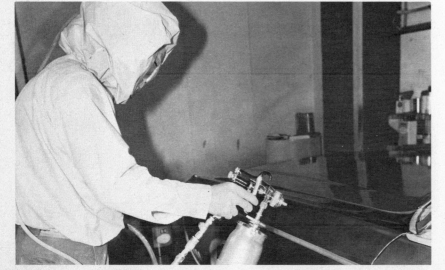

1. Spray Paint Hood Mask

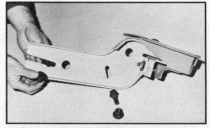

2. Special Serrated Bolts

3. Ford Shock-Absorbing Bumper

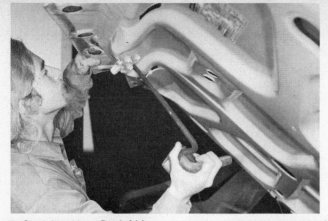

4. Straightening a Deck Lid

5. Frame Straightening

1. Newest wrinkle in painting—a hood mask with filter that inflates with air from the air pressure line and dispels toxic fumes from use of new enamel hardener additives.

2. Special bolts attach the Pontiac telescoping box sections to the frame. The bolts "crush" part of the frame and box into each other and have to be torqued to 80-100 ft.-lbs.!

3. Front bumpers on all 1973 cars use an impact-absorbing device to withstand up to 5-mph impact without damage. In the Ford bumper attachment device, an I-beam (1) rides inside a channel (2) and the two are bonded together with a special rubber that returns the I-beam to its original position after impact.

4. Picks in varying lengths, shapes and points are often used in places such as this deck lid where you can't reach the damaged area with a hammer to raise low spots.

5. Major collision repair, such as frame straightening, is best left to a professional with the proper equipment. Here a frame is being heated and pulled into shape on an alignment rack with the use of big chains and "come-along" pullers.

In addition to these tools, you may rent or borrow a welding outfit, disc sander, and paint spraying equipment. Such normally expensive equipment as this is a superb investment, but it is always possible to purchase equipment second-hand and save at least 50%. A good place to start looking for used hand and power equipment is the local body shop.

While the welding outfit is nice to have, you can repair the panel until welding is necessary, and farm the job out, then continue the repair. A disc sander is primarily a time saver, and the apprentice body man invariably finds he will learn the trade better if he concentrates on use of jack, hammer and dolly at first, doing all the finish work with a file. Lots of elbow grease is required with this type finishing, but an excellent job is easier to accomplish.

WELDING

Simple welding is an absolute requirement for any accomplished body repair man, although many repairs require little more than simple brazing. Because it is such an integral part of any body job, and actually attendant to most home vehicle repairs, the amateur should spend time becoming proficient with a torch. The best place for the young repairman to learn is high school or college auto shop, but an excellent alternative is the local garage.

Although they may seem rudimentary, there are certain precautions to observe when working with a gas welding outfit. First, always have a small fire extinguisher handy. There are many parts of a car that like to burn, and sparks from panel cutting or welding can get into the strangest places. Small extinguishers are available at low cost, but if nothing better is at hand, keep a water hose nearby. And never forget that a spark can smolder for hours in insulation before breaking out in flames.

Care and use of a welding outfit is explained in booklets available through parts and welding supply stores. They're mighty handy reading. They'll advise always mounting the welding bottles to a cart or chaining them to a work bench. A bottle can tip over and break off the regulator. When that happens either the bottle wants to go into orbit, or acetylene may catch fire. Either way, things get too exciting. Keep the hose connections tight, and turn off the acetylene and oxygen at the bottles after use.

One of the most common mistakes the amateur body man makes when welding is using the wrong torch tip. Because the sheetmetal is usually between 16 and 20 gauge, which means it is thin, a small tip is best (tip size designations vary with manufacturer). A large tip may work, but the heat generated will be transferred to the surrounding metal, causing warpage.

Different pressures are required for welding and cutting different thicknesses of metal. For sheetmetal welding, set the regulators at about 5 psi for acetylene and 10 psi for oxygen. For cutting the same thin sheetmetal, raise oxygen pressure to near 15 psi, and keep the acetylene at or lower than 5 psi. For ordinary work these same pressures will hold, but may have to be raised slightly when cutting frame members or very heavy steel. In no case should the acetylene pressure be above 15 lbs. since acetylene is dissolved in acetone. Too much pressure will cause the acetone to collect in the hoses and create a very dangerous situation. Normal hoses used for welding should never get more than 30 lbs. of oxygen pressure, and this high setting is used for cutting only.

After the regulator pressures have been set, which determines just how intense or harsh the flame will be, the torch oxygen valve should be opened approximately ⅛-turn and the acetylene valve approximately ½-turn. After the torch is lit, the acetylene valve should be opened until the flame begins to leave the end of the torch tip ("blows" away from the tip). Back the acetylene valve down slightly until the flame just touches the torch tip again. When first lit, the flame is a carbonizing type.

Gradually opening the oxygen valve will make the acetylene "feather" disappear and will produce a neutral flame. For body and fender repair, as well as most general welding, this neutral flame is desirable. To get the neutral flame, the oxygen valve is turned until the feather has been eliminated, and there is just a single small blue flame in the cone. Opening the oxygen valve further will make the flame hotter (known as an oxidizing type).

The intensity or harshness of a flame increases as the gas pressures increase. A flame which is too harsh may agitate the weld puddle violently, making good welding very difficult. A flame that is too soft may not have enough "push" to set the puddle for a good job. After becoming proficient with a welding torch, the body man learns many variations in the use of a single tip.

When welding body sheetmetal, the amateur will do best to tack-weld the separation in several places, making sure each surface is level at the separation. If one surface is lower, the final smoothing process is far more difficult. Keep in mind that metal will tend to "grow" as it is heated. Therefore, if a split in the fender is to be butt-welded, there should be a slight gap between the pieces. If the pieces touch, the welding heat will tend to create a small ridge down the weld, a ridge that must be heated and shrunk out.

When welding sheetmetal it is best to weld forward, ahead of the tip, rather than behind the tip. When welding backward, or moving along with the tip pointing back toward the already welded seam, the heat is increased in the panel, encouraging excessive warpage. When tilting the torch tip at a 45° angle and

Body & Paint

pointing it ahead of the weld, it tends to preheat the metal and make a smooth bead every time. The welding rod is held at 90° to the flame, or 45° from the seam in the leading direction, and the flame is played in a small arc (usually about ¼-in. diameter) as the seam proceeds. A good weld will have consistent ripples throughout.

To weld a break or tear near the edge of a panel (around the flange, etc., which is a common occurrence), first rough out the panel to its approximate shape with a hammer and dolly. If there is considerable stress at that particular point, a jack may be necessary to get reasonable alignment. Clamp the edge of the split panel with flange pliers or vise-grips and tack-weld the break every inch or so. This will keep the edges from creeping during the final welding stage. Start the final weld bead at the apex of the break, working steadily toward the edge.

If a small section, or panel, is to be welded into an existing panel, such as the front section of a straight fender to replace the crumpled part of a fender, the entire cut must be tack-welded as mentioned.

Hammer welding is not common to ordinary bodywork, being more attuned to customizing, but it can save time and effort of leading or epoxy filling. As the weld progresses, working with about ½-in. at a time, the weld is hammered flat with a hammer and dolly while still red. This flattens the entire welded seam and makes working with a pick hammer and file easy. Remember to wear a long glove on the dolly hand, and immerse the dolly in water regularly to remove heat buildup. Since this type of weld requires intermittent use of the torch, it is wise to build some kind of torch holder. In this way the torch will not have to be relit every 3 or 4 mins.

Brazing is simpler to master than welding, and some of the new low-temperature brazing rods are ideal for bodywork. However, the beginner will never know if he is doing a good brazing job or not unless he learns fusion welding also. There are many places where brazing is better than welding, particularly because of the low temperatures involved. At the same time, brass may be filed and ground smooth much as lead, so it is ideal as filler for small holes, etc.

Use of the cutting tip is abused by many amateur welders, simply because they have not considered the problems involved. In bodywork, the majority of cutting will be done on large sheetmetal panels. Because the metal is so thin, a small cutting tip should be selected, and seldom can a gas cut be made without some minor metal warpage immediately adjacent to the cut. For this reason, when a panel is being replaced, always make the initial gas cut 2 ins. from the final cut, then sever the remaining piece with snips or a power shear. Power shears are available that work off ordinary drill motors. As soon as the metal is ready to cut, tilt the cutting tip in the direction of the cut and move briskly. This procedure will cut sheetmetal with a

1. Aligning a Trunk Lid

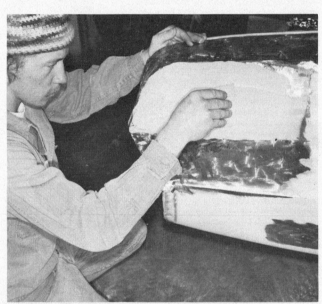

2. Using Body Filler

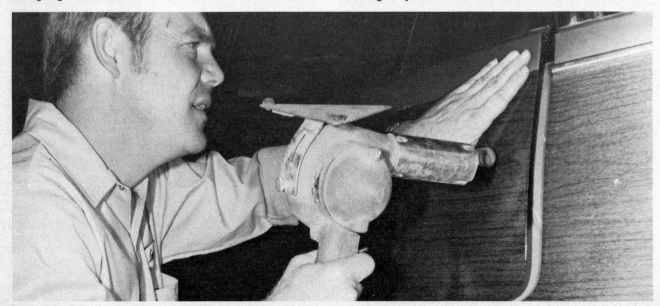

3. Transfer Film

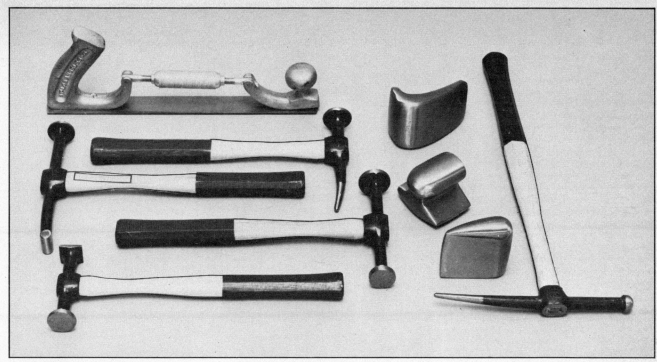

4. Hammers and Dollies

5. Pop Riveting

1. Sometimes a small job of panel alignment on hood, doors or trunk lid can be handled simply, without special tools or training.

2. There are two basic ways to fix minor collision damage. The quick and easy route is lots of filler.

3. Simulated wood grain on transfer film is today's counterpart of the wooden-bodied station wagon. Material comes in rolls, is cut to fit desired panel, and is adhesive-backed. Here a door panel is being replaced. Film backing is peeled off, then film is placed over panel wiped with detergent. Heater speeds drying process.

4. The professional must have a variety of hammers and dollies for his work, but you may find objects around your garage to do the job.

5. Blind pop rivet gun is greatest invention since the welding torch, but a heck of a lot less troublesome. Special rivet is inserted in gun chuck, shank inserted in proper diameter hole drilled in pieces to be joined, then handle squeezed. In one operation rivet is flared on back side, excess rivet shank cut off.

6. The best repairs take more time, of course. A good metalman will get the panel as straight as possible first, so that only a thin coat of filler is needed. After preliminary hammering on the dent, grinding the surface shows high and low spots that have to be worked on.

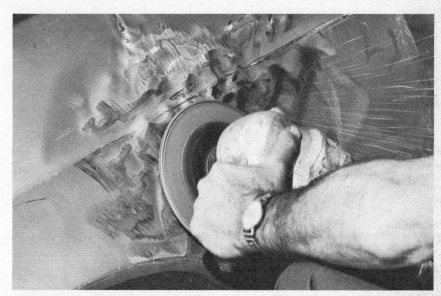

6. Working the Metal

minimum of warpage, but does not work well with heavier steel.

WORKING METAL

As we have pointed out, when straightening a bent panel, the work should start in reverse order from impact. When the pressure that causes subsequent wrinkles and buckled areas down a panel has been released (by pulling or pushing into rough shape), start at the ridge farthest away from the impact point and start working back. In many cases, the minute this last ridge is straightened, most of the other buckles will disappear also.

Take that hypothetical fender again. The front of the fender around the headlight is crushed and wrinkled, but farther aft there is a depression above the wheel opening and a ridge behind that. By placing a spoon on the rear ridge and slapping it with a mallet or hammer, the ridge will be driven inward and the depression will spring outward to near original contour. Localized stress points have been relieved, leaving only small areas to reshape with hammer and dolly.

The secret to good bodywork is to use the hammer sparingly. If a panel is repeatedly hit with a hammer and there is no support behind the panel, a series of individual valleys is created. On the other hand, if the panel is supported by a dolly and is repeatedly struck, the metal is stretched out of shape. The best procedure is to select a dolly with the same general contour as the original panel line, then slap the panel with medium hammer effort, moving the dolly around beneath all the high spots. When visiting a body shop, note how the accomplished body man strikes a panel with about 60 blows a minute, making a kind of glancing strike on the panel.

To raise a low spot in the metal, place the dolly at the apex of the dimple and

Body & Paint

strike the dimple edges with the hammer. This will raise the section. The kind of hammer used is very important. In the first place, body hammers are relatively light-weight, and they all have specially contoured faces. Using something like a ball-peen hammer to straighten a panel is the quickest route to the junkyard.

Spoons come in various sizes and shapes, but are primarily used on a big expanse of metal where the blow should be distributed over a wide area. They can also be used as backup dollies when space is cramped. Dollies vary in weight, shape and contour, but are nothing more than a hand-held anvil. Watch a professional body man and note how he will often use the dolly to tap up a low spot as he progresses, rather than resort to using a heavy and unwieldy body hammer.

Sometimes there will be small dents that are not easy to remove with a dolly, or perhaps a dolly cannot be squeezed into the area. These dents may be removed with a pick hammer. The pick end of a body hammer may be straight or slightly curved, but in either case the pick tip is rounded, not sharpened. When metal is tapped, the small rounded end will tend to stretch a tiny area, or cause little bubbles to raise. By striking metal from the underside with the pick, and placing a lightweight dolly on the outside panel surface, an area may be raised enough for final working. *Warning:* Never pick up a depression, such as a small dent that has been obviously stretched, and then grind or file the surface without working with a dolly in the normal manner. The little bubbles may be too high and when ground will cause thin spots in the metal, or may even allow the grinder to cut holes.

Obviously, when a severely crunched area is worked, there is lots of hammer and dolly work necessary. Despite the fact that this initial work might make the area seem beyond repair, you'll find that perseverance will prove the metal forgiving. As with that fender again, keep at it with light strokes and move the dolly around to get the proper contours—and soon the right shape will develop.

After the general contours have been reached, run the flattened hand over the surface. Any irregularities will be felt immediately and may be worked up slowly. Finally, file the area with a body file, holding the file flat and making even strokes. Remember that most automotive body panels have at least a simple curve, so do not file in one place long enough to cause a flat spot.

As the body file is shoved across the surface, it will take slight cuts off the high spots and leave the low spots untouched. Raise the low spots with the hammer and dolly, and continue until all the area is being filed with every stroke. A disc sander is faster, but the amateur will find the file gives a better result.

SHRINKING

Any crease type of damage will probably require metal shrinking for repair. As a crease or gouge is worked out with

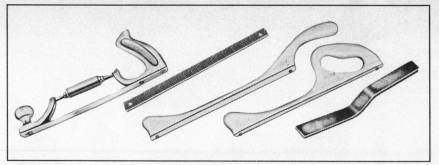

1. Body Files

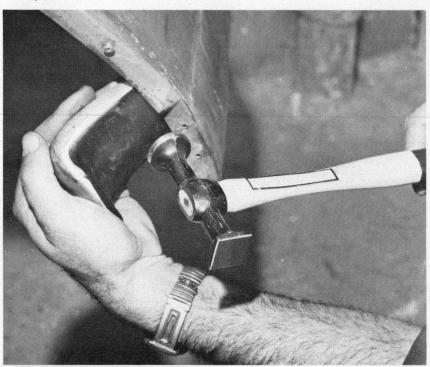

2. Using Hammer and Dolly

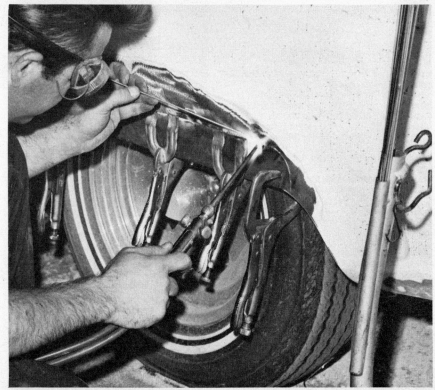

3. Welding a Patch Panel

4. Using Picking Hammer

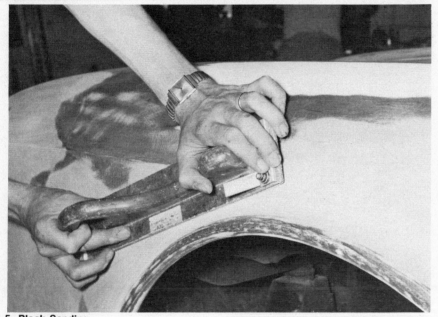

5. Block Sanding

1. Files of various grits are used in shaping both metal and filler.

2. A hammer and dolly are the most basic tools in bodywork. You should never hammer on a panel without a dolly to back up the other side.

3. With basic welding knowledge and some sheetmetal, you can easily patch rusted out fenders and rocker panels. After this, the welds are ground down and smoothed into the main panel with filler. This often makes a better repair than just filling rust holes with "bondo."

4. The pointed end of this "picking" hammer is useful for tapping up the backside of small low spots.

5. Block sanding of large, flat areas is best done with shaper that uses replaceable sandpaper strips.

6. Here's the secret of using a disc sander on reverse-crown metal where disc edge would dig in. With disc edge cut this way, it's limber enough to flex with the contour.

6. Modifying a Sanding Disc

a hammer and dolly, the stretched metal involved will not want to flatten out properly, staying as either a slight crater or bump. It may be shrunk out.

Shrinking consists of heating a small spot in the middle of the stretched area where the metal has been made thinner. This will make the metal thicker, and it is easier than you might think. Put a small tip on the welding torch and heat a spot (about the size of a silver dollar directly in the center of the stretched area) to a strong cherry red. Be careful not to burn a hole. Immediately discard the torch and strike a hard blow with a body hammer directly on the heated spot. This will upset the metal and form a crater. Now, while the metal is still hot, hold a dolly against this crater from the back and tap the rim of the crater down with a hammer. Work around the rim in a decreasing diameter as the area cools. Quench about a 6-in. diameter with a water soaked rag to draw the heat expansion from the area, and you should be through. However, if the original stretched spot is large, it may require several shrinkings to straighten the panel. This is one procedure best observed before tried.

LEADING

After welding, and sometimes because of excessive damage, a panel may need leading. This is a process of filling a sunken area to the surrounding metal height. The secret to leading is clean and properly tinned metal. The surface to be filled should be cleaned with a wire brush, extending at least 2 ins. beyond the rim of the indentation or welded area.

There are a number of leading fluxes, both liquid and powder, on the market, but as a general rule use whatever your local body man recommends. To apply the flux, warm the cleaned area and then spread the flux thoroughly. A ball of steel wool clamped in pliers can be used to scrub the surface and get a good tinning job. This is possible because the flux will dissolve the oxide present on any cleaned surface.

When the area has been cleaned and the flux applied, spread a small bit of lead solder to the surface, using a *soft* torch flame as with any kind of soldering. While the lead and metal surfaces are still warm, wipe the solder over the area with a clean rag. This will complete the tinning process, and any place that does not accept the tinning will certainly not accept lead.

Making lead stay on anything but a flat, horizontal panel can be a study in sheer frustration for the beginner. The only solution to this dilemma is practice and patience. Some lead is easier to apply than others, because of the metallic composition, so again let the local body man guide you.

In applying lead, use a soft flame and brush it across the tinned surface now and then to keep the metal warm (not hot!). Hold the lead stick near the tinned area and direct the flame over the stick end until the end begins to sag, much as a heated candle would. Quickly press the stick onto the surface. Keep this up

Body & Paint

until enough lead is on the surface to fill the depression or welded area. As you are depositing the lead, occasionally brush the soft flame back across the deposited lead just to keep the area warm and pliable.

Shaping the lead is done with a wooden paddle frequently dipped in beeswax. The flame is passed across the lead deposit and as the lead becomes plastic (it loses the "sugared" look and gets shiny—be careful, because it is ready to run on the floor!), the paddle is used to push the lead across the surface. Paddle the lead over the entire tinned area and build it up slightly higher than the surrounding surface, scraping excess off onto the floor. Feather the edges smoothly with the paddle to reduce filing effort. While working the lead, if it keeps the sugared brittle look, you're probably working it too cold.

After the leaded area has cooled, it may be worked with the vixen body file. Care should be observed to keep the file flat, as the lead is softer than the surrounding metal and will gouge easily at this stage. The surrounding metal is the guide as to how low the lead should be filed, and if the area was tinned properly the lead will feather into the metal perfectly.

EPOXY FILLERS

More common with amateurs is the epoxy filler, normally called 'glass. There is nothing wrong with this type filler, although it is not as strong as lead and should not be used where a stress build-up is likely or at an edge where it can easily chip.

These plastic fillers, highly refined over the past 20 years, are popular because they are applied without heat and will not shrink or crack if properly mixed and applied. Always use the best epoxy

fillers available as good insurance.

As with lead, the area to be treated with epoxy filler must be thoroughly cleaned. The filler is generally in a liquid form with a quick-setting hardener mixed just before application. Mixing must be thorough.

The mixture will set within 15-30 minutes, so work must go along quickly. Spread the mixture over the area with a wooden paddle or flexible rubber blade, as with putty.

The hardener added to the filler creates heat, and after an hour, the filler will be firm enough to be cheese-grated (roughly contoured with an open-cut plastic filler file).

After the rough shaping, which is easiest just before the filler gets superhard, the area is then sanded with a #80 paper, followed by 180 or 220 grit sandpaper, then cleaned and primed.

When either epoxy or lead has been used, always clean the area thoroughly with a cleaning compound such as

2. Mixing Fiberglass Filler

1. Some of the common tools used in body repairs include spray gun, hand riveter, and various fiberglass fillers and repair materials.

2. Body fillers are made by mixing fiberglass filler with a small "dab" of hardening agent, which should be mixed in thoroughly. By varying the amount of hardener used, you can mix the filler to harden slowly or in a hurry. Don't add too much though, or the filler will actually heat up and crack off the repaired surface.

3. Never apply body fillers this thick! Road vibrations will cause it to crack and fall out. Instead, work the metal enough so little filler is required to make a smooth repair.

4. After sanding bare metal with a grinder or heavy sandpaper, deep scratches are sometimes left that cannot be concealed with primer. In this case, more sanding with a lighter paper is required.

5. Corvette makes a number of replacement panels as well as molds. Local independent fiberglass companies offer panels also. Surprisingly, panel replacement of fiberglass is quite similar to sheetmetal repair.

6. Repair of fiberglass follows a set pattern as shown in Figs. 1–4. When metal is repaired (Figs. 5–6), edges must be flanged as indicated, fiberglass patch laminated to lips.

1. Bodywork Tools and Materials

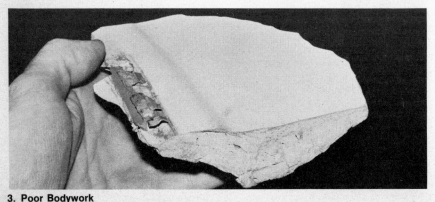

3. Poor Bodywork

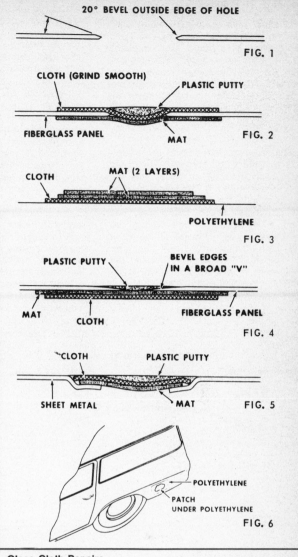

20° BEVEL OUTSIDE EDGE OF HOLE

FIG. 1

CLOTH (GRIND SMOOTH)   PLASTIC PUTTY

FIBERGLASS PANEL   MAT   FIG. 2

CLOTH   MAT (2 LAYERS)

POLYETHYLENE

FIG. 3

PLASTIC PUTTY   BEVEL EDGES IN A BROAD "V"

MAT   CLOTH   FIBERGLASS PANEL   FIG. 4

CLOTH   PLASTIC PUTTY

SHEET METAL   MAT   FIG. 5

POLYETHYLENE

PATCH UNDER POLYETHYLENE

FIG. 6

4. Grinding Marks

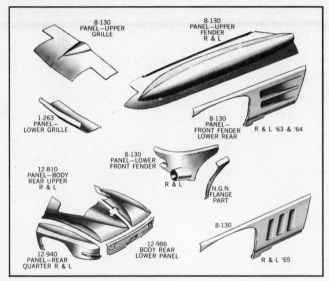

8-130 PANEL—UPPER GRILLE

8-130 PANEL—UPPER FENDER R & L

1-263 PANEL— LOWER GRILLE

8-130 PANEL— FRONT FENDER LOWER REAR   R & L '63 & '64

8-130 PANEL—LOWER FRONT FENDER   R & L

12-810 PANEL—BODY REAR UPPER R & L

N.G.N. FLANGE PART

8-130

12-940 PANEL—REAR QUARTER R & L

12-986 BODY REAR LOWER PANEL   R & L '65

5. Fiberglass Replacement Panels

6. Glass Cloth Repairs

Met-L-Prep, then apply primer.

Body glaze or putty comes in a tube and is actually like thick paint. It is extremely useful for covering small scratches, pinholes in epoxy fillers, and for filling small valleys in feather-edged areas. It isn't designed to be used like regular body filler, though, and should never be applied very thick. For best adhesion the area should be primered *before* applying putty. The putty flows on easily with a squeegee and watersands supersmooth.

REPLACING PANELS

It is often more expedient to remove and replace a badly damaged panel rather than straighten it. Because replacement panels from a junkyard sell for about 30% of new cost, exploring such a source makes sense economically. However, there are certain things to watch for during an R&R (remove and replace) operation.

Make sure the mounting area has been straightened and aligned, or the replacement panel will not fit.

Take that fender again. If the damage was heavy enough, the mounting near the door may have been bent. Surely the inner splash panel has been bent, and

the radiator-core support may also need straightening.

If the quarter panel must be replaced, then do a similar job to the crumpled panel. Often the replacement panel can be mated to the car beneath a beltline or fender molding.

If this is possible, overlap the top piece so water cannot slide down the joint and cause excessive rust, then braze each end of the mated joint. The overlap will be hidden by the chrome strip, so secure the joint with metal screws or (even better), use pop-rivets.

PAINTING

After all the bodywork has been completed, in preparation for a good paint job, every piece of chrome trim should be removed from the body. There are a few pieces that can't be taken off, for one reason or another, but the majority are removable. Reason for the extra work is to save extra work. That is, mask-taping the trim properly is a time-consuming project, and although it only takes about one-fourth the time of complete removal, there are other ramifications. In the first place, if you miscue with the tape, you can botch an otherwise good paint job. Secondly, if you

take the trim off, the entire body gets painted, under trim and all. Thirdly, the area around trim is a perfect place for wax and other types of film buildup, and if you're not very thorough with your preparation, this kind of film will ruin the paint. And finally, it's just a devil of a lot easier to prepare, paint, and finish a car that's minus trim. Incidentally, if the trim is held in place by stationary clips (the clip bolts to the body panel and the trim piece snaps away), don't go to great effort removing the clips. Just paint them.

In addition to the trim, take out the grille (so the cavity can be painted); remove the bumpers; remove the rubber bumpers from the hood, deck lid, and doors; and lastly, peel the rubber wind lacing seal away from the doors and deck lid. Be careful, for you'll want to reuse this seal if it's still good. If not, you can put on new rubber, either standard or universal type. In case you really want to be meticulous, remove the door upholstery panels and kick panels. These are difficult to tape off, and the little extra effort is worth it.

SANDING

It isn't important whether you feather-edge the repaired areas or sand the un-

Body & Paint

blemished paint first. Because water sanding is the fastest, cleanest, and easiest method of sanding, you'll probably do the overall sanding job first. This way, if the job stretches out over several days (nothing wrong with this), the slight surface rusting that's bound to cover the repaired areas will be taken off in the feather-edging step just before primer is applied.

Sandpaper for automotive use is available in both dry and wet-or-dry types, but for all practical purposes, the wet paper is far superior. The wet-or-dry type may be used either way, and costs about 10¢ per sheet, which means that you'll spend $1 for paper on the average job. Using water keeps the paper lubricated and the pores clean so that the paper will last much longer than if used dry. Wet-or-dry is available in a variety of grits, from 180 through 600, and you'll need several sheets of different rating. A couple of 180 grit, at least four of 220,

four of 320, and later some 600. In addition, pick up two sheets of dry #80, which is very coarse.

Obviously, it's wise to pick a place that will drain well for your sanding location. The residue from sanding actually acts like a mild stain, and it can discolor driveway concrete if left standing.

If possible, use a hose for water supply, with a bare trickle available at all times. If such is impractical, a bucket of water and good sponge will suffice. Thoroughly wet the surface before you start, and if possible, do the sanding in the shade, if for no other reason than comfort. Another hint, you might as well plan on getting wet, for you will before you're through.

The top is as good a starting place as any; work down to the hood and deck lid before attacking the side panels. Hold the hose in one hand, keeping the metal end from making new scratches, and sand with the other. Direct a small flow of water on the work as needed, which means a fine film of water at all times. You won't get too much water as far as

sanding is concerned, but too much will make it messier on you. When you're getting just enough water, the paper will glide without grabbing, but will have enough drag to tell you it's cutting.

The sanding pattern is extremely important and can have drastic effect upon the finished job. Work in one direction as much as possible, preferably lengthwise with the panel (much like the grain in wood), and never, never in circles. On many panels, such as the top rear windshield and rear windows, the lengthwise direction will not get around the windows well, so the direction must be changed to fit the circumstance, but the pattern here will be straight cross-grain effect.

The paper may be held either by hand or with a semi-flexible sanding block. The block is very good for large panels, but the hand conforms better to curves. If a block is used, tear strips from the sheet just wide enough for the block. Use 220, 280 or 320 for pre-primer sanding. If hand-held, the paper is torn differently. That is, the 9 × 11-in. sheet is

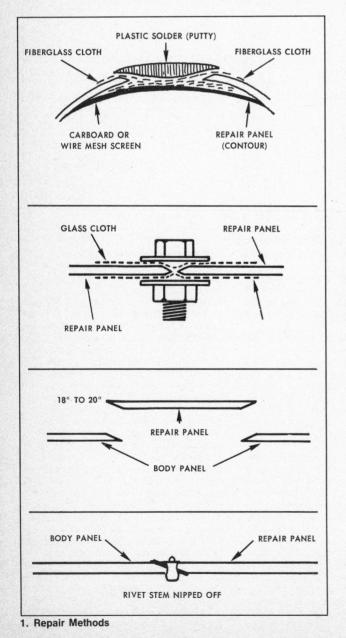

1. Repair Methods

PLASTIC SOLDER (PUTTY)
FIBERGLASS CLOTH
FIBERGLASS CLOTH
CARBOARD OR WIRE MESH SCREEN
REPAIR PANEL (CONTOUR)

GLASS CLOTH
REPAIR PANEL
REPAIR PANEL

18° TO 20°
REPAIR PANEL
BODY PANEL

BODY PANEL
REPAIR PANEL
RIVET STEM NIPPED OFF

2. Spraying Primer

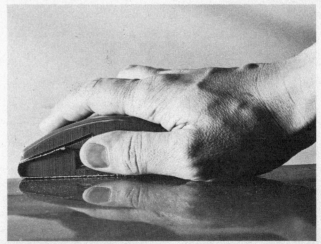

3. Using a Sanding Block

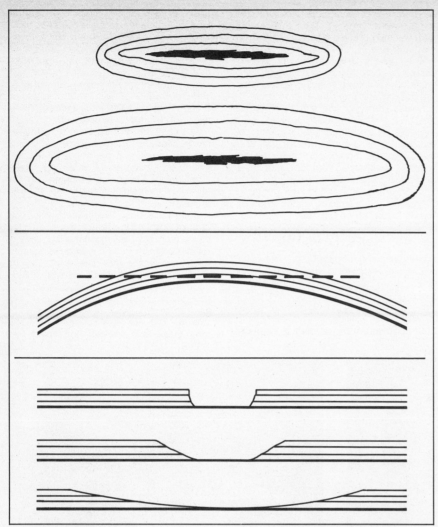

4. Featheredging

1. High-crown area damaged in collision can be replaced by using a supporting mold from inside. It may be necessary to bolt or rivet panels together to get them flush during initial repair.

2. When you think you have a panel pretty smooth, lay a coat of primer on it. Sanding the primer lightly will reveal if there are any high spots still left in the panel.

3. Sanding blocks like this made of hard rubber are inexpensive and do a much better job than using the flat of your hand.

4. These three drawings show how to featheredge sand a spot or chip. The larger the feathered circle. the better the result. Paint on a crowned surface will tend to sand flat, and must be radiused. Narrow scratches must be flared into area.

5. Thin putty or "glaze" spreads out almost like thick paint and is just the ticket for filling small sanding scratches or feathered-out nicks. The area must be primered before using putty, though.

6. Naturally, before any painting is done, the car must be masked off. This can be done for the most part with ¾-in. masking tape and sheets of newspaper. Narrow tape can be used on emblems like this, but the best results are obtained when all chrome is removed for preparation and paint.

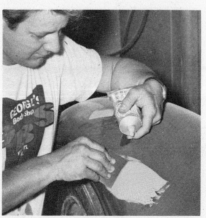

5. Spreading "Glaze" Putty

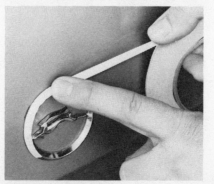

6. Masking Off Trim

turned on its side, folded together, and torn down the center. Each piece is then folded triple, leaving one face toward the paint, one toward the hand, and one folded between the two exposed faces.

When sanding by hand, keep the entire hand in contact with the surface, not just the finger tips or side of the palm. However, for specific areas, these two pressure points may well be used to advantage.

After the entire area has been sanded, let it dry and check to make sure every inch has been covered. Any streaks or corners missed must be touched up.

With the biggest part of the surface sanded, attention can be directed toward the repaired areas, scratches, and chips. Getting these places feather-edged properly is vital to a good finished product! This cannot be over-stressed.

Feather-edging a large area, such as around a straightened place on a fender, is much simpler than small chipped spots. This is where those pieces of 80 grit dry sandpaper come in. To speed up the job, attach strips of the #80 to the sanding block (or to an electric or air-powered "jitterbug" sander) and do the rough-edging first. This paper cuts very fast, and leaves deep scratches, so use caution until you're familiar with it. With the rough production paper, it's best to sand with the edge, much like walking around the shore of a lake.

After this initial fast cut, switch to 220 and the block, plus water, and repeat. The idea is to feather the break between paint and metal over a wide area. There will be at least two paint layers showing, the color coat and the primer/surfacer, and on older cars the number can be as high as eight or nine layers. The wider the band of each paint layer showing, the better the feather-edging job! A 1-in. band means a much better job than a ¼-in. band. Finally, sand the feather-edged area in the direction of the overall panel sanding job.

The scratches are easy to remove if they're only one coat of paint thick. Just a little more localized pressure on the paper will do the job, but the "trough" should be feathered as much as possible. The little minute rock chips along the car front and around the wheel openings are harder to remove, and because of their sheer number, it's best to use a block or electric/air jitterbug. You can rent one of the handy gadgets, incidentally, for $3 a day. When the rock chips are really numerous and deep, resort to an initial attack with #100 paper, then follow up with the finer grits before priming. When this happens, the entire area of color coat is usually removed, but the effort is absolutely necessary.

Chips on the rest of the car, such as around exposed hinges or door openings, or what have you, are really the hardest of all to feather-edge. This is because their size means the feather-edging will leave a sort of smooth crater. Although the paint may be thin, the crater will really show up (even if properly feather-edged) in the finished job if you're not careful. The best route to follow when fixing up chipped places is to make the feather-edging area several times bigger than the chipped size. If

Body & Paint

there were several coats of paint on the car, the crater might best be filled with a thin coat of putty after the primer is applied. The important point is, make a chip crater as smooth as possible, flowing gradually into the surrounding paint.

Be careful when sanding next to chrome, aluminum or glass, as the paper will cut these surfaces quickly. Next to chrome, slide the index finger (or little finger) off the paper and use as a guide. The same goes for the other materials, too. With a block, just be careful.

The edges of all opening panels, such as hood, doors, ect., should be sanded to bare metal with the block. This won't be hard; paint here is usually minimal.

The door jambs and door edges should be washed clean of all accumulated dirt and grease, then thoroughly sanded with both paper and #00 steel wool. The steel wool gets down into all the little irregularities the paper can't reach, otherwise the final paint might not bond securely.

Fenders should be loosened and the fender welt removed, then the mating edges very carefully sanded, especially chipped places. This is one location where shoddy preparation will quickly show up. New fender welt, which only costs 20¢ per foot, may be added after the color is on. Don't try to tape it off!

Finally turn to the repaired areas again. If a spot has been worked, sand the bare area well with 220 or finer paper, until all rough file or grinder scratches are no longer rough to the touch. The jitterbug can be used here, also. Don't use rough paper, and don't lay on the pressure. Lead isn't nearly as hard as the surrounding metal, and neither is 'glass, so be careful

FINAL PREPARATIONS

Should the fiberglass area have what appears to be blisters, some further repair is in order. This sometimes happens, so just peel out the blister air bubble with a knife blade and patch with more 'glass or resin.

Special attention is paid a repaired area before primer/surfacer is applied. If lead was used wash the entire area thoroughly with properly diluted Met-L-Prep, which removes the inherent acid and grease. Wash away the Met-L-Prep residue with water. With both 'glass and lead repaired areas, clean thoroughly with grease and wax remover (even though they've been well sanded), then spot with a good coat of primer.

At this stage of the game, a compressor is handy, which can be rented along with the paint gun for about $8 a day. You'll only need it for a day (actually much less). The compressor should be able to maintain a steady 60-80 lbs. pressure.

Build up a tank of pressure, drain the tank of any oil (the renter will show you how), then blow all the dirt and sanding residue from the car. Be especially careful to get all the little pieces of stuff in the cracks around windows, windshield, hood hinges, etc. Use a lint-free rag as you go along to clean the surfaces and all chrome and glass areas.

When the car is clean, tape off the trim, glass, and interior, and cover the

1. Paint Spray Booth

2. Gravity Feed Spray Gun

3. Marbles For Agitation

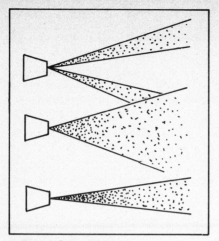

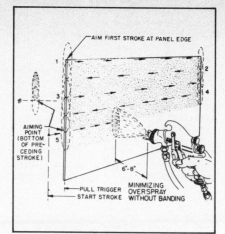

4. Proper Spray Pattern   **5. Overlapping Each Pass**   **6. Testing Spray Pattern**

7. Poor Pattern

1. You may not have a professional spray booth to paint in, but good jobs have been done by amateurs in a garage with floor wetted down, or outside on a calm day.

2. There are many kinds and brands of spray guns. Pressure, siphon and gravity feed (like this model) guns all have different capabilities.

3. When painting with metalflake or other metallic or iridescent paints, a few marbles or clean bolts in the paint gun will help to keep the metallic elements in suspension.

4. Spray gun pattern is critical in getting good results. Top pattern is too wide, gun needs adjusting. Middle pattern is just about right, at about 8 ins. from the gun. Bottom fan is much too narrow; this will load the paint on too heavily.

5. Practice making even strokes with paint gun, starting each pass "dry" and adding trigger at end of each stroke. Overlap must be just right or paint, especially any of the metallic types, will streak.

6. Before starting on the car, it's a good idea to test the spray pattern on something unimportant first.

7. This test spray pattern is too coarse or too wet, shows a need for an increase in air pressure of 5 lbs.

engine and the seats with an old piece of anything handy. Tape newspaper or wrapping paper around the engine compartment opening, and around entire door opening. Tape off the door upholstery panels and the glass molding if they haven't been removed. Keep all this paper as flat as possible, so debris can't fall into the folds and blow out later.

As you'll find, taping can be quite a maddening procedure. The best width to use on cars is ½ or ¾-in., which costs about 75¢ per roll. You'll need one or two rolls for the average car. When applying the tape, work over at least an arm-length stretch, rather than in short 3- and 4-in. distances. This makes following an edge infinitely easier, and the whole job much faster. For instance, to tape the long side molding, stick the tape end to one end of the molding, hold it there with the next finger, then unroll about 16 to 24 ins. of tape. Run the finger down this stretch, pushing the tape against the molding as you go. By sighting down the tape, you can get it exactly at the edge of the molding. If a little tape gets on the painted surface, run a razor blade parallel with the surface and cut away the offending tape. This tape must be removed, or an unpainted area, which shows up like a sore thumb, will be left!

When the entire car is taped, mix up the primer/surfacer. Always remember that neither lacquer nor acrylic will go

over enamel in color coat form! The only time this can be done is over a factory-baked enamel job, where the paint is dry clear through. Even baked enamel from local shops is likely to blister when covered with the hotter paints. This applies only to the color coats, and not to the primer, which will cover with no adverse effects.

SPRAY GUN TECHNIQUE

No matter what kind of paint will be finally used—enamel, lacquer, or acrylic—use a multi-purpose primer with the appropriate thinner. Mix according to the can directions, which is about two parts thinner to one part primer, and stir thoroughly. For primer, a good all-around spray gun head will do, something like a #30 on the DeVilbiss and #362 on the Binks. Adjust the gun so that the spray fan is about 8 ins. wide at a point 12 ins. from the gun head. If the fan is too wide, there will be a thin spot in the middle; if it's too narrow the pattern will appear as a tight band. The fan adjustment is the top knob above the handle. The second knob is for material adjustment, and won't concern you too much at this time.

Make several practice passes on a piece of cardboard, with the compressor setting at 60 lbs. constant. With the De-Vilbiss, keep the gun 8-12 ins. away from the surface; make it 10-12 ins. with the Binks. Notice that when the paint gun trigger is first depressed there is a moment when only air comes out. Following this, the paint comes. Practice making a smooth pass, keeping the gun a constant distance from the surface until the pass (which should average about 2 ft. per swing) is completed. Start the pass on one side, swing horizontally to the other limit, raise or lower the gun nearly a fan width and go back. Keep the gun parallel to the surface, so that one end of the fan isn't closer to the surface than the other.

As soon as you feel confident with the paint gun (don't worry too much, because primer dries relatively fast on the surface and it's easy to fix up a botched area), set it aside and get the car surface ready. Wash the entire car with a good wax/grease remover, then again blow away dirt, etc., from the cracks.

Start with the door, hood and deck lid openings. Spray the primer on evenly, in

Body & Paint

smooth strokes. When these are done, allow them to dry for 10 or 15 mins., then close the openings and start on the big outside metal.

The previously primed spots where metalwork was done must be sanded with 220 or finer paper, then wiped clean. Any small spots of putty should be treated likewise.

Start spraying on the top, which is the hardest to reach, and follow these handy hints. Throw the air hose over one shoulder and hold away from the car with your other hand; wrap a piece of rag around the gun/cap connection point to keep paint from dribbling out when painting with the gun in a horizontal position (such as for the top, hood, deck lid).

If the paint is going on right, it will appear smooth and wet for just a bit af-ter application. If it looks grainy, as if full of sand, the paint is too thick or you're holding the gun too far away from the surface. If the paint runs (you won't need anybody to show you what this panic is!), it is too thin or you are holding the gun too close. If the patch alternates dry-wet-dry, or wet-runny-wet, your pass is not constant. And don't stay in one place too long. It's just like a dance step—1-2-3, 1-2-3, etc.

If the gun doesn't seem to be making a constant fan, it may be clogged up. If so, soak the head (which unscrews from the handle) and make sure all the little mixing holes are clear. Pour thinner through the handle part of the head (not through the air delivery hole), and make sure the pressure-equalizing hole in the cup lid is open. When all this has been done, spray a little clear thinner through the gun first to make sure it's really clean. As you use a primer gun, the primer—which is very thick anyway— tends to build up and close the cup lid vent, so poke this open occasionally.

Primer is the necessary good base for a fine paint job, so don't skimp. It takes about 1 gal. of unthinned primer/surfacer for the average car, so keep going around the car until you're sure you've got it well covered. Cost is $10 per gallon for the primer, $3 per gallon for the thinner.

You don't need a special spray booth, so you can spray right out in the open. Naturally, don't spray next to a building, or in a windstorm, but don't worry about overspray. Primer dries before it's 5 ft. from the gun and will blow or wash off whatever it settles on. Don't spray under a tree that drips sap! Plan your time so that you're through spraying with at least 2 hrs. of sunlight left, and when the temperature is at least 40° or above. If spraying in the cold winter or inside when it's raining, use special thinner (the paint store will decide for you).

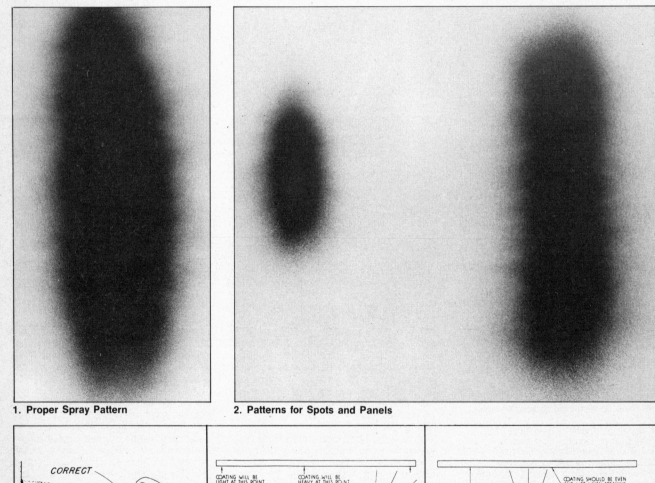

1. Proper Spray Pattern

2. Patterns for Spots and Panels

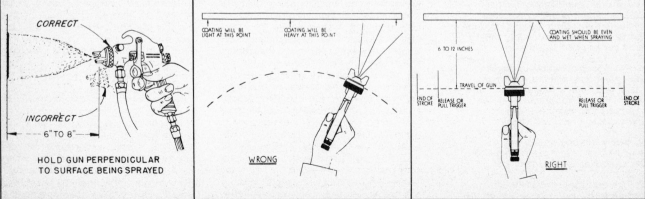

3. Holding Gun Properly

4. Cleaning Air Hole

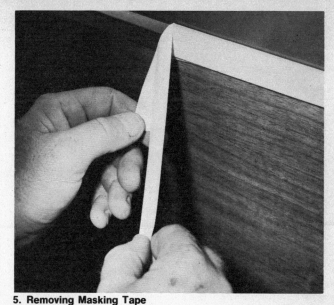

5. Removing Masking Tape

1. This is a normal spray pattern. Do not use excessive air pressure as it wastes material in the form of overspray, and ruins paint surface.

2. The small spray pattern here is used for spot repairs. The larger pattern is used for panel repair and complete refinishing jobs.

3. A spray gun is nothing more than an air brush and must be held same distance from panel throughout stroke. When adjustments and stroke pattern are learned, most of the painting battle is won.

4. With guns that have an air hole at the top, it's important to keep the air hole free by poking a wire through it occasionally. The rag is tied around to catch any paint drips.

5. When removing masking tape from any surface, it's best to pull it back over itself like this, and always pull down away from newly painted panel or paint may chip.

Finally, if the car has slight waves in the panels that might be taken out by block sanding, a good trick is to spray a final coat of different colored primer. For instance, if the major primer color was light gray, finish with dark gray, or vice versa. Then, later on when you block sand, the thin top coat will come off but the other color will still show in low spots.

After the primer has dried for 20 to 30 mins., the tape can be removed. If you are painting over bleeders like maroon or red, the primer must be sprayed with a bleeder sealer to insure an even tone. Although it is possible to go right ahead and sand the car (dry) and follow with the color coats of paint, it is best to allow the primer to cure for several days, even weeks. The primer will dry and shrink, so allow about four weeks' time for a good quality job. You can drive the car meantime.

Scratches don't come in the paint can or from the gun. So, take it easy during the surfacer sanding operation. The surfacer will sand very easily, either dry or wet, and it's advisable to use 320 or 400 grit paper on surfacer. Remember this is the base for the color, and use of a coarser paper will leave scratches too deep for the color paint to cover.

Next, use the wax and grease remover solution, completely washing the car, even the smallest cracks. This is vital, for any foreign substance will invariably ruin an otherwise perfect job. For instance, just the marks left by your fingers will leave dark splotches under the final color. When washing the car with the cleaning solution, always use clean, lint-free rags (don't use shop towels, as they often are cleaned with low-grade solvents that contain contaminants bad for good paint adhesion). It's wise to use the special cleanser always, but in a pinch you can use lacquer thinner, applied with a very wet rag and immediately wiped off with a dry rag. Don't wait even a minute if you use thinner, as it is "hot" and will quickly soften the surfacer and may cause other damage to the paint below.

FINAL PAINT COAT

The car is now ready for the final color, and this is the precise moment most amateur painters get the jitters. It's also the time when one step must follow the other in rapid succession, so having the procedures well established in your mind will ensure best results.

What you do from now on depends a lot upon the paint you're using—the type, not the brand. Lacquer is the easiest to spray for the novice, followed by acrylic, then enamel. This is simply because the lacquer and acrylic dry much faster, compensating for many application errors—or at least, for a few.

Enamel paint, although hardest to actually apply, requires the least amount of overall effort, and is an excellent choice where maximum toughness is required. It gets its glossiness (shine) from a varnish used by the manufacturer. This varnish is made of a solution of resins with alcohol, turpentine, or amyl acetate. You must use enamel thinner with enamel paint. Although acrylic has received a big boost in use as standard finishes by several auto makers, at least one major

company still uses baked enamel. A baked enamel job is superior to an air-dry job and is very durable, but unless you have a bake oven available, you're stuck with air-dry. For years now auto enthusiasts have considered lacquer the only way to get a superb paint job, but such is not always the case. It depends generally upon the painter. For the average person unable to afford a good lacquer expert, and not wanting to take the extra preparation pains necessary for lacquer, enamel is an obvious answer. It will cover scratches well, and can be used almost anywhere you desire.

Acrylic is like lacquer, in that it dries right away, but it is plastic-based (lacquer is cotton-based) and undergoes a chemical change as the paint dries and unites with oxygen. Acrylic must be sprayed differently and will not dry to maximum gloss if put on in one heavy coat.

Before starting the color spraying, it's wise to completely clean the spraying equipment, especially if it has come from the local rental emporium. You can rent perfectly good equipment, but make sure the compressor is in good shape (not pumping oil). Paint guns will differ, but all you're interested in is a good all-around nozzle (head).

Clean the paint gun thoroughly before any use, either with acetone or lacquer thinner. Acetone works faster. Remove the pot and nozzle, then soak everything for 20 mins. or so. Follow by brushing the pot inside, the top sealing lip, the sealing area on the pot cap (the sealing gasket must be good), the nozzle, and the gun head. Make sure all mixing holes in the nozzle are clean.

If enamel is to be used, thin it with two parts thinner to one part paint, pouring the paint into the cup through a strainer which will trap bits of foreign matter. Tighten the pot until secure, as paint might otherwise drip from the connection (the shop rag tied around this connection point will prevent drips).

Before blowing color on the waiting car, test the gun pattern. Start by opening the gun up by turning the spreader adjustment (top thumb screw above handle) all the way out, and backing off the

Body & Paint

fluid screw (right beneath the spreader adjustment) until the first thread shows. Adjust the air pressure regulator to give a constant 40 lbs. pressure for lacquer and acrylics, or 60 lbs. for enamel. Hold the gun 6 to 8 ins. from the test surface, parallel to such surface, and give the trigger one full pull, then release.

The color coat is sprayed exactly like the primer/surfacer. However, some extra preparation might be needed if lacquer or acrylic is being applied over enamel. Just as a precaution, if the old paint is enamel, spray on a coat of Du-Pont #22 sealer, which will help keep the enamel from raising due to the hotter lacquer thinner. If you're not sure, always spray a test patch first. The sealer is always a good idea.

All the previous hard work will come to nothing if the final color coat is sprayed haphazardly. Before actually spraying any paint, practice the proper spraying swing. At all times, the nozzle should be from 8 to 12 ins. from the surface (individuals vary in technique, thus the difference in distances). Picture yourself facing the door of a car. You want to paint each individual panel, or panel group, with a full stroke, thereby reducing the number of overlaps to a minimum on each surface.

With the gun held at the left edge of the door, and the nozzle distance correct, twist the wrist so the gun is actually pointed lengthwise to the car. As the trigger is pulled, twist the wrist back toward the door. This makes the initial application of each stroke blend together at the overlap. As the gun comes to point directly at the surface, begin the smooth stroke across the panel. Not too fast, and not too slow. If you go too fast, the stroke will look misty; if too slow, the paint will pile up too heavy and try to run. Remember that it is easier to do a job with several thin coats than with one heavy coat. At the end of each stroke, twist the wrist away from the car in the opposite direction (or direction of the stroke).

Although the technique differs, most painters spray the door jambs, hood edge, trunk jambs, etc., before starting on the rest of the car. If you're careful during this phase, only a small amount of overspray will carry around the edge and onto the outside metal. If too much overspray gets around the opening, it may make the overall blending job too difficult. For lacquer or acrylic the area may be lightly sanded, for enamel the best procedure is a wash job with thinner before the paint hardens.

Because panels are sprayed one at a time, get into the habit of spraying consistently. Don't spray heavily in one place and lightly in another. As a panel is started, try starting the stroke slightly inboard from the panel edge and ending slightly short. As the next panel is started, the resulting overlap will keep the depth of paint constant.

The biggest single problem the amateur painter experiences is stroke inconsistency. The paint must overlap everywhere, otherwise it will appear streaked when it dries. It sometimes helps to

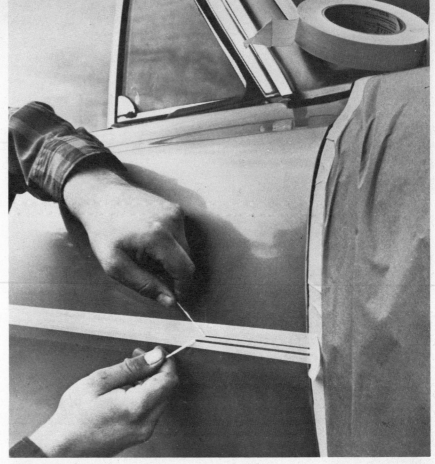

1. Taping for Pinstripes

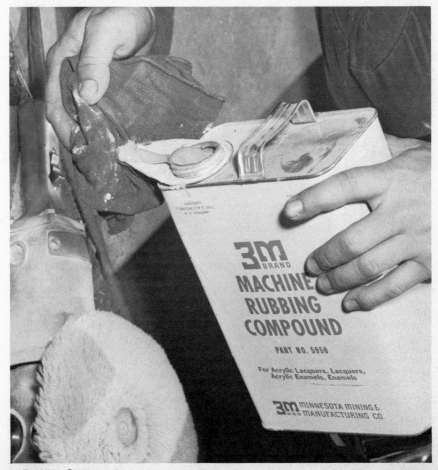

2. Rubbing Compound

3. Buffing With Rubbing Compound

4. Cleaning Clogged Buffer

1. Pin striping is an art in itself, but if you lack a steady hand, you can make straight stripes with this special tape which is scored so strips can be pulled out to paint through.

2. After a new lacquer or acrylic paint job has cured (usually a week or two), the paint must be rubbed out to achieve its final high gloss. Be sure you are using the right rub compound for the type of paint used.

3. Paint can be rubbed out by hand or with a buffer. Go cautiously if you use a buffing machine or you may buff right down to the metal!

4. When compounding with a buffer, the fluffy sheepskin becomes matted with hardened compound and should be cleaned with a "ticking wheel."

5. Touch-up paints in all stock colors are available in most auto parts stores. For small nicks and scratches, tubes of touch-up paint with applicators can be bought at your dealer's parts counter.

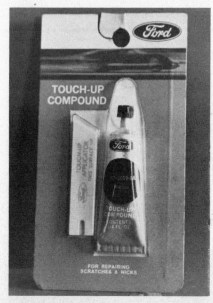

5. Ford Touch-Up Kit

make horizontal strokes first, then vertical strokes, etc. The idea is to apply the same amount of paint everywhere on the surface.

If lacquer is being used, the drying time is such that it may be applied at random. However, acrylic must be allowed to "flash" before the next coat is applied (surface harden). Enamel is a slow drier, therefore it should not be applied all at once. The first time around, a very light tack coat is applied. This will become sticky in a few minutes and helps make subsequent spraying easier by increasing adhesion. The second coat of enamel is sprayed normally, but the amateur should never try to get all the paint on the car in one pass (2 gals. required for the average sedan).

Starting with the top, spray each stroke evenly. If you load up a particular area, which is easy to do, the paint may sag or run. Don't panic, just continue with the spraying but stay away from that place. It is sometimes possible to stop a run in the early stages by simply backing away from the panel slightly and spraying nothing but air across the run. This will often give enough surface drying to hold the sag from advancing. When the first coat is dry, dip a tiny brush in enamel thinner and remove as much of the sag excess as possible. The idea is to soak up the excess rather than spread it around. After the sag has been carefully removed, fog a little paint over the area. If you do the job well, the little boo-boo won't be too apparent. On the next coat, go easy in the area of a run, again just spraying on a light fog coat.

An enamel job usually requires three coats—the tack coat, the first heavy color and the final color. After the last coat, wait a couple of minutes, check for sags and repair any if necessary, then leave the car to dry overnight. In fact, since enamel should be painted in a spray booth if possible, leave the car for a couple of hours before detailing.

A note about enamel and moisture. They just don't mix, so if the floor is washed down before painting to settle the dust, let it dry before spraying. Temperatures shouldn't be under 60° or over 100° F. when the car is being sprayed, otherwise special steps are required. Special additives are available to control the drying time, such as DuPont #3656 (rather than normal 366/g) for acrylic, which will slow drying if the temperature is too hot. If painting is done when the weather is wet or cold, the color can "blush." That is, moisture is trapped in the paint, so a slower thinner or special retarder may be needed. The paint store will guide you here. At all times, follow the mixing direction of the manufacturer explicitly!

Although the enamel job can be done at one spraying, lacquer and acrylic require more elapsed time for the best job. If you have the time, spray the latter in several good coats, then allow to dry for a couple of days. Water-sand with 600 sandpaper, then spray several more coats. Whereas enamel doesn't require any after-spray special attention, lacquer and acrylic must be color-sanded with 600 sandpaper before the final rubbing out process (buffing).

1. A scrape along the door sure doesn't look like much damage, but body shop estimates for repair (minus painting) could range from $88.50 to $99.25—something worth saving.

2. Without an awful lot of trouble, you can very easily restore partial shape and form to wheelwell dents by making a few well placed blows with an ordinary claw hammer.

3. The next step in this process of pulling out creases is to carefully drill ⅛-in. holes along the center of the panel crease. The holes should be spaced about 3-ins. apart.

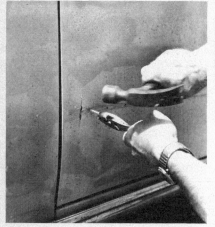

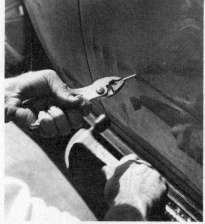

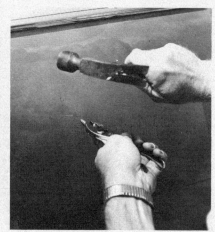

4. Thread a sheetmetal screw into first hole and pull it toward you. Use a pair of pliers and tug sharply. Then hammer above and below crease, while continuing to exert pull.

5. Continue pulling procedure along crease. By the time you're finished, it should be pulled back nearly to the original panel shape. Don't try for perfection at this point.

6. Check the panel carefully for any secondary damage. Here, there is a slight depression in the panel half-way between the major damage and the top of the panel on this car.

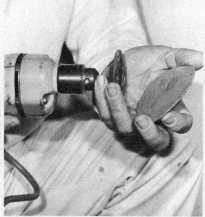

7. Once damaged areas appear near normal, run your hand over them. Don't worry about slight depressions. But raised surfaces should be detected and lowered to panel's shape.

8. Replace drill bit with a rubber pad sanding adapter. A #24 grit disc fits on the pad for grinding. Then apply firm hand pressure to the disc to make sure adhesive sticks.

9. Grind along the creased area to the bare metal. This helps to restore the panel contour by cutting off the high spots, and it prepares the surface for a body filler application.

10. Now, the next step is to go to work on the fender and the wheelwell damage. But be especially careful when you do the grinding so that you avoid cutting through the metal.

11. This particular dent was the most difficult. Hammering only restored contour about 50%; considerable cutting was needed to prepare it for the application of body filler.

12. Mix body filler and catalyst on fiber board or heavy cardstock. Follow directions on the can of filler. Work quickly because filler sets rapidly once catalyst is added.

13. Apply filler generously over the damaged area with a wide-blade putty knife. This is a rough application; its purpose is to fill low spots and to provide a base for shaping.

14. Fill all the other damage spots while you are waiting for the filler to flash off. When the filler is ready, use a "cheese grater" file to shape the contour to the original.

15. If you can't get the contour the first time around, apply more filler and refile. Once you do have it, a final application with a squeegee will fill any little pin holes or imperfections.

16. Hand sand with a folded sheet of fine grit paper. Be sure to feather the edges of the filler so that it blends smoothly into the undamaged area surrounding it in all directions.

17. Filing and shaping an area of heavy contour requires patience, but remember that the filler sets fast, and if you don't keep up with it, it may harden so much it can't be filed.

18. A coat of primer applied with a brush finishes the job. Total cost of the afternoon's work: $13.50. Before you spray a color coat, sand the primer lightly, and it's ready.

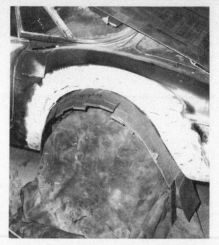

1. Fiberglass materials adapt as easily to customizing work as to repair jobs. Here's how to flare wheelwells on '62 Corvette. First, new opening is marked.

2. Ron Gauthe, of Fiberglass Specialists, 14761 Oxnard St., Van Nuys, Calif., cuts off old opening with sabre saw after sanding off the old paint.

3. Cardboard, the fiberglass worker's pal, is placed around the opening and blocked into place with pieces of wood put between opening and tire (covered).

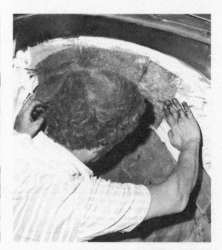

4. Slits are made in cardboard around outside edge to form a sloping curve, then masking tape is used to hold the desired shape of the new opening.

5. Since high strength is not a factor in wheelwells, Ron uses matte fiberglass instead of cloth. A standard paint roller applies resin mix to matte.

6. Resin-soaked matte is put right on body and cardboard, and Ron works the resin into the rough surface left by previous grinding of the wheelwell.

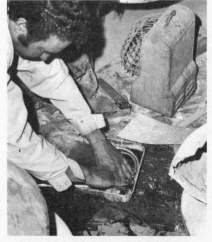

7. Once this first layer of matte is dry, Ron checks room around tire with blocks of wood removed, because car's owner wanted plenty of clearance.

8. When matte has hardened completely, cardboard can be ripped out from the wheelwell, and outside edge evened up with a grinder. Watch out for tire!

9. Strips of fiberglass "rope," which will be used to form inner lip of well, are soaked in mixture of fiberglass resin and catalyst, or hardener.

10. A large piece of cardboard is cut to shape of wheelwell and used as a support. Then fiberglass rope is worked between fiberglass and cardboard edge.

11. When the rope has hardened (a heater can be used to speed it up), small strips of resin-soaked matte are applied over the lip made by the rope.

12. Another handy fiberglass material is this "chopped" fiberglass which can be used to build up areas during bodywork, without adding very much weight.

13. The chopped fiberglass is used to blend the new fender extension into fender. About half of rope is ground away to make a flat lip on the outside.

14. Before applying any more matte, Ron brushes resin mix into the 'glass of body and fenderwell extension so last layer will lie flat and adhere well.

15. Ron rolls final layer of material over the whole wheelwell/body area, using lots of resin for smooth finish so that little filling will be needed.

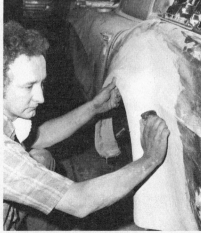

16. After the whole fenderwell has cured, a thin layer of body filler is applied over area and sanded. Ron uses a "cheese grater" file to rough-grind.

17. Here's a bodywork tip that applies to numerous jobs. Ron uses sandpaper, wrapped around piece of old radiator hose, for sanding inside curved areas.

18. With the sanding done, a primer coat is applied. All that's left before final painting is a thin layer of body "glaze," more primer for paint adhesion.

Caring for Your VW

Although VW shops probably offer the best service available in the U.S., it's not unusual for a VW owner to be tempted by the lower prices and immediate accommodation available at filling stations and independent garages. Unfortunately, it seems that about 99% of the mechanics found in these places are scared to death of foreign cars, and few of them have even bothered to buy their first metric tool, despite the fact that there are more VW's on American highways than many domestic makes. The driver who purchased a VW because he wanted an economical and easy-to-service vehicle is therefore more likely than most car owners to undertake routine service and repair operations himself.

LUBRICATION

Oil Changes. An oil change is often the first self-maintenance task undertaken by VW owners. Top brands of motor oil are sold in discount stores at prices far below those charged by service stations, and it is not unusual for the car owner to save at least a dollar on the cost of the oil alone. But the main reason for changing your own oil is to get the job done right! The VW manual states that the oil strainer in the bottom of the crankcase should be removed, cleaned, and installed with new gaskets at each oil change. Yet this is seldom done in service stations and is often skipped even at authorized VW garages.

The normal oil change interval listed in the owner's manual is usually adequate, but most conscientious owners will change oil more often in winter. To do it properly, warm the engine up thoroughly on the road before draining the old oil. Warm oil drains down quicker and will carry suspended sludge and carbon particles out along with it.

The crankcase strainer is held in place by six small nuts that require a 10mm wrench to undo. (Volkswagen owners will find it well worth the expense to purchase a set of metric wrenches for this and other repair and service operations.) Wash the strainer in gasoline to remove all dirt and sludge, then replace it using gaskets obtained from your VW dealer.

When pouring in the fresh oil, be especially careful not to overfill the crankcase. This can cause oil to be thrown out around the rear main bearing, and may lead to leaking gaskets and oil seals. Though the VW crankcase holds somewhat less than 3 qts., mechanics are sometimes tempted to pour in three cans and be done with it. This is both unwise and uneconomical. By saving the leftover oil for the next change you'll be able to get every fourth or fifth oil change for "nothing."

SAE 30 oil is recommended for temperatures above freezing, although many owners use multi-viscosity oil year-round. Below freezing an SAE 10W oil is used, and if temperatures stay below -13° F., SAF 5W is called for. Oil is changed the first 300 miles and then every 3000 miles thereafter.

Grease Jobs. A grease gun and a few cartridges of suitable lubricant will quickly pay for themselves. Service stations charge $1.50 to $2.50 for a grease job requiring about 25¢ worth of lubricant. It's easy to lube the VW's front suspension at home, although on models made before 1966 it is important that you jack the front wheels off the ground before greasing the kingpins. Keep pumping grease until fresh lube begins to seep out between the parts, then wipe away the old grease.

Gearcase Lubrication. Transaxle oil changes are required every 30,000 miles, and the oil level is to be checked each 6000 miles. The lubricant used must be SAE 90 hypoid oil. Not all service stations stock this grade, so be sure to check the labeling on their oil drum before turning the job over to them. SAE 80 should be used only where the temperature stays below 15°F.; however, many owners have found multi-viscosity SAE 80-90 hypoid oil to be entirely satisfactory.

Most service stations will be happy to sell you some of their gear lube if you provide the container. If you find that the oil level is low when you remove the side plug from the transaxle housing, it's easy to top it up using an ordinary trigger-type oil can filled with the SAE 90 lube.

The VW manual also states that the drain plugs should be removed at each level check and their magnetic inserts wiped clean of metal particles. This is of greatest importance during the early life of the car. You'll need a common thermos bottle cork that you can quickly jam

1. Volkswagen Cutaway

2. Oil Strainer

3. Wheel Bearing

4. Axle Nut

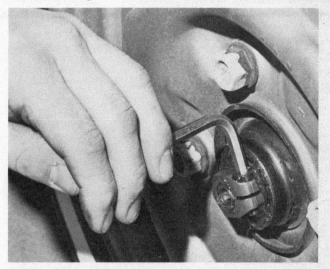

5. Roller Bearing Adjustment

into the hole as the drain plug is removed. If the filler plug is in place you will lose very little oil, but you will still want to have your trusty squirt can on hand to make up the loss. The same grade of oil can be used in the steering gearbox should its oil level become low.

Body Lube. A small can of lightweight dripless oil is adequate for lubricating the door hinges, carburetor linkage, hood hinges, etc. Since VW door hinges—particularly on the Beetle—are exposed directly to the weather, their frequent oiling is very important. Open the door and apply oil to the notches in the hinge pivot. Swing the door back and forth several times and repeat the oiling until the door moves with complete freedom. Neglected hinges can be "unfrozen" by applying Liquid Wrench before oiling them in the normal way.

A tube of white lithium grease is useful for lubricating the front seat rails, door latches, and hood catches. In cold climates it is important that a graphite-containing lock oil be applied to the door and ignition locks to prevent freezing. If this is not done, the starter lock-out in the ignition switch will freeze and prevent you from starting the car even though the ignition itself may work normally.

ROUTINE ADJUSTMENTS

Steering. Next to doing your own lube jobs, performing various routine adjustments is the most frequently required owner-maintenance operation. Keeping a close check on steering wheel play can be particularly rewarding for the "sporty" driver. The precise and quick VW steering is a real joy, and if never allowed to go slack, it will stay that way for the life of the car.

Although current VW manuals permit up to 1 in. of steering play (measured at the rim of the steering wheel with the front wheels pointed straight ahead), older manuals state that there should be absolutely no play up to a steering lock of 180° ± 30° to the left or right of center. The change is probably intended to take some work off the backs of VW service departments, since there have been no significant changes in the steering box which would dictate a change in actual specs. The conscientious Volks lover is therefore likely to adhere to the original "zero play" recommendation by making adjustments at home.

Usually your adjustments will be limited to setting the clearance between the worm and roller. To do this, take out the spare tire and remove the semi-circular panel located behind it. This will give access to the top of the steering box.

Turn the steering wheel 90° to the left or right (older manuals say 180°), then loosen the roller shaft adjusting screw lock nut. Loosen the adjusting screw approximately one turn, and then tighten

1. The VW is an intricate piece of machinery on the inside, despite its outward looks. If you don't have lots of VW know-how and metric tools, it's best to stick to easy tune-up.

2. Oil strainer is held in bottom of VW engine by six nuts. Remove and clean at each oil change. Forget about large plug in the middle.

3. VW's with 5-bolt wheels are equipped with ball bearings. When properly adjusted, this washer can be moved easily but firmly with the tip of a screwdriver.

4. Ball bearings on pre-1967 Bugs are adjusted by loosening lock nut, moving inner nut until washer slips with right "feel," then tightening lock nut again.

5. To adjust wheel bearings on VW equipped with roller bearings, loosen the cross-bolt in the clamp nut, using a 6mm hex key.

Caring for Your VW

it until you feel the resistance of the roller contacting the steering worm. Hold the adjusting screw at that point while tightening the lock nut, but be very careful not to overtighten it, since the steering box cover is aluminum and the threads are easily stripped. Eighteen foot-pounds is the correct torque figure—significantly less than the force you'd use to install a spark plug.

The steering can only be considered free of play when even the lightest movement of the steering wheel causes the front wheels to turn. However, if the steering does not return to within 45° of center after taking a corner at 10-15 mph, the roller is too tight and must be slacked off a bit to avoid eventual damage.

Older cars, and those that have been neglected or given hard use, will sometimes require adjustments to the worm. Jack up the front end and pull the left front wheel. Work the steering by grasping the steering coupling. If end-play is apparent in the steering gear input shaft, then it follows that the worm has excessive play.

The worm must be adjusted from under the car, and the job is awkward, to say the least. A large adjustable wrench can be used to loosen the lock nut. To tighten the worm adjusting screw, obtain a piece of scrap metal and cut it to a length that will engage the teeth on the inside of the nut. By holding this in the closed jaws of your adjustable wrench, the nut can be turned in until all play has been removed. Here again, be careful not to over-tighten, and be prepared to back off on the adjustment if tight spots are felt as the steering is turned.

Should the above adjustments fail to restore smooth and precise steering, it is likely that there is axial play in the steering roller. If such is the case, the car will have to be taken to an authorized dealer, since the steering box must be removed from the car and disassembled to correct the problem.

Wheel Bearings. Another common home maintenance job is adjusting the front wheel bearings. To do this, jack up each front wheel and remove the hub cap and wheel bearing dust cover. The cotter pin holding the speedometer drive cable must be removed before the left dust cover can be taken off.

Release the locking tabs, loosen the

lock nut, and tighten the inner nut with a 27mm wrench until all bearing play has been taken up. Do not force. Now tighten the locking nut and check the adjustment. The bearings are correctly adjusted if the large thrust washer behind the inner nut can just barely be moved sideways with the tip of a screwdriver. When this adjustment has been obtained, the locking tabs can be bent back into contact with the nuts and the dust cover replaced.

The 1966 and later VW's utilize a different type of front wheel bearing nut. Instead of separate locking and adjusting nuts, there is a single slotted clamp nut located on the spindle.

To adjust, loosen the screw in the clamp nut and spin the wheel by hand while slowly tightening the clamp nut on the spindle. When resistance is felt, back off the adjustment until free rotation is obtained. Tighten the locking screw. It is better to have the bearings on these later models slightly on the loose side than too tight. Removal and repacking of the front wheel bearings will be discussed later in the section under Running Gear.

Link Pins. On VW's built prior to 1966, the owner may wish to adjust the torsion arm links for side-play. Their condition

3. Link Pin Adjustment

1. Setting Bearing

2. Spindle

4. Setting Link Pin

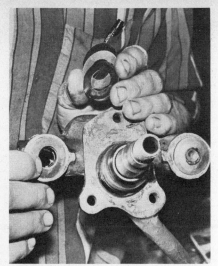

5. Wheel Camber Shims

6. Toe-in Correction

can be checked by jacking up a front wheel and shaking it at the top and bottom (with the front wheel bearings correctly adjusted). If there is any play felt, loosen the pinch bolts and fit a wrench to the flat sides of the exposed end of the link pins. Turn the pins until they are tight, then back off very slightly, lubricate the link pins via the grease fittings, and tighten the pinch bolts.

The toe-in of the front wheels may be altered by link pin adjustments, and this may be checked by measuring between the front edge of the wheel rims, marking the point with chalk on the tires, then rolling the car ahead one-half turn of the wheels and measuring between the marks which are now behind the wheel hubs. The distance should be about ⅛-in. greater. If not, loosen the locks on the tie-rods and turn the rods an equal amount on either side until the

1. VW specs are to adjust bearings until there is .001 to .006-in. of axial play measured with dial indicator. But you can set them by "feel" with a 24mm wrench.

2. Spindle and steering knuckle of pre-1967 VW link pin front end. This is the axle used in Formula Vee race cars, preferred by off-roaders.

3. To adjust link pins, loosen the clamp bolt, raise the car, and grease the link pins thoroughly.

4. Tighten link pins by fitting a wrench to their flat sides and turning clockwise. When tight loosen them very slightly and tighten the clamp bolts.

5. Worn link pins and bushings are easy and inexpensive to replace. Correct number of shims must be installed during assembly for proper wheel camber.

6. After adjusting link pins, it may be necessary to correct toe-in. What looks like two nuts on older VW tie-rods is really a lock nut and a drive-off clamp ring.

7. Super Beetle has MacPherson strut suspension which has only toe-in adjustment. It uses tie-rod clamps like those on domestic cars.

7. Super Beetle Suspension

correct toe-in is obtained. Some wheel alignment shops have a drive-over toe-in measuring machine for quick checks and will set this adjustment for you at a very low cost.

Brakes. Disc brakes require no adjustment, but drum brakes must be periodically taken up to keep a high pedal. VW brake drums have adjustment openings in their front surfaces, and the adjuster can be reached merely by jacking up the wheel and removing the hub cap. An ordinary screwdriver is used to engage the teeth of the starwheels.

Advance the adjuster until the shoes are just beginning to drag. Pump the pedal to recenter the shoes and recheck the adjustment. When the shoes continue to drag slightly after they have been centered, back off the adjusters until they are just clear of the brake drums.

The braking system of the VW is wholly conventional, and for additional details concerning brake work, the chapter on brakes should be consulted.

Handbrake. The VW handbrake is adjusted from inside the passenger compartment. Remove the rubber "boot" covering the back part of the handbrake lever and you will find two threaded cable ends projecting upward through loops welded onto the sides of the handle. There are two locking nuts and two adjusting nuts, all of which accept a 10mm wrench.

The only way to get a precision adjustment is to have both rear wheels off the ground. The lock nuts are loosened (there is a screwdriver slot in the end of the cable fitting to help you keep it from turning) and the adjustment nuts tightened until the rear wheels can just barely be turned by hand with the brake lever in its second notch. *Both sides must be equal.* With the lever in the fourth notch it should be impossible to turn the wheels by hand. Tighten the lock nuts, replace the boot, and the job is completed.

Clutch. Adjusting clutch pedal free-play is a very awkward job for a person with large hands and is almost impossible unless the car is on a lift. Usually it is well worth the expense of having it done in a

Caring for Your VW

VW garage, but if you are agile enough, here's how it works.

Release the small lock nut on the end of the clutch cable where it passes through the clutch operating lever on the side of the transmission bellhousing. Turn the larger adjusting nut until about ½-in. of free-play can be measured at the tip of the clutch pedal. Work the pedal several times and recheck. When the proper adjustment is obtained, tighten the lock nut. If clutch free-play is less than ⅜-in. or greater than ¾-in., adjustment is required.

Fan Belt Tension. Since a loose fan belt can also cause overheating, it is important to keep a close check on its tension and to carry a spare at all times. Firm pressure applied to the belt midway between the pulleys should cause it to yield approximately ½-in. If it is too loose or too tight, insert a large screwdriver through one of the slots in the rear half of the generator pulley and brace its tip

against one of the generator housing bolts. Loosen the nut at the center of the generator pulley and remove it. Rearrange the shim washers to increase or decrease the space between the inner and outer halves of the pulley, thereby causing the belt to ride higher or lower in the groove between them. Keep the extra spacers available for future adjustments by putting them on the outer end of the shaft before replacing the nut. Never over-tighten the belt adjustment, since this is likely to cause failure of the crankshaft pulley.

Door Latches. VW door latches can be adjusted to control the tightness of the doors as well as the effort required to close them. On pre-'68 models, a lock nut can be loosened on the striker plate and the adjusting screw turned with an ordinary screwdriver until the correct door action is obtained. After chassis No. 117,000,001, a new type of striker plate was used. It is adjusted by loosening the four Phillips-type screws and changing the angle or height of the striker plate and retightening the screws.

Headlights. Details on headlight aiming can be found in the chapter on lights. However, on 1966 and earlier VW's there is no need to remove the chrome bezel surrounding the lights when aiming the beams. Two Phillips-type screws are located in the bezel itself to control headlight aim. The upper one raises the beam when turned counterclockwise, and lowers it when turned clockwise. The lower screw moves the beam to the right when turned counterclockwise and to the left when turned clockwise. Although the Karmann Ghia does not have covered lights, its adjustment screws are also located in the bezel and can be turned without disassembly of the headlight.

When replacing a burned-out sealed beam in 1966 and earlier vehicles, remove the large slotted screw that is directly at the bottom of the headlight unit and the entire assembly will lift out of the fender. Detach the wires to the main and parking lamps and take out the spring clips that hold the sealed beam unit into the headlight assembly. When

1. Rear Suspension Bushing

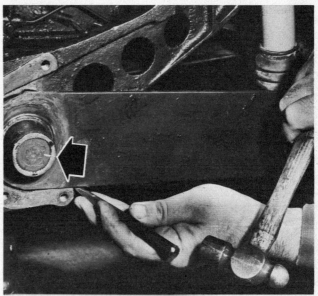

2. Torsion Arm Removal

3. Adjusting Brake

4. Fan Belt Adjustment

replacing the unit in the fender, be sure that the rubber seal is in good condition and properly in place. The aim of the headlight will have to be checked after such replacements are made.

Headlight aiming and sealed beam replacement in 1967 and later VW's and Karmann Ghias is a process identical to that on American cars. The bezel is removed by taking out a screw at the bottom to uncover the aiming and mounting screws. The aiming screws are at the top and side of the lamps. To change a sealed beam, remove the three mounting screws and lift off the lamp retaining ring.

RUNNING GEAR

Shock Absorber Replacement. The

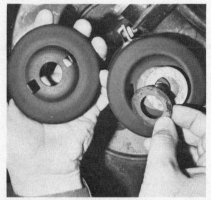

5. Removing Crank Pulley

1. Loose, noisy rear suspension on older Bugs can usually be corrected by replacing these large rubber bushings located on either side of torsion arm pivot.

2. When removing rear torsion arm or torsion bar, always mark original position of arm on bar and position of arm relative to car after prying it off its lower stop. This will help you get it back in same position.

3. You can reach the brake-adjusting star wheel through a small hole in front of the brake drum on VW's with 5-bolt wheels. Later cars have holes in back.

4. To adjust fan belt, insert screwdriver in notch in pulley back and brace it against generator bolt. This prevents turning. Loosen nut with spark plug wrench.

5. Split pulley comes apart so belt can be removed. This owner decided to install a degreed pulley on the crank, too, so a pair of screwdrivers were used to pull it.

6. Shims are removed from between generator pulley halves to tighten belt; they're stored under nut and washer. They'll have to be put back when new belt is installed.

7. The new aluminum pulley reduces engine power loss due to generator drive, permits exact timing because it is degreed for 360°, is lighter than stock, and adds to engine beauty. In adjusting fan belt, you should end up with about ½-in. give at each side, midway on the belt.

rear shocks can be removed by jacking up the car and taking off the rear wheels for easier access to the mounting bolts. You'll need one 17mm and two 19mm wrenches to remove them. Be sure you grease the bolts and nuts lightly with lithium grease before installing the new nuts, to make future removal easier.

The front shocks on 1966 and later vehicles are easier to remove—at least at the top. Front shocks get more road splashes and you are likely to find that at least some of the fasteners are locked with rust. If the shocks cannot be pulled off their lower mount, cut the rubber

bushing out with an electric drill so that the shock can be taken off. Then drill a hole in the metal bushing that is left on the lower torsion arm. Insert the tip of a punch and drive the bushing off the mounting stub of the shock absorber.

If the upper front shock bolt is frozen on pre-1966 models, apply "Liquid Wrench," hammer lightly on the bolt end, and apply heat to the shock tower with a propane torch. If necessary, the rubber bushings can be drilled out to get the shock off so that access to the stubborn bolt is improved. Needless to say, a good coating of long-lasting lithium

6. Generator Pulley Shims

7. Belt Adjustment

Caring for Your VW

grease should be applied to these parts before putting on the new shocks to avoid similar troubles in the future.

Wheel Bearing Repacking. The front wheel bearings are to be repacked each 30,000 miles with multipurpose lithium grease that is approved for wheel bearing use. Vehicles manufactured prior to 1966 were equipped with ball bearings, while later cars have the more usual roller bearings.

To remove the wheel, undo the lock nut (or loosen the locking screw) and take off the spindle nut(s). On disc brake models, the brake caliper must be dismounted from the steering knuckle. This is a simple job, and the caliper can be lifted aside with the hydraulic line still connected and the unit supported by a piece of wire hooked over the torsion bar tube to keep strain off the brake hose.

To remove the brake drum, back off the brake adjustments fully and pull the drum off the spindle. Be ready to catch the outer bearings should they fall out as the drum is removed. On ball bearing front wheels it is usually necessary to use a wheel puller. If you have no puller for VW wheels, use an ordinary type with a length of chain attached to three wheel lugs and looped over the cross bar of the puller.

It's necessary to pry out the grease seals to get the inner bearing race out of the drum. New grease seals cost less than 50¢, and it is always a good idea to replace them each time the bearings are repacked. Pry the old seals out with a screwdriver, and when installing the new ones (the last step before returning the brake drum to the spindle), coat their outside edge with grease to help them slide into place. A clean, flat piece of wood should be laid over the seal and tapped lightly with a hammer until the seal is driven home.

The procedure for cleaning and packing wheel bearings is described elsewhere in this book; however, the dust cover should not be filled with grease. Adjust the wheel bearings as described earlier, being careful not to get them too tight, which could destroy the grease film and lead to bearing failure.

Brake Lining Replacement. VW drum-type brakes are not unlike those found on American cars, and most of what is said in the chapter covering brakes will apply to the VW as well. However, removing the rear drums calls for some special equipment, and less experienced or under-tooled home mechanics may wish to leave relining work to their dealers. On the other hand, those who have adequate experience and the proper tools should encounter little trouble in doing the job themselves.

You'll need a good, strong 36mm (1-7/16-in.) socket wrench to take off the rear wheel nuts. The socket alone will cost between $5 and $10, which could go a long way toward paying for the job in a shop. You'll also need a 150 ft.-lbs. torque wrench with a half-length

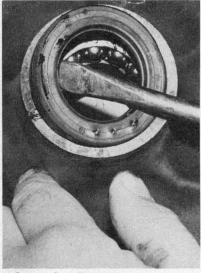

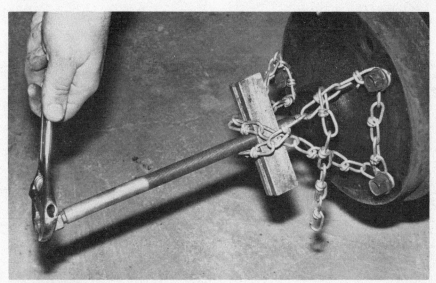

1. Grease Seal Removal

2. Homemade Puller

3. Marking Torsion Arm

4. Differential Snap Ring

adapter so that you can retorque these nuts to the required 217 ft.-lbs. A wheel puller is required to get the rear drums off the axle (after backing off the brake adjusters), but this can be a common heavy-duty type with a piece of chain looped over three wheel lugs to adapt it to the VW brake drums. Once you've gotten the brake drums off you'll find that the brakes are quite conventional.

The disc brakes used on VW's are also easy to service. When any one of the pads has worn down to a thickness of 2mm, all four pads should be replaced. All that's necessary is to remove the front wheel, drive out the brake pad retaining pin with a punch, remove the "H"-shaped spreader spring, and pull the old pads out with a hooked wire.

It's important to clean up the seating and sliding surfaces where the pads contact the caliper casting, and if the disc is badly scored or rusted within the swept area, it should be taken off and given to a machine shop for resurfacing. Insert the new pads and replace the spreader spring and retaining pin. Do not use the punch to drive the pin, since this can damage the clamp bushing in the caliper or the shoulder on the pin. Use a hammer only for reassembly.

Brake Bleeding. The VW's brakes are bled like any other car's, but the order in which they are bled is important. Cars with single-circuit drum brakes are bled in the following sequence: right rear, left rear, right front, and left front. All cars with dual-circuit brakes—including disc brake models—should have the front wheel circuit bled first. The order is therefore right front, left front, right rear, left rear. If the hydraulic system of dual-circuit cars is broken for repairs at either the front or rear, only the affected circuit needs to be bled after reassembly.

Rear Axle Boots. The rubber boots lo-

1. Rear brake drums and front drums on 5-bolt wheeled cars require a wheel puller to get them off. Ordinary puller can be used with help of a length of chain.

2. Front drums on a Beetle are a tight fit. The factory recommends a special puller, but a number of methods work, including light rapping with a mallet or this improvised puller.

3. Any time it is necessary to dismount a rear axle from the torsion arm, cut a notch in the arm that's in line with the one on the housing flange.

4. After axle housing is off, axle shaft is freed from differential by removing large snap ring. Alloy side plate need not be taken off for axle change alone.

5. Cylinder heads having a steel stud at this point should have their valves adjusted to .008-in. for the intakes and .012-in. for the exhausts.

6. Rocker cover gaskets were leaky on this engine, so a screwdriver is slipped under the retaining wire.

7. VW cylinder numbering will appear odd to domestic car mechanics. Here is proper numbering order. Distributor firing order is also shown.

5. Cylinder Head Identification

6. Removing Rocker Cover

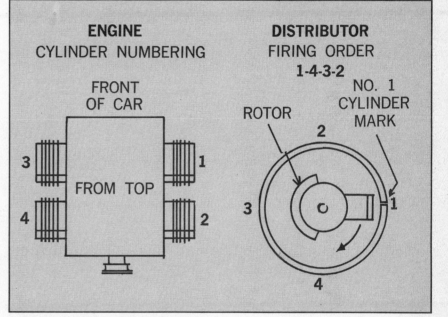

7. Cylinder and Distributor Numbering

cated at the inner end of the VW's rear axles must be in good condition to prevent road dirt entering the axle housings and transmission. Occasionally these boots will begin to crack and disintegrate due to age, oil leaks, or physical damage from flying stones. One-piece boots are installed at the factory, but split-type boots having six joining screws along their side are available to permit replacement without taking off the axle.

When installing the split boots, coat the joining surfaces lightly with trim cement, gasket cement, or other good sealer. Have the flange and joining screws pointed horizontally toward the rear of the car. Make sure that there is a snug fit between the boot and the transmission and between the boot and axle tube. Then tighten the retaining clamps that were left on the axle after cutting away the damaged boot.

CONTROL LINKAGES

Because of its rear engine, the VW has a number of control cables and rods which extend from the driver's seat to the rear of the car. These include heater controls, handbrake cables, the gearshift rod, throttle cable, and clutch. Trouble with at least one of these linkages is not an uncommon experience.

Heater Cables. Heater control problems are most frequent. If the heat will not turn off, the trouble is caused by stuck flaps or control arms on the engine itself and not by cable failure. If this trouble occurs, raise the car and treat all heater control bearings, pivots, and rubber surfaces with Liquid Wrench or some other rust-solvent preparation. Lubricate the affected parts with a long-lasting oil. Lithium grease and transmission oils have proven particularly effective.

Should it become impossible to turn the heat on, the trouble is probably a broken cable or a cable that has slipped out of its clevis at the rear of the car. Most breaks also occur at the rear, where the cable is exposed to weather. New cables are available at VW agencies and these should be coated with grease before installation. If the break is in an exposed part of the cable, solder-

Caring for Your VW

ing the broken ends into a small-diameter brass tube will make a satisfactory repair.

Throttle Cable. The throttle cable is next in line in order of trouble caused. New cables are easy to install by taking out the setscrew in the throttle arm pivot, compressing the spring inside the flared tubing beneath the carburetor, and taking off the slotted spring-retaining seat at the rear of the cable. The other end of the cable is then disconnected from the accelerator pedal and the new cable inserted from that end.

When the new cable reaches the rear of the chassis tube, you will have to crawl under the car and pull the plastic throttle cable hose out of the rubber boot in the "fork" of the chassis. Guide the cable into this hose and replace the hose in the chassis boot to prevent the entry of moisture.

Throttle cable breakage is usually caused by incorrect adjustment, so be careful how you install the new one. Open the throttle valve on the carburetor wide so that there is about 1mm clearance between the throttle lever and its stop. Have somebody press the accelerator completely to the floor and then tighten the setscrew holding cable onto the throttle arm.

Clutch Cable. Should the clutch cable break near the clutch arm, it is sometimes possible to back off the adjustment enough to overlap the broken ends and join them with a ⅛-in. cable clamp, but usually you'll have to install a new cable.

Take the lock and adjusting nuts from the rear of the cable (if this is necessary to extract the broken piece) and unbolt the pedal assembly from the car's floorboards. You'll have to take the pin out of the brake pedal to free it from the master cylinder pushrod. Remove the old cable by pulling the pedal assembly away from the chassis backbone until you can unhook the loop and withdraw the cable by hand.

When you buy the new cable be sure it has the same type of loop at the pedal end as the old cable did. Grease the new cable and slip it in from the front, hooking the loop onto the pedal arm and replacing the pedal assembly at the finish. It is a help to have someone under the car to guide the cable through the clutch arm as it emerges from the car's chassis. Recheck the clutch free-play frequently during the first few days of use, since new cables tend to stretch slightly after being placed in service.

Shift Rod. Most of the gearshift linkage problems encountered by VW drivers center around the coupling between the shift rod and the transmission. Access to this coupling is obtained by taking out the rear seat cushion and unscrewing the panel located on top of the "fork" area of the chassis tunnel. Broken or missing pins, loose setscrews, disintegrated rubber, or worn pivots are the usual problems.

TRANSAXLE TIPS

Major transmission repairs and overhauls require more equipment and skill than the average car owner is likely to have at his disposal. Should anything go wrong inside the gearbox, it is undoubtedly best to leave repairs to a VW shop. There are, however, several jobs that the home mechanic may decide to undertake after arming himself with a comprehensive VW repair manual. The following tips should help to make the job more successful.

Replacing Axles. On swing axle VW's made since 1961, it is possible to replace bent or broken rear axles without removing the transaxle and engine from the car. It is necessary, however, to unbolt the engine from the chassis and

1. Exhaust Valve Adjustment

2. Intake Valve Adjustment

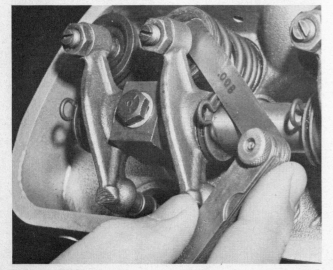

3. Feeler Gauge Check

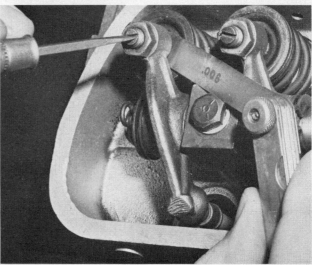

4. Exhaust Valve Checking

twist it in the car by jacking up the side on which the axle is being removed. After the brake drum, wheel bearing, and axle tube are removed, the snap ring holding the axle in the transmission can be reached through the opening uncovered by the removal of the axle housing and stamped steel axle housing retainer plate. Earlier cars that had "split" transaxle cases required that the entire transmission and differential unit be taken apart to get the axles 'out. Late "double-jointed" rear axles can merely be taken apart at the universal joints.

Your VW service manual will fill you in on most of the details concerning transaxle and rear end work, but here are some additional tips:

1) Whenever the axle housing is to be unbolted from the rear torsion bar radius arm, cut a mark into the top of the radius arm that is in line with the groove already provided in the top of the rear wheel bearing casting. Then when reassembling the parts, line these marks up carefully. Otherwise you will not be able to restore the proper toe-in/toe-out adjustment to the rear wheels.

2) Loosen the rear wheel nuts before any other disassembly, since they are torqued very tightly and require that the brakes be set to get them off.

3) If you obtain a replacement axle from a salvage yard, be sure it has the correct size tolerance for your car. Axle sizes are marked with paint bands around them. Yellow are smallest, blue middle-sized, and pink the largest.

Rear Wheel Bearings. Replacing rear wheel bearings is a cinch with the right tools—and a disaster without them. Do

not attempt it unless you have a bearing puller. Always replace the grease seals with new ones after installing new bearings. Late VW's with "double-jointed" rear axles should have their rear wheel bearings repacked with wheel bearing grease at least every 30,000 miles.

Clutch Shaft Trouble. The throwout shaft on which the clutch control arm mounts sometimes starts to bind in the bellhousing, or "freeze" due to corrosion. This can eventually lead to the ruin of both clutch and transmission, since clutch action is impaired. Any time your VW starts shifting hard, grinding gears on normal shifts, or creeping with the clutch pedal depressed, check the clutch throwout shaft for free movement. Pene-

5. Coating Rocker Cover

6. "Big" VW Engine

1. With No. 1 cylinder's exhaust valve wide open, it's time to adjust No. 3 cylinder's exhaust valve. In this way a "hot" cam or badly worn camshaft bearings cannot narrow the initial setting.

2. Intake valves on all engines except those with long rocker shaft studs should be set at .004-in., although some prefer .005 or .006-in. for engines rarely checked.

3. After adjusting a valve, try to slip in a feeler gauge .002-in. larger from the side. If it goes in, your adjustment hasn't been careful enough.

4. Set exhaust valves at .006-in. (except on long stud heads) instead of the .004-in. listed in most manuals; .004-in. is OK if you make checks weekly.

5. Use new gaskets when replacing rocker covers. Wipe away all oil on covers and heads, then coat both covers and gaskets with Gasketcinch, allowing it to set and get tacky before covers are replaced on heads.

6. "Big" engine used in VW 411 and latest busses and trucks is completely different in all its parts from earlier VW's. Outward-angled spark plugs revise wrench position.

7. Heat- and weather-cracked boots on the distributor cap are an invitation to trouble. Water and dirt will cause you many problems.

7. Heat-Cracked Distributor Boots

Caring for Your VW

trating oil will usually do the trick if the condition has not gone too far.

Oil Seals. Any time the engine is removed, check the inside of the transmission bellhousing for the presence of transmission oil. The grease seal around the transmission input shaft is cheap and easy to replace. A faulty one can cost you a new clutch.

THE ENGINE

Torque wrenches are an absolute necessity for working on the Volkswagen engine. The light alloy parts used throughout the VW are easily ruined by overtightening the threaded fasteners, so a wrench covering the 2 to 50 ft.-lb. range is indispensable. In addition, a 150 ft.-lb. torque wrench with a double-length adapter will be needed to tighten the flywheel nut to 217 ft.-lbs. Unless

these tools are available and unless fasteners are lubricated with anti-seize compound and tightened exactly to specifications *and no more*, "repairs" made to the V-Dub mill are likely to cause more eventual damage than whatever it was that originally prompted the work. We'll only touch lightly on complete engine disassembly here; the required information for such work should be obtained from a VW shop manual. There are, however, a number of owner maintenance operations that are within the scope of this chapter.

Adjusting Valves. It is highly important that VW valves be kept to prescribed clearances. The "early" 25- and 36-hp engines should have both intake and exhaust valve lash set at .004-in. Setting the No. 3 cylinder's exhaust valve at .006-in. is a common practice, however, and is recommended in the interest of reliability and longer valve life.

Beginning with the 40-hp engine in 1962 (square rocker arm shaft supports),

a new cylinder head design was introduced. This had long rocker arm shaft support studs that extended through the bottom of the rocker box and into the roof of the cylinder head. The intake valve clearance is .008-in. and the exhaust .012-in. in these "long stud" heads. Whenever you are working on a '62 or later 1200, early pancake 1500 or early transporter "1500," reach up between the rocker arm tubes on both heads and feel for these long studs. Many of these heads have been converted to short studs, which changes their valve setting specifications to those of the later engines. Occasionally you'll find a late "short stud" head installed on an early engine, or a "long stud" head installed on a later engine.

Some manuals list a clearance of .008-in. for both intake and exhaust valves on engines built from 1962 to 1964, but this should be disregarded in favor of the .008/.012in. settings on any head having the long studs. The specification change

1. New Alray Boots

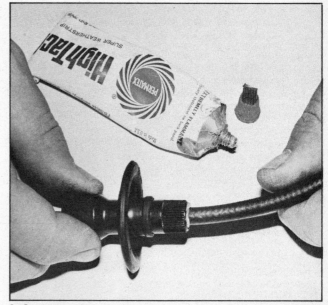

2. Cementing Plug Connectors

3. Adjusting Points

4. Cylinder No. 1 Firing Point

was made retroactive when it was found that these engines were encountering abnormal valve problems with the original .008/.008-in. setting. Unfortunately, many manuals and specification sheets had already been published listing the original specs.

From 1965 onward the manual specifies .004-in. settings for both intake and exhaust valves. However, the official policy in VW shops is to set intakes at .004-in. and exhausts at .006-in. Individual mechanics sometimes prefer a .005- or .006-in. setting for the intakes as well. The important thing is never to allow the lash to slip *below* .004-in. at any time between adjustments.

The early engines, including those having .008/.012-in. clearances, were to be adjusted only after the engine was completely cold—that is, after standing at least 2 hrs. and until no appreciable heat could be felt by placing your hand against any part of the engine. Late engines having the .004/.006-in. clearances can be adjusted so long as maximum oil temperature is below 122° F.

The best way to remove the valve covers is to loop an old leather belt or a length of cotton rope over the retaining bail and pull out and downward. This method saves a lot of scratched paint. There are two methods possible for adjusting the valves. The "factory" way is to snap off the distributor cap and turn the engine by hand until the distributor rotor is aligned with the No. 1 cylinder mark on the distributor body. The No. 1 cylinder is the front one on the right side of the car; No. 2 is behind it. No. 3 is the front cylinder on the left side of the car, and No. 4 the rear cylinder on that side.

After putting the rotor on the mark and adjusting the intake and exhaust valves of No. 1, turn the engine until the distributor points have closed and have just

1. Eelco makes these nifty Alray distributor boots that fit snugly over the cap towers. Center screw holds their high-performance wire in the boot for positive firing.

2. You can prevent spark plug cables from being accidentally pulled out of plug connectors by cementing them in place with trim cement or Goodyear Pliobond.

3. Adjust points to .016-in. by loosening lock screw and prying the stationary contact mount sideways by twisting a screwdriver between point mount and raised dots.

4. No. 1 cylinder's firing point is indicated by a notch in the distributor housing which aligns with one in the distributor rotor's tip.

5. VW's use a unique electric automatic choke heater. Hard starting may be caused by bad element (left) or broken thermal spring (right).

6. The correct plugs to use in all cases are 14mm and .472-in. reach. These should not be confused with more commonly seen 14mm/500-in. reach plugs on the market.

5. Electric Choke Heater

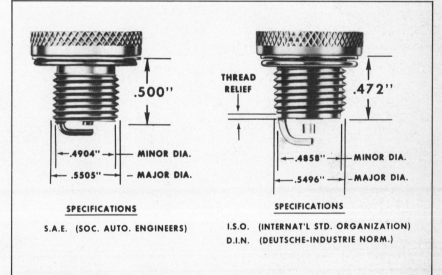

6. Plug Dimensions

started to open again. This will place the engine in the proper position to adjust the No. 4 cylinder's valves. Repeat this operation for No. 3 and No. 2—the next two cylinders in the 1-4-3-2 firing order. Valve adjusting procedures are shown in the photos and are essentially the same as those described elsewhere in this book.

A second valve adjusting method should be followed when working on high-mileage engines, pre-1965 engines which have the camshaft running directly in the crankcase instead of being carried in replaceable bearings, and on engines fitted with a high-performance camshaft. On such engines, it is imperative that adjustments be made when the lifters are at the lowest part of the cam lobe, and—in the case of worn engines—with all "slop" in the camshaft and valve train

directed toward the valve being adjusted. This adjustment procedure will guarantee that clearances will never fall below the minimum with the engine running and cause lost power and burned valves.

The alternate method is basically this: Since every lobe on the VW camshaft operates two valves on opposite sides of the engine, you can be sure that No. 1 cylinder's exhaust valve lifter is on the lowest part of the cam when No. 3 cylinder's exhaust valve is wide open. Adjust each of the engine's eight valves while the valve operated by the same cam lobe on the opposite side of the engine is wide open. Sharp VW tuners swear by this method.

Tune-ups. A typical tune-up should consist of adjusting the valves, checking and adjusting the ignition system, and adjusting the carburetor. Spark plugs for

Caring for Your VW

the VW have a reach of .472-in. and not ½-in. as is often stated. Plugs with ½-in. reach can be used, but sometimes they cause stuck plugs, combustion chamber hot spots, and cracks in the plug bosses. Champion and Bosch are the commonly available brands with the correct thread reach and clearances.

VW's deliver longer spark plug life than most modern engines, due to their relatively low cylinder pressures. New plugs every 12,000 miles (at every other tune-up) are therefore the rule. However, they should be removed and re-gapped at each 6000-mile check. Never install spark plugs in a VW with dry threads. Use an anti-seize compound or a light coating of lithium grease to prevent their "freezing" in the alloy heads. Don't over-tighten the plugs—20-25 ft.-lbs. is plenty.

VW plug connectors are excellent, but the resistance-type high-tension cables on early models have gotten a poor reputation. American-made resistance cables should be installed at the first sign of trouble. Late models have stranded wire cables with resistance built into the plug connectors and rotor. This system appears to be reliable and long-lasting.

The condenser and distributor rotor often last the life of the car, and there is little reason to replace them routinely. Similarly, a new distributor cap is rarely called for before 100,000 miles. Genuine VW points have plenty of meat on them and can be kept in service for at least 50,000 miles by periodically smoothing them with a fine stone. Make sure that the distributor cam and advance mechanism are properly lubricated to prevent erratic timing and premature wear.

After adjusting the breaker point gap to .016-in., the ignition timing should be adjusted. This can be done with a timing light, but it is "traditional" to time VW's with the engine turned off. Connect a non-powered test lamp to "ground" and to the distributor's primary terminal. Turn on the ignition and turn the crankshaft pulley clockwise until the first timing mark on the pulley lines up with the split in the center of the crankcase and the distributor rotor is pointed toward the No. 1 cylinder mark. Now loosen the distributor clamp bolt and turn the distributor slowly until the test light goes on. This will indicate that the points have opened. Tighten the distributor clamp and recheck the adjustment by turning the engine through two complete revolutions. The light should go on just as the mark on the pulley reaches the crankcase split.

The carburetor adjustments that will complete your tune-up should be carried out exactly as on any other car. On engines with fuel injection it is also wise to check several things which might cause trouble. First, make sure that the air tubes in the induction system are in good condition and free of leaks. Hard starting, misfiring and poor running are

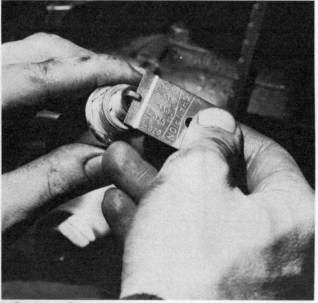

1. Gapping a Plug

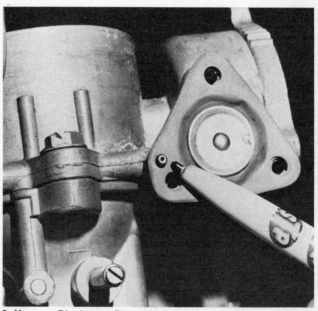

2. Vacuum Diaphragm Passage

3. Fuel Injection Multi-Connection

4. Installing Crankshaft

often caused by bent, loose, or dirty terminals on the many multi-connector plugs associated with the system. Clean them periodically with carbon tetrachloride, remove corrosion with crocus cloth, and make sure that they fit tightly and produce good contact. Lastly, the high-tension cable between the coil and distributor lies near wires serving the electronic injection system. A high-tension lead that is cracked or deteriorating may therefore allow a spark to arc into the injection system. This can cause some pretty hard-to-pinpoint troubles.

Electrical Systems. Aside from the fact that VW retained a 6-volt electrical system until 1967, there is little about it that is not similar to systems found on domestic cars. VW's have also retained fuses for all circuits while most other makes have switched to circuit breakers for at least some of them. The output of the charging system is rather marginal—especially on 6-volt models, which places a definite limit on the number of electrical accessories that can be added to the car. The following tips cover most of the "tricks" needed to keep the VW happy electrically:

1) Be careful never to overfill the battery. Its location under the rear seat makes overflows extremely damaging to the car.

2) Generator brushes can be changed without taking the generator out of the car. Just loosen the four 10mm fanhouse bolts and the generator retaining strap, then turn the unit to make the brush area accessible.

3) All electrical circuits can be tested from behind the dash. Open the hood and remove the fiberboard panel at the rear of the luggage area. Inside you'll find terminals on the back of the fuse panel for all electrical circuits. This panel also permits easy access to radio, instruments, dashboard controls and illuminating lights.

4) When installing the starter, be sure to pack the pinion bushing in the bellhousing with grease before inserting the starter driveshaft.

5) Although "official" VW manuals state that faulty voltage regulators should be replaced with new ones, most older

and independently published manuals will describe adjusting methods that will restore many malfunctioning units to service. A peculiar white powdery residue often forms inside VW regulators. Removing the cover and cleaning the contacts is often all that's required to correct a "no-charge."

6) VW windshield wipers that continue running after the switch has been turned off occasionally have loose pivots in the wiper mechanism, which allow the motor to coast past its automatic shutoff point. There is a magnetic brake in the system, however, which depends on the wiper's dashboard switch being solidly grounded. Wiper run-on can usually be corrected by restoring this ground.

Fuel System. Aside from those models equipped with fuel injection, the VW fuel system is completely conventional and should cause the home mechanic no trouble. Here are a few special pointers:

1) The VW fuel gauge installed prior to 1968 is mechanical and not electrical. It can be adjusted easily from behind the dash if it becomes inaccurate. A sticking gauge must be replaced, since it's united with the operating cable. The latter is

usually at fault. The terminal on the electric gauge sending unit is occasionally bent or knocked loose by loading heavy cargo in the front of the car. Check this if the gauge stays at the top or bottom of its scale all the time.

2) The many slip-on fuel hoses used throughout the VW fuel system can eventually cause trouble as hoses deteriorate and slip off. Keep a check on their condition, and add hose clamps if you intend to use your Bug in rough country or competition.

3) Tinkering with the electronic injection system—aside from the tune-up checks mentioned earlier—is taboo! "Computer" circuits are easily damaged by extraneous voltage introduced into the system by haphazard tests.

Basic Overhaul. Any engine work beyond that of a tune-up or routine maintenance nature requires the removal of the engine from the car. It seems a bother to go through for so simple a thing as grinding the valves, but that's the nature of the beast. The car must be lifted high enough off the ground that the engine can be lowered and pulled out from under the rear of the car. If

1. A spark plug gap tool such as this one by Champion will keep those plugs properly gapped at .030-in.

2. Other potential trouble areas on automatic choke are broken vacuum diaphragm or dirt lodged in this small-diameter vacuum passage.

3. Electronic fuel injection on Type 3 cars is sometimes upset by loose or dirty multi-connectors; the one on distributor is often bumped loose during ignition timing.

4. During assembly, the crankshaft (already fitted with connecting rods) is placed in one half of crankcase. Bearings and camshaft are also installed at this time.

5. One half of crankcase is lowered over assembled internals. Valve lifters in upper half can be kept in place with spring-type clothespins inserted backward.

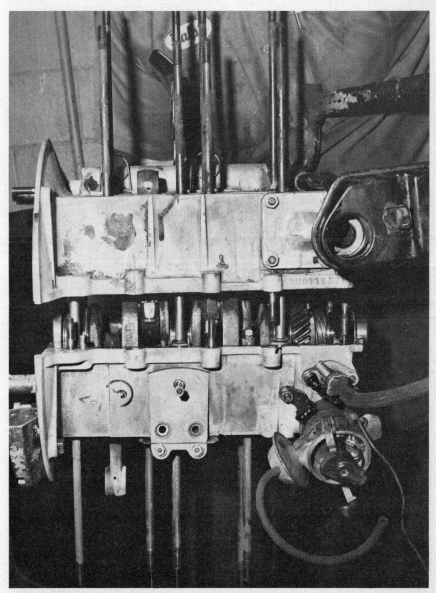

5. Assembling Crankcase Halves

Caring for Your VW

you're working with jack stands, you can considerably reduce the height it is necessary to raise a Beetle by removing the carburetor, manifold, fanhouse, generator, and oil cooler before taking the engine out of the car. This also makes it easier to get at the upper engine mounting bolts.

You'll probably need a transmission jack to handle the engine, although with a couple of helpers you might get by without one. Just lower the car until the engine rests on a wooden packing case (preferably on a wheeled furniture mover's dolly) before unbolting the engine. Slide the packing case (and the engine) to the rear until it is clear of the transmission input shaft, then have two men support the engine while the third slides the packing case out from under it. The engine may then be lowered to the floor. If your helpers haven't been doing their pushups lately, it'll probably go right through the floor!

Valve and ring work require only that the cooling shrouds, rocker shafts and nuts on top of the cylinder heads be removed so that the heads and cylinders can be slipped off the crankcase. Installing a performance-grind cam or replacing main bearings requires that the crankcase be "split," but if there's no crankshaft damage, a rod bearing can be replaced with the crankcase in one piece.

During reassembly, the halves of the crankcase must be coated with a sealer such as Permatex or Loctite "Fit-All Gasket." Rods are assembled on the crankshaft before it is installed in the crankcase. Main bearing studs are torqued first. All fasteners should have their threads and friction surfaces lubricated with anti-seize compound to assure accurate torque readings. Under no circumstances should you ever over-torque anything, particularly the cylinder head studs. Tensions increase greatly when the engine warms up and will often tear over-tightened studs right out of the crankcase.

The flywheel is removed and installed by unbolting the clutch assembly, then wrapping some heavy coat hanger wire between one of the clutch mounting bolts and one of the engine mounting bolt holes in the crankcase flange. The 36mm gland nut must be torqued to 217 ft.-lbs.; any less will eventually ruin the crankshaft and/or flywheel.

BEETLE HOP-UPS

Hopped-up and modified VW's are one of the country's fastest spreading automotive trends. A variety of performance and dress-up accessories is now available for VW's that rivals those built for domestic products. Space does not permit us to go into specifics, but from the repair point of view there are many improvements that can be made to the Bug by installing high-performance parts in place of worn or failing standard parts.

The Engine Modified. Carburetion improvements probably do the most to pep up the Beetle. Richer carb jets or a dual-throat carb on a ram-type manifold can make a noticeable improvement in acceleration and high-speed capability, especially when used with one of the better extractor-type exhaust systems. The next step up the performance ladder is the

1. Torquing Main Bearing Nuts

2. Generator Brush

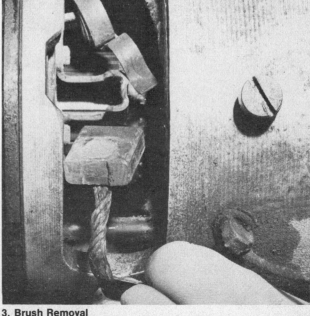

3. Brush Removal

4. Mechanical Fuel Gauge

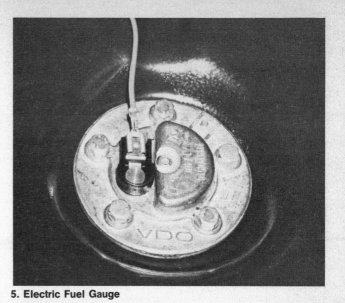

5. Electric Fuel Gauge

installation of a dual carburetor setup. A further boost for the conservative hop-up can be obtained by using a centrifugal-advance distributor from a VW transporter. Centrifugal-advance distributors from 4-cylinder Porsche engines are another possibility, but many of these have an advance curve that could "blow" a VW powerplant. Special high-performance distributors or distributors specifically modified for hopped-up V-Dubs are the safest way to go.

For the Volks enthusiast who wants a bit more in the performance department, there are late-model twin-port cylinder heads and similar heads built as accessories for earlier engines. Naturally, their installation calls for the removal of the engine from the car, and (if the cash is available) a set of big-bore pistons and cylinders should definitely be considered for installation at the same time. Custom heads and big-bore cylinders not only add displacement but raise the compression considerably.

Like most other engines, the Volks mill can benefit from special cam grinds, but the engine must be completely taken down and the crankcase "split" to install them. Once it has been decided to go ahead with a cam, installing a special crankshaft and connecting rods should

also be considered. These offer such features as increased stroke, larger bearings, roller bearings, sturdier flywheel mounting, and greater strength.

A VW oil pump in good condition is adequate for nearly all high-performance applications. Many of the oversize "heavy-duty" oil pumps on the market have so much clearance between their various parts that they actually pump less lubrication to the crankshaft than the stock pump. If you buy a larger pump, make certain its tolerances are at least equal to those of the stock unit.

Larger and sturdier oil coolers or even an additional oil radiator may be needed on exceptionally high-output engines that are operated for long periods at high temperatures.

Driveline. Increased engine outputs place greater loads on driveline parts. The main weak point is the clutch. VW transporter clutches are indispensable for nonslip performance even on many stock VW's. Various accessory clutches are also on the market that will help to make the Volks into a reliable grabber.

Gearsets with lower 3rd and 4th speed ratios can be obtained from EMPI, and these are a big help for pulling oversize tires with an underpowered engine. They also do the trick when top road or drag strip performance is desired from a high-revving modified engine.

Beetles and buggies that will be used off the road should have their stock rubber transaxle mountings replaced with all-steel types, or they should have heavy transmission support straps added to bolster up existing mounts.

Handling. Obtaining good roadability is every bit as important as cranking out extra power. In fact, handling improvements are absolutely vital for safety in VW's driven at high speeds. Padded racing-type steering wheels and custom shifters can add seconds by making it easier for the driver to "do his thing."

Special heavy-duty shock absorbers such as the famous Konis do a lot, but there are other items to be considered as well. Swing-axle Bugs need stabilization at the rear, and while later models with this type of suspension do have a rear anti-roll bar, a leaf-spring type stabilizer like the EMPI camber compensa-

tor will provide the most satisfactory improvement in establishing rear-end controllability.

Alterations to the rear wheel camber aid the handling of swing-axle cars, too. If you decide to change the camber, be sure to mark the original position of the radius arms on the torsion bars and also the angle to which the arms descend when slipped off their lower stops. The suspension can be decambered in very small increments by lowering the radius arm at the torsion bar's inner spline and raising it the same number of notches on the outer spline. The smallest possible decambering adjustment is one notch down on the inner spline and one notch up on the outer. The practical maximum is about nine up on the inner and nine down on the outer.

Changing wheels and tires can also improve performance. In general, wider rims on smaller diameter wheels are called for, but this depends a great deal on the type of driving to be done. If radial tires are installed, the front toe-in should be reduced to approximately zero—and many enthusiasts prefer to reduce front-end camber as well. This can be adjusted on VW's with ball-joint front ends, but can only be accomplished with shim changes on VW's having link pins. The change is considered unnecessary on the Super Beetle.

Obviously, it would be impossible to describe every possible repair operation for any particular make of car in the space of only one chapter. However, our intention has been to outline those things about working on the VW which are *different* from normal car procedures. A great many details helpful to VW owners can be obtained from the other applicable chapters of this book, and with the typical variations set forth in this chapter, the Volks enthusiast should be well prepared to carry out all common maintenance and repair tasks on his own. The VW is great fun to work on and its service simplicity is one of the things that makes it a truly economical car. Grab a fistful of small bills and dash off to the store for a set of metrics, then start slashing your personal gold drain to zero by doing your tune-ups, minor repairs, and routine servicing at home. 🐝

1. Main bearing nuts are torqued first, then flange bolts. Torque specifications must be met precisely for proper bearing "crush" and resulting clearance.

2. Generator brushes can be removed with dynamo still in car. Turn generator for easy access to inspection opening; remove screw as shown.

3. Brush is removed by lifting spiral spring tensioning clip to one side and pulling old brushes out by grasping their lead wire terminal.

4. Mechanical fuel gauges used from 1962 to 1967 can be adjusted for accuracy easily by turning this slotted lug on back of instrument.

5. Electric fuel gauge has been used since 1968. Check this terminal atop gas tank sending unit first if gauge fails to register.

1972 Tune-up Specifications

Cu. Ins.	HP[57]	Carb. (bbls.)	COMPRESSION (psi)	CYLINDER NUMBERING (front to rear)		FIRING ORDER	INITIAL TIMING[1] Std. Trans.	Auto. Trans.	DISTRIBUTOR ROTATION[2]
AMERICAN MOTORS CORP (Includes Jeep)									
232	100	1	9	123456		153624	5°	5°	C
258	110	1	9	123456		153624	3°	3°	C
304	150	2	9	L-1357	R-2468	18436572	5°	5°	C
360	175	2	9	L-1357	R-2468	18436572	5°	5°	C
360	195	4	9	L-1357	R-2468	18436572	5°	5°	C
401	255	4	9	L-1357	R-2468	18436572	5°	5°	C
BUICK DIVISION (GM)									
350	155[37]	2	17	L-1357	R-2468	18436572	4°	4°	C
350	180[38]	4	17	L-1357	R-2468	18436572	4°	4°	C
455	225[36]	4	17	L-1357	R-2468	18436572	4°	4°	C
455 GS Riv.	260	4	17	L-1357	R-2468	18436572	8°	10°	C
455 STG. 1	270	4	17	L-1357	R-2468	18436572	8°	10°	C
CADILLAC DIVISION (GM)									
472	220	4	165-185[11]	L-1357	R-2468	15634278	—	8°	C
500	235	4	165-185[11]	L-1357	R-2468	15634278	—	8°	C
CHEVROLET DIVISION (GM)									
140	80	1	140	1234		1342	6°	6°	C
140(L-11)	90	2	140	1234		1342	6°	6°	C
250	110	1	130[58]	123456		153624	4°	4°	C
307	130[46]	2	150[58]	L-1357	R-2468	18436572	4°	8°	C
350	165	2	160[58]	L-1357	R-2468	18436572	6°	6°	C
350	200[33]	4	160[58]	L-1357	R-2468	18436572	4°	8°	C
350	255	4	150[58]	L-1357	R-2468	18436572	4°	8°	C
400	170	2	160[58]	L-1357	R-2468	18436572	2°	6°	C
402	240[34][46]	4	160[58]	L-1357	R-2468	18436572	8°	8°	C
454	270[35][46]	4	160[58]	L-1357	R-2468	18436572	8°	8°	C
CHRYSLER CORP. (Plymouth, Dodge, Chrysler, Imperial)									
198	100[40]	1	13	123456		153624	2.5°	2.5°	C
225	110[41]	1	13	123456		153624	TDC	TDC	C
318	150	2	14	L-1357	R-2468	18436572	TDC	TDC	C
340	240	4	14	L-1357	R-2468	18436572	2.5°	2.5°	C
360	175	2	14	L-1357	R-2468	18436572	—	TDC	C
400	190[42]	2	14	L-1357	R-2468	18436572	—	5°	CC
400	255[42][43]	4	14	L-1357	R-2468	18436572	TDC	10°	CC
440	225[42][55]	4	14	L-1357	R-2468	18436572	—	10°	CC
440	280[42][56]	4	14	L-1357	R-2468	18436572	2.5°	10°	CC
440	330[42][46]	3-2	15	L-1357	R-2468	18436572	2.5°	2.5°	CC
FORD MOTOR CO. (Ford, Mercury, Lincoln)									
98	54	1	17	1234		1243	12°	—	CC
122	85[44]	2	17	1234		1342	6°	6°[18]	C
170	82	1	17	123456		153624	6°	—	C
200	90[45]	1	17	123456		153624	6°	6°	C
240	103[46]	1	17	123456		153624	—	6°	C
250	95[47]	1	17	123456		153624	6°	6°	C
302	139[48]	2	17	L-5678	R-1234	15426378	6°	6°	CC
351W	153[46]	2	17	L-5678	R-1234	13726548	—	6°	CC

NOTE: Footnote Explanations on Page 356

DISTRIBUTOR DWELL[28] (degrees)	DISTRIBUTOR POINT GAP[28] (ins.)	POINT SPRING TENSION[28] (ozs.)	IDLE SPEED (RPM)[3] Std. Trans. (in Neutral) NAT'L	CALIF.	Auto. Trans. (in Drive) NAT'L	CALIF.	FAST IDLE[4] (rpm) Std./Auto.	FUEL PUMP PRESSURE (psi)
31-34	.016	17-21	600	700	550	600	1600/1600[7]	4-5
31-34	.016	17-21	600	700	550	600	1600/1600[7]	4-5
29-31	.016	17-21	750	750	650	700	1600/1600[7]	5-6.5
29-31	.016	17-21	750	750	700[5]	700[5]	1600/1600[7]	5-6.5
29-31	.016	17-21	750	750	700[6]	700[6]	1600/1600[8]	5-6.5
29-31	.016	17-21	750	750	650	700	1600/1600[8]	5-6.5
30	.016	19-23	600	600	500	500	820/700[32]	3
30	.016	19-23	600	600	500	500	820/700[32]	3
30	.016	19-23	600	600	500	500	920/700[32]	4.5
30	.016	19-23	600	600	500	500	920/700[32]	4.5
30	.016	19-23	600	600	500	500	920/700[32]	4.5
28-32	[12]	[12]	—	—	600[5]	600[5]	—/1900[10]	5.25-6.5
28-32	[12]	[12]	—	—	600[5]	600[5]	—/1900[10]	5.25-6.5
31-34	.019	19-23	700[30 6]	700[30 6]	700[30 6]	700[30 6]	[29]	3-4.5
31-34	.019	19-23	700[30 6]	700[30 6]	700[30 6]	700[30 6]	[29]	3-4.5
31-34	.019	19-23	700	700	600	600	2400/2400[10]	3.5-4.5
29-31	.019	19-23	900[31]	900[31]	600	600	1850/2200[7]	5-6.5
29-31	.019	19-23	900	900	600	600	1850/2200[7]	7-8.5
29-31	.019	19-23	800	800	600	600	1350/1500[7]	7-8.5
29-31	.019	19-23	900	900	700	700	1350/1500[7]	7-8.5
29-31	.019	19-23	900	900	600	600	1850/2200[7]	7-8.5
29-31	.019	19-23	750	750	600	600	1350/1500[7]	7-8.5
29-31	.019	19-23	750	750	600	600	1350/1500[7]	7-8.5
41-46	.017-.023	17-20	800	800	800	800	2000/2000[7]	3.5-5
41-46	.017-.023	17-20	750	700	750	750	2000/2000[7]	3.5-5
30-34	.014-.019	17-20	750	700	750	750	1900/1700[7 62]	5-7
[16]	[16]	[16]	900[5]	900[5]	750[5]	750[5]	1900/1900[7]	5-7
30-34	.014-.019	17-20	—	—	700	700	—/1900[7 63]	5-7
28.5-32.5	.016-.021	17-20	—	—	700	700	—/1900[7 63]	3.5-5
28.5-32.5	.016-.021	17-20	900[5]	800[5]	750[5]	750[5]	1900/1900[7 64]	3.5-5
30-34	.014-.019	17-20	—	—	750	700	—/1600[7 65]	3.5-5
[16]	[16]	[16]	900	800	900	900	1800/1600[7 66]	6-7.5
[16]	[16]	[16]	900	900	900	900	1800/1800[7]	5.5-6.5
36-40	.025	17-21	900/500[23]		—		1700/—[7]	3.5-5.0
36-40	.025	17-21	750/500[23]		650/500[23]		1600/1800[7]	3.8-5.0
35-39	.027	17-21	750		—		1500/—[25]	4-6
35-39	.027	17-21	800/500[23]		600/500[23]		1750/2000[25]	4-6
35-39	.027	17-21	—		500		—/1650[25]	4-6
35-39	.027	17-21	750/500[23]		600/500[23]		1600/1600[25]	4-6
26-30	.017	17-21	800/500[23]		600/500[23]		1400/1400[25]	5-7
26-30	.017	17-21	—		600/500[23]		—/1500[25]	5-7

Cu. Ins.	HP[57]	Carb. (bbls.)	Compression (psi)	Cylinder Numbering (front to rear)		Firing Order	Initial Timing[1] Std. Trans.	Auto. Trans.	Distributor Rotation[2]
FORD MOTOR CO.									
351C	175[49]	2	17	L-5678	R-1234	13726548	6°	6°	CC
351C	262[22][46]	4	17	L-5678	R-1234	13726548	—	16°	CC
351CJ	248[50]	4	17	L-5678	R-1234	13726548	16°	—	CC
351HO	275	4	17	L-5678	R-1234	13726548	10°	—	CC
400	168[51]	2	17	L-5678	R-1234	13726548	—	8°[19]	CC
429	205[52]	4	17	L-5678	R-1234	15426378	—	10°	CC
429PI	NA	4	17	L-5678	R-1234	15426378	—	10°	CC
460	214[53]	4	17	L-5678	R-1234	15426378	—	10°[20]	CC
OLDSMOBILE DIVISION (GM)									
350	160[59]	2	17	L-1357	R-2468	18436572	8°	8°	CC
350	180[60]	4	17	L-1357	R-2468	18436572	8°	12°	CC
455	225[61]	4	17	L-1357	R-2468	18436572	—	8°	CC
455	250	4	17	L-1357	R-2468	18436572	10°	8°	CC
455	265	4	17	L-1357	R-2468	18436572	—	8°	CC
455	270	4	17	L-1357	R-2468	18436572	10°	8°	CC
455W30	300[46]	4	17	L-1357	R-2468	18436572	10°	10°	CC
PONTIAC DIVISION (GM)									
250	110	1	140	123456		153624	4°	4°	C
307	130	2	150	L-1357	R-2468	18436572	4°	8°	CC
350	160[54]	2	120-160	L-1357	R-2468	18436572	8°	10°	CC
400	175[54]	2	120-160	L-1357	R-2468	18436572	—	10°	CC
400	200[54]	4	120-160	L-1357	R-2468	18436572	8°	10°	CC
455	185[54]	2	120-160	L-1357	R-2468	18436572	—	10°	CC
455	220[54]	4	120-160	L-1357	R-2468	18436572	8°	10°	CC
455HO	300	4	120-160	L-1357	R-2468	18436572	8°	10°	CC

—=Equipment combination not available.
NA=Information not available at press time.
1 Disconnect and plug distributor vacuum lines when setting timing; all settings are BTDC.
2 C—clockwise; CC—counterclockwise; when viewed from the top.
3 Idle speed set by carburetor speed screw unless indicated otherwise.
4 Fast idle speed must be set with engine at normal operating temperature, idle speed correctly set, transmission in neutral, and fast idle screw on indicated step of fast idle cam.
5 Adjust by turning throttle stop solenoid.
6 Adjust by turning hex head of throttle stop solenoid.
7 On second step of cam.
8 On middle step of cam.
9 Variations between cylinders should not exceed 20 lbs.
10 On highest step of cam.
11 At cranking speed; 212-230 at 1000 rpm.
12 Due to close manufacturing tolerances, gap and point tension will be correct if dwell angle is set to 30°.
13 Not less than 100 psi; must not vary more than 25 psi between cylinders.
14 Not less than 100 psi; must not vary more than 40 psi between cylinders.
15 Not less than 110 psi; must not vary more than 40 psi between cylinders.
16 Equipped with electronic ignition system as standard equipment.
17 Lowest cylinder must be 70% of highest, and not less than 100 psi.
18 California vehicles, 9°.
19 California vehicles, 6°.
20 All 3.00 axles and California vehicles, 6°.
21 Manual, 0.020.
22 Available only on Cougar with 12-in. converter.
23 Solenoid energized/solenoid de-energized.
24 On second highest step of cam.
25 On kickdown step of cam (next to "V" stamped on cam).
26 Solenoid inactive.
27 Figures are approximate; no cylinder should be less than 80% of highest.
28 Applies to standard ignition only, electronic ignition does not use points.
29 Fast idle will be correct if curb idle is correctly set.
30 With air conditioning, 800 rpm.
31 950-C, K and G series for California only.
32 On lower step of cam.

DISTRIBUTOR DWELL[28] (degrees)	DISTRIBUTOR POINT GAP[28] (ins.)	POINT SPRING TENSION[28] (ozs.)	IDLE SPEED (RPM)[3] Std. Trans. (in Neutral)		Auto. Trans. (in Drive)		FAST IDLE[4] (rpm) Std./Auto.	FUEL PUMP PRESSURE (psi)
			NAT'L	CALIF.	NAT'L	CALIF.		
26-30	.017	17-21	750/500[23]	575/500[23]	625/500	1400/1500[25]		5-7
26-30	.017	17-21	—	650	650	—/NA		5-7
26-30	.017[21]	17-21	1000/500[23]	700/500[23]	800/500	1200/1200[25]		5-7
26-30	.020	17-21	1000/500[23]	—	—	1200/—[25]		5-7
26-30	.017	17-21	—	625/500[23]	625/500[23]	—/1500[25]		4.5-6.5
26-30	.017	17-21	—	600/500[23]	600/500[23]	—/1350[25]		5-7
26-30	.020	17-21	—	650/500[23]	650/500[23]	—/1900[25]		5-7
26-30	.017	17-21	—	625/500[23]	625/500[23]	—/1250[25]		5-7
30	.016	19-23	600	600	600	600	1000/1000[32]	5.5-6.5
30	.016	19-23	550	550	600	600	1100/1100[32]	5.5-6.5
30	.016	19-23	—	—	600	600	—/1100[32]	5.5-6.5
30	.016	19-23	600	600	600	600	1100/1100[32]	5.5-6.5
30	.016	19-23	—	—	550	550	—/1100[32]	5.5-6.5
30	.016	19-23	600	600	600	600	1100/1100[32]	5.5-6.5
30	.016	19-23	550	550	550	550	1100/1100[32]	5.5-6.5
32.5	.019	19-23	700[26]	700[26]	600[26]	600[26]	2400/2400[10]	4-5.5
30	.019	19-23	900[26]	900[26]	600[26]	600[26]	NA	5.5-7.5
30	.019	19-23	800[26]	800[26]	625[26]	625[26]	1500/NA [10]	5-6.5
30	.019	19-23	—	—	625[26]	625[26]	NA	5-6.5
30	.019	28-32	600[26]	600[26]	500[26]	500[26]	1500/1500[10]	5-6.5
30	.019	19-23	—	—	625[26]	625[26]	NA	5-6.5
30	.019	28-32	600[26]	600[26]	500[26]	500[26]	1500/1500[10]	5-6.5
[16]	[16]	[16]	600[26]	600[26]	500[26]	500[26]	1500/1500[10]	5-6.5

[33] Camaro, Nova and base Corvette option with engine code J; 175 hp.
[34] Chevrolet option with engine code S, 210 hp; if N10 dual exhaust is used, net hp is 260 and engine code is U.
[35] Wagon option only; engine code is V and net hp is 230.
[36] 250 with dual exhaust.
[37] 150 in California.
[38] 175 in California.
[39] 230 with single snorkel, dual exhaust; 245 with dual exhaust.
[40] 94 in California.
[41] 97 in California.
[42] Subtract 9 in California.
[43] Dual snorkel; 265 with Cold Air Pak.
[44] 86 in California.
[45] 91 in California.
[46] NA in California.
[47] 98 in California, applies to Maverick/Comet application; when used in Torino/Montego, 94 (95 Calif.); when used in Mustang, 98 (99 Calif.)
[48] 143 in California, applies to Maverick/Comet application; when used in Torino/Montego, 138 (140 Calif.); when used in Mustang, 138 (141 Calif.); when used in Ford, 140 (Calif. rating NA).

[49] 177 in California, applies to Mustang; Torino/Montego, 161; Ford/Mercury, 163; Cougar, 164.
[50] Mustang/Cougar application, 266.
[51] Ford/Mercury application, 172.
[52] Ford/Mercury application, 208; Thunderbird, 212.
[53] Lincoln Continental with A/C, 224; Thunderbird/Mark IV with A/C, 212.
[54] Base figure with single exhaust, varies 15 to 30 above base depending upon application and dual exhaust.
[55] Single snorkel and single exhaust; dual snorkel and single exhaust, 230; dual exhaust, 245.
[56] Dual snorkel; 290 with Cold Air Pak.
[57] SAE net.
[58] PSI at cranking speed, throttle wide open—maximum variation 20 psi between cylinders.
[59] 175 with dual exhaust.
[60] 200 with dual exhaust.
[61] 250 with dual exhaust.
[62] 1800/2000 in California.
[63] 2000 in California.
[64] 2000/2100 in California.
[65] 1500 in California.
[66] 2000/1800 in California.

Cu. Ins.	ENGINE HP[1]	Carb.	COMPRESSION (psi)	CYLINDER NUMBERING (front to rear)		FIRING ORDER	INITIAL TIMING[2] Std. Trans.	Auto. Trans.
AMERICAN MOTORS CORP (Includes Jeep)								
232	100	1-bbl.	8	123456		153624	5°	3°
258	110	1-bbl.	8	123456		153624	5°	3°
304	150	2-bbl.	8	L-1357	R-2468	18436572	5°	5°
360	175	2-bbl.	8	L-1357	R-2468	18436572	5°	5°
360	195[7]	4-bbl.	8	L-1357	R-2468	18436572	5°	5°
401	255	4-bbl.	8	L-1357	R-2468	18436572	5°	5°
BUICK DIVISION (GM)								
350	150	2-bbl.	11	L-1357	R-2468	18436572	4°[12]	4°[12]
350	175[10]	4-bbl.	11	L-1357	R-2468	18436572	4°[12]	4°[12]
455	225[10]	4-bbl.	11	L-1357	R-2468	18436572	4°[12]	4°[12]
455 GS Riv.	250	4-bbl.	11	L-1357	R-2468	18436572	10°[12]	10°[12]
455 Stg. 1	260	4-bbl.	11	L-1357	R-2468	18436572	10°[12]	10°[12]
CADILLAC DIVISION (GM)								
472	220	4-bbl.	18	L-1357	R-2468	15634278	—	8°
500	235	4-bbl.	18	L-1357	R-2468	15634278	—	8°
CHEVROLET DIVISION (GM)								
140 (L-4)	72	1-bbl.	140	1234		1342	8°	8°
140 (L-11)	85	2-bbl.	140	1234		1342	10°	12°
250 (L-6)	100	1-bbl.	130[24]	123456		153624	6°	6°
307 (L-14)	115	2-bbl.	150[24]	L-1357	R-2468	18436572	4°	8°
350 (L-65)	145	2-bbl.	160[24]	L-1357	R-2468	18436572	8°	8°
350 (L-48	175[21]	4-bbl.	160[24]	L-1357	R-2468	18436572	8°[25]	12°
350 (Z-28)	245	4-bbl.	150[24]	L-1357	R-2468	18436572	8°	8°
350 (L-82)	250	4-bbl.	150[24]	L-1357	R-2468	18436572	8°	8°
400 (LF-6)	150	2-bbl.	160[24]	L-1357	R-2468	18436572	—	8°
454 (LS-4)	245[22][23]	4-bbl.	160[24]	L-1357	R-2468	18436572	10°	10°
CHRYSLER CORP. (Plymouth, Dodge, Chrysler, Imperial)								
198	95	1-bbl.	34	123456		153624	2.5°[37]	2.5°[37]
225	105[29]	1-bbl.	34	123456		153624	TDC[37]	TDC[37]
318	150[30]	2-bbl.	35	L-1357	R-2468	18436572	2.5°[37]	TDC[37]
340	240	4-bbl.	35	L-1357	R-2468	18436572	5°[37]	2.5°[37]
360	170[31]	2-bbl.	35	L-1357	R-2468	18436572	—	TDC[37]
400	175	2-bbl.	35	L-1357	R-2468	18436572	—	10°[37]
400	185	2-bbl.	35	L-1357	R-2468	18436572	—	10°[37]
400	260	4-bbl.	35	L-1357	R-2468	18436572	2.5°[37]	7.5°[37]
440	215[32]	4-bbl.	35	L-1357	R-2468	18436572	—	10°[37]
440	220[33]	4-bbl.	35	L-1357	R-2468	18436572	—	10°[37]
440	245	4-bbl.	35	L-1357	R-2468	18436572	—	10°[37]
440 HP	280	4-bbl.	35	L-1357	R-2468	18436572	—	10°[37]

DISTRIBUTOR ROTATION[4]	DISTRIBUTOR DWELL[4] (degrees)	DISTRIBUTOR POINT GAP[4] (ins.)	POINT SPRING TENSION[4] (ozs.)	IDLE SPEED (RPM)[5] Std. Trans. (in Neutral)	IDLE SPEED (RPM)[5] Auto. Trans. (in Drive)	FAST IDLE[6] (rpm) Std./Auto.	FUEL PUMP PRESSURE (psi)
C	31-34	.016	17-21	700	600	1600/1600[9]	4-5
C	31-34	.016	17-21	700	600	1600/1600[9]	4-5
C	29-31	.016	17-21	700	750	1600/1600[9]	5-6.5
C	29-31	.016	17-21	750	700	1600/1600[9]	5-6.5
C	29-31	.016	17-21	750	700	1600/1600[9]	5-6.5
C	29-31	.016	17-21	750	700	1600/1600[9]	5-6.5
C	30	.016	19-23	600[13 14]	500[13 16]	820/700[17]	3
C	30	.016	19-23	600[13 14]	500[13 16]	920/700[17]	3
C	30	.016	19-23	600[13 15]	500[13 16]	920/700[17]	4.5
C	30	.016	19-23	600[13 15]	500[13 16]	920/700[17]	4.5
C	30	.016	19-23	600[13 15]	500[13 16]	920/700[17]	4.5
C	28-32	[19]	[19]	—	600	—/1900	5.25-6.5
C	28-32	[19]	[19]	—	600	—/1900	5.25-6.5
C	31-34	.019	19-23	700	750	[20]	3-4.5
C	31-34	.019	19-23	700	750	[20]	3-4.5
C	31-34	.019	19-23	700	600	[28]1800/1800[27 28]	3.5-4.5
C	29-31	.019	19-23	900	600	[28]1600/1600[26 28]	5-6.5
C	29-31	.019	19-23	900	600	[28]1600/1600[26 28]	7-8.5
C	29-31	.019	19-23	900	600	[28 26]1600/1300[27 28]	7-8.5
C	29-31	.019	19-23	900	700	[28 26]1600/1300[27 28]	7-8.5
C	29-31	.019	19-23	900	700	[28 26]1600/1300[27 28]	7-8.5
C	29-31	.019	19-23	—	600	[28]1600/1600[26 28]	7-8.5
C	28-30	.019	28-32	900	600	[28 26]1600/1300[27 28]	7.5-9
C	[36]	[36]	[36]	800[37]	750[37]	[38]	4-5.5
C	[36]	[36]	[36]	750[37]	750[37]	[38]	4-5.5
C	[36]	[36]	[36]	750[37]	700[37]	[38]	6-7.5
C	[36]	[36]	[36]	850[37]	850[37]	[38]	6-7.5
C	[36]	[36]	[36]	—	750[37]	[38]	6-7.5
CC	[36]	[36]	[36]	—	700[37]	[38]	4-5.5
CC	[36]	[36]	[36]	—	700[37]	[38]	4-5.5
CC	[36]	[36]	[36]	900[37]	850[37]	[38]	4-5.5
CC	[36]	[36]	[36]	—	700[37]	[38]	4-5.5
CC	[36]	[36]	[36]	—	700[37]	[38]	4-5.5
CC	[36]	[36]	[36]	—	700[37]	[38]	4-5.5
CC	[36]	[36]	[36]	—	800[37]	[38]	4-5.5

1973 Tune-up Specifications

Cu. Ins.	ENGINE HP[1]	Carb.	COMPRESSION (psi)	CYLINDER NUMBERING (front to rear)		FIRING ORDER	INITIAL TIMING[2] Std. Trans.	Auto. Trans.
FORD MOTOR CO. (Ford, Mercury, Lincoln)								
98	54	1-bbl.	46	1234		1243	12°37	—
122	85	2-bbl.	46	1234		1342	9°37	9°37
200	84	1-bbl.	46	123456		153624	6°37	6°37
250	88[39]	1-bbl.	46	123456		153624	6°37	6°37
302	132[40][41]	2-bbl.	46	L-5678	R-1234	15426378	6°37	6°37
351C	159	2-bbl.	46	L-5678	R-1234	13726548	—	10°37
351W[42]	156	2-bbl.	46	L-5678	R-1234	13726548	—	6°37
351CJ	246	4-bbl.	46	L-5678	R-1234	13726548	16°37	18°37
400	168[43]	2-bbl.	46	L-5678	R-1234	13726548	—	6°37
429	201[44]	4-bbl.	46	L-5678	R-1234	15426378	—	6°37
460	244[45]	4-bbl.	46	L-5678	R-1234	15426378	—	14°37
460 PI	274	4-bbl.	46	L-5678	R-1234	15426378	—	10°37
OLDSMOBILE DIVISION (GM)								
250	100	1-bbl.	48	123456		153624	6°	6°
350	160	2-bbl.	48	L-1357	R-2468	18436572	—	14°49
350	180	4-bbl.	48	L-1357	R-2468	18436572	8°	12°50
455 (L-74)	225	4-bbl.	48	L-1357	R-2468	18436572	—	8°
455 (L-75)	250	4-bbl.	48	L-1357	R-2468	18436572	10°	8°
455 (L-78)	270	4-bbl.	48	L-1357	R-2468	18436572	—	8°
PONTIAC DIVISION (GM)								
250	100	1-bbl.	55	123456		153624	6°	6°
350	150[54]	2-bbl.	55	L-1357	R-2468	18436572	10°	12°
400	170	2-bbl.	55	L-1357	R-2468	18436572	—	12°
400	200[54]	4-bbl.	55	L-1357	R-2468	18436572	10°	12°
455	215[54]	4-bbl.	55	L-1357	R-2468	18436572	10°	12°
455 SD	310	4-bbl.	55	L-1357	R-2468	18436572	10°	12°

1 SAE net.
2 Disconnect and plug distributor vacuum lines when setting timing; all settings are BTDC.
3 C=clockwise; CC=counterclockwise—when viewed from top.
4 Applies only to standard ignition. Electronic ignition does not use points.
5 Idle speed set by carburetor speed screw unless otherwise indicated.
6 Fast idle speed must be set with engine at normal operating temperature, idle speed correctly set, transmission in neutral, and fast idle screw on indicated step of fast idle cam.
7 With dual exhaust, 220.
8 Variations between cylinders should not exceed 20 lbs.
9 On second step of cam.
10 Add approximately 10% for optional dual exhaust.
11 Lowest must be 70% of highest, and not less than 100 psi.
12 ±2°.
13 With idle stop solenoid disconnected.
14 800 rpm with idle stop solenoid connected.
15 900 rpm with idle stop solenoid connected.

16 650 rpm with idle stop solenoid connected.
17 On low step of cam.
18 Lowest must be 70% of highest.
19 Due to close manufacturing tolerances, gap and point tension will be corected if dwell angle is set to 30°.
20 Refer to Vehicle Emission Control Information sticker on car for latest certified information.
21 190 in Corvette.
22 275 in Corvette.
23 215 in station wagons.
24 At cranking speed, throttle wide open. Maximum variation—20 psi between cylinders.
25 12° Corvette only.
26 With vacuum advance.
27 Without vacuum advance.
28 On high step of cam.
29 98 with N95 Emission Control package.
30 170 in Roadrunner.
31 163 with N95 Emission Control package.

DISTRIBUTOR ROTATION[4]	DISTRIBUTOR DWELL[4] (degrees)	DISTRIBUTOR POINT GAP[4] (ins.)	POINT SPRING TENSION[4] (ozs.)	IDLE SPEED (RPM)[5] Std. Trans. (in Neutral)	Auto. Trans. (in Drive)	FAST IDLE[6] (rpm) Std./Auto.	FUEL PUMP PRESSURE (psi)
CC	36-40	.025	17-21	900[37]	—	1700/—[9]	3.5-5
C	37-41	.025	17-21	750[37]	650[37]	1600/1800[9]	3.8-5
C	33-39	.025	17-21	750[37]	550[37]	1600/1600[9]	4-6
C	33-39	.025	17-21	750[37]	600[37]	1600/1600[9]	4-6
CC	24-30	.017	17-21	800[37]	625[37]	1250/1400[9]	5-7
CC	24-30	.017	17-21	—	625[37]	—/1500[9]	5-7
CC	24-30	.017	17-21	—	600[37]	—/1500[9]	5-7
CC	24-30[47]	.017	17-21	900[37]	700[37]	1300/1300[9]	5-7
CC	24-30	.017	17-21	—	625[37]	—/1500[9]	5-7
CC	24-30	.017	17-21	—	650[37]	—/1350[9]	5-7
CC	24-30	.017	17-21	—	600[37]	—/1350[9]	5-7
CC	24-30	.017	17-21	—	600[37]	—/1900[9]	5-7
C	33	.019	19-23	700[51]	600[51]	[53]/[53]	5.5-6.5
CC	30	.019	19-23	—	700[52]	—/900[17]	5.5-6.5
CC	30	.019	19-23	650	650[52]	1100/1000[17]	5.5-6.5
CC	30	.019	19-23	—	650[52]	—/1000[17]	5.5-6.5
CC	30	.019	19-23	750	650[52]	1100/1000[17]	5.5-6.5
CC	30	.019	19-23	—	650[52]	—/1000[17]	5.5-6.5
C	32.5	.019	19-23	700[58]	600[58]	[59]/2400[28]	3-5
CC	30	.016	19-23	900[58]	650[58]	[59]/[59]	5-6.5
CC	30	.016	19-23	—	650[58]	—/[59]	5-6.5
CC	30	.016	28-32[56]	1000[58]	650[58]	[59]/1500[28]	5-6.5
CC	30	.016	28-32[56]	1000[58]	650[58]	[59]/1500[28]	5-6.5
CC	30[57]	.016[57]	28-32[56][57]	1000[58]	750[58]	[59]/1500[28]	5-6.5

[32] 208 with N95 Emission Control package.
[33] 213 with N95 Emission Control package.
[34] Not less than 100 psi; must not vary more than 25 psi between cylinders.
[35] Not less than 100 psi; must not vary more than 40 psi between cylinders.
[36] Electronic ignition system is standard; no points or condenser.
[37] Data provided by manufacturer in advance of model year and may not apply to all of model run; refer to Emission Control label on vehicle for exact data for your car.
[38] Data not provided; refer to Emission Control label on vehicle for exact data for your car.
[39] 92 in Gran Torino Sport 2-dr. fastback.
[40] 135 in Torino wagons and Rancheros.
[41] 138 in Comet.
[42] NA in California.
[43] 163 in Torino wagons and Ranchero.
[44] 197 in Torino wagons and Ranchero.
[45] 208 in Mark IV; 219 in Lincoln.

[46] Lowest 75% of highest.
[47] Set manual transmission to 32-35°.
[48] Lowest 70% of highest, but not less than 100 psi.
[49] 12° with Delta 88.
[50] 10° with Vista Cruiser.
[51] Solenoid energized; adjust idle stop solenoid hex screw to obtain idle of 450 rpm with solenoid de-energized.
[52] Solenoid energized; adjust carburetor screw to obtain idle of 550 rpm with solenoid de-energized.
[53] Preset.
[54] Add approximately 15% for optional dual exhaust.
[55] Lowest 80% of highest.
[56] Only the dwell angle requires adjustment after replacement.
[57] NA if equipped with optional Unit Ignition System (electronic).
[58] Solenoid active, engine at normal operating temperature, choke open, air conditioner off, auto trans. in Drive, disconnected vacuum hoses plugged.
[59] Not specified by manufacturer; refer to Emission Control label under hood.

Factory Spark Plugs

AMERICAN MOTORS (Champion)

MAKE, YEAR AND MODEL	STD. PLUG	GAP
ALL MODELS		
6-Cylinder Engines 1971-73 232, 258 cu.in.	N-12Y	.035
1964-70....199, 232 cu. in.	N-14Y	.035
1962-64....196 cu. in. OHV (127-138 hp)	H-14Y	.035
1962-65....196 cu. in. OHV (125 hp)	H-18Y	.035
1962-65 196 cu. in. "I" head	H-10	.035
8-Cylinder Engines 1966-73 290, 304, 343, 360, 390, 401 cu. in.	N-12Y	.035
1970....390 cu. in. (340 hp)	N-10Y	.035
1962-66....287, 327 cu. in.	N-14Y	.035

MAKE, YEAR AND MODEL	STD. PLUG	GAP
JEEP (American Motors Corp.)		
1972-73....401 cu. in. V-8	N-12Y	.035
1971-73....304, 360 cu. in. V-8	N-12Y	.035
1971-73....232, 258 cu. in. 6-cylinder	N-12Y	.035
1969-71....350 cu. in. V-8	RBL-13Y	.035
1968....350 cu. in. V-8	BL-13Y	.035
1966-71....V-6 Engine	J-12Y/UJ-12Y	.035
1965-69....327 cu. in. V-8	H-14Y	.035
1965-70....232 cu. in. 6-cylinder	N-14Y	.035
1963-71....4-cylinder	J-8	.030
1963-66....Tornado Engine	L-12Y/UL-12Y	.030

CHRYSLER CORP. (Champion)

MAKE, YEAR AND MODEL	STD. PLUG	GAP
CHRYSLER		
1972-73....440 cu. in. V-8 (4-bbl. carb.)	J-11Y	.035
1972-73....440 cu. in. V-8 (2-bbl. carb.)	J-13Y	.035
1971-72....360 cu. in. V-8	N-13Y	.035
1966-71....440 cu. in. V-8 350 hp	J-13Y	.035
Police & Hi-Perf. Eng. 375 hp	J-11Y	.035
1961-64....361 cu. in. V-8	J-14Y	.035
1959-71....383 cu. in. V-8 (2-bbl. carb.)	J-14Y	.035
1966-67....383 cu. in. (4-bbl. carb.)	J-13Y	.035
Police & Hi-Perf. (4-bbl. carb.)	J-11Y	.035
1968-71....383 cu. in. V-8 (4-bbl. carb.)	J-11Y	.035
1959-65....413 cu. in. V-8:		
Two 4-bbl. carbs. (1963-64)	XJ-11Y	.035
Hi-Perf. 300 Series & Police	J-11Y	.035
Standard Engine	J-14Y	.035
COLT		
(Dodge) 1600cc	N-9Y	.030
CRICKET		
(Plymouth) 1600cc	N-9Y	.025
DODGE		
6-Cylinder Engines 1960-72 (OHV)	N-14Y	.035
1957-59 (L-head)	XJ-7	.035
V-8 Engines		
1972-73....400 cu. in. V-8 (4-bbl. carb.)	J-11Y	.035
(2-bbl. carb.)	J-13Y	.035
1972-73....440 cu. in. V-8	J-11Y	.035
1971-72....318, 360 cu. in.	N-13Y	.035
1973....340 cu. in.	N-12Y	.035
1968-72....340 cu. in.	N-9Y	.035
1966-71....426 cu. in. (2-4 bbl. carb.)	N-10Y	.035
1966-71....440 cu. in. 350 hp	J-13Y	.035
375, 390 hp.	J-11Y	.035
1965....413 cu. in. Standard Eng.	J-14Y	.035
Hi-Performance Eng.	J-11Y	.035
1964-69....273 cu. in. (2-bbl. carb.)	N-14Y	.035
Hi-Performance (4-bbl. carb.)	N-10Y	.035
1973....318 cu. in.	N-12Y	.035

MAKE, YEAR AND MODEL	STD. PLUG	GAP
1967....318 cu. in. 3/8" reach heads	J-14Y	.035
3/4" reach heads	N-14Y	.035
DODGE V-8 Engines (continued)		
1968-70....318 cu. in.	N-14Y	.035
1960-66....318, 361 cu. in.	J-14Y	.035
1960-71....383 cu. in. (2-bbl. carb.)	J-14Y	.035
1960-67....383 cu. in. (4-bbl. carb.)	J-13Y	.035
Police Hi-Performance (4-bbl. carb.)	J-11Y	.035
1968-71....383 cu. in. (4-bbl. carb.)	J-11Y	.035
1963-65....426 cu. in. (Do not use 3/4" reach plugs)	J-11Y	.035
IMPERIAL		
1972....440 cu. in.	J-11Y	.035
1970-71....440 cu. in.	RJ-13Y	.035
1966-69....440 cu. in.	J-13Y	.035
1959-65	J-14Y	.035
PLYMOUTH—VALIANT		
6-Cylinder Engines 1960-72 (OHV)	N-14Y	.035
V-8 Engines 1972-73 400 cu.in. (2-bbl. carb.)	J-13Y	.035
1972-73....400 cu. in. (4-bbl. carb.)	J-11Y	.035
1972-73....400 cu. in. V-8 (4-bbl. carb.)	J-11Y	.035
1971-72....318, 360 cu. in.	N-13Y	.035
1968-72....340 cu. in.	N-9Y	.035
1965-69....273 cu. in. Std. Engine:		
2-bbl. carb	N-14Y	.035
Hi-Perf. 4-bbl. carb.	N-10Y	.035
1967....318 cu. in. 3/8" reach heads	J-14Y	.035
3/4" reach heads	N-14Y	.035
1968-70....318 cu. in.	N-14Y	.035
1960-66....318, 361 cu. in.	J-14Y	.035
1961-71....383 cu. in. (2-bbl. carb.)	J-14Y	.035
1960-67....383 cu. in. (4-bbl. carb.)	J-13Y	.035
Police Hi-Perf. (4-bbl. carb.)	J-11Y	.035
1968-71....383 cu. in. (4-bbl. carb.)	J-11Y	.035
1966-71....440 cu. in. Police & Hi-Perf.	J-11Y	.035
1966-71....440 cu. in. Standard	J-13Y	.035
1966-71....426 cu. in.	N-10Y	.035
1963-65....426 cu. in.	J-11Y	.035

FORD MOTOR CO. (Autolite)

MAKE, YEAR AND MODEL	STD. PLUG	GAP
CAPRI		
1973....1.6 liter	AGR32	.030
1973....2.0 liter	BRF42	.025
1973....2.6 liter	AGR32	.030
1972....1.6 liter	AGR22	.030
1972....2.0 liter	BRF32	.025
COMET/MONTEGO		
1973....460 cu. in. Police	ARF42	.035
1971-73..6 cyl.	BRF82	.035
1971-73..302 C.I.D.	BRF42	.035
1971-73..351 C.I.D.	ARF42	.035
1972-73..400 C.I.D.	ARF42	.035
1972-73..429 C.I.D.	BRF42	.035
1971....429 C.I.D. S/T	ARF32	.035

MAKE, YEAR AND MODEL	STD. PLUG	GAP
COMET/MONTEGO (continued)		
1971....429 C.I.D. A/T	ARF32	.035
1970....302 C.I.D.	BF42	.035
1970....351 C.I.D.	AF42	.035
1970....429 C.I.D. Std. Eng.	BRF42	.035
1970....429 C.I.D. CJ	AF32	.035
1969....302, 351 2-bbl., 390 C.I.D.	BF42	.035
1969....351 4-bbl., 428 C.I.D.	BF32	.035
1968....302 C.I.D.	BF42	.035
1968....428 C.I.D.	BF32	.035
1967-68..427 C.I.D.	BF32	.035
1963-68..8 cyl. exc. 390 GT	BF42	.035
1966-68..390 C.I.D. GT	BF32	.035
1966-70..6 cyl. w/Thermactor	BF82	.035
1960-67..6 cyl. w/o Thermactor	BF82	.035

CONTINENTAL

Year	Model	Plug	Gap
1973	Mark IV	ARF42	.035
1972	Mark IV	BRF42	.035
1971	Mark III	BRF42	.035
1969-70	Mark III	BF42	.035

COUGAR

Year	Model	Plug	Gap
1971-73	351 C.I.D.	ARF42	.035
1971	429 C.I.D. S/T	ARF32	.035
1971	429 C.I.D. A/T	ARF32	.035
1970	302 C.I.D.	AF32	.035
1970	351 C.I.D. 2-bbl.	BF42	.035
	4-bbl.	AF42	.035
1970	428 C.I.D. CJ	BF32	.035
1967-69	289, 302, 351 C.I.D. 2-bbl., 390 C.I.D. exc. GT	BF42	.035
1967-69	351 C.I.D. 4-bbl., 390 GT, 427, 428 C.I.D.	BF32	.035

EDSEL

Year	Model	Plug	Gap
1960	292 C.I.D.	BF82	.035
1960	352 C.I.D.	BF42	.035
1959-60	6 cyl.	BTF6	.035
1959	292 C.I.D.	BF82	.035
1959	332, 361 C.I.D.	BF42	.035
1958	361, 410 C.I.D.	BF42	.035

FAIRLANE/TORINO

Year	Model	Plug	Gap
1973	429 C.I.D.	ARF42	.035
1973	460 C.I.D. Police	ARF42	.035
1971-73	6 cyl.	BRF82	.035
1971-73	302 C.I.D.	BRF42	.035
1971-73	351 C.I.D.	ARF42	.035
1972-73	400 C.I.D.	ARF42	.035
1972-73	429 C.I.D.	BRF42	.035
1971	429 C.I.D. S/T	ARF32	.035
1971	429 C.I.D. A/T	ARF32	.035
1968-70	302 C.I.D.	BF42	.035
1970	351 C.I.D.	AF42	.035
1970	429 C.I.D. Std. Eng.	BRF42	.035
1970	429 C.I.D. CJ	AF32	.035
1966-70	6 cyl. w/Thermactor	BF82	.035
1969	351 C.I.D. 2-bbl.	BF42	.035
1969	351 C.I.D. 4-bbl., 428	BF32	.035
1966-69	390 C.I.D. exc. GT	BF42	.035
1966-69	390 C.I.D. GT	BF32	.035
1966-68	289 C.I.D.	BF42	.035
1967-68	427 C.I.D.	BF32	.035
1965	289 C.I.D. exc. Hi.-Perf.	BF42	.035
	Hi.-Perf.	BF32	.035
1962-67	6 cyl. w/o Thermactor	BF82	.035
1962-64	8 cyl.	BF42	.035

FALCON

Year	Model	Plug	Gap
1963-70	8 cyl.	BF42	.035
1966-70	6 cyl. w/Thermactor	BF82	.035
1960-67	6 cyl. w/o Thermactor	BF82	.035

FORD

Year	Model	Plug	Gap
1973	460 C.I.D. Police	ARF42	.035
1971-72	6 cyl.	BRF42	.035
1972	302 C.I.D.	BRF42	.035
1972-73	351, 429 C.I.D. (18mm)	BRF42	.035
1972-73	351, 429 C.I.D. (14mm)	ARF42	.035
1971	302, 351, 390, 429 C.I.D. 2-bbl.	BRF42	.035
1971-72	400 C.I.D.	ARF42	.035
1971	429 C.I.D. 4-bbl.	ARF32	.035
1968-70	302, 351, 390 C.I.D.	BF42	.035
1970	429 C.I.D.	BRF42	.035
1966-70	6-cyl. w/Thermactor, exc. Police & Taxi	BF42	.035
	Police & Taxi	BTF6	.035
1968-70	427, 428 C.I.D. Police	BF32	.035
1966-69	289, 352, 390, 428 C.I.D. exc. 428 Police	BF42	.035
1966-67	6 cyl. w/o Thermactor	BF42	.035
1960-65	289, 332, 352, 390 C.I.D. exc. Hi.-Perf. 352, 390 C.I.D.	BF42	.035
1960-65	406, 427 C.I.D. Hi.-Perf. 352, 390 C.I.D.	BF32	.035
1963	260 C.I.D.	BF42	.035
1960-62	292 C.I.D.	BF82	.035
1959	332, 352 C.I.D.	BF82	.035
1955-65	6 cyl.	BTF6	.035
1955-58	272, 292, 312 C.I.D.	BF82	.035
1954	8 cyl.	AL7	.030
1952-54	6 cyl.	AL7	.030
1949-53	8 cyl.	AL9	.030
1949-51	6 cyl.	AL9	.030
1938-48	All	AL9	.030

LINCOLN

Year	Model	Plug	Gap
1973	460 C.I.D.	ARF42	.035
1971-72	460 C.I.D.	BRF42	.035
1968-70	460 C.I.D.	BF42	.035
1966-68	462 C.I.D.	BTF42	.035
1961-65		BF42	.035
1958-60		BF42	.035
1955-57		BF82	.035
1953-54		AL7	.030
1940-52		AL9	.030

MAVERICK

Year	Model	Plug	Gap
1971-73	6 cyl.	BRF82	.035
1972	302 C.I.D.	BRF42	.035
1970	6 cyl.	BF82	.035

MERCURY

Year	Model	Plug	Gap
1973	460 C.I.D.	ARF42	.035
1973	460 C.I.D. Police	ARF42	.035
1972-73	351, 429 C.I.D. (14mm)	ARF42	.035
1972-73	429, 460 C.I.D. (18mm)	BRF42	.035
1971	351, 429 C.I.D. 2-bbl.	BRF42	.035
1971-73	400 C.I.D.	ARF42	.035
1971	429 C.I.D.	ARF32	.035
1970	390 C.I.D.	BF42	.035
1970	428 C.I.D.	BF32	.035
1970	429 C.I.D.	BRF42	.035
1969	429 C.I.D.	BF42	.035
1968-69	390, 428 C.I.D. exc. Police	BF42	.035
1968-69	428 C.I.D. Police	BF32	.035
1961-67	352, 390, 410, 428 C.I.D. exc. Hi-Perf.	BF42	.035
1961-67	406, 427 C.I.D. Hi-Perf. 352, 390, 428 C.I.D.	BF32	.035
1961-62	6 cyl.	BTF6	.035
1960-61	292, 312 C.I.D.	BF82	.035
1960-61	383, 430 C.I.D.	BF42	.035
1959	312 C.I.D.	BF82	.035
1958-59	383, 430 C.I.D.	BF42	.035
1957-58	312 C.I.D.	BF82	.035
1957	368 C.I.D.	BF82	.035
1955-56	All	BF82	.035
1949-54	All	AL7	.030
1939-48	All	AL9	.030

MUSTANG

Year	Model	Plug	Gap
1971-73	6 cyl.	BRF82	.035
1972-73	302 C.I.D.	BRF42	.035
1971	302 C.I.D. 2-bbl.	BRF42	.035
1971	302 C.I.D. 4-bbl.	ARF32	.035
1971-73	351 C.I.D.	ARF42	.035
1971	429 C.I.D. S/T	ARF32	.035
1971	429 C.I.D. A/T	ARF32	.035
1970	302 C.I.D. exc. H.O. Eng.	BF42	.035
1970	302 C.I.D. H.O. Eng.	AF32	.035
1970	351 C.I.D. 2-bbl.	BF42	.035
1970	351 C.I.D. 4-bbl.	AF42	.035
1970	428 C.I.D.	BF32	.035
1970	429 C.I.D.	AF32	.035
1969	302, 351 C.I.D. 2-bbl.	BF42	.035
1969	351 4-bbl., 428 C.I.D.	BF32	.035
1969	390 C.I.D.	BF42	.035
1968	289, 302, 390 C.I.D. exc. GT	BF42	.035
1968	390 GT, 428 C.I.D.	BF32	.035
1967-70	6 cyl. w/Thermactor	BF82	.035
1965-67	6 cyl. w/o Thermactor	BF82	.035
1965-67	289 C.I.D. exc. Hi.-Perf.	BF42	.035
1965-67	289 C.I.D. Hi.-Perf.	BF32	.035
1967	390 C.I.D.	BF42	.035
1965	260 C.I.D.	BF42	.035

PINTO

Year	Model	Plug	Gap
1973	1600cc	AGR32	.030
1972	1600cc	AGR22	.030
1972-73	2000cc	BRF42	.035
1971	1600cc	AGR22	.030
1971	2000cc	BRF32	.025

THUNDERBIRD

Year	Model	Plug	Gap
1973	429 C.I.D.	ARF42	.035
1973	460 C.I.D.	ARF42	.035
1970-72	429 C.I.D.	BRF42	.035
1972	460 C.I.D.	BRF42	.035
1960-69		BF42	.035
1958-59	352, 430 C.I.D.	BF42	.035
1955-57		BF82	.035

Factory Spark Plugs

MAKE, YEAR AND MODEL	PLUG TYPE ACNITER	STANDARD	PLUG GAP
BUICK			
Centurion, Electra, Wildcat (thru 1970), Riviera, Estate Wagon, Riviera GS			
1973-72 V-8	R45TS	—	.040
1971-69 V-8	R44TS	—	.030
1968-67 V-8	R44TS	44TS	.030
1966-59 V-8	R44S	44S	.035
LeSabre, Sportwagon			
1973-72 V-8 350	R45TS	—	.040
1971-69 V-8 350	R45TS	—	.030
1968 V-8 350	R45TS	45TS	.030
1973-72 V-8 455	R45TS	—	.040
1971-70 V-8 455	R44TS	—	.030
Skylark, Century, Luxus, Regal, Luxus Wagon			
1971 6 Cyl. 250 1 Bbl	R46TS	—	.035
1970 6 Cyl	R46T	—	.035
1969 6 Cyl	R46N	—	.035
1968 6 Cyl. 250	R46N	46N	.035
1967-62 V-6	R44S	44S	.035
1967-65 V-8 300, 340, 2 Bbl Carb	R45S	45S	.035
4 Bbl. Carb	R44S	44S	.035
1973-72 V-8 350	R45TS	—	.040
1971-69 V-8 350	R45TS	—	.030
1968 V-8 350	R45TS	45TS	.030
1969 V-8 400	R44TS	—	.030
1966-65 V-8 400	R44S	44S	.035
1973-72 V-8 455	R45TS	—	.040
1971-70 V-8 455	R44TS	—	.030
CADILLAC			
Calais, DeVille, Fleetwood, Eldorado			
1973-70 V-8	R46N	—	.035
1969 V-8	R44N	—	.035
1968 V-8	R44N	44N	.035
CHEVROLET			
Bel Air, Biscayne, Impala, Caprice, Brookwood, Townsman, Kingsman			
1973-72 6 Cyl. 250	R46T	—	.035
1971 6 Cyl. 250 1 Bbl	R46TS	—	.035
1970 6 Cyl. 250	R46T	—	.035
1969 6 Cyl	R46N	—	.035
1968-62 6 Cyl. 230, 250, 194	R46N	46N	.035
1962-53 6 Cyl. 235	R45	45	.035
1957-55 V-8 265	R45	45	.035
1967-57 V-8 283	R45	45	.035
1968 V-8 307	R45S	45S	.035
1969 V-8 327	R45	—	.035
1968-62 V-8 327	R45S	45S	.035
1961-59 V-8 348	R44N	44N	.035
1973-72 V-8 350 2 Bbl or 4 Bbl	R44T	—	.035
1971 V-8 350 2 Bbl. (245 h.p.)	R45TS	—	.035
4 Bbl. (270 h.p.)	R44TS	—	.035
1970-69 V-8 350	R44	—	.035
1968-67 V-8 350	R44	44	.035
1969 V-8 396 (265 h.p.)	R44N	—	.035
1968-65 V-8 396 Normal Service	R44N	44N	.035
Light Service	R46N	46N	.035
1973-72 V-8 400 2 Bbl	R44T	—	.035
1971 V-8 400 2 Bbl. (255 h.p.)	R44TS	—	.035
1970 V-8 400 (265 h.p.)	R44	—	.035
1972 V-8 402 4 Bbl	R44T	—	.035
1971 V-8 402 4 Bbl. (300 h.p.)	R44TS	—	.035
1969 V-8 427 (335 h.p.)	R44N	—	.035
Bel Air, Biscayne, Impala, Caprice, Brookwood, Townsman, Kingsman			
1969 V-8 427 (390, 425 h.p.)	R43N	—	.035
1968-66 V-8 427 Cast Iron Head	R43N	43N	.035
1968-67 V-8 427 Aluminum Head	R43XL	43XL	.035
1973-72 V-8 454 4 Bbl	R44T	—	.035
1971 V-8 454 4 Bbl. (365 h.p.)	R43TS	—	.035
1970 V-8 454 (345 h.p.)	R44T	—	.035
1970 V-8 454 (390 h.p.)	R43T	—	.035
Camaro-SS-Rally Sport			
1973-72 6 Cyl. 250	R46T	—	.035
1971 6 Cyl. 250 1 Bbl	R46TS	—	.035
1970 6 Cyl	R46T	—	.035
1969 6 Cyl	R46N	—	.035
1968-67 6 Cyl	R46N	46N	.035
1969 V-8 302	R43	—	.035
1968-67 V-8 302	CR43	C43	.035
1973-72 V-8 307 2 Bbl	R44T	—	.035
1971 V-8 307 2 Bbl	R45TS	—	.035
CHEVROLET Cont.			
1970-69 V-8 307	R45	—	.035
1969 V-8 327	R45	—	.035
1968-67 V-8 327	R45S	45S	.035
1973-72 V-8 350 2 Bbl	R44T	—	.035
4 Bbl	R44T	—	.035
4 Bbl. (Z28)	R44T	—	.035
1971 V-8 350 2 Bbl. (245 h.p.)	R45TS	—	.035
4 Bbl. (270 h.p.)	R44TS	—	.035
4 Bbl. (330 h.p.) Z28	R44TS	—	.035
1970-69 V-8 350 (250, 300 h.p.)	R44	—	.035
1970 V-8 350 (360 h.p.)	R43	—	.035
1968-67 V-8 350	R44	44	.035
1969 V-8 396 Cast Iron Head			
(325 h.p.)	R44N	—	.035
(350, 375 h.p.)	R43N	—	.035
1969 V-8 396 Aluminum Head	R43XL	—	.035
1968-67 V-8 396 Normal Service	R44N	44N	.035
Light Service	R46N	46N	.035
1972 V-8 402 4 Bbl	R44T	—	.035
1971 V-8 402 4 Bbl. (300 h.p.)	R44TS	—	.035
1970 V-8 402 (396 SS)(350 h.p.)	R44T	—	.035
(375 h.p.)	R43T	—	.035
1970 V-8 454	R43T	—	.035
Chevelle, Laguna, Monte Carlo			
1973-72 6 Cyl. 250 1 Bbl	R46T	—	.035
1971 6 Cyl. 250 1 Bbl	R46TS	—	.035
1970 6 Cyl	R46T	—	.035
1969 6 Cyl	R46N	—	.035
1968-64 6 Cyl	R46N	46N	.035
1967-64 V-8 283	R45	45	.035
1973-72 V-8 307 2 Bbl	R44T	—	.035
1971 V-8 307 2 Bbl	R45TS	—	.035
1970-69 V-8 307	R45	—	.035
1968 V-8 307	R45S	45S	.035
1969 V-8 327	R45	—	.035
1968-65 V-8 327	R45S	45S	.035
1973-72 V-8 350 2 Bbl	R44T	—	.035
4 Bbl	R44T	—	.035
1971 V-8 350, 2 Bbl. (245 h.p.)	R45TS	—	.035
4 Bbl. (270 h.p.)	R44TS	—	.035
1970-69 V-8 350 (250, 300 h.p.)	R44	—	.035
1968-67 V-8 350	R44	44	.035
1969 V-8 396 Cast Iron Head			
(325 h.p.)	R44N	—	.035
(350, 375 h.p.)	R43N	—	.035
1969 V-8 396 Aluminum Head	R43XL	—	.035
1968-65 V-8 396 Normal Service	R44N	44N	.035
Light Service	R46N	46N	.035
1971 V-8 400 2 Bbl. (255 h.p.)	R44TS	—	.035
1970 V-8 400 (265 h.p.)	R44	—	.035
1972 V-8 402 4 Bbl	R44T	—	.035
1971 V-8 402 4 Bbl. (300 h.p.)	R44TS	—	.035
1970 V-8 402 (330 h.p.)	R44T	—	.035
1970 V-8 402 (396 SS) (350 h.p.)	R44T	—	.035
1970 V-8 402 (396 SS) (375 h.p.)	R43T	—	.035
1973-72 V-8 454 4 Bbl	R44T	—	.035
1971 V-8 454 4 Bbl. (365 h.p.)	R43TS	—	.035
4 Bbl. (425 h.p.)	R44TS	—	.035
Chevelle & Monte Carlo			
1970 V-8 454 (360, 450 h.p.)	R43T	—	.035
1970 V-8 454 (460 h.p.) w/Alum. Hd	R43XL	—	.035
Chevy Nova (Chevy II)			
1970-69 4 Cyl	R46N	—	.035
1968-62 4 & 6 Cyl	R46N	46N	.035
1973-72 6 Cyl. 250 1 Bbl	R46T	—	.035
1971 6 Cyl. 250 1 Bbl	R46TS	—	.035
1970 6 Cyl	R46T	—	.035
1969 6 Cyl	R46N	—	.035
1967-64 V-8 283	R45	45	.035
1973-72 V-8 307 2 Bbl	R44T	—	.035
1971 V-8 307 2 Bbl	R44T	—	.035
1970-69 V-8 307	R45	—	.035
1968 V-8 307	R45S	45S	.035
1969 V-8 327	R45	—	.035
1968-65 V-8 327	R45S	45S	.035
1973-72 V-8 350 2 Bbl	R44T	—	.035
4 Bbl	R44T	—	.035
1971 V-8 350 2 Bbl. (245 h.p.)	R45TS	—	.035
4 Bbl. (270 h.p.)	R44TS	—	.035
1970-69 V-8 350	R44	—	.035
1968 V-8 350	R44	44	.035

CHEVROLET (Cont.)

Make, Year and Model	AC	Niter	Gap
1969 V-8 396 (350, 375 h.p.)	R43N	—	.035
1970 V-8 402 (396 SS)(350 h.p.)	R44T	—	.035
(375 h.p.)	R43T		.035

Corvair
1969 6 Cyl. 164	R44FF	—	.030
1968-60 Std. Eng.	R46FF	46FF	.035
High Perf.	R44FF	44FF	.030

Corvette
1968-62 V-8 327	R44	44	.035
1973-72 V-8 350 4 Bbl.(260 h.p.)	R44T	—	.035
(LT1 or Z28)	R44T	—	.035
1971 V-8 350 4 Bbl. (270 h.p.)	R44TS	—	.035
4 Bbl. (330 h.p. LT1)	R44TS	—	.035
1970 V-8 350 (370 h.p.)	R43	—	.035
1970-69 V-8 350 (300, 350 h.p.)	R44	—	.035
1965 V-8 396	R43N	43N	.035
1969 V-8 427 Cast Iron Head	R43N	—	.035
Aluminum Head	R43XL	—	.035
1968-66 V-8 427	R43N	43N	.035
1973-72 V-8 454 4 Bbl.	R44T	—	.035
1971 V-8 454 4 Bbl. (365 h.p.)	R43TS	—	.035
1971 V-8 454 4 Bbl. (425 h.p.)			
Alum. Head	R44XL	—	.035
1970 V-8 454 (390 h.p.)	R43T	—	.035
1970 V-8 454 (460 h.p.) w/Alum. Hd.	R43XL	—	.035

Vega 2300 Sedan, Hatchback Coupe, Kammback Station Wagon, Panel Express Wagon
1973-71 4 Cyl. 140 1 Bbl. 90 h.p.	R42TS	—	.035
2 Bbl. 110 h.p.	R42TS	—	.035

OLDSMOBILE

F-85, Cutlass Supreme, Cutlass S Cruiser, Vista-Cruiser, Omega
1973 6 Cyl. 250 (Omega)	R46T	—	.035
1971 6 Cyl. 250 1 Bbl.	R46TS	—	.035
1970 6 Cyl. 250	R46T	—	.035
1969 6 Cyl. 250	R46N	—	.035
1968-66 6 Cyl. 250	R46N	46N	.035
1973-71 V-8 350 All 2 & 4 Bbl.			
w/Auto Trans. (Incl. Omega)	R46S	—	.040
4 Bbl. w/Man Trans.	R45S	—	.040
1970-69 V-8 350 Low Comp. 2 Bbl.	R46S	—	.030
High Comp. 4 Bbl.	R45S	—	.030
High Comp. 4 Bbl. Force Air	R43S	—	.030
1969 V-8 400 Low Compression	R46S	—	.030
High Compression	R44S	—	.030
Police Option	R43S	—	.030
1973-71 V-8 455 2 Bbl.	R46S	—	.040
4 Bbl. (Exc.4-4-2)	R46S	—	.040
4 Bbl. (4-4-2)	R45S	—	.040
4 Bbl. w30 option (4-4-2)	R45S	—	.040
1970 V-8 455 High Comp. 2 Bbl.	R45S	—	.030
High Comp. 4 Bbl. Vista Cruiser	R45S	—	.030
High Comp. 4 Bbl. Exc. Vista Cruiser	R44S	—	.030
1968 V-8 350 Low Compression	R46S	46S	.030
High Compression	R45S	45S	.030
1968 V-8 400 Low Compression	R45S	45S	.030
High Compression	R44S	44S	.030
Police Option	R43S	43S	.030
1967-65 V-8 400 High Compression	R44S	44S	.030
1967-64 V-8 330 Low Compression	R45S	45S	.030
High Compression	R44S	44S	.030

Delta 88, 98, Custom Royale, Cruiser, Toronado
1967-64 V-8 330 Low Compression	R45S	45S	.030
High Compression	R44S	44S	.030
1973-71 V-8 350 2 & 4 Bbl. Auto Trans.	R46S	—	.040
4 Bbl. Man. Trans.	R45S	—	.040
1970-69 V-8 350 Low Compression 2 Bbl.	R46S	—	.030
1969 V-8 350 High Compression	R45S	—	.030
1968 V-8 350 Low Compression	R46S	46S	.030
High Compression	R45S	45S	.030
1967-65 V-8 425 Low Compression	R45S	45S	.030
High Compression	R44S	44S	.030
Police Option	R43S	43S	.030
1973-71 V-8 455 2 Bbl. & 4 Bbl. w/Auto Trans.	R46S	—	.040
4 Bbl. w/Man. Trans.	R45S	—	.040
1970-69 V-8 455 Low Compression 2 Bbl.	R46S	—	.030
High Compression 4 Bbl.	R45S	—	.030
Police Options & Toronado Perf. Pkg.	R44S	—	.030
1968 V-8 455 Low Compression	R45S	45S	.030
High Compression	R44S	44S	.030
Police Option	R43S	43S	.030

PONTIAC

Bonneville, Catalina, Grandville, Grand Prix
Make, Year and Model	AC	Niter	Gap
1973-72 V-8 350 2 Bbl.	R46TS	—	.040
1971 V-8 350 2 Bbl.	R47S	—	.035
1970 V-8 350 2 Bbl.	R46S	—	.035
1966-63 V-8 389	R45S	45S	.035
1973-72 V-8 400 2 Bbl.	R46TS	—	.040
4 Bbl.	R45TS	—	.040
1971 V-8 400 2 Bbl. (265 h.p.)	R47S	—	.035
4 Bbl. (300 h.p.)	R46S	—	.035
1970-69 V-8 400 Grand Prix	R45S	—	.035
1970-69 V-8 400 Exc. Grand Prix	R46S	—	.035
1968-67 V-8 400	R45S	45S	.035
1966-63 V-8 421	R44S	44S	.035
1968-67 V-8 428	R44S	44S	.035
1969 V-8 428 Manual Trans.	R44S	—	.035
Auto. Trans.	R45S	—	.035
Auto Trans. (H.O.)	R44S	—	.035
1973-72 V-8 455 2 Bbl. or 4 Bbl.	R45TS	—	.040
1971 V-8 455 2 Bbl. & 4 Bbl.	R46S	—	.035
1970 V-8 455 Std. & H. O.	R46S	—	.035
1962-60 V-8	R45S	45S	.035

Firebird, Trans. Am. Esprit, Formula 350-400-455
1973-72 6 Cyl. 250 1 Bbl.	R46T	—	.035
1971 6 Cyl. 250 1 Bbl.	R46TS	—	.035
1970 6 Cyl.	R46T	—	.035
1969 6 Cyl.	R44NS	—	.035
1968-67 6 Cyl.	R44NS	44NS	.035
1967 V-8 326	R45S	45S	.035
1973-72 V-8 350 2 Bbl.	R46TS	—	.040
1971 V-8 350 2 Bbl.	R47S	—	.035
1970-69 V-8 350 2 Bbl.	R46S	—	.035
1969 V-8 350 4 Bbl.	R45S	—	.035
1968-67 V-8 350	R45S	45S	.035
1973-72 V-8 400 2 Bbl.	R46TS	—	.040
4 Bbl.	R45TS	—	.040
1971 V-8 400 2 Bbl. (265 h.p.)	R47S	—	.035
4 Bbl. (300 h.p.)	R46S	—	.035
1970-69 V-8 400 4 Bbl.	R45S	—	.035
1968-67 V-8 400	R44S	44S	.035
1973-72 V-8 455, LS 5, H.O.	R45TS	—	.040
1971 V-8 455 4 Bbl.	R46S	—	.035
4 Bbl. (H.O. 335 h.p.)	R46S	—	.035
1970 V-8 400 Ram Air III & IV	R44S	—	.035

Lemans (Tempest), Lemans Sport
1968-67 6 Cyl. 230	R44NS	44NS	.035

Lemans (Tempest), Lemans Sport
1966 6 Cyl. 230	R44S	44S	.035
1973-72 6 Cyl. 250 1 Bbl.	R46T	—	.040
1971 6 Cyl. 250 1 Bbl.	R46TS	—	.035
1970 6 Cyl.	R46T	—	.035
1969 6 Cyl. 250 OHC	R44NS	—	.035
1970-69 V-8 2 Bbl.	R46S	—	.035
1970-69 V-8 4 Bbl.	R45S	—	.035
1968-63 V-8	R45S	45S	.035
1973-72 V-8 350 2 Bbl.	R46TS	—	.040
1971 V-8 350 2 Bbl.	R47S	—	.035
1973-72 V-8 400 2 Bbl.	R46TS	—	.040
4 Bbl.	R45TS	—	.040
1971 V-8 400 2 Bbl. (265 h.p.)	R47S	—	.035
4 Bbl. (300 h.p.)	R46S	—	.035
1973-72 V-8 455 4 Bbl. & H.O.	R45TS	—	.040
4 Bbl., S.D.	R44TS	—	.040
1971 V-8 455 4 Bbl. (325 h.p.)	R46S	—	.035
4 Bbl GT (335 h.p. (HO)	R46S	—	.035

GTO, The Judge, GT-37
1973-72 V-8 400 4 Bbl.	R46TS	—	.040
1971 V-8 400 4 Bbl. (300 h.p.)	R46S	—	.035
1969 V-8 400 2 Bbl.	R46S	—	.035
1970-69 V-8 400 4 Bbl.	R45S	—	.035
1970-69 V-8 400 Ram Air III, IV	R44S	—	.035
1968-67 V-8 400 2 Bbl. Carb.	R45S	45S	.035
1968-67 V-8 400 4 Bbl. Carb.	R44S	44S	.035
1966-64 V-8	R44S	44S	.035
1973-72 V-8 455 4 Bbl. & H.O.	R45TS	—	.040
4 Bbl. S.D.	R44TS	—	.040
1971 V-8 455 4 Bbl.	R46S	—	.035
4 Bbl. (335 h.p. H.O.)	R46S	—	.035
1970 V-8 455 4 Bbl.	R46S	—	.035

Ventura II
1971 6 Cyl.	R46TS	—	.035
1973-72 6 Cyl.	R46T	—	.035
1971 V-8 307	R45TS	—	.035
1973-72 V-8 307	R44T	—	.035
1973-72 V-8 350	R46TS	—	.040

Electrical Testing Procedures

Some definite plan or procedure must be followed in order to perform chassis electrical tests efficiently and quickly. With all the different types of electrical circuits found in an automobile, it is impossible to establish one set procedure which would apply in all cases. However, the following basic procedure will provide a systematic approach to any testing problem:

1) If the fault is in a single unit in a multiple-unit circuit, start the test at the unit.

2) If the fault affects all the units in a multiple-unit circuit, start the test at the point where the circuit gets its power.

As an example, let's apply this procedure to the lighting circuit. If only one bulb in the circuit will not operate, start checking at the light bulb and check back along each part of the circuit until the defective element is found. If all the lights in a circuit do not operate, start checking at the point where the power is first introduced into the circuit and check each connection in sequence.

One of the first steps to take in diagnosing any electrical circuit problem is to perform a visual inspection of the affected components and/or wiring circuit. The most common problems revealed by visual inspection are a defective connection or a damaged wire. A loose connection can cause intermittent operation of the circuit or cause the circuit to open. Corrosion can appear as high resistance or as an open circuit. A damaged wire is obvious by its sharp kinks or frayed insulation. The wires should be moved around by hand when you make this test. A wire may be rubbing against a sharp sheetmetal edge or on the point of a screw and cause the insulation to be cut or worn through to the wire. If the bare wire comes in contact with the sheetmetal or screw, the circuit will be "grounded."

The visual inspection should be made quickly—but cautiously—of exposed, easy-to-reach parts. A visual inspection does not mean a disassembly of body parts to check the wiring harness.

If a known good part functions properly when substituted for a part that is not operating, the part which was removed is defective. If the part is a fuse or a circuit breaker and the part fails repeatedly, look for an overloaded circuit or a grounded circuit.

TEST FOR POWER: When a 12-volt test light lead is connected to a good ground and the other lead is connected to the circuit, there is power from the battery to the point where the test light is connected if the test lamp lights. If the test lamp does not light, there is no power in the circuit at the point being checked. This test can be made at any connection in the circuit.

A voltmeter, when properly connected between the circuit and a good ground, will show the voltage in the circuit at the point being tested. As with the test light, this is an indication of power in the circuit at this point. All switches in the circuit must be closed when you perform this test.

All electrical circuits must be complete from the source of power (battery) to the unit where the power is used, and back to the source of power again. A check at each connection in a circuit, starting at the battery, will locate an open circuit or will show that the circuit is complete.

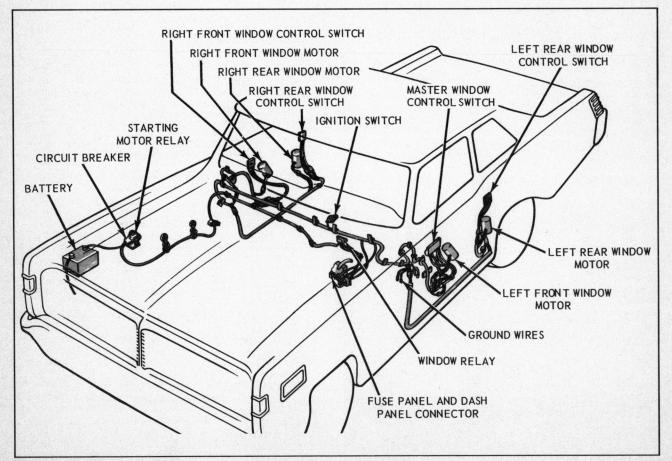

Power Window Circuit

A self-powered test light or ohmmeter, connected at any two points of a circuit with the power removed from the circuit, will show if the circuit between the two connections is open or complete. If the lamp does not light, the circuit is open. If the lamp lights, the circuit is complete.

In many cases when an electrical component stops operating, the trouble can be a blown fuse, and by replacing it with a good fuse the trouble may be eliminated. However, it can generally be assumed that something caused the fuse to blow other than just a bad fuse. If the second fuse blows soon after replacement, this is a sure sign of some other trouble.

Following are some examples of automotive accessories with various operating problems, along with an analysis of the possible trouble spots and suggested electrical testing procedures.

Power Windows

NO WINDOW OPERATION—ALL WINDOWS

If all windows are inoperative in all three positions of the bypass lockout switch, the problem most probably would be in the supply circuit, circuit breaker, or wiring. If the windows operate in the bypass position, the trouble would be in the window relay or circuit between the ignition switch and the relay.

1. Visually inspect the circuit breaker, wiring to the relay, and all wiring at the relay for loose or broken connection. Test for power (using a 12-volt test light) at the battery side of the circuit breaker. If there is no power, the trouble would be in the battery supply circuit.
2. Check for power at the output side of the circuit breaker. If there is no power, replace the circuit breaker.
3. If there is power, test for power at the center terminal (circuit breaker lead wire) of the window relay. If there is no power, the wiring from the circuit breaker to relay would be defective.
4. If there is power, turn the ignition switch to the "ON" or "ACC" position. Check for power at the ignition switch terminal of the window relay. If there is no power, the circuit from the ignition switch to the relay is at fault.
5. If there is power available to energize the relay, check for power at the output side of the relay. If there is no power, replace the relay.
6. If there is power at the relay output terminal, check for power at the master control switch. If power is not available, the circuit between the window relay and master control switch is faulty.
7. If voltage is available and the windows still do not operate, check ground wire circuit and assure a positive ground.

   NOTES: 1) In some power window circuits, the window motors are grounded individually.

   2) When diagnosing the problem on a car with a master control switch, it is suggested that the first step should be to check for power at the master control switch, and then if necessary to check for power at the window relay connector in the engine compartment.

ONE WINDOW WILL NOT OPERATE

For discussion purposes, assume the right rear door window will not operate. If the window will not operate from either the master control switch or the door panel switch, chances are the problem is in the motor and/or wiring in the door area.

1. Remove door trim panel and visually inspect the switch and motor connections to be sure they are properly installed. Inspect the window regulator mechanism for damage.
2. If window mechanism is satisfactory, test for power (using a 12-volt test light) at the motor disconnect in the UP and DOWN positions of the switch. If power is available, then the motor should be replaced.
3. If power is not available at the motor disconnect, test for power at the disconnect on the other side of the door panel switch. If power is available, replace the switch.
4. If power is not available to the door panel switch, check for power at the master control switch wiring connector. Check the door trim panel main feed wire connector. If power is available, the problem is in the wiring harness from the master control switch to the door panel switch.
5. If power is not available at the switch wiring connector or in the panel switch feed wire, inspect switch and wiring and repair or replace as necessary.

   NOTE: If the window will not operate from only one switch, the problem would be in that particular switch or switch feed circuit.

Dome, Courtesy and Pillar Lamps

DOME LAMP DOES NOT OPERATE FROM ANY OF SEVERAL SWITCHES IN DOORS OR ON DASH

If map lamp, clock, etc., operate, it can be assumed that the fuse is OK. However, if these items do not operate, check fuse.

1. Substitute a known good bulb and operate all switches. If the bulb lights, the old bulb is defective.
2. If the bulb does not light, check for power (using a 12-volt test light) at the dome lamp feed wire. If power is available, assure a good ground, inspect the dome lamp wire and socket assembly—repair or replace the parts as needed.
3. If power is not available at the dome lamp feed wire, check for power (using a 12-volt test light) at each door-operated switch.
4. If power is available at the switches, trouble is in the wiring between the switches and the dome lamp. Check for power at each connector in that part of the circuit between the switches and the dome lamp.
5. If power is not available, check circuit backwards from door-operated switches to power source.

DOME LAMP DOES NOT OPERATE FROM THE RIGHT DOOR-OPERATED SWITCH

1. Check for power (using a 12-volt test light) at the right door switch hot lead wire. If there is no power, check for power at each connection in the hot part of the circuit starting at the door switch. If there is power, connect a jumper wire between the leads at the door-operated switch. If the dome lamp operates, the switch is defective.
2. If the dome lamp does not operate, check for power at each connection between the switch and the dome lamp, starting at the door switch.

DOME LAMP DOES NOT OPERATE FROM THE LEFT DOOR-OPERATED SWITCH

1. Check for power (using a 12-volt test light) at the left door switch hot lead wire. If there is power, connect a jumper wire across the leads at the door-operated switch. If the dome lamp operates, the switch is defective.

DOME LAMP DOES NOT OPERATE FROM THE HEADLIGHT SWITCH

1. Check the operation of the dome lamp by operating each door switch. If the door switches operate the dome lamp, check for power (using a 12-volt test light) at the hot lead to the headlamp switch. If power is available to the main light switch, but is not directed to the dome lamp circuit when the dome lamp switch is operated, replace the headlamp switch.

Headlamps

ONE HEADLAMP DOES NOT LIGHT—ON LOW BEAM, HIGH BEAM, OR BOTH

When only one headlamp does not light, we can isolate the problem to the bulb, socket, or the wires leading directly to the bulb. The power source through the headlamp switch, foot dimmer switch, and up to the last common connection in the circuit must be good.

1. Disconnect harness connector from bulb. Visually inspect for loose or broken leads at the connector and the wiring between the connector and the main wiring harness to the other lights.
2. With the headlamp switch turned on, check for power (using a 12-volt test light) at the bulb wiring connector terminal(s). If there is power, connect the ground lead of the 12-volt test light to the connector ground terminal of the harness. If the test lamp lights, replace the bulb. If the test lamp does

Electrical Testing

not light, the ground circuit is bad.

3. If there is no power to the bulb wiring connector, the trouble is in the wire from the connector to the last common connection in the harness.

NOTE: On some installations, it may be faster and easier to substitute a known good bulb or to check for power at a wiring connector in the bulb circuit.

ALL HEADLAMPS DO NOT LIGHT ON LOW BEAM OR HIGH BEAM

If the headlamps do not light on low beam, or high beam, the problem can be isolated to the foot dimmer switch or to the wiring from the dimmer switch to the bulbs.

1. Visually inspect for loose or broken connections or damaged wiring in the circuit between the headlamps and the foot dimmer switch.
2. Pull back floormat to obtain access to foot dimmer switch. With the headlamp switch turned on, test for power (using a 12-volt test light) at the foot dimmer switch terminals. If either upper or lower beam operates, there will be power through the supply wire to the foot switch. If there is power through the switch to one terminal and not to the other, the foot dimmer switch is defective.

3. If there is power through the switch on both output terminals, there is an open circuit in the wiring somewhere between the foot dimmer switch and the headlamps.
4. Disconnect the wiring multiple connector at the dash panel which contains the headlamp circuit wires. With headlamp switch on, test for power (using a 12-volt test light) at the respective upper or lower beam wire at the firewall. If power is available, the trouble is in the wiring from the mating connector to the headlamps. If there is no power, the trouble is in the wire from the foot dimmer switch to the dash panel connector.

ALL HEADLAMPS DO NOT LIGHT

1. Visually inspect (where possible) all wires and connectors between headlamp switch and headlamps. Make sure the multiple connector at the dash panel is securely connected.
2. Test for power (using a 12-volt test light) at the headlamp switch source terminal. If power is not available, check power source circuit.
3. If power is available to the switch, turn headlamp switch on and check for power at the outlet terminal wire. If power is not coming from the switch, replace headlamp switch.
4. If power is available at the output terminal of the headlamp switch,

check for power to foot dimmer switch with the headlamp switch turned on. Check for power at the low beam and high beam terminals of the foot dimmer switch. If power is available to the dimmer switch, but not available to the output terminals, replace the foot dimmer switch.
5. If there is power from both terminals of the foot dimmer switch and all headlamps do not operate, check each wire circuit through the dash panel connector to the headlamps.

HEADLAMPS DIM AT IDLE

This problem may be the result of low battery voltage, poor connections or high resistance in the circuit. During the following tests, turn off all of the heavy-current-drawing accessories. Headlamp dimming at idle is normal when the charging system capacity is exceeded.

1. Check battery voltage to see that it is up to specifications. Correct if needed.
2. Visually inspect all wiring and connectors in the circuit for poor connection.
3. Check bulb ground wires for positive ground.
4. Disconnect a harness connector from one of the bulbs. With the headlamp switch turned on, check for applied voltage (using a voltmeter) at the high and/or low beam connector terminals. If an excessive voltage drop from battery voltage is indicated, repeat this test at next connector in the circuit.

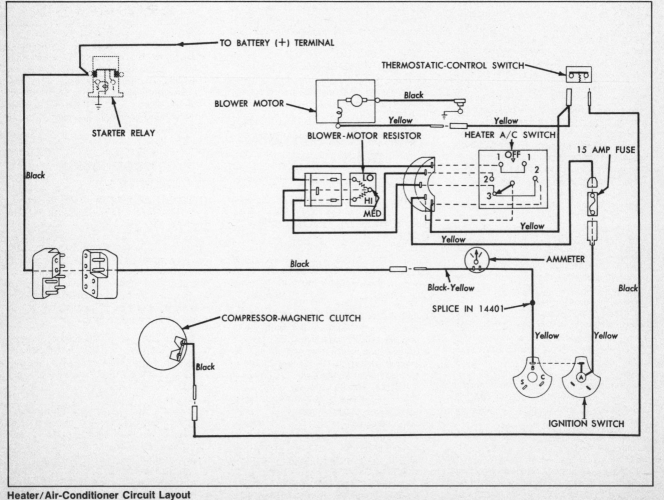

Heater/Air-Conditioner Circuit Layout

If the applied voltage at this point is near battery voltage, excessive resistance is indicated in the wiring from this terminal to the headlamp bulb. If the applied voltage at this point indicates excessive voltage drop, repeat this test at the succeeding connectors or components until the area of excessive resistance is located.

Instrument Panel Gauges

ONE INDICATOR GAUGE READS TOO HIGH OR LOW

1. Visually inspect wiring at the sending unit for loose or broken connections. In the case of the fuel tank sending unit, assure a good ground.
2. Disconnect the wire from the suspected sending unit and connect it to a substitute known good fuel tank sending unit for test purposes. Be sure the test unit has a good ground contact to the car. With the ignition switch in the "ON" or "ACC" position, place the tank sending unit float arm in its "empty," "half full" and "full" positions. Note the needle positions on the indicator gauge. If the indicator gauge reads as required, replace the sending unit.
3. If the indicator gauge does not read as required, inspect wiring connections at the indicator gauge for proper installation. Disconnect the gauge sending unit wire from the indicator gauge. Connect a short piece of known good wire between the indicator gauge and the known good fuel tank sending unit. Ground the sending unit. With the ignition switch "ON," place the tank sending unit float arm in the "empty," "half full," and "full" positions. Note the needle positions on the indicator gauge. If the indicator gauge reads as required, the trouble is in the wire from the indicator gauge to the sending unit. Test this wire for a short or open, using a voltmeter.
4. If the indicator gauge does not read as required, replace the indicator gauge.

ALL GAUGE INDICATORS READ MAXIMUM WHEN THE IGNITION IS TURNED ON

1. Check voltage at output terminal of constant-voltage regulator. If voltage oscillates between 0-10 volts, regulator is OK.
2. If voltage does not oscillate between 0-10 volts, replace constant-voltage regulator.

ALL GAUGE INDICATORS REMAIN ON LOW END OF SCALE WHEN IGNITION SWITCH IS TURNED "ON" AND ENGINE RUNNING

1. Check voltage at input side of constant-voltage regulator. If approximate battery voltage (12 volts) is available at input side, replace constant-voltage regulator. (Apparently an open

exists in the regulator.)
2. If no voltage is available to the input side of the constant-voltage regulator, check wiring from accessory terminal of the ignition switch to the input side of the regulator for continuity.

ERRATIC GAUGE INDICATOR OPERATION

The most probable cause of this condition is loose wiring connectors or a defective sending unit.

1. Clean and tighten all accessible connections (including ground) at the sending unit. If all gauges are erratic, check connections at the constant-voltage regulator. Recheck system operation.
2. If gauge indicator is still erratic, substitute the fuel tank sending unit reserved for testing purposes for the system at fault. Be sure the test unit has a good ground contact. Turn ignition switch "ON." Place the fuel tank sending unit float arm in its "empty," "half full" and "full" positions. If the indicator gauge reads as required, replace the sending unit.
3. If the erratic condition continues to exist, check all wiring connections back to the indicator gauge and check the operation of the indicator gauge with the test sending unit connected.

Horns

ONE HORN DOES NOT WORK

This problem can be isolated to the horn itself, wire leading to the horn, or a poor ground.

1. Connect a jumper wire from the battery positive terminal to the horn terminal. If the horn operates, the trouble is in the wire between the horn terminal and the point where the lead wire connects to the hot circuit.
2. If the horn does not operate, check and assure a positive ground. If ground is satisfactory and horn does not operate, replace horn.

BOTH HORNS DO NOT WORK

1. Check for power (using a 12-volt test light) on the power source wire on the harness connector at the base of the steering column. If power is not available, check the supply wire from the headlamp switch.
2. If power is available at the power supply wire, connect a jumper wire across the supply wire to the outlet wire. If the horns do not operate, the trouble is in the wire circuit from the connector at the base of the steering column to the horns. Test for power at each connector in horns' circuit to locate the cause of trouble.
3. If the horns operate when a jumper is connected across the supply wire and the outlet wires, the trouble is apparently in the steering column harness, brushes or horn button switching mechanism. Remove steering wheel. Check for power at the supply wire

brush. If power is available at the supply wire brush, connect a jumper across to the outlet wire. If the horns operate, trouble is in the horn button switch area. Inspect and repair as required. If the horns do not operate upon bypassing the horn button switch, trouble is in the outlet wire from the brush to the connector at the base of the steering column.

HORNS HAVE POOR SOUNDING QUALITY

The most probable cause of this problem is improper horn adjustment. High resistance in the circuit could also cause this problem.

1. Test the current draw of the horn. Connect a voltmeter and ammeter to the horn and to a battery source. The normal current draw for one horn at 12 volts is 4.0 to 5.0 amperes. If the current draw is outside specifications, turn adjusting nut or screw until the current is within the limits for the horn being adjusted.
2. If the horns are satisfactory, check voltage drop across the horn wire circuit. Connect a voltmeter between the positive terminal of the battery and the horn terminal. Operate the horns and note voltage drop. If voltage drop is excessive (high resistance), check horn circuit wiring to locate poor connections or high resistance.

Air Conditioning

The result of almost any air-conditioning malfunction is that the interior of the car will not cool down. In that case, the first thing to check is the airflow that is coming out of the air-conditioning outlets.

IF AIRFLOW FROM DUCTS IS NORMAL

Inspect system for obvious troubles, such as a broken compressor belt, blown compressor fuse, or damage from an accident. Then check the temperature of the air coming out of the ducts.
1. If air from ducts is cold: The problem is not the air conditioner, but in the unauthorized entry of hot air from outside. Look for air leaks in the car body, at the doors, windows, firewall, or fresh air ducts, including heater.
2. If air from ducts is warm or hot: Do not attempt further repairs. Take the car to an expert air conditioning serviceman.

IF AIRFLOW IS LOW OR NON-EXISTENT

1. Inspect the blower to see if it is working. If it isn't, the cause may be a blown fuse, a broken wire, loose connections, a bad switch, or even a bad blower motor. If the blower is working, look for leakage or blocked ducts. It could even be a clogged radiator core, caused by papers or dirt and dust. If ice is blocking the evaporator, take the car to an expert air conditioning serviceman.

Troubleshooting Guides

There are three ways that you can eliminate problems in an automobile. The first is to think about it, do a bit of testing and narrow the trouble down to one particular part or area. The second method is to replace everything on the car that might have anything to do with the problem in the hope that it can be eliminated. (A lot of shops do just this.) The third way is to sell the car. The first method is not used as much as it should be, as people just don't like to read. As they don't like to use their brains either, many jump quickly into the second method and start replacing everything on the car. There is one redeeming aspect to this approach—a lot of cars are eventually fixed that way.

We've seen complete rear axles replaced because there was a noise in the wheel bearing. We've also seen engines that wouldn't run correctly get loaded down with all new accessories—carburetor, distributor, spark plugs, wires, even

the battery was changed, because one of those units was probably the culprit. Unfortunately, you'll even find some mechanic among the pros who wants to replace a unit rather than analyze the problem. He's the one who'll accept any suggestion because he doesn't know what to do next. And then there's the poor soul, bless him, who will actually change the hood ornament or wheel covers to make the car run right, simply because these are the only parts he hasn't worked on already.

If you've got lots of money and time, that kind of hit-or-miss repairing is OK, but sadly, there's no guarantee of success, and you may end up with nothing else to do but sell the car. And if the fellow who buys it knows anything at all about making cars run, he's got the buy of a lifetime, because you've practically rebuilt it for him. That brings us full circle, right back to method No. 1, where you have to find the part that is causing the problem and either fix or replace it.

Almost anybody knows where to start the search. If the engine dies, you look at the carburetor. If it misses, you suspect the spark plugs. For an overheating problem, you check the radiator. But after you've checked the obvious and found nothing wrong, you should go to this troubleshooting list where you'll find causes you hadn't thought of before.

Admittedly, the troubleshooting lists are not absolutely complete, and any attempt to make them so would more than fill this entire book. But we've tried to pick the most common problems (and some that aren't so common) and lay them out for you. Reading these, you'll soon conclude that everything is arranged in helter-skelter fashion, but that's deliberate on our part. We figure that this is one way of forcing you to think while you're reading. These troubleshooting lists are really like the starting switch on your car—they're the first step in a process that should result in a good running automobile.

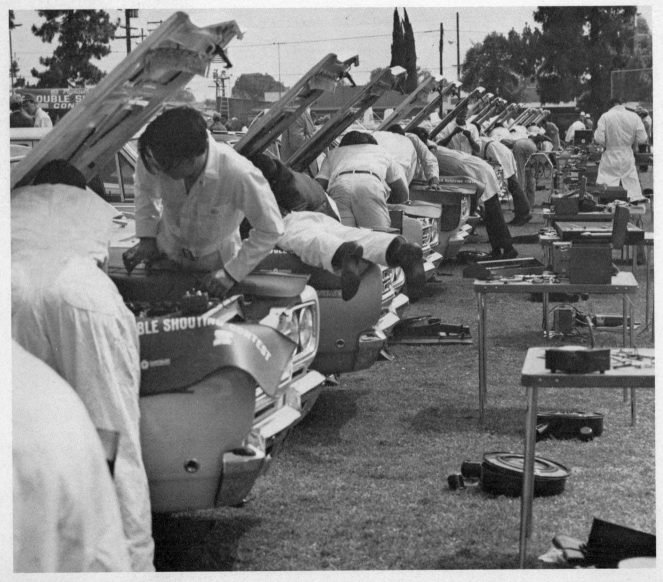

1. Engine

WILL NOT START

CONDITION	CORRECTION
(a) Battery is weak.	(a) Test battery specific gravity, and recharge or replace if necessary.
(b) Battery terminals loose or corroded.	(b) Clean and tighten; apply coat of petroleum to terminals.
(c) Faulty ignition cables, wires, or distributor cap.	(c) Check wiring for cracks or shorting, and replace if necessary; replace distributor cap.
(d) Faulty coil.	(d) Test and replace if necessary.
(e) Spark plug gap incorrect.	(e) Remove and regap to specs.
(f) Ignition timing incorrect.	(f) Reset timing to specs.
(g) Dirt or moisture in fuel line or carburetor.	(g) Clean lines and carburetor.
(h) Carburetor flooded.	(h) Adjust float level and check seats.
(i) Carburetor float setting incorrect.	(i) Adjust float level and check seats.
(j) Fuel pump faulty.	(j) Test output and replace if necessary.
(k) Carburetor percolating; no fuel in carburetor.	(k) Measure float level, adjust bowl vent and inspect manifold control valve operation.

ENGINE STALLS

CONDITION	CORRECTION
(a) Idle speed too low.	(a) Adjust carburetor.
(b) Choke adjustment incorrect.	(b) Adjust choke correctly.
(c) Idle mixture incorrect.	(c) Richen if too lean; lean if too rich. Use idle mixture screw on carburetor.
(d) Carburetor float setting incorrect.	(d) Adjust carburetor float level.
(e) Intake manifold has leak.	(e) Inspect intake manifold gasket; replace if necessary.
(f) Ignition wiring incorrect.	(f) Replace with correct wiring.
(g) Faulty coil.	(g) Test and replace if necessary.
(h) Burned or worn distributor rotor.	(h) Replace with new rotor.
(i) Tappet lash incorrect (6-cyl.)	(i) Adjust lash to specs.

LOSS OF ENGINE POWER

CONDITION	CORRECTION
(a) Ignition timing incorrect.	(a) Reset timing to specs.
(b) Burned or worn distributor rotor.	(b) Replace with new rotor.
(c) Distributor shaft worn.	(c) Remove distributor and repair.
(d) Dirty spark plugs or incorrect gap.	(d) Remove, clean, and regap or replace.
(e) Dirt or moisture in fuel line, carburetor, or filter.	(e) Clean lines and carburetor; replace filter.
(f) Carburetor float setting incorrect.	(f) Adjust float level.
(g) Fuel pump faulty.	(g) Test output and replace if necessary.
(h) Valve timing incorrect.	(h) Check and reset vave timing to specs.
(i) Cylinder head gasket faulty.	(i) Install new head gasket.
(j) Low cylinder compression.	(j) Remove plugs and test compression of each cylinder.
(k) Valves worn, pitted, or burned.	(k) Do valve job.
(l) Faulty exhaust system.	(l) Replace faulty components and replace.
(m) Faulty ignition cables, wires, or distributor cap.	(m) Check wiring for cracks or shorting, and replace if necessary; replace distributor cap.
(n) Faulty coil.	(n) Test and replace if necessary.

ENGINE MISSES ON ACCELERATION

CONDITION	CORRECTION
(a) Dirty spark plugs or incorrect gap.	(a) Clean plugs and reset gap to specs.
(b) Dirt in carburetor.	(b) Remove and clean carburetor.
(c) Ignition timing incorrect.	(c) Reset timing to specs.
(d) Weak acceleration pump in carburetor.	(d) Replace with new pump.
(e) Valves worn, pitted, or burned.	(e) Do valve job.
(f) Faulty coil.	(f) Test and replace if necessary.

ENGINE MISSES AT HIGH RPM

CONDITION	CORRECTION
(a) Dirty spark plugs or incorrect gap.	(a) Clean plugs and reset gap to specs.
(b) Distributor shaft worn.	(b) Remove distributor and repair.
(c) Distributor rotor worn or burned.	(c) Replace with new rotor.
(d) Faulty coil.	(d) Test, and replace if necessary.
(e) Ignition timing incorrect.	(e) Reset timing to specs.
(f) Dirt in carburetor jets.	(f) Clean jets thoroughly.
(g) Dirt or moisture in fuel line, carburetor, or fuel filter.	(g) Clean lines and carburetor; replace fuel filter.

NOISY VALVES

CONDITION	CORRECTION
(a) Thin or diluted oil in crankcase.	(a) Change oil.
(b) Low oil pressure.	(b) Check engine oil level; inspect oil pump relief valve and spring.
(c) Dirt in tappets.	(c) Clean tappets.
(d) Bent pushrods.	(d) Install new pushrods.
(e) Rocker arms worn.	(e) Replace, and check oil supply to rockers.
(f) Tappets worn.	(f) Install new tappets.
(g) Valve guides worn.	(g) Ream, and install new valve guides.
(h) Run-out of valve seats or valve faces excessive.	(h) Grind valve seats and valves to specs.
(i) Tappet lash incorrect (6-cyl.)	(i) Adjust lash to specs.

CONNECTING ROD NOISE

CONDITION	CORRECTION
(a) Oil supply insufficient.	(a) Check engine oil level.
(b) Low oil pressure.	(b) Check engine oil level; inspect oil pump relief valve and spring.
(c) Thin or diluted oil.	(c) Change oil.
(d) Bearing clearance excessive.	(d) Measure bearings for correct clearance.
(e) Connecting rod journals out-of-round.	(e) Replace crankshaft or regrind journals.
(f) Connecting rods misaligned.	(f) Replace bent connecting rods.

MAIN BEARING NOISE

(a) Oil supply insufficient.

(a) Check engine oil level.

(b) Low oil pressure.

(b) Check engine oil level, inspect oil pump relief valve and spring.

(c) Thin or diluted oil.

(c) Change oil.

(d) Bearing clearance excessive.

(d) Measure bearings for correct clearance.

(e) Excessive end-play.

(e) Check No. 3 main bearing for wear on flanges.

(f) Crankshaft journal out-of-round.

(f) Replace crankshaft or regrind journals.

(g) Loose flywheel or torque converter.

(g) Tighten to correct torque as per specs.

OIL PRESSURE DROP

(a) Low oil level.

(a) Check engine oil level.

(b) Faulty oil pressure sending unit.

(b) Replace with new sending unit.

(c) Clogged oil filter.

(c) Replace oil filter.

(d) Oil pump worn.

(d) Remove and replace worn parts or pump.

(e) Thin or diluted oil.

(e) Change oil.

(f) Bearing clearance excessive.

(f) Measure bearings for correct clearance.

(g) Oil pump relief valve stuck.

(g) Remove valve; inspect, clean, and reinstall.

(h) Oil pump suction tube loose, bent, or cracked.

(h) Remove oil pan, and install new tube if necessary.

OIL PUMPS AT RINGS

(a) Worn, scuffed, or broken piston rings.

(a) Hone cylinder bores and install new piston rings.

(b) Carbon in oil ring slot.

(b) Install new piston rings.

(c) Rings too tight in grooves.

(c) Remove rings and check grooves. If groove is not proper width, replace piston.

2. Starting System

STARTER WILL NOT OPERATE

(a) Battery discharged or defective.

(a) Check headlight operation; if dim or will not glow, charge battery. If battery cannot pass light-load test after charging, replace.

(b) Poor cable wire connections.

(b) Check connections at battery, solenoid, cowl connector, and ignition switch.

(c) Neutral start switch out of adjustment or defective.

(c) Move shift lever through all ranges with foot brake set and key in start position. If starter cranks in R and D, position shift lever in N with key off, remove neutral start switch, reinstall and try starting in N and P. If starter cranks in L2 and L1, replace switch.

(d) Fusible link burned out.

(d) Inspect condition of fusible link. If burned, replace and recheck starting.

(e) Ignition switch defective.

(e) Shift lever in neutral and turn ignition switch ON to see if wipers and turn signals operate. If not, check for disconnected cowl and/or ignition switch connector or burned fusible link. If all are OK, replace ignition switch.

CONDITION	CORRECTION	CONDITION	CORRECTION
(f) Solenoid defective.	(f) Connect voltmeter to solenoid "S" terminal and starter frame. Take your reading when trying to start the engine; if reading is 9 volts or more, replace solenoid.	(b) Starter drive clutch defective.	(b) Check drive clutch. Replace if necessary.
		(c) Missing teeth on engine ring gear.	(c) Replace engine ring gear and inspect teeth on drive pinion gear. Replace starter drive if necessary.

STARTER CLICKS BUT WILL NOT CRANK

CONDITION	CORRECTION
(a) Poor connections at battery and/or starter.	(a) Check and retighten connections.
(b) Solenoid or starter motor defective.	(b) Remove starter motor, check solenoid and/or starter and repair or replace.

STARTER CRANKS ENGINE SLOWLY

CONDITION	CORRECTION
(a) Battery discharged or defective.	(a) Check headlight operation as above.
(b) Poor connections at battery and/or starter.	(b) Check and retighten connections.
(c) Wrong starter motor on car.	(c) Check part numbers to insure that starter is correct for car; replace if incorrect.
(d) Starter is defective.	(d) Remove starter motor, inspect bushings and repair as necessary.
(e) Cranking voltage is low.	(e) Check cranking voltage at positive terminal of ignition coil; it should be at least 9.5 volts. If less, check condition of battery, cables and starter connections. If over 9.5 volts, low temperature or too heavy oil may be causing excessive engine drag.

STARTER SPINS BUT WILL NOT CRANK ENGINE

CONDITION	CORRECTION
(a) Armature shaft dirty or corroded.	(a) Clean armature shaft and lubricate with lithium soap grease.

STARTER CRANKS ENGINE BUT IS EXCESSIVELY NOISY

CONDITION	CORRECTION
(a) Drive pinion to ring gear clearance incorrect.	(a) Measure distance between tip of pinion tooth and root of two ring gear teeth with round feeler gauge at three locations around ring gear. Distance should be within .025 to .060-in. If distance is less than .025-in., shim starter away from engine block at both attaching bolts. If distance is greater than .060-in., shim to maximum of .30-in. at outboard attaching bolt. Recheck for correct clearance.
(b) Starter drive or ring gear is defective.	(b) Check drive and ring gear; replace if necessary.
(c) Starter bushing worn.	(c) Replace.

3. Fuel System

ENGINE CRANKS BUT WILL NOT START

CONDITION	CORRECTION
(a) Car is out of gas.	(a) Add fuel to tank and check fuel gauge for proper operation.
(b) Choke valve does not close sufficiently when cold.	(b) Adjust the choke thermostatic coil.
(c) Choke valve or linkage binds or sticks.	(c) Realign or replace the choke valve or linkage as required. Clean but do not oil.

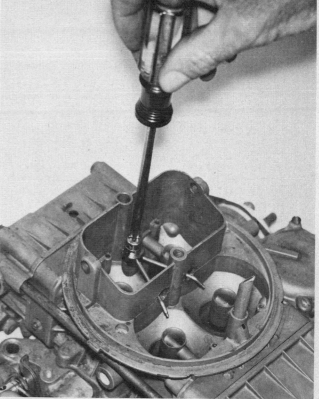

CONDITION	CORRECTION	CONDITION	CORRECTION
(d) No fuel in carburetor.	(d) Disconnect fuel line at tank and blow out with compressed air. Reconnect and check for proper operation. If not, replace fuel pump. Fuel filter may be plugged or carburetor float may require adjustment.	(d) Gasket between air horn and float bowl leaks.	(d) Torque air horn to float bowl to specs.
		(e) Carburetor loose on manifold.	(e) Tighten carburetor-to-manifold bolts to specs.
(e) Engine is flooded.	(e) Adjust throttle linkage and unloader if choke valve is not opening. If unloader works properly, disassemble and clean carburetor to remove dirt in carburetor float needle and seat. If engine still floods, check float for bent arm.	(f) Air valve sticks open.	(f) Free-up air valve shaft and align air valves. Check air valve spring for closing tension and replace if defective.
		(g) Secondary throttle valve lockout.	(g) Free-up and check for proper operation if binding, then adjust secondary throttle valve lockout.

ENGINE STARTS AND STALLS

NO POWER—HEAVY ACCELERATION OR HIGH SPEED

CONDITION	CORRECTION	CONDITION	CORRECTION
(a) Fast idle speed too low.	(a) Readjust fast idle to specs.	(a) Carburetor throttle valve not opening completely.	(a) Adjust linkage to obtain wide open throttle in carburetor.
(b) Choke vacuum break unit is defective.	(b) Replace diaphragm unit.	(b) Dirty or plugged fuel filters.	(b) Clean or replace filters.
(c) Choke coil rod out of adjustment.	(c) Adjust properly.	(c) Secondary throttle valves do not unlock once engine has warmed up.	(c) Free-up and adjust lockout.
(d) Choke valve or linkage binds or sticks.	(d) Realign or replace the choke valve or linkage as required. Clean but do not oil.	(d) Air valves bind, or are stuck open or closed.	(d) Free-up air valve shaft and align air valves. Check air valve spring for closing tension and replace if defective.
(e) Insufficient fuel in carburetor.	(e) Disconnect fuel line at tank and blow out with compressed air. Reconnect and check for proper operation. If not, replace fuel pump. Fuel filter may be plugged or carburetor float may need adjustment.	(e) Power system inoperative.	(e) Remove air horn and clean piston and cavity of dirt. Check power piston spring for distortion.
		(f) Float level too low.	(f) Check and reset float level to specs.
(f) Carburetor flooding.	(f) Check fuel filters and replace if necessary. If carburetor continues to flood, remove air horn and check float needle and seat for proper seal. If needle set leaks, replace.	(g) Float does not drop far enough in bowl.	(g) Check for bind in float hanger and arm; check float alignment in bowl.
		(h) Main metering jets or metering rods are dirty or plugged.	(h) Completely disassemble carburetor and clean thoroughly.

ENGINE IDLES ROUGH AND STALLS

ENGINE STARTS HARD WHEN HOT

CONDITION	CORRECTION	CONDITION	CORRECTION
(a) Idle speed setting incorrect.	(a) Readjust idle speed to specs.	(a) Choke valve does not open completely.	(a) As choke valve and/or linkage binds, clean or replace as required. Also check and adjust choke thermostatic coil.
(b) Manifold vacuum hoses disconnected, improperly installed or leak.	(b) Check all vacuum hoses, install or replace as required.		
(c) Carburetor loose on intake manifold.	(c) Tighten carburetor-to-manifold bolts to specs.	(b) No fuel in carburetor.	(b) Check fuel pump for proper operation and replace if necessary. Check and adjust float level.
(d) Dirt in idle channels.	(d) Clean fuel system and carburetor.		
(e) Secondary throttle valve out of alignment.	(e) Loosen screws, align valves and tighten screws.	(c) Float bowl leaks.	(c) Locate leak and repair.
(f) Defective intake manifold gasket.	(f) Replace manifold gasket.		

ENGINE SURGES OR RUNS UNEVEN

CONDITION	CORRECTION	CONDITION	CORRECTION
(g) Defective carburetor base gasket.	(g) Replace gasket.	(a) Fuel restriction.	(a) Check hoses and fuel lines for bends, kinks or leaks and straighten. Check fuel filter and replace if dirty or plugged.

ENGINE HESITATES ON ACCELERATION

CONDITION	CORRECTION	CONDITION	CORRECTION
(a) Accelerator pump system defective.	(a) Remove air horn and check pump cup. If cracked, scored or distorted, replace pump plunger. Check discharge ball for proper seating and location.	(b) Dirt or water in fuel.	(b) Clean fuel tank, lines and filters. Remove and clean carburetor.
		(c) Fuel level incorrect.	(c) Check for free float and float needle valve operation; free-up, adjust or replace as necessary.
(b) Dirt in pump passages or pump jet.	(b) Clean and blow out with compressed air.	(d) Main metering jets or metering rods are dirty, plugged or bent.	(d) Completely disassemble carburetor and clean thoroughly. Replace bent rods.
(c) Float level incorrect.	(c) Check and reset float level to specs. Make sure float needle is not sticking.	(e) Power system inoperative.	(e) Remove air horn and clean piston and cavity of dirt. Check power piston spring for distortion.

CONDITION	CORRECTION	CONDITION	CORRECTION
(f) Vacuum leakage.	(f) Tighten all hose connections. Torque carburetor to manifold to specs. Replace gasket if defective.		

4. Emission System EGR

EGR VALVE STEM DOES NOT MOVE ON SYSTEM TEST

(a) Hoses may be cracked, leaking, disconnected or plugged.	(a) Inspect all hose connections and leakcheck to confirm hoses are open. If any defective hoses are found, replace.
(b) EGR valve is defective, ruptured diaphragm or valve stem frozen.	(b) Disconnect hose from EGR valve and connect external vacuum source of 10 Hg or more to valve diaphragm. If valve does not move, replace. If valve opens about ⅛-in., pinch off supply hose to check for diaphragm leakage—valve should remain open for 30 sec. or more. If leakage does occur, replace valve.

EGR VALVE STEM DOES NOT MOVE ON SYSTEM TEST BUT DOES ON EXTERNAL VACUUM SOURCE

(a) Temperature control valve is defective.	(a) Verify that temperature in vehicle area is above that specified for particular EGR system, then disconnect hose from temperature control valve and plug hose. If EGR valve stem operates normally, replace TC valve.
(b) Defective control system—plugged passages.	(b) Remove carburetor and check vacuum passages in throttle bore. Use suitable solvent to remove any deposits and check for flow with light air pressure. Do not use drills or wires to clean carburetor control passages as these can upset calibration of precision control orifices.

ENGINE WILL NOT IDLE, DIES OUT ON RETURN TO IDLE, IDLE IS SLOW AND ROUGH

(a) EGR valve is stuck open.	(a) Disconnect hose from EGR valve and plug hose. Check idle. If idle is satisfactory, amplifier unit is defective (Venturi Vacuum Control System only).
(b) EGR valve leakage in closed position.	(b) Remove EGR valve and inspect to insure poppet is seated. Replace if defective.

POOR ENGINE RESPONSE AT ROAD SPEEDS BELOW 40° F.

(a) Temperature control valve is defective.	(a) Replace TC valve.

5. Emission System Air Pump

EXCESSIVE BELT NOISE

(a) Loose belt.	(a) Tighten belt to specs.
(b) Seized pump.	(b) Replace pump.

EXCESSIVE PUMP NOISE—CHIRPING, RUMBLING OR KNOCKING

(a) Leak in hose.	(a) Locate leak using soap solution and correct.
(b) Loose hose.	(b) Tighten or replace hose clamp.
(c) Hose touches other engine parts.	(c) Change hose position.
(d) Diverter valve does not operate.	(d) Replace.
(e) Check valve does not operate.	(e) Replace.
(f) Pump mounting fasteners are loose.	(f) Tighten mounting screws to specs.
(g) Pump failure.	(g) Remove and replace pump.

NO AIR SUPPLY AS ENGINE ACCELERATES ABOVE 1500 RPM

(a) Loose drive belt.	(a) Tighten to specs.
(b) Supply hose leaks.	(b) Locate leak, repair or replace.
(c) Leak at fitting(s).	(c) Tighten or replace hose clamps.
(d) Diverter valve leaks.	(d) Run car at idle; if air is expelled through diverter exhaust, replace valve.
(e) Diverter valve does not operate.	(e) Replace.
(f) Check valve does not operate.	(f) Replace.

6. Fuel Pump

PUMP LEAKS FUEL

(a) Diaphragm is worn, ruptured or torn.	(a) Replace pump.
(b) Diaphragm mounting plates are loose.	(b) Replace pump.
(c) Loose inlet or outlet line fittings.	(c) Tighten line fittings.

PUMP LEAKS OIL

(a) Cracked or deteriorated pushrod oil seal.	(a) Replace pump.
(b) Rocker arm pivot pin is loose.	(b) Replace pump.
(c) Pump mounting bolts loose.	(c) Tighten mounting bolts securely.
(d) Pump to block gasket is defective.	(d) Install new gasket.

INSUFFICIENT FUEL DELIVERY

(a) Vent in tank is restricted.	(a) Unplug vent and inspect tank for leaks.
(b) Leaks in fuel line or fittings.	(b) Tighten line fittings.
(c) Dirt or other restriction in fuel tank.	(c) Replace fuel filter and clean out tank.
(d) Diaphragm is worn, ruptured or torn.	(d) Replace pump.
(e) Gas lines frozen.	(e) Thaw lines and drain tank.
(f) Improperly seating valves.	(f) Replace pump.
(g) Pump pushrod worn.	(g) Replace pushrod.
(h) Vapor lock.	(h) Install a heat shield wherever lines or pump come near exhaust.
(i) Low pressure.	(i) Replace pump.
(j) Incorrect fuel pump affixed to car.	(j) Check part number and replace with correct pump unit.

CONDITION	CORRECTION	CONDITION	CORRECTION
(k) Dirty or restricted fuel filter.	(k) Replace filter.	(d) Low voltage regulator setting.	(d) Set up test as in (c) above but turn off all accessories. When engine is at normal operating temperature any reading between 13.5 and 15.0 volts indicates that regulator is OK.

NOISY FUEL PUMP

CONDITION	CORRECTION
(a) Mounting bolts are loose.	(a) Tighten mounting bolts securely.
(b) Rocker arm scored or worn.	(b) Replace pump.
(c) Rocker arm spring weak or broken.	(c) Replace spring.
(d) Stiff inlet hose.	(d) Install new hose about 3 ins. longer than old hose.

(e) High resistance in starting circuit or ignition resistor bypass. — (e) Connect jumper from negative terminal of coil to ground to prevent starting engine. Connect voltmeter to positive coil terminal and ground. Crank engine. Any reading below 9.0 volts requires a further test. Check voltage across battery posts during cranking. If voltage reading is within .5 volt of that at coil, circuits are OK but battery is too low for proper test.

BATTERY OVERCHARGED

CONDITION	CORRECTION
(a) Shorted battery cell.	(a) Perform battery load test to determine if battery cell is at fault.
(b) Voltage regulator setting too high.	(b) See Undercharged Battery (c) above. Set up test as in (c) and perform as in (d). If voltage is over 15.0 volts, replace regulator.

7. Charging System

GENERATOR LIGHT STAYS ON WITH ENGINE RUNNING

CONDITION	CORRECTION
(a) Belt is loose or broken.	(a) Replace belt if necessary; tighten belt tension to specs.
(b) No generator output.	(b) Connect test lamp to generator No. 1 terminal. If lamp lights dimly, generator receives initial field current but has no output. Ground generator field. If light does not brighten, remove and repair generator. If light does brighten, the generator is OK and voltage regulator is defective.

GENERATOR LIGHT ON WITH IGNITION OFF

CONDITION	CORRECTION
(a) Positive diode shorted.	(a) Replace diode bridge.

GENERATOR LIGHT OFF WITH IGNITION ON BUT ENGINE NOT RUNNING

CONDITION	CORRECTION
(a) Indicator bulb burned out.	(a) Replace bulb and socket assembly.
(b) Blown fuse.	(b) Replace fuse controlling indicator lights if all are off. If indicator lights do not come on with new fuse, check for an open in indicator light feed wire and correct.
(c) Open between bulb and ground in generator.	(c) Ground No. 1 terminal wire. If bulb lights, remove generator for repair. If bulb still does not light, check further for an open between bulb and generator.

UNDERCHARGED BATTERY

CONDITION	CORRECTION
(a) Continuous small drain on battery.	(a) Disconnect positive cable from battery. Connect test light between cable and battery post. If test lamp lights, trace and correct source of drain.
(b) Belt is loose or broken.	(b) Replace belt if necessary; tighten belt tension to specs.
(c) Low generator output.	(c) Connect voltmeter across battery and record voltage reading. Set carburetor on high step of fast idle cam, start engine, and turn on all continuous use accessories. If voltage across battery reads lower than the open circuit voltage just recorded, generator current output is low. Remove unit and repair.

8. Cooling System

ENGINE OVERHEATS

CONDITION	CORRECTION
(a) Belt tension is too low.	(a) Adjust belt tension to specs.
(b) Timing set incorrectly.	(b) Reset timing to specs.
(c) Timing retarded by faulty distributor vacuum advance unit or thermal vacuum switch.	(c) Check thermal advance for defective switch or distributor vacuum advance unit. Check hose for kinks, partial collapse or poor connections.
(d) Loss of system pressure.	(d) Test system and cap for pressure. If cap is not defective, inspect for leaks and repair when found.
(e) Radiator fins obstructed.	(e) Clean radiator fins of debris, bugs, etc.
(f) Cooling system passages blocked by rust or scale.	(f) Flush system and add fresh coolant.
(g) Reservoir hose is pinched or kinked.	(g) Replace hose and prevent kinking by rerouting if necessary.
(h) Lower radiator hose has collapsed.	(h) Replace.

COOLANT LOSS

CONDITION	CORRECTION
(a) Thermostat stuck in closed position.	(a) Replace thermostat.
(b) Leaking hoses or poor connections.	(b) Check hoses and connections. Tighten and/or replace if necessary.
(c) Heater core leaks.	(c) Replace heater core.
(d) Water temperature sending unit is leaking.	(d) Replace unit.
(e) Radiator leaks.	(e) Check radiator for leaks, especially bottom half.

ENGINE DOES NOT REACH NORMAL OPERATING TEMPERATURE

CONDITION	CORRECTION
(a) Radiator leaks.	(a) Check radiator for leaks, especially bottom half. Also check system for pressure.

CONDITION	CORRECTION
(b) Coolant reservoir/hose leaks.	(b) Replace reservoir or hose.
(c) Hoses or connections are loose or damaged.	(c) Reseat or replace hoses/clamps.
(d) Water pump seal leaks.	(d) Repair water pump or replace.
(e) Water pump gasket leaks.	(e) Replace gasket.
(f) Radiator cap defective.	(f) Test cap for pressure and replace.
(g) Radiator filler neck distorted.	(g) Use wooden block and mallet to reform neck evenly to fit cap.
(h) Cylinder head gasket leaks.	(h) Replace gasket.
(i) Improper cylinder head screw torque.	(i) Retorque screws to specs.
(j) Cylinder block core plug leaks.	(j) Replace core plug.
(k) Cracked cylinder head/block, or warped cylinder head/block gasket surface.	(k) Resurface if possible; replace if not.
(l) Heater core leaks.	(l) Replace core.
(m) Thermostat stuck open.	(m) Install new thermostat—make sure it's correct type and heat range.
(n) Heater water control valve leaks.	(n) Replace valve.
(o) Coolant level too low.	(o) Add coolant.

9. Turbo Hydra-Matic

NO DRIVE IN DRIVE RANGE

CONDITION	CORRECTION
(a) Oil level low.	(a) Top up to correct level. Check for external leaks or defective vacuum modulator. Leaking diaphragm will evacuate oil from unit.
(b) Oil pressure is low.	(b) Check filter assembly as O-ring may be missing or damaged; neck weld may leak or filter might be blocked. Check pump assembly for damage by converter. In rare cases, there might be porosity in intake bore of unit.
(c) Manual linkage is out of adjustment.	(c) Check and adjust linkage.
(d) Faulty control valve assembly.	(d) Reconnect manual valve to manual lever.
(e) Forward clutch not working properly.	(e) Check for cracked piston, missing or damaged seals, or burned clutch plates.
(f) Pump feed circuit to forward clutch faulty.	(f) Check for missing or broken oil seal rings, leak in feed circuits, pump-to-case gasket out of position or damaged. Clutch drum ball check may be stuck or missing.
(g) Broken spring or damaged cage in roller clutch assembly.	(g) Replace.

OIL PRESSURE TOO HIGH OR TOO LOW

CONDITION	CORRECTION
(a) High oil pressure.	(a) Vacuum line or fittings may leak; also check vacuum modulator, modulator valve, pressure regulator and oil pump for correct operation.
(b) Low oil pressure.	(b) Vacuum line or fittings may be obstructed; also check vacuum modulator, modulator valve, pressure regulator, governor and oil pump for correct operation.

1-2 SHIFT: FULL THROTTLE ONLY

CONDITION	CORRECTION
(a) Sticking or defective detent switch.	(a) Replace.
(b) Detent solenoid is loose, has leaking gasket or sticks open.	(b) Repair and/or replace as necessary.
(c) Control valve assembly faulty.	(c) Valve body spacer plate to cover gasket may leak. It can also be damaged or incorrectly installed. Check detent valve train for sticking and 3-2 valve for same.
(d) Porosity in case assembly.	(d) Replace.

NO 1-2 SHIFT: FIRST SPEED ONLY

CONDITION	CORRECTION
(a) Governor assembly faulty.	(a) Governor valve sticks. Driven gear may also be loose, damaged or worn. If driven gear shows signs of damage, check output shaft drive gear for nicks or rough finish.
(b) Control valve assembly faulty.	(b) Check 1-2 shift valve train to see if it's closed. Governor feed channels may be blocked, leaking or pipes out of position. Check valve body spacer plate-to-cover gasket as it may be leaking, damaged or incorrectly installed.
(c) Defective case.	(c) Replace leaking or blown-out intermediate clutch plug. Governor feed channel may also be blocked or governor bore could be scored or worn causing cross pressure leak.
(d) Intermediate clutch not working correctly.	(d) Replace clutch piston seals. Check center support oil rings as they may be missing or broken. Orifice plug could also be missing.

FIRST & SECOND SPEEDS ONLY, NO 2-3 SHIFT

CONDITION	CORRECTION
(a) Detent solenoid stuck open.	(a) Replace.
(b) Detent switch faulty.	(b) Replace.
(c) Control valve assembly faulty.	(c) Check 2-3 shift train to see if it's stuck. Also check valve body spacer plate-to-cover gasket as it may be leaking, damaged or incorrectly installed.
(d) Direct clutch defective.	(d) Replace center support oil rings. Also check clutch piston seals for damage and make sure that piston ball check is not stuck or missing.

DRIVE IN NEUTRAL

CONDITION	CORRECTION
(a) Manual linkage out of adjustment.	(a) Adjust linkage.
(b) Forward clutch does not release.	(b) Replace.

NO DRIVE OR SLIPS IN REVERSE

CONDITION	CORRECTION
(a) Oil level low.	(a) Top up oil to proper level.
(b) Manual linkage out of adjustment.	(b) Adjust linkage.

(c) Incorrect oil pressure.	(c) Replace vacuum modulator assembly.	**2-3 SHIFT SLIPS**	
(d) Control valve assembly faulty.	(d) Replace valve body spacer plate-to-gasket. Check 2-3 valve train to see if it's stuck open. Make sure low reverse ball is not missing from case and that reverse feed passage is correctly installed.	(a) Oil level low.	(a) Top up oil to proper level.
		(b) Incorrect oil pressure.	(b) Replace vacuum modulator assembly. Check for mislocated pump-to-case gasket and replace correctly if necessary.
(e) Rear servo piston seal ring damaged or missing.	(e) Replace ring.	(c) Accumulator piston pin leaks at swedge end.	(c) Replace.
(f) Reverse or low band defective or burned.	(f) Replace band.	(d) Direct clutch—piston seals leak.	(d) Replace seals and check for leak from center support oil seal rings.
(g) Direct clutch—clutch plates burned or damaged.	(g) Replace clutch plates. Check to see if caused by stuck ball check in piston. Also check outer seal as it may be damaged too.	**ROUGH 2-3 SHIFT**	
		(a) Oil pressure is too high.	(a) Modulator valve sticks or assembly is defective. Determine which and repair accordingly.

SLIPS IN ALL RANGES

		(b) Front servo accumulator spring missing or broken.	(b) Replace. Check for stuck piston.
(a) Oil level low.	(a) Top up oil to proper level.	**NO ENGINE BRAKING—2ND GEAR**	
(b) Incorrect oil pressure.	(b) Replace vacuum modulator assembly. Also check for plugged or leaking filter assembly, especially a damaged O-ring.	(a) Front band broken or burned.	(a) Replace and determine cause.
		NO ENGINE BRAKING—1ST GEAR	
(c) Forward and direct clutches burned.	(c) Replace burned clutches and locate cause.	(a) Low-reverse check ball missing from case.	(a) Replace.

1-2 SHIFT SLIPS

(a) Oil level low.	(a) Top up oil to proper level.	(b) Rear servo oil seal ring, bore or piston damaged.	(b) Replace.
(b) Incorrect oil pressure.	(b) Replace vacuum modulator assembly. Check pump pressure regulator valve at same time for correct operation.	(c) Rear band apply pin is short or improperly assembled.	(c) Replace correctly.
(c) Front accumulator oil ring damaged or missing.	(c) Replace.	(d) Rear band is broken or burned.	(d) Replace and determine cause.
(d) Control valve assembly bolts are loose.	(d) Torque valve body attaching bolts to correct specs if 1-2 accumulator valve train is not sticking. If valve sticks, replace.	**NO PART-THROTTLE DOWNSHIFT**	
		(a) 3-2 valve stuck, spring missing or broken.	(a) Free valve and/or replace spring.
(e) Rear accumulator oil ring damaged or missing.	(e) Replace.	(b) Oil pressure incorrect.	(b) Check operation of vacuum modulator assembly and replace if necessary.
(f) Mispositioned pump-to-case gasket.	(f) Replace gasket correctly.		
(g) Intermediate clutch plug in case leaking excessively.	(g) Replace. If leak continues, there may be porosity between channels.	**NO DETENT DOWNSHIFTS**	
		(a) 3-2 valve stuck, spring missing or broken.	(a) Free valve and/or replace spring.
(h) Intermediate clutch piston seals damaged.	(h) Replace. Clutch plates may also be burned and should be replaced if necessary.	(b) Detent switch out of adjustment.	(b) Adjust.
		(c) Solenoid inoperative.	(c) Replace.
		(d) Detent valve train sticking.	(d) Replace.

ROUGH 1-2 SHIFT

		WILL NOT HOLD IN PARK	
(a) Incorrect oil pressure.	(a) Replace vacuum modulator assembly. Check for loose fittings or restrictions in line.	(a) Linkage needs adjustment.	(a) Adjust linkage.
(b) Control valve assembly bolts loose.	(b) Torque valve body to case bolts to specs.	(b) Defective parking brake lever and actuator assembly.	(b) Replace.
(c) Valve body spacer plate-to-cover gasket damaged or mispositioned.	(c) Replace gasket.	(c) Parking pawl broken.	(c) Replace.
(d) Intermediate clutch ball missing or not sealing.	(d) Replace or ascertain why sealing is not taking place.		

10. 3-Speed Manual Transmission

NOISY IN FORWARD SPEEDS

(e) Rear servo accumulator assembly faulty.	(e) Remove unit and check for damaged oil rings, stuck piston, broken or missing spring or damaged bore. Repair accordingly.	(a) Low lubricant level.	(a) Top up as required.
		(b) Incorrect lubricant in use.	(b) Drain and refill with correct lubricant.
		(c) Transmission loose or incorrectly aligned.	(c) Tighten attachment bolts and check alignment.

(d) Main drive gear or drive gear bearing worn or damaged.

(d) Disassemble transmission and replace drive gear or bearing as required.

(e) Countergear or needle roller bearings worn or damaged.

(e) Disassemble transmission and replace as necessary.

NOISY IN REVERSE GEAR

(a) Reverse gear, reverse idler gear or shaft worn or damaged.

(a) Disassemble transmission and replace gears or shaft as necessary.

SHIFTS HARD

(a) Clutch improperly adjusted.

(a) Adjust clutch correctly.

(b) Shift linkage out of adjustment.

(b) Check linkage and adjust for smooth operation.

(c) Shift linkage bent; loose or damaged linkage.

(c) Replace damaged linkage; tighten loose linkage.

(d) Shift levers, shafts or forks worn.

(d) Disassemble transmission and replace components as required.

(e) Blocking rings worn or broken.

(e) Disassemble transmission and replace rings.

JUMPS OUT OF GEAR

(a) Shift linkage loose, worn or needs adjustment.

(a) Tighten loose linkage. Replace worn linkage, adjust.

(b) Transmission loose or incorrectly aligned.

(b) Tighten attachment bolts and check alignment.

(c) Bent or worn shift fork, lever and/or shaft.

(c) Disassemble transmission and replace parts as necessary for this and remaining causes.

(d) Pilot bearing worn.

(e) Detent cam spring weak or notches worn.

(f) Loose or broken bearing retainer, bearings on main drive gear and output shaft.

(g) Worn or broken blocking ring.

(h) Bent output shaft.

STICKS IN GEAR

(a) Clutch does not release fully.

(a) Adjust clutch properly.

(b) Low lubricant level.

(b) Top up as required.

(c) Incorrect lubricant in use.

(c) Drain and refill with correct lubricant.

(d) Tight main drive gear pilot bearing.

(d) Disassemble transmission and replace parts as necessary for this and remaining causes.

(e) Frozen synchronizing blocking ring on main drive gear cone.

(f) Damaged teeth on synchronizer sleeve and/or main drive gear.

FORWARD GEARS CLASH

(a) Clutch does not release fully.

(a) Adjust clutch to release fully.

(b) Springs in synchronizer assembly are weak or broken.

(b) Disassemble transmission and replace springs as required.

(c) Blocking rings and/or cone surfaces are worn.

(c) Disassemble transmission and replace worn components.

REVERSE GEAR CLASH

(a) Engine idle is set too high.

(a) Reset engine idle.

(b) Clutch needs adjustment.

(b) Adjust clutch.

(c) Clutch driven plate drags or is distorted.

(c) Adjust if possible; replace if necessary.

(d) Main drive gear bearing is tight or frozen.

(d) Disassemble transmission and replace bearing.

11. 4-Speed Manual Transmission

SHIFTS HARD ON DOWNSHIFT

(a) Downshifting at too great rpms.

(a) Shifting into low gear above 45 mph and second above 65 mph makes extra work for synchronizing assemblies. If low or 2nd is used constantly at high speeds, there is the danger of damage from overspeeding the engine.

DISENGAGES FROM GEAR

(a) Dirt between transmission case and clutch housing.

(a) Clean mating surfaces involved.

(b) Does not engage fully.

(b) Check linkage for interference and adjust or replace if damaged.

(c) Clutching teeth worn or defective and/or clutch hub spline worn.

(c) Replace gear, clutch hub and sleeve.

NOISY OPERATION

(a) Worn, scored or broken gears.

(a) Replace gears.

(b) Dirty or worn bearing.

(b) Flush transmission with kerosene. If noise is still there, replace bearings and examine gears—replace if worn or damaged.

(c) Clutch sleeve interferes with countergear.

(c) Replace worn shift forks, countergear and idler gear thrust washers to restore gears and clutch sleeve to proper location. Thrust faces on these gears should be checked for wear and replaced if necessary.

LEAKS LUBRICANT

(a) Too much lubricant in transmission.

(a) Drain to correct level.

(b) Main drive gear bearing retainer loose or broken.

(b) Tighten or replace retainer.

(c) Front main bearing retainer gasket damaged.

(c) Replace gasket.

(d) Cover loose or gasket damaged.

(d) Tighten cover or replace gasket.

(e) Operating shaft seal leaks.

(e) Replace operating shaft seal.

(f) Countershaft loose in case.

(f) Replace case.

(g) Lack of sealant on bolts.

(g) Coat bolts with sealant.

(h) Extension oil seal worn.

(h) Replace seal.

BACKLASH IN ALL REDUCTION GEARS IS EXCESSIVE

(a) Countergear bearings worn.

(a) Replace bearings and shaft.

(b) Too much end-play in countergear.

(b) Replace countergear thrust washers.

NOISY IN ALL REDUCTION GEARS

(a) Insufficient lubricant.

(a) Check and top up to correct level.

(b) Main drive gear or countergear worn or damaged.

(b) Replace gears.

SHIFTS HARD, UP OR DOWN

(a) Clutch binds or releases too slowly.
   (a) Adjust or repair clutch.

(b) Shift linkage binds.
   (b) Free linkage, lubricate and adjust if necessary.

NOISY IN ALL GEARS

(a) Insufficient lubricant.
   (a) Check and top up to correct level.

(b) Countergear bearings worn.
   (b) Replace bearings and shaft.

(c) Main drive gear and countershaft drive gear worn or damaged.
   (c) Replace gears.

(d) Main drive gear or mainshaft ball bearings damaged.
   (d) Replace bearings.

(e) Speedometer gears damaged.
   (e) Replace gears.

NOISY IN HIGH GEAR

(a) Front main bearing damaged.
   (a) Replace bearing.

(b) Rear bearing damaged.
   (b) Replace bearing.

(c) Speedometer gears damaged.
   (c) Replace gears.

NOISY IN NEUTRAL WITH ENGINE RUNNING

(a) Front main bearing damaged.
   (a) Replace bearing.

(b) Mainshaft pilot bearing damaged.
   (b) Replace bearing.

12. Clutch

FAILS TO RELEASE

(a) Linkage adjustment is incorrect.
   (a) Adjust linkage correctly.

(b) Pedal travel is wrong.
   (b) Trim bumper stop and adjust linkage.

(c) Linkage is loose.
   (c) Replace bushings.

(d) Pilot bearing is worn or damaged.
   (d) Replace bearing.

(e) Faulty driven plate.
   (e) Replace driven plate.

(f) Fork off ball stud.
   (f) Install correctly.

(g) Clutch driven plate hub binds on main drive gear spline.
   (g) Repair or replace main drive.

CLUTCH SLIPS

(a) No lash.
   (a) Adjust linkage.

(b) Driven plate contaminated with oil.
   (b) Install new driven plate; locate and correct oil leak.

(c) Driven plate facing worn or torn.
   (c) Replace driven plate.

(d) Pressure plate or flywheel warped.
   (d) Replace.

(e) Weak diaphragm spring.
   (e) Replace cover assembly.

(f) Driven plate not seated correctly.
   (f) Make 15-45 starts.

(g) Driven plate overheated.
   (g) Let cool then check lash.

CLUTCH GRABS

(a) Driven plate facing glazed, burned or oil contaminated.
   (a) Replace with new driven plate.

(b) Main drive gear splines worn.
   (b) Replace transmission main drive gear.

(c) Engine mountings loose.
   (c) Check and tighten or replace mountings.

(d) Pressure plate or flywheel warped.
   (d) Replace.

(e) Flywheel or pressure plate burned or resin-smeared.
   (e) Sand off if superficial but replace burned or heat checked parts.

RATTLING OR TRANSMISSION CLICK

(a) Clutch fork is loose on ball stud or in bearing groove.
   (a) Check ball stud and retaining spring—replace if necessary.

(b) Oil in driven plate damper.
   (b) Replace driven plate.

(c) Driven plate damper spring fails.
   (c) Replace driven plate.

THROWOUT BEARING NOISE WHEN CLUTCH IS FULL ENGAGED

(a) Improperly adjusted linkage.
   (a) Check and adjust linkage properly.

(b) Throwout bearing binds on transmission bearing retainer.
   (b) Clean, relubricate and check for nicks, burrs, etc.

(c) Tension between clutch fork spring and ball stud is not sufficient.
   (c) Replace fork.

(d) Fork improperly installed.
   (d) Remove and reinstall properly.

(e) Linkage return spring is weak.
   (e) Replace spring.

CLUTCH IS NOISY

(a) Throwout bearing is worn.
   (a) Replace.

(b) Fork is off ball stud causing a heavy clicking noise.
   (b) Remove and reinstall properly.

PEDAL DOES NOT RETURN WHEN CLUTCH IS DISENGAGED

(a) Linkage is binding.
   (a) Free linkage; adjust if necessary and lubricate.

(b) Pressure plate spring is weak.
   (b) Replace spring.

(c) Linkage return spring is weak.
   (c) Replace spring.

REQUIRES HIGH PEDAL EFFORT

(a) Linkage is binding.
   (a) Free linkage; adjust if necessary and lubricate.

(b) Driven plate is worn excessively.
   (b) Replace with new driven plate.

13. Front Suspension

POOR DIRECTIONAL STABILITY

(a) Stabilizer bar broken or missing link.
   (a) Remove and replace stabilizer and/or link.

(b) Shock absorber defective.
   (b) Install new shock absorber.

(c) Front wheel alignment (caster) is incorrect.
   (c) Align front wheels.

(d) Loose wheel bearings.
   (d) Adjust wheel bearings to specs.

(e) Ball joints and/or steering linkage need lubrication.
   (e) Lubricate suspension components.

(f) Steering gear not on high point.
   (f) Adjust steering gear on high point.

HARD STEERING

(a) Ball joints and/or steering linkage need lubrication.
   (a) Lubricate suspension components.

(b) Front tire pressure low or uneven.
   (b) Inflate tires to proper pressure.

(c) Power steering unit partially or completely inoperative.
(c) Check power steering unit for proper operation (See Power Steering).

(d) Front wheel alignment is incorrect (manual steering only).
(d) Check and align front wheels.

FRONT WHEEL SHIMMY

(a) Tire and wheel out-of-round, or out-of-balance.
(a) Check runout and balance tires.

(b) Wheel bearings worn or too loose.
(b) Adjust wheel bearings to specs.

(c) Tie-rod ends worn.
(c) Replace tie-rod end(s).

(d) Ball joints worn.
(d) Replace ball joints.

(e) Defective shock absorber.
(e) Install new shock absorber.

CAR PULLS TO ONE SIDE

(a) Tire pressure low or uneven.
(a) Inflate tires to proper pressure.

(b) Front or rear brake drag.
(b) Check brake adjustment.

(c) Front spring broken or sagging.
(c) Replace spring.

(d) Front wheel alignment (camber) is incorrect.
(d) Align front wheels.

TOO MUCH PLAY IN STEERING

(a) Steering gear parts worn.
(a) Overhaul gear and replace worn components.

(b) Steering gear incorrectly adjusted.
(b) Adjust steering gear.

WHEEL TRAMP

(a) Tire and wheel out-of-balance.
(a) Balance wheels.

(b) Tire and wheel out-of-round.
(b) Replace tire.

(c) Bump or blister on tire.
(c) Replace tire.

(d) Defective shock absorber.
(d) Install new shock absorber.

FRONT END NOISE

(a) Ball joints and/or steering linkage need lubrication.
(a) Lubricate suspension components.

(b) Worn or loose shock absorber bushings.
(b) Tighten bolts and/or replace bushings.

(c) Control arm bushings worn.
(c) Replace bushings.

(d) Stabilizer bar loose.
(d) Tighten stabilizer bar attachments.

(e) Tie-rod ends worn.
(e) Replace tie-rod end(s).

(f) Wheel bearings worn or too loose.
(f) Check wheel bearings and adjust to specs or replace.

(g) Suspension bolts loose.
(g) Torque to specs or replace.

(h) Wheel nuts loose.
(h) Tighten wheel nuts.

TIRE WEAR EXCESSIVE OR UNEVEN

(a) Tires improperly inflated.
(a) Inflate tires to proper pressure.

(b) Toe-in adjustment is incorrect.
(b) Adjust toe-in to specs.

(c) Wheels out-of-balance.
(c) Balance wheels.

SCUFFED TIRES

(a) Toe-in adjustment is incorrect.
(a) Adjust toe-in to specs.

(b) Tires improperly inflated.
(b) Inflate tires to proper pressure.

(c) Suspension arm is bent or twisted.
(c) Replace arm.

CUPPED TIRES

(a) Tire or wheel runout is excessive.
(a) Adjust or compensate for runout.

(b) Wheel and tire out-of-balance.
(b) Balance wheels.

(c) Wheel bearings worn or out of adjustment.
(c) Adjust wheel bearings to specs or replace.

(d) Ball joints worn excessively.
(d) Replace ball joints.

(e) Defective front shock absorbers.
(e) Install new shock absorbers.

ERRATIC STEERING WHEN BRAKING

(a) Tires improperly inflated.
(a) Inflate tires to proper pressure.

(b) Front wheel bearings worn or incorrectly adjusted.
(b) Adjust bearings to specs or replace.

(c) Brakes need adjustment.
(c) Check brakes for uneven or incorrect adjustment.

(d) Caster adjustment incorrect or uneven.
(d) Check and adjust caster to specs.

RETURNABILITY POOR

(a) Improper caster setting (negative).
(a) Check and adjust caster to specs.

(b) Power steering gear unit binding internally.
(b) Remove and overhaul steering gear.

(c) Steering gear out of adjustment.
(c) Adjust steering gear to specs.

(d) Worn idler arm bushing.
(d) Replace idler arm.

(e) Steering linkage needs lubrication.
(e) Lubricate linkage.

14. Driveline and Universal Joint

ROUGHNESS OR VIBRATION AT ANY SPEED

(a) Dented or bent driveshaft.
(a) Replace driveshaft.

(b) Undercoating on driveshaft.
(b) Clean driveshaft.

(c) Tires are out-of-balance.
(c) Balance.

(d) Universal joints are tight.
(d) Hit yokes with a hammer to free up. If it's impossible to free, or if joint feels rough when rotated by hand, overhaul.

(e) U-bolt torque excessive.
(e) Adjust to specified torque.

(f) Universal joints are worn.
(f) Overhaul and replace necessary parts.

(g) Companion flange has burrs or gouges. Check snap ring locating surfaces on flange yoke.
(g) Rework or replace companion flange.

(h) Unbalanced driveshaft or companion flange.
(h) Check to see if balance weights on driveshaft are missing. Remove and reassemble driveshaft to companion shaft 180° from original position.

(i) Slip yoke spline is too loose.
(i) Replace necessary parts.

(j) Driveshaft runout.
(j) Check runout at front and rear. This should be less than specified by manufacturer. If not, rotate shaft 180° and recheck. If still too much, replace shaft.

ROUGHNESS AT LOW SPEEDS WITH LIGHT LOAD

(a) U-bolt clamp nuts too tight.

(a) Check and torque to specs. If torque was too great and brenelled pattern is evident on trunnions, replace joints.

SCRAPING NOISE

(a) Companion flange, slinger or end yoke rubs on rear axle carrier.

(a) Remove interference by straightening slinger.

LEAK AT FRONT SLIP YOKE

(a) Splined yoke has rough outside surface.

(a) Replace seal if cut. Replace yoke if outside surface is badly burred; hone or smooth with crocus cloth if burring is slight.

(b) Transmission rear oil seal is defective.

(b) Replace seal. Top up transmission to proper level.

DRIVELINE KNOCK OR CLUNK WHEN OPERATED AT 10 MPH IN HIGH GEAR OR NEUTRAL

(a) Universal joints worn or damaged.

(a) Disassemble universal joints and replace worn or damaged parts.

(b) Size gear hub counterbore in differential worn oversize.

(b) Replace differential case and/or side gears as necessary.

PINGING OR CLICKING IN DRIVELINE

(a) Upper or lower control arm bushing bolts are loose.

(a) Tighten bolts to specified torque.

(b) Companion flange is loose.

(b) Remove and turn 180° from its original position, then apply white lead to splines and reinstall. Tighten pinion nut to specified torque.

15. Power Steering System

HISSING NOISE IN STEERING GEAR

(a) There's some noise in all power steering systems, one of the most common of which is a slight hiss evident at standstill or park.

(a) A slight hiss is normal and in no way affects steering.

RATTLE OR CHUCKLE NOISE IN STEERING GEAR

(a) Gearbox is loose on frame.

(a) Check gear-to-frame mounting and tighten bolts to 70 ft.-lbs.

(b) Steering linkage is loose.

(b) Check linkage pivot points for wear and replace if necessary.

(c) Pressure hose is touching another part of car.

(c) Adjust hose position but do not bend tubing by hand.

(d) Loose pitman shaft over center adjustment.

(d) Adjust to specs.

SQUAWK NOISE IN STEERING GEAR DURING TURN MANEUVER

(a) Dampener "O" ring on valve spool cut.

(a) Replace O-ring.

CHIRP NOISE IN PUMP OR BELT SQUEAL

(a) Loose belt.

(a) Adjust belt tension to specs.

GROWL NOISE IN STEERING PUMP

(a) Restriction in hoses or steering gear causing excessive back pressure.

(a) Locate restriction and correct, replacing part or hose if necessary.

(b) Scored pressure plates, thrust plate or rotor.

(b) Replace damaged parts and flush system.

(c) Cam ring extremely worn.

(c) Replace cam ring.

GROAN NOISE IN STEERING PUMP

(a) Low lubricant level.

(a) Fill reservoir to proper level.

(b) Air in the lubricant or a poor pressure hose connection.

(b) Tighten connector to specified torque. Bleed system by operating steering from right to left full turn.

RATTLE OR KNOCK IN STEERING PUMP

(a) Loose pump pulley nut.

(a) Tighten nut to specified torque.

(b) Vanes not properly installed.

(b) Remove and replace correctly.

(c) Vanes sticking in rotor slots.

(c) Free by removing dirt, varnish or burrs that act as a restriction.

SWISH NOISE IN STEERING PUMP

(a) Defective flow control valve.

(a) Replace valve.

WHINE NOISE IN STEERING PUMP

(a) Pump shaft bearing is scored.

(a) Replace housing and shaft and flush system.

POOR STEERING WHEEL RETURN TO CENTER

(a) Lack of lubrication in linkage and ball joints.

(a) Lubricate linkage and ball joints.

(b) Lower coupling flange rubs against steering gear adjuster plug.

(b) Loosen the pinch bolt and assemble correctly.

(c) Misalignment of steering gear to column.

(c) Align steering column.

(d) Tires improperly inflated.

(d) Inflate to specified pressure.

(e) Front wheel alignment incorrect.

(e) Check alignment and adjust to specs. Before aligning, disconnect pitman arm of linkage from pitman shaft of gear and turn front wheels by hand. If wheels will not turn easily, linkage or ball joints are also at fault.

(f) Steering linkage binds.

(f) Replace pivots.

(g) Ball joints bind.

(g) Replace ball joints.

(h) Steering wheel rubs against directional signal housing.

(h) Adjust steering jacket.

(i) Steering shaft bearings are tight or frozen.

(i) Replace bearings.

CAR WANDERS FROM ONE SIDE OF ROAD TO THE OTHER

(a) Front end out of alignment.

(a) Check front end and align to specs.

(b) Unbalanced steering gear valve, requires light effort in direction of lead and heavy in opposite direction.

(b) Replace valve.

MOMENTARY INCREASE IN EFFORT WHEN TURNING WHEEL FAST

(a) Low lubricant level in pump.

(a) Top up with power steering fluid as necessary.

(b) Pump belt slips.

(b) Check belt for wear; tighten or replace, and adjust to tension specs.

(c) High internal leakage.

(c) Check pump pressure; repair or replace.

STEERING WHEEL SURGES WHEN TURNING

(a) Low lubricant level. — (a) Top up as required.

(b) Loose pump belt. — (b) Adjust belt tension to specs.

(c) Steering linkage hits oil pan at full turn position. — (c) Correct clearance.

(d) Pump pressure is insufficient. — (d) Check pump pressure and replace relief valve if defective.

(e) Flow control valve sticks. — (e) Check for varnish or damage and replace if necessary.

EXCESSIVE WHEEL KICK-BACK OR LOOSE STEERING

(a) Air in system. — (a) Add power steering fluid to pump reservoir and bleed by operating steering, then check hose connectors for proper torque and adjust as required.

(b) Steering gear loose on frame. — (b) Tighten attaching bolts to specified torque.

(c) Steering gear flexible coupling loose on shaft; rubber disc mounting screws loose. — (c) Tighten flange pinch bolts to 30 ft.-lbs., if serrations are undamaged. Tighten upper flange to coupling nuts to specified torque.

(d) Excess wear in steering linkage. — (d) Replace loose pivots.

(e) Front wheel bearings worn or incorrectly adjusted. — (e) Adjust bearings or replace.

(f) Poppet valve (gear) worn. — (f) Replace.

(g) Thrust bearing preload adjustment (gear) loose. — (g) Adjust to specs with gear out of car.

(h) Excessive over-center lash. — (h) Adjust to specs with gear out of car.

HARD STEERING OR LACK OF ASSIST

(a) Loose pump belt. — (a) Adjust belt tension to specs.

(b) Low oil in reservoir. — (b) Top up to proper level. If excessively low, check lines and joints for evidence of external leakage. Tighten any loose connectors to 30 ft.-lbs.

(c) Steering gear to column misalignment. — (c) Align steering column.

(d) Lower coupling flange rubs against steering gear adjuster plug. — (d) Loosen pinch bolt and assemble correctly.

(e) Tires not properly inflated. — (e) Inflate to recommended pressure.

16. Drum Brakes

PEDAL GOES TO FLOOR

(a) Fluid level low in reservoir. — (a) Fill and bleed master cylinder.

(b) Air in hydraulic system. — (b) Fill and bleed system.

(c) Brakes improperly adjusted. — (c) Repair or replace self-adjuster.

(d) Wheel cylinders leaking. — (d) Recondition or replace wheel cylinder. It may be necessary to replace brake shoes.

(e) Loose or broken brake lines. — (e) Tighten all brake fittings or replace brake line.

(f) Worn or leaking master cylinder. — (f) Recondition or replace master cylinder and bleed system.

(g) Brake lining excessively worn. — (g) Reline and adjust brakes.

BRAKE PEDAL IS SPONGY

(a) Air in hydraulic system. — (a) Fill master cylinder and bleed hydraulic system.

(b) Contaminated or incorrect brake fluid. — (b) Drain, flush and refill with proper brake fluid.

(c) Brake drums excessively worn or cracked. — (c) Replace drums.

BRAKES PULL WHEN APPLIED

(a) Contaminated lining. — (a) Replace with new lining of original quality.

(b) Front end needs alignment. — (b) Check and align front end.

(c) Brake adjustment incorrect. — (c) Adjust brakes and check fluid.

(d) Unmatched brake linings. — (d) Match primary and secondary linings with same type on all wheels.

(e) Brake shoes are distorted. — (e) Replace shoes.

(f) Restriction in brake hose or line. — (f) Locate and replace plugged hose or brake line.

(g) Rear spring broken. — (g) Replace.

BRAKES SQUEAL OR CHIRP

(a) Brake lining glazed or saturated. — (a) Cam grind (glazed only) or replace lining.

(b) Brake shoe retaining spring weak or broken. — (b) Replace with new retaining spring.

(c) Brake shoe return spring weak or broken. — (c) Replace with new return spring.

(d) Brake shoes are distorted. — (d) Replace shoes.

(e) Support plate is bent. — (e) Replace with new support plate.

(f) Dust in brakes or scored brake drums. — (f) Blow out brake assembly with compressed air and reface drums—machine, do not grind.

(g) Drum or eccentric axle flange pilot out-of-round. — (g) Remove and replace—lubricate support plate contact areas.

BRAKES DRAG

(a) Wheel or parking brake adjustment incorrect. — (a) Adjust brakes and check fluid level.

(b) Parking brake engaged. — (b) Release parking brake.

(c) Brake shoe return spring weak or broken. — (c) Replace with new shoe return spring.

(d) Brake pedal binds. — (d) Free pedal and lubricate linkage.

(e) Master cylinder cup sticks. — (e) Recondition master cylinder.

(f) Master cylinder relief port is obstructed. — (f) Use compressed air to blow out relief port.

(g) Brake drum is bent or out-of-round. — (g) Reface or replace drum.

(h) Stop light switch needs adjustment. — (h) Adjust switch to allow for full return of pedal.

HARD PEDAL

(a) Brake booster is not working. — (a) Replace unit.

(b) Restriction in brake line or hose. — (b) Clean out or replace brake line or hose.

(c) Frozen brake pedal linkage. — (c) Free and lubricate linkage.

WHEEL LOCKS

(a) Brake lining is contaminated with oil or grease. — (a) Reline all brakes.

(b) Brake lining is loose or torn. — (b) Replace damaged linings.

CONDITION	CORRECTION
(c) Wheel cylinder cups stick.	(c) Recondition or replace wheel cylinders.
(d) Wheel bearings out of adjustment.	(d) Clean, pack and adjust wheel bearings to specs.

BRAKES FADE

CONDITION	CORRECTION
(a) Use of inferior linings.	(a) Replace with original quality linings.
(b) Brake drums overheat.	(b) Check for dragging brakes.
(c) Contaminated or incorrect brake fluid.	(c) Drain, flush, refill and bleed hydraulic brake system.
(d) Saturated brake lining.	(d) Reline all brakes.

SURGE BELOW 15 MPH

CONDITION	CORRECTION
(a) Rear brake drum bent or out-of-round.	(a) Reface or replace drum.

CHATTER FROM 40 TO 80 MPH

CONDITION	CORRECTION
(a) Front brake drum bent or out-of-round.	(a) Reface or replace drum.

SHOE KNOCK

CONDITION	CORRECTION
(a) Machine grooves in contact face of brake drum.	(a) Sand, reface or replace brake drum.
(b) Hold-down springs are weak.	(b) Replace with new springs.

BRAKES DO NOT SELF-ADJUST

CONDITION	CORRECTION
(a) Adjuster screw is frozen in thread.	(a) Clean and free all thread areas.
(b) Adjuster screw is corroded at thrust washer.	(b) Clean threads and replace thrust washer.
(c) Adjuster lever does not engage star wheel properly.	(c) Repair, free up or replace adjuster.
(d) Adjuster incorrectly installed.	(d) Check and reinstall correctly.

17. Disc Brakes

PEDAL TRAVEL IS EXCESSIVE

CONDITION	CORRECTION
(a) Air leak or insufficient fluid in hydraulic system or caliper.	(a) Check system for leaks and bleed.
(b) Shoe and lining assembly warped or excessively tapered.	(b) Install new shoe and linings.
(c) Disc runout excessive.	(c) Check disc for runout with dial indicator. Install a new or refinished disc.
(d) Rear brake needs adjustment.	(d) Adjust and check rear brakes.
(e) Wheel bearing adjustment is too loose.	(e) Readjust wheel bearing to specified torque.
(f) Caliper piston seal damaged.	(f) Install new piston seal.
(g) Contaminated or incorrect brake fluid.	(g) Drain and replace with correct fluid.
(h) Power brake unit malfunction.	(h) Replace unit.

BRAKE CHATTER

CONDITION	CORRECTION
(a) Braking disc has excessive thickness variation.	(a) Check disc for thickness variation with a micrometer.
(b) Lateral runout of braking disc is excessive.	(b) Check disc for lateral runout with a dial indicator; replace with new or refaced disc.
(c) Front bearing clearance is too great.	(c) Readjust wheel bearings to specified torque.

REQUIRES EXCESSIVE PEDAL EFFORT

CONDITION	CORRECTION
(a) Brake fluid, oil or grease on linings.	(a) Replace with new linings.
(b) Incorrect or faulty lining.	(b) Remove and replace lining with original quality lining.
(c) Seized or frozen piston(s).	(c) Disassemble caliper and free up piston(s).
(d) Power brake malfunction.	(d) Replace unit.

PULL, GRABBING OR UNEVEN BRAKING ACTION

CONDITION	CORRECTION
(a) Brake fluid, oil or grease on linings.	(a) Replace with new linings.
(b) Linings unmatched.	(b) Replace with correct lining.
(c) Seized or frozen piston(s).	(c) Disassemble caliper and free up piston(s).
(d) Tire pressure insufficient.	(d) Check and inflate tires to recommended pressures.
(e) Front end needs alignment.	(e) Check and align front end to specs.
(f) Rear spring broken.	(f) Replace.
(g) Restriction in hose or line.	(g) Check hoses and lines and replace.
(h) Caliper incorrectly aligned with braking disc.	(h) Check alignment and remove caliper if necessary to correct alignment when replacing.

BRAKE RATTLE AT LOW SPEEDS ON ROUGH ROADS

CONDITION	CORRECTION
(a) Inboard shoe anti-rattle spring either missing or not properly positioned.	(a) Install new anti-rattle spring or position properly.
(b) Clearance between shoe and caliper is too great.	(b) Replace shoe and lining assemblies.

SCRAPING

CONDITION	CORRECTION
(a) Mounting bolts are too long.	(a) Replace with mounting bolts of correct length.
(b) Wheel bearings are loose.	(b) Readjust wheel bearings to correct specs.
(c) Splash shield is deformed and rubs on rotor.	(c) Bend shield to provide proper clearance.

FRONT BRAKES HEAT UP AND FAIL TO RELEASE

CONDITION	CORRECTION
(a) Pedal linkage sticks.	(a) Free sticking linkage and lubricate.
(b) Seized or frozen piston(s).	(b) Disassemble caliper and free piston(s).
(c) Power brake unit malfunction.	(c) Replace unit.

LEAKING WHEEL CYLINDER

CONDITION	CORRECTION
(a) Worn or damaged caliper piston seal.	(a) Remove and disassemble caliper; install new seal.
(b) Scoring or corrosion on surface of cylinder bore.	(b) Remove and disassemble caliper; hone cylinder bore and install new seal.

PEDAL GOES TO FLOOR—NO BRAKING ACTION

CONDITION	CORRECTION
(a) Air in hydraulic system.	(a) Bleed hydraulic system correctly.
(b) Fluid leak past primary cup in master cylinder.	(b) Recondition master cylinder.
(c) Hose or line leak in system.	(c) Check hoses and lines for leak and repair or replace as required.
(d) Rear brakes need adjustment.	(d) Adjust rear brakes.
(e) Bleeder screw open.	(e) Close bleeder screw and bleed entire system.